The Habsburg Empire

The Habsburg Empire

A New History

PIETER M. JUDSON

The Belknap Press of Harvard University Press

CAMBRIDGE, MASSACHUSETTS
LONDON, ENGLAND

First Harvard University Press paperback edition, 2018
First Printing

Design by Dean Bornstein

Library of Congress Cataloging-in-Publication Data

Names: Judson, Pieter M., author.
Title: The Habsburg empire : a new history/Pieter M. Judson.
Description: Cambridge, Massachusetts : The Belknap Press of Harvard
University Press, 2016. | Includes bibliographical references and index.
Identifiers: LCCN 2015036845 | ISBN 9780674047761 (cloth : alk. paper) |
ISBN 9780674986763 (pbk.)
Subjects: LCSH: Habsburg, House of—History. | Nationalism—Europe,
Central—History. | Imperialism—Social aspects—Europe, Central—History.
Classification: LCC DB36.3.H3 J83 2016 | DDC 943.6/04—dc23 LC record
available at http://lccn.loc.gov/2015036845

FOR CHARLES

CONTENTS

NOTE ON NAMES AND PLACES

The subject of this book is a state that was known by many different names over the period 1770–1918. I refer to this state as the Habsburg Monarchy or Habsburg Empire. From 1804 until 1867 the state was known as the Austrian Empire. After the Settlement of 1867 the new dual monarchy was called Austria-Hungary. I refer to the western half of the dual monarchy as Austria, even though its official name was not Austria but rather "The Kingdoms and Lands Represented in the Parliament [*Reichsrat*]" (sometimes referred to as "Cisleithania," while Hungary became "Transleithania").

Writing about Habsburg central Europe in a way that does not reinforce a nationalist frame of reference is next to impossible. In recognition of this challenge, I try to refer to places with no common English names in the two or three languages their inhabitants used to name them. This practice may seem a cumbersome one, and nationalists may dispute the order in which I list those names, but it helps to challenge the assumptions that each of these places had a single authentic national identity. For places with common English names such as Cracow, Prague, Trent, or Vienna, I use the English version.

I try to avoid using normative terms like "Czechs," "Germans," "Poles," or "Slovenes," preferring instead descriptive terms like "Czech speakers," even though this practice does not adequately describe the linguistic practices of many of its peoples. It does, however, return a modicum of agency to people who are otherwise often categorized in ways they might not have recognized. I use the term "Hungarian" and "Hungarianization" in places where others might use "Magyar" and "Magyarization." Some scholars distinguish between a state-based concept of nation (Hungary) and a more ethnically inflected concept (Magyar), but this fundamental distinction makes little intellectual sense to me, especially in the context of the nineteenth century. For reasons of historical context I generally use the terms "Ruthene" and "Ruthenian" to denote the peoples and language that today are generally known as Ukrainian, although it is the case that by 1900 the term Ukrainian was becoming used more widely.

Except where cited in English-language works by other authors, all translations are my own.

LIST OF MAPS AND ILLUSTRATIONS

Maps

Illustrations

The Habsburg Empire

Introduction

On Tuesday the thirteenth and Monday the nineteenth of June 1911 in villages, towns, and cities across Imperial Austria, over four and a half million voters turned out to elect a new parliament.[1] Campaigns in individual constituencies were hard fought, and party agitators did their best up until the very last minute to rally their voters. From Vorarlberg to Bukovina, Prague to Dubrovnik, party rallies, bombastic programs, endless pamphlets, even clever satires, dominated public space in the weeks leading up to the election.[2]

Party newspapers urged readers who had not already done so to hurry to the local government office with official identification documents. Here they could pick up their voter-identification cards (*Legitimation* in German), which they should keep handy after they voted, in case their district held a run-off election. All warned against last minute chicanery devised by their opponents. Christian Social newspapers in Graz and Linz implored campaign workers to continue campaigning in every street and neighborhood of every district until voting ended. In Czernowitz/Cernăuți/Cernivci the bourgeois German, Romanian, Ukrainian, and Polish nationalist parties rallied their communities to unseat a Socialist incumbent. In Pettau/Ptui the Slovene-language *Stajerc* exhorted its readers as "Voters! Farmers, Workers, and Craftsmen," urging them to unity behind its favored candidates in South Styria.[3]

Prognosticators and candidates like to exaggerate the political stakes in any election. In retrospect, the stakes of this election in 1911 may not have been exceptional, but the level of excitement expressed in regional newspapers as well as the high turn-out rate on election day appear to reflect a high level of significance attributed by individual voters to the act of voting. One Social Democratic newspaper captured the essence of this significance, proclaiming, "When you cast your ballot in the urn, you decide your own future."[4]

As Austrians swarmed to their polling places to decide their own futures, they were well aware that they were also determining the future of their empire. Some of them even paid the ultimate price for their determination to vote, as shocked newspaper readers across the monarchy learned on 20 June, the day after the end of the voting. An election-day massacre had taken place the day before in the Galician oil town of Drohobych/Drohobycz.[5] A crowd of Jewish and Ruthenian- or Ukrainian-speaking Galicians gathered in the town square determined to exercise their right to vote at the end of a bitterly contested parliamentary campaign. Many worried with good reason that the local authorities would try to fix the outcome in favor of incumbent Nathan Löwenstein and prevent them from voting for their candidate, Zionist Gershon Zipper. The former was the candidate of the town's Jewish powerbrokers and of the conservative elites of the Polish Club who effectively ruled the crownland of Galicia.

For this election the town bosses set up a single polling station to accommodate close to 8,000 potential voters. During the day the local police prevented anyone but known Löwenstein supporters from entering to vote. Several times mounted police drove restless crowds away from the voting station. Instead of doing their expected brisk sales from the presence of a festive crowd of voters, local shop owners experienced broken windows and collateral damage from the increasingly frustrated mob. Then, in the afternoon, the town bosses encouraged troops brought in from the Rzeszów garrison near the fortress at Przemyśl to fire on the crowd. Twenty-six people died immediately, including women, the elderly, and children. Investigators later determined that most of the dead had been shot in the back, suggesting that they had been fleeing the troops.

This dramatically disturbing story does not simply illustrate the lengths that local political authorities were willing to go to maintain their power in an age of mass voter mobilization. It can also be read as a sign of the sheer intensity with which people in an industrial town far from Vienna and Budapest engaged politically and emotionally with their empire. This was only the second election held since the adoption of universal manhood suffrage for parliament in 1907, and only the third since the enfranchisement of men without property in 1897. Precisely for these reasons people treated the hard-fought right to vote as critical to their lives. Elections in the crownland of Galicia generally had a reputation for corruption at the time. The inhabitants of Drohobych/Drohobycz knew well that the men who ran their town would devise every possible form of chicanery to control the outcome of the poll.[6] Nevertheless, an ethnically, religiously, and linguistically diverse crowd of working-class people was determined to elect its agreed-upon candidate. Zionists and Ruthene peasants may seem like unlikely allies, especially since we are used to hearing about conflict in Imperial Austria that pitted national or religious groups against each other. Both groups, however, cared deeply about this election to the parliament in far-away Vienna, even though this institution had much less influence over their daily lives than did the Galician government in Lemberg/Lwów/Lviv and the local bosses who represented that regime. Why were the stakes so high, in both symbolic and real terms, for everyone in Drohobych/Drohobycz that day? What does this tell us about the place of the Habsburg Empire and its institutions in people's lives?

For many Austrians the empire constituted an alternative source of symbolic and real power that might not outweigh the power of local elites, but could at least temper it. When Zionist and Ruthene political leaders complained to the Ministry of Interior in Vienna about local corrupt electoral practices, for example, they did receive some legal redress, even if Vienna could not fully rectify the fundamental unfairness of local political conditions. On 19 June the crowd in Drohobych/Drohobycz used its imperial right to vote as a point of leverage—however small—against the people it perceived to be its local oppressors.

Parliamentary elections held immense cultural and social significance to people across the empire. Resident men over the age of twenty-three may have been the only ones officially entitled to vote in these elections, but the presence of women and children among the casualties at Drohobych/Drohobycz testifies to the degree to which empire concerned everyone on that day, not simply the enfranchised, and not simply the powerful. Franchise restrictions did little to prevent women, youths, and even children from participating in this political, cultural, civic, and often celebratory ritual that brought thousands of people together, connecting their community to the rest of the empire.

An examination of the boisterous events of June 1911 in villages and towns across Imperial Austria would reveal similar socially, religiously, and often linguistically diverse groups of people asserting their voices— often in unexpected alliances—to construct the future of their empire. The same was often true in the Hungarian half of the dual monarchy, despite the narrow franchise that limited the electorate there. Nevertheless, by the 1890s crowds of the unenfranchised in Hungary often mobilized to support a particular position or candidate on election day, even though they could not vote. On election day the empire functioned for all of them as a screen on which to project their beliefs, values, hopes, frustrations, and above all, their visions for the future. Election day constituted a critical ritual of empire in which people of all social classes shared. People held common expectations of the election process as well, expectations that officials would guarantee their fairness and legality, expectations that the authorities in Drohobych/Drohobycz so egregiously and tragically violated.

This book is about how countless local societies across central Europe engaged with the Habsburg dynasty's efforts to build a unified and unifying imperial state from the eighteenth century until the First World War. It investigates how imperial institutions, administrative practices, and cultural programs helped to shape local society in every region of the empire, from the late eighteenth century until the first decades of the twentieth century. It also examines how citizens in every corner of the empire engaged with these various practices and institutions, often appropriating them for their own purposes or reinterpreting them to fit their interests. Taken as a whole, these complex processes of empire building gave citizens in every corner of the empire collective experiences that crossed linguistic, confessional, and regional divides.

The violence at Drohobych/Drohobycz in 1911 is only one of countless examples that demonstrate how an approach to imperial history from the point of view of shared institutions, practices, and cultures challenges and rewrites the nation-based narratives to which students of the Habsburg Empire are accustomed. Placing empire at the center of the investigation, rather than seeing linguistic groups or ethnically defined nations as the building blocks of history, foregrounds a different kind of narrative for central and eastern Europe's history. Regional, linguistic, religious, or ethnic—what contemporaries around 1900 often called "national"—differences in society did not determine politics in Habsburg central Europe in easily predictable ways. The crowd in Drohobych/ Drohobycz at which the soldiers took aim, for example, was in fact multiconfessional and multilingual in character. As they asserted their right to vote, on that day at least, people did not interpret their political differences primarily in conventional ethnic or national—Jews versus Ruthenes versus Poles—terms. The struggle on June 19 was a populist one that pitted the people against local bosses who were unfairly trying to rob them of their rights as imperial citizens. Other situations saw other kinds of alliances.

To be sure, rulers, statesmen, bureaucrats, military advisors, or scientific experts helped ensure the rise and success of an imperial Habsburg state. But it was also an ongoing project that engaged the minds, hearts, and energies of many of its citizens at every level of society. This book focuses on the relationship between the state and society by analyzing the mutual construction of a Habsburg empire from several directions: state building from above and state building from below. Here I understand the state as far more than a discretely defined realm of politics, or a set of formal institutions separated from society. Instead, the state I discuss refers to a broad range of diverse cultural, religious, and social practices while society constitutes an equally important site where politics functions.

In the eighteenth century Habsburg rulers sought to apply a unified and centralized set of institutions to the collection of diverse territories over which they ruled, many of which functioned largely according to their own particular laws, institutions, and administrative traditions. Centralization and unification of the new empire were critical to project great power status and effectively withstand the military attacks of its many enemies. At the same time, however, this Habsburg state—like other developing states in Europe—had to be capable of inspiring an emotional attachment among its peoples by encouraging them to link their individual or group interests to imperial interests.

The book opens by describing and analyzing a broad range of administrative and institutional experiments inaugurated by eighteenth-century monarchs Maria Theresa and her sons, Joseph II and Leopold II, from diminishing the forced labor burdens on the peasantry to taxing the nobility. These measures elicited strong support for empire from peasants in several regions of the empire. Later chapters turn to subsequent state-building maneuvers carried out by their imperial successors— liberal absolutism in the 1850s, constitutional experiments in 1848 and the 1860s, the dualist settlement of 1867, experiments with other so-called "national settlements" after 1900, universal manhood suffrage in the Austrian half of the monarchy in 1907, federalization in October 1918, and the adoption by successor states of some Habsburg laws and practices in 1919 and 1920.

Each of these landmarks in Habsburg history is well known, and with only one real exception the book follows a fairly conventional periodization. What is different here is how I explain those landmark moments, where I locate causal factors, and above all, how they engage—and are even often produced by—initiatives and support from society. In each of these familiar historical periods the Habsburgs continued their efforts to forge a unified empire with a unified purpose. They did so, however, in ways that demonstrated remarkable creativity and flexibility in practice while rhetorically maintaining that the power of their empire remained unchanged and unbroken. Imperial state building took place under and necessarily responded to radically changing local, empire- and European-wide conditions, which demanded nimble strategies, dependent upon the support of different allies in society.

By themselves the imperial regime's visions, policies, tactical retreats, or strategic compromises reveal little to us about the meanings of empire in local society. From the first, however, Habsburg state-building policies sought implicit and sometimes explicit support from a very broad array of groups and social actors. In the eighteenth century, for example, the peasantry and the educated middle classes—for very different reasons— saw themselves as the indirect beneficiaries of Habsburg reform. They often responded actively and opportunistically to the spaces imperial policy created in public life—as with the end of feudal agrarian institutions or the creation of an imperial bureaucracy—to pursue their interests vigorously. In doing so, they signaled their qualified support for empire and its institutions.

Thanks to creative developments in law, economy, and education before the outbreak of the French Revolution in 1789, the Habsburg regime developed a model of common imperial citizenship that implicitly promised legal equality and equal obligations to its subjects (soon-to-be citizens). This concept of a universal citizenship was to some extent the inadvertent consequence of Habsburg efforts to create a more productive class of independent taxpayers out of the enserfed peasants under the rule of the local nobility. A free tax-paying peasantry would constitute a far greater resource to a cash-strapped state with great power ambitions. Freeing the peasantry, however, also meant diminishing the local powers of the nobility and leaving many nobles without the necessary resources to work their lands. Both peasants and noble landowners understood the stakes of the Habsburg efforts at reform.

In the early nineteenth century the Habsburgs extended the promise of legal civic equality to men and women of all social classes in the various law codes it proclaimed, culminating with the Civil Code of 1811 that applied to much of the empire. Of course legal equality did not imply social equality or cultural equality. Status based on refined hierarchies of education and class remained ubiquitous in public life and was reflected in the complex grades of civil service employment increasingly open to members of the educated middle classes and made visible by the uniforms those civil servants wore. The eighteenth-century Habsburgs also developed social policies that reinforced a sense of equal citizenship by promoting patriotic feelings for the state and respect for the social order. Universal primary education in vernacular languages, the creation of an imperial bureaucracy drawn largely from the educated middle classes, the establishment of an independent judiciary, and the promotion of free trade within the empire would also break the power of the regional aristocracy and promote Austria's great power status. Moreover, these policies gave their beneficiaries in Austrian society a more palpable stake in the empire. At the end of the Napoleonic Wars, from Trieste/Trst in the west to Brody in the east, the evidence demonstrates that many social groups already identified strongly with their empire, from landless peasants to merchants engaged in interregional trade, from local priests to district bureaucrats. Imperial patriotism too became a growing force in the Austrian Empire founded in 1804, even as local patriots defined empire in terms of their own regional interests.

By the mid-nineteenth century, many people defined their particular economic visions or political programs specifically in terms of the benefits to be had from the common framework of empire, including, of course, many nationalists. Constitutional reform spurred the mobilization of local society to participate directly in imperial institutions, channeling their dynamic activism into remarkably similar political, civic, and cultural institutions throughout the empire. The implementation of elected municipal councils run by citizens themselves in the mid-nineteenth century, to say nothing of regular elections for regional diets and the imperial parliament, brought more and more people into a public life whose specific character was determined by imperial institutions.

The reform of primary, secondary, and university educational systems across the empire in the 1850s and 1860s also reinforced the potential benefits a unified empire could bring to several populations. Among academic and amateur practitioners of the natural and social sciences, the fundamental idea of a regularized and integrated imperial space shaped research questions and methodological approaches in the nineteenth century. As historians of science have recently demonstrated, attempts to justify the spatial dimensions and demographic diversity of the Habsburg Empire in natural terms influenced the development of several scientific fields, from meteorology to seismology to anthropology.[7] In 1883 under the patronage of Crown Prince Rudolf, the government of Austria-Hungary initiated a vast project to make visible the diversity and dimensions of empire. The goal was to collect studies of the empire's highly diverse geology, flora, fauna, and populations in a set of illustrated volumes to be made available for public subscription: the so-called *Kronprinzenwerk*. This scientific labor did not merely reflect empire; it actively forged an explicit vision of a particularly Habsburg empire, one that united different cultures as it promoted their autonomous development.[8]

What about Nations?

By the last third of the nineteenth century the empire of the Habsburgs increasingly asserted its unique ability to create a productive unity out of the cultural diversity of its peoples. Why did this issue matter? Was the Habsburg Monarchy fundamentally more culturally or socially diverse than other contemporary European states? The second half of the nineteenth century saw the rise of powerful nationalist political movements across Europe. They increasingly explained their nations' distinctiveness in cultural terms symbolized by their different language use and religious practice—ideas they owed largely to popularized versions of the writings of Johann Gottfried Herder (1744–1803). By 1900 many nationalists argued that national differences were in fact unbridgeable and that national communities should have autonomous rights of self-cultivation and political organization in a manner reminiscent of liberal arguments about the natural rights of individuals.

In the Habsburg Empire, nationalist arguments often developed in relation to specific institutional spaces such as the courts or schools created by the empire. Many nationalist political battles in the late nineteenth century, for example, focused specifically on linguistic usage and language rights in public life. In doing so, they built at first on Habsburg traditional functional practices of publishing decrees or providing primary education in vernacular languages. When Austrian and Hungarian legislatures passed constitutional laws in the 1860s, however, they anchored the traditional expectations about language use in constitutional law. This in turn created many rich sites for developing a politics based on the implementation of promises around equality of language use.

This book treats political nationalism in Habsburg central Europe as a product of imperial structures and regional traditions, not as sui generis expressions of transhistorical ethnic groups the way that nineteenth century activists argued. Historians have of course long ago rejected such explanations, but they have been less successful in developing explanations that relate the concepts of empire and nationhood in a productive fashion. Concepts of nationhood and ideas of empire depended on each other for their coherence. As intimately intertwined subjects, they developed in dialogue with each other, rather than as binary opposites. By 1900 many ideologists of empire harbored nationalist beliefs, and nationalists regularly sought political solutions within the legal framework of empire. Nationalist movements organized around ideas of cultural difference played a key role in many of the empire's political and social institutions. Still, their prominence in high politics was not necessarily reflected in their centrality to daily life concerns. Nations mattered most to people when it appeared that their fundamental cultural rights were under threat (usually by another nation). But before they could matter, nationalists had to explain these rights, make them relevant to local social life, and warn when they were threatened.

Nationalism may have stirred up passions in group situations—as in rituals surrounding the taking of the decennial census or on election days—but its centrality often faded once an event had ended and more quotidian concerns took over. Nationalist movements did not always influence the concerns and rhythms of everyday life in more than a passing manner.[9] Attempts to persuade people to pattern their economic behaviors or educational goals along nationalist lines often failed to gain much popular traction. The mere existence of linguistic, religious, and regional differences among the citizens of empire did not by themselves determine the course of imperial history. Nor did these differences alone create a sense that the world was divided among ethnic nations with equal claims on political power. At the dawn of the twentieth century, the insistence that all people belonged to ethnic or national communities must be understood partly as a product of political work accomplished by nationalist activists. It was also, however, a product of the ways agents of the empire categorized its diverse peoples in order to govern them more effectively.[10]

Considering the Experiences of Empire

In the past thirty years dedicated scholars of central and eastern European history have revised—often radically—many of the public's most cherished presumptions about the history of the Habsburg Empire. They no longer see the empire as an anachronism among states in the nineteenth century, nor do they see nationalist conflict in simple and unchanging terms. Their studies have proposed exciting interpretations of local or regional phenomena, particularly in their focus on vibrant political cultures in the empire. The very multilingual character of empire itself spurred historians of the Habsburg Monarchy to adopt creative transnational and interdisciplinary approaches to studying the empire. It has made the empire's historians into innovative leaders in the field of European history. Their work has also begun to make historians of self-styled nation-states think more creatively about cultural differences that may lurk just below the surface of assertions of national homogeneity. At the same time, however, very few authors have used these revisionist works to retool our broad narratives of the empire as a whole.[11]

If among scholars of Europe, Habsburg history has become known as a laboratory for creative innovation in historical studies, this news has also been slow to reach nonspecialists within and beyond the academy. General studies of Europe and modern history treat the region as an exceptional corner of Europe, often due to the presence of several ethnic and religious groups in its societies, but also because of its problematic economic development, often characterized as "backward."[12] As insightful an historian as the late Tony Judt could write in 1996, for example, that:

> Certainly the centers of economic and cultural gravity moved around quite dramatically . . . But they rarely moved very far East, and never beyond Vienna. Whatever the passing brilliance of the civilizations of Prague or Vilna, they were never capitals of something definably European in the way that was at different moments true of Florence, Madrid, Amsterdam, Paris, London, or Vienna.[13]

As Peter Bugge points out, not only does Prague lie to the east of Vienna on Judt's mental map of Europe—a common geographic error among historians—but he also presumes that the reader will understand implicitly why in fact Prague (or for that matter Vilna) should not be considered definably European in their history.[14]

European historians may express their sense of the region's difference in the more objective sounding language of economic development or attribute it in part to the effects of the Cold War. Moreover, as several scholars have argued lucidly, central and eastern Europe's imagined difference from the West has often served to confirm the rest of Europe's comforting normalcy.[15] This trend is particularly clear in the spate of books on the First World War written in the last decade, some to mark the centenary of its outbreak. Almost all continued a tradition of pathologizing the Habsburg Empire as teetering on the verge of collapse thanks to nationalist conflict.[16]

We need not gravitate to an opposite extreme by asserting central and eastern Europe's blanket similarity to the rest of Europe. Rather, we need to understand the history of this region—its institutions and its economic, social, political, and cultural development—within, not outside of, a broadly comparative European context. This book underscores just how similar the Habsburg Empire was to other European states while highlighting moments when it pioneered new ideas about nationhood and new practices of governance. Like every European state, however, it also developed distinctive institutions and practices that make its history unique.

Above all, this book is an argument about the character, development, and enduring legacies of empire in central and eastern Europe. It does not claim to offer an exhaustive history of the Habsburg Monarchy. Some readers may not find significant material on important regions or events in which they have a particular interest; others may wish for more coverage of foreign policy and great power politics—both admittedly subjects of critical importance to Habsburg history. Such lacunae are inevitable in a book driven by revisionist arguments about why empire and its institutions mattered so much to so many for so long, rather than by an encyclopedic impulse to describe the empire's vast and varied histories. Nevertheless, as the author, I am keenly aware of significant gaps in the text, of left-out events—some critical, and some which could perhaps modify the arguments of the book—and of the tendency to simplify when writing a synthetic work. *The Habsburg Empire* is clearly indebted to superb work by other historians, especially in the ways it builds on their attempts to move the focus of history writing in this region away from questions of nationhood. It is limited, however, by its changing focus on particular regions and developments.

Since the collapse of the Habsburg Monarchy at the end of the First World War in 1918, narratives of nationhood have dominated its history.[17]

Less often have scholars made the empire itself the focus of their interpretations. In an oft-cited attempt to push scholars to take a less nationally and more socially oriented approach to the region, for example, historian István Deák argued in 1967 that "there were no dominant nationalities in the Austro-Hungarian Monarchy. There were dominant classes, institutions, interest groups and professions."[18] Several influential historians of the region in the 1980s followed this line of argument. In 1980 Gary Cohen and John Boyer published influential studies of politics and society in Prague and Vienna, which abandoned traditional presumptions about the primacy of nationhood in the region.[19] In Cohen's analysis, national belonging was a socially contingent factor, not given at birth or determined by descent. Especially among Prague's working classes in the nineteenth century, a sense of national identification often depended on the presence or absence of social institutions that promoted those identifications. Boyer analyzed the rise of Christian Socialism in Vienna in terms of ward politics, testing the ways in which broader ideological constructions and political cultures grew out of specific neighborhood concerns and situational alliances.

At the same time, influential studies by Austrian scholar Gerald Stourzh and several of his students (most notably Emil Brix, Hannelore Burger, and Maria Kurz) interrogated the specific ways in which Habsburg imperial institutions such as schools, the judicial system, or the Austrian census managed practical issues surrounding linguistic diversity.[20] These scholars' ability to tack between local examples and imperial politics undermined the notion that the existence of linguistic differences had somehow determined social relations and institutional development in the region. Instead, they showed for the first time how imperial institutions and administrative practices shaped nationalist efforts. Toward the end of the Cold War, scholars in economics, anthropology, political science, and literary studies also began to examine more critically and productively the surviving presumptions about economic backwardness or unbridgeable cultural difference that allegedly made central and eastern Europe somehow different from the rest of Europe.[21]

Since the late 1990s historians of the Habsburg Monarchy have often been in the forefront of European historians in developing cultural, transnational, or comparative approaches that question some of the most tenacious binary concepts that have traditionally structured most accounts of Western versus Eastern Europe: "civic nationhood" versus "ethnic nationhood," "developed" versus "backward," "democratic" versus "authoritarian," "ethnic homogeneity" versus "ethnic mosaic." Their work shows that these supposed oppositions largely fail when tested against evidence drawn from local society.[22] Today the field of Habsburg history flourishes as a site of remarkable creativity and innovation.

Historians of the Habsburg Monarchy have in fact taught their colleagues who study other regions in Europe a great deal about how to think about subjects like nationhood, multilingualism, indifference to nation, and perhaps most importantly, their typologies of empire and nation. What remains odd, however, is that few historians or editorial collectives have produced broader narrative histories that focus on empire rather than on nations as the moving force in the region's developmental trajectory. Several volumes in the remarkable project *Die Habsburgermonarchie 1848–1918* series published by the Austrian Academy of Sciences, for example, organize and structure their subjects by national categories. There are of course good reasons for maintaining such schemas. Until recently historical research and training in Europe and the United States has remained organized largely by national schools, making it difficult to imagine an effective alternate model for a large collective project.[23]

This book asks historians to make the Habsburg Empire itself the subject of historical inquiry by foregrounding the common experiences of empire. It investigates how shared imperial institutions, administrative practices, and cultural programs helped to shape local society in every region of the empire, from the late eighteenth century until the first decades of the twentieth century. It examines how these collective elements gave imperial citizens in every corner of the empire experiences that crossed linguistic, confessional, and regional divides, as well as chronological boundaries. Even after the Habsburg Monarchy formally ceased to exist in November 1918, common elements of imperial practice continued to shape many people's expectations, whether they were about welfare benefits, military conscription, or the question of how political life should function. Prominent nationalist politicians in the successor states, from Thomas Masaryk (1850–1937) in Czechoslovakia to Alcide De Gasperi (1881–1954) in Italy or Anton Korošec (1872–1940) in Yugoslavia were also heavily influenced by their formative experiences as important actors in imperial politics. They often adopted familiar laws, practices, and institutions for their new states. At the same time, however, they loudly rejected any legacy of empire as incompatible with democracy and national self-determination.

As we shift our lens farther away from the nation-states that today dominate the map of central and eastern Europe to focus instead on empire as our subject, we desperately need new general narratives around which to organize our findings. We do not need a single narrative, but we do need large-scale alternative stories with the capacity to serve as branches on which we can array the superb new work of the past few decades. We cannot continue to ask students of history to read and profit intellectually from that work, if at the same time we continue to fall back on basic narratives that contradict the new work. With this book I hope to offer one possible set of alternative narratives around which to organize our changing field.

CHAPTER ONE

The Accidental Empire

*The Greek or Roman father did not merely bring up a son
for the family; he brought up a citizen for the Republic. The young
man was quickly made aware of the advantages it conferred, learning
to perceive in it a perfection wanting in other states, and was
naturally moved by such perfection.*

— *Joseph von Sonnenfels,* Über die Liebe des Vaterlandes, *1771*

To Make a State

In 1770 the government of Empress Maria Theresa (1717–1780) sought to make an accurate count of the population in the western regions of her realm and to apply a new system of house numbers to "all towns, markets, and villages, even in the most scattered localities."[1] Obtaining an accurate picture of the population was critical to the process of conscripting troops for the military. More importantly, however, it was crucial to accomplishing the main goal of Maria Theresa's reign: forging more effective institutions of rule to create a state. Previous attempts at obtaining an accurate count of the population in the 1760s—generally provided by parish priests or local administrators—had yielded such widely divergent and useless numbers that one of the empress's privy counsellors had exclaimed in frustration that he doubted that "with these tables a state could be made."[2] Nevertheless, for pressing reasons we will learn more about below, Maria Theresa had to make a state.

The Habsburg government decided to remedy the deficit in its knowledge by using the military to carry out both the count and the house numbering. This option did carry with it some risks. When the military ventured into the countryside, it usually met with open hostility from local populations desperate to protect their young men from a form of military service that could last as long as twenty years. In some villages families would hide their men or send them into the forests. In other cases young men might mutilate their bodies—usually breaking a leg or an arm—in order to avoid the fate of forced conscription. In still other cases a mistaken belief that the military would spare married men produced sudden waves of local marriages. Anticipating this kind of trouble, the government instructed local priests in 1770 to quiet such fears wherever they could. The priests should assure the population that this census was not tied to military conscription. The government, however, doubted the effectiveness of this measure.

Much to everyone's surprise, local populations in 1770 behaved in some radically unexpected ways. In general they treated the appearance of the military in their villages as a positive event, often greeting the soldiers with enthusiasm. Why? The government had assigned the military a critical third task as well, beyond simply counting the population and numbering its houses. It had also charged the military to investigate the "condition" of the local population—that is, its health, level of literacy, and the quality of local living conditions (types of housing, sanitary conditions, effectiveness of teachers, state of the local economy). Once people understood that the military would report their condition— and their grievances—to the empress, they welcomed the soldiers, treating them as representatives of the ruler with whom they hoped to register their particular complaints.[3] As one officer reported from the crownland of Carniola, the people had generally behaved "in a peaceful and willing manner, not for any love of a soldier's life, but in the hope that their *Robot* [forced labor] and dues in kind would be diminished."[4]

These surprisingly positive encounters between local peasantries and a developing Austrian state capture three critical themes of this book. In the first place, these encounters offer typical examples of an eighteenth-century imperial regime seeking to consolidate its control over several very different territories by mapping their geographies, counting their people, numbering their houses, and for the first time, learning more about their people's living conditions. More than generating mere accounting, these state-building practices sought eventually to replace traditional local relationships of power with new loyalties that tied individuals to the central state. To do so, however, meant breaking the traditional political dominance exercised by regional powerbrokers, the local nobility. In 1770, for example, the central government purposely avoided delegating the tasks of counting and description to the local nobility or even to the local clergy. Rather, the regime sent its own loyal instrument, the military, to ascertain the truth. In doing so, it bypassed the local nobility to strengthen an incipient bond between the local population and the empire.[5]

Second, Maria Theresa's enumerative project reflects some fundamentally new thinking by the Habsburg dynasty and its advisers about the proper relationship between a government and its subjects, both aristocrats and commoners alike. This new relationship between ruler and ruled saw the people of the empire in essentially comparable and interchangeable terms, rather than in terms of traditional hierarchies of privileged and less privileged classes, each with different sets of rights.[6]

A third theme that we repeatedly encounter arises from how local peasants engaged with the men sent to count and describe them. In towns and villages across the monarchy, peasants repeatedly demanded access to the visiting military representatives to complain to them about local conditions. What is important here is not the specific content of the complaints—even some representatives of the military in 1770 doubted that what they heard was completely true—but rather the popular belief that one could complain to state officials, not local notables, to redress grievances. Peasants did not harbor naïve beliefs in the innate goodness of a far-away ruler who would rectify local injustices, once brought to her attention. The peasants who complained to the military appear to have been well aware of the strained relations between their empress and their local landlords. They took good advantage of this situation by casting their lot most enthusiastically with the central state and demonstrating a hopeful confidence in its ability to act on their behalf. Here we have an early example of local people making empire their own by using its emerging structures to argue for their own agendas.

From Marginal to Global

A centralized Habsburg state emerged in the second half of the eighteenth century out of various territories acquired by the Habsburg dynasty since the thirteenth century. Where exactly was this emerging new state located, and what kinds of populations did it encompass in the eighteenth century? In the 1780s the Habsburg dynasty's holdings stretched from today's cities of Innsbruck in the west to Lviv in the east, from Milan and Florence on the Italian peninsula to Antwerp on the North Sea and Cluj in the Carpathian Mountains, from Prague in Bohemia to Vukovar and down to Belgrade in the south. The Habsburgs held territories that today are located in twelve different European countries and that in the late eighteenth century included speakers of languages known today as Croatian, Czech, Flemish, French, German, Hungarian, Italian, Ladin, Polish, Romanian, Serb, Slovak, Slovene, Ukrainian, and Yiddish.[7] This diversity extended to religious practice as well. Although the Roman Catholic Church traditionally held a privileged place in the Habsburgs' lands, their subjects also included Orthodox Christians, Greek Catholics or Uniates, Calvinists, Lutherans, Jews, Armenian Christians, and Unitarians.

This linguistic and religious diversity was typical for larger states in early modern Europe, from the Spanish or French Empires in the west to the Polish-Lithuanian Commonwealth or the emerging Russian Empire in the east. Because of the ways in which states gained or lost territories in war, through dynastic marriages, or thanks to negotiated trades, their lands did not necessarily have any historical or cultural relationships to each other, nor were they necessarily even geographically contiguous. European dynastic states also did not rest on unified administrative institutions or unified cultural practices (such as common language use), and certainly not on a shared sense of identification among a ruler's subjects. Instead, Europe's dynasties treated territorial units as family possessions or as the fruits of military conquest to be traded at will. In most of those units, however, powerful noble families generally controlled taxation, the local administration of justice, and military conscription. Their representatives met irregularly in diets, or regional parliaments. The Habsburg rulers depended on negotiations with these diets for tax revenues and military conscripts.

The Habsburgs had started out as a relatively minor noble family with lands and a castle in what is today the Swiss canton of Aargau.[8] From this small territory the first Habsburg to achieve political fame, Count Rudolf IV (1218–1291), was elected German king and Holy

Remains of the Habsburg castle in Canton Aargau, Switzerland. 1903 color print by J. Lange. Credit: HIP/Art Resource, NY.

Roman emperor in 1273.[9] At the time—and until its collapse in 1806—the Holy Roman Empire was a loose confederation of large and small sovereign political states, stretching from the Italian peninsula in the south to Jutland in the north, and from contemporary France in the west to today's Poland in the east. Its nominal head, an emperor elected for life by the empire's most powerful princes, or "electors," enjoyed some international prestige, social status, and cultural influence with this title.[10] However, his largely ceremonial position gave the emperor little authority over the more than three hundred political units that made up the empire. In fact, by choosing the unassuming Rudolf of Habsburg over his more impressive rivals in 1273, the electors had prevented other more powerful claimants from threatening the balance of power in central Europe.

By the end of Rudolf's reign as Holy Roman emperor, however, the Habsburgs had managed to become key political players in central Europe. They had added considerably to the family's territories and moved the geographic center of their holdings eastward by winning the duchies of Lower and Upper Austria (including Vienna), Styria, Carinthia, and the Margraviate of Carniola from the Babenberg family. Later, in the next century, the Habsburg family added the principality of Tyrol to this new cluster of territories. As the family's new power base, these territories—which roughly match today's Austria and Slovenia—became known collectively as the Habsburgs' "hereditary lands" because the family established a right to permanent succession in them, while losing its Swiss holdings. Afterwards the term "Austria"—from two of the duchies—came to be used for these lands.

Following Rudolf's death in 1291, it was not until 1452 that another Habsburg, Frederick III (1415–1493), was elected Holy Roman emperor.[11] During his lifetime Frederick managed to have his son Maximilian I (1459–1519) elected his successor as emperor, establishing a practice that kept the imperial title in the family (with only one short exception in the eighteenth century) until the dissolution of the Holy Roman Empire in 1806. Both Frederick and Maximilian expanded the family's fortunes by arranging a series of brilliant dynastic marriages. Maximilian's marriage to Mary of Burgundy brought the family the resources of one of Europe's wealthiest states. The same strategy gained for two of Maximilian's children, Philip and Margaret, the newly united kingdom of Spain with its overseas empire. Maximilian's grandson (Philip's son) Charles V (1500–1558) inherited an empire that spanned the globe, from Spain and its holdings in the Americas to Burgundy, Austria, and the Holy Roman Empire. In yet another marriage coup, Maximilian betrothed two of Charles V's siblings, Mary (1505–1558) and Ferdinand (1503–1564), to King Louis II of Hungary and Bohemia and to his sister Anne, respectively. When in 1526 young King Louis of Hungary and Bohemia died in battle against the armies of the Ottoman Empire, the Hungarian and Bohemian estates, or parliaments, elected his brother-in-law Ferdinand of Habsburg to be the next King of Hungary and Bohemia. The Hungarian crown gave the Habsburgs a powerful claim to two regions historically linked to Hungary: the Kingdom of Croatia in the southwest and the principality of Transylvania in the east. Habsburg rule in Hungary, however, remained little more than a claim, since most of Hungary and Transylvania remained under Ottoman—or Ottoman-allied—rule for the next 175 years.

At the end of his reign in 1556, Charles V divided an unwieldy global empire between a western, or Spanish, branch of the family under his son Philip II (1527–1598) and an eastern, or Austrian, branch under his brother, who became Emperor Ferdinand I.[12] For the next 150 years the Spanish and Austrian branches of the Habsburg family remained closely allied, reinforcing their special relationship with frequent intra-family marriages. When the Spanish branch of the family died out for lack of a male heir in 1700, the French king, Louis XIV, claimed the Spanish throne. A war over the succession to the Spanish throne pitted the Austrian Habsburgs and their allies against France. When the war finally ended in 1714, the Austrian Habsburgs had lost the Spanish throne to a junior branch of the French royal house.[13] In part the loss of the Spanish territories would facilitate the building of a territorial Habsburg state in central Europe in the next century.

Sex and the Empire

The origins of a unified Habsburg state in Central Europe, unofficially called "Austria" after the dynasty's core territories, date to a specific series of laws promulgated in the early eighteenth century and later known collectively as the "Pragmatic Sanction." Ostensibly, this bundle of laws dealt with the most intimate of family affairs: the worrisome lack of a male heir. Unlike the situation in Britain, for example, where women of the Tudor and Stuart dynasties had inherited the throne, traditions originating in the so-called Salic law restricted the succession to males in many continental European states. No woman could be elected to lead the Holy Roman Empire, although there was no reason why a woman could not rule in the territories the Habsburgs held directly. In formal terms, however, the Habsburgs held their core Austrian lands as a fief from the Holy Roman emperor, and if that position passed out of the family, would another emperor challenge their rule in their own territories?[14]

Given that his two sons, Joseph I (1678–1711) and Charles VI (1685–1740), had so far fathered either daughters or no children at all, Emperor

Leopold I (1640–1705) feared that the Austrian branch of the dynasty would die out the way its Spanish counterpart had in 1701. In 1703 Leopold decreed the *pactum mutuae successionis* that forbade the monarchy's partition and allowed that in the absence of a male heir, a female descendant could rule the core Habsburg lands. In 1713 Charles VI altered Leopold's agreement to place his own two daughters ahead of his deceased elder brother's daughter. The various diets ratified this agreement swiftly. Fears that the end of the Habsburg dynasty could bring war and instability to the region made this Pragmatic Sanction more attractive to the diets, which might otherwise have rejected it as an encroachment on their prerogatives. They all agreed that barring the miraculous appearance of a male heir, when Charles VI died, they would confirm his elder daughter Maria Theresa as their ruler. Charles then spent considerable political and financial capital trying to persuade the other European powers to accept the arrangement, while paradoxically doing nothing to prepare his daughter Maria Theresa for her impending royal responsibilities.[15]

As intimately bound up with problems of reproduction as these laws may have been, they turned out later to have had another more critical aspect. The Pragmatic Sanction was the first significant piece of legislation that treated what could be called a "composite monarchy"—the diverse territories under Habsburg rule including the kingdoms of Bohemia and Hungary—as "indivisible and inseparable," that is, as a single political unit.[16] At this time, the Habsburgs' territorial holdings were indeed geographically more consolidated than they had been a century earlier, although they still included some noncontiguous territories in the Netherlands and on the Italian peninsula. After 1700, contemporary cartographers had begun to refer more frequently to a greater "Austria" (meaning more than simply the duchies of Lower and Upper Austria) and to the Habsburgs as the "House of Austria." Mirroring Charles VI's and Maria Theresa's state-building efforts, maps of central Europe increasingly centered their depictions of the Habsburgs' lands on Austrian Vienna rather than on the Holy Roman Empire with its capital at Frankfurt, although the latter remained the source of their most illustrious title.

Yet if contemporaries gradually came to view the Habsburgs' territories as a single state called Austria, this statehood was hardly rooted in

institutional realities. Accustomed as we are to the institutional and administrative homogeneity claimed by territorial nation-states today, we
might be tempted to see the Habsburgs' territories on those maps around
1700 as forming a coherent whole. This presumption would be erroneous.
The character and extent of Habsburg rule differed substantially from
place to place within the borders of their lands.

The Habsburgs exercised direct control over fiscal, administrative,
and judicial institutions in their hereditary lands (Lower and Upper
Austria, Styria, Carinthia, Carniola, and Tyrol) through an Austrian
chancellery located in Vienna. By 1700 they wielded almost as much
control over their Bohemian crownlands (Bohemia, Moravia, Silesia).[17]
They did not seek to exert such systematic control over their territories
on the Italian peninsula. They exerted the least amount of control over
Hungary, whose nobles resisted Habsburg efforts to incorporate it into a
larger common state after its conquest from the Ottomans.

Although in the long run the Pragmatic Sanction became the legal
basis for a unitary Habsburg state, in the short run, Charles VI's efforts to gain its acceptance by Europe's opportunistic powers failed
dramatically. When Charles died in 1740, his twenty-three-year-old
daughter, Maria Theresa (1717–1780), immediately found herself under
attack by rapacious neighbors. Seeing a rare opportunity, Frederick II
of Prussia (1712–1786; known as "the Great") invaded the rich and
highly populated province of Silesia. At the same time, Elector Charles
Albert of Bavaria (1697–1745)—with the support of the French, the
Saxons, and a part of the Bohemian nobility in the diet—laid claim to
neighboring Bohemia and had himself elected Holy Roman emperor
as Charles VII over Maria Theresa's husband, Francis Stephen of
Lorraine (1708–1765).[18]

With no other available option, the beleaguered Maria Theresa
began her reign by making concessions to the Hungarian nobility. She
needed funds, she needed troops, and she needed both immediately. In
1741 she had herself crowned King of Hungary, and at a meeting of the
Hungarian Diet in Pressburg/Poszony she sought financial and military assistance.[19] Dressed in white and gold—the Hungarian colors of
the time—and contrary to later depictions and descriptions, without her

Maria Theresa and her children in 1776. Painted by Heinrich Füger. Credit: Gianni Dagli Orti/The Art Archive at Art Resource, NY.

six-month-old son, Joseph present (she exhibited him to the diet nine days later), Maria Theresa made an emotional appeal, swearing to uphold the diet's privileges[20]:

> The very existence of the kingdom of Hungary, of our own person, of our children and of our crown are now at stake. Now that we are forsaken by all, our sole resource is the fidelity, arms, and long-tried valor of the Hungarians. In regard to ourself [sic], the faithful Estates and Orders of Hungary will enjoy our hearty cooperation.[21]

Her entreaty elicited offers of "life and blood to our king Maria Theresa" by the assembled notables, although less well-known was the hard bargaining that preceded this outpouring of loyalty.[22] Thanks largely to

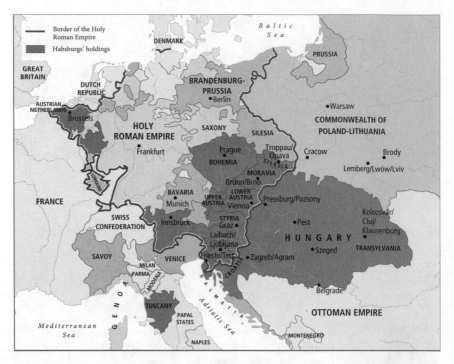

Habsburg Territories at the end of the War of the Austrian Succession, 1748

Hungarian support, Maria Theresa swiftly changed the fortunes of war, turning the tables on the Bavarians by capturing their capital of Munich at the end of 1741. The Austrians regained Bohemia, Moravia, and a small part of Silesia, as well as defeating the Bavarians and the French, whose harsh occupation policies had in any event alienated their would-be Bohemian allies. In 1745, with the death of Charles Albert of Bavaria, Maria Theresa had her husband, Francis Stephen, elected Holy Roman emperor. In 1748 the Treaty of Aachen officially ended the War of the Austrian Succession. Maria Theresa had successfully held off all challenges to her rights, but she had lost most of Silesia, her most economically valuable province, to Prussia.

Her country's military and financial unpreparedness for war made it clear to Maria Theresa that she must reform her state, and quickly too, if it was to remain a great power in eighteenth-century Europe. She would also need a new series of alliances to help her win back Silesia from Prussia. She would have to create a standing army that could compete effectively with Prussia's reformed military, and she would have to integrate her territories into a far more effective, unitary state. Maria Theresa never did regain Silesia, but certainly not for lack of trying. In the 1750s she and her foreign minister, Count (later Prince) Wenzel Anton Kaunitz (1711–1794), orchestrated something of a diplomatic revolution in central Europe.[23] Abandoning Britain, Austria allied itself to its traditional enemy, France, for the first time in centuries, an alliance that was eventually embodied—literally—in the marriage of Maria Theresa's youngest daughter, Maria Antonia (1755–1793), to the future King Louis XVI of France. This strategic transformation was aimed especially against Prussia. Only Maria Theresa's obsessive desire to regain Silesia allowed her to overcome her powerful anti-French prejudices. The failure to regain Silesia in the Seven Year's War (1756–1763), however, left Austria with a nominal French alliance, and with far greater concerns in the east where Imperial Russia sought aggressively to expand at the expense of its neighbors, the Ottoman Empire, Sweden, and the Polish-Lithuanian Commonwealth.[24] In fact it was on the eastern front that Maria Theresa eventually gained territorial compensation for the loss of Silesia. In 1772 she partook—albeit reluctantly—with Frederick II of Prussia and Catherine II (the Great) of Russia in the first partition of the Polish-Lithuanian Commonwealth.

Using that state's alleged internal disorder as a pretext, these three neighboring powers divided about 30 percent of the Polish-Lithuanian Commonwealth's territory among themselves. Although Maria Theresa had originally criticized Russian and Prussian intentions with respect to the commonwealth ("The word 'partition' repels me!"), her foreign minister, Kaunitz, nevertheless made certain that she received a significant share of the spoils. The new territory was christened (in Latin) the "Kingdom of Galicia and Lodomeria," after the medieval Rus principalities of Halych and Vladimir, which the Hungarian crown had claimed in the twelfth century.[25] Along with her state-building impulses, Maria Theresa clearly knew the value of mobilizing her family's mythic history to overcome any scruples about taking new territories.

State Building and Reform

In 1748, immediately following the War of the Austrian Succession, Maria Theresa implemented a barrage of administrative reforms to strengthen her military and to create a more effective and centralized state. Her state chancellor, Count Friedrich Wilhelm von Haugwitz (1702–1765), forced the diets of the Hereditary Lands to increase their tax contributions to the military budget, while creating a standing army of some 108,000 men. Additionally, Haugwitz compelled the individual diets of those lands to grant the government these funds for ten-year periods rather than annually, thus diminishing their ability to bargain with the state when it needed military funds.

Continuing the institutional process of making formerly autonomous kingdoms into provinces of a central state, local and provincial administrators were increasingly made responsible to Vienna rather than to the various diets. In 1749 Haugwitz merged the Bohemian Chancellery with its counterpart that administered the Hereditary Lands.[26] In 1751 Maria Theresa created a single supreme court located in Vienna for both the Bohemian and Austrian lands. Over the next decades the government continued to experiment with institutions designed to centralize administration of the state. Vigorous provincial opposition often forced Maria Theresa to modify or postpone implementing these proposals, but her government doggedly kept up its efforts, often proposing yet new sets of institutions.

In their pursuit of territorial integration and centralization, the eighteenth-century Habsburgs and their advisers did not follow a single model of state building. The remarkable reform rulers of the eighteenth century—Empress Maria Theresa (1717–1780) and her sons, the Emperors Joseph II (1741–1790) and Leopold II (1747–1792)—developed ad hoc ideas about how best to unite their territories more effectively. All three shared fundamental long-term goals: to stabilize state finances by taxing the nobility; to raise productivity among peasant producers by relaxing—or ending—feudal relations; to encourage the expansion of domestic industry, trade, travel, and communication networks; to diminish regional guild restrictions on manufacture; to promote the moral and practical education of their subjects; and to reform the Catholic Church by bringing religious practice under state control.

Like some of their contemporaries in Europe, these three ambitious Habsburg rulers have often been called "enlightened despots." The term refers in part to their assertions of absolute centralized power as the means to reform the state and to transform the societies over which they ruled. Absolutism (or despotism) for these monarchs specifically references their refusal to share power with the nobility. The term "Enlightenment" refers to a loose set of intellectual networks and cultural movements across Europe in the late seventeenth and eighteenth centuries that celebrated the growth of knowledge and encouraged its explicit application to social institutions and political structures in order to improve the condition of humanity. The eighteenth century saw a veritable explosion of published works of literature, science, history, religion, and philosophy in the territories ruled by the Habsburgs. Eighteenth-century European society also experienced an explosion in literacy rates and an increase in public social settings—and not simply elite ones—where such ideas might be openly read, discussed, and debated. The Enlightenment interest in science and in humanist studies also made explicitly secular approaches to governing more possible in a world still dominated by religious institutions and cultures. At the same time, however, religious and moral questions remained at the heart of Enlightenment concerns. While Maria Theresa and her sons debated policy with their advisers in far more utilitarian and functionalist terms than had their predecessors, and while they sought advice from a range of educated secular experts, they nevertheless continued to acknowledge the fundamental value of religion to society.

The rise both of literacy and of interregional networks of humanistic and scientific research made it possible for all kinds of people to comment on or argue publicly and privately with the broader processes of reform undertaken by the monarchs. Although noble-dominated diets and noble commentators had long been able to make their varied opinions known, it was in the eighteenth century that people from the commercial, administrative, and entrepreneurial professions also began to articulate their interests and attitudes publicly toward state policies. During the second half of the century, local society in cities and towns like Vienna, Prague, Brünn/Brno, Kaschau/Kassa, and Pressburg/Pozsony created new kinds of sites of public discussion, from coffee houses to semipublic salons to museums. Here members of middle-class society met or might occasionally rub shoulders with aristocrats while exchanging opinions about the religious, philosophical, and artistic questions of the day. Soon after the municipal government of Kaschau/Kassa erected a town theater in 1781, for example, the city fathers undertook alterations specifically to establish a coffee house on the north side of the building.[27] By the 1790s, sites of sociability like coffee houses or scientific societies in towns or agricultural clubs in the countryside enabled their members to debate and develop original policy ideas. As we will see, these settings served as models for the many voluntary associations that exploded on the urban scene in the early nineteenth century.[28]

Equally important, when it came to the transformation of Enlightenment ideas into political, social, economic, or cultural programs, were the many Freemasons' lodges that sprang up in the Habsburg lands starting in the 1740s. Thanks in part to the support of Maria Theresa's husband, Francis Stephen, who was himself a Mason, lodges with thousands of members established themselves during this period despite the vocal disapproval of the papacy.[29] The lodges were not exactly sites of social equality, nor were they particularly secular in character: by the 1770s a good number of Austrian Masons were themselves priests who wanted to see the Catholic Church purged of what they termed "old-fashioned" or "intolerant" attitudes.[30] The lodges also afforded their members settings where they might debate and test all kinds of reform ideas. In Hungary it was largely Protestant religious thinkers, writers, and aristocrats who engaged with Enlightenment ideas to develop and promote reform programs. Thus, it was not simply urban-based Freemasonry that offered sites for sociability and debate. In Bohemia, for example, local notables organized agrarian societies designed both to spread knowledge about modern agricultural techniques to ordinary peasants and to circulate information about new technologies or new crops among their wealthier members.[31]

The contemporary theories of political economy whose merits were debated in pamphlet literature, in salons, and in agrarian societies and

Freemason lodges offered the Habsburgs many possible models for reform. The physiocrats, for example, located prosperity specifically in the agricultural wealth produced by a prosperous peasant population. Mercantilists, on the other hand, promoted local industries and (regulated) international trade through a policy of protective tariffs. Cameralists sought to reorganize government institutions by dividing and designating specific functions for them (such as ministries in a cabinet) to make them more efficient and effective. Central European Jansenists promoted improved public morality through the spread of a vigorous, reformed, and far less Jesuitical form of Catholicism. The point that matters is this: new social actors engaged in fierce intellectual debates about politics, economics, and society and in so doing, produced an ideological apparatus in service of reform-minded monarchs.

If the scale of the reform programs contemplated by the Habsburg rulers seemed challenging for such a large empire, at least they could now call upon self-proclaimed men of science to conceptualize and justify specific reform programs by referring to empirical studies of real conditions. As we saw at the beginning of this chapter, the eighteenth century was not simply an age of philosophy and science; it was also an age of information gathering, of mapping, of statistical studies of all kinds. The ultimate function of all of these applied forms of knowledge—like that of the enlightened despot—was to serve the general well-being of state and society.

The expanding and increasingly centralized bureaucracies of the eighteenth century continued to employ many of the regional nobles who might otherwise have lost political influence as the diets gradually ceded more areas of competence to Vienna. In the case of Bohemia, for example, Maria Theresa even retained the services of several Bohemian nobles who had momentarily abandoned her for the Bavarians in 1741, installing them in both the provincial and central bureaucracies.[32] The ambitious character of the reform programs produced a sharp increase in civil servants' administrative reach into society. It also produced a growing demand for new servants of the state to take on a rapidly expanding workload. In Hungary during Maria Theresa's reign, the ruling council saw its workload rise by 400 percent, while the numbers of officials who dealt with correspondence alone rose from fifty to over one hundred twenty! Clearly administrative change required more and better educated state employees to manage reform. Although nobles and aristocrats usually occupied the highest echelons of this expanding bureaucracy, educated sons of the middle classes were increasingly filling positions at the middle and lower levels. Moreover, Maria Theresa handed out more patents of nobility than ever before to commoners who earned distinction through their service to the state. During her reign almost 40 percent of all the people who gained a patent of nobility came from the expanding bureaucracy.[33]

At the same time, the need to maintain an expanded military forced Maria Theresa to end the tax exemptions enjoyed by the nobility and the church in her Bohemian and Austrian lands in 1748. This critical measure undermined the traditional social privileges enjoyed by the nobility, even though the state assessed noble and church lands at a lower rate than peasant-owned lands. Maria Theresa also used fiscal policy to promote interregional and international trade. She maintained the privileged tax status that her father had conferred upon the towns of Trieste/Trst (really a fishing village) and Fiume/Rijeka on the Adriatic in 1719. This status freed the towns' merchants from liability for normal duties on goods exported and imported through the city and thereby gave them an incentive to bring their businesses there. With the loss of most of Silesia to Prussia in 1741, Maria Theresa's government also hoped to redirect more commerce away from northern trade routes (through Hamburg) as far possible southward through Trieste/Trst and Fiume/Rijeka. As a result both towns grew rapidly into cities over the course of the eighteenth century, and both competed with Venice for Mediterranean trade in the 1760s.[34] By the end of the century a third of the monarchy's exports passed through Trieste/Trst alone, and the town's population surpassed 30,000. Eventually Trieste/Trst became the fourth-largest city in the monarchy and one of Europe's busiest commercial ports.

Meanwhile, in 1779, at the eastern edge of her lands, Maria Theresa conferred free trade privileges comparable to those enjoyed by Trieste/Trst and Fiume/Rijeka on another critical entrepôt, the Galician town of Brody. Brody's incorporation into the Habsburg Monarchy as part of the new Kingdom of Galicia had at first threatened the town's status as a wealthy trading post in a critical east-west network that stretched from

View of Trieste's/Trst's very busy harbor in the eighteenth century. Engraving by Desmaisons after a drawing by Louis Cassas. Credit: Photo © Tallandier/ Bridgeman Images.

Leipzig to Odessa and the Crimea. As a result of Brody's incorporation into Austria, its merchants—mostly Jews—now had to cross several new borders in order to maintain their former trading relationships, and each border crossing required payments of import and export duties. Not wishing to weaken the town's comparative economic advantage, the Habsburg government conferred the special status of a free-trade zone on Brody and its surrounding villages, enabling merchants to exchange their goods there without having to pay duties. In making this decision, Vienna officials had explicitly debated whether to treat Brody as a "free seaport" (*freier Seehafen*) similar to the monarchy's existing Adriatic free ports of Trieste/Trst and Fiume/Rijeka.[35] Their thinking on the issue rested on larger questions of empire-wide economic development, and not simply on the parochial interests of Galicia. Vienna worried that without a favorable tax status, Brody's merchants would decide to move their businesses across the border to neighboring towns in what remained of the Polish-Lithuanian Commonwealth. At the same time, however, the new Galician administration protested vigorously against the privileges granted to the town because it hoped to tax Brody's lucrative trade for itself.

Many of Vienna's economic policies also reinforced the regime's political goal to integrate the Habsburgs' diverse territorial units more effectively into a larger whole. In 1775, for example, after years of planning, negotiation, and wrangling, the government united the Hereditary Lands with the Bohemian lands under a single tariff regime at their borders, allowing complete freedom of trade inside the new borders for the first time. Galicia was next in line for this common tariff regime, but Vienna worried that its comparative economic weakness, and the necessity to reorient regional trade networks and relationships after the partition, made it too vulnerable as yet to participate in a large free trade zone.

Political thinkers in eighteenth-century Europe frequently argued that the military capabilities of a state depended directly on society's economic prosperity. So we cannot understand the full range of Maria Theresa's reforms if we view her state-building policies purely in terms of administrative and fiscal reform. She also sought to improve peasant productivity, to introduce new industries by diminishing local guild powers, and to expand Austria's share of international trade. Since economies in eighteenth-century continental Europe ultimately rested on the productivity and wealth of the peasantry, and because the peasantry bore most of the tax burden, the state took an increasing interest in improving the situation of the peasantry. Countless contemporary observers blamed the fiscal instability of the Habsburg state precisely on the economic inefficiency of the existing organization of rural society.

In most of the territories Maria Theresa governed, peasants were legally and practically bound to the local estate owners. Not only did landowners demand cash or produce from the peasants who leased their lands, but landowners also claimed a certain number of days' labor from the peasants per week (the hated institution known as the *Robot*). The exact number of such days varied considerably by territory, but in many parts of Galicia and Hungary it was more than three days a week, creating a situation that, as one contemporary noted, "makes it impossible for the peasant to cultivate his own plot."[36] None other than Maria

Theresa's son Joseph II made the crucial observation on his first trip to Galicia in 1773 that "the people are so busy with *Robot* that their corn remains un-harvested and is totally neglected and lost."[37] In some regions the law also prevented peasants from migrating elsewhere and even forbade them to marry without the landlord's consent. Moreover, if a peasant wished to challenge his treatment at the hands of his landlord, it was usually the latter who served as the local judge. Taken altogether, one could argue—as did many of Maria Theresa's advisers—that the peasants lacked fundamental control over their own bodies, something the religiously inclined empress also worried must eventually twist their moral character as well as limit their life chances. These constraints on peasant freedom and productivity might best be viewed comparatively in the context of a broad variety of contemporary forms of unfree labor, ranging from serfdom in Imperial Russia to plantation slavery in Europe's American and Caribbean colonies.

Still, it was first and foremost fiscal need, rather than moral outrage, that drove the Vienna government to take on the improvement of agricultural productivity in the territories it governed. Financial considerations also led to perhaps the most unintentionally radical of Maria Theresa's reform efforts, and one that was only fully realized by her sons Joseph II and Leopold II after her death: the modification—if not the complete abrogation—of the institutions that bound most peasants to the landed nobility. Believing that nobles, peasants, and state would all benefit from making peasants into more productive and independent individuals, Maria Theresa sought to transform the labor and crops that peasants owed to their lords into fixed cash payments to be shared by the landowners and the state. Independent peasants should control their own destinies as legally, economically, and morally free individuals. They should eventually own their own plots of land wherever possible. Nobles who needed peasant labor to farm their estates would eventually be able to hire landless peasants for a wage. Noble landowners would give up personal control over the peasantry, along with their rights to unpaid peasant labor, to the administration of local justice, and to their own tax-free status.

Maria Theresa could not simply impose such a radical change on society anywhere in Austria. Nor was it her intention to act radically. She preferred a process of negotiation and compromise. Still, she implemented as much of this model reform as she could, especially on those lands she and her family owned directly. Although she failed to impose a full change on all of her lands, even the fact that she limited the amount of unpaid labor the nobles could demand from the peasantry began to undermine the very logic behind traditional social hierarchies. Pamphlet literature and public debates in the 1760s and 1770s increasingly asked what the rights and obligations of a future free peasantry would look like. In doing so, the authors helped to shape debate over what was possible or desirable. The government also began work on a new civil law code that wrestled with the concept of the peasant as a free individual.[38] By the 1790s, as we will see, the logic of reform pushed the regime ever closer to adopting a single concept of equal and active legal citizenship for all inhabitants of the realms, regardless of their social rank. In 1799—after the demise of all three of the Habsburg reform monarchs—a draft law for Galicia could state that "Every citizen, regardless of rank, estate *[Stand]*, or sex is obligated to promote the general wellbeing of the state through careful obedience to its laws."[39] This formula straddles two very different concepts of society. One version was divided socially and culturally by estate or privileged class; the other, still in the making, was a world of citizens who would be equal in their obligations to the state and in the rights they received from it.

Peasants Speak

As we saw at the opening of this chapter, the state had traditionally depended for information about the population on irregular reports of births, marriages, and deaths generated by parish priests. Given the succession of wars fought by Maria Theresa, military demand for ever-increasing numbers of healthy recruits drove the development of new census technologies for determining the size of local populations as well as their distinctive qualities. The military leadership of the mid-eighteenth century emerged as a powerful and influential source of support for a range of social, political, and economic reforms in part because it too was interested in more than simply raising the numbers of recruits. The physical condition of recruits was as much a concern as their numbers.

For this reason several military leaders shared Maria Theresa's skepticism about the economic inefficiency and low productivity levels engendered by traditional relations on the land, and instead strongly supported her ideal of a legally emancipated and economically free peasantry.

When a census was taken in 1770 to determine the size, health, and educational levels of local populations in the Hereditary and Bohemian lands or when Habsburg territories had to be mapped—often for the first time—it was the military that developed new techniques. Only the military could draw on large enough numbers of men to carry out such projects successfully. The armies of civilian bureaucrats and civil servants that would later blanket the central European landscape did not yet exist. Thanks largely to their active participation in local recruitment and data gathering projects, both the military leadership and many rank-and-file officers also developed a profound sympathy for the plight of the peasantry throughout Austria. The *Hofkriegsrat*, or War Ministry, claimed in 1770 that its broader aim in taking the census was to aid "the servile people to become more rational, more sober, cleaner, more affluent and happier."[40]

One innovation introduced in 1770 was the imposition of house numbering systems in villages and towns to maintain more accurate records about their inhabitants in the long term. Military assessors who traveled to each locality did not simply count the population, dividing it by sex and age; nor did they simply assign numbers to the smallest huts and largest town houses depending on the route they took as they traveled through a town. More important by far, the assessors also served as eyes and ears for the central government, collecting information from each locality about fourteen different topics of potential interest, including health and hygiene, education levels, degree of religious piety, level of affluence, and the general public mood.

The officers who carried out the census in 1770–1771 were explicitly ordered not to encourage peasant complaints. Nevertheless, as we saw at the outset of this chapter, they heard an earful. In Styria the assessors reported: "A general complaint is the high amount of *Robot* that makes it impossible for the peasant to work his own plot of land and to pay his dues both to the government and to the landowner." Around the town of Cilli/Celje in south Styria, conditions were so bad that the assessors noted, "Many houses are empty and much land has been deserted." Peasants in this region had found themselves forced to "abandon house and land and to seek a living with their families as farmhands in [neighboring] Croatia."[41] In Carniola, just to the west, the population generally cooperated willingly during the census, "from the hope of gaining a reduction in the *Robot* and the dues in kind."[42] In Bohemia, tenants on the estates of Count Palm complained specifically about the severity of the *Robot* requirements: "In the winter season they must give three days every week, but in the summer they owe work every day with the oxen, and in addition to this another one or two persons must perform manual labor." In the district of Leitmeritz/Litoměřice "complaints only came to us in secret." There, the assessor hinted that an objective investigation would bring to light many misdemeanors by landowners.[43]

Local authorities were quick to defend themselves from peasant complaints, accusing peasants of gross exaggeration and general willfulness. In the southern Bohemian town of Klattau/Klatovy, for example, one officer reported that peasants clearly would have made even more complaints to him had not a local order suddenly come down "that they were not to turn to any military officer with complaints." In Styria officers objected that in one district the local landlord himself sought to hinder their questioning of the peasants. In fact, in both Bohemia and Moravia, where peasant rebellions broke out sporadically in the 1770s, officials on local estates complained that the military census and process of house numbering fostered a dangerous sense of freedom and emancipation from local authorities among the peasants.

In 1770, it seems, many peasants thought of the central state or imperial power as a handy counterweight to the authority of the local nobility. Although in institutional terms, that state barely existed as yet at the local level, it clearly held great symbolic meaning to peasants who aggressively asserted their desires to its military representatives. Peasants in many regions invested a deep commitment—at least situationally—to the Habsburg dynasty and its central institutions, seeing in them a means to protect and further their social interests. Thus the distance of the empire from its many constituent territories, along with the diversity of those territories, could paradoxically produce new kinds of attachments to it, as the empire's agents appeared to stand between local notables and peasants.

The emancipation of the peasant from the direct influence of the local nobility also demanded the creation of educational institutions. Peasants required training both in the latest agricultural techniques and, perhaps more importantly, in moral strictures, so that under transformed circumstances, they would remain orderly, respectful of authority, and diligent in carrying out their duties. That same military survey of 1770–1771 repeatedly highlighted peasant illiteracy as a cause of much poverty and social misery. Illiteracy in turn was blamed on the neglect of schools by local authorities, on the insufficient numbers of teachers, or on the impossible burdens with which the teachers were charged. In South Styria in 1771 the surveyors observed:

> In each of the parishes a school teacher has been funded and hired, but the immense spread of the parishes, the dispersal of houses in the parishes, and the fact that the schoolteacher is also employed by the parish and the church for other tasks, leaves him too little time to give the children their necessary lessons. Thus very few peasants can actually read; in fact quite a few of them do not even know their names or their ages.

Similarly, surveyors in Bohemia noted with disapproval that "too little thought is given to the schools; they do not make a priority of hiring qualified schoolteachers. Thanks to the heedless neglect of the parents, the young children go bad in several ways."[44]

In 1774 (1777 in Hungary) Maria Theresa established a general education requirement for children of both sexes. From then on, all children between the ages of six and twelve throughout the monarchy would have to attend school. At least on paper, if not in practice, this system of mandatory public schooling suddenly placed the Habsburg state at the forefront of European developments in education. This legislation focused more on the education of Austria's least enlightened classes, however, than on developing Austria's institutions of higher learning. Maria Theresa's initiative did not generally aim to create intellectual academies or to expand existing university faculties. In larger towns and provincial centers, the government did add teacher-training programs. Maria Theresa also created some new Latin high schools and technical training schools in fields such as mining and metallurgy as well as an Oriental Academy in Vienna to teach languages and train interpreters—mostly to produce potential officials and experts for her expanding bureaucracy.[45] But on the whole her education policy aimed to reach the lowest classes. She hoped to provide the peasantry the requisite moral and economic training to become productive and orderly members of society, but she did not want to give them so much education that they themselves might question the order of religion or the state. The law's main accomplishment was to establish several one- or two-class primary schools in vernacular languages across the monarchy. Given the relatively modest goals of these schools, the use of the vernacular was deemed appropriate and necessary, since few children would have understood other languages.

In the eighteenth century most of the teachers who staffed these new primary schools—when they were established at all—were local members of the clergy. It could hardly have been otherwise anywhere in Europe, given that local priests were often the only individuals with even a smattering of education, especially in more remote rural villages. Nevertheless, the reliance on the clergy for the provision of a basic education to all children forces us to consider the role of the church in determining the content of education as well as the Habsburgs' broader institutional relationship to the church in the eighteenth century. How did the clergy understand this additional responsibility, given that the state already relied on local clergy for onerous burdens of official record keeping of birth, death, marriage, and conscription?

Making local priests into the instrument of educational reform did not necessarily mean that mandatory primary education would be steeped in the conservative strictures of baroque, counter-reformation Catholicism, as it undoubtedly would have a century earlier. In the sixteenth century the Catholic Church had introduced highly emotional, highly visual, and ritually demonstrative forms of Catholic worship as tools to combat the growth of popular Protestantism in Austria. Two centuries later, however, many Catholics rejected this kind of overt religiosity. Instead they sought far simpler forms of devotion that focused more on internal personal piety and good works than on dramatically externalized ceremonial forms of devotion. Maria Theresa's personal religious practice shared a great deal with this form of simpler Catholicism that spread both in Hungary and Austria during the eighteenth century. This Catholicism emphasized simple, modest, and pietist virtues in everyday life, while avoiding the overtly emotional excesses of baroque ritual practice. During Maria Theresa's reign, many Catholic thinkers, officials, and orders supported the government's increasing interference in church policy. Thus the precise character of church influence on public education depended a great deal on the attitudes of the local priest, who might well engage at a rudimentary level with this or that development in the humanities, natural sciences, and jurisprudence or with Enlightenment attitudes toward education in general.

Maria Theresa's more radical advisers gradually convinced her to impose state supervision over the church in all matters save the purely spiritual, from the education of priests in state-run seminaries to the appointment of bishops. The regime attacked the influence of the Jesuit order in the universities, but more importantly, it took over the task of censorship from the church in 1752. As a result, the government index of banned works soon differed substantially from the church's index.[46] The government drastically reduced the number of recognized religious holidays and dissolved contemplative orders whose members did not serve a charitable purpose in the community, appropriating their property to help fund local educational and welfare institutions. On the whole, the government reduced many—but by no means all—of the Catholic Church's privileges, increasingly treating it as one of many legitimate private associations that demanded some regulation by the state. At the same time, however, her personal sympathies for reformed Catholicism prevented Maria Theresa from sympathizing with the radically secular logic propounded by many of her advisers and later by her sons Joseph II and Leopold II. Throughout her reign, for example, she vigorously opposed the principle of religious toleration for Protestant or Eastern Orthodox sects, much less for Jews. As a devout Catholic, she did not see how the toleration of other religions could possibly improve her subjects' moral character. And members of the Catholic Church retained considerable privileges over other religions, such as the rights to worship publicly, to build churches with towers, and to ring church bells.

Maria Theresa was not beyond contradicting her own preferences when it suited a critical policy objective, such as the encouragement of commerce in the free port city of Trieste/Trst. There she promoted immigration by merchant communities, including specifically Jews, Greek Orthodox, Armenians, and Greek Catholic Uniates. After the empress's death, her son Joseph extended this policy to Protestants.[47] Starting with the Jews in 1746, each of these religious minorities in the city was permitted to form a corporate body, to organize worship and schools among its members, and to enjoy the same civil and economic rights as local Catholic merchants.[48]

Whatever her narrower intentions had been in the 1740s, by the 1770s Maria Theresa's reform efforts had in some way reshaped almost every conceivable aspect of public life and policy, from religious practice to education to the administration of justice, from farming techniques to the creation of new manufactures, from the construction of more effective networks of roads and canals to the encouragement of sea and overland trade.

Hungary and the Habsburgs

For over two hundred years the Habsburgs had spent many of their resources trying to conquer Hungary from Ottoman occupation, defending themselves from further Ottoman attacks, and, after finally defeating the Ottomans, trying to establish greater political control over Hungary, Croatia, and Transylvania.[49] Eventually, their conquest of Hungary gave the Habsburgs an opportunity to redraw somewhat the constitutional balance of power between themselves and Hungary's powerful nobility. In 1687, in recognition of Habsburg efforts to liberate Hungary, the diet conceded to the Habsburgs a hereditary right of succession to the throne. The Habsburgs also created a zone of direct administrative control for themselves in a long strip of territory that ran along the border with the Ottoman Empire in Southern Hungary, Croatia, and Transylvania, known as the "military frontier." They populated this frontier with largely Eastern Orthodox Christian refugees from Ottoman rule who received tax privileges in return for their commitment to defend the frontier against attack from the south.[50] Yet in the eighteenth century, the Habsburgs lacked the financial resources to establish full administrative control over Hungary. One clear sign of this weakness was their inability to root out the considerable pockets of Calvinist, Lutheran, and Unitarian communities (and their aristocratic supporters) that continued to flourish in Transylvania and Upper Hungary. In consequence, Hungary remained religiously far more diverse than the dynasty's other holdings. Periodic local rebellions in Hungary until 1715, continued sporadic wars against the Ottomans until 1739, and the dynasty's dependence on the surviving Hungarian nobility to serve as local administrators also meant that Hungary retained a distinctive place among the Habsburgs' holdings.

In Hungary it was not simply the diet that regularly asserted independence from the Habsburgs, but also the local administrations run by noble-elected county governments. During the long Ottoman presence, when a central government had all but vanished from most regions of Hungary, these county governments had shouldered the difficult burdens of local administration, justice, and even military defense. Throughout the period of administrative reorganization that followed the Habsburg conquest of Hungary, neither the dynasty nor the Catholic Church had the necessary resources to impose completely new political or religious structures on Hungary, despite their redistribution of property and encouragement of resettlement in central Hungary and their establishment of the so-called military frontiers in the south. In fact, during the eighteenth century, county governments in Hungary became critical bastions of opposition to the Habsburg administration, and even consulted each other to develop common strategies of resistance to the king.[51]

On what ideological grounds did Hungarian institutions justify their opposition to their king's attempts at centralization? In the eighteenth century both the diet and county governments referred to themselves collectively (in Latin—their traditional language of business) as the *natio Hungarica*, or "Hungarian Nation." They argued that this historic "nationhood" gave them certain shared rights. At the coronation ceremony, every king of Hungary had to swear an oath to respect the collective rights of this Hungarian "nation." But what did the term "nation" mean to an eighteenth-century public? In Hungary "nation" referred to a small minority of the king's subjects indeed. The *natio Hungarica* was constituted from those members of the nobility who sat in the two chambers of the diet, those who had the right to elect its deputies, and those who also, by definition, remained exempt from taxation. Most subjects of the king of Hungary, however, and indeed most people who lived within Hungary's borders, were not considered members of the Hungarian nation.

In its arguments against the king, the nation championed a vision of Hungary as an independent state whose ruler coincidentally happened to rule several other separate territories as well. Hungary, the nation argued, was most definitely not a component part of a larger Habsburg state, just as it did not belong to the Holy Roman Empire the way Bohemia did, for example. Nor, claimed the Hungarian Nation, did Hungary desire to be part of any administrative structures common to other lands the Habsburg king ruled. Thanks in part to specific references made by the French political philosopher Montesquieu in his 1748 *Spirit of the Laws* after a visit to Hungary, the eighteenth-century Hungarian nobility also began to claim that taken together, its traditional "national rights" made up an age-old unwritten constitution. The diet cited this revered, ancient, and invented constitution to lend even greater legal persuasiveness to its arguments against full incorporation into a Habsburg state.[52] The Habsburg kings, on the other hand, sought to coordinate the administration of Hungary with the rest of their monarchy. The kings thus cited other ancient Hungarian constitutional traditions that gave them broad executive and judicial powers and an undisputed right to raise an army for the country's defense. When the king fought Hungary's enemies, his military constituted a single coordinated force and not separate Austrian, Bohemian, or Hungarian armies. Hungarian diets had traditionally accepted this claim.

With the exception of educational reform, Maria Theresa treated almost every matter of governance differently when it came to Hungary. Her personal relationship to Hungary was tinged most obviously by the gratitude she felt throughout her reign for the critical support the Hungarian Diet had offered her in her moment of abject weakness. She expressed great pride in her Hungarian title of king which, unlike her other titles—such as that of empress—she shared neither with her husband, Francis Stephan, nor her son Joseph. These considerations tempered Maria Theresa's centralizing efforts, made her willing to leave Hungary somewhat separate from the rest of her state, and encouraged her to seek negotiated solutions with Hungary, rather than forcing her cause. Structurally at least, during a half century of intensive reform projects, Hungary remained somewhat peripheral to the institutional developments that unified the rest of the Habsburg state.

To be clear, this period also saw considerable state-building activity *within* Hungary. As in her other lands, Maria Theresa expanded state services in Hungary, centralized the administration, and managed it more professionally. In Hungary, however, where administrative offices remained restricted to the nobility, the expansion of the central bureaucracy did not diminish the powers of the local nobility by empowering a cadre of commoner bureaucrats. Hungarian aristocrats also occupied the administrative positions in Vienna that governed Hungarian affairs. With only one notable exception—the military—administrative reform in Hungary tended to reinforce that society's separateness from the rest of the Habsburg Monarchy.

Maria Theresa constantly needed funds for her reforms and for her wars. Yet in her forty years on the throne, she summoned the Hungarian Diet to meet only three times, thereby avoiding potentially difficult conflicts with the elite Hungarian nation. In 1767, however, Maria Theresa did introduce the radical urbarium laws to regulate the treatment of peasants by their lords in Hungary. Uncharacteristically, she took up this thorny issue in Hungary before she took it up in the rest of the monarchy, in part because severe agrarian revolts had broken out in western Hungary in the early 1760s and in part as a way to impose her will on a recalcitrant diet. Maria Theresa's sentimental attitude toward the gallant Hungarians who had rescued her in 1741 certainly did not cloud her judgment about their treatment of their peasants. With regard to peasant revolts, she opined that it was "only the cruelty of their lords which has driven these wretched people to such extremes."[53]

Her decision to raise the peasant question at this particular time also grew out of other strategic considerations. In 1764 her government had faced bankruptcy after the Seven Years' War and had sought a voluntary fiscal contribution from the Hungarian Diet. She and her advisers also sought some tax relief for those people who actually paid Hungary's taxes—all non-nobles!—and who made up the military's rank and file as well. Suspicious of Vienna's increasingly absolutist tendencies, however, the diet refused the financial contribution to the government and instead presented its female king with 228 of its own complaints. Largely in response to this affront, Maria Theresa had decided to place the material condition of the peasantry firmly on the diet's agenda.

The urbarium of 1767 imposed a fixed system of dues and obligations, adjusted for local conditions, on the peasants and their landlords. On her royal lands in Hungary Maria Theresa went even farther, transforming all peasant labor and crop dues into cash rents for land. Despite these far-reaching reforms, however, Maria Theresa failed to impose general taxation on the nobility in Hungary the way she had in Bohemia and in the Hereditary Lands. Hungary's irregular contributions to the military budget also remained relatively small, given Hungary's size, and a matter of some complaint especially among Bohemians who paid the lion's share of the military budget. Claims of Hungarian separateness counted little, however, when it came to the recruitment, provisioning, and commanding of troops. Even before the Pragmatic Sanction, a law in 1715 had authorized the recruitment of Hungarian forces into a combined Habsburg military. From then on, Hungarian regiments had regularly been incorporated into the Habsburg armies, and by the mid-eighteenth century Hungarian soldiers saw combat not simply in Hungarian or Transylvanian theaters of war (as they had during the Ottoman Wars), but all over Europe.[54] By merging Hungarian units with other Habsburg forces, Maria Theresa made the military into one of the few sites where Hungarian non-nobles could achieve a significant degree of social mobility by rising through the ranks.[55] The military reforms themselves, however, unwittingly increased the powers of the local county governments by making them responsible for the recruitment and supply of their military units.[56] The very backbone of resistance to Habsburg absolutism in Hungary lodged in these local organs of government that absolutism now fed and expanded.

Toward Statehood, Citizenship, and Patriotism

Maria Theresa's ambivalence about Hungary's relationship to the rest of her realms throws into relief some larger questions about the nature of the Habsburg state under construction during this period. Hungary's elite maintained a specific identity for itself based largely on claims about its role in Hungary's national history and its mythological constitution. The nobles cited this national identity to legitimize their opposition to the absolutist pretensions of their ruler. Although this claim to nationhood in fact excluded close to 95 percent of Maria Theresa's Hungarian subjects from membership, it nevertheless provided the small elite with a rhetorically useful tool for asserting that it alone acted in the interest of all Hungarians.

To what extent did contemporary ideologists elsewhere recognize in the Habsburgs' emerging state a meaningful object of personal or popular identification? And to what extent had this new state become real in the eyes of both literate and nonliterate publics? Was it on a par with traditional objects of identification, such as the village or the region, or with the kind of universalist projects of the Roman Catholic Church or the Holy Roman Empire? The new concept of a territorial Habsburg state also contradicted the family's symbolic claim to be heirs to the universal Roman Empire. In earlier centuries, gaining control over any territory had served to expand not only the dynasty's resources but also its symbolic glory on a European or global stage. The dynasty's territorial holdings had also reinforced Habsburg claims to the title of Holy Roman emperor. According to this older way of thinking, Habsburg dynastic power had not been rooted in the existence of a particular Habsburg territorial state, since territories could be traded at will for political gain. There was also therefore no need to make these territories' internal structures conform to a unified model of administration.

In the eighteenth century the Habsburgs continued to protect their universal symbolic status as Holy Roman emperors, with the election of Maria Theresa's husband in 1745 as Emperor Francis I and of her sons Joseph II in 1765 and Leopold II in 1790. Nevertheless, by 1750 several practical concerns had forced a shift away from the symbolism of universal empire and more to the stabilization and strengthening of the Habsburgs' own state, increasingly known as "Austria." In 1741 the very survival of the dynasty had demanded it.

As the Holy Roman Empire declined in relative importance for the Habsburgs during the reign of Maria Theresa, some publicists began to write about the new Habsburg state using the terms "nation" and "fatherland" and to treat this state as an object of patriotic devotion. We have already encountered the term "nation" defined as an elite community with political rights in Hungary. In the late eighteenth century, the term also came to describe the generality of people who held a kind of equal membership within a single state.

This newer concept of nationhood derived its meaning from membership in a community defined by common borders, by subjection to common laws, by a common government, and of course by a common dynasty. This state-based understanding of nationhood is as different from the linguistic or ethnic concepts of nation that became popular in nineteenth-century Europe as it is from the elite concept inherited from earlier centuries. This definition of a community united by common borders and institutions broke with the older understandings of political community that rested on hierarchies of privilege and power. In part this new understanding of nationhood derived from emerging claims that subjection to the law applied to everyone equally, and not simply to some.

Maria Theresa and her advisers did not enunciate a specific vision of equal citizenship, but many of their policies pointed unmistakably in this direction. Other thinkers, politicians, and indeed Maria Theresa's eldest sons intentionally drew the radical conclusions at which she had only hinted. If peasants were eventually to be freed from personal servitude and treated as morally and economically capable individuals, it would indeed be difficult to continue to justify legal privileges for the nobility. If education and merit were required for service to the state, then the privilege of aristocratic birth would lose much of its social significance. As historian R. J. W. Evans has asserted about the centralizing policies of this period, "The whole attack on privilege, on corporations, on provincial status, etc. undertaken by 'enlightened despots' like Maria Theresa and Joseph II involved a new stress on citizenship." In turn, he observes that "the language of government, especially its myriad administrative enactments, becomes peppered with talk of the *Bürger* and *Bürgertum* or with references to the *Volk* as an object of policy."[57]

In his 1771 *Über die Liebe des Vaterlandes* (On Love for the Fatherland) jurist and novelist Joseph von Sonnenfels (1732–1817) urged all ranks of society to take up civic responsibilities together to promote greater patriotic love of something he called "the fatherland." Just as this kind of patriotic idea sought a cultural justification for the new concept of citizenship, it also offered another powerful way to identify most of society with the reforming efforts of the Habsburgs and their emerging state.[58] The populace might come to view its interests specifically in terms of an imperial program promoted by reforming monarchs and reject the particularism articulated by local lords.

How would this emerging feeling of patriotism for a larger fatherland relate to existing regional loyalties or to those forms of identification espoused by Austria's noble elites? The challenge of expressing society's relationship to the new state in terms of cultural or emotional identification, the question of encouraging personal identification with the state through patriotism (admittedly a dynastic patriotism), the difficulty of integrating noble nations like Hungary or Poland into a larger unified state remained to be debated and tested under Maria Theresa's successors.

In this regard, the Habsburg state resembled its European counterparts more than it differed from them. No European state could be considered a centralized, unified, compact unit in the 1770s. Most states also ruled over populations characterized by their considerable linguistic diversity as well. A comparison with contemporary Britain reminds us that Scotland, Wales, and England had different legal systems and Ireland a separate parliament. A comparison with Prussia shows that different estate bodies governed different regions. A comparison with France reveals the presence of several linguistically diverse populations. If Austria's situation was indeed more extreme in both the diversity of its institutions and numbers of official languages, then this was a difference of quantity rather than of quality.[59]

At her death in 1780 Maria Theresa bequeathed to her son Joseph II a Habsburg state that was administratively far more unified and integrated than it had been a half-century before. It was also a state onto which increasing numbers of groups in society, from the peasants in 1770 to the new class of bureaucrats, projected their own visions and desires. Maria Theresa's achievements were rooted both in her dogged intent to pursue the cause of reform over several decades and in her efforts to realize progress through compromise wherever she could.[60] How much more compromise could be achieved by her successors if they were to pursue centralization and reform to their logical ends? And to what extent could the increasingly vocal and empowered supporters of empire tolerate compromise to the imperial reform projects?

CHAPTER TWO

Servants and Citizens, Empire and Fatherland, 1780–1815

An individual earns the full enjoyment of his rights through his citizenship in the state.

— Allgemeine Bürgerliches Gesetzbuch, *1811*

Maria Theresa had planted the seeds of a crucial reform that her sons and grandson brought to fruition: the reconceptualization of subjects *(Untertanen)* as citizens *(Staatsbürger)*—that is, as individual men and women with common legal rights and obligations anchored in their unmediated relationship to a central state. This radical transformation of the individual—from a link in a corporate hierarchy to a citizen whose legal relationship to the state was the sole determinant of his (and sometimes her) legal position—had profound consequences for thinking about populations. It implied that at least in theory, all citizens, from serfs to powerful aristocrats, shared the same legal position. They must all, according to Maria Theresa's son and successor, Joseph II (reigned 1780– 1790), "work for the general good according to their wealth, their strength, and their capacity to be useful."[1]

Without enduring a revolutionary upheaval like the one that roiled French society at the end of the eighteenth century, Habsburg society was also fundamentally transformed in legal terms during this period. Ironically, however, it was not Joseph II who brought this vision to fruition in a new Austrian state. Rather this distinction lies unexpectedly with Joseph's unimaginative and conservative nephew Francis, who reigned first as Francis II of the Holy Roman Empire and after 1804, as we will see, as Francis I, Emperor of Austria. Twenty years of unrelenting and mostly unsuccessful warfare against the French frequently brought the monarchy close to economic and social collapse, but it also forced the creation of a new state whose General Civil Law Code *(Allgemeines Bürgerliche Gesetzbuch* or AGBG) of 1811 largely validated Joseph II's radical visions of citizenship.

Joseph II repeatedly drew a connection between the ability of a free individual to pursue a productive life and the resulting benefits that would accrue to society and to the state. This was powerfully illustrated by the text of his 1782 law that regulated the legal status of Jews in Lower Austria and Vienna:

> One of [our] principal concerns [is] that all our subjects, without distinction of nation and religion . . . should take their share in the public prosperity that we desire to increase by our solicitude, should enjoy a legally guaranteed freedom, and [should] encounter no hindrance when seeking in every honorable way to make their living and to contribute by their industry to the general prosperity.[2]

This desire to unleash the capacities of the individual for the benefit of the state guided Joseph even more fully than it had his mother, Maria Theresa. It also produced two larger problems that plagued the monarchy during and after Joseph's brief reign.

The first of these was Joseph's tendency to forge ahead with reform—often regardless of the advice he received. This inevitably provoked conflict with powerful interests in society whose privilege rested on their traditional rights to exploit others economically. Joseph waved their protests aside in the belief that the privileges exercised by local nobilities over the peasantry violated the very strictures of natural law itself:

> Where a small minority set themselves up as rulers of the country and treat the great majority—namely the workers and producers— merely as a means to their own financial needs and pleasures, and where this minority makes all the laws or interprets them in such a way as to maintain their own immunity and independence, there is no hope of any lasting and permanent remedy, for humanity is oppressed in violation of its natural sentiments.[3]

In Joseph's view the law should ultimately replace the arbitrary conventions and customs of traditional hierarchic society. Enormous differences in social and economic status continued to characterize Habsburg society, but the law increasingly trumped all other forms of authority in its universal application. In fact, the sovereign came to be understood primarily as the giver, protector, and implementer of laws.

Joseph's single-minded determination to impose what he saw as rational standards of rule, however, often bordered on ruthlessness. An impatient reformer, he held his bureaucrats to the highest standards, regularly excoriating their inability to live up to his exacting principles, yet keeping most of them in their positions for lack of better alternatives. During his short reign Joseph inspired fanatical loyalty among his admirers, especially within the expanding state bureaucracy. Still, admirers who came too close to the man often found themselves alienated by his controlling martinet-like qualities. Not surprising in one who valued rationality, centralization, and discipline, Joseph was also a lover of the military, and he frequently applied a military way of thinking to domestic policies. Unlike the purposeful wheedling and tactical compromise that had characterized Maria Theresa's reform efforts, once Joseph had decided on a course of action, he simply imposed his sweeping plans, rarely permitting discussion or compromise. By the second half of his brief reign, the question became just how much he could transform his realms before his opponents fought back effectively.

The second problem produced by his determination to reform society at all cost was in fact the question of cost. Joseph cut costs ruthlessly in all departments at the same time that he imposed countless new mandates for local government to fulfill. Moreover, even as he oversaw the expansion of imperial and regional bureaucracies, he also expanded their responsibilities so that these increased at a much faster rate than did bureaucratic budgets and resources. If reform provoked rebellion, it also strained fiscal limits and created more work for servants of the state at every level.

By the time of his early death in 1790 Joseph's legislation sparked rebellion in both the Austrian Netherlands and in Hungary, as well as serious unrest in other parts of the monarchy. His brother and short-lived successor, Leopold II (1747–1792), Grand Duke of Tuscany, was left to pick up the pieces and to restore confidence among the rebellious nobility while nevertheless continuing to pursue the family's reform program. Within two years Leopold himself died, leaving the unfinished legacy of

Habsburg Territories in 1772

reform to his eldest son, Francis (1768–1835). Although Francis was not a reformer by temperament or ideology, as we will see, it was nevertheless his declaration of an Austrian Empire in 1804 that finally transformed the Habsburg's diverse holdings into a single state. It was also his publication of the AGBG in 1811 that transformed his subjects into equal citizens before the law. All of this took place in the shadow of a ruinous twenty-year war against revolutionary France, led by the upstart Emperor Napoleon.

Servants of Society

After 1780, a new sense of urgency invigorated the Habsburg project of administrative centralization. At the helm of these sped-up efforts was Joseph II, a new style of ruler who more than any of his contemporaries embodied the sober epithet "the first servant of the state."[4] The epitome of what contemporaries and later historians called an "enlightened ruler,"

Joseph earned his reputation thanks to his ceaseless devotion to work, his restless travel to every corner of his vast realms, his mania for gathering detailed information about all manner of social phenomena, his unrelenting reform of traditional institutions, and his habit of micromanaging his administrators with volumes of detailed orders. Not surprisingly, given this particular list of traits, Joseph also alienated almost everyone he encountered in the short decade of his reign.

At the same time, Joseph also became an object of intense veneration or demonization long after his death. During his lifetime, for example, peasants across the monarchy, from Bohemia and Moravia to Galicia celebrated Joseph as a folk hero who more than once had tried his hand at plowing a field, most famously in 1769 at Slavíkovice Moravia, and who later, they believed, had "freed" the serfs. Peasants increasingly referred specifically to Joseph whenever they challenged the demands of their noble overlords in the half-century after his death. Later in the nineteenth century liberal Jews also mythologized Joseph as the ruler most responsible for their legal emancipation. Moreover, many progressive educators saw in Joseph's example an embodiment of the principle of freedom of thought, and democrats saw him as a great social leveler. By contrast, even during his reign, critics from the nobility and the church reviled Joseph as a cold and stubbornly shortsighted tyrant who trampled on what they referred to as their "traditional" or "national liberties"—what others might call their "traditional privileges."

Joseph's person offered later generations a potent symbol for other causes as well. A century after his death German nationalists in Austria willfully misinterpreted his effort to make German the administrative language for the entire monarchy as a nationalist act and memorialized him with countless statues. By contrast, many nineteenth-century Czech and Hungarian nationalists loathed Joseph as a Germanizer whose language policies had allegedly robbed the monarchy's diverse peoples of their precious linguistic heritages.

All of this creative mythmaking tells us far more about later political conflicts than about the emperor's intentions or vision. Joseph was anything but a nineteenth-century liberal, despite the fact that many of his emancipatory policies resembled critical aspects of later liberal programs for society. Nor was Joseph a nationalist intent on destroying regional or

Nineteenth-century depiction of Joseph II taking a turn at the plow in Slavíkovice Moravia on 19 August 1769, by Emil Pirchan. Credit: Österreichische Nationalbibliothek.

local linguistic cultures by Germanizing his realms. In fact, some of his less well-known reforms encouraged a greater use of regional vernacular languages—especially Czech—in local schools, publications, and administration.[5] On the whole, Joseph aimed to give his subjects more opportunities to achieve a better life for themselves because he saw this as the most effective means to increase the overall well-being of the state. At the same time, however, he insisted that he alone was the best arbiter of what was actually good for them.

When Joseph took full power in 1780, his mother and her advisers had already spent over thirty years experimenting with reforms that challenged a range of social and political traditions. During those years, the optimum welfare of state and society had gradually become the new standard by which the Habsburgs and their advisers measured policy outcomes. No longer did they think primarily in terms of promoting the glory of the dynasty. Now the reputation of the dynasty depended increasingly on its ability to provide its subjects with prosperity. The health of the state—and of the society over which it ruled—became significant ends in themselves.

With the death of his father, Francis Stephen, in 1765, the twenty-four-year-old Joseph had been elected Holy Roman emperor, while his mother had made him her "co-regent" of the Habsburg lands. Maria Theresa, however, retained a tight control over policy formation, often keeping important intelligence from her son and limiting his participation in major decisions. So Joseph sought other outlets for his tireless energies during the fifteen years he shared the throne with his mother. He traveled obsessively throughout her realms, meeting with people from all classes, regions, and religions, asking endless questions about local conditions, and collecting countless petitions from his subjects, especially from peasants. By the time of his mother's death in 1780, Joseph II self-consciously inhabited a role as first servant of the state. If his mother had often been this kind of ruler in practice, she had nevertheless justified her position in more traditional ceremonial and representational ways.

Depictions of Maria Theresa during her lifetime either highlighted her many royal, imperial, or religious titles—as if to emphasize her legitimacy—or constructed a symbolic role for her as mother of her peoples by placing her at the center of a large family in domestic scenes.[6] Joseph clearly believed in a different kind of rulership. Both his official and unofficial portraits show a man in military dress, usually holding a field marshal's baton, never wearing a crown or the robes of office, and often in conversation with simple people.[7] The childless Joseph never appeared in any formal portraits with either of his spouses.[8] Instead, it was his younger brother and successor, Grand Duke Leopold of Tuscany, who continued Maria Theresa's genre of Habsburg domestic symbolism, surrounding himself in portraits with his wife and children, thirteen of whom survived to adulthood.

Joseph's rejection of traditional ceremony and symbolism—his biographer Derek Beales described his court as "the meanest, most masculine, and the least attractive in Europe"—did not mean that he believed any less in an absolutist system of rule than his recent ancestors had.[9] In his view only the ruler and his close advisers were informed enough to

Pietro *Leopoldo*

Maria Theresa's son Grand Duke Leopold of Tuscany, later Emperor Leopold II, surrounded by his family in Florence. Through the window the cupola of Santa Maria del Fiore is visible. Copper engraving by Giovanni Battista Cecchi, 1785. Credit: Österreichische Nationalbibliothek.

perceive the general good for the whole of society. But he took this same logic of state that had driven Maria Theresa's reform efforts and made it his explicit program, cutting away the cultural, religious, and symbolic trappings of imperial rulership and replacing them with a functionalist state ideology informed by reason and logic. Of course Joseph was not necessarily any more rational or logical in his thought processes than anyone else. For Joseph, however, abstract concepts of reason, rationality, and natural law, not religion or imperial tradition, shaped policy debates and justified decisions during his reign.

One instrument of Joseph's determined will was the growing bureaucracy, already under construction during the reign of his mother. In piecemeal fashion she and her advisers had established a new concept of bureaucratic service, one that rested on loyalty to the state, rather than loyalty to the dynasty or to the noble court. Aristocrats and magnates at court served as the empress's highest functionaries. Exclusive academies like the Theresianum, founded in 1745, or the Consular Academy for future diplomats catered to the sons of the aristocracy, reserving for them careers at the very highest levels of state service. Lower down on the scale—but not too much lower—the sons of the middle and commercial classes entered this expanding bureaucracy in increasing numbers. With the exception of Hungary, where noble status remained a requirement for state service, a career in the bureaucracy promised social advancement to non-noble candidates who obtained the requisite education for such posts.

In the 1770s most middle-class candidates for bureaucratic positions that carried with them decision-making responsibilities studied law at one of Austria's universities.[10] Study at these institutions in itself was not necessarily an expensive proposition, especially for those who already lived in a university town. Moreover, the availability of scholarships also made it possible for sons of lesser means to study, even if the scholarships barely paid their living expenses.[11] The period 1780 to 1848 saw both an absolute and a proportional increase in the numbers of non-noble men who served at the higher levels of the bureaucratic service. During this period a bureaucrat's success depended increasingly on proof of his individual merit. A bureaucratic post could be considered neither hereditary nor venal. The candidate who earned it became an active participant in the very construction of the new state. In this sense, as Waltraud Heindl has argued, the expansion of the bureaucracy as the executor of state policy rested on an Enlightenment ideal of dedicated citizenship. "[The bureaucrat's] job presupposed a concept of citizenship, and to be a citizen meant, according to the Enlightenment . . . active participation in the construction of the nation state. His post could neither be hereditary, nor for sale [venal], nor could it depend on the caprice of the prince [monarch]."[12] In turn, the rapid expansion of non-noble membership in this bureaucracy produced a workplace ethos that by 1800 had incorporated new habits, new social behaviors, and new cultural practices among bureaucrats both at the office and in domestic settings with their families.[13]

The middle-class conquest of the bureaucracy was both subtle and profound, as middle-class rhythms of work and family life and even work-place spatial arrangements gradually replaced aristocratic norms for the service as a whole. During Maria Theresa's reign, for example, several new buildings had sprung up in Vienna and in the crownland capitals to house the offices where her bureaucrats came to work every day.[14] Although some aristocrats continued to work from home (as late as the post-Napoleonic period Metternich frequently received colleagues at home in his pajamas), the new trend demanded a strict separation of workplace from home. One Viennese observer in 1787 described seeing at half past nine daily "an army of ca. four and a half thousand men marching; it is the army of the bureaucrats. After these follow three hundred wagons. . . . All of these headed for the Department of State, the Imperial Chancellery, the Department of War, the Austrian-Bohemian Chancellery, the Hungarian-Transylvanian Chancellery, the Netherlandish Chancellery, the Town Hall, etc."[15] After the 1780s, bureaucrats worked at home only in times of emergency—during the Napoleonic Wars—when the regime wanted to save on light and heat costs.

Bureaucratic service also meant keeping specific hours at the office (in Vienna usually 9 to 12 and 3 to 6) and demanded punctuality. Although punctuality gradually became understood as a particularly bourgeois virtue during the early years of the nineteenth century, both middle-class and aristocratic bureaucrats were forced to adhere to its demands at work. The mixing of aristocratic and middle-class men in a single office space also demanded challenging adjustments in outward behavior, and not surprisingly, members from different class backgrounds looked upon each other with considerable suspicion. Middle-class bureaucrats, for example, watched jealously for signs that their aristocratic colleagues received unfair privileges, while aristocrats bemoaned the allegedly narrow money-grubbing social outlook of their bourgeois colleagues.[16] Nobles and commoners maintained status differences outside of the office in their domestic arrangements. Especially in Vienna, but also in regional capitals like Prague, Lemberg/Lwów/Lviv, and Graz, the "first society" of nobles strictly separated itself from the "second society" of bureaucrats, businessmen, intellectuals, or artists. Even marriages that bridged the two societies—usually made for financial considerations—rarely united the two families themselves.

The bureaucracy became an object of obsession for Joseph who explained his passionate ideals for state service in a so-called pastoral letter issued in 1783:

> Whoever agrees with me, and who, forsaking all other concerns, will devote himself to being a true servant to the state, he will understand the preceding sentences [the rules governing a bureaucrat's life]. Carrying out their strictures will seem as little burdensome to him as it seems to me. However, he who serves in order to earn money or honors, and whose devotion to the state is merely a side concern, he should be aware of it now, and should leave a post for which he is not worthy, and for which he is not made, a post whose administration demands a burning enthusiasm for the good of the state and a complete renunciation of himself and of every comfort.[17]

This ascetic vision that renounced personal concerns for the sake of a burning commitment to the state was heady stuff, especially for young men of the middle classes seeking to make their mark on Austrian society.

Through his many regulations for the bureaucracy and its procedures, Joseph sought to establish a unified and equal set of norms throughout the monarchy and to create what often sounds like a secular priesthood. During his ten-year reign he issued a steady stream of regulations to micromanage its every aspect of a bureaucrat's career, from his education to rules for his hiring, promotion, salary levels, punishments, and vacations, as well as to prohibit him from accepting gifts. Joseph was the first to establish personnel files (the so-called *Konduite-Listen*), for example, requiring heads of departments to report unsatisfactory employees to him.[18] Joseph insisted that a principle of social equality should permeate the bureaucracy. To this end he established rigorous seniority rules in employment and promotion. "Whether a candidate had bourgeois, knightly, gentry noble, or even princely standing," he wrote, the candidate was nevertheless subject to strict rules of seniority.[19] The seniority principle became an important instrument for breaking the earlier domination of state service by the nobility and laying a foundation for the advancement of members of the middle classes. They, it was assumed, would be far more loyal to the state that had advanced them than to regional interests or class privilege.

A critical aspect of Joseph's bureaucracy was its growing cultural identification with the imperial center in Vienna and specifically with an *Austrian* state. Ideally, patriotic bureaucrats—like Joseph himself—devoted their lives to state service. But to which state should their patriotism attach? Not to Bohemia, Moravia, Hungary, or Croatia—all entities that had earlier histories as independent states. In his 1771 treatise on "Love for the Fatherland," mentioned in the conclusion of Chapter 1, Maria Theresa's adviser Joseph von Sonnenfels had written that the fatherland is the "land in which a man has made his permanent abode." To this bland characterization he added other qualities, including the common laws of the land, its form of government, and all the other people who inhabit the land and are equally subject to its laws. For Sonnenfels, a reformed state based on rational principles did not need traditional patriarchal loyalties or even loyalty to a dynasty. Rather, he argued that such a state required patriotism, a necessary sense of emotional attachment that linked citizens to their state. Sonnenfels's account of patriotism was grounded firmly in the present, and it emphasized attachment to shared laws or what we might today call a constitution. It avoided any reference to a shared past or to a common culture or language. Instead Sonnenfels's patriotism evoked rational choice to explain the emotional quality that should motivate patriotic attachment, rooting emotional attachment—or patriotism—in a kind of utilitarian calculation of advantage:

> The feelings of happiness imparted to us in that land under the protection of such laws, through such a form of government and in the society of such fellow-citizens—all these produce a sense of attachment that is the foundation of our love of the Fatherland. . . . To this must still be added the conviction that we could not find such happiness . . . in any other land, under any other law or form of government, or with any other fellow-citizens than these. . . . In every loss suffered by the Fatherland, we see our own loss; in its very gain we see an increase in our own advantage.[20]

"Fear of losing these advantages," he wrote, "will make us actively fight to save the Fatherland." But would it? Sonnenfels believed that education would eventually root love for an Austrian *patria* in the people. To produce patriotism required teaching about the fatherland in local schools as well as in the universities. A Czech-language primary schoolbook from the reign of Joseph II explained, for example, that

> By "fatherland" [vlast] we understand the place where we were born, but also the land—that is the fatherland—in which we live and enjoy security and protection. All lands above which one emperor, king, or other higher lord reigns are to be held as one fatherland. Thus not only Bohemia, but also Moravia, Austria, Hungary, and other lands belonging to our Monarch are our fatherland.[21]

In this textbook formulation, as in Sonnenfels's patriotic formula above, the common fatherland where people enjoy security, protection, and equality under the law is nevertheless linked in the public mind very closely to a dynasty that embodies it.

In 1788–1789 Gottfried van Swieten (1733–1803), Joseph's director of the State Education Commission (and later of the State Censorship Commission) initiated the first-ever lectures at the University of Vienna on the history of what he called "Österreich," or "Austria" (rather than the Holy Roman Empire or the individual crownlands that made up the monarchy). Joseph II's persistent budget cutting soon put an end to Swieten's Austria lectures, and these early attempts to legitimate empire through education probably made little emotional difference to anyone, except to some servants of the state.[22] Yet, as we have seen with the examples of the peasantry, by the end of the eighteenth century more and more Austrians chose to position themselves on the side of this larger imperial whole. As we will see, a short generation later, in 1815, following the trauma of the Napoleonic Wars, "Austria," the imperial whole, indeed gained emotional meaning as a fatherland or home nation for people of many social classes and geographic regions.

Reform

Under Joseph, the numbers of imperial decrees increased exponentially compared to the last years of Maria Theresa's reign. In 1780 the empress had issued eighty-two decrees for the non-Hungarian regions of her state. In the next year alone, Joseph published 402 decrees for the same regions.

Among the first of these were laws to end censorship as it had been practiced and to substitute radical new guidelines for censors. Maria Theresa had already removed responsibility for censorship from the Catholic Church and created a government commission to rule on the suitability of every work for publication. While not ending the commission, Joseph transformed its function dramatically. In the future, all serious academic works were to be published without question. Moreover, instead of approving every book, the Censorship Commission would rule only on the suitability of a few books that did not appear to pass the new standards. Members of the clergy were no longer allowed to criticize government decrees openly in writing. Other authors, however, were practically invited to criticize Joseph's policies.

Joseph appears to have believed that a policy that blocked every dangerous book and inadvertently ended up excluding many good ones "thereby block[ed] a vital aspect of commerce" and was detrimental to society. Joseph did, however, maintain strict rules against publications that criticized the rulers of other states. Anti-Christian works also remained illegal, and Joseph controlled theatrical productions more carefully than he policed books and pamphlets. This was because Joseph worried more about how such works might influence a largely uneducated public than about their availability to educated individuals. One must, he wrote,

> come down strongly against works that contain unbridled obscenities, from which no learning or enlightenment can ever arise; and to be all the more indulgent in the case of those in which learning, knowledge, and coherence are to be found, since the former are read . . . by the multitude and by weak souls, while the latter come into the hands only of those with well-prepared minds and well-established principles.[23]

The change in censorship rules immediately reduced the number of prohibited books from 5,000 to 900. It also produced a veritable flood of pamphlet literature—over a thousand brochures in the first eighteen months of Joseph's reign. One of these enthusiastically—if somewhat inaccurately—opened with a panegyric to Joseph that claimed: "The wisest, the best of monarchs has given us the freedom to write what we think."[24] The new censorship policy, however, elicited protests from the papal nuncio and other Catholic dignitaries, as well as a cynical response from many aristocratic observers. One of these, Joseph's friend Princess Eleonore Liechtenstein, noted in a letter to her sister, "We are in quite a new world. Isn't it enough to tolerate everything, must we also publish it?" Like several of Joseph's critics, Liechtenstein saw his censorship policy as a sign of disrespect for traditional hierarchy and for the Catholic religion. "Everything is to be feared from the emperor's spirit in this field, from his love of novelty, his perversity, his mania for rousing subordinates against their chiefs, and still more from the hardening of his heart and, finally, abandonment of God."[25]

From the very beginning of his reign Joseph sought to expand his mother's policies to promote popular education. There had never been anywhere near enough schools to realize Maria Theresa's principle that primary schooling should be compulsory for all Austrian children, both boys and girls. Nor was there any effective way to compel families to send their children to schools. Funding for this ambitious goal was entirely inadequate. Joseph's micromanaging bent made him eager to make specific budget cuts for existing institutions in order to balance the increased funding he proposed to give to primary schools. Joseph's emphasis on increasing literacy among the lowest classes led him to shift funds away from secondary and higher institutions of learning. However, his own Education Commission fought Joseph's repeated attempts to downgrade some of the universities and to rid them of subject areas he considered to be of little worth.

Eventually Joseph concluded that no amount of cuts to university budgets could possibly fund the compulsory elementary school system at an adequate level. Instead he enacted a law in 1785 that required a school to be established in every parish.[26] Schoolteachers would be considered civil servants, but given the job description of local sacristan for the church, thus forcing the church to pay most of their salaries. Local property owners and the church would also have to share the costs of the school building and of housing the teacher. It fell to the hapless underpaid teacher to ensure that all local children actually attended school for six years and that they paid minimal school fees. If, however, a family did not have the means to pay the school fees for their children of either sex, they could be relieved of the obligation to pay. Finally, universities would pay a tax to help fund primary schools.[27]

In 1812 the government published regulations that had been accruing since 1785 and touched on every conceivable aspect of schools in the Austrian Hereditary Lands, from their particular locations (on good dry land—no swamp!) to the optimal layout of classrooms to the ideal characteristics of teachers. Each teacher in the school should have his own classroom, which should be bright (with placement of windows specified) and heated by an oven in the winter. There should be double benches on each side of the room set up in such a way that the children would have enough room to sit and to write (exact measurements prescribed). The teacher should sit at a small table on a platform at the front of the room, next to a large blackboard "which can be seen by all the children." The school should be arranged so that the "domestic business of [the teacher's] wife, his children, and his servants do not disturb the pupils and [so] that the schoolroom is not used for any purpose other than teaching." Moreover, extraneous items that have nothing to do with the lessons, such as "spinning wheels, reels, or parts of beds," should not be visible. A special cabinet should store the schoolbooks used by those children who were too poor to buy their own, and extra stools on which school visitors and observers could sit should be provided. New school buildings should also include a separate chamber (1788 law) to accommodate an older sick teacher or a younger assistant, as well as the tools needed by the children who had to learn spinning and knitting outside of regular school hours.[28]

In the same year that had seen the end of traditional forms of censorship, Joseph also issued edicts of toleration for non-Catholic Christians, and later for Jews. Advisers like Kaunitz had consistently urged such a policy of toleration on Maria Theresa, but as a devout Catholic, she had worried that toleration of other sects might harm the moral constitution of the common people. Joseph had very different ideas about religion. He did not oppose the Catholic Church, but he saw religious practice as a personal issue that should not impact civic policy. Moreover, he rightly suspected that newly tolerated groups might prove to be especially loyal to the state. A 1781 order by Joseph stated, "In no matter, except with regard to public religious worship, is a distinction to be made anymore between Catholic and Protestant subjects."[29] Many of the disabilities that had affected his Protestant, Eastern Orthodox Christian, or Greek Catholic subjects—from discrimination in state employment or the right to own land to the right to educate their children—now ended. Protestant children, for example, had to be tolerated in Catholic schools. In communities with more than five hundred Protestant children, the Protestant community gained the right to organize its own schools. These, like their Catholic counterparts, were subject to government regulation. Non-Catholic Christians faced continued limitations on their ability to worship publicly—they could not build steeples with bells, nor generally call attention to their places of worship. Still, the tolerance laws decisively changed the situation of Protestants, Eastern Orthodox Christians, Greek Catholics, and Unitarians decisively. It gave them more legal rights—to join guilds, attend university, or serve in government employ—than members of Protestant sects (to say nothing of Catholics) enjoyed in England at that time.[30]

Joseph's policies toward his Jewish subjects ultimately proved to be far more radical than what his advisers counseled. With the acquisition of Galicia in 1772, the Jewish population of the monarchy more than doubled from about 150,000 in the Habsburgs' hereditary, Bohemian, and Hungarian lands, and by 1780, it stood at around 350,000. Habsburg policy had forbidden Jews (like Protestants) from settling in the central duchies of Lower and Upper Austria, Styria, Carinthia, and Carniola. But as we saw in Chapter 1, even the severely anti-Semitic Maria Theresa had nevertheless encouraged Jewish merchants to settle in the port of Trieste/ Trst. In fact, during her reign Jews had even been encouraged to settle as so-called colonists in depopulated regions of Hungary like the Banat or in Transylvania. Altogether about six hundred Jews had the privilege of living in Vienna, including the important banking families of Arnstein, Eskeles, and Wertheimer, who often served as agents and lenders to the Habsburg government. Bohemia and Moravia had a combined Jewish population of 60,000 in 1780. Here, in return for toleration of their presence, the government subjected Jews to punitive tax levels, as well as to severe restrictions on movement, marriage, employment, and many kinds of property ownership. In Hungary there were about 75,000 Jews in 1780, in Transylvania about 1,000.[31]

Between 1781 and 1785 edicts for each Habsburg territory with a significant Jewish population—Bohemia, Galicia, Hungary, and Moravia—removed several restrictions on Jewish life, opened commercial professions, artisanal crafts, and government service to Jews, and required them to obtain a secular German-language education.[32] (In Hungary, teaching for Jews could be in German, Hungarian, or in a local Slavic language.) The edicts required that Jewish legal and business documents would in future have to be written in German (Latin and Hungarian were also possible in Hungary).[33] Although the edicts did not mention military service, they nevertheless immediately sparked a pamphlet debate in the Holy Roman Empire about Jewish service in the military. Many "enlightened Gentiles" and Maskilim, or "Jewish enlighteners," who participated in these eighteenth-century debates, considered the obligation of military service to be a major obstacle to potential Jewish citizenship and one that either should be or could not be overcome.[34]

When the governor of Galicia proposed a draft Edict of Toleration for his crownland in 1787, he also suggested conscripting Galician Jews into the transport corps. The War Council demurred, citing an alleged Jewish inability to serve on the Sabbath, not to mention the difficulties presented by Jewish dietary laws. Joseph waved aside these objections and ordered the conscription of Galician Jews into both the transport corps and the artillery.[35] Four months later he extended the order to cover Jews in every region of the monarchy. Jewish communities across Galicia vigorously protested the edicts and petitioned to allow Jews to provide paid replacements for military recruitment. Among their arguments, they claimed that Jewish recruits would always be disadvantaged since, unlike their gentile counterparts, they could never gain advancement in the military, no matter how well they served. Some military officers made a similar argument from the opposite perspective: that it would be dishonorable to the military if Jewish subjects, who in civilian life were excluded from several professions, were to assume positions of command over Christian soldiers.

Michael Silber's analysis of these debates demonstrates that at least for Joseph, the earlier Edict of Toleration for non-Catholic Christians had already solved this question. That edict had confirmed that military advancement depended solely on competence. Chancellor Leopold Count

Kollowrat (1727–1809) cited this point indirectly as a reason to reject the Galician Jewish petitions against service: "Since your majesty has graciously granted that Jews like Christians can be qualified for every public office, it therefore follows that in the military profession as well, they can look forward to all promotions which men of other faith can claim to merit."[36]

One remarkable result of these decisions was that during the quarter century of war that dominated Europe from 1788–1815, only the Habsburg Monarchy and revolutionary and Napoleonic France conscripted significant numbers of Jews into the military. In wars fought first against the Ottoman Empire (1788–1791) and later against France (1792–1815), the Habsburgs mobilized thousands of Jewish soldiers. Toward the end of the Napoleonic Wars, for example, Jews made up between 15,000 and 19,000 of the half-million men conscripted in 1814. Altogether, 35,000 Jews may have served the Habsburgs during the twenty-five year period of wars against the French.[37]

Despite the emancipatory elements in Joseph's Jewish legislation, Jews remained subject to a considerable range of local civic and social restrictions in the Habsburg Monarchy. Unlike other citizens Jews did not gain the freedom to migrate and settle anywhere within the monarchy at this time. In particular they could not settle in most of the Hereditary Lands outside of Lower Austria. And everywhere in the monarchy only the eldest son of a Jewish family could marry, and then only after paying a substantial tax; the rule produced a range of negative social effects. In some provinces Jews still required specific permission to settle in particular regions or towns, such as Brünn/Brno in Moravia.[38] Finally, as we have seen with regard to military service, Jewish responses to Joseph's legislation were often ambivalent, largely because Joseph's decrees seemed to define emancipation in terms of a kind of general assimilation (especially the linguistic requirements for education and for legal and financial documents).

At the same time that Joseph increased official toleration for other religions, he also sought to place Catholicism under greater government control, making it, in effect, a state-run church. He continued his mother's policy of closing cloistered communities whose purpose did not directly involve education or hospital work and using their endowments to help pay for the expansion of elementary education. In response to protests by Catholic bishops, Joseph decided to extend state control over education for the clergy. In 1784 Joseph created state-run seminaries in each crown-land capital, and assigned theological faculties to the existing universities.[39] Thanks to Joseph, Catholic bishops in Austria were allowed little formal contact with the pope or with international Catholic institutions. True to his micromanaging impulses, Joseph also imposed specific changes on the Catholic liturgy, cut the number of feast days that could be celebrated, abolished religious brotherhoods, and regulated everything from religious processions and pilgrimages to burial practices. These measures were anchored as much in practical or economic considerations (the numbers of feast days on which workers were excused from working, money spent on processions and church ornamentation, burial and public hygiene) as they were in ideological considerations (rejection of practices Joseph believed to be based on superstition). Among the most radical of these decrees was one in 1784 that regulated marriage as a civil contract and took the power to determine appropriate marriages—for example, among related or divorced individuals—away from the Catholic Church and gave it to the secular courts. Marriage among Christians remained a religious sacrament celebrated by a priest or pastor, but now the state stepped in to regulate an institution that had previously been regulated solely by the church.[40] This legislation did not create a form of civil marriage, but it appeared to lead in that direction.

From 1781 to 1784 Joseph also issued decrees limiting the physical powers nobles could exercise over the serfs who worked their lands. This decisive intervention became known as the abolition of *Leibeigenschaft*—personal bodily servitude or serfdom. From now on, peasants would be free to marry without the permission of the lord, they would be able to move freely, and they could choose an occupation without the lord's permission.[41] The decrees also limited the ability of the lord to punish peasants physically or to fine them. Several economic elements of what was known as "serfdom," however, remained in force in many parts of the empire until the Revolutions of 1848, especially the hated labor service, or *Robot*.

Joseph also intended to provide the emancipated peasantry with land. With regard to his legislation ending serfdom for Bohemia, he noted how much greater "the advantage of this change for the state would be . . . if, at the same time as the abolition of *Leibeigenschaft*, the Bohemian peasant could be granted ownership of his land [on the Austrian model]."[42] But in undertaking a reform of noble-serf relations, Joseph also encountered energetic and powerful opposition. Nowhere was this more the case than in Hungary, where Joseph's attempts to reform the position of the peasants and to tax noble estate owners met with a violent storm of obstruction.

Empire, Integration, and Settlers

The process of building a unified Austrian state included imperial expansion, especially to the east against Poland and the Ottoman Empire, and it was in the newly colonized territories that the Habsburgs believed centralization and administrative reform could assume their purest forms. By participating in the partition of Poland with Russia and Prussia in 1772, the Habsburg regime had picked up a large territory it named the "Kingdom of Galicia." In appropriating the area, however, it also multiplied the administrative and institutional challenges to its goal of territorial integration. Especially in the case of Galicia, the imposition of new borders on the region also required a complete reorientation of its communication, trade, and travel networks, away from what remained of Poland (and the territories taken by Prussia and Russia) and toward Austria.

Joseph and his successors frequently treated the newly invented Kingdom of Galicia as a blank slate on which they could more easily impose enlightened institutions of government. The myth of Polish chaos that had justified the first partition did not recognize the legitimacy or even the prior existence of Polish legal institutions. Instead the Habsburgs and their crusading bureaucrats saw their mission in Galicia as the provision of order, laws, beneficial institutions, and education to an allegedly primitive, lawless, and badly ruled society. As Joseph himself wrote to his mother on his first visit to Galicia in 1773, "I already see in advance that the work will be immense here. Besides the confusion of affairs there already reigns here a partisan spirit that is frightful."[43]

In Galicia the Austrians hoped to showcase the kind of centrally-imposed institutions that had remained challenging if not impossible to impose elsewhere in their monarchy. The problem was, however, that Galicia was anything but a blank slate. Its landowning nobility had traditionally exercised enormous power over local and regional society, as part of a highly de-centralized state, the Polish-Lithuanian Commonwealth. No amount of so-called enlightened laws and institutions in the region could change that fundamental fact. Traditional local power relations made it extremely difficult to create a new Galician society without an enormous investment of resources, and that was something the Habsburgs—especially budget-cutting Joseph—could not afford. Later on, as it became clear that enlightened policies had failed to Austrianize (or according to some bureaucrats, to "civilize") Galicia, the failure was said to be a result of the enormous extent of backwardness, disorganization, and chaos in Galician society. These allegations in turn demanded the imposition of new, firmer forms of centralized rule, which, when they too failed, produced new allegations of backwardness.[44]

Galicia was not the only territory to be integrated into the Habsburgs' Empire with new and enlightened institutions. In 1774 Austrian forces occupied a northern slice of the Ottoman principality of Moldavia, seeking to create a territorial link between Transylvania and the freshly annexed Kingdom of Galicia. The Austrians named this region, which had been the site of several recent wars, "Bukovina" ("Beechland") in reference to the many beech forests that covered its terrain. Like Galicia, Bukovina constituted a newly invented territorial unit. Unlike Galicia, however, Bukovina did not have much of a population and hardly anything of a native landowning nobility to challenge Habsburg plans. This made it far easier to establish new regulations and institutions of rule there, although its depopulated condition meant that Bukovina could hardly pay for its upkeep, given its nonexistent tax receipts. Almost immediately after acquiring this border territory, Maria Theresa and Joseph II sought to recruit a new population for it and to encourage economic development, which, in turn, would defray the costs of maintaining security. Together, however, the goals did not necessarily produce a coherent policy.

When the Habsburg administration first set up shop in Bukovina in the 1770s, Russia, the Ottoman Empire, Poland, and Austria had been fighting incessant wars in the region for over a century. During the most recent wars many peasant communities had simply fled to neighboring Moldavia to seek refuge. Their constant need to be mobile when this or that army swept through the region also influenced peasant agricultural choices in Bukovina. They tended to raise sheep for trade while cultivating only those short-term crops they needed to sustain themselves. They rarely produced an agricultural surplus for trade or for paying taxes.[45] The region's geography did not allow for easy agricultural settlement anyway, especially in the foothills and higher ranges of the Carpathians.

The military sought to establish settled peasant communities that could provide for the military's food and material needs, so it strongly encouraged peasant communities to return from Moldavia once Austria had established order. Joseph II and his bureaucracy in Vienna, however, had more ambitious plans for the region. They hoped to speed Bukovina's economic development by populating it with farmers and artisans from elsewhere in the monarchy and the Holy Roman Empire. Such migrants, who came to be known as colonists, received some land, periodic tax exemptions, farm animals, and seed as incentives to move to this largely unknown land. Under Joseph II, the non-Catholic Christians among them also received official assurances of religious tolerance. Since this new territory was neither dominated by a landowning nobility (as was Galicia) nor by a powerful church, it was at least easier to imagine that the addition of colonists would produce Joseph's ideal society of a free, productive, landowning, tax-paying, and patriotic peasantry.[46]

German nationalist activists in the nineteenth- and early twentieth-centuries often referred to the migrations from the Holy Roman Empire (including Bohemia) or from Transylvania to Bukovina and Galicia as part of a cultural transfer from West to East. According to them, it was not simply agricultural knowledge, or more generally customs and traditions that was transferred, but rather German civilization itself (which they liked to compare with fertilizer for an otherwise barren east). Some of these writers claimed that the same settlers had supposedly provided the East with a greater respect for order, education, and hygiene, all of which could be seen as markers of more advanced levels of civilization. In this way, Austria's population policies in Galicia and Bukovina could be seen in the nineteenth and twentieth centuries as part of an age-old mission undertaken by German or Hungarian nationalists to civilize eastern Europe and the Balkans. With this interpretation nationalists self-consciously invoked the imperialist language of Western superiority articulated by proponents of global colonialism that we will encounter in Chapter 6.

Nationalist narratives about the east gained credence for later observers because many contemporaries—including Joseph II—used the term "colonists" to characterize migrants to Bukovina and Galicia. Moreover, the cultural arguments the regime used to legitimate its role in the partition of Poland—namely, that Austria had entered Poland to bring order, stability, and economic prosperity to what was repeatedly described as a neglected, disorganized, backward, and badly governed society— could be seen to correspond with later arguments about relative levels of civilization. However, it is critical to differentiate between eighteenth-century views about a Habsburg dynastic mission and later nationalist claims of ethnic or even racial superiority. We also have to question claims made by nationalist historiographies that Habsburg rule subjected Galicia, for example, to a form of extractive imperialism comparable to Britain or France's treatment of their colonies in the Americas. Policy debates within the Habsburg government about migrants to the east did not center on arguments about Western cultural or racial superiority. Nor was the effort to populate Bukovina with peasants and artisans from the west part of a goal to Germanize the region, however much later nationalists liked to portray that effort as such when they linked it to Joseph II's German language policies.

Instead, contemporary eighteenth-century debates about colonists covered a range of practical issues about the relative utility of different kinds of migrants. Would it, for example, be more useful to bring in peasant farmers from Bohemia? Or perhaps Szekler farmers from Transylvania? Or should Bukovina instead be repopulated by peasants brought in from neighboring (Ottoman) Moldavia to the east? Under Joseph II the Vienna bureaucracy seems to have favored the former programs, while the military actually argued for the latter. In neither case, however, did the debate revolve around concepts of civilization. Rather, the arguments centered on whether security or economic needs predominated in Bukovina, and thus on the relative utility of the different skills that various populations might bring to the region. In every case, the regime also had to learn from earlier mistakes. Maria Theresa, for example, had sought to import skilled artisans to Galicia and Bukovina out of a general concern about the lack of crafts in those territories. It swiftly became clear, however, that simply importing artisans would not of itself transform local economies. Subsequently, Joseph II developed a more serious and detailed program of migration based on his own observations of conditions in Galicia and Bukovina, advocating bringing peasants to specific regions and even to specific villages in the area. Not surprisingly, given his style of rule, he also had a lot to say about exactly the kinds of houses the migrants should build, at what time of year they should build them, and from what materials. Joseph also accommodated the military's needs by building new villages whose sole role was to serve the local needs of the military.

Subjects to Citizens?

In 1823 Elizabeth Hausner migrated from Bavaria to work as a domestic servant in Vienna. In the following decade Hausner not only worked as a servant, but also managed to become something of a successful jewelry maker on the side.[47] She never married—an important fact in her story—but thanks to her jewelry business, she managed to save up a considerable sum with which she hoped to open a shop. Because she was a resident alien, however, local law prevented her from attaining this aim. So in January 1833, Hausner applied for imperial citizenship. The government took up her case and obtained a police certificate vouching for her morality. Four weeks later she found herself on the steps of Vienna's city hall hearing a lecture on the rights and duties of citizenship, repeating an oath in front of two witnesses, and receiving a certificate that identified her officially as an Austrian *Staatsbürgerin*.

This story, typical for so many migrants to Austria in the eighteenth and early nineteenth centuries, demonstrates the Habsburgs' general openness to immigration from across Europe into all of their lands. They sought not only to repopulate areas of Hungary, Galicia, and Bukovina that had been ravaged by war, but also to raise levels of productivity by importing knowledgeable farmers and artisans with skills in a range of new industries.[48]

As they regularized citizenship requirements across the empire, the Habsburgs made access to state citizenship relatively easy for both male and single female foreigners and resident aliens to obtain. A decree of 1784, for example, advised: "Those foreigners who have lived here for a full ten years are to be considered locals *[Inländer]*." Two years later, the first volume of Joseph II's *Reformed General Civil Code* for the monarchy stated that, "all those who live united in the hereditary lands under the princely power should be considered locals *[Inländer]* and subjects."⁴⁹ The final and perfected version of the ABGB issued in 1811 confirmed the relative ease with which foreigners could become citizens. And as the story of Elizabeth Hausner demonstrates, the code did not differentiate between male and female immigrants' applications for citizenship in the case of single women workers. This quasi-universal character of citizenship with regard to gender did not rest on an emancipatory attitude toward women; rather, it reflected the supposition that women were generally wives and daughters rather than unmarried and independent. A single woman like Elizabeth Hausner qualified for citizenship in a case like this precisely because as a woman she did not conform to the presumed norm.⁵⁰

Along with the thousands of decrees issued during Joseph's reign, the AGBG decisively transformed the social and legal position of the emperor's subjects in relation to each other and to the newly developing Austrian state.⁵¹ Paragraph 16 of the AGBG proclaimed that as citizens of this state Austrians enjoyed innate rights according to the dictates of natural law.

> Every human being has innate rights, which are already obvious according to reason, and is therefore to be regarded as a person. Slavery and servitude, or the use of power to achieve them is not allowed in these territories.⁵²

The code went on to catalog and explain subjects' rights and obligations, which in almost every case tended toward equalization, while terminating corporate or group privileges enjoyed by the nobility and Church institutions. Even though customary noble and Catholic privilege remained substantial when it came to cultural attitudes, and many Galicians and Hungarians complained that servitude had hardly been abolished, the increasing use of a new term—*Staatsbürger,* or state citizen—implied a kind of equality of all before the laws of the central state.[53]

This very mention of citizenship in the new law codes also underlined the ways in which a person now belonged to the empire as a whole, and not simply to a locality or to a particular territory such as Bohemia or Galicia. Such a concept of common citizenship superseded the many different rules of "subjecthood" imposed by the various territories and their diets.[54] It foregrounded the common obligations and privileges of all and implicitly diminished the powers exercised by local or regional authorities. Paragraph 11 explained, for example, that provincial and districts laws were valid after the publication of the ABGB only if the ruler specifically confirmed them. At least in imperial legal terms, subjects of the Habsburg Monarchy were becoming citizens of the state well before the French Revolution had established a model of national citizenship in Europe.

Qualified foreigners like Elizabeth Hausner may have easily obtained imperial citizenship, but even after the publication of the Civil Code, local laws often continued to influence other aspects of one's legal place within the empire. The most critical issue in the eighteenth and nineteenth centuries for citizens and resident aliens alike, one that indirectly challenged the new concept of imperial citizenship, was the requirement that each citizen have a *Heimat.* This was a home locality, where she or he was officially registered and where she or he qualified for public or church assistance. Normally *Heimat* membership was proven by birth registration in the parish records. The problem was that with the decline of serfdom and the rise of more manufacture and industry, increasing numbers of people migrated more frequently, especially from rural to urban areas. Their residency in these expanding towns, however, did not entitle them to welfare benefits or often even to charity there. When workers fell on hard times, they faced the practical necessity of returning to their original *Heimat* if they wanted to qualify for public aid. Those applicants for aid who did not want to return—or who indeed might never have seen their *Heimat* since birth—could be removed by an official policy of forcible deportation, or *Schub.*

In the nineteenth century the rapidly expanding cities and towns increasingly hid behind local *Heimat* requirements as a way to avoid having to dole out welfare or charity to a growing urban working-class population. Local officials also were quick to invoke laws that expelled beggars, petty criminals, and those dependent on public aid to their legal *Heimat*. Clearly the problem here was not so much the foreignness of a person but rather the person's poverty, since only the demand for aid could start the legal process of expulsion, or *Schub*. In the eighteenth century, therefore, local borders and local laws were far more critical to migrant working-class populations than were the more permeable state boundaries or friendly imperial laws. At the same time, when local officials moved quickly to expel paupers and their families to their *Heimat*, regional and imperial officials to whom these unfortunates often appealed put the brakes on the process in order to conduct their own investigations, as Harald Wendelin's illuminating study of *Schub* practices in Vienna in the first half of the nineteenth century demonstrates.[55] Although they usually sided with the local authorities in the end, state authorities showed considerable empathy to the workers and their families who were forced to return to faraway villages where they may have had neither relatives nor social connections, and where they could not find appropriate employment for their particular skills. Wendelin's study also offers quantitative evidence for the surprisingly large distances traveled by many of Austria's poorest citizens during the first half of the nineteenth century in their ongoing search for work that could support them.[56]

The lasting legal importance of *Heimat* in the nineteenth century and the willingness of the local authorities to resort to *Schub* raise the question of the degree to which the Habsburgs succeeded in articulating the dimensions of a shared citizenship in a cultural sense as well as a legal sense Did people of different classes come to see themselves as part of a larger whole? And if so, what were the particulars of a common shared citizenship? How did they conceptualize their relationship to the whole and to each other? Before considering possible answers to these questions, we need to examine the territory where the notion of a common citizenship and loyalty worked least well: Royal Hungary.

From Opposition to Open Rebellion

After the death of Maria Theresa, Joseph avoided subjecting himself to coronation or installment ceremonies in any of his territories, thereby evading a commitment to work with their diets.[57] A coronation diet in Hungary, for example, would have forced Joseph to hear Hungarian demands for a redress of grievances. Given that Maria Theresa had not summoned that diet since 1764, by 1780 the list of potential grievances was daunting. Better not to have the diet meet at all. Since Joseph never convoked the diet, Hungary's sixty-three county assemblies gradually and informally took over from it, formulating grievances and organizing opposition to the king. In 1785–1786 he therefore eliminated their right to meet without his explicit permission, as well as making county governments answerable to a new set of royal commissioners whom he himself appointed.

The next policy of Joseph's that raised opposition was an inevitable product of centralization—namely, his attempt to impose a new administrative language on Hungary. In 1780 the Habsburg state generally used four different languages for official purposes: German in the Hereditary Lands, the Bohemian lands, and in Galicia, Latin in Hungary (including Croatia and Transylvania), Italian in Lombardy, and French in the Austrian Netherlands. At the local level primary schools might use other languages such as Czech in Bohemia, Polish in Galicia, or Hungarian or Slovak in Hungary. But for bureaucratic purposes Joseph decreed in 1784 that German should replace Latin as the official language of administration in Hungary. Local officials who did not already know German would have three years to learn the language if they wished to retain their posts.

Joseph's reasoning had nothing to do with ethnic nationhood, or even with the goal of creating greater social unity through the imposition of a single bureaucratic language. His concern was efficiency. In his view, because the archaic Latin language could hardly keep up with the scientific, technological, and institutional innovations of the eighteenth century, it was incapable of communicating the needs of a modern state. But there were few obvious candidate languages with which to replace it. French and Italian were common in aristocratic circles and at court in the eighteenth century—even Maria Theresa's letters crossed unselfconsciously and frequently from French to Italian to German. The German language seemed a more practical choice as a replacement lingua franca for Latin in Hungary. It was taught throughout the monarchy, and it was also becoming one of the literary and scientific languages of Europe.

Traditionally, most members of the Hungarian elite themselves had little knowledge of the Hungarian language. Hungarian was largely a peasant language, although during Joseph's reign, it gained proponents among the noble elite and the gentry. In 1784, however, Hungarian would not have been a realistic choice with which to replace Latin. Hungary's elite—even those who were less educated—shared in an informal multilingual tradition that encompassed knowledge of several languages: perhaps a Slavic language learned from Slovak-, Croat- or Serb-speaking servants and nursemaids, French and Italian for the higher nobility with some education or experience at court, Latin among the diet and county officials, and sometimes German as well. The Croatian elite that were counted part of Hungary's nobility, for example, were far more likely to use Slavic, Latin, or German than Hungarian. Most people in Hungary's cities at this time spoke German, especially the politically under-represented merchants and artisans of Pressburg/Pozsony, Buda, and Pest. Finally, German already served as the interregional administrative language for many other parts of the Habsburg state and the military. Its introduction would be yet another means for helping to integrate Hungary more fully in the rest of the monarchy.

All of this may have made good rational sense in the mind of a dedicated reformer like Joseph. But the new language policy provoked a completely different reaction among Hungary's elite, particularly at the local level. Hungary's nobles, whether rich or poor—and the income of many local gentry families barely distinguished them from common peasants—shared two fundamental privileges that set them apart from the rest of the population. One was the exclusive right to serve as local or royal administrators. In Hungary, unlike the rest of the monarchy, only nobles could be administrators. The other was not having to pay taxes, a privilege that nobles in many other parts of the monarchy had recently lost under Maria Theresa. Joseph's language reform threatened the first of these privileges. If local gentry administrators did not learn German within three years, they would forfeit the extra income from their service in administrative posts, income many counted on to ensure their survival.

The historical timing of Joseph's decision to impose German as the favored lingua franca of imperial administration was problematic in another way, and not simply in Hungary. Joseph favored German because of its new status as a literary and scientific language in the eighteenth century. At the same time, however, this period saw efforts in Bohemia and Hungary by regional patriots to revive, modernize, and promote the Czech language and the Hungarian language as well. Several new journals appeared in Czech and Hungarian in the 1780s, precisely when officials began to encourage improvements in peasant agriculture by publishing pamphlets in these vernacular languages. Those sympathetic to the government's program could argue, as did the Hungarian Györgi Bessenyei, that "the key to culture is a national language . . . and the cultivation of that language is the first duty of the nation." While the new strength of German in literature and the sciences hardly eclipsed other languages at this time, as Robert J. W. Evans has noted, it did serve as an example of how other vernacular languages might themselves be updated and increased in use. This development in turn upset the neutral character of Joseph's linguistic program, which in the face of attempts to promote vernacular languages came to appear Germanizing and thus to deserve resistance.[58]

Joseph's next initiatives threatened the other major privilege enjoyed by Hungarian nobles, their freedom from taxation. When he imposed a census to coordinate military conscription in Hungary with conscription in the rest of the monarchy, his action aroused suspicions that his deeper purpose was to impose taxation on Hungary's nobility the way Maria Theresa had on nobility in the Bohemian and Hereditary Lands thirty years earlier.[59] Indeed, another of Joseph's plans—to carry out a land survey (cadastre) throughout the entire monarchy in 1785—raised objections from the nobility everywhere who saw it as a prelude to new taxes.[60] In fact the new survey did create the basis for a simplified future land tax, and in February of 1789 the announcement of a new "Tax and Agrarian Regulation" confirmed the worst fears of nobles across the monarchy. The law imposed the system that Maria Theresa had adopted decades earlier for her own lands in Bohemia and Hungary. From now on, all hereditary tenants (so-called rustical peasants) would pay a single tax of 30 percent on their yearly produce.[61] This single cash tax would be divided between the central state, which would receive 12.2 percent of peasant income, and the local landowner who would receive 17.8 percent. The law ended all other peasant obligations, including the hated compulsory labor (Robot) that most tenants still owed their lords. Theoretically this single tax payment incorporated the value of that labor in its calculations.

Most nobles feared that this reform would drastically reduce their income, and with good reason. In the Hereditary Lands, for example, landlords already took in anywhere from 25 percent to 42 percent of the value of their tenants' annual produce rather than the 17.8 percent to which this legislation would limit them. In Galicia their potential loss was higher.[62] It would be even worse for the nobility in Hungary, who had been completely free of taxation. For the nobility with large estates, the ending of unpaid serf labor, or Robot, spelled disaster for a way of life that for years had depended on relations that approached those of slavery.

Although this legislation applied only to hereditary peasant tenants, most nobles with landed estates feared that once the other peasants—those who worked directly for their landlords (the so-called dominical peasants)—learned about these reforms, they would demand a similar deal.[63] In any case, given Joseph's views on citizenship and the importance of independent production, it would only be a matter of time before he applied the same arrangement to the dominical peasants. This, estate owners feared, would completely destroy the necessary conditions for their economic survival.[64] Indeed, had this legislation been implemented, many nobles in Hungary and Galicia would have been forced to sell their estates. Without forced labor contributions from the peasantry they would have lacked the necessary labor to farm their lands. This outcome might have produced a society of arguably more efficient small landowners of the kind that reformers had been seeking to create since the 1740s. But it would have spelled disaster to many nobles.[65]

The shock of this legislation, combined with anger about so many of his other reforms, brought the empire closer to disaster than at any time since Frederick of Prussia's invasion of Silesia in 1741. Several of Joseph's own advisers protested vigorously against the 1789 regulation whose implementation Joseph was forced to delay until 1790, when the land survey would be complete. Meanwhile peasants in several parts of the monarchy simply withheld their tax payments altogether in anticipation of the new law. In the Austrian Netherlands (today's Belgium), Joseph's reforms met with massive displays of civil disobedience, and local opposition leaders began to organize an armed revolt. In Hungary the tax reform, along with administrative centralization and the imposition of German, produced a perfect storm of opposition. Moreover, thanks to an alliance with Catherine the Great of Russia against the Ottoman Empire, Joseph had found himself unwillingly forced into war in 1787, when the Ottomans declared war on Russia. While an Austrian army of 200,000 was tied down in the Balkans, Joseph faced danger from another quarter.[66] The new king of Prussia, Frederick William II (1744–1797), had negotiated an offensive alliance with the Ottomans in 1790. Sensing Habsburg weakness, Prussia sent agents to both the Austrian Netherlands and Hungary and appeared to be preparing an invasion of Bohemia.[67] In Hungary many nobles in the county opposition demanded the convocation of a diet to replace the Habsburg dynasty. Since Joseph had never been crowned king, they argued, all of his legislation was null and void, and since the diet had traditionally elected the King, it could certainly elect one from another dynasty.

Now is the place to mention another institution that Joseph had developed during the last years of his reign: a secret police. Under the direction of Count Johann Anton von Pergen (1725–1814), who had previously served as Galicia's first governor, Joseph established a so-called *Geheime Staatspolizei*, or secret state police. The exact purpose of this force remains somewhat unclear even today. Secret police agents paid by the state were nothing new, nor particularly Austrian. Joseph allegedly wanted this force to monitor public opinion and to keep an eye on suspicious persons and foreigners, as well as on the conduct of his own officials. According to his biographer, Derek Beales, however, Joseph had a low opinion of spies, asserting that "they only did it for the money without giving true service . . . and often made a mess of things." Joseph's lack of enthusiasm was also reflected in the miserable budget with which he provided Pergen, who had only enough money to employ two assistants.[68]

This minimal force could tamper with mail, for example, but according to Joseph, its actions should not "damage the reputation of the post and civil freedom." Moreover, Joseph repeatedly emphasized that people ought to be allowed to criticize the government, as long as they posed no threat to security. In fact, Beales argues that this new force was more a product of Joseph's relentless desire to know what was going on everywhere than an attempt to police society. Nevertheless, in the last year of his reign, as rebellion brewed in Hungary and the Netherlands, the role of this force grew. Joseph started reviving some other forms of censorship as well. Essentially what he learned from Pergen's secret police was just how pervasive political discontent among the elite had become by 1789.[69]

It was not only Pergen's spies, but also many of Joseph's closest advisers who feared the political consequences of the agrarian reform among the nobility. In the Austrian Netherlands the recent revolution in France seemed to inspire great enthusiasm as well as minor revolts among the nobles. Joseph's minister there reported to him that "our situation becomes more critical with every day that passes."[70] In this moment of considerable danger to the dynasty, Joseph, who was badly ill, began to backpedal. It was too late to save the Austrian Netherlands for Austria, but he promised to convoke a diet in Hungary. When that failed to quell the opposition, he renounced most of the policies he had imposed on Hungary during his ten-year reign and promised to return the crown of St. Stephan from Vienna to the castle in Buda.[71] "It is my will," he wrote, "in order to meet every imaginable and half plausible complaint from the Hungarian and Transylvanian Estates, that all the generally applicable laws and orders made since the beginning of my reign shall be repealed, and everything put back to the condition in which it was at the time of Her Late Majesty's death.[72] Joseph stipulated certain exceptions to his renunciation. Both the toleration patent (for non-Catholic Christians and for Jews) and the patent abolishing the physical servitude of serfs were to be maintained. "I wish from my heart," wrote Joseph in the same document, "that Hungary may through this decree enjoy as much happiness and good order as I desired at all times to bestow on her through my legislation."

To his brother and heir, Grand Duke Leopold of Tuscany, Joseph wrote privately that he had been "unfortunate in everything" he had undertaken. Characteristically he added that "the appalling ingratitude with which my good arrangements are viewed and I am treated" filled him with doubt. "I dare not defend my own opinion and haven't the strength to impose it and argue for it."[73] Within three weeks Joseph was dead, barely a month before his forty-ninth birthday. Leopold was left to pick up the pieces.

Opposition and Nationhood

When Leopold arrived in Vienna from Florence, he had his hands full trying to restore peace to his rebellious subjects and to protect the fragile integrity of the state. In order to salvage the monarchy from the dramas of his brother's turbulent reign, Leopold made several tactical retreats, listened politely to endless litanies of complaints, and forced himself to express sympathy for aristocrats and their provincial concerns. To establish some measure of trust, he immediately agreed to coronations in both Hungary and Bohemia, something Joseph had always refused to do. Coronations gave provincial diets the opportunity to make demands of their sovereign as he swore oaths to uphold provincial traditions. In this case Leopold did not simply anticipate diet demands. The new emperor went out of his way to invite the provincial diets—or "nations" as many called themselves—to submit their complaints to him. Throughout the monarchy the noble estates in the diets took the opportunity offered by a new reign to try to assert—or regain—several lost elements of their privileged standing.

As in the past, Hungarian leaders claimed the most far-reaching rights of their elite "nation" against the encroachments of Joseph. Elsewhere in the monarchy, other diets, which had not met in decades, now deployed the rhetoric of nationhood to shift a fluctuating balance of power in their favor. Their use of this rhetoric reflected some relatively new and subtle shifts in understandings of the meaning of "nation." We have already encountered two very different political understandings of the term, with one, in the case of traditional Hungary and Poland, being applied to those with political privileges (the noble nation) and the other, promoted by men like Sonnenfels, being simply the fatherland of all the state's citizens. In yet a third meaning of the term, rulers or administrators sometimes treated different crownlands as distinct nations, as in

"Bohemia," "Moravia," or "Hungary." Maria Theresa's political testament of 1750–1751, for example, referred critically to the ways in which her administrators had too often sought the good of their own "nations," in this case meaning their home crownlands (Bohemia or Hungary), as opposed to the good of the whole fatherland. But elsewhere, in discussing her administrative reforms, she had also referred to Bohemia and Moravia as part of her Hereditary Lands, as opposed to her treatment of Hungary as a distinct "nation." In Maria Theresa's mind, Hungary always occupied a special place. Hungary, after all, had been key to her very survival as ruler in 1741. Joseph II, on the other hand, had refused to see Hungary in that way and had refused to be crowned there.

In yet a fourth use of the term "nation," both Maria Theresa and Joseph II mentioned informally the many "peoples," or "nations," that made up their larger state, referring in this instance to the different languages those peoples used. A 1747 patent of Maria Theresa, for example, had referred to the *böhmische Landessprache,* or Bohemian provincial language, by which she meant Slavic Bohemian, or what we would call Czech. When Hungarians protested his imposition of German as an administrative language, Joseph wrote in 1784: "The German language is the universal language of my *Reich.* Why should I use the national language when treating the laws and public business in one single province?"[74] Here Joseph's characterization of Hungarian as a specific "national language" emphasizes its provincial character, in contrast to his conception of German as an imperial or universal language. This latter usage, however, was further complicated by the Habsburgs' position in the Holy Roman Empire. Did Joseph mean that German was the universal language of the Holy Roman Empire or of an emerging Habsburg state? Such a distinction would not always have been very clear to contemporaries (the way it might be for us), since many writers often blurred the Habsburgs' nominal position at the head of the old Holy Roman Empire with their position as rulers of an emerging Austrian state. In still other contexts Joseph called German the true mother tongue and *Landessprache* of the whole monarchy.

Just as the French revolutionaries used the assertion of French nationhood to unify their state, the Habsburgs too sought to use a common national citizenship as a way to impose uniformity on their diverse realms. Their opponents used the term "nation" in order to pursue a kind of federalism that would maintain different rights and privileges against imperial centralization. This logic became much more apparent when Leopold agreed to convoke many of the individual territorial diets in order to restore stability after Joseph's death. Several diets asserted their "national rights" as a way to restore their diet's privileges. One diet's assertion of its "national" rights, however, could draw opposition from another diet that defined nationhood differently. In 1790, when Leopold agreed to undergo coronation rituals in Hungary and Bohemia, the Bohemian diet claimed Moravia and Silesia as integral parts of the lands belonging to their crown, which was known as the crown of St. Wenceslas.[75] Members of the Moravian Diet, however, balked at their inclusion in the Bohemian coronation ceremonies in Prague. Arguing that they constituted a separate "nation" from the Bohemian or Czech nation, the Moravians petitioned for some kind of equivalent ceremony in Moravia to complement the coronation in Prague. The Moravian petition demonstrated the degree to which many people understood nationhood in purely political or historic terms (historical Bohemia versus historical Moravia) or regional terms (the Moravians constituted a regionally different nation from the Bohemians, despite linguistic similarities between the peoples of the neighboring crownlands) rather than in other terms such as language use or ethnicity.[76]

Yet a fifth concept of nation is evident from arguments the Bohemian Diet made to Leopold as it tried to renegotiate its relationship to the crown. In lobbying for a new treaty to be drawn up between the king and the nation, the diet used the term "nation" to refer to the traditional elite estates represented in the diet: usually nobles, the church, sometimes the towns. In this case, however, some members of these privileged estates positioned themselves as the representatives of every inhabitant in Bohemia, calling themselves the voice of all the people vis-à-vis the ruler. To reinforce this claim, the Bohemian Diet used the Czech language for part of the coronation ritual for both Leopold (1791) and his son Francis, who succeeded him in 1792. The particular form of Czech used in certain coronation speeches was an extremely formal, archaic language, carefully prepared for the occasion by Slavic philologist Joseph Dobrovský (1753–1829). It bore little resemblance to the Czech language used by most peasants or townspeople in Bohemia.[77]

This symbolic act of linguistic inclusion hardly implied that Bohemian nobles necessarily wanted to make Czech their language of daily conversation. According to František Martin Pelcl (1734–1801), a tutor in aristocratic Bohemian households, generally the clergy used Latin, the nobility spoke French, merchants, burghers and civil servants communicated in German, and "a part of the burghers, the crowd [Pöbel] and the peasants" spoke Czech. Dobrovský also argued in 1791 that Czech was "the spoken language of the ordinary man, but at the same time in no way the spoken and written language of the most moral and enlightened part of the nation." In fact, those nobles who preferred French also considered German to be almost as rough and primitive as Czech. At this point in history, we are still over a decade away from educator Joseph Jungmann's efforts to persuade Bohemian society that the Czech language had the requisite qualities to become an interregional language on the level of French, Italian, or German, and that its use should not simply be limited to the communicative needs of the lowest classes. In the context of the coronation ceremonies its use both conveyed a self-conscious link to the medieval Kingdom of Bohemia and implied that the diet spoke for all Bohemians, not simply the traditional political nation.

In Vienna's late eighteenth-century centralizing policies, the Czech language (whether used or not) was gradually being adopted as a symbol for Bohemian autonomy and its *political* nationhood by elites who claimed to represent all the people. Vienna's dual policies of using German as an imperial bureaucratic language on one hand, while encouraging the use of vernacular languages for local usage and education on the other, drew increasing attention to an emerging and unintended hierarchy of languages and by extension, as could be argued, of the people who spoke them.[78] The equality of citizenship—and the idea of the nation as all the people—would thus require that all languages in use in the empire be considered equal as well.

What did those diets that claimed to speak for nations actually demand of Leopold? In general, they sought a return to the status quo that predated both Maria Theresa's and Joseph's many reforms. The Bohemian

Diet even sought to make kingship elective again, to divide legislative power between the king and an annual diet, and to revoke the measures that had taxed the nobility and had diminished peasant obligations to their local lords. The Hereditary Lands demanded much the same in terms of restoring noble privilege and reviving the *Robot*. Leopold did revoke some of Joseph's most radical reforms (including the new cash tax system to replace *Robot* and dues on kind), but on the whole he tried to maintain the more centralized structure of his mother's and brother's state.

War and a New Austrian State

Starting in 1789 a revolution in France that became increasingly radical in tenor began to cause concern among the other rulers of Europe, especially Leopold II, Queen Marie Antoinette's brother. The revolutionary regime declared war on Austria and Prussia in the spring of 1792, and its army unexpectedly defeated the Austrians and Prussians at the Battle of Valmy in September 1792. Revolutionary France now plunged Europe into a quarter of a century of ongoing warfare. Earlier in that same year in March, Leopold himself had died unexpectedly, well before he had fully resolved the dangerous situation bequeathed to him by his brother, Joseph. Leopold's eldest son, Francis (1768–1830), who began his reign as Francis II of the Holy Roman Empire and ended it as Francis I of the Austrian Empire, was no scion of the Enlightenment like his father and uncle. Moreover, the first two decades of his long reign (1792–1835) were overshadowed by the need to stave off recurring military challenges from France that threatened the very survival of his dynasty's patrimony. This left few options for creative initiatives in state building. When combined with Francis's particularly cautious personality traits, all of these unexpected demands produced a conservative and defensive approach to maintaining the existing state.[79] Like both his uncle, Joseph, and father, Leopold, however, Francis did see himself as a devoted servant both of the state and of the law. Like both of them, he also pursued a fundamentally centralizing agenda. Unlike his father, however, Francis was unsympathetic to even limited ideas of constitutional reform. Unlike his uncle, Francis had a very limited imagination. His bureaucracy was not there to reform society. Rather, the bureaucracy served to maintain order and legality in society.

Francis's image of the ideals that his bureaucrats should embody also differed from Joseph's. Not only did they have to live up to the exacting standards of work laid forth for them by Joseph II, and for less pay in a time of terrible wartime inflation, but increasingly their private lives also became objects of state interest. A bureaucrat's private life had not particularly interested Joseph; he had cared only about how well a man did his job. Contemporaries, however, often interpreted the social upheavals caused by the French Revolution as products of private moral decay. Thus under Francis, an Austrian bureaucrat's private life came to outweigh his particular knowledge or accomplishments when he applied for a post. Now a bureaucrat's (and his family's) morals and religiosity counted more than his education and experience.[80] This had implications well beyond death or gender, since a bureaucrat's widow had to remain morally "above reproach" if she hoped to receive a pension and his daughter likewise had to be considered virtuous if she hoped to qualify for a scholarship to a young lady's academy.

Francis's attitude toward the very purpose of his state service created considerable problems once the long wartime emergency had ended. Unlike both his father and uncle, he also believed that the interests of the crown and the crownland aristocracies were essentially one. Thus, despite the fact that many Josephenists remained in their positions, one historian has called Francis's system "absolutist and centralist in its institutions, but usually aristocratic and ultra conservative in the conduct of them."[81]

After the first few years of war, when surprisingly good harvests had kept food prices low, war began to cause inflation and food shortages in many parts of the monarchy, especially in the cities and towns. By 1795 the government was printing paper money to cover the added costs of war, and by 1797—as a result of a panic caused by fears that Napoleon would take Vienna—silver was completely withdrawn from circulation, and state employees and state creditors had to accept paper bills as their payment.

Conditions for urban working people deteriorated drastically during the war for a variety of reasons, while the city and town populations nevertheless continued to grow.[82] In the first years of the war Viennese journeymen in the textile industry protested openly against their employers' increasing use of unskilled female and child labor.[83] The protestors, however, tended to blame their employers and not local women. Almost twenty years later, crowds attacked bakeries, took paper money from the till, and tore it up to general jubilation. Meanwhile, the gentlemen of the textile industry throughout the monarchy often profited handsomely from the war, thanks to military contracts for uniforms and other supplies, and later thanks to Napoleon's blockade of British goods from the European continent.[84]

War also produced mounting fears of subversion on the part of the regime. Starting in 1800, the state for the first time required bureaucrats to swear an annual oath of loyalty. The regime also acted to limit those spaces in society where it believed that subversion might develop. It closed down Freemason associations and cracked down harshly on the alleged "Jacobin conspiracies" it unearthed in Vienna, Tyrol, Hungary, Carinthia, and Carniola. These so-called "Jacobin conspiracies," named after the radical French political party of the mid 1790s, tended to involve civil servants, educated men who had served Joseph II and Leopold II and who hoped to inject more of a reform orientation into the reign of Francis II. Many of them generally supported programs that were hardly radical by the standards of the 1790s. Indeed, among the plans developed by the most radical of the conspirators was one to convoke an empire-wide people's parliament (Volksrat), suggesting that even they did not question the existence of the empire; they questioned merely its particular style of rule.[85] Nonetheless, those conspiracies that the police managed to uncover were treated with incredible severity, and several ended in executions. Still, the war saw no diminution of the popular eighteenth-century coffee houses and other social meeting places in towns and cities throughout the monarchy. If anything, in the towns at least, coffee houses took on new roles as sites where the latest news about the war could be exchanged and debated.

On the other hand, Emperor Francis opposed mobilizing popular patriotism for his empire during most of the two decades of war. While a few other central European monarchs—especially the King of Prussia— embarked on significant experiments with reform programs to rebuild their military and create popular support for war, Francis did so only with the greatest reluctance. Anything that promoted social reform or worse still, popular enthusiasm, once unleashed, might not be so easily contained. So it fell to others to advance the wartime popularity of the emerging Habsburg state and of the new Austrian Empire that Francis eventually proclaimed in 1804. Already in 1796, for example, as French armies in northern Italy neared the Austrian border, the governor of Lower Austria, Count Francis Joseph von Saurau, commissioned poet Leopold Haschka to write a text to encourage patriotic enthusiasm for Austria's cause. Saura then persuaded composer Joseph Haydn to set the text to music. Haydn referred to his composition specifically as the "peoples' song" *(Volkslied)*. On February 12, 1797, on the occasion of the emperor's birthday, this now famous "Emperor's Song," or "God Save Our Emperor," was first performed in theaters across the empire (the emperor himself heard it in the Court Theater).[86] The song, translated into all the vernacular languages of the monarchy, would become Imperial Austria's official anthem later in the nineteenth century.

Finally, after losing three consecutive wars against France (in 1793, 1799, and 1805), and with several Austrian territories under foreign occupation (the Bavarians occupied Tyrol, while the French took parts of the empire's new Adriatic holdings), Emperor Francis reluctantly approved some cautious efforts to reform Austrian society to build wartime patriotism. This brief reform period was nothing like that engaged in by Prussia during this time, and we should keep a clear sense of proportion in mind when examining the changes themselves. Nevertheless, it is apparent that the few reforms the government did propose helped to build a greater sense of common purpose and identification among the emperor's subjects. The emperor's brother Field Marshal Archduke Charles (1772–1847) carried out the most far reaching of these administrative reforms: he dismissed twenty-five generals, worked to humanize military discipline, implemented the new idea of reserve battalions, and promoted plans to create a popular "people's militia." For his part, the emperor proclaimed his intention to allow society a freer intellectual life (including support for literature) and to establish more schools, but expectations that he would abolish censorship were disappointed, as were expectations that he would reform the scope of the secret police (whom Francis had spy on his popular brothers as well as on ordinary Austrians).[87]

As Austria prepared for the War of the Fifth Coalition against Napoleon in 1809, the emperor's popular—and some have argued more capable—brother Archduke Johann (1782–1859), about whom we will hear more in Chapter 3, organized Austrian men into a home militia (*Landwehr*). The militia was compulsory for all men between the ages of eighteen and forty-five who were not already serving in the military and was instituted in the hereditary provinces and the Bohemian lands. At the same time, the government also created a comparable institution in Hungary called the *insurrectio*. In Galicia, however, where the regime rightly suspected the Polish nationalist elite of harboring sympathy for Napoleon's promise to reconstitute an independent Poland, the regime created a reserve instead.[88]

The home militia, or *Landwehr*, attained considerable emblematic significance as an interregional all-Austrian patriotic institution. Symbolizing the universal mobilization of all Austrians and their commitment to an interregional defense, the militia demonstrated that the war was not waged on behalf of far-away rulers and that it instead involved the "Austrian people"—all classes, all generations, sometimes even both genders—sacrificing to defend their common interest. In 1813, only four years after the creation of the militia, during the War of the Sixth Coalition, also referred to as the War of Liberation, painter Johann Peter Krafft portrayed a determined young man dressed as a militiaman, with rifle in hand, leaving his family for the war in *The Departure of the Militiaman*, a popular painting that represented the militiaman in general as the embodiment of the Austrian people's sacrifice and of their enthusiasm for the common cause.[89]

The setting of the painting is domestic, depicting the interior of a modest rural hut that nevertheless contains several articles of furniture and décor that indicate the solid prosperity enjoyed by the family. The scene is also intergenerational, showing the parents of the militiaman weeping and praying, while his wife and three children are saying goodbye. Another militiaman accompanies the subject of this painting, and through a small window we see many others departing in a hilly landscape. There is nothing forced about the militiaman's attitude. His

The Departure of the Militiaman (1813) by Johann Peter Krafft. Credit: © Belvedere, Wien.

determined expression captures his alleged willingness to defend the fatherland, while his family voluntarily makes their sacrifice, even as they understand the terrible consequences war might bring. Although the militiaman's mother hides her face in tears, his wife clasps his hand and does not cry or look away (nor do the children). The centrality of the wife in the picture suggests to me the degree to which Krafft wished to depict the universality of a cause that demanded sacrifice of Austria's women as well as of its men.

No patron had commissioned *The Departure of the Militiaman*. It was entirely Krafft's inspiration, and it garnered him immediate praise and served as a model for many other artists in the next half century. Emperor Francis bought the painting in 1815 and had it exhibited publicly before housing it in the imperial picture gallery. The picture also gained great popularity when two well-known engravers sold etched versions to Austrians across the empire, ensuring Krafft a broad reputation as premiere painter for the fatherland.[90] The themes of the popular painting were also repeated in other forms of contemporary material culture such as painted porcelain or glass and commemorative medallions.[91]

The militiaman may have been a universal figure in the empire, but it was often regional conditions that shaped his reasons for fighting. At the same time, what makes this moment critical to the history of the empire is the way in which those regional imperatives often became connected to the imperial cause in highly particular ways. Nowhere perhaps is this clearer than in the case of the "Tyrolean nation" and the popular mythology that developed around the figure of the insurrectionary leader Andreas Hofer. When French forces first threatened invasion in 1796, the degree to which the national defense mobilized men of all classes from across the region against a common enemy can be gathered from popular songs of the period. "Up brave Tyrolers!" exhorted one song in dialect, and ended by proclaiming, "Everyone's heart burns for love of the fatherland" and "We favor only one Lord, only Francis the Second." The popular understanding of the relationship between Tyrol and the empire, however, was still expressed through a traditional concept of mutual obligation, not an idea of organic unity. Francis II protected the traditional rights and freedoms of the political nation Tyrol, and in turn, Tyrolers fought loyally for their emperor.

In 1805, however, the Treaty of Pressburg, which ended Austria's role in the War of the Third Coalition, attached Tyrol to neighboring Bavaria. Bavaria's attempt to impose its centralized constitution on Tyrol, along with new religious laws, raised considerable opposition within the population. In April of 1809 Austria again declared war on the French. The following declaration to the troops composed by Friedrich Schlegel for Archduke Charles framed the Austrian cause specifically in terms of Austrians' freedom: "Europe seeks freedom beneath your standards. Your victories will loose her bonds." The declaration aimed to remind Tyroleans, who suffered under Bavarian rule, that Austria was prepared to liberate them. Napoleon meanwhile, sought to undermine the unity of the empire by issuing his own counter-proclamation directed at Hungary, inviting the Hungarians to rise up against Austria; as one historian put it, the invitation "fell almost flat."[92]

At that moment Andreas Hofer also led a successful rebellion against Bavarian rule in the Tyrol, after having secretly negotiated with Vienna

for money and arms. Hofer was an innkeeper from just north of Bozen/
Bolzano who spoke both German and Italian and who had formerly
served as an elected deputy to the Tyrolean Diet. Under Hofer, Tyrolean
militiamen and sharpshooters swiftly drove out the Bavarians and reestablished Austrian rule (and more importantly, Tyrolean customs) in
Innsbruck. In May Emperor Francis promised the reestablished Tyrolean
Diet that he would not sign any peace treaty that did not reunite Tyrol
with Austria. After losing to the Archduke Charles at Aspern in June, the
French nevertheless defeated the Austrians at Wagram in July, not far
from Vienna. In the subsequent Treaty of Vienna, concluded in October,
Austria was forced to pay an enormous indemnity to the French, to reduce the size of its military, and to cede its Adriatic territories, along with
Trieste, Istria, and Carniola to France. Austria also agreed to return Tyrol
to the Bavarians.

In relinquishing Tyrol, Francis treated that crownland according to
an older tradition of imperial horse-trading we saw in Chapter 1, but Tyroleans treated Francis as far more than a sovereign and now clearly
regarded Austria as their state or fatherland. In this case the regional
loyalties and interests of the Tyroleans in remaining part of the Austrian empire outstripped the callous state-building considerations emanating from Vienna. As a result, the Tyroleans continued a sporadic gue-
rilla war effort against the French, but eventually, in January of 1810 the
French captured Hofer and took him in chains to the fortress in Mantua.
There Napoleon had him tried and shot in February, despite an attempted intercession by Metternich.[93] Hofer's tenacious engagement
against the French and Bavarians may have proved ineffective in 1810, but
his death—soon framed as martyrdom in the extremely Catholic Tyrol—
created powerful myths of Tyrolean resistance to tyranny and exceptional loyalty to Austria, myths that contributed to Austrian patriotism
and imperial glory during dark times.

Over time, the Hofer myth came to serve two interrelated but very
different claims. The first strengthened the notion of Tyrolean particularism by mythologizing the distinctive bravery and independent spirit
of a "Tyrolean nation." The second and related claim, however, placed
Tyrol in the first place of honor in terms of bravery, piety, and patriotism
among the different lands that made up the empire. Tyrol's distinctive-

ness, many argued in subsequent decades, lay precisely in its exceptional and special loyalty to the dynasty and thus to the imperial order.[94] This suggests also that despite Sonnenfels's emphasis on a patriotism determined by loyalty to law, in fact the dynasty continued to occupy a central place in the mythologies of the common empire.

Common Empire in Peace

In June of 1814, with Napoleon exiled to Elba, Emperor Francis returned to Vienna in triumph from Paris. Celebrations greeted Austria's emperor along the way in central Europe, often in towns that had only recently been part of the Holy Roman Empire over which he had once reigned, at least symbolically. Banners in the streets, on houses, and on hastily erected triumphal arches alternately hailed him as the prince of peace, a glorious conqueror, the liberator of the pope, the father of the people, or as the German emperor. On 15 June Francis reached his suburban palace at Schönbrunn, and on the following day he set out for Vienna. He was greeted at the city's Carinthian Gate (Kärntner Tor) by the mayor and an assemblage of 547 boys and girls dressed in the Viennese colors of white and red, the girls wearing flower garlands over their dresses and the boys laurel wreaths.[95] From here the emperor made his way along narrow flower-strewn streets that twisted through the old city until he reached St. Stephen's Cathedral where he heard a *Te Deum*. In the evening, Vienna's residents illuminated their houses, using images, metaphors, and slogans—many drawn from classical mythology—that celebrated Francis's alleged qualities as victor and as bearer of peace.

Theatergoers at the Kärntner Theater that night were treated to an allegorical drama by Joseph von Sonnleithner. In the play the goddess of peace, having vanquished the demons of war, decides to settle in Austria under the "most just Emperor." To celebrate her decision, fifty couples dressed in diverse folk costumes representing all the "peoples" of Austria—defined by their historical crownland identities—form a semicircle around the goddess. She exhorts them to unity, and the Hungarian, the Bohemian, the Tyroler, and the Lower and Upper Austrian each swears allegiance to her in the name of all Austria's peoples. The allegory replaced the martial exhortations to patriotism that had only recently

Johann Peter Krafft's depiction of the triumphant return of Emperor Franz I to Vienna, 16 June 1814, painted for a cycle in the Hofburg Palace, 1828–1832. Credit: Erich Lessing/Art Resource, NY.

dominated an Austria constantly at war for over two decades with a new image was of unity defined by a common commitment to peace. At the same time, however, as Brian Vick points out, in their allegory the organizers also spoke of *Freyheit,* or freedom, to conjure a more active concept of the citizenry.[96]

We know about these festivities in exacting detail thanks to the diligent work of one Joseph Rossi, a Viennese civil servant who documented the celebrations in the form of a two-volume book.[97] Rossi's first volume contained descriptions and drawings of house illuminations created by men and women in Vienna and its suburbs. In it we learn, for example, how the Jews of Vienna celebrated the emperor's return "in a less opulent but nevertheless tasteful and clever manner."[98] Rossi's second volume recounted in comparable detail the quasi-spontaneous celebrations and illuminations that broke out in the rest of the empire, not only in cities and towns, but also in the tiniest of villages. These celebrations were not created, designed, imposed, or even suggested by the central state, which had in any case long ago run out of the kind of money such an undertaking would have required.[99] Instead, local businessmen, civil servants, and landowners initiated and financed these ceremonies. Local volunteer committees that organized the patriotic festivities often used them to raise money for hospitals for the war wounded. At the very least they reflect the existence of a common legitimating understanding of empire shared by thousands of regionally dispersed Austrians. They also demonstrate the existence of a distinctive and shared culture of imagery, slogans, and ritual practices around the idea of empire.

Rossi had begged officials from every crownland to send him accounts of local festivities so that his book could present subscribers with a complete picture of the celebrations that had greeted the final end of the war and the return of the emperor. What he learned tells us both about local understandings of empire and about a festival culture whose common norms, practices, slogans, and images transcended differences in geography, history, and language use. Despite their far-flung regional, geographic, and cultural locations, and despite often being communicated in different languages, the festivities in the larger towns resembled each other as well as those held in Vienna to an extraordinary degree. Although reports by local officials also emphasized particular details that lent local decorations a unique character, nevertheless, the erection of triumphal arches, the speeches held at town halls, the parades with bands by veterans and militiamen in town squares, the singing of the "Emperor's Song," the holding of a *Te Deum* at the church, followed by evening illuminations—all record a remarkably similar culture of imperial celebrations held in even the most far-flung corners of the Austrian Empire. The powerful impression of similarity is all the more noteworthy precisely because Rossi made certain to include in his accounts detailed descriptions of celebrations among diverse Eastern Orthodox Christian, Greek Catholic, Protestant, and especially Jewish religious communities. Additionally, his accounts of celebrations held in smaller villages noted carefully whether the sermons or speeches had been made in German, in "Slavic" (a term Rossi used for languages spoken in Bohemia, Carniola, Croatia, Galicia, Bukovina, and Southern Styria) or in Italian.[100]

Rossi attempted to depict the totality of Austria's territories and peoples as simultaneously engaged across space and time in a common patriotic celebration. Yet the spatial and chronological dimensions of this simultaneity depended completely on the rate at which news traveled in different parts of the empire in June of 1814. Celebrations in the larger towns of Bohemia and Moravia took place on 16 or 17 July, while smaller villages in those crownlands organized their festivities closer to the end of the month. Farther to the east, the festivities in Lemberg/ Lwów/Lviv took place on 29 July; those in Czernowitz/Cernăuți/Cernivci on the thirty-first. The impression to be gained from Rossi's catalog, however, is nevertheless one of simultaneity and cultural uniformity. Even though different towns celebrated on different days, they nevertheless all celebrated at the moment in time when they first received news of the happy event.

The elements of cultural diversity mentioned by Rossi also tend to reinforce a larger common framework of social and cultural unity. In Rossi's depiction, the emperor's subjects may worship differently and they may use different languages in some regions of his realm, but they use their different languages to convey unified feelings of loyalty to the Austrian state and to its dynasty in surprisingly similar ways. This sense of unity is thus reflected in the common culture of celebration shared in the diverse regions of Habsburg central Europe.

As we consider the popularity of the new Austrian state born officially at the dawn of the nineteenth century, we should also note another important element of social unity that Rossi's account conveys, however unintentionally. The similarity of forms of celebration dominated by Austria's burgher classes in socially extremely diverse regions suggests the prior existence of a recognizable inter-regional culture of sociability that drew on very particular symbols, texts, and images to produce common points of reference among participants. These common points of reference in turn rested on shared elements of post-primary school education, especially the myriad references to classical history, mythology, and literature. It also rested on common European imagery, discourses, and symbols of patriotism and civic virtue—flags, cockades, forms of dress, national hymns—all made popular by the French Revolution. Moreover, it was Austria's burgher social classes, and not the bankrupt state, that had organized and produced the celebrations from Trieste/Trst to

The Austrian Empire in 1815 after the Congress of Vienna

Lemberg/Lwów/Lviv. Across the empire, house owners, religious communities, and voluntary associations deployed the same slogans, metaphors, poems, mythological references, and images when they illuminated their houses, their town squares, and their streets for this occasion. Together it seems that this common culture that celebrated empire constituted a different but equally important legitimation of empire, as did the many peasant communities that viewed empire—or the dynasty—as their protector against the arbitrary power of the local lords.

The question remained, however, to what extent a defensive and conservative government under Emperor Francis would actively pursue the potential benefits of empire for peasants, the educated, or the manufacturing classes. Would the common empire of Maria Theresa, Joseph, and Leopold flourish under Francis's defensive stand? If the imperial center avoided taking up the kind of activist reform policies Francis's predecessors had pursued, could a pro-empire public take its place as an engine for reform? The ensuing decades, known alternately as the "Metternich years" (after Francis's main adviser), or as the *Vormärz* or "pre-March" (in reference to the revolutions of March 1848) saw popular hopes rise, and for the first time it was society as such that promoted the advancement of a common imperial project whose popular potential the emperor himself feared.

CHAPTER THREE

An Empire of Contradictions, 1815–1848

It is therefore a high service to the Fatherland when private
persons at least partly and gradually accomplish what
the state is not now able to accomplish.

— *Moriz von Stubenrauch*, Statistische Darstellung
des Vereinswesens im Kaiserthume Österreich, *1857*

The year 1814 saw a remarkable series of spontaneous popular celebrations of empire following the defeat of Napoleon. If a specifically
Austrian empire had emerged only recently in the shadow of Napoleonic
conquest, it nevertheless appears to have successfully engaged the imagi-
nations of a good many of its citizens. The institutional foundations laid
by Maria Theresa for this emerging state had immediately earned for it
the loyalties, however strategic in character, of several interest groups,
particularly the peasantry. Under Joseph II, this evolving state had also
become the particular property of segments of a growing educated middle
class who saw in it considerable possibilities for economic advancement
and social mobility. In his attempts to subject all religious communities
equally to state control, Joseph had also earned the loyalty of several minority religious communities for his empire. With the publication of the
civil law code (*Allgemeines Bürgerliches Gesetzbuch* or ABGB) in 1811, the
empire had succeeded in translating the varied legal statuses of its subjects into a form of legal citizenship whose promised equality breached
traditional norms of class or culture.[1]

After establishing a lasting peace in 1815, the Habsburg regime maintained its centralizing efforts, but it did not return to the socially trans-
formative agenda of the eighteenth-century reform monarchs. Even in a
time of greater peace and stability, and despite their continued interest

in institutional rationalization, Emperor Francis I and his most influential advisors shied away from experimentation with socially significant changes. Decades of war had taught them the lesson that any kind of social change should be treated with suspicion. Unlike other monarchs who believed reform could diffuse revolutionary potential, Francis believed the opposite. For him reform could too easily upset a delicate balance in society and provoke the kind of popular mobilization that had brought revolution to France.

The dynamic society over which this fearfully conservative regime presided, however, demanded innovation. Having survived a quarter century of almost continuous warfare, every region of the Austrian Empire now experienced a significant rise in agricultural output, in population size, and in trade and manufacture. Technological innovation and new corporate practices changed the character of local businesses. Roads, bridges, canals, smokestacks, rails, and new agricultural practices transformed local landscapes. Many of the social reforms through which Maria Theresa and her sons had hoped to transform economic life in their empire finally bore fruit after the intervening decades of war.[2] And although the end of Napoleon's blockade of British manufactured goods may have doomed some of its protected industries, Austria nevertheless experienced considerable industrial growth, often—as elsewhere in Europe—in irregular bursts and busts, and not uniformly across regions.

A lot of this restless economic activity produced new challenges to the fabric of local governance, particularly with regard to public health and social welfare. No longer the active instigators of social and economic change in the eighteenth century, however, Austria's post-Napoleonic governments often struggled to catch up to society in the first half of the nineteenth century. In fact, during the period 1815–1848 it was precisely independent elements in local society—farmers, entrepreneurs, technicians, academics—who took up the imperial visions promoted by those enlightened despots, Joseph II and Leopold II, and became their strongest proponents, often against the wishes of the regime.

Both middle-class and noble Austrians initiated new forms of activism in order to solve local social problems that the paralyzed government seemed unwilling to address. They organized civic associations to improve the cultural, educational, moral, and economic status of their fellow citizens—men and women—in this rapidly changing society. They built educational institutions to replace those that the state had stopped funding, founded scientific and literary societies, and created local natural history museums. They invented new technologies or sought to apply the inventions of others in agriculture, business, and manufacture. In doing so, these champions of local society pursued their own vision of empire, one shaped in many ways by the promise of state activism made in the late eighteenth century.

Not surprisingly, the regime treated such initiatives with caution and often with suspicion. On the one hand, Austria's fiscally strapped rulers tolerated and occasionally encouraged independent civic engagement that worked to solve expensive social problems. On the other hand, many in Francis I's government suspected that any associations formed independently by citizens to promote the public good constituted potentially subversive threats to public order. Metternich was not alone in reportedly referring to civic associations in the Hereditary Lands as "a German plague," while during the French Revolution Francis I had outlawed the Freemasons and dealt brutally with Austria's incipient Jacobin societies.

After revolutions in 1848 brought the regime to a dramatic end, liberal historians especially castigated its short-sighted and narrow minded practices of repression. In an effort to shore up their own whiggish version of history, they tended to portray the 1830s and 1840s as a tragic period of lost opportunities. Continuing this tradition, Cold War historians located the origins of what they perceived to be the economic and political backwardness of east central Europe precisely in this period. They blamed an oppressive Habsburg regime for having suppressed the market forces and democratic developments that they believed differentiated western Europe from eastern Europe at that time. This chapter argues, however, that Austrian society itself took up the challenges of creating social and economic change where enlightened despotism had left off.

Strong State, Weak State

The regime's anxieties about social activism among its peoples did not mesh well with the powerfully reforming ethos of intervention in society that Maria Theresa and her sons had cultivated only a half-century before. Those rulers had designed the expanded bureaucracy to serve precisely as a powerful engine to create change against the entrenched powers of the regional nobilities. They had encouraged their bureaucrats to initiate new social and economic practices at every level of society. Now, however, the Habsburg regime charged its servants with preserving—some said petrifying—the status quo. And although a few elements in the bureaucracy continued actively to support a productive transformation of Austria's economy and society, the regime became well known across Europe for its paranoid aversion to change and its propensity to censor and even to spy on its citizens.

While many histories portray Metternich's regime as a dictatorship that successfully repressed all demands for enhanced participation in civic life, Metternich's police state was never the totalizing dictatorship that both he and his opponents liked to claim that it was.[3] Austrian society was hardly isolated behind what derisive contemporaries and later historians referred to as a "Chinese wall" of censorship, police spies, and general repression. And although this regime regularly sought to quash initiatives from civil society, as well as to limit the influence of so-called "foreign ideas" in Austria, it could hardly muster the financial resources or the manpower to do so effectively–not with the daunting fiscal crisis the regime inherited from the period of the Napoleonic Wars and the limits on technologies of social control in the period after 1815. Moreover, many of the dangerous so-called "foreign ideas" that Metternich hoped to prevent from circulating in Austrian society were in fact products of homegrown Austrian thinking in the first place.

But there was another critical and underappreciated power that put a brake on the repressive efforts of the regime: the force of law. Despite recurring complaints about arbitrary state repression, Austria was a full-fledged *Rechtsstaat*—that is, a state that functioned according to the rule of law, and not according to the arbitrary whims of its ruler or local notables. This fact alerts us to yet another set of contradictions that often remain unexplored in histories of the period 1815–1848. The very idea of arbitrary rule contradicted the rationalizing and integrating elements of the Josephenist system on which Francis I based his rule. The regime's adherence both to the centralism and the legalism of the Josephenist legacy forced it to favor consistency, systematization, and the implementation of common administrative systems in every region over which it ruled, including Hungary. This emphasis on the unity of common institutions and procedures in turn made administrators throughout the empire extremely sensitive to issues of formal legality.

Austria fostered, as one historian has called it, "a legal system that was scrupulous in the extreme in upholding the rule of law."[4] When local nobles complained about the intrusion of the central government, local administrators responded by citing the universal applicability of imperial law. The government might initiate secret monitoring procedures, it might censor newspapers and magazines, it might prosecute individuals for political crimes, but it had to do so legally and according to recognized procedure. In the Austrian, Bohemian, and Galician crownlands, the government also had to adhere to the provisions of the ABGB. In the first half of the nineteenth century Austrians were as much citizens of the empire as they were the emperor's subjects when it came to legal process.[5] Vienna promoted respect for legal process precisely because of the state's ambition to achieve a more centralized, rationalized relationship to the territories over which it ruled.

Not surprisingly, however, the reorientation of purpose from carrying out reform to maintaining the status quo demoralized many of those who loyally served in Austria's bureaucracy. Some who occupied the highest offices in Vienna or the crownland capitals simply turned their eyes away from serious infractions of the censorship laws, for example, embarrassed by their new charge to watch over society. Several high-level bureaucrats also criticized the regime bitterly in anonymous pamphlets that they published (abroad of course), especially in the 1840s. They castigated the regime's petrification and its treatment of them as mindless enforcers, rather than as creative problem solvers. Thus it was that in a highly ironic twist of perceptions, much of Austrian society in the 1830s and 1840s (including many bureaucrats) held the bureaucracy itself responsible for thwarting potential progress and prosperity. This self-castigation reached a high point later in the nineteenth century when, as Waltraud Heindl alleges, one might have imagined that the bureaucracy had been responsible for the outbreak of revolution in 1848.[6]

It was not simply their narrowly prescribed function that demoralized the bureaucrats, however. Their own downward social mobility also provoked considerable bitterness in their ranks. During more than two decades of war, the bureaucracy, like many sectors of Austrian society, had seen its real earnings decline drastically thanks to uncontrollable inflation and stagnant wages. In the two decades following the war, these servants of the state never regained their prior level of financial security, except for a privileged few at the very highest level. Nor did those families who hoped to see their sons advance socially by joining the state service appreciate the limits that a penny-pinching regime placed on higher education after 1815.[7]

Fiscal limitations also made it harder than ever for the state to realize its long-term centralizing ambitions as fully as its policymakers desired. We can usefully think of this state during this period as strong in terms of ambitions (and promises), yet weaker than ever in terms of its ability to translate those ambitions into an effectively centralized system of rule. What appears to be hesitation or fear regarding the possible political dangers of engaging in innovative industrial or social policy often turns out to have been the product of limited resources. And as we will see, when faced with a lack of resources, Austria's rulers during this period often preferred no change at all to engaging in half measures. Francis I's regime was as indifferent as it was hostile to initiatives in areas like public education or industrial development. Now and then government ministers recognized that Austria's business and academic middle classes had specific needs that had to be met if they were to spur economic growth. Francis himself frequently expressed personal sympathy for the plight of Austria's poorest classes. Often it was the regime's fiscal prudence—the war had put Austria in serious long-term debt—that shaped important policies, as in the case of higher education. Enrollments in university preparatory schools (*Gymnasien*) and in the universities, for example, actually fell between 1815 and 1848. Although some interpreted this as a sign of the regime's overt hostility to universities (as a potential breeding ground of political opposition), or even as an attempt to put a brake on social mobility, the policy was largely the product of short-sighted austerity measures. At the same time, however, the undeniably restrictive mood that at times pervaded the gymnasia and universities themselves resulted far more from the regime's political fears than from the budgetary axe.[8]

Historians still debate how exactly to measure the effects of the apparent contradiction between the regime's struggle to limit the effects of social change on the one hand, and the increasing dynamism of the society over which it ruled on the other. As far as the economy is concerned, however, it is no longer possible to assert, as many once did, that fear of industrial social conflict caused the regime to oppose new economic initiatives. Austrian absolutism most definitely did not retard economic growth during this period, as some Cold War historians claimed; the economies in this part of central and eastern Europe did develop apace. In fact, as we will see, from 1815 to 1848 the government was often a major player in expanding the domestic transport infrastructure—from roads and canals to railways and shipping lines. Moreover, the regime deployed tax policies, reformed patent law, and liberalized trade, all to encourage the founding of new industries.[9]

When it came to social or civic life, however, it is more difficult to assess the effects of the government's relentless conservatism. Like their counterparts elsewhere in Europe, both bourgeois entrepreneurs and a growing educated elite in Austria (often bureaucrats employed by the state) increasingly sought a share in political responsibility. Moreover, the regime's regular dependence on access to loans from a few large banking houses to cover its recurring deficits meant that eventually those banking houses would also claim a role in influencing the government's budgetary priorities. The regime had no satisfactory answer to such claims, except to assert its traditional authority even more aggressively. This in turn raised the hackles of business and educated elites, who often joined with regional noble elites to express their dissatisfaction with the ways in which a petrified regime ran roughshod over the specific needs of their locality. In doing so, they continued to use the eighteenth-century rhetoric that had asserted traditional legal forms of local or crownland autonomy—often couched as "nation"—against the encroachment of a centralizing imperial state.[10]

In 1835, the accession of Francis I's mentally weak son, Ferdinand I (reigned 1835–1848), worsened the situation considerably by creating a serious power vacuum at the top of the system. Increasing political stagnation—the growing inability to respond satisfactorily to new political and economic challenges like strikes or food riots—coupled with active opposition to any social or political innovation incurred the anger of many otherwise patriotic subjects.

This political stagnation and the opposition it engendered among the rising business and educated classes across the monarchy was hardly the regime's only weakness, although it was the most obvious one. Throughout this period the dynamic economic developments experienced in some regions and sectors masked the essentially feudal economic and social relations that continued to survive in others, especially in more agricultural regions like Galicia and many parts of Hungary or Dalmatia. Problems in those regions often resulted from the poverty of the local landed elite, as well as from their narrow understanding of their economic options. By contrast, in economically more dynamic regions like Bohemia, Lower Austria, or Moravia a prosperous nobility often took the initiative to invest its considerable capital to promote economic change. Noble families with large estates often led the way, experimenting with technical innovations on their own lands and developing new rural industries such as food processing or energy production. In many parts of Hungary and in most of Galicia, however, local estate owners calculated their economic survival purely in terms of the added value from labor they could squeeze out of the peasantry. Peasants subjected to substantial labor obligations often responded with violence, especially in Galicia, where recurring local peasant rebellions punctuated the 1820s and 1830s. Peasant rebels understood the dynamic of imperial centralization and looked strategically to the regime in Vienna for aid. By the mid-1840s, Galicia balanced dangerously between the threat of large-scale peasant violence and severe repression. Perhaps ironically, this deteriorating situation ultimately had the effect of popularizing the cause of empire among the peasantry at the expense of claims for regional autonomy or noble nationalism.

Unlike the estate owners of Galicia, Hungary's noble elite did develop a reform movement in the 1830s that openly debated how to strengthen its economy.[11] Framing their positions largely in Hungarian patriotic terms, the debaters tried to explain why, according to almost every contemporary measure of productivity, Hungary's economy appeared to lag behind that of the rest of the monarchy and of those parts of Europe to which the Hungarian elite liked to compare its situation. Many Hungarian patriots blustered that Austria's tariff frontier kept Hungary in a quasi-colonial condition of relative economic backwardness. In 1830 and 1831, however, the aristocrat Count István Széchenyi transformed the parameters of debate about Hungary's economy in two books, *Hitel* (Credit) and *Világ* (Light). Széchenyi argued vigorously that Hungary's comparative economic backwardness and its specific weakness in trade could not be blamed on the Austrian tariff system. Instead, he claimed that Hungary's traditional feudal system of production was responsible for its problems.[12]

In *Hitel* Széchenyi argued that Hungary's agriculture remained unproductive because of its reliance on the unpaid labor of serfs. If they wanted to raise production, landowners should instead employ wage labor on their estates. But in order to afford large numbers of wage laborers or the luxury of experimenting with new technologies, Hungary would also have to rid itself of the legal tradition of entailed estates. Entail prevented the estates of the magnates—the highest aristocrats—from being partitioned or sold. It required that land be passed down undivided according to specific inheritance rules. An entailed estate could not be used as collateral for raising mortgage loans, nor could any of it be sold off to raise funds. These laws made it impossible to use land as a resource for raising the money needed to invest in new technologies or to develop a system that paid wages to free peasant laborers. Széchenyi pointed out that while nobles owned more than two thirds of the arable land in Hungary, a surprisingly high percentage of that land remained uncultivated. And this in a time where 920,000 peasant families in Hungary were registered as "landless." If nobles could sell or mortgage their lands for credit, they could invest in new technologies of production, and they could pay wages to peasant workers. If they could raise credit, nobles could also fund new manufactures that could employ landless peasants. Széchenyi criticized many other aspects of the feudal system in Hungary, especially the nobles' continued immunity to taxation, the inability of most peasants to own land, the restrictions that the guild system placed on the free development of manufactures, and the lack of legal equality for the vast majority of the population.[13]

Széchenyi's ideas generated considerable interest and debate in Hungary, and, as we will see, they helped to produce a powerful reform movement there in the 1840s. Yet this movement remained largely rhetorical in quality. Even if some of Hungary's land-owning elite sought to promote capitalist growth in the 1830s and 1840s, social conditions there nevertheless continued largely unchanged. Peasant violence on the scale of Galicia did not break out in Hungary, but refusal to perform the *Robot* or labor service, for example, was a frequent occurrence.

Once again, it was largely fiscal austerity that prevented the central state from intervening in Galicia, Hungary, or several smaller rural crownlands such as the coastal province of Dalmatia. Nor did it invest in developing transport and communication infrastructures in those regions. During the first half of the nineteenth century the government appears to have fulfilled just enough of its ambitious promises to make the imperial state an ongoing object of hope among peasants, local entrepreneurs, and the educated classes.[14]

Economic Growth and Social Change

In the immediate aftermath of the Napoleonic Wars, Imperial Austria counted some 30 million people inside its new borders. During the next thirty years the population grew rapidly at an annual rate of at least 1 percent as increased agricultural productivity especially in the Hereditary Lands and Bohemia made it possible to feed an expanding population. Austria's cities increased in size as well. The populations of administrative centers like Vienna or Prague, for example, exploded rapidly, although the second half of the century would see far more spectacular growth rates. Vienna's population increased from around 250,000 in 1817 to 357,000 in 1848; Prague's rose from 65,000 to 115,000 during the same period. But the population growth of these cities is perhaps less instructive than the growth rates of several provincial towns where Austria's economic development tended to be located.[15] Pest, for example, grew steadily from 22,417 during Joseph II's reign to 35,349 in 1810, to around 44,000 in 1830 to over 100,000 by the late 1840s, easily making it the largest city in Hungary. In the 1840s, the Pest market fairs attracted some 30,000 participants. Already in 1821 one guidebook quoted by Robert Nemes in his history of Budapest noted how rapidly the town had changed its look:

There, where marshes, reeds, and devastating quicksand once covered the land . . . is now the central point of the annual markets' enormous traffic. . . . A most beautiful arrangement of houses has formed the new square, which surpasses all its cousins in the Austrian Empire (excepting St. Mark's in Venice) and deserves to be compared with the greatest and most beautiful squares in Europe.[16]

The port of Trieste/Trst at the head of the Adriatic experienced a similarly dynamic rate of growth, transforming from an eighteenth-century fishing village into a world-class port with a population of 43,000 in 1820 and, only twenty years later, of more than 80,000.[17] The population of the Moravian capital, Brünn/Brno—probably the most industrialized town in the monarchy during the period before the development of the railways—approached 30,000 in 1830 and 45,000 a decade later. Economically booming towns like Pest, Trieste/Trst, and Brünn/Brno owed their rapid growth to the merchants and manufacturers (often foreigners) who founded or expanded businesses there, and who employed increasing numbers of workers in their shops, factories, warehouses, and in the case of Trieste, on their docks.

Brünn/Brno's growth was still something of an Austrian exception, since it derived specifically from the rise of industrial work in textile mills. Already in 1840, close to 15,000 people worked in mills that had sprung up in its suburbs, earning for Brünn/Brno the name "Manchester of Austria." Journalist Jan Ohéral left a powerful description both of the new landscape in Brünn/Brno and of the speed with which the transformation had taken place. "The look of Brünn has changed completely in just a few years' time," he wrote in 1838. Describing its former appearance in static terms, as "a picturesque still-life painting," Ohéral drew a stark contrast with the city's new landscape and constant movement, especially in the industrialized outskirts.

Overnight, a new power, a new type of employment has lent its colors to this painting and has set its stamp firmly on the town, a new power that has transplanted us from quiet, dreamy peacefulness to the uproar of the workshop; this new power has chosen the suburbs as its battlefield, and built huge palaces there with monumental chimneys, which point like a petrified finger from the earth to the heavens and veil the old, many-towered town with their dark clouds of smoke.

"Traverse the streets of the town center," added Ohéral, and even here among the staid aristocratic palaces and government offices the perceptive observer "would notice busy, relentless activity emanating from the warehouses," as well as the "relative isolation of the idler who stands out among the feverish majority of people" who are engaged in the relentless demands of their business.

> But when you encounter row upon row of factories and workshops in the outskirts of town, or when you hear the groaning din of the steam machines or the monotonous noise of the hammer and loom at every step, when in the evening you see rows of lit windows and behind them hundreds of people diligently working late into the night, or when in the pale gaslight you see masses of machines of all kinds set up for every purpose running uninterruptedly, you will no longer doubt that the manufacturing system, of which factories represent the most developed version . . . in many parts of the world . . . has established itself here as well.[18]

In most other parts of the monarchy it would be another fifty years before large-scale industries attracted factory labor from the countryside to the cities in such high numbers as in Brünn/Brno. By comparison, for example, Prague, with a much larger population of 100,000 in 1840, had only about 4,000–5,000 industrial workers.

Industry and trade in cities like Brünn/Brno, Pest, and Trieste/Trst also benefited from new links created by Austria's growing transportation infrastructure, which in turn stimulated increased economic growth. New highway projects, canals, river regulation, and mountain pass systems produced a rapid increase in continental transport and trade, as well as cutting the time it took to travel between economically linked destinations, often by over 50 percent.[19] Between 1815 and 1848 the state constructed 2,240 kilometers (almost 1,400 miles) of roads, while local town governments or noble landowners added another 46,400 (28,830 miles) of privately funded roads.[20] In Hungary, several projects increased the navigability of the Danube and Tisza Rivers. By the 1830s a Danube Steamship Society offered regular service between Vienna and Pest. In

1847 the society's fleet of forty-one ships transported over 900,000 passengers.[21]

In the 1830s a new Adriatic shipping line created the first regular link between Trieste/Trst and the coastal towns of Dalmatia and Ottoman Mediterranean ports like Constantinople, Alexandria, and Salonica. The Austrian Lloyd Company was born in the merchant coffee houses of Trieste/Trst as an insurance conglomerate in 1833. It soon became a shipping company that sought to speed the movement of goods and information across the Mediterranean and eventually around the globe. The Austrian Lloyd primarily served ports across the eastern Mediterranean, making it the most important transport company for the Ottoman Empire as well as Austria. The Lloyd gradually extended its reach, however, to East Asia and Latin America as well. Within a decade of its founding, the Lloyd had already helped to make Trieste/Trst into one of the ten largest ports in the world.

For the first time, Trieste/Trst's merchants could rely on a regular and predictable schedule of local vessels to ship their wares and passengers throughout the Mediterranean region, from Marseilles to Salonica to Alexandria to Constantinople. In 1851 the Lloyd transported 222,000 passengers, over half a million letters, and over a quarter million packages.[22] For Dalmatia, whose many ports were generally surrounded by impassable mountainous terrain, the ships of the Austrian Lloyd offered sea connections that made travel faster and far more comfortable than over-land travel. In March 1848, for example, it was a Lloyd steamer rather than the overland mail coach that brought the first news of revolution in Vienna to Dalmatia's capital, the port city of Zadar/Zara.[23]

Immediately following the Napoleonic Wars, several influential political figures, private investors, and a few Austrian military officers had lobbied the emperor and his advisors to introduce railways—at first horse-drawn and later steam-powered—for the swifter transport of goods, travelers, and troops within the empire. In 1816, after returning from a trip to England, the reform-minded Archduke Johann urged his brother Emperor Francis to emulate the English promotion of railroads. In 1825 the Archduke championed a specific rail line to connect Trieste/Trst to Hamburg (through his homeland of Styria, by the way, and

An Austrian steamship of the mid-nineteenth century arriving in Trieste/Trst. Painting by P. Kappley. Credit: Gianni Dagli Orti/The Art Archive at Art Resource, NY.

bypassing Vienna).[24] By the 1830s Archduke Johann's views had gained support among several influential bankers (Rothschild, Sina) and industrialists.

The earliest proposals for railway lines were made by private parties, and they tended to duplicate existing and well-traveled trade routes. The very first line built in Austria was meant to solve a series of engineering challenges that earlier experts had hoped to work out by constructing a complex series of canals. Since the reign of Maria Theresa, both the Austrian government and influential merchant interests had sought a way to link traffic from the Moldau/Vltava River in Southern Bohemia—connected to the north-south Elbe/Labe River network as far north as Hamburg—with east-west traffic on the nearby Danube River. Engineer Francis Joseph Gerstner (1756–1832) suggested in 1807 that a railway might cover the difficult terrain far more easily and far less expensively than a series of canals.[25] Gerstner and his son Francis Anton pioneered a technology to build graded rail lines through mountainous terrain, and in 1824 Francis Anton sought a fifty-year concession from the government for a 139-kilometer (80-mile) horse-drawn railway that would connect Budweis/Budějovice on the Moldau/Vltava river in Southern Bohemia with the Danube port of Linz in Upper Austria, forty-eight miles to the south. A concession gave the petitioner the sole right to run a railway line for a specific period of time, and often obligated the state to guarantee the original investors a fixed rate of return.[26] To create public interest in the project, Gerstner even built a 250-meter test rail line in Vienna's Prater Park.

When construction started on the Linz Budweis/Budějovice line, it was the first rail project on the European continent.[27] By the 1830s, however, several other European states were building railways. In particular the small- and mid-sized states of the German Confederation rushed to build railroad lines in order to avoid being bypassed by major trade routes that might otherwise run through neighboring states. This anxiety to control where the emerging trade routes would be located undoubtedly made the building of rail lines a far more urgent matter in those smaller German states than it was in Austria. Nevertheless, in 1829, while the horse-rail line linking the Moldau/Vltava and the Danube was still under construction, Gerstner and engineer Francis Xaver Riepl (1790–1857) joined banker Salomon von Rothschild to request a government concession for a more ambitious steam-powered locomotive railway project. This one would connect Vienna to the iron- and coal-mining regions of northern Moravia and to salt fields farther east in Galicia.[28] Although penny-pinching Emperor Francis declined to give the concession, five years later his son Ferdinand granted Rothschild a concession for the joint-stock Emperor Ferdinand Northern Rail Company (Kaiser Ferdinand Nordbahn Gesellschaft), which eventually linked Vienna to Moravia, Silesia, Galicia, and later Bukovina. In 1838 the very first passenger train left the Viennese suburb of Floridsdorf on this line and traveled some eight miles northeastward to the town of Deutsch Wagram near the Moravian border. In July of 1839 the new company inaugurated full service to Brünn/Brno, capital of Moravia.[29] In its first year of service the Nordbahn transported more than 228,000 people to Brünn/Brno; a

The railway bridge leading to Brünn/Brno, with the city in the distance. This was part of the Kaiser Ferdinand Nordbahn. Credit: Erich Lessing/Art Resource, NY.

year later, in 1840, it transported over 29 million kilos (64 million pounds, or 32,000 tons) of goods.[30]

Historians have tended to interpret the history of Austrian railways according to the railroads' changing terms of ownership: private versus public. The first phase of building in Austria involved mostly private ownership, and it allegedly ended in 1841 when the government published a long-term plan for an entire network that it would build itself, still mobilizing private capital to fund the individual projects. This next phase of direct government ownership ended in the mid-1850s, however, when the sky-rocketing cost of the railroads forced the state to return to a system of private concessions. Finally, toward the end of the nineteenth century, the state once again took up a more direct role in building and running railroads. Historians who saw the terms of ownership as the decisive factor in the development of Austrian railways presumed that the state and private capital held fundamentally divergent interests. On its own, many historians imagined, a free market would have dictated far different priorities in terms of routes than did the state. Proponents of this approach claimed that during the first period of state ownership (1841–1854), it was the Austrian military that had dictated the shape of the rail network, to the detriment of business and industrial interests. The military, they claimed, built lines to strategic sites that were of little economic value. These historians concluded that in Austria, unlike the British or French cases, the railways had *not* successfully stimulated general economic growth, precisely because they had been forced to serve military or state purposes instead of private ones. Some historians even thought that state ownership of railways had actually retarded economic growth and contributed to long-term "economic backwardness" in "eastern" Austria, when compared to the character of economic development that railway construction in "western" France, Belgium, and the German states had powered.[31]

This argument fit well with a range of other traditional beliefs we have already encountered, alleging that a general backwardness in eastern Europe resulted from excessive state intervention, according to a model whose Cold War origins are undeniable. An eastern system of quasi-military despotism harnessed a weak indigenous entrepreneurial class to its imperial designs, thereby preventing a free market approach that allegedly characterized the West, where the entrepreneurial classes supposedly determined rail policy. Both characterizations of East and West are well off the mark, but traditional stereotypes—particularly those that frame larger arguments—do not die easily. It is only more recently that historians have decisively disproved these characterizations of the relationship between the railroads and Austrian economic development.

Independent market-based priorities, it turns out, did not differ substantially from those of the state in the 1840s. In fact, market priorities appear to have driven the construction of specific lines in Austria far more than military interest did. It is true that Emperor Ferdinand declared in 1841 that all lines could be nationalized if wartime circumstances demanded it. Nevertheless, his military simply could not imagine *how* it might use the railways. Military strategists worried that rail lines would be too vulnerable to enemy artillery to be of much use in wartime, and they saw little potential in railways until after the 1846 crises in

Galicia proved their efficacy for transporting troops and supplies rapidly and cheaply. Even following this positive experience, however, and even after the railroads' successful use by Field Marshal Radetzky (1766–1859) during the revolutions of 1848, the military never initiated railway projects, nor did it insist that specific rail lines be built. Rather, the military seems to have supported those rail projects in which business had *already* shown a prior interest.[32] If anything, civilians in industry or banking cited alleged military needs in order to justify building their desired new lines. In 1839, for example, when deputies to the Galician Diet petitioned the state to finance a project that would connect Bochnia to the Galician capital of Lemberg/Lwów/Lviv, they argued that the military would also reap unspecified "strategic benefits" from this line.[33]

More important than the question of state or private ownership is the question of how decisions that favored some rail links or networks over others were made. After an initial decade of private initiatives that sprang up in different regions of the monarchy, the central state (but not the military) did assume the dominant role in determining the shape of a broad network, which private investors could then develop for the entire empire. In 1838 the regime even removed the right to give railroad concessions from regional crownland authorities, guarding this right for the central state.[34] The state-determined network did in turn decisively influence cultural and economic developments later in the nineteenth century, consigning some regions to the economic periphery and making others into flourishing regional centers of economic development.

In the case of Brünn/Brno, for example, which was already a booming textile manufacturing center before 1840, the advent of the Kaiser Ferdinand Nordbahn boosted local industry even further. It brought an even greater influx of textile workers from the countryside, which expanded the city's population to over 47,000 in 1850. Routes and specific links could play a crucial role in determining local economic and demographic development.[35] This was certainly the case when the state planned a challenging trans-alpine route to link Vienna to the empire's main port city of Trieste/Trst. By 1849 this Southern Railway (Südbahn) successfully linked Vienna to Laibach/Ljubljana, the capital of Carniola. After overcoming several further engineering challenges, the entire route between Vienna and Trieste/Trst was completed in 1857.[36]

Popular Visions of a Strong State in Galicia and Dalmatia

While improved transport and communication spurred industry and manufacture in several regions of Austria, their novelty masked the unchanging relations, misery, and grinding poverty that continued to characterize many agricultural regions of the empire. Given the images of profound transformation associated with the term "industrial revolution," it is important to recall that the changes wrought by nascent industry in its early years were neither consistent nor did they immediately and directly affect the lives of most people on the European continent. Even within the same country, one district might experience rapid social transformation, while a neighboring region maintained centuries' old traditional ways of life. And those regions where the early industrial revolution was concentrated were often subject to wild pendulum swings of a business cycle that might create enormous demand for factory labor in one year and then send workers packing six months later. Still another jarring and visible effect of industrialization was its tendency to produce fantastic new levels of wealth for some and new depths of poverty for others, often in the same town.

The Habsburgs were not directly responsible for the rise of industry in places like Brünn/Brno, but their regime was responsible for the failure of administrative and social reform in several poverty-stricken agricultural regions. And in the first half of the nineteenth century there was no region the Habsburgs ruled where traditional feudal society lived on in all of its misery as tenaciously as it did in Galicia, Austria's slice of the partition of Poland. There, despite the hopes of Maria Theresa and Joseph II to create a model enlightenment society, peasants remained firmly tied to the land, subject to crushing labor requirements from their lords and obligated to pay in-kind dues as well. The system continued to work thanks largely to the threat of force regularly deployed by landlords against peasants. But it also lived on in the daily humiliations to which both the lords and their agents subjected the peasants. Moreover, the system survived thanks to the tacit, if unwilling, support lent it by the central state, which frequently sent in the military to quell an increasing number of peasant revolts in the first half of the nineteenth century, even as it bemoaned Galicia's backwardness.

The state had developed ambitious plans to reform Galicia dating from the first partition of Poland in 1772, treating the province as something of a blank slate for enlightened policy experiments. But as many writers observed during the period since then, Austria had apparently accomplished very little there. The Galician nobility recognized no obligation to improve its peasants' lot, and few positive incentives might have produced significant change in this system. Maria Theresa and Joseph had formally ended the legal physical ownership of peasants by their estate owners (the *Leibeigenschaft*) and thereby won a degree of peasant loyalty for the empire. In consequence of this reform, for example, the estate owners technically could no longer personally whip their peasants or prevent them from marrying. The same reforms had also limited peasant labor obligations to the lords to a maximum of three days a week, down from five or six on some estates. In addition, Joseph II had sought to restrict the vast legal powers of estate owners by making it possible for peasants to bring lawsuits against them.[37] Yet despite reforms that introduced legal technicalities like these, the system continued to function much as it had in the past, with floggings, illegal labor requirements, and no realistic option for redress. This was the case because the state, for all of its interfering legislation, once again lacked the necessary resources to influence local relations on estates in Galicia. Moreover, in Galicia the state had no local allies on whose support it could depend in its reforming efforts—no nascent middle or educated class to whom its bureaucrats might turn for support, or whose members might supply the bureaucracy with new recruits. Galician Jews, who fulfilled some functions of a local commercial middle class as small business owners, moneylenders, or estate managers, were under the firm control of noble estate owners. And as the region's most powerful figures, the nobles successfully influenced or bribed the local officials whose duty it was to enforce imperial law.

Not surprisingly, frustrated reformers and moralizing commentators from Vienna explained this ongoing situation by elaborating extreme myths of Galician backwardness whose causes they increasingly attributed to the cultures, if not to the very inborn natures, of the Galicians themselves.[38]

One significant obstacle to enforcing peasant rights against noble power was an exceptionally low literacy rate in Galicia. Unlike the situation in other parts of the empire, state efforts in the eighteenth century to improve education had barely registered at the village level in Galicia. Even in those localities that boasted a parish school, children rarely attended with any consistency. Austrian statistics for the year 1842, for example, show that officially at least, only 15 percent of school-age children in Galicia attended a school, compared to 94 percent of school-aged children in Bohemia.[39] Meanwhile, in the Stanislau/Stanisławów (later also Stanyslaviv) district in Eastern Galicia, 73 percent of the local children had never attended a school. Of the 27 percent who had actually visited a school, only a quarter had attended classes with any regularity. Frequently it was the local church organist or parish priest (himself sometimes barely literate) who served as a teacher in these schools in order to earn an extra income. As a result, it is perhaps not so surprising that as late as 1865 only 4.5 percent of all military recruits from Galicia could read and write. In fact some landowners regularly ensured that those peasant sons who did manage to pick up some education in the village—and sometimes even teachers in the parish schools—were the first locals to be taken as recruits by the military.

Without the ability to read the estate inventories that catalogued their legal obligations, peasants could hardly pursue successful lawsuits against their lords. Clearly the Galician nobility had every interest in preventing literacy. When in 1840 the Uniate Bishop of Przemyśl/Peremyshl' proposed that the Galician Diet found more public elementary schools in the villages, the deputies rejected his legislation almost unanimously. They opined with some sarcasm that more schools would only encourage peasants to draw up more petitions to the district authorities.[40] As this example indicates, regional or provincial authorities were responsible for funding the schools mandated by the central government since the time of Maria Theresa.

Apparently, Galician peasants were well aware that little love was lost between their noble masters and the imperial regime in Vienna. This specific knowledge fed their view of the Habsburg ruler as an almost mythological power who exercised a fatherly concern for their wellbeing. If the emperor had known what exactly was going on in Galicia, according to peasant lore, he would not have allowed things to continue. This attitude was hardly a manifestation of peasant isolation or naiveté, as some today might see it. Far from it. This view of the emperor was highly useful to peasants who used it to justify their refusals to carry out noble demands or their determination to lodge legal complaints against their masters with the local authorities. In this sense, the myth of the good emperor, which was confirmed by the legislation of the 1770s and 1780s, lent peasants a symbolic form of agency in the brutal ongoing struggle against their masters. Peasants frequently legitimated their revolts in early nineteenth-century Galicia by citing alleged decrees from the emperor. Many in fact believed that the Habsburgs had already ended all servile obligations and that corrupt officials and conniving landlords had withheld this vital information from them.

In John Paul Himka's masterful study of Galician village life, peasants consistently evoke imperial authority to challenge their lords or to legitimate acts of rebellion:

> When in January 1784 Przemyśl circle [district] Commissioner Rutkowski read peasants the Imperial Patent of 1 October 1781 reforming serfdom, they told him that part of the patent was indeed composed by the emperor but the part that obliged them to do corvée *[Robot]* and road work was written by the landlords. In 1819 peasants of Komarno refused to give fodder, chickens, and capons to the lord until they heard from the emperor. "When the emperor writes to us in response to our petition, then we will do and give whatever he tells us."[41]

The trope of peasant devotion to the Habsburg dynasty is frequently invoked today in a simplistic and nostalgic pro-Habsburg fashion that mistakes the fundamental nature of peasant views about power and authority for a particular love of the Habsburg dynasty. Above all, Galician peasants mistrusted *all* officials, whether they represented a local estate owner or even the emperor in Vienna. As we will see in the next chapter, many peasants knew quite well that their situation had generally improved after the partition of Poland, when Austrian had replaced Polish rule. So peasants opportunistically cited the authority of the Austrians whenever they could, to counterbalance the authority claimed by their masters. Added to that was the experience to which some peasants could refer: that Austrian district officials or courts occasionally had helped them to win legal challenges against their lords. This too gave them the opportunity to justify their arguments on the basis of a higher authority in Vienna.

By the 1820s, however, the economic situation in Galicia was worsening for the peasants. Nobles seeking to augment their own declining incomes—thanks to the ravages of wartime inflation—contrived elaborate subterfuges for lengthening the workdays the peasants owed them, or for increasing the size of their own estates at the expense of lands traditionally used in common by peasant villages. In the latter case, the lords simply seized neighboring lands that peasant communities had used for grazing their animals or for keeping a wood supply in the winter. When their complaints and petitions about this practice remained unredressed, peasants frequently refused to carry out the *Robot* or to deliver their dues in kind. Or they responded to the desperation of their situation with violence. In such cases the landlords could count on the imperial military to discipline the peasants and restore order.

But in Galicia, the Austrian military constituted a double-edged sword for the local nobility. This part of previously independent Poland had only recently been incorporated into the monarchy in 1772. A few decades later during the wars against France, the local nobility had witnessed Napoleon's creation of an allegedly independent Polish state, the "Duchy of Warsaw," to the north of Galicia, from 1807–1815. Although the Congress of Vienna had not reestablished an independent Poland after the war, it had confirmed that the tsar's slice, so-called Congress Poland, would enjoy quasi independence with linguistic and cultural autonomy. These promises were eventually abrogated. Hopes to revive an independent Poland had not died among democrats and among members of Poland's leading noble families. Many of them either sympathized with or continued to participate in conspiracies against the three partitioning powers (Russia, Prussia, Austria), especially during uprisings in Russia in 1831 and 1863. An Austrian military presence in Galicia could just as easily be used against the rebellious Polish nobility as its recalcitrant peasants.

Another territory where the ambitious designs of the centralizing state were repeatedly thwarted far more by its lack of fiscal resources than by local noble opposition was Dalmatia. The Congress of Vienna had assigned to Austria this economically troubled strip of coastal territory on the Adriatic, which stretched from Istria and Carniola in the north to Montenegro in the south. Dalmatia's geographic profile isolated it from the rest of the monarchy, thanks largely to the mountain ranges that separated its coastline from the neighboring hinterlands (Croatia, Hungary, and Ottoman Bosnia). Dalmatia's coastal towns lived on small local trade or fishing, while isolated peasant communities below the mountains struggled to grow crops on poor quality land. Most of Dalmatia, with the exception of the town of Dubrovnik/Ragusa, had been ruled by Venice until 1797, and Napoleon had governed the entire territory from 1809–1813 as part of his creation of a French province of "Illyria."

In 1818 Dalmatia had a population of 296,800, most of whom spoke a Slavic language (later codified as Croatian and Serb), and a small urban minority (under 5 percent) who spoke Italian. Of the Slav-speaking population 20 percent practiced an Eastern Orthodox rite, while the rest were Roman Catholics. There were also some four hundred Jews living in the coastal towns of Dubrovnik/Ragusa and Split/Spalato. As late as 1848, Dalmatia's port towns were relatively small both by Austrian and general European standards. Split/Spalato was the largest with a population of 10,687, while Dubrovnik/Ragusa counted 5,462 people, and Zadar/Zara the provincial capital, counted 7,280.

Unlike Galicia or Hungary, Dalmatia had no powerful and privileged noble landowning class that traditionally dominated society. Moreover, the Napoleonic regime had abolished all titles of nobility in Dalmatia, and when the Austrians took over, they too had refused to recognize most Dalmatian titles of nobility. The nobles in Dalmatia, who had largely served as administrators under the Venetians, found themselves cut off from lucrative administrative positions under the Austrians. They took little interest in economic activity, and except where they could derive some wealth from land rents, they lived in relative poverty. The local elite in Dalmatia consisted of merchant oligarchs in the coastal towns, a few state administrators, and some few landed estate owners. Also, unlike Hungary and Galicia, Dalmatia had no provincial legislature or diet that might have served as a central focal point for a provincial elite to give voice to its common interests. This too ensured that the nobility had less social influence than in other crownlands.[42]

In theory, imperial reformers should have found it easier to transform Dalmatia than to bring change to Galicia, for example. But the province remained poor and badly integrated into the rest of Austria, and it was a site of sporadic famine and rebellion throughout the nineteenth century. Later Croatian nationalist historians would assert that an allegedly Austrian colonial policy had somehow retarded economic development in Dalmatia. Recent historical work, however, argues the opposite. In fact, Austria invested proportionately far more in developing Dalmatia's economy and society than it did in the rest of the monarchy. Nevertheless, despite concerted state efforts, illiteracy remained stubbornly high, and basic consumer demand for almost everything except food was minimal. Without local demand, there was little impetus to develop local trade or agricultural innovation. In fact, it was state salaries that tended to finance what little consumer demand was to be found, especially in administrative towns like Zadar/Zara or the naval base at Kotor. The Dalmatian countryside saw little social differentiation, very few handworkers providing artisanal crafts, no new technical advances in agricultural practices, and very little access to education. And since the terms of their incorporation into the empire in 1815 had freed Dalmatians from the obligations of military conscription (a popular measure indeed!), military careers—often a means for gaining a measure of education and social advancement elsewhere in the Empire—were closed off to them. Furthermore, linguistic barriers separated literate coastal townspeople, who often spoke and read both Italian and Slavic, from rural inland Dalmatians, who used only Slavic.

Thanks to all of these factors, but especially to poor agricultural productivity and infrastructure, the state actually had to transport food to Dalmatia to prevent the recurring possibility of famine. The Austrian state played a highly visible role in trying to keep Dalmatia afloat. And this in turn created increased expectations among Dalmatians about the possibilities of empire that the state could hardly fulfill. At least in the first half of the nineteenth century many educated Dalmatians projected their hopes for their region onto the very concept of empire embodied by Austria. Their new membership in this empire would be their salvation, and it was their obligation to bring their region's specific needs to the attention of the regime in Vienna. Several contemporary observers after 1815 asserted enthusiastically that Dalmatia's powerful new Austrian rulers had the potential to transform society through targeted intervention.

In an 1821 *Memoria Statistica sulla Dalmazia* (*Statistical Memorandum on Dalmatia*), engineer Frane/Francesco Zavoreo of Split/Spalato urged Dalmatia's new rulers to develop the region's infrastructure, to improve agriculture by increasing the size of individual land parcels, and to improve education. Zavoreo appealed specifically to the powerful qualities he attributed to empire: "All we need is an effective stimulus to shake us out of our lethargy, *and this can come only from a government that unites in itself the necessary knowledge and power.*"[43] Other contemporaries also looked to the imperial regime to implement an effective elementary school system, something the French during their occupation had tried and failed to accomplish. Gymnasium teacher Pietro Bottura in Split/Spalato wrote in 1830 that the level of a nation's civilization (in this case he meant a "Dalmatian nation") was measured not by its literary output, but rather in "the perfecting of *all* classes of people in their respective arts or professions" through education. Local Austrian officials agreed. In 1847 the district administrator in Dubrovnik/Ragusa wrote that only an increase in elementary schools could imbue Dalmatians with a necessary moral sensibility.[44] Indeed, by contrast to Galicia, where powerful local interests opposed state attempts to transform society, Dalmatia seemed to offer a far more welcoming environment for state-sponsored educational, agricultural, and commercial projects.

Nevertheless, despite the hopes placed in empire, the example of Dalmatia shows us something critical about the character of the Austrian state that is less clear from the Galician example because of ongoing political conflict there. It is that given a choice, the Austrian regime preferred to spend its limited resources on achieving administrative centralization in its newly acquired provinces, rather than target resources to raise economic or cultural standards there. More precisely, when it did consider investing in infrastructure or education or in the local economy, the state always sought to create centralized empire-wide institutions first, which added decades onto the time it took to establish new institutions. In consequence, many Dalmatians in the 1830s and 1840s could not understand why such a powerful state, which had the potential to accomplish a great deal, could be so frustratingly slow and even neglectful when it came to addressing Dalmatia's needs.

Education policy illuminates the troubled logic of this regime whose need to construct centralized administrative structures undermined the successful accomplishment of its policy goals. Despite his social and political conservatism, Francis I vigorously pursued the eighteenth-century reform vision of Maria Theresa, who had sought to give every child from every social background a basic education. Indeed, under Francis this vision became far more of a reality in most territories of the Habsburg state.[45] Moreover, no one in Vienna, much less in Zadar/Zara, doubted that local primary schooling could be enormously effective in helping to raise the economic productivity of the Dalmatian populace.[46] Yet when it came to implementing specific policies, the emperor and his advisors spent their time devising one-size-fits-all structures for all the Habsburg realms. They spent far less time thinking about Dalmatia's specific needs or how to accomplish specific educational goals there. From the perspective of Vienna it was far more important to root the *same* educational administrative structures in Dalmatia as those that already existed in the Austrian and Bohemian lands, for example, than that it was to actually build good schools or to train effective teachers.

From 1815 until 1848 reforms in education and in religious and economic policy all took a back seat to implementing an administrative centralization that would reproduce in Dalmatia the organizational systems that already existed in the hereditary and Bohemian crownlands. The imperial order of 1818 that established an education system in Dalmatia captured this set of priorities in the specific wording of its title: "The *organization* of elementary schools in this province, and [then] their gradual *introduction*" ("Organisierung der Volksschule in diesem Lande und deren allmählige Einführung").[47] Introduction could only follow successful organization. Practical measures could be implemented only *after* larger structures had been established. In the meantime, however, schools, teachers, and pupils languished. When individual Dalmatians requested permission to found local private elementary schools before the organization of the new system had been completed, they were regularly refused, even if provincial administrators supported such requests.

Once a comprehensive system was implemented, it took little account of important local traditions that made Dalmatia different from the hereditary and Bohemian crownlands. For example, teacher's salaries elsewhere in the monarchy were customarily set at a very low rate—200 florins annually—because the local priests who functioned as teachers normally had access to supplementary forms of income. In Dalmatia, however, local priests did not enjoy the options for extra income that their counterparts in Lower Austria or Bohemia and Moravia enjoyed. In Dalmatia more than elsewhere, meager state salaries were completely inadequate to a teacher's basic survival. In 1827 the archbishop of Zadar/Zara complained to Vienna that teachers everywhere in his archdiocese lacked rudimentary shelter and the means to obtain basic subsistence. Ultimately, reported the archbishop, the teacher

> finds himself in humiliating dependence on crude and impoverished parish children who only pay him what he is owed with great unwillingness, [and then] only when forced to do so, [and this] makes it morally and physically impossible for him to carry out his [local] spiritual office as a shepherd of souls.[48]

The government also learned to its dismay, that its imposition of requirements for teaching credentials from the Hereditary Lands and Bohemia-Moravia made it impossible to hire any teachers in Dalmatia. The provincial administration had to petition Vienna to lower the requirements. Still other rules imposed from the rest of Austria placed the financial burden for building schoolhouses squarely on the community itself, a factor that also slowed the establishment of schools, and not only in Dalmatia.

Despite these conspicuous failures, and precisely because the Austrian state was not as laissez-faire in its attitudes toward intervention as was its British counterpart, it continued to intervene just enough to make its presence known and to raise repeated hopes that it could accomplish more. State policy also ensured that Dalmatians, unlike their Irish counterparts, did not starve in times of famine. Still, Dalmatia ultimately constituted an extremely expensive burden on the Austrian state, which regularly ran a steep deficit there. Income derived from the province never came close to covering the costs of its civil administration.[49]

Policing and Censorship

The argument that the Austrian state during this period combined an almost limitless thirst for administrative centralization with financial means that could never match its administrative reach can also be applied to the character and effectiveness of what many have called Metternich's "police state." As we have seen earlier, the regime feared the kinds of popular mobilization that the French Revolution had produced, both during and after the Napoleonic Wars. But while the strict imposition of censorship and spying might be more understandable in the context of war, it provoked opposition and criticism once normal peacetime stability had been reestablished. The regime's efforts to spy on its subjects and its determination to prevent any manifestations of popular politics demanded an intensification of policing, not its relaxation in the years following the war. The regime charged the police especially with monitoring the comings and goings of foreign travelers to Austria through a system of passport control and local hotel registration (with which today's travelers will likely be familiar). In addition the police carefully watched foreigners' contacts in Austria. Together with the work of the censors, these measures sought to prevent dangerous foreign ideas from taking root in Austria.

The underfunded police could not possibly have developed as wide-ranging a spy network as historians have often claimed they did, while also carrying out all of the other roles the regime demanded of them. Officers gathered information for the government about local events that shaped the public mood, and they often spied on local public functionaries, such as teachers and priests. However, as David Laven's study of the police in Venetia during this period demonstrates, the government's anxieties about local functionaries had less to do with their political reliability than with their moral character. After the Napoleonic interlude in northern Italy, for example, the regime was not above hiring its former political opponents as a way to harness their talents and ensure their loyalty to the regime. "On the other hand," Laven writes, "a drunken professor, a womanizing priest, or a homosexual director of police stood to discredit the regime. Scandal was perceived as a bigger danger than conspiracy."[50] In other words, because the police were often charged with watching over the efficiency and respectability of other branches of the bureaucracy, they rarely concerned themselves directly with an alleged threat of revolution.

The role of the police officer as information-gatherer for the regime betrays another unexpected phenomenon that we encounter repeatedly in the nineteenth and twentieth centuries—namely, that when the police reported on local social conditions, their bulletins frequently sympathized with local public opinion. Police reports often criticized government policy and did not shy away from proposing specific reforms that police believed could most effectively aid the local populace. Since these reform suggestions were often rooted in parochial perceptions about local conditions, they rarely took into account the broader ways they might have impacted neighboring district or larger regions. In this very regard, the police ironically provided the government with the kind of feedback that one might have expected to hear from local political representative institutions.[51]

When it came to policing and censorship, the regime could rarely match its ambitions with appropriate measures any more than it could in the case of developing infrastructures or educational policies. The government could not afford to staff the police or the censorship office with anything like the workforce it would have needed to carry out its charge effectively. Financial constraint meant, for example, that the men who were hired at relatively low wages to censor books, pamphlets, and newspapers, often had little understanding themselves of the documents they were charged with censoring. They might miss the cleverly disguised metaphors embedded in many literary critiques of the regime. Some censors might also sympathize with the allegedly subversive points authors made. Moreover, some cities became known as friendlier sites for the publications of works on specific topics, religious, political, economic, or cultural. According to Michal Chvojka, authors and publishers were well acquainted with the individual tastes of censors in different towns or regions and chose their publication sites accordingly.[52]

While censorship may have kept some books and especially newspapers from public places where a reading public might easily access them, it could not as easily keep those works out of private libraries and reading club rooms. The fact that several high-level members of the government and of the bureaucracy belonged to Vienna's Legal-Political Reading Association, for example, may account for the government's occasionally lax supervision of that association's library. When police officials did stage periodic raids of the library, they found that the association owned over sixty forbidden titles, many of which had apparently been smuggled into Austria by its members or by high-level foreign guests. The police subjected similar reading clubs in Graz and Innsbruck with wealthier or noble members to comparable oversight, reporting "irregularities" at Graz's Johanneum in 1846 and confiscating several journals in the same year from the Innsbruck *Lesekasino*.[53]

At the same time, censors themselves frequently issued contradictory rulings, or reversed their rulings about the status of a given periodical or book. In 1843, for example, the police granted the Reading Association permission to subscribe to the previously banned *Leipziger Zeitung* and the *Grenzbote*, both left-leaning journals published in Saxony. In 1844 the association gained the right to subscribe to *Le Constitutionel* and *Le Siècle*, two moderate liberal newspapers from France that the censors had also formerly banned.[54]

The uneven quality of censorship did not, of course, prevent urban Austrians from complaining about it, nor did it build any popular credit for the regime. But if contemporaries and later historians denounced the particularly reactionary nature of the Austrian regime, we should keep in mind that Metternich's own views on society and politics were hardly exceptional among conservatives across Europe.[55] The period following 1815 was characterized by conservative fears everywhere in Europe about the chaos the French Revolution had recently unleashed, first on French society and later on all of Europe, thanks to Napoleon. Conservatives everywhere feared that the spread of revolutionary ideas about social equality might upset the precious stability that could be maintained only by adhering to traditional social hierarchy. The same held true for foreign policy as well. Metternich's attempt to maintain the Congress of Vienna settlement against any changes in subsequent decades obligated Austria to at least consider intervening in almost every major European crisis between 1815 and 1848, from rebellions in the Ottoman Empire to revolutions in France. Metternich's ambitious intention was less to cut Austria off from the rest of Europe than to police both Austrian and European society with the help of conservative allies across Europe, in order to prevent the spread of those dangerous ideas that could threaten social stability. But he could rarely realize these intentions in consistently effective policies. And when it came to domestic policing, William L. Langer pointed out long ago that while King Louis Philippe of France could muster 3,000 municipal guards, 84,000 national guards, and 30,000 troops in Paris in 1848, and Queen Victoria of Great Britain could count on a force of 3,000 well-trained policemen, 50,000 troops, and over 150,000 special constables in London, the Habsburgs in 1848 could rely on no more than 1,000 policemen, a municipal guard of 14,000 (consisting mostly of brass bands), and a military force of 14,000 for protection in Vienna.[56] In regard to policing, Austria was hardly exceptional in mid-nineteenth-century Europe.

Civic Initiative, Social Obligation, and Bourgeois Cultural Life

What did this civil society that Metternich and his colleagues feared so much look like? Traditional accounts of Austrian society during the period 1815–1848—especially of its middle-class elements—used terms such as "quiescence" or "a-political" to describe a society that allegedly offered little or no resistance to dictatorial rule. In the arts, this period in Austria has been called "Biedermeier," a term that traditionally connoted an upright and earnestly respectable bourgeois society, which was primarily inward-looking and small-minded in its concerns and not at all socially engaged beyond the limits of the parlor. Biedermeier painting or furnishings are often characterized by what at first glance appear to be idealized bourgeois domestic scenes or rural idylls. In part, this vision of a fundamentally a-political society held in check by fear of the police, spies, and censors rested on a later liberal critique of the Metternich era, one that celebrated the overtly liberal values of the 1848 revolution that overturned Metternich's rule. Later historians also drew on this view of an apolitical society as a way to explain what seemed a surprising lack of political activism especially among Austria's emerging bourgeois classes. After all, these very same social groups in France had been influential in sparking and then containing the revolution of 1830, and in Britain, they were openly agitating for electoral reform.

Did this alleged political quiescence also reflect the fundamental economic backwardness of Austrian society compared to more dynamic developments in western Europe during this same period? The fact that revolutionaries toppled a reactionary regime in 1830 in France, or that agitation for reform of Parliament succeeded in 1832 in Britain, allegedly reflected the new assertiveness of those countries' growing capitalist classes. But when it came to Austria, many historians attributed the apparent absence of liberal activism to an alleged weakness or even absence of those bourgeois capitalist classes that should otherwise have projected a confident liberalism. Austria's allegedly backward economy, claimed many analysts, had prevented the development of a self-conscious and assertive economic middle class there.

In important ways, historians' claims for the regime's far-reaching police powers confirmed Austria's supposed lack of a real civil society that could resist such a dictatorship. Metternich, it was asserted, had succeeded in preventing the rise of both a middle class and a factory working class that might have challenged the legitimacy of his regime. Society itself allegedly proved the validity of this claim by not developing strong independent voices of dissent, by not offering alternative visions to the existing dictatorship, and ultimately, by not rebelling. Yet, the whole idea of an apolitical Biedermeier style, to stay with the artistic term for a moment, the whole idea of bourgeois domesticity, of a middle-class world unto itself, also suggests the very opposite of political and social quiescence. The artistic style also pointed to an emerging middle-class society that defined itself and its values increasingly aggressively in its own terms, separately from the traditional aristocratic or feudal social hierarchies embodied by the current regime.

The historians who have offered a more nuanced reading of Austrian civil society during this period remind us that the Metternich regime ended in revolution across the Habsburgs' lands. They point to the economic dynamism we encountered earlier in this chapter, which transformed Austrian physical landscapes, brought thousands of men and women from the countryside to Austria's new urban centers of industry and trade, and created new networks of trade and transport. In their considerations of civil society, these historians examine the ways that middle-class Austrians organized independent civic associations as a means both to effect change in local society and to improve themselves. Historians also point out that the moral impulses of self-improvement derived largely from dynamic new visions of how society ought to be organized more effectively, more fairly, and more profitably. Middle-class and noble Austrians often asserted these visions out of frustration with the state's compulsion to maintain the status quo at all costs and its inability to effect the changes it would have liked to bring about in other areas of policy. If we examine local contexts we find plenty of assertions of alternate visions, and in some cases, of political opposition.

In 1835 Faustin Enns (1782–1858), a native of Troppau/Opava, capital of Austrian Silesia in the very north of the empire, published a four-volume account of the history, natural environment, and social life of his hometown.[57] His project was reminiscent of efforts to map, describe, categorize, catalogue, and illustrate Austria's many different regions in the eighteenth century, when Joseph II had sought to gather information to carry out his centralizing and reform efforts. Yet by the early nineteenth century this kind of informational project had assumed some new meanings and new functions.

In his introduction Enns expressed his intention to write a history of Troppau/Opava that would help the reader to understand the town's current situation, not only as the product of beneficent Habsburg rule, but also as a product of its citizens' accomplishments. For Enns empire and local cultural activism were inextricably related. Enns depicted the town's current prosperity as the product of an imperial rule that had actively encouraged local citizens' initiatives, especially under Maria Theresa and her sons. Thanks to them, he said, "the dawn of reason ended many local superstitions." Joseph II had "raised the level of education and guarded the rights of the citizens with vigilance."[58] Consequently, the citizens of Troppau/Opava were free to pursue "the gradual fashioning of the intellectual, cultural, and *bürgerlich* world in this principality," which Enns saw as "the main theme of my story."[59] According to him, this self-fashioning of the rising bourgeois class in Troppau owed everything to the town's place in the larger Austrian Empire. *Imperial* care empowered common citizens to improve their quality of *local* civic life.

Although emperors and generals dominated much of his narrative, Enns reserved his most enthusiastic praise for the civic accomplishments of his own fellow citizens, whether they hailed from noble or bourgeois, German-speaking or Slavic-speaking backgrounds. What counted most to Enns was their ongoing engagement with the civic, social, and moral community in Troppau/Opava. It was this commitment to civic engagement, not their individual accomplishments or their social, familial, linguistic, or ethnic heritages that made these citizens into the true natives of Troppau/Opava.[60]

In particular Enns praised both the citizens' industriousness and their civic-mindedness in the past half century, 1785–1835. Like many towns in Austria, Troppau/Opava had actually flourished economically during the Napoleonic Wars. Thanks to Napoleon's continental blockade, which removed British competition, cloth manufacturers in Troppau/Opava had expanded their businesses. In this time of growing affluence, the town's appearance had changed considerably. The old gabled rooftops had been replaced by full-scale second stories. The interiors of the houses had also received more attractive and comfortable furnishings, "and great progress was made even in the design of the kitchens."[61] For Enns, such improvements, while of course desirable in themselves, were actually individual reflections of important community developments that took place during this time of affluence. Enns noted that during this period the townspeople had actively improved the quality of life for all citizens, in part through a program of urban beautification and in part by organizing institutions to serve the town's citizens. The town built a theater along with a new police station. It added street lighting and a new park outside the old town walls. Moreover, "during this time of increased enjoyment and [better] quality of life, the people did not forget their disadvantaged brothers and sisters." They also founded a hospital for the poor, which soon gained recognition as a model institution. And, added Enns, it was very lucky that the citizens had built these institutions when they did, because after the war, Troppau/Opava's cloth manufacturers and merchants had to struggle against revived competition from English cloth goods.[62]

Enns reserved his greatest praise, however, for three private citizens who in 1814 founded a public museum and library in Troppau/Opava. As an initiative undertaken by private citizens to increase knowledge in

View of Troppau/Opava. Painting by Georg Fritsch, 1820. Credit: Collection of Slezské zemské museum/Silesian Museum.

the community, this project embodied the highest form of civic virtue. It was especially praiseworthy because it served the youths who attended the local gymnasium. They would be able to use the library and experience the museum's natural history collection first hand, from its stuffed birds to its gems and minerals. Enns explained that the library and natural history collections would give students the kind of practical knowledge that they might not have developed in the classroom. "They could now experience physically the objects of their study," and this empirical experience would in turn "protect them from the lure of false ideas." Visiting the museum and library would also awaken in students and other town dwellers a desire to further study nature. It would provide all who visited it with "a new respect for the basic natural principles of order, love, thrift, harmony, and peace."[63]

Here we have a celebration of virtues that may at first glance seem to have reinforced the dominance of the state by promoting quiescence, but that in fact offered a powerful alternative vision of society. The benefit of the imperial order according to Enns lies in its ability to enable citizens to develop their individual capacities. The harmony produced by this order is not one imposed from above, but one constructed by the individual members of the community from the bottom up, one might say. Thrift, among other virtues, enables the individual citizen to participate in projects that benefit the welfare of all. And indeed, with the help of financial donations and diverse collections from local thrifty towns-people (including, ironically, 272 volumes donated by another Troppau worthy, Count Joseph von Sedlnitzky, Imperial Austria's chief censor), the museum and library opened its doors to the public in 1817. Teachers at the gymnasium could borrow books from the library collection, and the museum instituted regular visiting hours for students. The local newspaper, the *Troppauer Tagblatt,* reported daily on the museum and its exhibitions. In 1818 the museum was incorporated as an independent association with a board of directors. And in 1821 the Silesian Diet funded an endowment from which a permanent curator could be paid.[64]

In a period when the imperial government had actually reduced access to secondary and higher education, many comparable civic initiatives throughout the empire promoted the diffusion of knowledge, self-cultivation, and a pride in regional history. Faustin Enn's story of the public museum and library in Troppau/Opava is hardly unique. At the time of its founding, civic-minded nobles in Moravia, Bohemia, Galicia, Salzburg, and Styria had already established many similar institutions. Local notables with an amateur's interest in science and technology and a patriotic concern for the education of their fellow citizens founded museums of natural history or endowed scientific libraries specifically to benefit the public or made private collections of art available to public viewing.[65] As with their collections of historical and natural objects, aristocratic collectors now treated their art objects more in terms of their educational function than their dynastic-representational character.[66] They published amateur scholarly journals that featured the latest research on items in the museums and collections, and in Bohemia they often did so in the Czech language, thereby promoting the development of a scholarly and scientific vocabulary.

Stories about these emerging institutions reveal much about the character of an emerging bourgeois society in Habsburg Austria, its values, and the developing forms of urban sociability that took shape on the heels of the Napoleonic Wars. By 1815, despite the regime's deep mistrust of public initiatives and its almost paranoid fears of political mobilization, its bankrupt finances forced it to tolerate the founding of a range of independent civic associations that could assume some of the economic, charitable, or educational functions that the government could not afford.[67] Such for example was the case with the remarkable and spontaneous celebrations across the empire in June 1814 discussed at the end of Chapter 2, which had also served to raise money for impoverished veterans. Increasingly by the 1830s, groups of leading citizens in towns and cities across Austria had formed organizations to promote their general interests such as manufacture and trade, agricultural improvement, charity, reading, education, or local history. Such initiatives provided their bourgeois and noble founders with independent public spaces for the open and legitimate discussion of public issues.

These highly respectable activists understood their organizations to function independently of government supervision and according to rules and models of behavior that drew from the citizenship model of the emerging *Rechtsstaat*. In particular, they located moral value in the public exchange of ideas among idealized equals, and they believed that a greater diffusion of knowledge would somehow benefit their vision of community, whether local, regional, or national.

Industrial associations, for example, grew out of local initiatives to pressure the government to support business interests more actively. They brought together broad coalitions of artisans, merchants, manufacturers, and industrialists to demand a comprehensive reform of restrictive banking, credit, tariff, and guild laws. Given their diverse memberships, the industrial associations could not always agree on specific policies. Where they were united, however, was in their common demands for representation in economic policy formation. In other words, they sought an institutionalized political voice for business, commercial, and manufacturing interests.[68] Following an 1845 exhibition sponsored by the Lower Austrian Industrial Association of Vienna, for example, one frustrated economist expressed the hope that this event would "finally awaken an awareness by the state that industry is useful" and an appreciation "of the value of private enterprise in terms of the state's interests."[69]

Industrial associations produced studies of local or regional conditions that served as ammunition in policy debates. They initiated industrial exhibitions not simply to influence government policy makers, but also to acquaint foreign buyers with Austrian products and technologies.[70] The industrial association in Graz also made credit and new technologies available to members at lower rates.

Others organizations brought new local and regional newspapers into being, newspapers that for the first time reported local events along with international or court news. And more often than not, the middle classes were reading and discussing the contents of those newspapers not simply in their own Biedermeier parlors or drawing rooms, but also in a growing numbers of public sites (clubs, cafés, and restaurants) where social and civic life increasingly took place. Each of these diverse institutions—the museum, the library, the newspaper, the club, the café—had its roots in the seventeenth or eighteenth century, but only in the first half of the nineteenth century did their numbers proliferate significantly, and not simply in the few large cities of the empire like Vienna, Prague, or Milan. As smaller towns grew in size, the character of public life there gradually changed as well. In the late eighteenth century the Austrian Freemason Johann Pezzl had already observed that cafés not only were associated with urban life, but "as everyone knows, are considered nowadays to be one of the indispensable requirements of every large town."[71]

There are a few key points to be made about the character and quality of this developing engagement in public life. In the first place, these organizations were products of specifically urban forms of sociability, even if some of them were founded in rural villages or towns or promoted rural causes. In Bohemia, the Patriotic Economic Society sought to improve general knowledge about agricultural technologies among the peasantry, but it was an urban society whose members met in Prague.[72] In the mostly rural Adriatic provinces of Dalmatia and Istria, at least sixteen reading societies, often called "casinos," sprang up during the period 1814–1848, but only in the coastal towns—one Istrian exception being the inland town of Mitterburg/Pisinio/Pazin, where the leading (Italian-speaking) citizens organized a Casino di Società in 1844.[73] The casinos were generally sites where the local educated or merchant elite socialized, although they were also often the only places where the educated of Dalmatia or Istria could find books.[74] According to one contemporary observer, their newspaper offerings resembled those of a well-stocked Viennese coffee house.[75]

The kinds of organizations I have mentioned so far usually limited their membership to a local urban elite who could afford membership fees or charitable contributions. They were hardly democratic in terms of their appeal. The *Társalgási egylet* (*Geselligkeitsverein*) or Great Casino in Kaschau/Kassa (today's Košice) founded in 1828 next to the town's theater, lecture hall, and café, charged its members the enormous membership fee of twelve gulden. This had the effect of making the club into a site of defined social exclusivity.[76] Some such casinos had even started as informal groups of noble friends before they opened their membership to the local middle classes. But their particular values rested on new concepts of community. The casino in Pressburg/Poszony, for example, offered members food, cigars, a library, and most of all a congenial setting for informal conversation.[77]

Moreover, while they may not have been democratic in terms of their appeal or their memberships, these organizations nevertheless posed an alternative to the traditional public hierarchies that had earlier been dominated by the aristocracy, clergy, or local gentry. In this newly emerging elite society, nobles and non-nobles often rubbed shoulders with each other and interacted on terms of growing social equality, even if middle-class members continued to show a certain deference to their noble colleagues.[78] Within these organizations or discussion circles members cultivated forms of sociability based on democratic models of participation. They elected boards to govern their associations and regulated participation using rules that applied to all members equally. Unspoken rules of social hierarchy certainly influenced who might be elected to the board or who exercised decisive influence within a local club. But the official rules reflected a new vision of society. In his study of Pest and Buda in the 1830s and 1840s, Robert Nemes notes how social clubs brought the Hungarian nobility "into contact with a relatively wide range of social groups" for the first time, and he quotes an Austrian journalist who observed favorably of Pest's clubs that "one can be admitted without regard to rank, religion, and national origin."[79] Anna Millo points out that business accomplishment, not social status or language use, determined membership in clubs in Trieste/Trst, where even the so-called German club (Casino Tedesco) in 1831 wrote its revised statutes in Italian.[80] The intermingling of the upper and middle social classes in such organizations, especially in Hungary, helped to create a new understanding of a broader elite class that included members of the business, educated, and noble classes together. This intermingling also helped to produce a sense of common goals around which a general political opposition to the regime had crystalized by the mid-1840s.

This phenomenon of social mingling also characterized the well-known Legal-Political Reading Association in Vienna (established in 1841), and the Lower Austrian Industrial Association in Vienna (established in 1838). In 1847, for example, the Reading Association counted a dues-paying membership of over two hundred men, largely middle-class lawyers, civil servants, professors, and businessmen—some Jewish—but also some notable aristocrats. University students—including those from relatively poor backgrounds—could buy associate memberships at a reduced rate. In Graz, the Inner Austrian Industrialists' Association counted a socially diverse membership of 2,391, including those who belonged to corresponding branches in Klagenfurt and Ljubljana/Laibach. A similar industrialists' association had been founded in Prague in 1828.[81] In Hungary, a so-called Protective Association agitated for independent industrial development in Hungary. Its members—not all nobles—promised, for example, to purchase only domestically produced manufactures (they meant manufactures produced within Hungary's borders). Hungarians founded over 140 branches of this organization.[82] There were two hundred casinos, or discussion clubs, in Hungary by the 1840s, which also brought together local people of diverse social, religious, and linguistic backgrounds to participate in a new, more self-consciously Hungarian national elite.

Although participation in these new forms of public sociability were understood in gendered terms that typically relegated middle- and upper-class women firmly to the home, this did not prevent the occasional appearance or participation of women at the margins of such organizations, especially those founded for charitable purposes. In Vienna, for example, a Charitable Association of Jewish Women (*Wohltätigkeitsverein der israelitischen Frauen*) came into being in 1842, the only exclusively female association founded during this period in the city.[83] But already in 1814 a Society of Noble Ladies for the Promotion of the Good and the Useful (*Gesellschaft adeliger Frauen zur Beförderung des Guten und Nützlichen*) could boast over two thousand members in branches in Lower and Upper Austria with "contributing members of all estates" (that is, middle-class members) in many local branches.[84] On the other hand, an activist like teacher and Hungarian nationalist Klara Lövei, whose life is documented by Robert Nemes, was frustrated to find on her arrival in 1843 in Pressburg/Poszonyi (where the Hungarian Diet met) "that few women are interested in the affairs of the homeland, and many cannot grasp the questions of the day."[85]

The slow expansion of their public and civic roles along with their increasing intrusion in various civic contexts were often the products of middle-class and noble women's creativity in justifying their appearance in public life. This was particularly evident—despite Lövei's frustrations—in the Hungarian nationalist movement in the 1840s, as well as in the monarchy during the revolutions of 1848–1849.[86] Reflecting public ambivalence about women's increasing appearance in places considered to be public, the owner of a café on the Stephansplatz in Vienna's first district decided to offer women their own space (smoking forbidden!), but located it upstairs where the women could not be seen from the street, thereby essentially maintaining the fiction that they were not present in public.[87]

This brings us to the question of the values embodied in the programs and structures of the budding organizations. They were not democratic in terms of their class appeal. But the values they asserted rested on new concepts of community that existed next to and sometimes competed with older values based more explicitly on birth and social rank. These new values, while celebrating the theoretical equality of all male citizens, established some new hierarchies of their own. People who joined these organizations increasingly viewed their activism as a public reflection of their private economic, cultural, or social contributions to society. According to this emerging worldview, one's perceived ability to contribute meaningfully to the good of the community gave one a measure of social status that entitled one to a voice in public. Social organizations offered the people who saw themselves as society's "productive"—and therefore its best—classes a growing forum where their voices might influence public policy, at least indirectly. Particularly in towns like Trieste/Trst or Brody whose economies rested completely on the success of commerce, it was one's professional accomplishment defined in terms of business success that conferred membership—and a right to a public voice—in the most influential associations.[88]

Languages of Nation, National Languages

In this context of changing values, an emerging concept of nationhood played an increasingly critical role. In Pest, for example, activists linked intellectual, technical, educational progress to the progress of the nation. In Bohemia the founding of a "national museum" sought to put the collected knowledge embodied in its exhibits at the service of the nation. In the 1840s nationhood referred primarily—but no longer exclusively—to historically defined entities like Hungary, Bohemia, Poland, or Austrian Silesia.[89] (The empire was the fatherland.) However, this historic understanding of nationhood embodied the changes we observe in public socializing that brought the classes together, at least notionally. The nation no longer connoted simply the privileged elite who participated in the diet; in its ideal form, it included members of all classes. The purpose of an agrarian organization like the Patriotic Economic Society was, in the words of Rita Krueger, "the socialization of the rural population and the creation of citizens, or *Bürger*, out of the rural population." "Both the people and the land," she adds, "needed to be reclaimed." In practice this meant distributing almanacs to peasant communities stressing the importance not only of three-crop rotation but also of cultivating good habits in their children that would make them useful to society. Both the living standard and the educational and moral character of the peasantry mattered to the well-being of the nation.[90]

Greater numbers of people in the 1830s and 1840s participated in policy debates thanks also to a rapid rise in literacy rates and to the dizzying increase in newspapers and magazines. Although heavily censored by the regime, these publications nevertheless promoted interregional discussions about many economic and social issues. While Hungary's first newspaper had appeared in 1705 (in Latin) and its first German-language newspaper in 1764, the first Hungarian-language newspaper debuted in 1780, followed by a Slovak-language newspaper in 1783. All had been published in the western city of Pressburg/Poszony (today's Bratislava), Hungary's capital during and after the Ottoman occupation. By the 1840s, as newspapers increased their readerships and journalism became a paid profession for the first time, newspapers constituted a growing mass urban public forum for the propagation and exchange of elite opinion. And since Hungarian censors were generally considered to be looser than their counterparts elsewhere in the monarchy, many writers from other parts of Austria chose to publish their work in Hungarian journals.

The spectrum of publications included scientific and academic journals, literary reviews, specialty journals in fields ranging from medicine to agriculture, almanacs, and fashion magazines. Some were published monthly or weekly, a few appeared as many as four times a week, and most appeared in the rapidly expanding town of Pest. In 1847, 103 of a total of 191 newspapers, periodicals, and magazines published in Hungary, appeared in Pest alone while another eighteen appeared across the Danube in Buda. These numbers both reflected and produced a vibrant urban public culture of discussion and debate in these towns in the 1840s. Other periodicals in Hungary were published in towns in Transylvania, the Banat, and Croatia and in several different languages (Croatian, German, Hungarian, Romanian, Serb).

In 1841, when Louis Kossuth (1802–1894) became its founding editor, the newspaper *Pesti Hirlap* (Pest News) started out with sixty subscribers. In only six months' time, however, its circulation reached 4,000. By 1845 *Pesti Hirlap* regularly printed 5,200 copies, which reached an estimated 100,000 readers (this out of a total of 136,000 enfranchised nobles and an estimated million literate people in Hungary). The rapid success of *Pesti Hirlap* is also notable because it appeared in the Hungarian language at a time when a majority of newspapers and magazines in Hungary appeared in the German language.[91] The developing public culture of reading and discussion was clearly happening in more than one language, and often in the same place, partly because a majority of town dwellers in Hungary during this period spoke German at the same time that many of them were learning Hungarian for patriotic reasons.[92] As Robert Nemes points out, many readers in Pest probably subscribed to both German- and Hungarian-language papers.

In other urban centers of the monarchy the situation was similar both in terms of growing potential audiences for newspapers and in terms of multiple language use. In the Hereditary Lands and Bohemia, German-language newspapers predominated in the developing urban centers, although in Bohemia one also found several bilingual Czech and German periodicals and German-language journals translated directly into Czech. The first Czech-language newspaper had appeared in 1719, followed by many more in the 1780s. From the 1790s through the 1820s several German-language magazines were translated and published in Czech as well. In 1824 the Prague firm of Gottlieb Haase's Söhne received a government concession to publish both Czech- and German-language newspapers. Its *Pražské noviny* (Prague News) employed some of the most important Czech-language literary figures of the 1840s including poet Karel Havlíček. As we have seen in Chapter 2, some important enlightenment organizations such as the Bohemian Museum increasingly published their scientific and academic journal articles in the Czech language as well.[93]

The few regular publications in Trieste/Trst, Istria, or Dalmatia were generally published in Italian, either in Venice or in the larger coastal Adriatic towns. Here, with the exception of Dubrovnik, use of the Italian language predominated among the educated urban public. Austrian Dalmatia's first regular newspaper was the 1832 Italian-language *Gazetta di Zara* published in Zadar/Zara. Around this time, when historian Ivan Katalinic sought to publish a one-volume summary in "Slavic" of his three-volume history *Storia della Dalmazia*, he had to abandon the project for lack of potential subscribers. A decade later, however, a market for slavic publication in Dalmatia had materialized, and in 1844 the *Gazetta di Zara* was joined by the "Illyrian"-language weekly *Zora Dalmatinska*, also published in Zadar/Zara.[94]

Thanks in large part to the regime's commitment to offering primary education to all Austrian children in their various regional languages, and thanks to the efforts of the men who sought to codify and regularize their grammars and vocabularies, increasing numbers of periodicals

The port of Zadar/Zara in Dalmatia, ca. 1845. Lithograph by Johann Högelmüller and Matthias Trentsensky. Credit: Österreichische Nationalbibliothek.

were printed in local or vernacular languages. Their success and the size of their readerships depended largely on factors such as the degree of urbanization in a region, the literacy rates, or the existence of trade or administrative networks linking small towns. What were the social profiles of the audiences to which these local periodicals sought to appeal? Publications in a language like Czech, for example, found a strong market in Bohemia among a socially diverse group of educated readers ranging from aristocrats and academics to businessmen, civil servants, artisans, and shopkeepers. Publications in Hungarian had the support of a growing number of bourgeois subscribers in Buda-Pest and Pressburg/Pozsony who self-consciously defined themselves as patriots and treated their subscription to Hungarian-language papers as a public affirmation of their loyalties (even if they used German in everyday interactions). Publications in the emerging languages or dialects that were known as "Illyrian," "Alpine Slav," or "South Slav," however, carried a limited appeal in part because of the largely agricultural profiles of the societies in which these languages were spoken. This made it more challenging to establish successful newspapers or periodicals in these languages, since their publishers could not rely on support from a ready-made literate urban audience. On the other hand, the work of the vernacular schools in some of these regions, along with the growth in the number of educated teachers and clergy who read and wrote in these languages, meant that more rural towns and villages harbored potential readerships. Such periodicals, of course, would need to appeal explicitly to rural interests.[95]

An illuminating example of these challenges, and one that brings together the new associational life with the phenomenon of newspaper readership, is that of the first "Alpine-Slav," "Carniolan," or "Slovene" language newspaper, *Novice*. This journal, published in Ljubljana/Laibach, first appeared in 1843 and gained a modest circulation of five hundred subscribers, mostly in Carniola and Lower Styria. The journal came into being thanks to the efforts of the Carniolan Agricultural Society, an association that sought to promote new agricultural techniques among Carniolan peasants. Archduke Johann, the same entrepreneurial brother of Emperor Francis who had championed the railroad, served as patron of the society. At its annual meeting in 1838, he chided the members, arguing that as an agricultural society they needed to appeal far more effectively to the rural population. "Our membership is lacking those for whose very benefit the society was founded in the first place; we are lacking peasant members." The leaders of the organization attributed this deficiency to the fact that most Carniolan peasants did not generally understand the business language of the organization, which was German. Given that for fiscal reasons the state had long preferred to educate peasants in their own languages rather than to support a more expensive bilingual education (and bilingual school books), the only solution was to address the peasantry in the so-called Carniolan language (Krajnski or Krainisch). Within a year of its founding, the *Novice* had gained a circulation of 1,000 and in 1848 it surpassed 1,500. Given its paternalist combination of loyalty to the empire with a pragmatic approach to practical everyday issues of rural life, the *Novice* had little problem with the censors.[96]

But did this newspaper in fact appeal to peasants? An analysis of *Novice*'s sales in 1847 suggested that most subscribers were in fact recognizable types in the rural landscape, people who certainly interacted frequently with peasants, but were not themselves peasants. Almost half of the sub-scribers, 48.7 percent, were local priests. Another 9 percent were artisans or in trade, 8.7 percent were estate owners, 8 percent were teachers or students, and 6 percent were civil servants. Only 5 percent of subscribers were listed as peasants (Bauern).[97] This does not mean that peasants remained outside the growing network of Novice readers. Historian Joachim Hösler calls the Novice "a newspaper for readers, whose occupations gave them the task of reporting things to others," especially the clergy whose own social background and linguistic competence was close to that of their peasant charges and who enjoyed relatively high respect among them. In Carniola it was largely members of the clergy who had put together the very first "Alpine Slavic" or "Carniolan-language" grammars, dictionaries, schoolbooks, and songbooks in the period 1815–1848. They had done so not as a nationalizing project—these activists did not see themselves as part of a Slovene nation—but rather as a regional literacy project. The same clergymen also sat on rural district school committees or served as local censors for the regime. They not only communicated the word of God to the people, but also constructed and conveyed normative social ideologies through their other functions. We may conclude that the ideas expressed in Novice undoubtedly reached peasant listeners. These same peasants, however, were not a part of the social network or imagined community constructed by subscribers to the newspaper.

While at first the Novice's publishers referred to it as a newspaper "in Carniolan"—named for the crownland—they very soon began to refer to this language as "Slovene." In doing so, they redefined their prospective audience in transregional terms. "Carniolan" would not have been very attractive to people who spoke related dialects of Alpine Slavic in neighboring Styria, Istria, Görz/Gorica/Gorizia, or Trieste/Trst. The use of the term "Slovene" made a claim to an interregional community defined by shared language use rather than by administrative, institutional, or even historic boundaries. The term "Slovene" also asserted that all of these related dialects constituted a single language in the same way that the supporters of a Czech language subsumed Moravian, Silesian, and Bohemian dialects under this term, or the way supporters of German did the same.

Nationhood and Politics

By the 1840s oppositional politics seemed to infuse all kinds of social and civic institutions and situations in cities and towns throughout the Habsburg realms, thanks both to the rise of associational life and to the expansion of a press, however much it was censored. Diaries and observations by urban contemporaries noted this increase in political discussion. "Without our ever having heard much about freedom," wrote educator Leopold von Hasner of this period in Prague, "a spirit of freedom took root in us."[98] In 1842 Eduard von Bauernfeld noted of his fellow Viennese in one of those many works published outside of Austria that "there is almost no important trend . . . in which the Viennese middle class does not take part. More is being read in Vienna in recent years. The masses of books and pamphlets that the capital city consumes, especially those dealing with politics and belles lettres, is astounding." Contradicting a common stereotype of the Viennese public as interested only in food and entertainment, Bauernfeld asserted that "a people who create industrial associations and build railroads has little time for grilled hens, vaudeville, and Strauss."[99]

But it was in Pressburg/Poszony and Pest in Hungary where rudimentary political parties mobilized an urban public in the mid-1840s. When revolution came swiftly and suddenly in early 1848, the prior existence of such parties helped to produce more coherent and effective political programs that served as instructive examples for revolutionaries in the rest of Austria.

In terms of politics, developments in Hungary during the period 1815 to 1848 moved in a different direction from the rest of the Habsburg territories. Hungary was the only part of the larger Habsburg state where a self-conscious, broad-based political opposition to the regime developed, one rooted both in Hungary's major cities and in its self-administering counties. While there were plenty of political complaints against centralization and overbearing bureaucrats in other parts of the monarchy, nowhere else did these complaints become articulated as specific oppositional programs, either in civil society or in the diets.

Both the Hungarian aristocracy and the lesser gentry had largely cooperated with the Habsburgs during the Napoleonic Wars, fearing social revolution and invasion. Both had also done well economically, thanks to the increased need for grain during the war and the lack of competition from British goods under the Continental System. But in the decades after 1815, Hungarian political opposition to increasingly centralized rule from Vienna grew. Hungary's relatively autonomous counties did not necessarily contribute their share of taxes and military recruits, and their intransigence forced the Vienna government to convoke diets in order to deal with—or suppress—opposition issues. Starting in 1825, the King unwillingly called diets regularly through 1847. These so-called reform diets became the objects of all kinds of political hopes for establishing greater autonomy from Vienna, all projected by different elements of elite Hungarian society. By the 1840s the diets served as highly effective soapboxes from which Hungarian politicians might galvanize a literate public as well. At the same time, the diets regularly disappointed the hopes placed in them, in part because they became staging grounds for both factional posing and effective manipulation from Vienna.

The political issues of this period were far more complex than a simple juxtaposition of Hungarian patriotic opposition versus Habsburg centralization. For one, the gentry and aristocracy in Hungary needed Habsburg protection from potential peasant uprisings or foreign invasion. Aware of this, the Vienna government frequently took the wind out of the sails of the Hungarian opposition by proposing legislation to reform the oppressive situation of the peasants, as Maria Theresa and Joseph II had sought to do in the eighteenth century. The Hungarian nobility claimed to make up the nation, but if one defined nation in the broader terms of the French Revolution or even in the terms articulated by the Bohemian Diet of 1792—as a "people" whose interests the diet merely represented—then the Hungarian nobility would have to legitimate its power in more democratic terms. When the reform diets proclaimed their defense of the rights of the historic Hungarian nation, this did not include rights for the peasantry or the unrepresented towns. Every time the Hungarian noble opposition demanded autonomy, the government threatened social reform.

The Hungarian noble opposition also courted new dangers in the ways it sought to redefine the nation in the 1840s, by asserting its "national patriotism" against what it called "foreign" Habsburg aggression. What had seemed like a relatively narrow issue in the 1780s—that of language use in the diet or the administration (see Chapter 2)—now stirred up another set of potential problems. Joseph II's imposition of German to replace outmoded Latin had provoked strong political opposition, especially locally in the counties. The issue of administrative language use symbolized the assertion of the nation's rights in the reform diets of the 1830s and 1840s. Use of Hungarian, however, also implied the co-membership of the peasantry in a national community, peasants having constituted the main group of Hungarian speakers in eighteenth-century Hungary. How would this linguistic—albeit symbolic—definition of Hungarian nationhood affect the majority of Hungarians who, after all, spoke other languages?

There are two ways to understand this problem. First, in terms of elite rights, as long as Latin had been the official language of the kingdom, Hungary's political classes had all participated at an equal disadvantage, so to speak. Latin was no one's "first language." Once Hungarian became increasingly asserted as Hungary's official language in the 1830s and 1840s, however, Croat nobles insisted on their right to use Latin in the diet, as did non-Hungarian-speaking Transylvanians and Serbs later on. Thus the choice of the Hungarian language to define the nation created serious rifts within parts of the Hungarian elite. Second, if the choice of the Hungarian language was meant to unify a broader national society behind an elite assertion of national rights, then making language use a defining quality of the nation implied that the nation was constituted not just from the elite, but also from the rest of Hungary's inhabitants who spoke Hungarian. This again raised the question of representing nonelite interests, a question that the Hungarian nobility did not want to address, and one that the Habsburgs exploited wherever they could. As in the rest of their territories, the Habsburgs generally supported the use of vernacular languages in education and public life. That support posed an increasingly attractive alternative to the diet's growing insistence on replacing Latin and local languages administratively with Hungarian. In the short run the assertion of patriotic independence through linguistic practice seemed to mobilize greater support in Hungary for opposition to the regime in Vienna. But in the longer run this assertion undermined the way in which many non-Hungarian-speaking Hungarians understood their own identities, as well as threatening to divide Hungary.

*

During the decades following the Napoleonic Wars the concept of empire as it should be became articulated more fully in society and less and less by the state itself. After a half century of pursuing radical structural reform to achieve an integrated and prosperous state, the Habsburg regime abandoned enough of its former goals so as to remove any meaningful reform content from its practices of centralization. After 1815, state building from above was often about preserving what could be saved and no longer about realizing an ideal. A demoralized imperial bureaucracy found its raison d'être shorn of deeper meanings. Its purpose became the protection of a status quo, rather than the creation of a new society.

The visions of what the Habsburg state might be, however, remained alive in several parts of society. Among the peasantry, especially in Galicia, the Habsburg state still symbolized hope for full emancipation from the depredations of the landed estate owner and his administrators. For the middle-class society that was coming into its own, the imperial state often symbolized the possibilities of social mobility and a fatherland geared toward the good of all of society and not simply the nobility. On the other hand, crownland nobilities, especially in Hungary, took advantage of the state's partial retreat to reassert their traditional powers, often using a new rhetoric of national rights to legitimate their cause among the people. And all the while Austrian society was rapidly changing in ways that made any return to traditional ways extremely unlikely.

CHAPTER FOUR

Whose Empire? The Revolutions of 1848–1849

Wounded, [our brothers] lay on the streets, ignoring their pain,
thinking only of their fatherland; but they had accomplished the[ir]
work, and . . . their holy blood binds all the peoples of the Empire
to each other even more firmly, just as it binds them to the throne. . . .
Let their blood also constitute a tie of fraternal love among us.

— *Karl Hickel*, Die Opfer des 13. März 1848 (ein Erinnerungsblatt)

In the spring of 1848, when a series of revolutions broke out across Europe, activists in Austria risked persecution and blood to realize their visions of a renewed empire. In revolutionary clubs, newspapers, town councils, and parliaments, they debated bold new experiments in political and social policy and in the process, created the basic terms of political struggle that dominated imperial society for the next half century. In the past, political struggles had pitted crownland diets and regional nobilities against the imperial state, while the rest of society could only look on. In 1848, however, peasants and middle-class activists forced their way onto the political stage, promoting their programs and elaborating new political discourses. Meanwhile the former tenants of that stage scurried to catch up and to adapt their own rhetoric to the demands of the new times.

The revolutions that convulsed the empire—indeed all of Europe in 1848—built on the forms of public organization and communication that we encountered in Chapter 3. They did not constitute a single phenomenon, but rather many revolutions, some of which were more successful than others. In one of these revolutions, noble elites tried to expand their local power against the bureaucratic state by demanding political autonomy within the empire, or even by establishing their full independence from Austria. Another revolution in the cities and towns sought to subject the imperial bureaucracy to the will of society by creating a constitutional empire to oversee it. Both of these first two revolutions created spaces for a new politics in which the revolutionaries could negotiate with the state and influence its policies more effectively. Yet a third and often violent revolution swept away the vestiges of agrarian feudalism in the countryside. None of these three revolutions would have stood a chance if it had not successfully engaged the imagination and activism of a broad and politicized public.

In 1848 the question of the ideal role for empire—or even the very idea of empire—lay at the heart of each of these three revolutions. Most revolutionaries rejected neither the Austrian Empire nor even the rule of the Habsburgs (except notably in parts of the Italian peninsula and Hungary). On the contrary, they fought for the right to reshape the structure and the purpose of the existing empire. Bohemian historian and Czech nationalist activist František Palacký (1798–1876) was hardly alone when he famously opined that "had the Austrian State not existed for ages, it would [assuredly] have been in the interests of Europe, and indeed of humanity to endeavor to create it as soon as possible."[1] In 1848 those people who believed that they benefited from the empire's very existence hastened to make known their desires about whom it should serve and how.

For this reason, many revolutionaries portrayed themselves as caretakers of the true Habsburg imperial idea as it ought to be practiced, using a language that emphasized their desire to *return* to an imperial legality that they claimed had been abandoned in the recent past. These men and women justified rebellion by claiming that the bureaucratic regime had strayed too far from the respect for law and due process, which had defined the empire in earlier decades. Their ostensibly pro-imperial attitudes, however, did not make their diverse demands any less radical, disruptive, or unpalatable to the Habsburg dynasty. Renewed respect for the law and due process could mean many things to different people, from increased administrative self-rule to a complete rejection of the central state altogether. Conversely, they could also mean deploying the powers of the central state to enforce politically radical ends, such as the full emancipation of the peasantry or finally giving a vote in the diet to non-noble citizens.

A Disquieting Prelude in Galicia

On 22 February 1846, rebel Polish nationalists in the free city state of Cracow across the Vistula River from Austria boldly announced the resurrection of an independent Poland. Hoping to incite uprisings, they crossed the river and took their message of nationalist liberation into the Austrian province of Galicia. Events there, however, did not proceed according to plan. The revolt ended in crushing defeat, but not at the hands of the Austrian government. The uprising failed spectacularly because peasants in the villages of West Galicia rose up and massacred the rebels in a series of grisly incidents that resulted in 700 to 1,000 casualties.[2] These bloody massacres offered a gruesome reminder of peasant anger, and more importantly, they demonstrated that imperial authority played a critical symbolic function for peasants during a time of revolutionary upheaval.

Before the uprising the rebels had decided *not* to enlist the support of the Galician peasantry for their cause, knowing that any gesture to end feudal relations they might offer the peasants would alienate too many in their own privileged ranks, especially the landowning gentry.[3] Galician peasants, however, attacked the rebel lords, often while proclaiming their own loyalty to Emperor Ferdinand. In so doing they demonstratively performed their allegiance to an imperial regime that they believed was far more likely to support their interests than were the Polish nationalists. The peasants who massacred their lords in 1846 made it abundantly clear that they did not see themselves as "Poles," given the negative meanings they attached to this term and the historical memory of the Polish state they had constructed for themselves. When Polish nationalists in one village sought to persuade the peasants that their situation would improve dramatically if the Austrians could be expelled, the peasants replied:

> No, Honorable sir, it will not be that way. You [only] want to drive the most merciful Lord [the Habsburg Emperor] from the land, in

order to bring ruin upon the country, because, as my grandfather told me, [back] in the time of the [Polish] Commonwealth, lords were allowed to beat the peasants. There was no one to whom the peasant could complain. . . . If you could expel the Emperor from the land, then each of you would want to play the King, and you would beat the peasants as you did [back] in the days of the [Polish] Commonwealth.[4]

Instead of merely withholding their support from the rebellion, peasants actively attacked rebels, their families, and their estate managers, and then turned the corpses and the survivors over to the Habsburg authorities. They also destroyed feudal documents where they could find them, hoping thereby to abolish the basis for their servitude. In some cases they even divided noble lands among themselves. The Habsburg military had to intervene to stop the violence, ironically to protect the nationalist rebels from the wrath of Austria's patriot peasants.

The grisly events of 1846 in Galicia, however extreme, offer us one gauge—however situational—of peasant attitudes toward the Austrian Empire. Polish Democrats and the nationalist nobility portrayed their rebellion as an attempt to gain national freedom from a repressive Austrian regime. Galician peasants, however, preferred a Habsburg emperor who stood between them and the harsh tyranny of the landowner's whip to an independent Polish state. No broad feelings of national solidarity impelled Galician society to follow its nobility into battle against the Habsburg state. The bloody outcome of this revolt demonstrated both the narrow social appeal of Polish nationalism in the mid-nineteenth century, and the degree to which peasants rendered the idea of the Habsburg Empire instrumental to their own ends.

In the wake of the failed uprising, both Polish nationalists and the Metternich regime waged a relentless propaganda campaign for the sympathies of the rest of Europe.[5] Thanks largely to this campaign, the most significant element of the incident—the peasants' proactive defense of empire—was immediately lost to public view. Polish nationalists claimed effectively that Habsburg blood money had purchased the support of gullible peasants who otherwise would of course have supported their national leaders. And, as the preserver of Europe's social and political status quo, Metternich could hardly admit that peasant violence—even in service of the empire—was in any way justifiable.[6]

Immediately following the rebellion, neither the empire nor the Polish nationalists in Galicia did anything concrete to ameliorate the desperate condition of the peasantry. Only in later decades would Polish nationalists largely change their strategy and offer peasants a stake in the nationalist cause. For its part, the imperial regime claimed it could do nothing until it had developed a workable solution for all crownlands where feudal agrarian relations remained at issue. This solution posed an impossible challenge for a state with few fiscal options: the compensation of landlords for the potential loss of forced peasant labor. Nevertheless, the Galician revolt did produce one significant political change: it gave Austria an excuse to annex the free city-state of Cracow to Galicia.

The events of 1846 alert us to some critical patterns in the revolutions that would explode across most of Europe only two years later. In the first place, social misery by itself, although severe, had not produced the 1846 revolt in Galicia, nor would it cause the European revolutions two years later. Instead, it was socially privileged groups who sought a greater voice for themselves in policymaking, especially in their own crownlands, who orchestrated the uprisings when they saw an opportunity. In 1846 a Polish nationalist elite had sought to restore its power by recreating an independent Polish state. In 1848 Hungarian elites would seek the same for Hungary, asserting their state's independence from the rest of the empire. Noble activists in other Austrian crownlands also used the revolution of 1848 as an opportunity to assert—or in their language, to restore—their influence over policy formation, directing their anger against a centralizing imperial regime that had robbed them of their former privileges. At the same time, however, the educated and entrepreneurial classes in provincial towns and cities also demanded a role in running public affairs. In 1848 they often lined up at the outset with the nobility against the central state, only to part company with the nobility soon thereafter over issues of citizenship rights, political representation, and the local exercise of power. As with Galicia in 1846, elites who sought to restore their own powers in 1848 unleashed a revolution that unexpectedly empowered other social groups.

If privilege as much as misery underlay the outbreak of revolt and revolution in 1848, the two issues were nevertheless closely intertwined throughout the empire. Once rebellion by privileged groups had toppled the old regime in March of 1848, the effects of social misery—and a powerful sense of the unfairness of the system—often brought peasants and industrial workers into the picture, thus radicalizing the original revolutions. In 1848 it was peasant and working-class unrest that persuaded the imperial regime to accede to the political demands of the more privileged rebel groups and to let those groups try to restore order. Of course the working-class or peasant riots had little to do with the political questions that exercised the original rebels. Riots were about peasant access to land, peasant opposition to the *Robot,* urban anger at severe food shortages and inflated prices, or industrial workers' hostility to the introduction of machines or female labor. Their combined effects scared the regime—the bulk of whose military forces were busy elsewhere on the Italian peninsula—into granting noble and middle-class revolutionaries the power to write constitutions and to implement new forms of rule.

This dynamic expressed a critical point regarding the relationship of the rebels to the imperial regime. The lowest classes might have heaped outrage on their noble masters or their industrial employers, but they generally held a positive image of their Habsburg ruler. Many privileged rebel groups therefore found it expedient to include expressions of loyalty to the person of the emperor in their revolutionary rhetoric. They portrayed their efforts as attempts to *rebalance* a fundamentally decent system that had become unhinged, thanks to the untoward influence of some scapegoat, usually Metternich, or a reactionary conspiracy surrounding the unwitting—and in this case mentally incapacitated— emperor, dubbed the "court *camarilla.*" To cite the term that Hungarian revolutionaries applied to their own actions, they claimed to engage in a "lawful revolution."[7]

Events in Galicia also highlighted the importance of recent technological developments that influenced more than a few outcomes in 1848. Both the Polish rebels and the government in 1846, for example, sought actively to win over popular opinion through the use of propaganda, especially in the developing print media. And in 1846 Austrian military leaders also learned to their great surprise just how effectively the modern railway moved troops and weapons.[8] These instruments—popular press and railway—were still in their infancy, and yet many actors in 1848–1849, from Hungarian revolutionary Louis Kossuth to Field Marshall Radetzky, successfully manipulated their powerful potential to change the outcome of events.

Of the many elements of 1846 that reappeared in 1848, what of the rhetoric of nationhood that had accompanied the failed Galician revolt? In 1848–1849 Hungarian revolutionaries used nationalist rhetoric to legitimate their break from Austria. In other parts of the monarchy, however, the appeal of nationhood was neither as clear, nor necessarily as popular as it was in Hungary. Although much political rhetoric in 1848–1849 was expended on the ideal of achieving "nationhood" or of "emancipating nations," or even of "unifying a German [or Italian] nation," nationhood held highly diverse meanings for the many people who invoked it. Was the nation, for example, limited to the privileged classes represented in the crownland diets, as traditional usage implied? Or did the nation include people of all classes combined in some kind of universal community of shared language and culture, as middle-class activists increasingly asserted? Most nationalists in 1848 argued for the latter, more socially inclusive vision of nationhood, while exponents of the older elite view hastened to popularize their own usage, modifying it to imply that the nobility spoke for a more populist whole.

This broadening tendency did not, however, settle conflicting questions about nationhood, some of which we have already encountered. Was there an Austrian nation? Or did a nation encompass the inhabitants of a specific historic territory such as Bohemia or Styria or the Kingdom of Hungary? Or did some kind of common linguistic heritage that crossed traditional crownland borders define nationhood? Did Czech-speakers in Bohemia, for example, constitute a single nation with Czech-speakers in Moravia and Silesia? Or did historic Bohemia and Moravia constitute separate nations? Was it possible for a single person to belong to more than one nation? Or was membership in a nation exclusive in nature? Were relations among nations to be fraternal in character, as many nationalists presumed in the first weeks of revolutionary exuberance, or did nationalist claims rest on a zero-sum game that inevitably pitted nations against each other for access to state resources or territorial claims? Above all, how should individual nations relate to Austria, the imperial fatherland?

Peasants meanwhile had every reason to remain suspicious of or simply to ignore nationalist programs in 1848. Those programs usually sought to expand the political influence of privileged citizens, while stabilizing an economic status quo that peasants hoped to change. Moreover, as we will see, few nationalist leaders made peasant demands a serious part of their programs, except for vague promises to end the feudal system.

Uproar in the Towns

Several rebellions broke out in January 1848 on the Italian peninsula, first in Sicily, and then farther to the north. The Metternich government sent troops to defend the monarchy's Italian Lombardo-Venetian territories from any potential spillover from these revolts. Then, however, the news that a revolution in Paris had deposed French King Louis-Philippe late in February 1848 suddenly made revolution in Austria seem possible.

In fact, the revolutionary fuse had already been lit during an increasingly public struggle between Metternich and the Hungarian Diet late in 1847. The immediate issues, not surprisingly, were fiscal in nature. How to reform Hungary's fiscal system and stabilize its relationship to the rest of the monarchy? In fact, nearly all the political players from Metternich to the cautious Széchenyi, to the more radical Kossuth or the pragmatic Deák agreed that these fundamental issues must be solved. They disagreed far less on the particular solutions than about who had the right to solve them. In theory it might have been possible to bridge the relatively small policy gaps that separated the various sides in order to reform the feudal system, promote tax reform under which nobles would finally be liable for payment, improve communication and travel networks, hasten the economic modernization of Hungary, and bring Hungarian law into closer accord with that of the rest of the empire.[9] But the sticking point remained the question of competence: Who ultimately had the right to decide these issues, the Hungarian Diet or the central government in Vienna?

In the 1840s, this debate had been played out in Hungary's nascent urban public sphere of coffee houses, newspapers, and discussion circles. Hungarian activists had increasingly framed the conflicts between the king and the diet (or between the king's government and the self-administering counties, with their 6,000 public employees) as struggles between "outsider Vienna" and "patriotic Hungary." The self-styled patriotic media consistently exaggerated every politician's invocation of Hungarian history, use of the Hungarian language, or even decisions to dress according to an emerging "Hungarian national style." Every time Vienna made a concession, as it did in its 1847 decision to replace the customary Latin with the Hungarian language in the diet, the action produced only new conflicts over symbols and alleged slights to the nation.

In the 1840s the Metternich government's strategy to weaken Hungarian noble opposition to the crown involved invoking fears of peasant discontent.[10] Metternich often replied to opposition demands in the diet by threatening unilaterally to emancipate the Hungarian peasantry. Normally this had been sufficient to wring a grudging short-term compromise from the diet's more conservatives and moderate majorities. Yet following the 1846 Galician rebellion, even Metternich pulled back from this brink. Instead of threatening peasant emancipation, he tried to trump the opposition's program by introducing legislation that realized most of its reform demands.

Calling the diet into session, however, also meant holding elections. Even if only a tiny number of Hungarians had the right to vote, the elections mobilized far more public interest in 1847 than ever before, spawning veritable orgies of patriotism. Avid discussion of politics dominated social life in urban Hungary. In Pest, the election campaign became a more popular affair than usual, even if the numbers of eligible voters in the city—14,000 out of a population of 600,000—remained minuscule.[11] Supporters of the opposition celebrated several victories, including the elections of the radical newspaper editor Kossuth, of the more moderate Ferenc Deák, and Széchenyi.[12] Yet the number of votes cast reminds us of the limited character of this politicized public: In Pest, for example, even given the extraordinary publicity around the campaign, Kossuth won only 2,948 votes to 1,314 for his opponent, despite the much larger number of eligible voters who never showed up at the polls.

When the diet opened in Pressburg/Pozsony in November of 1847, it would have been difficult to say whether the government's program or that of the opposition was ideologically more revolutionary.[13] In much of the Hungarian public mind, of course, the opposition stood for a patriotic, specifically Hungarian point of view that contrasted with a "foreign" and Vienna-centric imperial state. Still, despite rousing support for the opposition from students who crowded the observers' galleries at the diet sessions, the government quickly succeeded in parrying the opposition program. Soon the session threatened to bog down completely, as had so often been the case with past diets.

It was at this point that the shocking news of revolution arrived from France, lending a new energy to the opposition at the Pressburg/Pozsony Diet. On 3 March, at an unofficial meeting of the deputies, Kossuth gave a speech that radicalized events. Calling for a separate Hungarian cabinet responsible to an elected parliament (the diet), Kossuth also demanded the taxation of the nobility, an end to peasant forced labor, compensation for the landlords, enfranchisement of the urban middle classes and better-off peasants, the reorganization of the Habsburg military to reflect Hungarian interests, and the creation of a constitution for the rest of the Habsburgs' lands as well.

The speech created an immediate sensation. Translated into German, it soon appeared as a pamphlet in Vienna where it was read in the main auditorium of the university and later to crowds in the city streets. The Viennese public turned its own attention to the upcoming meeting of the Lower Austrian Diet scheduled for 13 March.[14] Members of local reading and professional clubs vacillated between taking some political initiative and expressing fear about the potential volatility of the lowest classes. On 4 March, for example, the elite Legal-Political Reading Association demanded an overhaul of the entire system of government and administration, as well as the arming of the citizens to police the city. It also sought to curtail official police powers, to end censorship, to institute religious, educational, and judicial reform, and to create a central parliament in Vienna to legislate for the entire empire. At the same time, however, one prominent club member also warned of the perils of fomenting open revolt among the unemployed textile and machine workers who crowded Vienna's suburbs.[15]

When Monday 13 March arrived, the high level of public interest was clear from the throngs of curious Viennese who gathered in the narrow streets surrounding the Landhaus where the diet was to meet. Earlier that morning, before the fearful government had thought to close the city gates, workers celebrating their traditional "Blue Monday"[16] had managed to enter the inner city in order to join a planned student demonstration.[17] By the time the noisy band of students arrived at the Landhaus from the nearby university, crowds had blocked the neighboring streets. Cries of "They're coming!" greeted the students, and several people watching above from open windows (it was an unusually warm March day) threw down bouquets, ribbons, wreathes, and, in a few cases, jewelry.[18]

While the crowd waited for the deputies to emerge from the Landhaus, a young Jewish physician from Buda, Adolf Fischhof (1816–1893),[19] made an impromptu speech. Giving coherence to the desires of the crowd, Fischhof demanded an end to censorship and freedom of instruction at the university. After someone read aloud Kossuth's speech of 3 March, demands for Metternich's fall spread. A hurriedly organized committee of students and physicians took the crowd's demands inside to the diet. Alarmed by the restless throngs, the diet members in turn sent a deputation to the Hofburg with a petition for reform. At the same time, however, the Hofburg called up troops and finally closed the city gates.

In the confusion that followed, the military attempted to clear the streets near the Landhaus, shooting five people and wounding several more. Contemporary illustrations depict the horror expressed by the bourgeois men and women, solid citizens who suddenly found themselves under fire from the military. Among the first to fall was Karl Heinrich Spitzer, a Jewish polytechnic student from Moravia, later hailed as the original martyr of the revolution.[20] In the confusion and chaos that followed the shooting, bands of workers attacked troops, and Vienna's mayor begged the government to arm the propertied citizens (on which it had so recently fired!) and deputize them to take over the task of pacifying the city from the unpopular military. As the situation worsened, the government capitulated completely, withdrawing the military and allowing the arming of the citizens.[21] It also allowed the students to create an armed Academic Legion to be led by Fischhof. By 15 March, 30,000 men had joined either the Civic Guard or the Academic Legion and received arms.[22] Meanwhile, in something of a palace coup, a desperate group of archdukes—Ferdinand's uncles and cousins—had fired Metternich (who left Vienna immediately in disguise), along with the unpopular

Emperor Ferdinand on 15 March 1848, acclaimed by an enthusiastic Viennese crowd after his promise of a constitution. Painting by Johann Nepomuk Höfel. Credit: bpk, Berlin/Deutsches Historiches Museum/Arne Psille/Art Resource, NY.

police and censorship chief, Count Sedlnitzky, and the Hungarian chancellor, Count György Aponyi.

With open revolution now preoccupying Vienna, Kossuth and his allies in Pressburg/Pozsony easily persuaded the Hungarian Diet to endorse the constitutional demands articulated in his speech of 3 March and to send them in the form of a petition to the emperor.[23] A delegation in gala dress immediately set out for Vienna by Danube steamer to present its address to the throne. At the same time, demonstrations in Pest led by a young group of students and radical writers (the so-called Young Hungary movement) endorsed Kossuth's 3 March demands. On 15 March the radical poet Sandor Petöfi publicly recited a "National Song" he had composed at the Café Pilvax in Pest. The song's refrain aggressively asserted:

"We swear by the God of the Hungarians/We swear, we shall be slaves no more."[24] That afternoon Petőfi addressed thousands of demonstrators at the National Museum in Pest, after which the crowd marched on city hall. There, its leaders demanded the formation of a revolutionary "Committee of Public Safety" (using, as was often the case in 1848, a symbolic name taken from the first French Revolution) to govern Buda and Pest, as well as the creation of a national guard to police the city. Later in the day a crowd estimated at 20,000 people crossed the Danube and forced the Vice-Regal Council in Buda (the emperor's local representatives) to abolish censorship, call off the army, and release all Hungarian political prisoners (of whom there was exactly one).[25]

Back in Vienna, more demonstrations on 15 March forced Emperor Ferdinand's advisors to promise a constitution, a move that immediately elicited copious expressions of gratitude and loyalty to the emperor. On that same day, a group of fifty citizens met to select a provisional city council to run municipal affairs until the citizens of Vienna could elect a council. The men chosen represented solidly conservative economic and social interests—small businessmen, factory owners, professors, and one representative of the Jewish community.[26]

It was also on 15 March that the Hungarian deputation arrived in Vienna to wild public acclaim. Contemporary accounts report that thousands of people greeted the Hungarian deputation as heroes of the revolution. Enthusiastic supporters unhitched Kossuth's carriage and pulled it through Vienna's streets, stopping frequently on the way to the palace to allow him to make speeches. In the next two days the government frantically negotiated with the Hungarian deputation to reach an agreement. In the end it capitulated to every one of the diet's demands, including the formation of a separate Hungarian cabinet to be headed by Count Lajos Batthyáni (1807–1849).[27] For these Hungarians, revolution had meant establishing (or "reestablishing") an independent Hungarian state ruled by its Habsburg king, but separate from the other Habsburg territories. Elsewhere in the monarchy—including in Vienna—revolution held other meanings.

Most cities and towns received the news of these sudden events with public demonstrations of support for a newly reformed regime, and occasionally with personnel changes in local administration. Only in two major cities, Milan and Venice, did the news provoke uprisings against Habsburg rule.[28] Most middle- and upper-class Austrian citizens ostentatiously celebrated the granting of a constitution as a way of claiming powers for themselves, while creating local civic or national guards to help to contain the revolution and prevent other social groups from gaining power. In fact, it is striking how uniformly citizens across the Austrian half of the empire (and in some parts of Hungary like Croatia) responded to the news of the March revolution in Vienna by openly linking their own claims to a voice in local institutions to the emperor's offer of a constitution that created a more participatory vision of empire. The creation of local guard units expressed the citizens' claim to a voice in local affairs, while their celebration of the promise of a constitution projected that claim (in an abstract sense) onto the level of empire.

In the Upper Austrian capital, Linz, an industrial city with a significant working-class population, the leading citizens organized demonstrations, a celebration at the provincial theater, and the Association of Industrialists sponsored a torchlight parade on 15 March. Middle-class citizens and students in Linz also hurried to join a new national guard to watch over the city's security. A local observer noted with satisfaction the absence of any violent working-class excesses in Linz of the kind experienced by the Viennese, tellingly emphasizing that the revolution had not "interrupted the normal functions of local industry."[29]

In the Styrian capital, Graz, like Vienna also a university city, the impending meeting of the diet had provided a focus for petitions and demonstrations similar to those in Vienna. At a performance of Schiller's *Don Carlos* on 14 March, the moment in the play when the Marquis of Posa begs King Phillip II of Spain to grant his subjects freedom of expression elicited a thunderous ovation from the bourgeois audience. The next day, a deputation presented the Styrian Diet with a petition signed by six hundred citizens, demanding that the city government be elected "by all citizens from the business and industry communities." It also demanded for these same citizens the rights to formulate tax policy, to appoint and dismiss public officials, to set education policy, to implement freedom of speech, thought and conscience, to form a citizens' militia to replace the police, and to end censorship, corporal punishment, and the local "influence of the Jesuits," who had been banished over half a century earlier, on education. On 16 March the Graz city government distributed five hundred guns and three hundred sabers to those it judged "worthy of the general trust."[30] In the next few days, bourgeois observers proudly noted the way members of the nobility rubbed shoulders with simple citizens, students, and lesser civil servants in the ranks of the new militia.[31]

News of the promise of a constitution and of Metternich's flight arrived in the Lower Styrian town of Cilli/Celje on 16 March from Graz via the newly completed southern rail line. "Joy knew no bounds," reported a local newspaper. Accompanied by martial music and canon shots, people "of all classes" gathered at the train station, which had been decorated in the Styrian colors, white and green. From there the crowd marched to the local church and then to the district commission, where it cheered Ferdinand I and sang the emperor's hymn. The town magistrate hung a banner above his office proclaiming "Long live Ferdinand I, freedom of the press, the people's parliament."[32]

To the west, the news reached the Carinthian capital of Klagenfurt by mail on 16 March. The local newspaper reported that Klagenfurters received the news "with a general sense of joy." Citizens crowded the streets around the main square, most wearing a white cockade, cheering the emperor, but also applauding the citizens of Vienna. As in Linz, the paper reported with pride that despite the excitement generated by the news, nothing illegal took place, and no one disturbed the peace. The city was illuminated for several nights running. Bands of musicians marched through the town streets, often surrounded by crowds, and the local statue of Maria Theresa was decorated with a white flag. On 19 March, citizens organized a provisional national guard. At a gala theatrical performance the local men's choral association performed several works including what was reported to be a popular rendition of the "German hymn." The public singing of a German hymn (there were in fact several such German hymns composed in 1848) reflects Austrians' intimate knowledge of similarly tumultuous events across central Europe. One expected result of revolution at this early phase was the possible creation of a "free" new German state, whatever that might turn out to mean in practice.[33]

A traveler from Vienna brought the news of revolution to Laibach/Ljubljana, the capital of Carniola, some fifty miles southwest of Cilli/

Celje, (since the Südbahn link to Vienna had not yet been completed). Within hours many had donned the same white ribbons to demonstrate their support for the constitutional transformation promised by Emperor Ferdinand. In the evening the wealthier citizens gathered for a festive celebration in the hastily decorated city theater, where a crowd cheered the emperor several times. Outside in the streets, and well into the night, a local newspaper reported, some students, apprentices, and workers had regrettably engaged in "tumultuous excesses," demolishing tollbooths, breaking windows, and tossing a portrait of Metternich in the river. The Mayor of Laibach/Ljubljana, a man described by the same newspaper as "unpopular with the citizens," fled to the suburb of Oberlaibach/Vrhnika, some ten miles to the west, never to return.[34]

The news arrived by ship in Dalmatia's capital, the Adriatic coastal town of Zadar/Zara, on the evening of 20 March. A local official there, not knowing his boss had already been fired, reported to security chief Sedlnitzky in Vienna:

> The streets were lively the whole night long until five in the morning; masses of people carried bottles, jugs, and the like filled with wine, which they drank publicly on the streets, encouraging the acquaintances they met to drink with them. For this reason there were many drunken people well into the night among whom one heard here and there, cries of . . . "Viva the constitution, viva the national guard of Dalmatia, viva liberty, viva me, viva you, viva everybody!" . . . Many were heard asking each other just what a constitution was, and no one was prepared to give an accurate answer.[35]

From Zadar/Zara the news moved southward by steamer along the coast until it reached Kotor/Cattaro at the Montenegrin border on the twenty-seventh.[36]

Local officials in Dalmatia's coastal towns also encouraged the populace to form national guard units—undoubtedly viewing them as useful tools for the maintenance of order. They promoted the election of new city councils and later elections to the Austrian Parliament and to a new diet for Dalmatia. In all of these places both the leading citizens and the local bureaucrats framed the revolution in terms of loyalty to a regenerated Habsburg Empire. Soon thereafter, however, Dalmatians also learned

Nineteenth-century engraving depicting the Venetian uprising. In the fore-ground citizens tear out paving stones to throw as Austrian troops advance in the background in the Piazza San Marco, 18 March 1848. Credit: De Agostini Picture Library/A. Dagli Orti/Bridgeman Images.

of a revolt against Habsburg rule in Venetia that had broken out on 23 March. The fact that Dalmatian-born Niccolò Tommaseo (1802–1874) led the secession of the break-away Republic of Venice created enormous interest in the revolt among Dalmatia's urban and Italian-speaking public.[37] Sympathy for the Venetians drove some younger Dalmatians and Istrians to volunteer for the Venetian military. At the same time, however, like Tommaseo himself, most Italian-speaking Dalmatians and Istrians nevertheless believed that their own home territory should remain a part of the empire.

Events in Trieste/Trst provided evidence for similar sentiments. Here, reports of the Vienna revolution had arrived on 17 March. The stunning news of revolt from nearby Venice a week later encouraged a few groups to attempt a similar revolt in Trieste/Trst. Their efforts, however, were quashed immediately, thanks largely to the actions of Italian-speaking Habsburg loyalists who had also organized a national guard in the city.[38] As Dominique Reill has shown, Trieste/Trst's influential citizens believed that their city depended for its prosperity on its vital commercial connections to the rest of Austria. Many Italian nationalists in Trieste/Trst also insisted that their city was fundamentally multinational in character—if Italian in leadership—and that its interests placed it firmly in the Habsburg camp. Arguing that "commercial Trieste's" geographic position had "brought people here of every nation," one Italian nationalist journalist warned that if Trieste/Trst joined a Venetian-style rebellion, "Our prosperity would vanish and we would return to the status of any other small Istrian municipality, while our new buildings [palazzi] would remain deserted."[39]

To the north of Trieste/Trst in Southern Tirol, with its substantial Italian-speaking population, the news of the revolution arrived in the towns on the 17 and 18 March by mail. As it coincided in Trent with the arrival of peasants around an annual regional market, news of the revolution produced a short-lived anti-(consumption) tax protest by peasants and some townspeople of the poorer classes. For their part, civil servants, shop keepers, most artisans, and students at the local secondary school joined together to celebrate the idea of a constitution for the empire and to protect "la causa della legale libertà." To do so they too rapidly constituted a civic guard to protect their newly found liberties from the potential disorders "di quell proletariat."[40]

Further to the north, Prague, like Vienna, Graz, and Pressburg/Pozsony, witnessed several local political initiatives in early March, despite the fact that the Bohemian Diet was not scheduled to meet. Many among the highest Bohemian nobility hoped somehow to forge a more independent political place within the empire for the traditional lands of the Bohemian crown (including Moravia and Austrian Silesia), one comparable to Hungary's relative autonomy. They sought a separate chancellery to administer purely Bohemian affairs in Vienna, comparable to the Hungarian Chancellery, and they sought the appointment of a Habsburg archduke to serve as a viceroy in Prague. Yet in Prague noble diet-based politics did not foment the kind of broad-based public opposition that had developed in Hungary. With much larger industrial, commercial, financial, and educated middle classes than in Hungary, the politicized public in Bohemia worried far less about restoring the so-called "ancient rights of the Bohemian Diet" than about what it saw as government incompetence in handling riots by unemployed textile workers, not to mention the threat of rising food prices to social stability.[41] When a diverse group of citizens met on 8 March to draw up a petition to the emperor, their efforts quickly overshadowed the behind-the-scenes activities of the diet nobility. This petition demanded the creation of a citizen's militia to protect society from the dangers of "proletarian disorder," in addition to an increased use of the Czech language in schools, increased municipal autonomy, and the abolition of censorship and forced labor *(Robot)*.[42] When news of the emperor's promises of a constitution and an end to censorship reached Prague on 15 March, citizens and students there also rushed to form a civic guard and an academic legion.

The 8 March petition had included the signatures of Bohemians who used both the Czech and German languages and who identified themselves as both Czech and German Bohemians. To them, the argument for greater Bohemian rights, or for the protection of the "Bohemian nation," did not necessarily apply to one language group or another, although more activists probably understood these terms in a specifically Czech nationalist sense. In Prague, the most politically active Bohemian citizens in 1848 were often recruited from the growing Czech-speaking intelligentsia, because in Prague the formation of middle-class demands for citizenship rights proceeded in tandem with the active creation of a self-consciously Czech nationalist community. Still, while events in Prague and a few other Bohemian towns produced some early conflicts between Czech- and German-identified activists in 1848, the vast majority of Bohemians did not see themselves as part of a transregional, linguistically defined Czech or German nation. For some who *did* identify their loyalties in these terms, this allegiance did not always prevent them from occasional identification with Bohemia's other nation as well. In fact many political activists early in 1848 continued to speak of "Bohemian patriotism," referring to a regional commitment whose boundaries problematized purely linguistic definitions of loyalty.

The students of Prague, like many elsewhere in Bohemia, organized impressive public ceremonies to commemorate those who had fallen in

Vienna's March uprisings. Although Prague had suffered no casualties at this point (and would not do so until the siege of the city in June by General Alfred Windischgrätz), Praguers nevertheless commemorated the Viennese "fallen martyrs of liberty" in an impressive mass held in the Tyn Church on the old town square on 21 March. In his speech, Augustin Smetana emphasized that the dead were "brothers, who sacrificed their lives for love of liberty and the fatherland."[43] A Czech-language pamphlet signed by Prague University students calling for unity and fraternity asserted: "Your blood has tied the peoples of Austria together more firmly."[44]

When news of revolution in Vienna reached the Galician capital Lemberg/Lwów/Lviv on 18 March, it unleashed competing maneuvers by Polish nationalists on the one hand, and Habsburg Governor Count Francis Stadion (1806–1853), on the other. With the events of 1846 in mind, each side tried to outflank the other by mobilizing for itself the support of a suffering peasantry. Both Polish nationalists and Habsburg officials also feared the potentially dangerous effects that mass starvation of the year before could bring to the region. A group of Polish nationalist Democrats immediately drafted a petition to the emperor demanding constitutional freedoms and the abolition of compulsory peasant labor. In less than a day, these activists had collected over 12,000 signatures within the city, thanks largely to publicity from local nationalist newspapers. At the very same time, however, Governor Stadion pressured Vienna to let him be the first to announce an end to the remaining feudal relations as the emperor's new gift to the peasantry.

The abrogation of what remained of feudalism proved a challenge to both the government and the Polish nationalists. In return for their renunciation of forced labor, for example, Polish nationalists insisted on the abolition of "common lands," those fields and woods the peasants had traditionally used to pasture their animals, to collect wood, or to forage for food. Nobles asserted their legal ownership of these lands in order to end their usage by peasants. In particular, many nobles worried that the abolition of compulsory labor would leave the peasants no motivation to sell their labor to the lords, even for a wage. Ending access to these so-called common lands" would help to make peasants more dependent on waged labor for their survival and maintain a pool of cheap labor for the lords.[45] Habsburg bureaucrats for their part worried about how best to compensate the lords for the peasant labor they would lose, preferring to develop a comprehensive plan for the entire monarchy before publicly announcing an end of the *Robot* in Galicia.

On 13 April following a month of intense negotiation, Polish nationalist members of the newly organized Central National Council (Radowa Narodowa Centralna) agreed that noble landowners across Galicia would simultaneously and very publicly renounce the use of forced labor on Easter Sunday, 23 April. However, Governor Stadion unexpectedly announced the end of all peasant obligations one day earlier on 22 April, thus beating them at their own public relations game. Although the government did not actually issue the official decree that ended feudal relations for the whole monarchy until 15 May, so important was this public relations coup that Stadion obtained special permission for an early announcement in Galicia. To the dismay of Polish nationalists, the peasants experienced the abolition of forced labor as a gift from the Habsburg emperor and not from the Polish nation.[46]

The issue of ending feudal relations was most salient in Galicia, given the recent bloody events of 1846, but many peasant communities across the monarchy simply presumed that after March 1848 their various obligations had ended. Many stopped delivering dues in kind or money to estate owners, many stopped performing their labor obligations, and many acted as if they now owned the land they inhabited outright.[47] By the summer of 1848 peasants in the west had also ended what remained of agricultural feudalism there. In his memoir, Josip Vošnjak recalled returning to his Carniolan village from a Graz boarding school for the summer vacation and learning to his surprise that back in March, peasants there had attacked the administrator of the local castle and announced their emancipation from all feudal dues.[48] This was hardly an isolated event. On the evening of 21–22 March, for example, 300 to 500 hundred people had stormed the castle at Burg Sonnegg/Sonnig, a few miles to the south of Ljubljana/Laibach. The peasants plundered the castle and burned the urbarial record books in which their obligations to Joseph Count Auersperg were inscribed.

For many peasants, the revolution meant the definitive end to their obligations to estate owners, and it also gave many an opportunity to settle some old scores. Peasant violence was so massive in Carniola and Lower Styria that local administrators and estate owners begged for military reinforcements.[49] Peasants in many parts of Hungary duplicated this kind of behavior. In April 1848 rumors of impending emancipation produced rioting by Hungarian peasants who believed that the king had freed them from their obligations, but that the nobles, the officials, the priests, or the Jews in many cases were hiding the news from them. In June the new Hungarian cabinet found itself obliged to proclaim a state of siege, to arrest peasant ringleaders, and even to organize vigilante squads to repress peasant uprisings.[50]

We can conclude from their actions in the spring of 1848 that Austrians across most of the empire recognized in the news of revolution both opportunities to influence policy and opportunities to realize long-held local goals. Austrians made sense of the revolutionary events they experienced by connecting their particular interests to larger and more abstract forms of imperial power. Local activists took steps to control local political developments where possible by organizing guard units, and then projected their interests forward onto the future constitution as a means to influence their place in the empire and indeed to determine the very shape of empire. As with the celebrations of victorious empire in 1814, local meanings assigned to revolutionary celebrations in the spring of 1848 created a level of popular engagement with empire that helped to ensure its survival. The formerly bureaucratic regime was becoming what it should have been all along: their empire.

Revolutionary Public Culture, Ritual, and Transparency

With the swift end to censorship, new newspapers sprang up (or collapsed) with remarkable speed. Increasing numbers of citizens, it seems, could not wait to express their opinions publicly, whether in newspapers, at club meetings, in street demonstrations, or at theater performances. Discussions at public coffee houses and pubs became more open—they often provided the new newspapers for public consumption—and men and women in several towns demonstrated their revolutionary commitments ostentatiously by adopting new forms of dress and of address, and

Depiction of the first uncensored newspapers sold in the streets of Vienna in 1848. Watercolor by Johann Nepomuk Höfel. Credit: Erich Lessing/Art Resource, NY.

sometimes even by adopting new names. Many communities swiftly created rituals to commemorate, and thereby interpret and control, the meanings of recent revolutionary events.

Above all, as we have seen, townspeople asserted their new influence on local public affairs by joining new civic guard units that patrolled streets to protect neighborhoods from unrest and instability. Formerly, civic guards had been small ceremonial organizations, membership in which was seen as a corporate privilege limited to the wealthiest property owners in a town. In 1848, by contrast, guard units swiftly came to symbolize an active, masculine, general form of citizenship—or self-rule—that applied to the self-reliant men who constituted the broader community. Just how broad that community should be in practice, however, remained a matter of local debate. Guard units embodied the pride of a local middle class, a group that saw itself as lacking social privilege and now asserted responsibility for governing. This critical symbolic importance of the guards is reflected in the fact that even communities untroubled by social unrest organized them. The arming of "the citizens," proclaimed a March 17 pamphlet in Troppau/Opava, gave "the people" the power to protect their rights themselves.

> The honor of the Civic Guard rests on the honor of the citizen. From now on he counts for something [er ist kein Null mehr]. He is as valiant as his ancestors were through the centuries, [only now] he feels he has won back his honor, his strength. The people raise their weapons only [in defense of] a pure cause, for the protection of justice, of the law.[51]

As with the ABGB, such statements used universalist language to conceive of the *people* and the *citizens* as the same group, even if in practice activists applied qualifications of property ownership and social independence to construct guard membership and active citizenship. Contemporaries liked to describe the formation of guard units as a veritable "arming of the people" to protect its universal interests. The old regime had treated "the people" as immature, incapable of participating in public affairs, whereas the new guard units asserted the people's ability to rule itself. Guard companies everywhere proclaimed their intention actively to "protect newly gained freedoms" while "enforcing peace, security and order," although against what enemy—except possibly a resurgent counterrevolution—remained unclear.[52]

In practice, however, the term "the people," as elsewhere in 1848 Europe, referred to a particular portion of the population, one ready (on its own account) to participate in public affairs. Although pamphlets and speeches praised the guards in universalist terms as the "arm of the people," in fact, the Civic Guard or Academic Legion units armed classes of men who simply claimed to represent the interests of all the people. As the same Troppau/Oppava pamphlet proclaimed, it was a man's "intellect, education, honor, and respectability"—all virtues measured in terms of property ownership or degree of higher education—that qualified him to join the guard.[53] Most revolutionaries believed that their position as stakeholders in the community made property owners the only legitimate executors of the general will. This explains why, in the rush to create guard units, the new authorities had tried so hard to prevent un-propertied citizens from obtaining arms. Urban workers or apprentices, they believed, could not be trusted to pursue the larger community good. Left to their own devices, uneducated or property-less workers would impose their short-sighted, selfish, narrow group interests on the community, rather than unselfishly recognizing the general good.

In some towns, other questions about inclusion in the new revolutionary community emerged in the context of guard membership. Were Jews—specifically Jewish property owners—to be considered part of the "the people," for example, or were their interests antithetical to the good of the entire community? Far to the east in Galician Brody (known at the time as Austria's "most Jewish city"), the Civic Guard was in fact a Jewish one.[54] In Vienna, many Jews served in the National Guard, and a Jew (Adolf Fischhof) led the Academic Legion. There also, ceremonies presided over by a priest and a rabbi in March had honored the Moravian Jewish student Karl Heinrich Spitzer as the first martyr of the revolution.[55] In Prague, however, where violence against Jews had erupted as recently as 1845, Jews found it necessary to form their own guard units. This may also help to explain the aggressive appropriation by Prague Jews of Spitzer's memory in their commemoration ceremony on 23 March. A service held in the Old Synagogue included the participation of many Christians, both students and members of local associations. A large catafalque rested in the center of the synagogue surrounded by candles. At its head was a depiction of the Bohemian lion with the words "God give him eternal happiness," while on either side Jewish students with drawn swords stood guard, lending the scene a masculine military character. The Jewish community in Prague clearly hoped to win emancipation from the revolution, and Rabbi Saul Isaak Kämpf repeatedly reminded his audience that liberty meant nothing without equality for all members of society:

> Are we not *Bürger* of one city, children of one country, subjects of one King? Are we not all equally animated by love for our dear fatherland? . . . Whether we descend from Germans or Slavs—whether we descend from Semites or Japhet [Europeans]—we remain Bohemians together. Verily, we [Bohemians] offer a sensible example to the inhabitants of this country [Austria], that they too—as different as they may be as individuals from each other in descent and language—still

form an unbroken unity. This unity, however indispensable for the wellbeing of our fatherland, can be realized only when the sun of liberty, which has now risen, gives light and life-bringing warmth to all of its children.[56]

In Pest, when Jews had tried to volunteer for local guard units in March 1848, their Christian fellow citizens had barred them from doing so. During subsequent anti-Semitic riots in Pest and Pressburg/Pozsony, the government even ordered that weapons be collected from Jews, thus punishing the victims of the riot, as contemporary critics noted.[57] Radical poet Sandor Petöfi responded by organizing an all-Jewish national guard company in Pest, but his example constituted an exception in Hungary, where the April Laws, Hungary's new constitution, failed to include a full emancipation of Jews. In some towns in Moravia Jews served together with Christians in guard units, sometimes even assuming leadership positions. "We Jews," wrote a drill sergeant in Boskowitz/Boskovice, "live here in peace and harmony with our Christian brethren, who even accepted us most amicably into the honorable ranks of the local National Guard."[58] In Moravian towns with recent histories of Jewish-Christian tensions, however, Jews often had to establish separate guard units.[59] In July 1848, for example, a Jewish guard deputation from Ungarisch Brod/Uherský Brod petitioned the Vienna government for help:

> Since Christian intolerance did not include us in their ranks, we formed a separate company with approval from the commander-in-chief and outfitted ourselves with weapons and uniforms at our own cost. But for several days the attitude toward us has become more infuriating; they insulted many members of our community because they were wearing the national guard insignia. We implored the officials in vain; they afforded us no protection.[60]

Even as they joined civic guard companies, local activists simultaneously created elaborate community rituals to highlight their critical symbolic function in a changed world. In doing so, communities expressed pride in more active forms of citizenship that they did not limit to guard members. Middle-class women in several communities, for example, created a significant place for themselves in the guard narrative of citizenship by creating flags for local companies, organizing auxiliary associations to raise funds for company needs (such as uniforms or weapons), and helping to organize elaborate ceremonies around the donation or consecration of company flags. Such ceremonies may have involved women for the first time in official public roles, and they clearly reinforced functional distinctions between the sexes, by casting the patriotic women of a community in the symbolic role of so-called "flag mothers" (*Fahnenmütter* in Vienna) of guard units. The oaths sworn by guards to freedom, to the fatherland, and to the nation also promised to protect the honor of the women of the community and in so doing, helped to create a new type of citizen-masculinity defined by its defense of women. The flags created by women served specifically as symbols of the male citizen's commitment to protect the dignity of the (implicitly) middle-class female population. At the same time, the creation of flags gave women an active role in civic rituals through their manual work. As one "patriotic woman of Vienna" maintained in a letter to the newspaper *Volksfreund*, "Flags made by our hands should lead the troops in the future whenever there is a question of defending our freedom."[61]

Emotional and pathos-ridden songs, poems, and odes by National Guardsmen and Academic Legionnaires in 1848 also testify to the centrality of the so-called "flag mothers" who served as symbols for all that was considered virtuous and for all that demanded male protection.[62] Occasionally songs and pictures gave women a more active role in the revolution.[63] A popular Czech song "The Hero's Love: A Scene from the Battle for Liberty in Berlin, 18 March 1848" not only dealt with events outside of Austria, but even more interestingly, told the story of a heroic woman who actively joined the battle when her lover died on the barricade. The song ended with her death and a call to Bohemian (Czech) women to join their patriotic men in the nationalist movement, and if necessary, to give their lives in battle for liberty, justice, and the fatherland. This image should remind us that while gender stereotypes usually demanded that women serve the cause from the safety of the home, twenty women were in fact killed in the March days and over forty in the bloody Viennese uprising of October 1848.[64]

In the early months of the revolution, men and women also demonstrated their enthusiasm for the revolution by adopting particular dress codes. In Hungary when the new government officially adopted the red, white, and green tricolor as the national flag, many residents of Pest and Pressburg/Pozsony incorporated these colors into their daily dress to demonstrate their patriotic commitment.[65] Members of a Pest organization called Radical Hungarian Women underlined the importance of such symbolic action, adding that their sisters should always "speak Hungarian, purchase domestic goods, wear national costumes, and dance national dances" like the czardas. This reminds us that most urban Hungarians typically spoke German, not Hungarian, and that in 1848 this fact in no way detracted from their patriotic or nationalist feelings for Hungary. Still, it did lead several German-speaking Hungarians to learn Hungarian. Individuals with German- or Slavic-sounding names in Buda and Pest often adopted Hungarian-sounding names to demonstrate their loyalty to the new Hungary. Many of those who changed their names were patriotic Jews. One of the organizers of the Jewish guard unit in Pest, for example, gave all of his recruits Hungarian-sounding names.[66]

Colors and style of dress served as potent markers of revolutionary commitment elsewhere in the monarchy as well, as was the case with the crowds that had decorated themselves with white cockades or ribbons to show their immediate support for the revolution. In the weeks leading up to the March revolution in Vienna, for example, women at balls (it was the carnival season after all) had enthusiastically demonstrated support for constitutional monarchy by "tearing . . . their veils and decorating the men with white scarves, sashes, bows, or cockades."[67] Like their sisters in Pest, middle-class and aristocratic women in Vienna often modified their dress as a means to make their political sympathies more transparent. "For the sake of our beloved fatherland and for the good of all classes, especially the unemployed," declared one street pamphlet directed at the women of Vienna, "let us pledge not to buy any materials of foreign origins."[68] French hats were especially to be avoided since they were not only foreign, but also smacked too much of aristocratic superficiality. Instead, suggested a letter from one woman to the newspaper *Constitution,* patriotic women should don functional straw hats decorated with a ribbon in the German national colors (black, red, gold).[69] In fact, by the end of March, white ribbons had largely disappeared from people's clothing, often to be replaced by nationalist or regional colors. For German nationalists in Austria excited by the prospect of a new united Germany, this might mean wearing items in black, red, and gold, while for Czech or Slovene nationalists this meant red, white, and blue. The red-black-gold color combination derived from the anti-Napoleon movement in the German states in the early nineteenth century. Now it reemerged across revolutionary central Europe as a transregional symbol of freedom and liberty and of support for a united Germany. The revolutionary Viennese newspaper *Schwarz-Roth-Gold* (Black-Red-Gold) explained the current significance of the colors as follows: the revolution had taken Austria "out of the [black] night of destructive fragmentation and isolation, through the [red] dawn of joyous consciousness of national unity, to achieve the [gold] light of spiritual unity among all peoples and races that inhabit central Europe."[70]

All this emphasis on the transparency of individual revolutionary commitment (reflected in outward manifestations such as dress, name, form of address) followed scripts based largely on middle-class revolutionaries' romanticized understanding of events and personalities from the first French Revolution sixty years before, and especially from its so-called Reign of Terror phase. That revolution had in turn borrowed many of its conventions and practices from examples in Classical and Roman antiquity. Ironically, given the patriotic Austrian mobilizations against the French and their revolution fought barely half a century earlier, many Habsburg 1848ers self-consciously cast themselves or their contemporaries as updated versions of Robespierre, St. Just, or Danton.[71] Viennese and Pest radicals also invoked the French example by reorganizing their local municipal governments as "Committees of Public Safety" (organizations that did not in the least resemble their French namesake).

These scripts were most pronounced in the practices developed inside the new urban political clubs that sprang up in the spring of 1848. The clubs constituted a critical organizational and social setting that developed and promoted public ideas about colors, dress, address, song, and especially the political issues of the day. Like guard units, political clubs offered sites where like-minded people came together locally to develop, discuss, and try to implement political agendas. This was especially the case in Vienna, where from March to October democratic clubs worked to drive the revolution in more radical directions, and more conservative clubs sought to put the brakes on revolutionary impulses.

The clubs promoted their favored issues in speeches, petitions, and pamphlets. Meetings offered a kind of training in parliamentary process to their members who learned rationally organized, rule-based forms of interaction that contrasted vividly with the perceived arbitrariness of the old regime. Like the organization Radical Hungarian Women in Pest, a First Viennese Democratic Women's Association, led by Baroness Caroline von Perin, was formed following riots in August over pay cuts to women workers. An anonymous pamphlet invited concerned "noble German women" to wear the German cockade on the left breast and to attend an organizing meeting in Vienna's *Volksgarten*. "We do not want to appear as amazons," claimed the pamphlet, "but rather to follow our calling and to heal wherever there are wounds: we are not judges but mediators." Whatever the women's intent, however, Viennese caricaturists quickly satirized them as modern-day amazons, and male hecklers gleefully disrupted their first meeting. Nevertheless, the club soon became a site where women of both the upper classes and the working classes met to debate how to elevate the miserable lot of Vienna's poorest women. Not surprisingly, members of the club frequently fought over social issues. In September 1848 they debated whether landlords should be forced to postpone the collection of rents from artisans hard hit by economic crisis. When Perin, like many politically moderate men, argued that such a postponement was tantamount to assaulting a landlord's property, one young worker answered, "You all pull the bedclothes over your heads and pretend to sleep whenever the poor are starving."[72]

Activists in several other cities in the monarchy organized political clubs in 1848, and some organized specifically nationalist clubs. The government also promoted organizations that might support its local agenda. This was the case in Galicia, for example, where behind-the-scenes support from Governor Francis Stadion encouraged early Ukrainian nationalists to organize a Ruthene council (*Holovna Rus'ka Rada*) in Lemberg/Lwów/Lviv under the leadership of the Greek Catholic bishop of Przemyśl. This does not mean that Ruthene nationalists might not have staked out their interests on their own in 1848, especially in response to Polish nationalist claims on Galicia. Rather, it underlines the degree to which Vienna sought to control events in Galicia by undermining wherever possible the local influence of the Polish nationalist nobility and intelligentsia.

This same Ruthene council published its proclamation to a "Ruthenian nation" in Galicia, demanding increased peasant education and linguistic parity for the Ruthene language with Polish. On 10 May, the council called upon Ruthenes to found local district councils, the membership of which should include village elders, townspeople, educated peasants, and priests. Most often the local Greek Catholic priest took the initiative in organizing and chairing these district councils, whose memberships varied considerably in terms of size and social composition.[73] Not surprisingly for largely peasant organizations, their program emphasized loyalty to the dynasty above all, and a rejection of Polish nationalist "revolutionary goals." Peasants quickly came to view the local councils as potential arbiters in their struggles against noble landlords over common lands or feudal obligations, and they swamped the new organizations with petitions for help. This in turn forced the councils to support and represent peasant interests more explicitly and after 1848, to frame the Ukrainian nationalist cause increasingly in terms of peasant social interests.

In terms of shaping public opinion, newspapers reached far more people than did clubs in 1848. During the revolutionary year hundreds of new periodicals sprang into existence, taking advantage of changes in censorship law and practice. Their veritable explosion in numbers took place largely in the cities and sizeable provincial towns. Most of them survived for only a few editions since competition became especially fierce.[74] Some newspapers were really little more than cheap brochures, pamphlets, or street flyers. One contemporary estimated that two hundred new publications appeared in Vienna alone in 1848, of which thirty-four appeared only once.[75] Newspaper culture also changed significantly. With the sudden abolition of the censorship regime, for example, many newspapers began to rely as much on street sales as they had previously on private subscriptions. Printing editions in far greater numbers than their subscriptions demanded, publishers clearly expected to sell more papers in cafés and pubs or on the streets.

Newspapers often chose names to convey revolutionary commitment and thereby increase sales. Many added popular terms such as "constitution," "reform," "the people," "freedom," and "progress" to existing names. These newspapers carried far more political news than ever before, often reproducing parliamentary or town council debates on the pressing issues of the day and sometimes printing cartoons as well. They also promoted rumors, gossip, and shameless slander against local public figures. As a result, it was not long before both the revolutionary governments of Hungary and Austria drew up press legislation to regulate the content of the new journals. Like the shocked followers of Joseph II years before, liberals experienced the end of censorship with great ambivalence. They often framed the need for some forms of restraint in terms of a division between appropriate reporting on public issues and the inappropriateness of private or personal attacks on individuals. A pamphlet from Silesia tried to explain this difference:

> It is up to the people to use this precious gift wisely. A free press addresses only public life, that is, the state and local administration. One's family life and private character should remain out of bounds of the press. Liars and those making dishonorable accusations will still have to face legal punishments.[76]

In terms of language use and reading publics, in Bohemia the government officially registered one hundred newspapers and journals in 1848, of which forty-one appeared in the Czech language and the rest in German. In Moravia, the government recorded twenty-eight publications, of which nine appeared in Czech.[77] Trieste/Trst proved to be something of an exception to the trend in the rest of the monarchy. The city did not experience the founding of new newspapers in 1848, perhaps because its residents already had access to so many established and respected independent newspapers, many of them from abroad. In Galicia, where literacy rates were far lower than in Vienna, Bohemia, or Trieste/Trst, three noteworthy newspapers had existed before the outbreak of the revolution. After March 1848, however, another thirty-seven Polish-language newspapers and at least one Ukrainian-language publication were established. Of these, twenty sprang up in Cracow, and twelve in the Galician capital of Lemberg/Lwów/Lviv.[78]

West Galician gentry from Cracow also created a Polish-language press specifically aimed at the peasantry. Not surprising, given the bloody events of 1846, such papers preached nationalist solidarity. While urban Polish-language papers may have sported the French motto "Liberty, Equality, Fraternity" on their own mastheads, newspapers aimed at peasants trumpeted safer mottos such as "Vigilance" (against interfering bureaucrats, as in 1846), "Unity," and "Harmony." Papers directed at the peasantry used ancient legends, stories, and poems to promote a nationalist patriotic education among the peasant classes, whom they addressed in highly didactic tones. They expressed loyalty to the emperor (who they claimed was surrounded by evil advisors) and promoted religion as the most important unifying social institution.[79]

In the major cities in 1848, newspapers were increasingly important not simply for the dissemination of news, but also to the very construction of public opinion on the major issues of the day. As early revolutionary unity in March gave way to conflict among the revolutionaries over how the empire should be organized, newspapers and clubs became the primary sites for the elaboration of differing political visions. Generally in Austria these visions divided into three overlapping positions represented as (1) pro-government, (2) liberal, and (3) self-styled democratic or radical. In Vienna, for example, the democratic newspapers, like the democratic clubs, actively sought to drive the revolution farther to the left during the summer and fall of 1848 by demanding universal manhood suffrage for all elected bodies, the provision of urban social welfare through public works, and the regulation of food prices and establishment of controls on rents. The Vienna democrats succeeded in achieving many of their demands in the summer of 1848 (expanded suffrage, welfare public works, rent control). In response, liberal papers, which had begun life sympathetic to the interests of workers and democrats, now began to side increasingly with the government the more they worried that the revolution threatened property rights and public order. Vienna's daily *Constitution,* for example, considered its primary function to be to serve as "a guide to the culturally uneducated public regarding its interests."[80]

In the Hungarian towns Pest, Pressburg/Pozsony, and Kolozsvár/ Cluj in Transylvania, several new papers sprang into existence also representing highly diverse political positions from liberal, to radical, to working-class.[81] One of the most radical newspapers directed specifically at the working-class, *Munkások Ujsága* (Workers' Newspaper), had a subscriber base of around 600, but regularly printed 3,000 copies, distributing them at markets for people coming to town from the countryside.[82] In Hungary, several newspapers printed in the Slavic languages used by Croatian (usually Catholic), Serb (usually Orthodox), or Romanian (Orthodox or Unitarian) patriots also sought to mobilize a nascent public to oppose a growing Hungarian nationalism that seemed increasingly bent on imposing the Hungarian language on all Hungarians.

The journalists who wrote about the news in 1848 often belonged to the very same narrow circles of people who made the news. Especially in a crownland such as Galicia with a small, educated public to start with, journalists and political activists were usually the same people. The western parts of the monarchy (including Hungary) generally boasted more independent literary or academic figures capable of making independent careers as journalists, just as Kossuth had in Hungary in the 1840s. A typical case was that of the young writer Karel Havlíček in Bohemia whom we met in Chapter 3. In 1846, thanks to a recommendation from historian František Palacký, Havlíček had been appointed editor of the official *Pražské noviny* (Prague News) and had swiftly raised its quality, its profile, and its subscription numbers. During the revolution, in April of 1848, Havlíček took over the new liberal *Národní Noviny* (National News), through which he and his colleagues had the chance to translate their liberal revolutionary ideals openly into a language that would persuade an educated public.[83]

"We Are Free Citizens of a Constitutional State"

The most dynamic evidence for the revolutionary nature of events in 1848 was the appearance of new legislatures where for the first time popularly elected representatives met to determine the future shape of empire.[84] Already starting in March, the diets that had been in session had hastily recruited non-noble townsmen and peasants into their ranks so that they could more fairly claim to speak for all the people in their crownland. In Upper Austria, for example, the Linz city council, "informed of the lively desire of the local citizens . . . to participate . . . and reminded of the reward due them for having maintained peace and order during the recent agitated days," asked the Linz *Bürgertum* to elect ten responsible deputies from its ranks to attend the diet.[85] The Styrian Diet determined, meanwhile, that henceforth the towns and the rural communes would each elect a third of the deputies.[86] In all of these cases provincial diets simply recognized new social categories (urban *Bürgertum*, peasantry) in addition to traditionally represented social categories such as noble landowners or church officials, thus augmenting traditional corporate practices of election and deliberation with new social categories.

The Hungarian Diet had already produced constitutional laws after working feverishly throughout March and early April, when the emperor's government had been too preoccupied with revolution in Vienna to influence what was happening in Hungary. The resulting April Laws had established Hungary as an independent constitutional kingdom ruled by a Habsburg king in conjunction with a Hungarian cabinet responsible to a Hungarian Parliament (the old diet renamed). The April Laws left open key questions about the relationship of Hungary to the Austrian Empire, particularly regarding the common imperial military and the common national debt. Clarity continued to be elusive in the summer of 1848 as the dynasty used uncertainty about Hungary's future relationship to Croatia and Transylvania, both of which had histories of autonomous relations to the rest of Hungary, to gain political leverage.

For the first time the Hungarian April Laws extended the right to vote for the diet, or parliament, beyond the noble class to all men age twenty or over who had been born in Hungary but who nevertheless owned a fairly substantial amount of property. Nobles who did not own property (and there were many) retained the vote on the basis of their titles, while several categories of citizens with specific educational degrees but too little property to qualify (professionals, teachers, clerics) also gained the right to vote. On the other hand, voters had to belong to a recognized religion, which in Hungary excluded Jews from voting. In all, the law enfranchised about 25 percent of adult males, or 6 percent of the entire population.[87] These provisions brought Hungarian practice into line with constitutional practice elsewhere in Europe. For, while the April Laws enfranchised a higher percentage of the populace than did the British Parliamentary Reform Act of 1832, the French electoral law of 1830, and

Entitled "Our Motion is Carried!" this late nineteenth-century image depicts the moment on 2 July 1848 when the Hungarian Parliament voted to create a military force to fight the invading army of Ban Joseph Jelačić. At the rostrum is an impassioned Louis Kossuth. Color lithograph by Antal Gorosy. Credit: Private Collection/Archives Charmet/Bridgeman Images.

the Belgian law of 1831, revolutionary France and Austria enfranchised much higher percentages of their citizens in 1848.

Meanwhile in Vienna, the emperor issued a temporary constitution for the rest of the empire on the day after Easter. Prime Minister Pillersdorf had written the draft after consulting Belgian and South German examples, which he had circulated among several high bureaucrats and archdukes. This constitution asserted the indivisibility of the Austrian lands ("All lands belonging to the Austrian Imperial State form an indivisible constitutional monarchy") but immediately conceded a separate status for Hungary and Lombardy-Venetia. It foresaw a central parliament (with a veto for the emperor), regional diets to deal with provincial interests, and civil liberties including "the inviolability of nationality and language," but left many issues unaddressed, such as the emancipation of Austria's Jews. It was assumed that once elected, the new parliament would modify the constitution—a challenge that many regional groups later took up with a vengeance.[88]

Complicating matters, earlier that spring, Austrians from Lower and Upper Austria, Styria, Carniola, Carinthia, Tyrol, the littoral, Trieste/Trst, Bohemia, Moravia, and Silesia, all regions officially part of the loose German confederation, had elected deputies to another kind of legislative body, the so-called Frankfurt Parliament. This parliament, with the same Archduke Johann as its titular head, or *Reichsverweser,* was charged with determining the shape of a united Germany. During the next year the Frankfurt Parliament struggled to decide the form a new united Germany should take, and whether that Germany should include the Austrian empire and the lands—such as Hungary, Croatia, and Galicia—that had not previously been part of the Confederation.[89]

In July, on the basis of a broad manhood suffrage, Austrians of all kinds elected a Parliament, which would determine the future political structures of empire and the nature of Austrian citizenship. Suffrage provisions for this Austrian Imperial Parliament enfranchised all "independent males" over the age of twenty-four who were Austrian citizens and domiciled in a single locality for at least six months. This decision enfranchised more than 50 percent of Austrian men twenty-four or older, or about 10–15 percent of the total population. To minimize the voters' alleged lack of political education, the government also created a two-stage, or indirect, system of election. Voters would first elect delegates from their electoral district who in turn would elect the district's deputies to Parliament.[90]

The requirements of independence and of a six-month domicile for the right to vote were meant to diminish the possible influence of day laborers on the outcome, since most of them could not prove a six-month residency. These requirements, along with the two-tiered election system, paralleled the local property requirements for membership in the new civic guard units. In fact, these diverse conditions created a functional difference between active and passive forms of Austrian citizenship for the first time. More importantly, the government, like the local authorities, never resolved what was meant by the term "independence." Clearly this requirement excluded those who received public charity from voting, but what about domestic servants who depended on employers for room and board? The relationship between perceived degree of independence and the right to vote remained highly controversial both during and after the revolution, as we will see below with regard to communal and crown-land voting.

These suffrage provisions for Parliament did not result in great masses of Austrians flocking to the polls in June 1848 to elect their first parliament. Rates of participation in the elections to the Austrian Parliament remained well below 50 percent both in the towns and the countryside.[91] In larger towns and cities, election committees and local clubs nominated and campaigned for candidates who they trusted would represent their general ideological positions. In cities, democrats appealed to working-class and artisanal voters who shared immediate concerns about controlling rents or food prices, issues that meant little outside the cities. Moderates did their best to counter the electoral efforts of the radical democrats. In Graz, for example, a liberal club urged local voters not to elect workers, since they lacked the necessary worldly experience, far-sightedness, and conviction necessary for political life. Instead, the local liberal newspaper advised voting for men who would follow a path of "steady and sober progress."[92] In Brody, a Jewish majority of seventy-seven and Christian minority of seven electoral delegates unanimously chose Rabbi Isaak Noah Mannheimer of Vienna to represent their town, an outcome that suggested both the imperial (as opposed to Galician) and German (as opposed to Polish nationalist) loyalties of Brody's Jewish voters. At the same time, however, the delegates published a statement justifying their election of a Viennese Jew, perhaps in order to placate local Polish-speaking Christian voters. The committee had sought to "claim an oppressed and forgotten religious minority's [the Jews'] holy rights as well as to recognize the rights of the long oppressed Polish nationality which has our sympathy."[93]

One thing that urban democrats, moderate liberals, and even many government ministers and bureaucrats agreed on was that peasants had little understanding of politics and cared only about abolishing what remained of the feudal system. One Styrian newspaper bitingly characterized the peasant voter's world view as: "One God, one Emperor, one religion, no *Robot*, no tithe, no chickens, no eggs [referring to feudal dues in kind], no burdens—otherwise things can remain the as they are."[94] Usually urban committees of notables nominated candidates for election to nearby rural districts. Peasants were willing to elect educated men from the city as long as they mentioned the issues that concerned them most: ending feudal dues and maintaining loyalty to the emperor.

In fact, of the newly elected parliamentary deputies from across Austria (a socially more diverse group than those elected to any later parliament!), a quarter belonged to the rural bourgeoisie of non-noble property holders—many were better-off peasants—while a quarter were urban middle-class professionals. Still another quarter was made up of state or private officials, both with university training, while 5.75 percent of the deputies were religious officials, and 6 percent were merchants or factory owners. Only 12 percent of the deputies had noble titles, most of them of a lesser degree.[95]

Galicia elected by far the largest bloc of peasant deputies (around 40 percent). Galician peasants were certainly not going to vote for their social betters, whether noble land owners, estate managers, or civil servants. Unlike the peasants in the west who had been free from most direct forms of serfdom for several generations and could be persuaded to elect local urban notables, Galician peasants expressed hatred toward local elites with devastating force through much of the nineteenth century. When Galician peasants agreed to participate in the elections at all—and they often refused, believing elections to be part of a noble plot—they voted for other peasants. Of Galicia's one hundred parliamentary districts, thirty-five to forty (the estimates vary) actually sent peasant deputies to the Parliament in Vienna. Of the remaining deputies, however, fifty were members of the Polish gentry or nobility, thus making Galicia exceptional in yet another way, given how few nobles were elected in all other crownlands.[96]

The fact that several Galician districts elected peasant deputies in 1848 while in several others peasant voters intentionally abstained from participation demonstrated a fierce peasant determination to enforce their political will, particularly in districts hard hit by violence in 1846. At the same time, however, Polish nationalists were quick to claim that imperial officials had somehow manipulated the electoral behavior of the peasantry in order to prevent the election of more Polish nationalist candidates. This claim was untenable, not least because imperial officials also feared the effects of electing illiterate peasants.[97] In fact, close to half of the peasant deputies elected to the Parliament from Galicia and Bukovina were indeed illiterate. Additionally, only those with some history of military service understood enough German to enable them to follow the debates in Vienna. Polish nationalists sought to marginalize the effect of peasant deputies on legislation wherever they could. When a Galician peasant deputy to Vienna requested translations (blaming Polish noble exploitation and oppression for his ignorance), a Polish nationalist deputy immediately opposed his motion. Not until October 1848 did Parliament undertake to make official translations of the daily protocols available. Clearly peasant deputies from Galicia did not slavishly follow the orders of the noble conservatives, as many other deputies of the left (and Polish democrats) also later charged.[98]

The Austrian Parliament spent most of the summer of 1848 debating initiatives on the abolition of feudal structures and the question of compensation for landowners. In the summer of 1848 a young peasant's son from Silesia, the deputy Hans Kudlich, moved that the remaining feudal relationships between owner and peasant be abolished without compensation. Although the Parliament eventually decided by a vote of 174 to 144 to compensate landowners for the loss of free peasant labor, nevertheless on 9 September it did vote to end the *Robot*. This was undoubtedly its most important accomplishment, and one that the resurgent counterrevolution later on would not reverse.[99]

The Parliament also elected a constitutional committee, which created two important subcommittees to draft a bill of rights for the citizens and to outline the future constitutional structure of the empire.[100] How did deputies in the first subcommittee conceive of the future rights of citizenship? Did they disagree much about these? In August, Bohemian Czech nationalist deputy František Rieger (1818–1903) offered a strongly democratic draft text, which was based largely on the French revolutionary constitutions of 1789 and 1791 and which German nationalist liberals on the committee strongly supported.[101] This draft, passed by acclamation in committee, went before the entire Parliament on 4 January 1849. The draft asserted the novel concept that all state power originated with the people—an assertion that the imperial government immediately disputed and forced the committee to withdraw.[102] This was the only statement in the draft, however, that the Imperial government bothered to challenge, and the Parliament did not accept the modification without a fight. The rest of the draft outlined an impressive range of rights for individual Austrian citizens (many of which were also consistent with a Josephenist state tradition).

The bill of rights guaranteed all citizens equality before the law, and it explicitly abolished all traditional forms of social privilege. Henceforth, for example, the state would neither confer nor even recognize titles of nobility, and it would fill all offices purely on the basis of individual merit.[103] Individual freedoms guaranteed in the draft included those of privacy, belief (religion), speech, assembly and association, and movement. No church, for example, would enjoy any state-conferred privileges that were not enjoyed by all churches under this proposal, and obligatory civil marriage would have to precede all religious marriage ceremonies.[104] The draft also promised the creation of an independent judiciary and the abolition of the death penalty. It stated that except in time of war, the military was subject to civil laws and judicial procedures. The bill also promised to implement a system of public education to be paid for by the state. Article 19 took up linguistic diversity in Austrian society, promising that

> all the peoples [Volksstämme] of the empire are entitled to equal rights. Every people has an inviolable right to residence and cultivation of its nationality in general and of its language in particular. The equality of all languages used in a given province [landesüblich] in schools, official offices, and in public life is guaranteed by the state.

Political moderates and democrats alike (not to mention Slav and German nationalists) in the Parliament shared a common vision that confirmed the particularly Habsburg notion of equal citizenship under the law that had been articulated in the civil code of 1811, the ABGB. This part of the draft confirmed Joseph II's vision of a rationalized state structure that ruled over citizens who shared equal rights with each other. Education had also been a favorite issue of Maria Theresa and her sons, although none had managed to realize in practice the universal education they had guaranteed in theory. So too was the proposition that education should take place in local languages rather than in a single national language. By guaranteeing the churches autonomy from state control, however, the draft departed considerably from Joseph's vision of state control over all of them.[105] Moreover the draft guaranteed freedoms of teaching and scientific inquiry in institutions of learning to an extent that went well beyond Josephenist reform.

Where the concerns of political moderates and state Josephenists— already burned by their experiences with unruly Viennese radicals in the previous summer and fall—crept into the document was in the way the draft proposed to implement the rights of association and freedom from censorship. While promising that no form of censorship might limit the abstract right to free speech, the draft nevertheless added the proviso that misuse of this right could lead to punishment and that a future press law would regulate the question of what exactly defined such misuse. And although the draft gave Austrians "the right to assemble peacefully and without weapons," it added that such meetings in public had to have the advance permission of a public official, and that permission might be revoked in case of concerns for public safety, as defined by the state. Citizens could also organize associations, but again, only as long as these were not judged by the police to pose a danger to the state.

Back in the early months of the revolution many Austrians had also demanded a greater voice in governing their communes and regional diets, bodies that often determined local economic development, town planning, and welfare policies. When the reconstituted diets and town councils met, they too debated the parameters of local citizenship rights, but in far less abstract form than did the Austrian Parliament. At this level of governance, questions of participation were understood in terms of everyday face-to-face relationships. Moderate revolutionaries used these forums to remove their more radical local opponents from active participation by redefining voting qualifications. Although they spouted an emancipatory language that applied to all citizens in the abstract, when it came to local suffrage qualifications, the revolutionaries set the bar relatively high. In Vienna, for example, the city council originally gave all citizens who paid taxes in 1848 the right to vote. Following riots in September and a violent uprising in October, however, the council changed its mind and imposed a minimum annual tax threshold of five florins for the right to vote, thus disenfranchising hundreds of small property owners.[106]

City councils and diets also imposed voting systems that divided the voters into two or three classes called "curias," each of which elected the same number of deputies. The wealthiest few voted in one curia, while the many who paid far less in taxes or who qualified to vote only thanks to their level of education (often teachers or civil servants) voted in a second or third curia. On the surface these systems resembled the traditional systems of voting by estate or social status (aristocracy, gentry, clergy) that had elected the traditional diets. But in fact these newer curial divisions were economic (tax requirements) and cultural (educational requirements) in nature, as well as being the product of growing fears among liberals about the dangerous potential of the lowest classes. Through the spring of 1850 local debates about voting rights repeatedly revisited earlier debates about the degree to which one's personal degree of "independence" qualified a person for the right to vote. Moderates continued to claim that personal independence was a key prerequisite for being able to perceive the common good. Dependence, by contrast, was defined by poverty, reliance on charity, and even by criminality, and could, it was believed, lead to political support for short-sighted sectarian causes (such as socialism). Deputies to the Upper Austrian Diet asserted, for example, that "we should prevent only those individuals from voting who live from a daily wage or who enjoy contributions from a charitable institution . . . in short, those who are not independent."[107]

Urban democrats and radicals fought these claims where they could, and did not allow them go unquestioned. One democratic newspaper in Tyrol, for example, mocked the moderates' apparent obsession with the principle of independence, arguing that it served the cynical goal of limiting participation in elections. Why, after all, should higher civil servants be considered independent when they clearly owed their employment to the government? And why, asked the *Innsbrucker Zeitung*, should the franchise be withheld from allegedly dependent property-less workers— or even from women!—when "state bureaucrats, despite their unconditional subordination to their superiors all the way up the cabinet ministers, are nevertheless considered independent enough to be elected to the representative bodies" or to exercise the vote?[108] Why indeed? This newspaper was not the only one to cite the example of women and the right to vote either. As we saw earlier, the civil code of 1811 had not created distinct male and female forms of citizenship despite the ways it had instituted different gender roles within the family. Nor in fact did the constitutional draft bill of rights do so (although voting in parliamentary elections was defined as a male right). Now that the right to vote was under discussion at the more intimate village, town, or provincial level, gender concerns appeared openly in some debates about local rights of participation. If, for example, voting rights depended on property, income, or educational qualifications alone, then why should not women who met those qualifications gain the right to vote in their communes? In Styria, where the diet of 1848 turned extensive powers over to communal taxpayers, one deputy asked:

> Why since we decided that an individual is a member through ownership of either landed property, a house, a business, or the equivalent, should not women who are often in possession of these qualifications, qualify to vote, albeit by [male] proxy? Since ownership of taxable property makes someone a full [voting] member of the community, I believe that in writing the paragraph this way we have enfranchised women.[109]

In 1848–1849 the question of women's right to vote in local elections remained ambiguous in several crownlands, and when representative institutions were revived in the 1860s and some women did indeed vote (albeit by male proxy), the question would have to be resolved in a permanent fashion.

Springtime of the Peoples?

In 1848 much political rhetoric conjured the awakening, the renewal, or the apotheosis of what revolutionaries called "the nation." Contemporaries and later activists—among them many historians—celebrated the revolutionary year for having, in their opinion, given birth to mass nationalist movements. To them, 1848 was the moment in history when many nations, having slumbered for centuries under imperial rule, awakened to claim their rightful place on Europe's political stage. Many political movements in Austria justified their programs using a rhetoric that promoted so-called national rights. But what did they mean by "the nation?" And did any such nations exist in 1848?

Claiming the nation as the source of political legitimacy was hardly a new phenomenon, especially in Galicia or Hungary, where for decades noble opponents of empire claimed to speak for a wronged Polish or Hungarian nation against the centralizing efforts of the Austrian state. In 1848, however, what was generally meant by "the nation" in public discourse changed its character radically, from a sociopolitical unit that promoted the rights of a ruling elite to a mass-based phenomenon defined in broadly cultural, Herderian terms. The nation was no longer the nobility represented in the diet, but rather the totality of a people bound together by shared language, cultural traditions, and sometimes, it was claimed, even by shared blood.[110]

Hungary, where nationalists had a long tradition of asserting the rights of the nation against the encroaching dynasty, offers an especially interesting example of this transformation. The April Laws' insistence on defining a unified Hungarian citizenship in terms of Hungarian ethnic nationhood, as well as its insistence on expanding the official use of the Hungarian language, gave Croatian and Transylvanian elites who spoke other languages (to say nothing of non-elites) good reason to mistrust the new Hungarian constitutional laws. As Romanian, Serb, German, and Slovak speakers came under increasing and unaccustomed pressure in 1848 to assimilate to the Hungarian nation, they risked suffering further political marginalization if they did not. Before 1848 it had been possible to imagine an independent Hungarian state that housed political and religious elites who spoke different languages but who saw themselves as Hungarians in a political sense. The nationalist emphasis on language, however, made it difficult for those who spoke different languages to consider themselves loyal Hungarians. It also made it impossible for them to serve as deputies in the diet since the regulations now stated that "such persons are electable as can satisfy the provision of the law whereby Hungarian is the exclusive language of legislation."[111]

This problem was almost inevitable, given the tendency in urban Hungary of the 1840s to couch patriotic opposition to "foreign Vienna" in symbolic cultural demands, such as the use of the Hungarian language in the diet instead of Latin. By making the use of Hungarian into a patriotic symbol, however, nationalist activists had almost inadvertently created an exclusively linguistic or cultural definition of nationhood. As long as Latin had been the administrative language in the diet and the counties, speakers of all languages had experienced the same comparative disadvantage, since no one was a native speaker of Latin.

Now, not only were elites in regions with histories of administrative autonomy like Croatia or Transylvania disadvantaged; so were communities within Hungary proper where Slovak, Serb, or German were spoken. These languages were not linked to administrative entities like Croatia or Transylvania, which had traditionally enjoyed some historic rights in their relationship to Hungary. Nevertheless, the diet's choice to link Hungarian citizenship to the formal use of the Hungarian language suddenly raised previously unexamined questions about what it meant to be a citizen of Hungary, especially since a majority of Hungarians actually spoke languages other than Hungarian. Citizens of Pest or Pressburg/ Poszony who did not speak Hungarian, as we have seen, may have demonstrated their revolutionary ardor by subscribing to Hungarian newspapers or adopting Hungarian names, but what of Hungarians outside these urban centers of patriotic ferment?

Ironically, educated Hungarians who did not speak Hungarian but rather other languages (Croatian, Romanian, Serb, Slovak, but not generally German) soon framed their own cultural or political demands in comparable ways. In 1848 Romanian and Serb nationalists in Transylvania and the Banat and Batschka regions, for example, demanded linguistic and administrative autonomy for the speakers of their languages within Hungary, something the Hungarian nationalists who had just gained their independence from Vienna were loath to concede. Very quickly, the original fraternity of nations had given way to brand new enmities, as Serb nationalists in the south rebelled against the Pest government.

The issue of nationhood, however, was rarely defined simply in terms of one language versus another. This was merely one dimension of a complex network of potential loyalties and commitments. The largely urban nationalists of 1848 often interpreted even the cultural-linguistic model of nationhood in ways that could differ as much as apples and oranges. A nation might connote anything from one's hometown or region to internationally dispersed people who all happened to use a similar language. Nationalist commitments were not comparable, uniform phenomena when central Europeans articulated them in 1848. At the same time, however, whatever the word "nation" meant in a given situation, people in 1848 used it with an almost universal confidence in its legitimizing power. With the exception of the weakened dynasties and their counselors, everyone, it seems, accepted that a nation should be a critical object of primary loyalty and a key principal for reorganizing state structures.

To a great extent, it was the empire's centralizing impulse that had produced concepts of nationhood that rested on ideas about common language use. Thanks to the increasing administrative reach of the central state, issues of regional decision-making, linguistic usage, and linguistic fairness occupied a central place in most political programs in 1848. Activists increasingly articulated their local interests in terms of language usage by officials and educators, especially given the progressive codification of vernacular languages like Slovene or Slovak, as well as growths in popular literacy. Should not speakers of these languages have the right to communicate their needs to the state, represent their interests, and invoke their legal rights in their own languages? It was not simply local priests, educators, businessmen, or journalists who demanded that official policy take better account of local linguistic practice. Civil servants, too, complained that their frequent inability to communicate in vernacular languages with the people they administered compromised the imperial system's effectiveness. For functional reasons alone, they argued, the state must communicate with people in their own languages. As one civil servant posted to Dalmatia advised in frustration, "We should finally give up the idea of forcing Italian-language schools on villages or districts where no one knows a word of Italian."[112]

In Carniola, Carinthia, Istria, or Styria, activists and their newspapers had for some time asserted the existence of a Slovene nation united by a common language. In 1848 the chaplain of the Klagenfurt/Celovec cathedral, Matija Majar-Ziljski, who had occasionally written articles for the Slovene-language *Novice* in the 1840s, circulated a typical draft petition among what he called his "Slovene patriot" colleagues, which explicitly connected language use to an emerging concept of Slovene nationhood. Of Majar-Ziljski's eight suggested demands, a full five dealt specifically with questions of administrative language use in regions where Slovene was spoken. One demand urged that "only men who truly love our people be appointed, our nationality, and our language" while another asked that the Slovene language receive the same rights "in Slovene regions, that the German language enjoys in German regions."[113]

In Bohemia, Czech nationalist activists linked issues of language use to Bohemian history. Long before 1848, Bohemian patriots seeking autonomy for their crownland within Austria had begun associating a medieval Bohemian state specifically with a linguistically defined Czech nation. The flourishing Czech language culture of the Middle Ages and the Renaissance, they claimed, had been gradually forgotten, thanks to Austria's counterreformation policies after 1620 and attempts to impose German as the sole administrative language on Bohemia. Even more complex than these efforts, however, were the vague claims made for a so-called "Illyrian" nation among Slav activists in Dalmatia, Croatia, and occasionally in Carniola. The precise territorial, linguistic, or orthographic definition of an Illyrian nation, however, differed radically according to the particular activist groups in Zagreb or Zadar/Zara who invoked it. The stakes were high, since greater official recognition of a language increasingly justified activist demands for more local or regional power over educational, judicial, administrative, and political institutions.

In 1848, this idea that a cultural or linguistic nation might demand an autonomous political existence for itself produced several unforeseen local and regional dilemmas. What was important to nationalists in 1848 often depended on specific local conditions. People in some rural regions, for example, might not want to belong to the urban-based national movement that claimed them. Or cultural nationalists might shy away from the demands of political nationhood because they believed that administrative autonomy could adversely affect their region's economy or traditional culture. This was the case when activists in the Croatian capital of Zagreb sought to attach Austrian Dalmatia to a greater Croatian (or greater Illyrian) state, claiming that the peoples of the two regions were in fact one people, based on their alleged common language, customs, and religious practice. Croatian nationalists further hoped that this enlarged Croatian state would become autonomous within or even fully independent from Hungary, to which Croatia was historically attached. A police report from Zadar/Zara, however, documented the reluctance of local Slav nationalists to take such a step: "In the last few days the idea that Dalmatia should be united with Croatia and Hungary has been generally discussed, and many complain loudly that if it should happen, this province [Dalmatia] and in particular Zara would lose a lot." Not only urban Italian speakers in Dalmatia rejected Croatian claims. Local Slav nationalists in Zadar/Zara feared that by attaching themselves to a larger Croatian state entity their own city would lose its administrative importance, since it would no longer rank as crownland capital. "The idea that the number of civil servants in the city would be greatly diminished (and civil servants are the city's main resource) . . . has had a dampening effect on the mood of Zara's populace."[114]

A comparable situation developed to the north among Slovene nationalists active in Carniola, Carinthia, Istria, and Styria, as well as those from these regions who were studying in Vienna. In the first weeks after the revolution, these students witnessed multiple deputations from different crownlands petition the emperor for increased linguistic rights or administrative autonomy. Where, wondered the students, were their own Slovene-speaking countrymen?[115] In a letter to the newspaper *Novice,* the students urged their brothers to send a popular deputation to the emperor, since "the same blood flows in the veins of Carniolans, Styrians, Carinthians, and Istrians." "We all are brothers," they wrote,

> and we beg the gentle Emperor, our father Ferdinand, to unite us, so long [administratively] separated, under one ruler. In these times, everyone who is part of a single nation desires to be united, and will be united. It is terrible to separate by force those who according to blood, their hearts and their language are united.[116]

These Slovene nationalists wanted the emperor to create a brand new crownland to unite all Slovene speakers within its borders. This concession would, of course, mean breaking apart existing crownlands and including other linguistic groups in the imagined new entity. Other Slovene nationalists rejected this proposal precisely because it would destroy the traditional crownlands to which they felt strong emotional ties.

One of the very first petitions sent from Prague to the emperor had demanded political autonomy for a new administrative creation that would unify Bohemia, Moravia, and Silesia[117] on the basis of their having belonged to the historical lands of the Bohemian Crown. These same three crownlands also happened to be the three regions in the empire where Czech was spoken. The proposed result would thus be a political nation made up of Czech- and German-speaking citizens in which the Czech speakers, however, formed a clear majority. This amalgamation of arguments based on history (the borders of the historic Bohemian crownlands) and language (the majority position of Czech) undergirded future Czech nationalist demands for both linguistic rights for Czech speakers and territorial autonomy for historic Bohemia-Moravia-Silesia. Czech nationalists in neighboring Moravia, however, reacted with suspicion directed against what they saw as an attempt by their Bohemian neighbors to abolish Moravia's historically independent crownland status. When the Moravian Diet sent a deputation to the emperor in April 1848, it used a traditional, diet-oriented rhetoric to protest any attempts at a merger of Moravia with Bohemia. "Moravia is a land independent of Bohemia, belonging only to the whole union of the Austrian Monarchy." The deputation argued that Moravia was itself a nation with historic rights, although closely related to Bohemia. ("Between the two lands there has always been a close union based on the same nationality and one sovereign.") The Moravian deputation concluded with the hope that "under the protection of this [promised] constitution, the national specificities and individuality of the whole people of Moravia" would be protected. Here, as so often in 1848, we see two completely different conceptions of nationhood at work within the same program: one nation is historic Moravia, and one nation is the community of Czech-speakers.[118]

How did different nationalists imagine that the empire should be reorganized in order most effectively to guarantee their nations' future development? In the first few weeks after the retreat of the old regime, most nationalist activists rejoiced in what appeared to them to be a grand fraternity of nations in central Europe that would now forge a new Europe. When activists in Prague, for example, commemorated the

March revolution in Vienna, they emphasized the common action taken by different nations: "Slavs fell in Vienna with Germans for a greater common cause," proclaimed one Czech-language pamphlet. "Let us follow their example, let their blood also constitute a tie of fraternal love among us."[119] In the first weeks after the March revolution, as nationalist deputations from across the monarchy presented their demands for political autonomy and increased linguistic rights to the emperor, the demands of one nation did not appear, at first, to clash with those of other nations.[120] Many nationalists in Vienna (often students) or those who were visiting Vienna as part of the deputations treated the first revolutionary weeks as a new golden age of fraternal unity among all nations. "Teach your children that they are not simply Hungarians, Germans, Slavs, [or] Italians," advised one Viennese journal, "but rather citizens [Bürger] of a constitutional Austrian state." This same article, however, also suggested that unity in the form of a common Austrian nationality should supersede all other differences. "On that day [March 13] we were one people. . . . Therefore let us have only one nationality and no national divisions!"[121] It was precisely on this issue, however, that the golden age of fraternity soon foundered.

From the first days of the revolution, a range of nation- and state-building projects jostled against each other, often overshadowing celebrations of the proclaimed unity of nations. A very few nationalist programs even demanded complete separation of nations from the empire for their realization. Some Italian nationalists in Lombardy, for example, looked to King Charles Albert of neighboring Piedmont to unify the diverse territories on the Italian peninsula in an Italian federation. Meanwhile, the Hungarian April Laws essentially divided the Austrian empire by establishing a separate Hungarian state that shared only a common Habsburg ruler with the rest of the empire. Others, especially many Slav nationalists, developed more of a "zero-sum strategy" that sought a redistribution of state resources in their favor, not an exit from the empire. Those Austrians who supported the creation of a unified Germany, meanwhile, are even less easily categorized because they sought to create a unified Germany that nevertheless included the Habsburg territories that had formerly been part of the Holy Roman Empire. If successful, all of these nationalist state-building projects—from those based on separation to those based on redrawing—could easily have destroyed the imperial unity on which most 1848 nationalist activists in Austria nevertheless insisted.

These apparent contradictions—expressing loyalty to empire while building new nations—rest in part on the fact that both the empire and the dynasty generally remained popular. Most activists would not have seen a contradiction in building their nation within the political context of an empire. Claims that nations united in culture, history, and language use embodied a collective will to form individual states, remained rare. It is also useful to recall that in 1848, with the exception of Hungary, most nationalists who supported one of these ambitious transregional national unification projects generally expected that future nation states would be organized as loose federations with considerable rights of autonomy— linguistic and administrative—for member regions. This is the only way to understand early support in Austria for an imagined unified Germany or Italy.

On the other hand, simply the publicity alone surrounding plans for the Frankfurt Parliament to develop a unified Germany elicited negative responses from nationalists who desired a very different future for the Habsburg Empire. In petitions and newspaper articles, for example, many Slav nationalists whose territory had been part of the Holy Roman Empire rejected membership in the German confederation outright and urged their countrymen to boycott elections to the Frankfurt Parliament in April 1848. Why should Bohemians, Carniolans, or Istrians be subject to some new Germany when they were loyal subjects of the Austrian emperor? Publicity around the Frankfurt Parliament also encouraged some Slav nationalists to go even farther and to develop an alternate concept of Austria's place in Europe: Austro-Slavism. When in the spring of 1848 the planning committee for the Frankfurt Parliament invited the famous Bohemian historian František Palacký to attend (Bohemia had been an important part of the Holy Roman Empire), Palacký declined, underlining his claim to belong to a Czech Slav nation that he argued was historically separate from the German nation.

> The Czech nation, affiliating itself with the German nation as an equal, and entering into the closest unions with it for more than a

thousand years, has to the present day defended its nationality. And no matter how many German things it has adopted and experienced spiritually, it has not on that account ceased to be a Slav nation.[122]

Palacký staked out a position that would have been as difficult for many Bohemians to wrap their minds around as was the idea of their joining a German nation state. He argued that within what had been thought of as a "Bohemian nation," there were in fact two nations defined by different language usage, a Czech majority and a German minority. The historic differences between Czechs and Germans, he claimed, were actually far more consequential than were any claims for a bilingual and unified Bohemian nation. At the same time, however, Palacký went farther than simply asserting the existence of mutually exclusive Czech and German nations in Central Europe. He argued that Austria should assume a Slavic identity and pursue a more Slavic-oriented politics. In his reckoning, Austria was critical to the survival of all the smaller nations, "none of whom is sufficiently powerful itself to defy successfully their superior neighbor to the east," or a united Germany to the west. "They could only do so if a close and firm tie bound them all together as one."[123]

Palacký combined traditional diet-based patriotism that demanded autonomy for Bohemia within a federal Austria with a newer Czech ethnic nationalism that sought linguistic parity—or hegemony—in the administration of Bohemia. If Austria's various Slav "nations" made comparable demands, the empire would have to orient itself to their common program. In order to develop and spread this Austro-Slav vision, Palacký and several other Slav nationalists organized a Congress of Slavs in June 1848 in Prague.[124] In one sense the short-lived congress (it ended prematurely with the siege of Prague by General Windischgrätz) offered a symbolically influential counterpoint to the Frankfurt Parliament. Although many of the Slav nationalist participants did not share an especially Austro-Slav vision (particularly the Polish nationalist participants), Palacký and his allies nevertheless offered a compelling logic for restructuring the empire, one that questioned the assumption that Austria's natural role lay in leading a united Germany.

František Palacký (1798–1876), noted historian of the Bohemian Lands and political leader of the Czech nationalist movement in the mid-nineteenth century.
In his famous 1848 "Letter to Frankfurt," he insisted on the Slav character of the
Austrian empire. Credit: Private Collection/© Look and Learn/Elgar Collec-
tion/Bridgeman Images.

Many German nationalists in Austria, however, interpreted such Slav
nationalist programs as a zero-sum challenge to their own national rights
in multilingual regions like Bohemia. For one side to gain greater recognition and rights, the other side would necessarily have to give up power.
More than this, German nationalists interpreted Slav opposition to

German hegemony as a politically reactionary rejection of the goals of the revolution—indeed as a counterrevolutionary brand of politics. To German nationalists, their nation stood for the liberal virtues of humanity, progress, education, and economic development. Those who rejected these virtues were rejecting the gifts brought by the revolution.[125] German nationalists, who uncritically thought of Slavs as largely uneducated and lacking the potential for high culture, were baffled by Slav rejections of Germanness. Why would cultivated Slavs not want to learn German (as many already did, often to achieve social or economic advancement) and also *become* German. Why not join a highly cultivated national community with world-class universities, literature, and science? Someone like Palacký who had written his earlier volumes of Bohemian history in German, for example, constituted a mystery to German nationalists for precisely this reason.

Here we also see the relative openness of such nationalists to what we might call national conversion. German nationalists in Austria who defined their nation largely in terms of its cultural superiority left the door open for other, upwardly mobile peoples to join their nation. When a group of German nationalists in Vienna organized the political Association of Germans in Austria, for example, they made membership open to all "Austrians with German sympathies," not necessarily to Germans.[126] This was a different concept of nation, although one that was also vitally dependent on concepts of language use for its coherence.

For these reasons, the more radical Vienna Democrats especially blasted Czech nationalist deputies in the Austrian Parliament as closet reactionaries. The Czech rejection of German hegemony constituted a betrayal of liberal ideals. In point of fact, however, German and Czech nationalists shared far more politically than members of either group wanted to admit. As Peter Bugge has argued, during the mid-nineteenth century, nationalists of both stripes from Bohemia generally knew both languages, shared common social backgrounds and educational experiences, and supported similar reform visions. And as we will see, these unacknowledged commonalities became critical when it came time to write a constitution for Austria. However, we should still consider how exactly those emerging German nationalists within the Habsburg state balanced their enthusiasm for a liberal, unified Germany with their loyalties to a liberal Habsburg Empire.

Most Austrian deputies to the Frankfurt Parliament did not conceive of the future rights of German citizenship in purely ethnic terms, given their cultural understanding of their own nationhood. German citizens would be those who lived inside the borders of the new state. In debates on the Frankfurt constitutional committee's first draft, deputies voted to replace the phrase "Every German possesses the general German citizenship" with the phrase "Every citizen [jeder Staatsangehörige] possesses the general German citizenship." This, they believed, would signal to non-German speakers that they could expect fair treatment in a future Germany as fellow citizens.[127] The shared liberal standpoint of most of the deputies meant that they endorsed cultural rights in a future united Germany for those citizens who, as individuals, spoke other languages. On the other hand, however, the deputies were far less comfortable with conceiving of these non-German-speaking citizens in terms of particular groups, than as atomized individual citizens who happened to speak other languages. Even the ardent supporters of a Germany led by Prussia without Austrian participation believed that a new Germany had to be a federal state.[128] The question was, to what extent would this federalism cover cultural or linguistic differences?

Over time in 1848, the allure of a united Germany began to fade for many Austrians who did not want to give up any of their particularly Austrian cultural identity—or their traditional link to Austria's territories outside of the German Confederation—as the price for becoming citizens of a united Germany. If a united Germany included only the Austrian lands that belonged to the Confederation (essentially everything except for Hungary, Galicia, and Dalmatia) what would Austria's structural relationship to those other territories be? On the other hand, many German nationalists at Frankfurt balked at including the entire Austrian empire in a newly united Germany (the so-called 70-million solution), precisely because the many other non-German language groups would allegedly dilute the Germanic cultural quality of a new Germany. Many German nationalists also tempered their original enthusiasm for a united Germany for economic reasons. Austrian manufacturers worried that they could not compete successfully against German wares in an open market. Thus, a petition from the Prague Handworkers' Association asserted:

The experience of England and France has taught us that so-called freedom of industry and trade, the unlimited application of machines, the super power of big capital, only crushes the *Mittelstand* and acts as midwife at the birth of the fearsome proletariat.[129]

Above all, German nationalists in Austria came to see that enthusiasm for a united Germany only weakened their position at home. Creating a liberal political structure for a future Austria was a far more urgent project ultimately than participating in an increasingly questionable project to create a united Germany. This impulse became imperative in the fall of 1848 with the resurgence of conservative dynastic forces after the regime crushed a radical uprising in Vienna in October. With the removal of the emperor and Parliament to Moravia (the former to Olmütz/Olomouc, the latter to Kremsier/Kroměříž), German nationalist parliamentarians recognized that they had to work more closely with other nationalists to save what they could of the liberal revolution.

The Constitutional Committee of the Austrian Parliament now wrestled with the challenge of devising a coherent administrative and political structure for Austria, which both the Parliament and the dynasty would accept. How could they mediate the competing demands made by ethnic nationalists, crownland patriots, civil rights liberals, and bureaucratic centralizers (sometimes multiple perspectives shared by the same individual)? Bohemian deputies Palacký and his lawyer son-in-law Rieger, proposed a highly federalist draft solution for the empire that gave considerable autonomy to individual crownlands, treating them almost as mini-states. They argued that the constitution should first specify the (limited) future powers of Austria's central government and then leave everything else to the diets. Tipping the balance of power in favor of the individual diets would in turn enable Czech nationalists, for example, to control most questions of provincial life in Bohemia and Moravia. Polish nationalists clearly agreed with this position, since it would give them far more influence over policy in Galicia. Most German nationalists on the other hand favored a more centralist solution under which the powers of the crownland diets would first be enumerated, and everything else would be left to the central government.[130] They preferred to give more power to the central state, in part because German speakers constituted linguistic minorities in many crownlands. But they also feared that empowering the diets in a federalist structure could hinder the realization of progressive reform across the empire since some crownlands would adopt liberal reforms, but others would fail to do so.[131]

Late in January Palacký offered a revised draft that now divided the empire into eight autonomous entities organized purely along linguistic lines: German, Czech (including Slovaks), Polish, Slovene, Italian, Serbo-Croat, Hungarian, and Romanian. Thus, for example, in this version Palacký separated the German-speaking territories of Bohemia from the Czech-speaking ones. This draft, which adhered more fully to a twentieth-century concept of nationhood, was even less acceptable in the world of 1848; both centralists and diet-based conservative federalists rejected it, and Palacký resigned from the committee.[132] Instead the majority on the committee adopted a more centralist draft by Silesian Cajetan Mayer as the basis for further negotiation. Despite its centralist thrust, Mayer's draft offered several compromises to federalists. It also left unclear what role Hungary might play in a reconstituted empire. What is perhaps most critical about these developments is that all sides in the Austrian Parliament remained committed to forging a common constitution for the empire.

Popular Nationalism?

Reading contemporary speeches or reform programs, one can easily imagine that nationalist rhetoric suffused the popular mood throughout central Europe. Journalists, politicians, government figures, and other public commentators all spoke as if nationhood were a primary form of loyalty or commitment among Austria's citizens. In fact, nationalist loyalties and ways of thinking could be found only among a relatively narrow, and usually literate and urban, public. That public did indeed debate nationhood in every part of the monarchy in 1848–49, also using nationalist terminology to articulate both their demands and their accomplishments. Yet we should keep in mind the sobering words of gymnasium student Josip Vošnjak from Carniola who spoke about a much different Austria when he recalled that "the year 1848 was in a nationalist sense completely meaningless to the great mass of the people, namely to the peasant population."[133]

Contrary to their own claims, nationalists there and across Europe sought in practical terms primarily to create national communities. They might speak movingly about their nations, but it appears doubtful from the evidence that masses of people in 1848 believed that they belonged to national communities, particularly those defined specifically by ethnicity or language use. Political commitment to this kind of national idea remained a fundamentally urban phenomenon in 1848, one largely limited to literate activists and traditional elites. If sociologist Rogers Brubaker is correct that ethnically or linguistically based nations are not "things in the world" but rather "perspectives on the world," then it is fair to say that in 1848 relatively few people shared such a perspective, and then only in limited situations.[134] It remained for nationalists to create the very nations whose interests they claimed to represent. Of course nationalists did not express their activism in these terms. Instead, they spoke of themselves as representatives of already existing nations, nations whose millions of members it was their task to awaken to full-blown national commitment. At bottom, however, their claim to speak for existing popular nations constituted little more than hopeful rhetoric, rhetoric that elicited surprisingly little resonance among millions of inhabitants of the empire.

Nationalist ideas rarely touched the landed population, and they barely touched many people in small towns and even some cities. Peasant commitments had everything to do with ending the remaining feudal obligations or obtaining and confirming their direct ownership of the land. In 1848 activists tried to awaken (as they called it) feelings of authentic national identity by inculcating peasants with a nationalist spirit at mass meetings. "In our days," wrote Slovak nationalist journalist and poet Ľudovit Štúr (1815–1856), "after centuries of drowsiness the Slavic tribes have awakened to spiritual life as if called by the trumpet of an archangel. And the Slovaks too were awakened and began to see themselves as a nation."[135] These may have been heady times for nationalists, but we should keep in mind that more often than not, they failed conspicuously in their roles as awakeners. In fact, they frequently met with open hostility from peasant audiences. To take only one example from Carniola, 500 to 700 peasants who attended an open-air meeting sponsored by Slovene nationalists in Pöltschach/Poljčane grew restless when the middle-class speakers began discussing the alleged oppression of the Slovene nation rather than the future ownership of the land. When one speaker told the peasants they should peacefully await the outcome of legislation about land distribution, the assembled group shouted down the speaker, denouncing him as an enemy of the peasants.

In a speech to the nationalist Slovene Association of Ljubljana in May 1848, association director Heinrich Martinak echoed complaints he had heard from nationalist colleagues across Styria and Carniola that the peasant population cared not a whit for nationality and was motivated only by material interests. "The intellectuals and priests," concludes Joachim Hösler, simply "did not want to accept [the fact] that their national-political solutions gave the peasants no real answer to their social concerns and problems."[136] We should also reject the verdict of many urban nationalists that peasants were simply too hopelessly ignorant on this score. As we have seen from the Galician example, many peasants rejected the concept of nationhood outright for good reason. Still others saw no obvious link between their particular interests and those of the national community being described to them.

At the same time, however, there is no question that the rhetoric of nationhood could inspire passion and motivate sacrifice among its true believers. If most people in the Habsburg Monarchy knew little and cared less about the abstract idea of the nation, this did not detract from nationalism's salience as an emerging language of politics. The independent Hungarian state, for example, quickly built up a fervent culture of nationalism in the cities, where it gave popular support to the new regime during its war of independence from Austria. The Austrian military attack on Hungary later in the fall of 1848 and again in 1849 roused the patriotism—and by extension the nationalist ardor—of many urban Hungarians even further, and several expressed a willingness to sacrifice everything, even their lives, for the nation.

Back in the Saddle

By the summer of 1848, the balance of power between the liberal revolutionaries and the Imperial Court already began to change, imperceptibly
as far as contemporaries could see, but significantly when examined in
hindsight. Eventually, by the end of the year, the court found itself in a
position to roll back some of the revolutionaries' accomplishments. Already in June Field Marshal Alfred Windischgrätz had besieged Prague,
successfully ending a radical student uprising there. By early August Field
Marshal Johann Joseph Radetzky had defeated King Charles Albert of
Piedmont at Custozza and had retaken Milan from the rebels. Both
these victories elicited fevered support from revolutionaries in Vienna—
especially the German nationalists among them—who saw them as patriotic triumphs against foreigners. In fact, it was to celebrate Custozza
that Johann Strauss premiered his "Radetzky March" to a jubilant Viennese crowd.[137] In September of 1848, Ban (or Viceroy) Josip Jelačić of Croatia marched an imperial army against fraternal Hungary. In October
the same Windischgrätz who had subdued Prague in June successfully
laid siege to revolutionary Vienna, long since abandoned by the court, the
Parliament, and most political moderates. In a final sign of dynastic con-
solidation, on 2 December the court replaced the faltering Emperor Ferdinand (who was implicated personally in too many concessions to the
revolution) with his more vigorous eighteen-year-old nephew, Francis
(1830–1916), who took the name Francis Joseph I. Endowed with the inevitable charisma attached to his title, but with little obligation to carry
through the many promises made by his Uncle Ferdinand, Francis Joseph
moved decisively against some aspects of the revolutionary order he had
inherited. In March of 1849, with final victory in Italy in sight, the new
emperor believed his position strong enough to have his prime minister,
Felix Schwarzenberg (1800–1852), disband the elected Parliament in
Kremsier/Kroměříž, and impose a constitution of his own devising on
Austria. In 1847 most Austrians would probably have greeted this imposed constitution with enthusiasm; by 1849, however, many viewed it
with suspicion.

In April of 1849 the Habsburg strategy for Hungary of divide and
conquer—especially the appointment of the Croatian Ban Jelačić to

command the imperial forces there—provoked the Hungarian revolutionaries to declare full independence from Austria. As the Habsburg military pursued war against the rebels, it purposefully exploited their alienation of regional elites in Croatia, Transylvania, and the Banat. Under some circumstances those elites might have sympathized with Hungary's new constitutional regime, but the Hungarian nationalization policy had alienated them decisively. After several months in which the forces of independent Hungary frequently outsmarted the imperial armies, and with the help of a large Russian force, the Austrians finally managed to defeat the rebels in August of 1849. Once the revolutionary events of 1848–49 had definitively ended, the numerous sieges, rebellions, and especially the bloody Italian and Hungarian wars had cost the lives of over 100,000 Austrians.[138]

Where the empire and its new young emperor would go from here was not at all clear to contemporaries. Whether Austrians would accept the undoing of some of their revolutionary accomplishments also remained uncertain. However, in 1849, most contemporaries did not in fact believe that the imperial military victories meant that Austria would abandon constitutionalism. Rather, it seemed that the new emperor would impose some kind of conservative constitution of his own making on the empire to replace those written by Austria's and Hungary's elected deputies. Many signs indeed pointed in this direction. While the regime treated the Hungarian rebels harshly, imprisoning and executing many, while marshal law reigned in Hungary and other parts of Austria, and while harsh censorship regained its sway, the regime nevertheless proceeded in the fall of 1850 to hold elections to the new municipal councils.

Despite the despair felt by many revolutionaries who ended as prisoners or exiles, the uprisings that had felled the Metternich regime in March 1848, the attempts to establish a constitutional empire, and the later rebellion in Hungary all permanently transformed Austrian society. The revolution ended what remained of the manorial system for good, while validating a revolution in political values that had already taken root among an increasingly educated transregional public in the 1830s and 1840s. While many in the upper echelons of the military or the nobility continued to press for reactionary social programs as a necessary response to revolution, it was impossible to deny society what was perceived to be its right to participate in governing itself after 1848. The survival of empire would require some degree of popular legitimation. The regime that emerged from the wreckage of 1848 may have stood for many things that even moderate revolutionaries reviled, but it tacitly accepted the revolution in values asserted by the revolutionaries of 1848. As in contemporary France and Prussia, so in Austria, the question remained: To what extent, under what limited conditions, and in what narrow contexts could institutions of self-rule be permitted to develop? More than ever before, the empire of the Habsburgs demanded society's engagement; it had to be understood as society's empire.

CHAPTER FIVE

Mid-Century Modern: The Emergence of a Liberal Empire

On New Year's Eve of 1851, young Emperor Francis Joseph I announced to his peoples:

> After careful consideration of every aspect, we find ourselves pressed by our duty as sovereign to declare the . . . constitutional document of 4 March 1849 to be annulled. The equality of all citizens before the law, as well as . . . the laws regarding abolition of all peasant serfdom with compensation . . . remain in force.[1]

With these words the emperor withdrew the constitution he had recently granted in March 1849, while conspicuously committing himself to maintain its arguably most popular achievement, the emancipation of the peasantry. The decree also sought to reassure Austrians by reminding them of the dynasty's commitment to maintaining the equality of all before the law, a commitment whose origins long predated 1849. In two accompanying decrees, however, the emperor canceled the list of specific civil rights guaranteed in his imposed constitution of 1849, while promising to maintain the legal status of Austria's recognized religions and announcing new judicial and administrative structures for the empire. Above all, Francis Joseph's message emphasized the organic unity of his empire in words far stronger than any previous Habsburg had used in stating that "the lands, which under their old, historic, or new titles are united with the Austrian imperial state form the inseparable elements of the Austrian Imperial hereditary Monarchy."[2]

Having made these decrees, Austria's new ruler embarked on an ambitious and in many ways forward-thinking program of economic, social, and cultural renewal. This program sought to overcome revolutionary instability by strengthening the empire domestically and at the same time to enhance its international standing in central Europe. The program of the 1850s built on some of the economic, social, and legal accomplishments of the revolutionaries, but it did so in a politically absolutist fashion, reminiscent of the most radical centralizing aims of Joseph II. With this naked bureaucratic absolutism the dynasty abandoned the last remaining shreds of its ancient political function—that of mediating the different needs of the varied crownland nobilities. Instead, the emperor used the bureaucracy and military forcefully to impose his program throughout the empire from Vienna. The price for this style of reform was the imposition of a police state.[3]

The creators of the liberal empire forged in these years balanced dynamic transformation with authoritarian control. Later historians interpreted this period largely in terms of that control—the harsh ban on political activity of any kind, especially in Hungary, and the return of censorship—some even seeing it as a return to the illiberalism of the reactionary Metternich system. It may therefore seem counterintuitive to refer to this police state as a liberal empire. In fact, however, as in other European states from France to Prussia, a modernizing program in the 1850s accomplished quite a lot of exactly what liberal reformers in the Habsburg Monarchy had desired in 1848. The new regime confirmed the final establishment of capitalist relations in the countryside by abolishing what remained of the feudal system. It ended the exceptional privileges of guilds to regulate access to local trades, it confirmed freedom of property ownership, of movement, and of profession, and it asserted equality under a unified legal system for all citizens. The regime implemented comprehensive reforms to improve education, especially in the universities, and it also made efforts to bring trade policies in line with the demands of Austrian business, while investing heavily in Austria's developing railroad infrastructure. Where it departed from the liberal canon was in the new treaty, or concordat, the empire negotiated with Rome to increase the rights and influence of the Catholic Church while diminishing the rights gained in 1848 by religious minorities, especially Austria's Jews.

This bureaucrat's utopia lasted barely a decade. By 1859 the regime's high-risk gambles had produced short-term disasters. Defeat in war and fiscal collapse destroyed this experiment in transformation through radical centralization. Furthermore, the regime's authoritarian measures proved ineffective against Hungarian resistance (especially to paying taxes), while its legal, economic, and educational reforms won it precious little praise from the intended beneficiaries, the educated and business-oriented liberal middle classes. Peasant opposition, at least, was generally neutralized (except in Galicia), thanks to the abolition of feudalism.[4] But Vienna's hope that an economically strengthened Austria would play a more influential role in Europe was dashed, first by an expensive mobilization during the Crimean War (1853–1855), which won Austria no friends and alienated its former ally Russia, and later by a disastrous war against Piedmont and France (1859), which lost it the wealthy crownland of Lombardy. For the first time in memory, even the positive reputation of the dynasty suffered, thanks to the emperor's decision to assume personal command of the troops in northern Italy, just in time to lose the decisive battle at Solferino.[5] When Francis Joseph's uncle and mentally impaired predecessor Ferdinand I heard of the Italian defeat in his Prague retirement, he remarked, "Even I could have done as well as that."[6]

By 1860 the empire teetered on the brink of fiscal collapse, its impressive cultural and infrastructural gains outweighed—at least in the short term—by the ruinous monetary practices that underwrote its adventurous foreign policy. The capital markets refused to make more loans without some kind of responsible oversight of the budget. As Anselm Salomon Rothschild, founder of the Creditanstalt Bank, allegedly told the emperor, "No constitution, no money."[7]

By 1867 another major military defeat and more financial crises forced Francis Joseph to stabilize the monarchy by negotiating independence for Hungary, thereby creating Austria-Hungary out of Austria. In the same year he also sanctioned liberal constitutional laws for the rest of his lands. What followed, however, was a continuation of liberal empire under slightly altered terms. The absolutism of the 1850s had laid several of the critical foundations for the constitutional systems that replaced it in the 1860s. The liberal thinking of the 1850s that produced innovative changes in economy, education, and the sciences continued to dominate policy in both halves of the new dual monarchy long after 1867. Liberal policies continued to fuel rapid economic expansion (the so-called *Gründerzeit* of 1867–1873), as well as creating new publically financed school systems and independent judiciaries. Additionally, municipal home rule was implemented, a rapid expansion of communications and transport infrastructures was effected, and ambitious development plans for cities, ports, towns, and villages in both Austria and Hungary were put forth. The Austrian and Hungarian bureaucracies retained their critical roles as mediators between state and political society, albeit in somewhat altered forms. Even the Vienna stock market crash of 1873 and resulting decade of recession did not slow the pace of development, although it did detract from the political credibility of the dominant liberal parties in the Austrian half of the empire. Moreover, as in France, Britain, or the new Germany, lingering fears about the dangers of social unrest in Austria-Hungary caused parliamentary liberals to pursue some highly illiberal social and policing policies of their own, which continued several high-handed bureaucratic practices of the 1850s.

In the 1860s liberals developed a triumphalist historical narrative in which they portrayed themselves as the final victors in an epic Manichean struggle against the powerful forces of ignorance and reaction embodied in the aristocracy, as well as in the unrestrained bureaucratism of the 1850s. Believing that their historical time had come at last and imbued with a smug self-confidence bordering on arrogance, the liberals treated "their" accomplishments—a universal secular education, economic development, scientific progress—as the keys to Austria-Hungary's future greatness. Later, as we will see, they would add to this litany of accomplishments a new liberal and imperial civilizational mission for Austria-Hungary in eastern and southeastern Europe. The dominant understanding of empire expressed in the liberal media, by diet and parliamentary representatives, and in local town councils and schools rested in fundamentally liberal understandings of the world. Both the failed constitutional experiments of 1848–1849 and the bureaucratic development regime of the 1850s shaped this understanding of the world. It was a view that eagerly embraced economic development and the empowerment of property-owning, liberal civil society, even as it limited the degree to which all citizens could participate in public life.

Laying the Foundations for a Liberal Empire

The primary aims of the court circle that installed the young Francis Joseph as emperor back in 1848 had been to reaffirm both the dynasty's power within the empire and its preeminence in central Europe.

Recognizing the importance of economic and technical development to accomplishing these goals, Francis Joseph and his closest allies sought to adapt the most useful aspects of liberalism to a politically authoritarian framework. One remarkable difference between the absolutist regime of the 1850s and Metternich's system in the 1840s was the way the new regime dispensed with the services of the aristocracy and nobility. The new prime minister, Prince Felix Schwarzenberg—himself an aristocrat—claimed that he did not know a dozen men of his class "with enough political vision or enough knowledge to whom one could entrust a substantial share in power without fear that they would rapidly lose it." As if in reply, Bohemian Count Richard Belcredi complained bitterly that everything was now being "handed over without protection to the bureaucrats," adding of the new order that "what conservative institutions the revolution from below left intact, the revolution from above has continued to destroy."[8]

A different kind of elite staffed this new order, one that drew its inspiration from the age of Joseph II's activist bureaucracy. Many of the new men had themselves participated in the revolutions of 1848–49 in its early phases, although during that year they had all come to mistrust the social revolutionary influence of the streets. They now believed that a reformed bureaucracy could achieve the thoroughgoing modernization of state and society that popular politics had failed to accomplish. Organized participation by the citizenry, they decided, should be strictly limited to what they believed was the least political of forums: the local municipal councils. The same man who had been responsible for drawing up the imposed constitution of March 1849, Interior Minister Count Francis Stadion (1806–1853), developed the concept behind the autonomous municipal councils and their consultative relationship to the government.

The man who gave his name to this so-called neo-absolutist period—Alexander Bach (1813–1893), who succeeded Stadion in 1849—was a lawyer who in 1848 had served on Vienna's revolutionary Committee of Public Safety and later as minister of justice.[9] As interior minister in the 1850s, Bach developed ambitious plans for a centralized, rational, effective, but also comparatively humane administration. Before 1848, most observers had targeted the bureaucracy as the problem rather than the solution in

Austria. Especially in its failure to connect its sense of professional duty to the society it was meant to serve, this demoralized body had lost all sense of purpose. Bach wanted a bureaucracy that could deal effectively with the specific problems faced by a rapidly developing industrial society, problems far different from those faced by the patrimonial society of the eighteenth century. He wanted the state to be able to intervene positively and as rapidly and efficiently as possible in every corner of the empire. Bach streamlined the bureaucracy's command structure starting at the local level—the community, or *Gemeinde*—and then moving up to the district *(Bezirk)*, then to the crownland, and finally to the individual cabinet ministries.[10] The crownland governors *(Statthalter)* became direct servants of the crown, no longer semi-independent agents who represented the interests of their region as defined by the diets to the imperial center.[11]

Bach gave special attention to the complete administrative integration of Hungary into the imperial system. He often referred to it as the "former Kingdom of Hungary," and he expressed confidence that if the experiment could have twenty-five years to take root, "we [will] have won the game forever."[12] To facilitate this extreme process of integration, the government abolished Hungary's traditional administrative unit, the self-administering counties, and replaced them with Austrian-style districts *(Bezirke)* with new boundaries. This not only made Hungary's districts comparable in size and population to the rest of Austria's administrative units, but also allowed the government to replace the local elites who had traditionally administered the counties with bureaucrats appointed from Vienna. These German-speaking administrators were usually Austrians of Czech-, German-, or Slovene-speaking background. They came to be known contemptuously by Hungarian nationalists as "Bach Hussars," a term that connoted both the punitive military force with which many Hungarians associated their authority, as well as their oddly conceived uniforms meant to embody what was imagined to be "Hungarian elements" of dress.[13] Clothing, by the way, was not the only area where Bach demanded outward and inward conformity of his bureaucrats. Regulations also demanded, for example, that civil servants everywhere shave their chins, since full beards were associated with a revolutionary masculinity.[14]

Minister of Justice and of the Interior Alexander von Bach (1813–1893) underwent a personal transformation from revolutionary to architect of the authoritarian regime imposed by Francis Joseph in 1851. Credit: Private Collection/Bridgeman Images.

The explicit task of these so-called Bach Hussars was to coordinate Hungary structurally with the rest of the empire and to do so using the German language, thus reintroducing Joseph II's earlier model of a single language of administration for the entire empire.[15] How and in what situations the bureaucrats were to use the German language show that this linguistic policy was more a product of systematic centralization efforts than an ambitious scheme to Germanize local populations. German was the official language of the "inner administration" throughout the empire, that is, the language local bureaucrats used to communicate with each other in the various crownlands and with Vienna. At the same time, however, the state continued to use vernacular languages for what was known as the "outer administration," where civil servants dealt with petitioners, plaintiffs, and the general public. In Hungary, the conduct of that outer administration might include several languages other than Hungarian such as Romanian, Serb, Slovak, or German. Given the ways that many 1848ers had effectively made questions of official language use into potent political issues, the role now accorded German in the administration and the military could easily be perceived as a privilege exercised by an entire, if imagined, *nation* rather than simply by certain educated speakers of a given *language*. The imperial logic behind this administrative language policy often provoked complaints about alleged Germanization, and not only in Hungary. The fact that many Habsburg bureaucrats posted to Galicia were scorned as "Germans," even though as individuals they as frequently came from Czech-speaking backgrounds, demonstrates the ways that nationalists after 1848 framed individual language capability in terms of the government's allegedly nationalizing policy.[16] This reflects the high degree to which nationalist claims at mid-century depended largely on imperial policy for their political coherence.

At the same time that Bach imposed an increasingly authoritarian and centralist regime after 1851, he also sought to make his bureaucrats more popular. By responding effectively to the needs of local society, they would, he hoped, earn the public's trust. Lorenz von Stein, newly appointed to a professorship at the University of Vienna, theorized administrative practice in terms of successive historical stages that he believed had culminated in the Bach system. The first two types of administration, he argued, had applied to past historical ages: a corporatist/feudal phase, and a police/security phase. Currently, however, Austria found itself in a phase where the bureaucracy furthered the "development of the independent activity of the people" by which he meant the development of their economic diligence, their industrial capacities, and their taxable incomes.[17] According to instructions from one crownland governor, district authorities should "look out for the needs of the inhabitants" and care for "the welfare of every class of the population."[18] A powerful and effective bureaucratic structure, populated by hard-working, intelligent, and beardless bureaucrats loyal to the state but also sensitive to the populace, could, it was hoped, unite Austria's socially and culturally diverse society. The government took other steps to increase public trust as well, establishing new courts in each of the local districts *(Bezirksgerichte)*. This act was meant to give the courts a visible measure of independence from local powerbrokers in the eyes of the people, and make them appear to be a forum for popular redress instead of a tool of the local nobility.

The regime was not tone-deaf to the realities of cultural and social diversity, at least outside of Hungary. This is particularly evident in the thinking and work of the Bohemian aristocrat Count Leo Thun (1811–1888), who was put in charge of restructuring Austria's educational system and its university curriculum. A pious Catholic, a harsh critic of the Enlightenment natural law theory so beloved of Josephenists, and anything but a political liberal, Thun nevertheless believed that raising academic standards in Austria required greater freedom of intellectual inquiry. Austria's universities, he argued, ought to be research institutions to promote the development of knowledge and not simply professional training schools. Thun worked closely with liberals like professor of law and 1870s cabinet minister Joseph Unger (1828–1913) to revise the training of bureaucrats, who he believed needed an education in practical subjects like history or Roman law.[19] As we saw in Chapter 2, eighteenth-century thinkers like Joseph von Sonnenfels had argued in favor of an abstract, utilitarian ideal of patriotism for Austria. In his 1771 *Love for the Fatherland,* Sonnenfels had avoided basing patriotism on shared elements of culture because Austria's crownlands included such different peoples, states, languages, and traditions. In the natural law tradition Sonnenfels argued that the current state and its laws that should elicit the love of rational people who understood that it best served their interests. Thun, however, saw this natural law tradition as too narrowly abstract to answer Austria's needs, particularly with regard to education.

Many emerging nationalists would have agreed with him. Thun himself was an aristocrat who ultimately favored a federalist system that gave more attention to crownland traditions. His critical point of view (especially toward the predominance of natural law training) could easily be transformed by nationalists into an argument for greater administrative sensitivity to regional differences of tradition, language use, or even nationhood.[20] Other cabinet ministers were highly sensitive to the potential dangers that linguistic diversity might produce, believing that the politicization of such issues had needlessly radicalized the revolutions in 1848–49. The cabinet hoped to depoliticize national feeling altogether by maintaining a general policy of "inter-linguistic equality" when such a policy did not contradict the need for a single bureaucratic language. Thus the government maintained the traditional use of vernacular languages in primary schools, while requiring the study of German in secondary schools across the empire. In theory, speakers of all languages could pursue their own cultural development insofar as it was not political in nature, but in practice this was tricky to do. Even bilingual secondary schools treated languages differently as German often became the only language of instruction in the final years.[21]

While Thun worked to make Austrian educational standards more competitive with those in the rest of Europe, especially Prussia, he also sought to maintain stability in society by fostering improved public morals and a greater respect for Catholicism. This effort may seem contradictory to the modern reader for whom academic freedom and an increased institutional power for Catholicism do not easily appear to go hand in hand. And indeed, as Gary Cohen has pointed out, Thun trod an extremely delicate line, "trying to find a workable compromise between free inquiry and respect for conservative political and religious principles."[22] For Thun, the purpose of the universities "must lie in the cultivation of as thorough a scholarliness as possible inspired by a genuine religiosity."[23] His education reforms ultimately produced a massive overhaul of secondary school and university structures and curricula, which promoted far greater academic freedom. This policy, of course, inadvertently facilitated the rapid spread of liberal thought and values in educational institutions. At the same time, however, the regime negotiated a major treaty, or concordat, with the Vatican, one that contradicted Josephenist tradition of state control by restoring to the Catholic Church its control over clerical appointments, marriage, and education.

Unlike its 1840s predecessor, this regime actively initiated several policies designed to improve agriculture, industry, infrastructure, and trade. Peasants finally gained ownership of the land they had previously held under feudal arrangements, and the dues they owed were canceled. The government stepped in to organize compensation to the lords for lost labor, according to a complex formula based on estimates of the lords' financial loss over a twenty-year period. Outside of Hungary, the state set the value of lost peasant labor at one-third the value of free labor and calculated the value of dues in kind according to how those goods were assessed in local tax lists. The government then reduced the value of this total by a third, arguing that the local lords were no longer responsible for the cost of judicial and administrative functions, which the state had taken over. The full amount of compensation outside of Hungary came to 290 million gulden. In Hungary the government set compensation at one-third the value of the land occupied by the peasants, or 304 million gulden. In Hungary, Galicia, and Bukovina, the government itself paid the entire amount of compensation, while in the rest of Austria, the peasants and crownland governments were required to share the costs. This meant an enormous expansion of credit in the countryside. In Bohemia alone, peasants were responsible for paying 56 million florins of the total compensation while in the territories that make up today's Austria, they had to come up with 41.5 million. To repay the loans they took to cover their share of the compensation, peasants had to produce increasingly for a cash-based market as well. In all cases the government paid the lords their compensation in interest-bearing forty-year bonds.[24]

In Galicia, feudal relations had exercised an unusually tight hold on the peasant population, and the emancipation did little to ease the bitter relationship between peasant and lord. Emancipation also produced conflicts over peasant use of traditionally common lands, an issue that had already provoked local rebellions in the decades before 1848, as well as exercising peasants throughout Europe. Increasingly, local lords asserted full property rights over lands that peasants had traditionally used "in common" to pasture their animals or to gather wood or other resources to help them survive the winter months. Having lost *Robot* labor, many lords claimed ownership over the common lands as a means to force peasants to return to work for them, this time for wages, while offering the village the use of a small part of the formerly common land. Galician peasants in turn often feared that if they returned to work for the lord, they would be trapped in a new *Robot* relationship.

An 1853 law allowed the lords to purchase common lands from village communities or from individual peasants. These could be cash transactions, or more commonly, the lords could assign a small piece of the formerly common fields or forest back to the peasant community as payment for the rest of the land they took. In 1855 the government set up a commission to adjudicate conflicts in individual cases; it did not fully complete its work in Galicia until 1895! The commission usually assigned the peasant community at least a small portion of the land in question—on average of 8 percent—in return for peasants giving up their traditional rights of usage.[25] Most Galician peasants, however, refused to accept the loss of what they considered to be their pastures and forests, and many continued to use these lands illegally. This in turn invariably led to police or military intervention on the side of the lords, but does not seem to have compromised the popularity of the dynasty among Galician peasants at least.[26] The latter often reverted to their trusted strategy of sending a deputation to the emperor in Vienna. This ongoing conflict indicates that emancipation and legal equality did little to diminish peasant suspicion that the lords were plotting to revive their feudal privileges.[27] We will see that this suspicion shaped peasant political activism and early Ukrainian nationalism in Galicia after 1867.

In Bohemia, to take a contrasting example, the reform increased capitalist developments in agriculture and benefited the more well-to-do peasants. With the added time they gained thanks to the cancellation of the *Robot,* they expanded their planting, and thanks to a steep rise in grain prices between 1850 and 1870, most of these peasants paid off their share of the costs of the compensation within a decade. Given that the communal voting laws of 1849 favored larger property owners, these peasants also gained control over administration of community property such as common lands as well. They frequently used this control to privatize that property, usually by selling it to themselves. Poorer peasants in Bohemia generally left the land for industrial work, unable to make the necessary payments or to compete with wealthier peasants. The abolition of patrimonial relations also meant that traditional informal welfare arrangements—ranging from provision of seed to social support in lean years—were now a thing of the past. Noble large landowners in Bohemia, meanwhile, may have lost their exclusive corporate identity and their sovereignty over many local communities, but unlike the situation in Galicia, the groundwork for economic success under the new system had already been laid.[28] "In the period after the revolution," one historian of this period tells us, "the [Bohemian] nobility found many ways to combine (to great effect) bourgeois principles of property and profit maximization with their attempts to restore their earlier political influence."[29]

Other economic policies designed by the talented, if mercurial, Finance Minister Karl Ludwig von Bruck (1798–1860) sought to integrate markets within the empire more effectively by creating a single free-trade zone and to increase trade with Austria's neighbors by diminishing tariffs. A tariff wall had long divided Hungary from the rest of the empire, despite Maria Theresa's and Joseph II's desire to transform the empire into a single free-trade zone. They and their successors had left the barrier in place, however, to compensate for the fact that the Hungarian nobility remained exempt from direct taxation. Since tariff policy was outside the control of the noble-dominated Hungarian Diet, the barrier had allowed Vienna to collect much-needed income. After putting down the Hungarian Revolution in 1849, however, the Austrian government simply eliminated the Hungarian nobility's tax-exempt status and imposed an income tax. In 1851 the government also removed the tariff barrier between Austria and Hungary. It then liberalized foreign trade by lowering or removing several tariffs, and in 1853 negotiated a trade treaty with the states of the German Customs Union (*Zollverein*). These moves demonstrated Bruck's willingness to subject Austrian industry to European competition, something his less radical predecessors—along with many Austrian industrialists—had feared to do.[30] These policies, however, fit very well with Prime Minister Schwarzenberg's political ambitions to make Austria the leading power in Germany by challenging Prussia's economic clout within the German Confederation.

The most influential economic policies of the 1850s, however, were those that rapidly expanded Austria's railroad network and created an institutional means to finance such large-scale ventures. Up until 1854, the Austrian government itself owned and managed 70 percent of the railroads.[31] The state recognized the vital importance of railroads both for economic and military purposes. Field Marshal Radetzsky, for example, never tired of advocating for new railroad lines, having experienced their efficacy in his northern Italian campaigns of 1848–49, although, as pointed out earlier, military considerations alone had little effect on railroad policy in the 1840s. In the first years of the new regime, the Commerce Ministry mapped out an ambitious network of future rail lines, proposing to invest staggering sums to build them. Annual budgetary concerns and other pressing priorities, such as the renovation of existing railroad stations and track, repeatedly forced the government to postpone much of the new building it hoped to accomplish. In 1853, during the Crimean War when the neutral Austrian government engaged in a costly mobilization, Francis Joseph himself complained that the railway system had failed the military's expectations. The combination of fiscal crisis and the perceived inadequacy of the existing rail lines produced a reluctant decision to privatize the system.

With a new railway concession law in 1854, the state began selling off lines to private companies, while offering their stockholders attractive guaranteed rates of return on investment in new lines. Stockholders of the new *k.k. priv. Österreichische Staatseisenbahn-Gesellschaft*, for example, received a minimum annual return of 5.2 percent interest on their investments, along with generous tax subsidies for a line that would connect Austria with eastern Hungary.[32] Given such favorable terms, it is not surprising that by 1859 the empire had succeeded in divesting itself of almost all of its railroad holdings. Many of the companies that bought existing lines took advantage of beneficial terms to win concessions for new rail lines in the 1850s and 1860s.

In the 1860s the Südbahn, which had connected Vienna to Trieste/Trst, expanded northwards into Tyrol and eastwards into Hungary. In 1854 a new company using German and Austrian capital built the Kaiserin Elisabeth Westbahn to connect Vienna with Linz, Salzburg, Passau, and Munich. During the 1850s alone, rail lines in the empire increased by almost 2,000 miles.

None of this mobilization of credit for railway expansion would have been possible without a simultaneous overhaul of Austria's banking system. Since the founding of an Austrian national bank in 1816, the empire had monopolized the bank's resources for its own borrowing needs, making it impossible for the bank to meet the credit needs of any but a few other wealthy private clients. The services of some international banking families (Rothschild, Sina, Arnstein Eskeles) were available to Austrian borrowers during this period, but in the 1850s Austria's finance

Photograph from an album by Johann Bosch commemorating the completion of the Südbahn railway line between Laibach/Ljubljana and Trieste/Trst in 1857. This 1855 photograph shows the construction of a viaduct in Franzdorf/Borovnica, about 12 miles southwest of Laibach/Ljubljana, which would be completed in 1856 at a cost of two million gulden. Credit: Österreichische Nationalbibliothek.

ministers addressed the problem of capital shortages by creating new banks that could make much larger amounts of credit available to private borrowers. These new institutions could, it was believed, take the lead role in financing infrastructure projects like the railways (as did the Crédit Mobiliers in France, for example).[33] In 1855 the government permitted the establishment of the independent Creditanstalt Bank for Commerce and Industry by a consortium that included several wealthy aristocrats and Anselm Salomon Rothschild. Organized as a joint-stock company, the Creditanstalt's capital of 100 million gulden easily exceeded the value of the national bank's holdings by a third, and its size allowed the Creditanstalt to initiate large development projects. The founding of the Creditanstalt probably meant little to average Austrians, but within twenty years it had worked enormous effects on their lives, especially through its role in the rapid development of Austria's rail infrastructure, which connected formerly isolated provincial local economies. By making it possible to transport perishable goods much greater distances, for example, the railroads helped create new commercial opportunities that otherwise could never have been imagined. At the same time, the rise of large bank-initiated projects created more joint-stock companies in which increasing numbers of small investors participated, especially, as we will see, during the heady years of Austria's *Gründerzeit* (1867–1873).

In March 1850 Commerce Minister Bruck founded regional chambers of commerce, institutions designed to facilitate public discussion of local matters of economic interest.[34] The fifty-six chambers (including one for each crownland capital city) regularly supplied the Ministry of Commerce with reports about local economic conditions, regional transport, policy evaluations, and suggestion for future policies. The chambers also acted as referees in disputes between firms or between employers and employees. Their elected members had to be Austrian citizens at least thirty years of age who had owned or managed a business for at least five years and who were legal residents of the district the chamber served. Members elected their peers to serve three- (later four-) year unpaid terms. Any independent business and trade owner or manager in the district had the right to vote in elections to the chambers.[35] After the one-time communal elections for town councils held in 1850, these chambers of commerce constituted the only state institutions that regularly held elections during the 1850s. Additionally, we will see that when constitutionalism was revived in 1861, the chambers of commerce gained the right to elect their own deputies to the crownland diets, imperial parliament, and to some city councils. They thus went from serving as advisory bodies to constituting official interest groups whose legitimacy was considered so critical that they gained corporate voting rights when a more liberal parliamentary system replaced the bureaucratic absolutist regime in 1861.

Selling the Dynasty

While government experts built new systems, the dynasty also sought new ways to increase its popularity among its recently rebellious peoples. In 1849 only the Hungarian and northern Italian rebels had actually repudiated the Habsburgs outright. Many Austrians—especially the peasants among them—had remained loyal to the dynasty or had attempted to appropriate it for their particular vision of empire. As early as 1850 the new emperor ordered a series of reforms and personnel changes to revitalize the court and its public ceremonies. Later throughout the 1850s the imperial court intentionally revived, reconstructed, or invented a range of public ceremonies with an eye to more actively mobilizing popular opinion in favor of the empire. As part of a new public relations campaign, Francis Joseph traveled far more extensively throughout his realms than had any of his predecessors since Joseph II. In the 1850s alone he led so-called inspection tours to Galicia, Bukovina, Bohemia, Moravia, Lombardy, Venice, Trieste/Trst, Tyrol, and twice to Hungary.[36]

Although early in the emperor's reign the recently rebellious local elites in Hungary, Galicia, and Lombardy rarely offered him a particularly warm welcome, district officials reported enthusiasm among the peasantry for the Galician tour of 1851. With the railroad line to Galicia not yet completed at that time, the emperor and his retinue had traveled slowly by carriage from west to east across the crownland, often giving peasants along the route a chance to see their ruler up close. In every village and town crowds welcomed the imperial conveyance, often swarming around it with petitions for the ruler. Bach's spies reported that the emperor's visits "have given rise to the fullest satisfaction from the public," while district officials in Galicia noted that the emperor was "especially joyfully received by the rural population."[37]

As historian Daniel Unowsky tells us, the Galician tour revealed just how carefully the court calibrated its efforts when it came to handling conflicting social, confessional, and nationalist claims made by the local nobility, clergy, and educated classes. Most of Francis Joseph's activities in Galicia, for example, involved inspecting military installations. However, he did on occasion tour sites important to Polish nationalist mythology such as the tombs of Polish kings in the Wawel Castle in Cracow. While in the Galician capital of Lemberg/Lwów/Lviv, however, Francis Joseph also laid the cornerstone for a Ruthenian (Ukrainian) national institute, an act that clearly challenged the local hegemony of Polish nationalists while thrilling local Ukrainian nationalists. Those

Ukrainian nationalists (generally of the Uniate or Greek Catholic religion) had earned the nickname "Tyroleans of the East," thanks to perceptions of the unquestioned loyalty they had offered the dynasty in 1848,
in contrast to their rebellious Polish nationalist counterparts in Galicia.
They were even allowed to present the emperor with a petition asking
him to divide Galicia into two, between a Polish and a Ruthene national
crownland.[38]

The inspection tour of Galicia illustrates another set of potential contradictions raised by Francis Joseph's intentional reshaping of monarchic
symbolism. In particular the concordat with Rome had renewed the dynasty's traditional symbolic role as defender of the Roman Catholic
Church. Along with negotiating the concordat, Francis Joseph also revived or invented several specifically Catholic public rituals such as the
annual Corpus Christi parade that culminated in the emperor's demonstrative washing the feet of ten beggars. These rituals portrayed Francis
Joseph as a model of piety to the empire's Catholics. At the same time,
however, the demands of empire required that his people view the sovereign as "everyone's emperor" and thus as protector of all legitimate
faiths. Starting with the Galician inspection tour of 1851 and increasingly throughout his reign, Francis Joseph went out of his way to visit
Jewish, Greek Catholic, and Eastern Orthodox sites of worship along
with the usual Roman Catholic ones. In the twentieth century he also
became—ironically given his family's history—protector of the Muslim
faith in Bosnia-Hercegovina as well. Practitioners of these other religions
increasingly claimed Francis Joseph as protector, and they lobbied openly
for his personal patronage. On the Galician tour, for example, the Jewish
community in Cracow erected a triumphal arch honoring the imperial
visit and displaying the motto: "The Thankful Israelites to the Emperor."
Rabbis in the crowds lifted Torahs as the emperor passed by, and Jews in
towns and villages across Galicia vociferously welcomed the emperor
whose reign, many hoped, would bring their full emancipation. Although
Francis Joseph actually postponed full Jewish legal emancipation for almost twenty years, (in fact reversing the accomplishments of 1848), his
popularity among Jewish communities eventually became legendary.
With Jews, Orthodox, Greek Catholic, and even Protestant Austrians
treating this emperor who revived Catholic power in Austria as the

special patron of their own religions, the dynasty's commitment to protecting the rights of religious minorities was solidified from below.[39]

In 1853 Francis Joseph also improved the dynasty's tarnished reputation when he married his young cousin Elisabeth of Bavaria (1837–1898). This event created countless opportunities to celebrate the dynasty, as well as to create popular mythologies around its newest addition, the sixteen-year-old empress, popularly known later as "Sisi." Despite Elisabeth's lifelong troubled relationship to the Vienna court, she occasionally served as a formidable weapon in the court's efforts to popularize both dynasty and empire. Unlike her husband, who for many Hungarian patriots had the blood of national martyrs on his hands, Elisabeth became immensely popular in many parts of Hungary, largely because of her demonstrative efforts to learn the Hungarian language and her insistence on employing Hungarian aristocrats in her retinue, as well as the popular belief that in 1867 she had personally interceded with her husband in favor of the Hungarian national cause. For the rest of her life Elisabeth remained a subject of fascination and nationalist projection in Hungary, and in 1894 rumors circulated that she had even secretly laid a wreath at the grave of the recently buried Louis Kossuth.[40]

In May of 1857 Francis Joseph brought Elisabeth with him for the first time on a tour of Hungary. Stepping off the steamer in Buda, Elisabeth caused an instant sensation as observers noted that she had made the Hungarian national colors (at this point, red, white, and green) a key part of her attire. During the royal visit observers commented repeatedly on the pro-Hungarian symbolism of the young queen's fashion choices.[41] Unexpectedly during the trip, the imperial couple's infant daughter, Sophie, died from a case of measles. In an example of the renewed Catholic ritual typical of the 1850s, after the funeral the imperial couple made a public pilgrimage to the shrine to the Virgin at Mariazell in Styria. Thirty thousand Hungarians showed their sympathy for the couple—or their appreciation of Elisabeth—by also making the trip to Mariazell. Apparently the imperial visit and its aftermath succeeded in at least moderating Hungarian popular antipathy to Francis Joseph.[42]

The court manipulated the public image of the emperor and his family primarily through its ability to control reporting about the dynasty in

Empress Elisabeth of Austria on horseback, one of her favorite activities. Engraving by Thomas Lewis Atkinson, 1882, from a painting by John Charlton. Credit: Österreichische Nationalbibliothek.

networks of newspapers throughout the empire. The newspapers in turn were eager to publish any and all details of imperial life for public consumption. When strict government censorship ended in the 1860s, this particular dynamic did not necessarily change. The court continued to control carefully the image of the imperial family, even occasionally doctoring official photographs to suggest a happy domestic idyll, and the family remained the object of intense popular interest. For this reason, newspapers of all kinds, Catholic, nationalist, liberal, or socialist, had to report on the family and thus participated, at least indirectly, in promoting its popularity.[43]

The imperial family in 1860. Court photographer Ludwig Angerer was supposedly the only one to photograph the Empress Elisabeth (front row left) together with her children and husband. Normally Elisabeth and Francis Joseph attended Angerer's studio separately. This photograph also features Francis Joseph's brothers and parents. Credit: Adoc-photos/Art Resource, NY.

Visualizing a Liberal Empire

In 1857 newspaper editor and former liberal 1848er Ernst von Schwarzer (1808–1860) published a paean to Austria's absolutist regime entitled *Geld und Gut in Neuösterreich* (Money and Property in the New Austria). In it he documented not the virtues of the imperial family, but rather the remarkable economic, social, and cultural strides made by the empire under the neo-absolutist system.[44] His statistical study of land, people, and production levels celebrated the empire's distinctive geographic, cultural, and economic achievements, placing its recent advances in the context of general European progress in the mid-nineteenth century. Schwarzer's report trumpeted the benefits of liberal cultural ideology as well as its imperialist goals in Austria. Arguing that because their "rare multiplicity of character, of customs, and needs" made Austrians different from other Europeans, Schwarzer stressed the positive benefits that a strongly centralized state had conferred upon Austria's peoples in just seven short years.[45] These peoples, although legally equal to each other, were not exactly cultural equals. Only a unified regime like Austria's, he argued, could have helped "the eastern peoples [of Austria] to make even greater progress, and to jump over whole developmental periods, as for example Hungary had done, thanks to the [introduction of the] railway." Schwarzer claimed that "in every part of the monarchy one now finds merchants, shipping agents, manufacturers, and [large] tradesmen; speculation finds its way into the farthest corners, takes possession of hidden mineral wealth, and conveys it to the global market."[46]

The former 1848er, whom one historian recently called Austria's "ideologue of capitalism," drew both political and civilizational lessons from the progressive economic developments that he argued had blessed Austria in the 1850s.[47] In terms of politics, it was thanks to the unified state's program of reform that all Austrians had experienced material and spiritual benefits. The revolution of 1848 had failed tragically to bring Austrians progress and happiness. The surprise was that the same progress and resulting happiness could be created by other means. "The truly obtainable aims that malcontents and utopian dreamers had once tried to gain by means of political and social revolution are now being realized with the help of the government, through legal and economic reform."[48] State activism, he claimed, had ultimately achieved more of the reform goals of the 1848 revolutions than could any amount of political activism.

Schwarzer's argument was as much about a civilizing mission as it was about the economic benefits of empire. One thing the painful experience of revolution had revealed to many ideologists of empire, thanks in part to nationalist activism in 1848 and in part to the complexities of ending feudalism in such different regions, was the exceptional diversity of the empire's peoples. Writers like Schwarzer understood this diversity not simply in terms of the multiple languages Austrians used, but also in terms of the radically different social and economic conditions that they believed characterized Austria's different peoples. Schwarzer interpreted these differences largely in terms of relative levels of modernity, which in

turn he framed as signifying different levels of civilization. This generalized discovery of the different levels of civilization that characterized the
peoples of the empire, a discovery that had long been the ideological
foundation of imperial policy in Galicia, for example, became a critical
justification for the renewal of the Josephenist program of radical bureaucratic centralization at mid-century. Thanks to the spread of capitalist
relations, Schwarzer tells us, "Oriental conditions are coming to an end
in Hungary."

Writers like Schwarzer trod a challenging path with regard to these
arguments. On the one hand, their legitimation of empire rested increasingly on the tropes of alterity with which they characterized the different
populations of the empire. Indeed, for many European observers, it was
its people's very differences—both linguistic and cultural—that made
Austria an empire by definition, rather than a nation-state. Austria's
people "belong, as in no other European state, to every level of civilization and to the four main tribes of European people, the Roman, Germanic, Finnish, and Slav."[49] Of course contemporary travelers in rural
parts of France, Italy, Spain, or Britain made similar observations about
the civilizational levels and linguistic practices of the allegedly savage
peoples they encountered far off the beaten track. In France alone, as
Eugen Weber's classic study tells us, in 1863 at least a quarter of the population spoke no French, and many more understood very little.[50] The
fact remains, however, that nineteenth-century observers increasingly
saw Austria, with the high degree of linguistic differences of its peoples,
as an exception in Europe.

On the other hand, this emphasis on ethnic and civilizational difference made it harder for authors like Schwarzer to assert the organic
cohesiveness of this empire when they discussed Austria's other characteristics such as its geography, trade routes, and climate. Even more
problematic, however, was the new way in which the very erasure of difference that had served as a structural goal of empire since the 1780s had
changed. In Joseph II's day, the challenge to state-building had been to
unite *different legal codes or institutional practices* in regions that had
once existed independently from each other and from the Habsburg dynasty. Now, however, the empire was viewed increasingly as a collection
of *ethnically different peoples* who also allegedly occupied different

"levels" of civilization (ethnic Hungarians, Czechs, Croatians). It was no longer an empire made up of different states and their institutions (Hungary, Bohemia, Croatia). In fact, as we will see in Chapter 6, many nationalists now argued that distinctive institutional differences derived from ethnic or linguistic differences among peoples.

In the mid-nineteenth century, Schwarzer's reference to different levels of civilization was also bound to raise comparisons between Austria and Europe's other empires. In a lecture to the Austrian Academy of Sciences on the occasion of its fifth anniversary in 1853, for example, Ottoman scholar and orientalist Joseph Hammer-Purgstall praised Austria's legal system, comparing it favorably to what he called the "oppressive" systems of the British and Russian Empires. Those two states, he argued, had acquired their empires through violent conquest. Austria by contrast, had emerged from a series of friendly treaties and dynastic marriages. Treaties and dynastic marriages may have brought these various regions together in a dynastic empire, but Hammer-Purgstall's point was more about the legal system that resulted from this process of empire-building. He was particularly interested in the ways in which Austria took account of its people's linguistic diversity, while nevertheless treating them equally as citizens. Hammer-Purgstall asserted that in north and south Asia, for example, imperialist Russian and British colonizers had forced people to abandon their own languages and to use those of their new overlords. Austrian multilingualism, on the other hand, was itself a measure of the distinctive way that Austria promoted unity, not subordination or hierarchy, among its citizens. This policy also made sense because Hammer-Purgstall firmly believed that globalization (or Europeanization) would soon demand increased multilingualism of all Europeans. When that happened, Austria would be far ahead of the rest of Europe.[51]

In making this comparison among Austria, Russia, and Britain, and in celebrating Austria's multilingualism, Hammer-Purgstall never questioned the privileged use of the German language in Austria's interregional civil service or in the military. To him this resulted simply from its rational utility, not from a policy designed to privilege one people over another. Moreover, even though civil servants would always need to know German, he also believed that they would need to learn the languages of the regions in which they served. Similarly, while German remained the language of military command, all officers would have to learn enough of the regional languages spoken by their recruits in order to serve effectively and to advance through the ranks. Linking ideals of multilingual practice to an emerging form of identity, Hammer-Purgstall asserted that "the more languages of the monarchy one learns, the more one becomes a true Austrian."

Hammer-Purgstall's argument for Austrian multilingualism also constituted an argument about imperial patriotism. While they may have spoken different languages, Austrians nevertheless shared a common love of "the entire fatherland," a love reminiscent of the kind of (noncultural) rational patriotism articulated by Joseph von Sonnenfels in the 1780s. This love for Austria was rooted in the empire's unified form of citizenship. "In Austria," claimed Hammer Purgstall, "the essence of citizenship is its guarantee to every people of the same rights." In a final swipe at the British Empire he added that "in Austria there is no difference between Brahmin and Pariah before the law." For Hammer-Purgstall, nothing better captured Austria's distinctiveness than its peoples' usage of differing languages and the equal relationship among those languages. Equality of language use symbolized a unity of peoples that was anchored in their fundamental interchangeability as citizens.[52]

Another important ideologist of empire during this period was Karl von Czörnig (1804–1889), civil servant, statistician, early ethnographer, and former 1848er. In his early career Czörnig had actively promoted Danube shipping and the expansion of Austria's railways. In 1848–49 he had served as a deputy to the Frankfurt Parliament that negotiated German political unity. During the 1850s, among other positions, Czörnig directed the office of administrative statistics for the Commerce Ministry. In this capacity he undertook two massive studies that powerfully influenced public understandings of the new, unified Austrian Empire. One of these, the three-volume *Ethnographie der österreichischen Monarchie* (Ethnography of the Austrian Monarchy, 1855–1857), detailed the populations (with their languages and religions) that inhabited the various crownlands of the empire. The other, *Österreichs Neugestaltung* (Austria's New Organization, 1858) was a statistical survey of Austria's transformation since 1848 and similar to Schwarzer's work. Both volumes asserted new visions of empire and its raison d'être, and both addressed the significance of its people's linguistic diversity.

Austria's New Organization begins with a paradox: Europe's oldest dynasty, the Habsburgs, ruled over what was technically one of its youngest states. For centuries the Habsburgs had collected territories with different laws, traditions, and peoples. With the Pragmatic Sanction of the early eighteenth century, Charles VI had decreed the inseparability of those territories. But according to Czörnig that law had not created a unified state. A unified Austrian state was not born officially until the creation of the Austrian Empire in 1804. And not until the 1850s did a truly united Austrian state come into being, since neither the Kremsier/ Kroměříž constitutional draft nor the imposed constitution of 1849 had applied to Hungary.

Given his ethnographic work, Czörnig offered a more sophisticated argument than Schwarzer's about the relative qualities of Austria's peoples and the cultural benefits they gained from being part of an empire. Czörnig did not imagine an East that was by nature backward and that required civilizing from the West, as had Schwarzer. Rather Czörnig pointed to the ways in which purely regional political relations had allowed one group (Poles) to prevent another (Ruthenes) from developing fully, a situation that demanded the intervention of imperial institutions to guarantee legal equality.

Not surprisingly, Czörnig located the empire's distinctive character precisely in terms of the many natural, cultural, and social forms of diversity it harbored. From climate to agriculture, from industry to language use, Austria was exceptional in its remarkable diversity. His greatest contribution to imagining empire, whether intended or not, was Czörnig's elaborate ethnography of Austria with its colorful attendant maps that represented linguistic and ethnic groups geographically. Instead of focusing on the historic boundaries of Austria's crownlands (Bohemia, Dalmatia, Hungary, Galicia, and so on), the maps charted the territories where particular languages were spoken and where different religions were practiced. Czörnig's research concluded that every crownland in the empire was in fact linguistically and culturally heterogeneous, thanks to historical processes of migration and resettlement. In his view, no single language group could make an authentic or exclusive claim to any crownland. Moreover, his linguistic maps illustrated graphically the fact that any territorial separation of people along linguistic lines in Austria was fundamentally impractical. In this, Czörnig helped to shape an antinationalist approach that typified early Austrian ethnography as compared to its more nationalist western European and particularly its German counterparts.[53]

In terms of relations among linguistic groups, Czörnig asserted that overall in the empire the main national groups balanced each other "in numbers and inner strength, as well as in [differing] levels of civilization." Most importantly, with reference to the imperial regime itself he noted like Hammer-Purgstall that "in their [Austria's many peoples'] unity, and not in their subordination, they constitute the foundation on which the state rests."[54] As we will see, however, in the 1880s, nationalists would begin to use such linguistic maps to argue in favor of a very different position from Czörnig's—namely, the possibility of discrete nation-based territories within the empire.

Empire and People in the 1850s

Popular reactions to the new regime were both more complex and more practical in nature than the theoretical musings of liberal intellectuals like Czörnig, Schwarzer, or Hammer-Purgstall. For peasants in Galicia, for example, heated conflicts over use rights to common lands quickly replaced traditional battles with local gentry over the *Robot*. In these conflicts peasants continued to look to imperial officials as arbiters, but not uncritically. They did not simply trust in the emperor's authority but sought actively to advance their own preferred outcomes through petitions and sometimes by resorting to violent actions. Austrians engaged in small- or large-scale manufacture and trade welcomed the gradual return of stable conditions after 1849 and the end of revolutionary inflation. Less than a year after the military had put down uprisings in Prague and Vienna, for example, many business owners apparently agreed with Prague textile merchant Heinrich (later Jindřich) Fügner, who remarked of the new regime that "everyone who is involved in any kind of practical business is satisfied."[55] Bach and Bruck both hoped to undercut the twin dangers to their centralization schemes posed by political nationalism and social radicalism with promises of economic expansion for all of Austria's peoples. Bach reported confidently about "the masses" to Francis Joseph in December 1851 that they had little interest in political affairs "and busy themselves far more with improving their material conditions."[56] One newspaper reported from Vienna in 1850:

> Material advantage[s] will prove a much stronger force binding the peoples of the different crownlands more closely to each other. . . . Nationality is a noteworthy, but hardly the dominating factor in [achieving] the common good. . . . In the worst case, things will develop in Bohemia as they have in Galicia, where the people, not the government keep the nationalists in check. The people want peace in order to strengthen their material lives.[57]

Likewise, Leopold von Sacher Masoch, police chief of Lemberg/Lwów/ Lviv during the 1846 rebellion and now stationed in Prague observed in 1852 that "the characteristic type of our age lies in this yearning for peace."[58] One year earlier, a local official in Pilsen/Plzeň reported to Governor Mecséry of Bohemia what many officials must have hoped to learn, that

> at least according to what I hear, up until now people don't seem to have bothered much about losing constitutional civil rights. The property owning classes especially reckon that a successful revival of imperial power will accomplish a moral strengthening of the state's condition as well as strengthening their individual property.[59]

Many former revolutionaries who were not exiled or jailed (and even some who were) focused on making money in the 1850s, quite consciously placing their political convictions on hold while joining expanding sectors of the economy such as the railways.[60] Like Prague law professor Leopold von Hasner, who wrote that during the 1850s "I belonged almost completely to my teaching and research activities and not at all to the events of the outside world" they claimed to have abandoned their public activism.[61] Middle-class activists clearly understood that the government's infrastructure policies offered their communities great potential for growth. They often characterized developments in communications, transport, or trade using the same liberal terminology of "progress" and "modernity" trumpeted by ideologists of empire like Schwarzer or Czörnig. Some parroted the regime's rhetoric of imperial unity and central European hegemony when they lobbied the government to add a rail line to their particular region. Arguing for the potential benefits that a rail link between the Tyrolean capital and Munich might bring, for example, Innsbruck's vice mayor claimed that "[if] Austria wants to establish the unity and power of the Monarchy, a railroad in Tyrol is of the highest importance for the material fortification of this unity."[62] The local liberal newspaper similarly characterized the railroad specifically as "a means to reach the unification of Greater Germany, both commercially and politically."[63]

Of course not all former revolutionaries—even the moderates among them—accepted the political changes so easily. Prague businessman Richard Dotzauer, himself a moderate liberal, later recalled of this moment that "the abrogation of the constitution affected me deeply. I became downright sick and did not understand how most people could just treat such an important event with indifference."[64] Others, who endured exile or who had been banned from exercising their chosen professions because of their activism in 1848, reflected with bitterness on their treatment, but they did not necessarily lose their passion for a constitutional Austria. Some, like the Moravian law student Carl Giskra, who had studied in Vienna and sat on the left in the Frankfurt Parliament, scraped by on odd clerking jobs provided by former colleagues.[65] Many who like Hasner had suffered no consequences after 1848 and who appear to have readily abandoned their political activism for career advancement nevertheless swiftly rejoined the bandwagon of liberal constitutionalism when it became safe to do so in 1861.

By the late 1850s few middle-class liberals shared the unbridled enthusiasm for the regime expressed by a Schwarzer or a Czörnig. They might appreciate the fine points of the regime's self-justification, they often benefited materially from economic development, and it was largely from their families that the revitalized bureaucracy was recruited. But as the decade wore on, they chafed under the regime's abrogation of their political rights and its often harsh media censorship. In fact, the more success they experienced in the economy, the more they believed that success justified their right to a voice in shaping public policy. Many might have agreed with former revolutionary Adolf Fischhof that the regime rested on the support of a standing army of soldiers, a kneeling army of worshippers, and a crawling army of informants.[66]

Former liberals may also have welcomed the chambers of commerce, the end of the guilds, and the investment in infrastructure, but by 1860 they gave the state little credit for such reforms. Conservatives of different stripes, meanwhile, had their own reasons to oppose the absolutist regime, despite its socially conservative policies such as the concordat with Rome. Regional nobles and gentry resented the unbending centralism that removed them from exercising their accustomed influence over local policy or even social relations. And in Hungary, opposition to the absolutist regime remained widespread, grounded both in the regime's denial of Hungarian statehood and in the brutal reprisals it had carried out against the so-called Hungarian rebels. The government's radical restructuring of Hungary and its harshly centralized administrative policies had the unintended consequences of uniting even conservative aristocrats in Hungary with gentry and urban liberals with regard to the liberal nationalist program embodied in the laws of April 1848.

Signs of local dissatisfaction with the regime were already visible in 1850 with the first elections to village and town councils, well before the regime had even withdrawn the constitution it had imposed on Austria in March 1849. That so-called imposed constitution (Oktroyierte Verfassung), like the Kremsier Parliament's draft, had treated political participation at the level of the local commune (Gemeinde) as the critical foundation for all responsible political participation and fruitful civic initiatives.[67] In many communes, however, those first elections went very badly for the regime and its bureaucrats. During the 1848 revolution, for example, many districts had elected state employees to serve as their deputies to the Austrian parliament, to the diets, and on the city councils. In the communal elections of 1850, however, property-owning voters in many part of the empire decisively rejected the notion that state bureaucrats could represent the public will. In relatively conservative Innsbruck, for example, a local liberal newspaper rejoiced that despite election rules that gave bureaucrats considerable electoral advantages, not one of the city's three voting classes, or curias, in 1850 elected a single state employee—and this in an election that had attracted a voter participation rate of between 75 percent and 100 percent in all three curias![68]

In part, election results like this heralded a significant shift in liberal politics that would become much clearer in the 1860s and 1870s, as artisans, manufacturers, and other members of the economic middle classes entrusted their political fates no longer to the bureaucrat with his legal education, but rather to another legally educated white-collar professional: the lawyer. "The lawyer," argues Thomas Götz, "embodied the prototypical educated citizen *(Bildungsbürger)* like no other; his specialized knowledge and fluent speaking abilities gave this professional enormous potential usefulness for the new legal functions assigned to the newly set-up civic communes."[69] Although the bureaucrats and lawyers shared much in common, particularly a common educational background, they occupied professions that related quite differently to the public. In Innsbruck, for example, those communal elections of 1850 constituted a breakthrough for lawyers who, as an occupational group, now replaced state bureaucrats—also educated in law—as the acknowledged political voice of the middle classes. When constitutional life resumed in the 1860s, lawyers would dominate elected institutions at all levels of government, from village councils to Imperial Parliament.

The regime also often subverted its own political program. By retaining elected town councils but indefinitely postponing any new elections throughout the 1850s, and by creating elected chambers of commerce to advise the government on economic policy, the government kept the issue of elections and popular political participation in the public eye. In turn, middle-class, and especially educated, Austrians found increasingly public ways to display their dissatisfaction with political absolutism. During the 1850s the numbers of public voluntary associations not affiliated with religious groups or charity efforts continued to grow. In industrial associations, rifle clubs, singing associations, and gymnastics associations, Austrians came together, however informally, to discuss and disapprove of public policy.

In 1859, many Austrians also vented their public dissatisfaction with the authoritarian political system by participating in festivals organized locally to mark the centennial of poet and playwright Friedrich Schiller's birth. In Prague, this anniversary brought former exponents of both

Czech and German nationalist politics together to stress the importance of a free public sphere by celebrating a poet whose work more than that of any other symbolized freedom and emancipation to educated Europeans. Writer Fritz Mauthner recalled of the Schiller celebrations in Prague that "if one had not otherwise known that . . . this celebration grew out of a political mood of longing for freedom, one could have guessed it from the participation of [both] the Czechs [and the Germans]." In Budapest in October, centennial celebrations of the author Ferenc Kacinzcy (1759–1831), a tireless activist for the use and reform of the Hungarian language, turned into comparable popular demonstrations of Hungarian nationalism.[70] After these celebrations ended, the men and women who had served on their organizing committees often remained active, setting up new associations, especially gymnastics societies and student clubs. The Schiller year also inaugurated closer connections between activists in different regions of Austria, as communications and rail networks offered greater opportunities to participate in an increasingly interregional festival culture.[71]

Imperial Ambitions in Europe

It was, however, its ambitious foreign policy initiatives that eventually brought down the absolutist regime. Francis Joseph's original decisions to pursue an agenda of economic and social reform had grown out of his desire to challenge Prussia's increasing economic hegemony among the German states. Austria's impressive development at home, however, did not produce an equivalent improvement in its international status. Ill-conceived foreign policy decisions outweighed any political capital the regime gained from its policies of economic development, and this fact eventually gave proponents of constitutionalism new leverage against the dynasty.

The fiscal consequences of Austria's foreign policies originated largely in the state's hunger for currency during the upheavals of 1848, when Austria's decision to issue paper money had destabilized the international value of its currency. From 1850 through 1867 each new finance minister struggled to establish fiscal stability while budgeting enormous outlays for infrastructural projects and military buildup.[72] At the same time, however, each finance minister sought to stimulate rapid economic growth in order to raise revenues. This dual set of fiscal goals explains, for example, the simultaneous decision to privatize the railroads while nevertheless encouraging their expansion through overly favorable concessions. Yet these long-term efforts to create financial stability were repeatedly foiled by military mobilizations in 1853, 1859, 1862, and 1866.

Since the time of Maria Theresa's wars against Frederick the Great, and certainly since the humiliating collapse of the Holy Roman Empire in 1806, Prussia had increasingly challenged Austria for leadership among the states of the German Confederation. In the 1820s and 1830s Prussia had steadily increased its political influence in central Europe by organizing a German Customs Union (*Zollverein*) to which Austria did not belong and which gradually came to include almost all of the small and midsized German states. In 1848 many Austrian manufacturers had balked at the idea of a united Germany that would have required them to join this German Customs Union and expose their goods to dangerous competition. Increasingly, however, the lessons of recent history suggested that if Austria wanted to compete successfully with Prussia in the future, it would have to demonstrate a comparable degree of economic power.

While competition with Prussia underlay Francis Joseph's support for economic development, other pressing foreign policy concerns also sapped the budget. To the east and south, the same Russian Empire that in 1849 had saved Austria by putting down the rebellious Hungarians now took advantage of the weakening Ottoman Empire by supporting— or instigating—rebellions in the Balkans and even taking territory for itself. Neutral Austria sought through an expensive mobilization during the Crimean War in 1853 to send a clear message to Russia to stay out of the Balkans. But Austria's mobilization only angered the Tsar who saw it as a gesture of ingratitude and even betrayal. In the west, meanwhile, the Kingdom of Sardinia (Piedmont) plotted with the secret help of France to gain control over more of the Italian peninsula, as it had sought to do in 1848. In 1859 Austria fought a losing war against France and Piedmont to prevent precisely this development. Then in 1862 Austria joined Prussia in mobilizing its forces against Denmark in order to help the German Confederation to retain the provinces of Schleswig and Holstein against Danish claims and to make sure that Prussia did not reap the public relations benefits of having won a victory against Denmark by itself. Finally, in 1866, Prussia challenged Austria directly in a lightning war that ended any hopes Austria entertained to unite Germany under its auspices. Each of these mobilizations also plunged Austria back into fiscal crises that weakened its currency and raised the deficit. By 1859 the regime's domestic achievements were completely overshadowed by a monetary and fiscal crisis of immense proportions.

"No Constitution, No Money"

After the 1859 peace of Villafranca, which required Austria to cede the wealthy north Italian province of Lombardy to France and Piedmont, the defeated Emperor Francis Joseph understood that to reaffirm his legitimacy and restore the state's credit, he would need to concede to some kind of power-sharing arrangement. Francis Joseph still believed that a superficial reform would be sufficient to renew the regime's popularity. In 1860 he wrote to his mother, "We shall indeed have a little parliamentary government, but the power remains in my hands."[73] How little this turned out to be the case shows just how badly Francis Joseph and his advisors understood his empire. What started as a controlled exercise in "window dressing" quickly snowballed into a free-for-all among conservatives and liberals, aristocrats and bourgeois professionals, noble gentry and capitalist entrepreneurs to seize the opportunity to construct their own particular vision of empire on the ashes of the failed system of bureaucratic centralism.

The unpopular architect of the absolutist system, Alexander Bach, resigned, and Francis Joseph retreated openly from his absolutist program. But with whom would the emperor share power? He needed desperately to gain political backing from two very different social groups who had both chafed at their lack of political influence in the 1850s: the crownland aristocracies and the increasingly influential capitalist middle classes (including Vienna's banking community). Francis Joseph's "little parliamentary government" unleashed a fierce competition between these social groups (later joined by others) over the shape of the new system that would replace the absolutism of the 1850s. The contests over power-sharing that ensued lasted eight years and were not fully resolved until the empire had lost yet another costly war in 1866. Even then, as we will see, Austria remained divided in both political and cultural terms until well into the 1880s, when all sides at least tacitly accepted the parameters of the new constitutional system.

In 1860 the regional aristocracies demanded a federalist system that would end bureaucratic centralization and return full control over regional policy and politics to them. In particular they demanded that legislative power be given (or in their language "restored to") the crownland diets, which they fully expected to dominate. The crownland aristocracies did not necessarily oppose the idea of a central parliament for Austria, but they wanted its competence strictly limited to a narrow handful of matters such as the imperial budget. Meanwhile, the capitalist and educated middle classes demanded the creation of an elected and powerful central parliament for the entire empire. Unlike the aristocrats, many middle-class liberals were not unhappy with a strongly centralized state, but they wanted to organize it on their terms. Thus, they supported aspects of Joseph II's centralist legacy, viewing state power as the most effective means to impose the rule of law on any surviving forms of feudal and religious privilege in Austrian society. At the same time, though, they also demanded a constitution with a bill of rights, the repudiation of the concordat with Rome, the separation of the judiciary from the administration, and the subjection of the bureaucracy to the oversight of an elected parliament.

When it came to electing Austria's new institutions however, be they regional diets or a central parliament, both the aristocratic federalists and the liberal centralists did not want a repeat of the popular excesses of 1848. They agreed that the electorate should be restricted to the responsible property owning classes (that is, to themselves). Where they disagreed was on how exactly to weigh the relative influence that landowning nobles as opposed to urban capitalists would exercise in elections.

In 1860 the emperor first turned to the federalist nobility. Appointing Galician aristocrat Count Agenor Gołuchowski to head a ministerial cabinet, Francis Joseph issued the "irrevocable" October Diploma. This document promised to reinstate the crownland diets, which would then elect deputies to an Austrian parliament whose sole job was to review the annual budget.[74] This solution devolved considerable power from the centralized bureaucracy to the local diets, over which the regional nobilities confidently assumed they would exercise decisive influence. Despite its federalist promises, however, the October Diploma failed to satisfy most Hungarian politicians, since it treated Hungary as one of many components in the larger empire and refused to recognize Hungary's April Laws of 1848. The October Diploma also frustrated many liberals outside of Hungary who saw it as a step backward from the parliamentary system they themselves had briefly created in 1848–49. For liberal nationalists outside of Hungary, of whom the Czech nationalists were the only real representatives, the October Diploma also created a fundamental dilemma. On the one hand, its federalist provisions went a long way toward fulfilling their nationalist demands for greater Bohemian autonomy. On the other, it did little to liberalize society in terms of civil rights and judicial practices.

Both the Hungarian and Austrian liberal media fomented so much criticism of the plan that Francis Joseph—still seeking support from the reluctant credit markets—soon found himself forced to modify the "irrevocable" diploma. Dropping the aristocratic federalists in December 1860, the emperor appointed a centralist bureaucrat and former 1848er to head his cabinet, Anton Ritter von Schmerling. With the help of a small circle of bureaucrat colleagues, Schmerling devised the so-called February Patent (1861), creating a central parliament *(Reichsrat)* whose consent was required for more kinds of legislation than simply the budget. This parliament would also exercise more power than the crownland diets over domestic policy, although its deputies were to be elected by the individual diets and not directly by the voters.[75]

The new election system divided eligible voters into four unequal voter lists called "curias": (1) large estate owners, (2) chambers of commerce, (3) urban constituencies, and (4) rural constituencies, with a relatively high tax minimum for voting in the last two.[76] As a gesture to the Hungarians, Schmerling divided this parliament into two potential bodies, one, the so-called narrower parliament *(engerer Reichsrat)*, which would legislate for all of the non-Hungarian crownlands, and the other, a parliament that included Hungarian deputies and would take up only common empire-wide issues.[77]

In 1848 the Austrian Parliament had consisted of a single chamber of deputies that had set its own rules and had legislated on a full range of issues. Deputies to that body had enjoyed rights of legal immunity, and cabinets had fallen when they lost the support of a parliamentary majority. The February Patent, however, added a House of Lords to moderate the actions of the Chamber of Deputies. Members to this upper chamber were either princes of the Habsburg dynasty or prominent individuals appointed by the emperor. Successful legislation had to win support from both houses and from the emperor. Deputies to this Parliament and to the revived diets enjoyed no legal immunity from prosecution, and they had no formal influence on the composition of the cabinet. There was no constitutional guarantee making officials responsible for implementing legislation. Under these daunting conditions it seemed doubtful that the deputies would be able to assert their wishes against the power of the regime.

Following the first elections held in over a decade, the reconstituted diets met in the spring of 1861, and with the exception of the Hungarian and Croatian diets, they each elected deputies to the central Parliament in Vienna. When the newly elected deputies gathered in the hastily erected Parliament building near Vienna's Schottentor in April 1861, however, they unleashed a vigorous game of tug-of-war with the regime, which did not end until the 1870s. The deputies and their allies in the press willfully ignored the limits the emperor and Schmerling had placed on the new institutions. Buttressing their claims with popular intellectual and legal arguments, they consistently referred to the new institutions as "constitutional" in the sense of 1848 and not as "consultative" as Francis Joseph saw them. The cabinet endured constant and often embarrassing demands made by deputies in the form of critical interpellations and unwanted legislation. In turn, the cabinet responded defensively, struggling to limit the effects of Parliament's more radical demands.[78] The emperor's earlier confidence that "all power stays in my hands" turned out to be woefully naïve in this new and unpredictable world of popular politics.

Both liberals and conservatives alike (in 1861 those positions were generally defined in terms of centralism and federalism) were determined to bring about a truly constitutional, if not democratic, age. They attacked what they viewed as the constitutional shortcomings of the system from both federalist and centralist perspectives. They tried to legislate into being the powers that this Parliament lacked compared to its 1848 predecessor, especially with regard to the issue of ministerial responsibility. Their main tactic, however, entailed acting as if they already exercised the very rights they were trying to attain. Thus in the earliest sessions—all avidly reported in the daily press—several deputies described themselves as "representatives of the people," despite the fact that neither the October Diploma nor the February Patent mentioned "the people" or even the term "representatives."

Lawyers dominated debate in the earliest sessions, using legalistic and technical arguments to justify their far-reaching claims to power. In the second session lawyer Eduard Mühlfeld (Lower Austria) proposed that the Chamber of Deputies free itself from the rules imposed on it by the government and write its own order of business.[79] In the same session lawyer Carl Giskra (Moravia) argued that the Parliament should draw up a formal reply to the address with which the emperor had opened the session.[80] By replying to the emperor's address, the deputies could articulate their own agenda while shaping public perceptions about the most important issues of the day. Many deputies used the debate over how to reply to the emperor's address as a way to publicize their differences with each other as well.[81] For example, federalists and centralists clashed vigorously over the competence of the Parliament as opposed to the individual diets, thus helping to establish the basis for cross-regional alliances among early parties.

Having laid out their agendas in their reply to the emperor, the deputies now unleashed a full frontal attack on the new system.[82] On 15 May 1861, Giskra introduced legislation to make the cabinet directly responsible to Parliament for the execution of legislation. Each responsible minister would have to co-sign legislation when it passed both houses and had received the emperor's sanction. Parliament could take action against any minister who did not execute the new law. The measure would curtail the traditional independence of the imperial bureaucracy, which as an instrument of the crown had historically functioned independently. Now the liberals sought to restructure the empire by making the bureaucracy responsible to the legislature.[83]

In justifying his proposal, Giskra cast the Austrian people themselves as the basis for parliamentary legitimacy, arguing that it was they and not the deputies who desired this reform of constitutional procedure. "Public opinion . . . clearly recognized deficiencies and mistakes in the constitution, and it demands their remedy as an urgent necessity."[84] Giskra also attempted to reconcile the contradiction that constitutional empire created between the absolute nature of Habsburg kingship on the one hand and constitutional rule on the other. Constitutional theorists throughout Europe in the nineteenth century, he argued, faced this paradox, not simply the Austrians. "Theory and praxis," he argued, "have long recognized the axiom: 'The King cannot be wrong.'" For Giskra, this was "a necessary legal fiction that places the occupant of the throne above any attack" in a constitutional monarchy. "In such states," he added, "theory and praxis have supplemented this legal fiction with a second institution," and that second institution, ministerial responsibility, required the crown's servants to uphold parliamentary legislation.[85] Ministerial responsibility would harmonize the absolute prerogatives of the crown with the rights of the people to legislate.

If a frustrated Francis Joseph rejected the radical presumptions of Giskra's discourse, much of the newspaper-reading public accepted these assertions, partly because the uncensored press repeated them with gusto. After twelve years of absolutism, Austria's newspaper readers followed parliamentary speeches and debates with heightened interest. Many of the leading deputies cultivated close relationships with reporters and newspaper editors in an effort to shape public perception. Journalist Heinrich Pollak of the *Morgenpost* recalled, for example, that deputies had mixed freely with journalists in the buffet area of the Parliament building, often slipping journalists advance copies of upcoming speeches. Moravian Giskra and Bohemian law professor Eduard Herbst were on especially close terms with Pollak, while Bohemian Ignaz von Plener cultivated a close relationship with August Zang, editor of Vienna's *Die Presse*.[86] In his memoirs Schmerling lashed out against these relationships, blaming them for undermining his program and his relationship with Francis Joseph. He attributed the deputies' cultivation of relationships with reporters to their addiction to favorable press coverage. This common character flaw, he thought, regularly impelled deputies to leak secret information to the press, so that confidential "decisions which had been negotiated in committee the evening before appeared for all to read in the next morning's papers." "When a committee meeting ended,"

Schmerling observed, "the reporters who lurked near the door received notes from various committee members, on which they based their stories." Of course Schmerling was not above using his own publicists to popularize government positions in the press; nevertheless he blamed his opponents' relationships with the press for an unseemly lack of discretion. Over time, the more public the processes of imperial decision-making became, the more the emperor's direct influence over events diminished, as the views of the deputies and their reporter allies became normative in the media.[87]

As Schmerling increasingly lost control over his Frankenstein creation, his relationship to the emperor also collapsed.[88] This collapse was due less to the threat posed by liberal constitutionalism, however, than to Schmerling's failure to persuade the Hungarians and Croatians to attend the Vienna Parliament.[89] Their representatives insisted on the restoration of the April Laws of 1848 before they would participate in any common imperial institution, and as a result Francis Joseph closed down the Hungarian Diet and reimposed martial law in Hungary. At the same time federalist resistance to the new system also increased, especially among Czech nationalists in Bohemia, Polish nationalists in Galicia, and Catholic conservatives in the Tyrol. From the point of view of the central Austrian state, Schmerling's constitutional system had produced on every front exactly the opposite effect that its creator had intended for it.

Nationalism, 1860s-Style

With the revival of constitutional life in 1861, a vigorous—if still socially limited—politics organized around largely federalist forms of nationalism developed in some crownlands and consequently in the Vienna Parliament. During the period 1861–1880 nationalist political movements remained largely—but not exclusively—a top-down phenomenon, as an examination of political life at the communal level in Chapter 7 confirms. Not surprisingly, nationalist thinking in the 1860s returned to the ideas and experiences of 1848 for its specific programs. Elements from 1848 such as a revival of an Austro-Slav ideal, the restoration of an independent Polish state, or increased crownland federalism underlay most nationalist demands. Nationalist programs—if not ideologies—remained products of specific crownland political conditions rather than of empire-wide conditions. In other words, when German speakers spoke of themselves as part of a nation in the 1870s, they tended to understand that nation and its interests in terms of identification with their individual crownlands rather than in terms of identification with an empire-wide national community or national interest. One could barely speak of empire-wide Czech, German, Italian, or Slovene nationalist movements in imperial Austria, for example. Rather, one would have encountered a Czech nationalism in Bohemia quite different from Czech nationalism in Moravia, a Slovene nationalism in Carniola different from its counterpart in Styria, or an Italian nationalism in Tyrol that differed substantially from its counterparts in Istria, Trieste/Trst, or Dalmatia.

During this period, nationalist political programs tended to refer to older models of a federalized empire based on historical crownland units like Hungary, Galicia, or Bohemia. The Polish Galician vision of nationhood, often dominated by a conservative gentry, opposed participation by the peasantry or by emerging Ruthene nationalists in politics, and remained firmly wedded to the restoration of an independent Poland. Until the old Polish Lithuanian Commonwealth could be restored, however, Polish nationalists sought an autonomous federal status within the Austrian state. And while peasants managed to elect several deputies to the first Galician Diet *(sejm)* of 1861, they failed to elect or reelect any peasants again until 1889. In the intervening years, conservative Polish nationalists used every trick at their disposal to keep peasant representatives out of the diet.[90]

Bohemian Czech nationalists also lobbied Vienna for autonomy for their crownland. At the beginning of the constitutional revival in 1861, Czech nationalist leaders Palacký and Rieger negotiated a political alliance with the federalist Bohemian nobility under Prince Heinrich Clam-Martinic. Their common program sought to "restore" Bohemia's historic state rights by recognizing the primacy of the diet and treating the Vienna Parliament as a collective diet where individual crownlands simply negotiated matters of common importance among themselves. The alliance with the federalist nobility obliged Palacký and Rieger to moderate their—and their followers'—political liberalism and to exchange the arguments they had made in 1848 for the Czech nation's natural right to self-determination for an argument that rested on historic crownland traditions. Over time this alliance between bourgeois activists and federalist nobility produced considerable internal dissension, since Czech nationalist liberals often held positions on social and economic issues that placed them closer to their centralist liberal opponents than to their noble allies. In 1863, following the Hungarian example, Bohemian Czech nationalists decided to boycott the Vienna Parliament. In 1864 they were joined by Moravian Czech nationalists who nevertheless distanced themselves from the claim that Moravia belonged to a common kingdom with Bohemia.[91]

Settlement

By 1865, sensing that a reasonable agreement with Hungary might yet be obtainable outside of the current system, Francis Joseph changed tactics and replaced the centralist Schmerling with a conservative federalist, Count Richard Belcredi of Moravia. Belcredi in turn suspended the Vienna Parliament and called new elections, hoping to return federalist majorities to the diets, which would then approve a federalist reform of the system. At the same time, completely outside of this constitutional framework, Francis Joseph also negotiated with Hungarian leaders.

Once again, however, it was defeat in war, this time against Prussia in 1866, that forced Francis Joseph to make even more radical concessions than he had originally envisioned, both to the Hungarian nationalists and then to the Austrian centralist liberals. Defeat at the hands of Prussia ended all hope of some kind of federalist unification of Germany under Austrian auspices. Instead, Austria was formally expelled from the German Confederation and forced to cede Venice to France (which receded it to Italy). Francis Joseph could at least be grateful that Hungarian society had remained loyal during the war and had not chosen this moment to agitate for full independence. In the spring of 1867 the emperor negotiated a settlement with moderate liberal Hungarian activists led by Ferenc Deák, which would restore almost all of Hungary's 1848 April Laws.

Under the terms of the settlement Hungary gained full independence from the rest of the Austrian Empire with regard to domestic issues.

Ferenc Deák (1803–1876) in mid-life. Along with Julius Andrássy, Deák largely negotiated the 1867 settlement for the Hungarian national side. Nineteenth-century French engraving. Credit: Private Collection/Bridgeman Images.

Delegations from the Hungarian and Austrian parliaments would regularly negotiate the division of the state debt, tariffs, and other common questions. Francis Joseph consented to a coronation ceremony for himself and Elisabeth that took place on 8 June. On that day in Buda's Coronation Church of Matthias Corvinus, Francis Joseph received the ancient crown of St. Stephen that embodied the "ancient Hungarian nation." Outside the church, on horseback and with his sword drawn, like Maria Theresa (at Pressburg/Pozsony) and his uncle Ferdinand before him, he spoke an oath directed in the four directions of the compass.

In Austria, meanwhile, Francis Joseph reconvened the Parliament on 15 May, this time with its centralist liberal majority. As a sign of recon-

Count Julius Andrássy (1823–1890) leads the homage paid by the assembled Hungarian notables to Francis Joseph and Elisabeth after their coronation as King and Queen of Hungary in the Mathias Church, 8 June 1867. Copper engraving by Jenö (Eugen) Doby, 1877, after a painting by Eduard Engerth completed in 1871. Credit: Österreichische Nationalbibliothek.

ciliation with the liberals, he reluctantly appointed the self-dramatizing and highly popular Moravian lawyer and former 1848er, Carl Giskra as its president. In return for their eventual passage of the Settlement with Hungary, Francis Joseph permitted the liberal deputies who dominated this session to draw up a series of fundamental laws that would serve as a constitution, this time including a bill of rights based largely on the Kremsier/Kroměříž draft voted in 1849. Many centralists reluctantly came to terms with the Hungarian Settlement, which they had previously opposed. Many did not like the way it divided the unitary empire, and some protested to no avail that this compromise had been imposed on them without their participation.

On 21 December 1867, when the emperor sanctioned the new constitutional laws, three new entities officially, if not practically, replaced the Austrian Empire of 1804: a creation known as Austria-Hungary that existed in some situations—diplomatic, military, finance—but not in others; a Kingdom of Hungary; and an imperial state officially known until 1916 as "the Kingdoms and Territories Represented in the Parliament" but which for the sake of convenience we will call "Austria."[92] From now on Hungary and Austria shared only a common Habsburg ruler, who was king of Hungary and emperor of Austria, a common military, a common foreign policy, and limited common financial arrangements. Both Hungary and Austria became constitutional monarchies, with very different constitutions, different administrative and judicial systems, and even different qualifications for citizenship.[93] Delegations from both parliaments would meet annually to set budgets for common matters and every ten years would renegotiate the fiscal terms of the agreement that had created Austria-Hungary. Neither state could change the arrangement without the agreement of the other.

In consenting to this new system, Francis Joseph had retained his prerogative to determine a common military and foreign policy himself. But even in these two critical areas, the emperor-king could not necessarily rule as he pleased. Budgetary limits after 1867 repeatedly constrained him, requiring him to forge a broad political consensus on most military and foreign policy issues. Given his personality as consummate—some might say pedantic—bureaucrat, Francis Joseph eventually learned the intricate rules of each constitutional system far better than did most of his cabinet ministers. By adhering closely to these rules, and by demanding formal adherence to them from others, his behavior tended in the long run to strengthen constitutional practice in both Hungary and Austria rather than to weaken it. It was more than a little ironic that the man who opened his reign by shutting down the Kremsier/Kroměříž Parliament, abrogating the April Laws, and harshly executing Hungarian rebels now became the most reliable executor of their constitutional legacies.

In Austria the settlement was generally understood to constitute a temporary victory of German- and Hungarian-oriented state centralism over crownland federalism. Many federalist nationalists accused the 1867

The Austrian Empire, 1859–1867

Settlement of enshrining Hungarian and German national domination over the other nationalities in each half of the empire. Luka Svetec—later the first deputy to deliver a speech in Slovene to the Carniolan Diet— warned his colleagues during the debate over the settlement that it would constitute the opposite of a solution to the nationality question. The settlement, he argued, would in fact divide Austria into two separate camps, "those [nations] who ruled through no merit of their own, and those [nations] who served through no fault of their own."[94] Indeed the successful passage of the settlement seemed to encourage other parties to demand federalist concessions for their own crownlands. The most influential of these, Bohemian and Galician federalists, strongly opposed a dual monarchy that gave ultimate power to Budapest and Vienna at the expense of Prague, Lemberg/Lwów/Lviv, Agram/Zagreb, Laibach/ Ljubljana, or even Innsbruck. At the same time, many of them treated the 1867 Settlement as an example that could be copied. They nurtured hopes—not unreasonably as it turned out—that they might be able to conclude their own comparable settlements with the dynasty in the near future. Although Galician Polish and Bohemian Czech nationalists never gained the kind of official status enjoyed by independent Hungary in the dual monarchy, they did achieve high levels of autonomy for their crownlands particularly with regard to questions of language use in the local civil service and in questions of control over education and welfare policy.

Independent Hungary

One of the earliest tasks of the new Hungarian cabinet was to create a comparable settlement—or *Nagodba*—with Croatia (now to include much of the former military frontier as well). The new Hungarian government under Prime Minister Andrássy negotiated this 1868 agreement with a largely pro-Hungarian party in the Croatian Diet, or *Sabor* (whose election the more nationalist Croatian parties had boycotted). The agreement recognized Croatia's historic position as an independent kingdom allied with Hungary, giving Croatia limited cultural and administrative autonomy, retaining an elected *Sabor,* and granting Croatia the right to independent representation in the Hungarian Parliament when that body dealt with issues of common interest. From now on Croatia sent forty deputies out of the 442 in the Budapest Parliament who had the right to speak Croatian in parliamentary debates. A Croat minister without portfolio was also meant to represent Croatia's interests in the Hungarian cabinet. The Hungarian prime minister recommended the appointment of the Croatian viceroy, or *Ban,* to the king, and the *Ban* was technically responsible to the *Sabor* although in practice he was widely viewed as subservient to Hungarian interests. Croatia was empowered to retain 45 percent of taxes collected there for purely Croatian purposes.[95]

The specifics of the *Nagodba* typified the approach of the Hungarian political class to the 1867 Settlement in general. Above all, the larger settlement recognized what that class argued was Hungary's historic independent existence, which had always been legally separate from the other lands ruled by the Habsburgs. The *Nagodba* simply codified the historic constitutional relationship of the Croatian state to the Hungarian state. In both cases, however, the political demands of modern nationhood soon overwhelmed and reformulated traditional arguments about national sovereignty. Constitutional questions became increasingly bound up with national cultural concerns, which were increasingly expressed in ethnic terms to make them more persuasive.

The 1867 Settlement had created two states in which no language was the language of a majority and no ethnic nation could claim to be the majority. Not surprisingly, the two states immediately parted company in terms of how they handled issues of multilingualism and national identification. Constitutional rulings in the next thirty years—if not legislation—continually reinforced the Austrian state's status as fundamentally multinational. In Hungary, however, Hungarian nationalists mixed traditional state patriotism with emerging ethnic nationalism in an attempt to create a specifically Hungarian nation that sought increasingly to assimilate ethnic non-Hungarians to an ethnic Hungarian identification. These two routes of development will be taken up in Chapter 6, but for now it is important to understand how the particulars of the 1867 Settlement set the structural parameters for these contrasting developmental trajectories.

The 1867 Settlement gave birth to a lasting political situation in Hungary in which constitutional questions about Hungary's relationship to Austria, rather than social, economic, or political policy questions, constituted the ideological bases for Hungarian political parties and their relations to each other and to their king. Until the end of the First World War the core question that animated Hungarian politics was one's position on the 1867 Settlement. Either political parties supported the fundamentals of the settlement (and thus were considered by the king to be capable of forming a parliamentary cabinet, or *Regierungsfähig*), or they agitated for a return to the April Laws, which would limit the link to Austria to a purely "personal union" embodied in the Habsburg ruler. According to the parties who followed this latter so-called 1848 program—and who thereby alienated their king—Hungary should gain its own army (not to mention the right to use Hungarian as the language of command) and control of an independent foreign policy. There would no longer be a need for the meetings of the parliamentary delegations and no decennial renewal of the economic terms of the settlement agreement. Support for the 1848 position generally emanated more from local county politicians, while state employees and bureaucrats tended to support the government parties.

At this point it is important to note a few points about the constitutional obsessions of Hungarian parties. First, the remarkable economic, social, and demographic transformation experienced by Hungary in the decades after 1867 may have produced pressing social problems, but it was not these issues that divided Hungary's political parties in ideological or policy terms. Formal divisions among parties always rested on their differing approaches to national(ist) issues and never on their approaches to social issues. For this reason all Hungarian parties considered themselves to be "liberal" either in the tradition of 1848 or of 1867. There could be no formal conservative parties because conservatism was associated with Habsburg absolutism.[96] Second, the ongoing prominence of constitutional questions kept the issue of nationhood and its meanings at the center of Hungarian politics. This in turn continually narrowed the governments' options with regard to its treatment of Hungarian citizens—often patriots—who nevertheless spoke other languages (Romanian, Serb, Slovak, Ruthene, German, Yiddish). It produced policies of linguistic Hungarianization that successive governments pursued with more or less intensity. Ongoing battles over the 1867 Settlement forced several of these cabinets to preempt their critics by favoring an increasingly ethnic definition of Hungarian-ness. This in turn alienated broad sectors of Hungarian society from the state. Despite the prominence of Hungarian chauvinist nationalism in the 1860s, however, this kind of policy was certainly neither inevitable nor even fully predictable, given the liberal character of Hungary's language and nationality laws legislated in 1868.

The Law of the Nationalities was largely the creation of Baron Joseph Eötvös (1813–1871), minister of religion and education, a well-known progressive who had also served in the same capacity in 1848. It provided a very liberal, if very generalized framework that guaranteed a range of linguistic rights to non-Hungarian speakers as individuals. It did not foresee collective rights attached to groups like nations.[97] The law's details, however, were vague; they would have to be worked out in different areas of law and administration in subsequent decades. But starting in the 1870s, subsequent legislation and specific applications of the law abandoned Eötvös's liberal construction of national minority rights at every level of government and public life. Thus, for example, Article 20 of the law gave communes the right to choose their language of administration, Article 22 stipulated that the communes had to communicate with the county administrations either in Hungarian or in their own language. In practice, however, the county governments—which supervised communal budgets—forced the communes to communicate with them in Hungarian and to provide only Hungarian-language versions of all documents. Many communes gave way to these demands in order not to have to duplicate their administrative work.[98] As a result, even non-Hungarian communes tended to hire Hungarian-speaking clerks and bureaucrats. The state in turn increasingly expected those low level clerks to function as local "representatives of the Hungarian state idea." As in many Galician villages—or French villages for that matter—local village councilors often found themselves signing documents that they themselves could not read. As early as 1872, and in a sign of things to come, county courts in Transylvania that had only recently started accepting petitions in Romanian now rejected them.[99]

Finally, the importance of constitutional questions and the formal slide into an increasingly but not fully Hungarian ethnic chauvinist policy meant that unlike governments in Austria, governments in Hungary did their best to avoid reforming the franchise either for communal and county institutions or for the Hungarian Parliament. Universal manhood suffrage of the kind introduced in elections to the Austrian Parliament in 1907 would have meant both a proportionate increase in the numbers of deputies elected by linguistic minorities and an intolerable diminution of the influence of the Hungarian gentry classes. The landed nobility's 64 percent of deputies to the Hungarian Parliament in 1861 may have been typical for European parliaments in the mid-nineteenth century, but by 1914 the fact that this social group still constituted 41 percent of the deputies made the Hungarian Parliament an outlier in Europe and radically different from its Austrian counterpart.[100] Successive Hungarian governments' intransigence on the issue of suffrage reform—in fact the government actually added more restrictions to the suffrage in the 1880s—aggravated social protest in both rural and urban Hungary already in the 1880s and 1890s and contributed as well to the rise in popular anti-Semitism.[101] It also gave the king a wedge issue with which to threaten stubborn Hungarian cabinets in conflicts over constitutional questions as he did in 1906 during debates on the military language of command.

*

This chapter opened with the confident proclamation of an imperial dictatorship in 1851 and closes, less than two decades later, with an examination of the lively party political activism that now dominated the governments in both halves of the new dual monarchy. In a very short time the various practitioners of liberal politics had managed successfully to assert their vision of liberal empire against the activist absolutist politics of their Habsburg emperor, who himself had adopted several liberal tenets to his program. The locus of decision-making shifted during this period, but the particular content of most political decisions changed very little. The radical discourse of the various liberals who asserted the moral supremacy of their values against those of the system that governed in the 1850s did not produce policies that differed all that much from the predecessors whose system they so loudly rejected. Their reliance on the asserted superiority of their system's values, however, anticipated new kinds of political arguments and discourses that would come to dominate Austrian and Hungarian politics for the next half century. As a society experiencing increasing regional industrialization, urbanization, literacy, bureaucratic specialization, internal migration, and political participation, Austria-Hungary was typical of nineteenth-century Europe. The particular arguments made by its politicians, however, and the particular cultural values they asserted, appear unique, even as they faced the common European challenges of managing increased social mobilization and increased social conflict.

CHAPTER SIX

Culture Wars and Wars for Culture

By virtue of its ethnographic depictions and by virtue of its political
character, it will be a monument to the solidarity that ties the people of
the Monarchy to each other, to the unifying feeling, which after all of this
opacity and inhibition will once again emerge victorious.

— *"Erkennet euch selbst" (Recognize Yourselves)*
in Neues Wiener Tagblatt, *27 March, 1884*

This chapter traces the ways in which activists of all stripes in Austro-Hungarian society increasingly invoked the authority of what they called *culture* to assert their visions of empire, to build political and social movements, to sharpen their differences with opponents, and to discredit competing visions. From 1867 until the fall of the empire, advocates of all kinds of political positions in Austria-Hungary increasingly justified their demands, proposals, and programs by making sweeping cultural claims about whole populations. From secular liberals to ultramontane priests, from sectarian nationalists to imperialist propagandists, they framed their visions in Manichean terms. Their subjects were whole cultures allegedly separated from each other by unbridgeable differences.

The increasing turn by politicians and activists to cultural references, illustrations, terminologies, and arguments was clearest in the rise of new forms of political nationalism in Austria-Hungary. Nationalists based their increasingly populist definitions of nationhood on what they interpreted to be the obvious facts of different language usage. The fact that citizens of the empire used many languages to communicate among themselves and with the state already lent itself to the argument that several defined cultures or nations made up Austro-Hungarian society.[1] This assertion in turn produced arguments that cultural or national differences were fundamental in nature and could not be bridged. Claims about national difference anchored some groups' political assertions that the very function of the imperial state was to rectify the historic victimization of one nation by another.

The legitimation of political entitlements based on cultural differences, however, was hardly limited to nationalists. After 1867 religious activists exploited similar claims of cultural victimhood in both Austria and Hungary. State and dynasty also legitimated Austria-Hungary's existence by touting the beneficial unity it provided to the allegedly different peoples, cultures, or nations over which it ruled. One argument of this chapter is that the work of ideologists of nationhood and ideologists of empire in the late nineteenth century rested on parallel suppositions and produced similar outcomes. The imperial state facilitated a cultural turn in politics by increasingly justifying its existence in terms of its ability to promote the development of its constituent nations. The self-appointed representatives of the different national communities in turn fought to gain a better place for themselves within the framework of the empire.

Nation in Austria-Hungary's Culture Wars

Many histories of post-1867 Austria-Hungary focus their attention on what they call the "nationalities conflict." This conflict manifested itself in everything from parliamentary obstruction to street riots to economic boycotts to political assassinations. For some contemporary observers like Hungarian sociologist Oscar Jászi (1875–1957), who published the influential *Dissolution of the Habsburg Monarchy* (1929) as well as for historians whose work built on Jászi's insights, these ongoing conflicts demonstrated the dual monarchy's increasing incapacity to govern a multinational society. In an age of growing mass politics, they argued, the coexistence of different language groups or nations within a single empire inevitably led to social conflicts that produced what Jászi termed a powerful centrifugal political effect. Many historians following Jászi have posited implicitly or explicitly a causal relationship between the existence of deep cultural differences in society, on the one hand, and the political conflicts these differences allegedly produced, on the other.[2]

My own approach reads such struggles in Austria-Hungary as primarily political in nature rather than as natural products of the multilingual character of this society. In place of the term "nationalities conflict"—which implies conflict among whole populations—I use the term "nationalist conflicts" to emphasize instead their specifically political character and context. This allows us to make sense of what appears to be a paradox in Austro-Hungarian society in the second half of the nineteenth century—namely, the critical importance of nationalism in many public situations and its irrelevance in others. Nationalism unquestionably dominated public discourse in the mass media, controlled the organization of most nonreligious civic life, and dominated political activity at election time. Yet testimonies from individuals about many other kinds of daily life situations, along with the testimonies of some frustrated nationalists, indicate that people often simply ignored nationalist demands for their loyalty.

We should also recall that both social conflict and linguistic diversity were typical of many nineteenth-century European societies. Austria-Hungary was not so completely distinct as a polity. By itself, sporadic and extreme political conflict was not a sign that Austria-Hungary suffered from more structural problems than did other states. Almost every European society in this period found itself torn by political and social struggles that were often cast in cultural terms, as political activists attempted to both manage and take advantage of the entrance of larger numbers of people into political life. Serious comparison with other societies also suggests that Austria-Hungary's distinctive cultural make-up was more a question of relative than absolute difference. After all, from Wales to Ireland to Catalonia, to East Prussia, to Sicily, how linguistically or culturally homogeneous were other European societies? Did not France, Britain, Germany, Italy, and Spain struggle to integrate linguistically and culturally heterogeneous peoples into national societies in the second half of the nineteenth century?[3] In 1861, when Piedmont's Massimo D'Azeglio (1798–1866) made his oft-quoted observation "We have created Italy. It remains for us to create Italians," this signified his recognition that the serious cultural challenges that hampered the legitimacy of the new self-styled Italian nation-state would need to be overcome. The challenges faced by state-builders in Austria-Hungary were often qualitatively similar to those faced by state-builders in the rest of Europe even if Austria-Hungary handled these challenges distinctively.

What made Austria-Hungary, and especially the Austrian half of the dual monarchy, unique was not so much its ethnic make-up but rather the legal and administrative structures it developed to manage questions of linguistic and religious difference. The particular character of imperial law, of imperial administrative practice, and of traditional claims for crownland autonomy taken together made it more likely that when people in Austria-Hungary became civically engaged, it was through institutions that demanded fairness or parity in official linguistic practice. By the late nineteenth century in Austria and Hungary it was impossible to escape these issues in public life. Nationalist activism became the dominant means through which entire populations—often including working-class Socialists—were mobilized into public life and specifically into politics. Nationalist conflict was not an inevitable result of the multilingual quality of Austrian and Hungarian societies but was a product of institutions. The history of Habsburg Austria may also remind us that political solutions can in fact manage and shape the kinds of ethnic conflicts that often appear to divide societies.[4]

With this in mind, my narrative of Austro-Hungarian history reverses its accustomed terms. Instead of seeing political conflict as the inevitable product of underlying ethnic differences in society, I ask instead how political conflicts may have produced a greater sense of national differences among people. In doing so, I analyze people's experience of mobilization into local and regional political movements as a kind of prerequisite for (rather than a product of) understanding the world in terms of discrete nations. In my account, claimed cultural differences are not necessarily experienced as such in local society—but they gain meaning when they become the basis for political agendas. Thus, people in the same village may not necessarily think of each other as belonging to different cultures just because they speak different languages. A political program that demands legal, social, or institutional rights for speakers of one of those languages would, however, encourage the people in a locality to see themselves and others largely in terms of language-based categories. My approach does not minimize people's social experience of sharing language use or religious practice. It does not question the emotional power of the nationalist or religious feeling people may experience in particular situations. It does, however, question the all-too-easy association of what we might call objectively common traits with specific forms of political identification.

What follows are three closely related points of departure for under-standing nationalist politics in Austria-Hungary. First, the growing frequency and intensity of nationalist conflict in Austria-Hungary after 1867 was primarily a political phenomenon clothed in the language of culture. Extreme conflicts over ethnic-cultural issues generally played themselves out within political institutions over specifically political questions. The articulate protagonists in almost all of these conflicts turn out to have been elected officials, political activists, and political journalists who claimed to represent national masses. When nationalists obstructed the work of Parliament, vandalized a local schoolhouse, or provoked a riot over the naming of a village square in Austria-Hungary, they engaged in organized political responses to specific issues.

The turn to cultural arguments developed because politics after 1867 became increasingly popular and more democratic in character. In the Austrian half of the dual monarchy every decade after 1867 saw an expansion of the suffrage, culminating with the institution of universal manhood suffrage for Parliament in 1907. Suffrage reform repeatedly challenged existing political movements either to absorb and mobilize new classes of voters into their ranks or to risk obsolescence. Early on, nationalist activists turned increasingly to broad cultural-nationalist arguments partly to unify voters from different social classes for their programs. Voters, they believed, identified more easily with broad common cultural attributes like language use than with narrower occupation- or class-specific programs. Activists naturalized their particular political agendas by expressing demands in the more inclusive language of ethnic nationhood. This language made cultural commonalities the basis for group identification. It appealed to imperial fairness to achieve redress for past and present victimization.

Second, if we do not start from the presumption that Austro-Hungarian society was made up of culturally different and warring nations, we still need to explain how a belief in the existence of different nations became such a popular article of faith, capable at times of mobilizing different publics. Here we should examine more fully the daily labor engaged in by nationalist activists as they struggled to popularize a coherent sense of national belonging among local populations. What tools enabled them to make their arguments more persuasively? In what contexts were their arguments more likely to persuade? What kinds of situations produced feelings of national belonging among people in Austro-Hungarian society?[5]

Nation-building, like political party-building, did not come naturally. It was hard work, and it often produced false starts or failure. A citizen might vote for a local nationalist candidate after a particularly hard-fought election campaign, but this did not necessarily make him a committed member of a national community once the excitement of the campaign had ended. Another citizen might participate in an economic boycott promoted by local nationalists of a particular village store. But she might also hire a domestic servant who spoke another language or send her children on an informal exchange with another family to perfect their knowledge of the region's other local language—both actions that nationalists opposed. People's daily level of commitment to nationalist demands was rarely reliable or even predictable. This is why we need to think in terms of "event-driven" or "situational" nationalism.

Third, we also need to take the role of empire seriously in the construction of ideas of nationhood. Imperial institutions, laws, and administrative practices played crucial roles in giving shape to the more successful forms of nationalism. Distinctive nationalist movements developed in response to and operated very much within the idiosyncratic institutional, legal, and constitutional structures of the Austro-Hungarian Empire. The character of these structures made possible the elaboration of some kinds of arguments about nationhood at the expense of others. The precise concepts of nationhood that developed during the 1880s and 1890s owed a great deal to the particular spaces for them created by empire. If we examine how existing laws, imperial structures, and political institutions shaped beliefs about nations or cultures, we may gain a clearer understanding of the dynamics that repeatedly reproduced nationalist conflict.[6]

At the same time, we can place the ideologists who promoted empire—ethnographers, scientists, artists, explorers, and dynastic propagandists—in close conversation with contemporary nationalist activists rather than seeing them as part of a completely different world. The men and women who sought to legitimate the existence of empire by giving it a clearer mission during the late nineteenth century paid very close attention to the cultural ideologies articulated by nationalists. They too reinforced the idea of the empire's many forms of cultural diversity by promoting them as objects of study. They sought to assert more effectively the many ways in which imperial unity improved the social and economic viability of these component cultures, especially those in the empire's poorer and predominantly agricultural regions.

This kind of argument for empire, when projected outward, also produced a more coherent sense of imperial mission to the Balkans and especially to Bosnia-Herzegovina, Austria-Hungary's sole colony from 1878 to 1908. If this empire was good at fostering diverse cultures and promoting their improvement at home, then it was well suited to bringing stability, development, and eventually prosperity to the multiple cultures in Balkan societies. Nation and empire, two polar opposites in the early twentieth-century imagination, repeatedly constituted each other in terms created by and for each other.

Early Culture Wars and Liberal Players

After 1867, the first culture wars to preoccupy the Austrian and Hungarian publics had little to do with nationalism and everything to do with the new constitution. What would the imposition of a liberal constitution mean for Austria's and Hungary's traditional governing classes? How would liberals exercise their new power? In January 1868, only one week into the rule of Austria's new cabinet (dubbed in the popular German press the *Bürgerministerium*, or Burgher Cabinet), the satirical magazine *Kikiriki* carried a telling political cartoon. Playing on the 1848 notion of the beard as symbol of revolutionary masculinity—and Bach's and the emperor's subsequent proscription of it for their bureaucrats in the 1850s—the cartoon depicted the new minister of the interior, a bearded Carl Giskra, entering a room of astonished (and beardless) bureaucrats. The latter cry out in fear and confusion: "There he is! Gentlemen, a cabinet minister with a full beard—Austria is lost!"[7] As the cartoon implied, Austria's new liberal governing class faced plenty of opposition not simply from Austria's traditional social elite of nobles and

Cartoon in the satirical magazine *Kikeriki*, 9 January 1868. The bearded Carl Giskra meets the beardless bureaucrats. Credit: ANNO/Österreichische Nationalbibliothek.

church princes, but also from a wary bureaucracy. The division was not just political. The highest bureaucrats feared that a radically different culture of political values and practices—represented culturally by the revolutionary's beard and legally by the new constitution—threatened to replace the recent presumption of bureaucratic rule.

In their actions—and especially in their rhetoric—Austria's first constitutional ministers and their allies in the press did everything in their power to confirm those fears, repeatedly declaring war against those who might conspire to keep Austria in a dark age of ignorance and absolutism. However, the Manichean drama that pitted rational modernity against arbitrary custom was complicated by the contradictory roles imagined for the state bureaucracy, a contradiction captured in the *Kikiriki* cartoon. On the one hand, this was a profession whose members, even at the highest levels, had increasingly been appointed from the same common culture of educated men from which liberal activists emerged. Bureaucrats had long symbolized for many liberals the historic victory of meritocracy over aristocratic privilege under Joseph II. Most liberal leaders had themselves at one time been employed as servants of the state, from government administrators to university professors. Yet this same bureaucracy had served an absolutist state in the 1850s. Would the bureaucracy transfer its loyalty—as the liberals of the 1860s and 1870s demanded—from the emperor to the Parliament, from the dynasty to the constitution? Would it join a culture of light that claimed to stand on the side of the people in making the laws?

There was no simple answer to this question, in part because the response of many higher-level bureaucrats depended on signals given by the emperor himself, and in the first years after 1867 these were highly ambiguous. Francis Joseph viewed the reforms of 1867 as his final concessions to liberalism and not as the dawning of a bright new era of reform. Almost every new piece of liberal legislation faced initial disapproval from the emperor. Then there were the emperor's own cultural prejudices: in contrast to Hungary, where aristocrats whom he found socially congenial dominated his liberal cabinet, in Austria, his new ministers were in his view far too assertive, too legalistic, too argumentative, and culturally far too bourgeois. They dressed like the lawyers they were, not in military uniforms but in black suits. More than one wore that full beard of the revolutionary rather than the side burns combined with a clean-shaven chin that Francis Joseph favored.[8]

Importantly, however, for the role of the bureaucracy in a new constitutional age, the liberals acted as if their popular political support was so great that they could reject the need to build some kind of consensus with their political opponents—many of whom could have become useful allies. This shortsighted attitude roiled Austrian politics and occasionally created social instability. Some crownland governors hesitated to implement the more controversial aspects of the liberal legislation regulating public education or the place of the church in Austrian society, fearing the public backlash that enforcement might provoke. Some enforced only parts of the new laws, or slowed their enforcement. The very novelty of the new constitutional system allowed them some space to moderate or even to undermine it its effects.

Intent on pursuing the victory of enlightened progress at all costs, the liberal cabinet ministers threatened harsh measures against subordinates who hesitated to administer the new laws. Giskra, for example, instructed all civil servants to treat clerical opposition to the confessional reforms of 1868 and 1869 "with utmost severity," warning them against even the smallest disloyalty to the constitution. Justice minister and former law professor Eduard Herbst wrote legislation enabling him to discipline civil servants in his department who might undermine the new legislation.

A highly vocal interregional liberal press egged on the ministers, creating a cult around them. By repeatedly referring to the new cabinet as the "*Bürgerministerium*" (Burgher or Citizens' Ministry), the liberal press kept the powerful symbolic social and cultural dimensions of the liberals' recent victory in the public eye. The fact that elected commoners in dark suits—not military dress—suddenly occupied positions that had previously been reserved for aristocrats, generals, and high-level bureaucrats signaled that Austrians were witnessing something much greater than a mere political change.[9] Newspapers repeatedly characterized the burgher ministers' meteoric ascent in cultural rather than political terms. Thus, they were celebrated as upright commoners, whose ability to rise to the highest ranks of government symbolized the new political muscle of the *Bürgertum*, a class, the press claimed, whose members worked for the general good rather than for the interests of an elite few. In particular the newspapers hailed the appointment of that same 1848 revolutionary Carl Giskra to be minister of the interior (in charge of the police no less!). He was "at every time the very embodiment of . . . Austrian liberalism." Leaving little doubt where the division between the two cultures lay, one newspaper opined that appointment to high office would not change Giskra's simple manner or honest outlook. "He has the confidence of the people."[10] The newspaper might well have said, "He is the people."

Eager to take charge and to assert their vision for Austria after twenty years in the political wilderness, the liberal ministers and their allies adopted a combative, uncompromising manner as they tackled an enormous range of complex issues. At least history, the liberals believed, was on their side. Ignorance in Austria remained to be conquered, and their absolute confidence in their historic mission made them frame political conflicts as cultural clashes and pit their forward-looking policies against shadowy forces of reaction that wanted to return Austria to a medieval past.

Their parliamentary opponents—federalists who sought increased power for the crownland diets or clerical conservatives opposed to diminishing the church's social influence—fought bitterly against liberal reforms. What was new to this constitutional era, however, was the role played by local political organizations in fanning the flames of these political conflicts. New laws permitting the organization of political associations led to small-scale recreations of this Burgher Ministry drama throughout the empire. Local mayors, town counselors, do-gooders, philanthropists, concerned citizens, and opportunists founded political, philanthropic, and social clubs in cities, towns, and even villages across Austria. They saw themselves as the tools of a revolution that would transform local society according to grand liberal visions. Their programs avoided a politically partisan tone by articulating their agenda in broadly shared cultural terms such as "the encouragement of spiritual and material progress."[11] Culture for them referred above all to the particular form of social capital—specifically to the level of education—that for middle class citizens justified their local claims to power.

In particular, the clubs promoted education so that all of Austria's citizens would be able to discharge their civic duties for the good of the entire community, and not simply for shortsighted sectarian interests.

"The securest basis of any constitutional state and the most important task for liberalism," wrote the editor of the St. Pölten Wochenblatt, "is to achieve a healthy practical education for the people."[12] Often the achievement of these goals meant founding a local village reading room with a small lending library of educational works for adults and children alike. One liberal politician from Moravia even suggested that the long winter months of enforced idleness created a perfect opportunity for farmers to educate themselves further by reading.[13] Realizing liberal goals meant educating fellow citizens—in local newspapers, published pamphlets, and farmers' almanacs—about their rights and duties under the new constitutional laws.

The positive arguments for improving life in the empire through a diffusion of knowledge constructed a negative view of those who opposed this program, usually attributing their opposition to a refusal of the benefits of enlightenment. Those unfortunates were oppressed by the backward-looking forces of reaction. Their misguided opposition to the new school system, for example, contributed to the continued ignorance of Austria's citizens. In the 1870s, especially in the western and northern regions of Austria, liberals projected this idea of an enemy culture specifically onto the Catholic Church hierarchy, engaging in what they referred to as a cultural war (Kulturkampf), a term they borrowed from Bismarck's contemporaneous campaign in Germany against the Catholic Church.[14] But the liberals could just as easily tar their opponents as the nobility's misguided allies in the bureaucracy and the military.

The liberal war on the pillars of traditional society—the church, the aristocracy, the absolutist bureaucracy, the military—was not limited to building schools, training teachers, organizing clubs, or publishing newspapers. From roughly 1860 to 1890 Austria's German liberals creatively deployed a variety of cultural symbols, erecting monuments to Habsburg rulers such as Maria Theresa and Joseph II in public places, naming streets and squares for admired historic figures, and even, as we will see in Chapter 7, deploying specific architectural styles to express liberal values in new public buildings. Nationalists in other cities did the same.[15] Statuary in public spaces, as well as names chosen for new streets and squares in the expanding cities, made spatial claims by evoking greater and lesser heroes of modern liberalism and nationalism.[16]

Other elements of changing cityscapes also served as symbols to popularize liberal narratives of local history. In 1861 the liberal town council in the Tyrolean town of Bozen/Bolzano organized a "Shooting Competition of Light" for local sharpshooters *(Schützen)* in order to celebrate both the new law tolerating Protestantism *and* the introduction of a system of gas lighting in the town. The Tyrolean liberals linked a powerful symbol of regional identification from the days of the Napoleonic Wars and the recent mobilization against Italy—the heroic Tyrolean sharpshooter battling foreign invasion—to its new system of street lights to galvanize popular support for their program. Texts produced for the festivities repeatedly connected the symbolism of light to the liberal concept of enlightenment. A parade through the town showed off individual figures representing science and knowledge surrounding a large golden candelabra. The town's liberal mayor made sure his audience grasped the symbolic point: "The light on our streets, which from now on will turn night almost into day . . . calls to mind . . . the emancipation of conscience from every kind of unworthy confinement."[17]

The liberal regimes in both Austria and Hungary mobilized words, rituals, clothing, public art, architectural styles, and redesigned civic spaces to transform their visions of modernity into the stuff of everyday life for their citizens. This was an essential part of the political re-education—or emancipation—of men and women who must be trained, paradoxically, to accept their new freedoms and prepared eventually for their future right to vote.

Crusades

In the fall of 1870 as Laurence Cole tells us, a school inspector charged by the regime with ensuring local compliance with the new liberal education laws set out to assess conditions at a schoolhouse in the South Tyrolean village of St. Peter im Ahrnthal. When he arrived in the village, however, he found the school entrance barred by an angry crowd yelling that "this Lutheran fiend" would not be allowed inside. What accounted for this spontaneous rebellion to defend the local school against the liberal gift of enlightenment? And why was a Catholic inspector tarred as a Lutheran fiend?[18]

In the previous weeks the prince bishop of nearby Brixen/Bressanone had forbidden local clerics from cooperating with the new system of school inspectors and encouraged local priests to speak out against the laws from the pulpit. This gave local parents in this agricultural region who opposed much of the new school law for practical reasons—its eight-year requirement robbed them of valuable child labor at the harvest—license to vent their opposition using language and symbols provided for them by an increasingly militant Catholic Church. The reference to Luther derived in part from the ongoing refusal by Tyrol's political and clerical leaders to recognize the government's legalization of Protestant communities and their strategic association of liberalism with Protestantism in their sermons.

Several Burgher Ministry initiatives sought to transform the relationship of organized religion to family life and primary education. In 1868 three so-called May Laws decisively altered the public role of the Catholic Church in Austria by transferring jurisdiction over marriage, burial practices, and record-keeping from local parishes to civil authorities and by creating the option of civil marriage for Austrians of different faiths. The three laws also confirmed the equality of all recognized confessions—including Judaism—and transferred oversight of the school system and its curriculum from the Catholic Church to the crownland governments.[19] The laws evoked bitter opposition from church officials, sympathetic politicians, and often crowds like the one that gathered in St. Peter im Ahrnthal. Many liberals, however, argued that the laws did not go far enough, and they insisted—unsuccessfully as it turned out—on introducing obligatory civil marriage.

A year later, a school law created a new system of public school financing that made the crownland governments and municipalities jointly responsible for building school houses where necessary and for funding teacher salaries. The law required all Austrian boys and girls to attend school for at least eight years. It outlined curricular requirements, the local regulation of the new public school system through elected school boards, and the creation of crownland teacher training institutions and accreditation procedures. Students might attend religious schools as an alternative to the new public schools, but even religious schools had to follow guidelines that included the eight-year attendance requirement and a minimum of classroom hours devoted to secular subjects.

Liberal newspapers jubilantly described the laws as the final victory of an enlightened society over the dark forces of reaction that had kept people "mired deep in superstition, ignorance, sloth, . . . and destitution."[20] To celebrate the passage of the laws, those with liberal sympathies in Vienna illuminated their houses and businesses—a sight that Francis Joseph, on a trip to Budapest, was spared.[21] As one newspaper explained, the laws augured well for a bright future since historically societies always "began to progress at an amazing rate as soon as they freed themselves from clerical tutelage."[22] Not everyone agreed. The laws provoked disapproval from the cabinet's federalist, clerical, and conservative political opponents in Parliament, in many of the regional diets, and in the upper reaches of the bureaucracy. Federalists and conservatives asserted that the crownland diets should have the right to implement a shorter school requirement that took into account the labor needs of local agriculture at harvest time. Having struggled successfully to obtain provincial autonomy for Galicia in the 1860s, Polish conservatives now successfully reduced the school requirements from eight years to six in 1873.[23] But it was Catholic officials and local parish priests especially in the western crownlands (Tyrol, Upper Austria, Salzburg) who fought the implementation of the new laws most tenaciously. In Tyrol, the clerical-dominated diet postponed full implementation of the eight-year schooling requirement until 1892.[24]

The battles over control of education—or indeed over values themselves—coincided with two critical transformations in the international Catholic Church that helped to create popular culture wars out of what might otherwise have remained dry policy debates. The first transformation was a popular revival of Catholic practice and piety that had been underway since the 1840s. In many regions of Europe, including Austria, men's and women's participation in local Catholic associations, pilgrimages (made more accessible by growing railway connections and falling ticket prices), and new forms of popular devotion to Mary, to particular saints, and in the Tyrol, to the Sacred Heart of Jesus, increased dramatically.[25]

Austria's liberals were hardly alone in their increasingly aggressive ideological use of public spaces, invocation of symbols, and in exploitation of popular practices like shooting contests to reinforce their cultural legitimacy. If, as we saw earlier, the liberals of Bozen/Bolzano sought to link their program to Tyrol's popular resistance to Napoleon by organizing a "Shooting Competition of Light," local Catholic activists soon responded effectively in kind. In 1870 the prince bishop of nearby Brixen/Bressanone organized a celebration in Bozen/Bolzano of the Catholic Conservative Peoples' Association in which he pointedly renewed Tyrol's symbolic bond with the Sacred Heart of Jesus—also a potent symbol from the Napoleonic Wars—to mobilize popular support for Catholicism against godless liberalism.[26]

In the 1850s and 1860s Catholic Church officials began a spate of public building of their own, intentionally seeking to reinforce Catholic values among the public. They raised funds to build impressive neo-Gothic churches primarily in new, often working-class neighborhoods of Austria's growing cities. In 1855 the activist bishop of Linz, Francis Joseph Rudigier (1811–1884), about whom we will learn more below, celebrated the popular new doctrine of the Immaculate Conception by planning an enormous new cathedral in Linz that would take seventy years to complete. The new and newly renovated churches that increasingly dotted the suburbs of provincial cities and towns in the countryside sought to reinforce the critical significance of the church to a changing society. They constituted a visible part of what we might call a Catholic revival whose architectural avatar was neo-Gothic. Soon, this Catholic revival produced highly popular Catholic political parties in several Austrian crownlands.

The second critical transformation in the Catholic Church was the international rise of a combative ideology known as "ultramontanism," an aggressively conservative doctrine that emphasized strict hierarchy and asserted the absolute primacy of the pope, both within the Catholic Church and over secular institutions. The essence of ultramontanism was captured in Pope Pius IX's 1864 *Syllabus of Errors,* which condemned, among others, arguments for religious freedom or for the separation of Church and state.[27] In Austria ultramontane ideology took root especially among an activist generation of clergy from modest social backgrounds who dominated seminary society in the 1840s and 1850s and were among the earliest non-nobles appointed to key bishoprics.[28]

As liberals across Europe restructured traditional church state relations to reduce the influence of Catholicism, it was ultramontane priests and bishops who fought this trend most effectively. They deployed an increasingly radical rhetoric of combat in their pastoral letters, local organizations, and especially in new Catholic newspapers. Unlike more traditional church leaders such as Vienna's Cardinal Joseph Rauscher (1797–1875), who preferred to work discretely behind the scenes for change, these activists openly incited popular opinion against the liberal government. They treated the confessional laws as an outright declaration of war on the faith, and—just like their liberal opponents—they would be satisfied with nothing but the complete defeat of the enemy. "For the present ruling class, we want humiliation, comprehensive humiliation" fulminated the Catholic and federalist newspaper *Vaterland* in its declaration of war on liberalism in 1868.[29] These ultramontane radicals understood how key elements of contemporary life—from newspapers and illustrated pamphlets to consumer markets and railways—could serve their ends. In fact, they often used them far more effectively than did their liberal opponents.

In September 1868 the same Bishop Francis Joseph Rudigier who planned the cathedral in Linz published a pastoral letter denouncing the May Laws in explosive terms as "lies." The Upper Austrian government quickly confiscated the letter, indicted the bishop, and placed him on trial. Finding him guilty, the court sentenced Rudigier to fourteen days in jail. In a letter to his son Ernst, Finance Minister Ignaz von Plener explained that the proceedings had been "unavoidable," since the "cabinet had to draw the line somewhere" to demonstrate that "church officials are subordinate to the state." In July 1869, however, the emperor pardoned the law-breaking cleric, thus demonstrating—in Plener's words—just "how little his Majesty agrees with the new laws . . . and how little he actually sympathizes with the present government."[30]

Pope Pius IX condemned Austria's new laws as "destructive, abominable, damnable, absolutely null and void," and a breach of the 1855 concordat.[31] Precisely at this juncture, from December 1869 through July 1870, an ecumenical council that met at the Vatican reached decisions that further enflamed the burgeoning culture war. Not without internal disagreement, the council endorsed a document that declared the pope's word to be infallible on questions of Catholic dogma.[32] Alleging that the assertion of infallibility had changed the legal relationship between the two parties to the treaty, the liberal minister for religion and education used the excuse of the new doctrine to revoke the concordat.[33]

The issue of papal infallibility was hardly as clear-cut as cultural warriors on both sides loudly proclaimed it to be. Most Austrian bishops (including their titular head, Cardinal Rauscher of Vienna) had opposed papal infallibility in an initial vote, and Austro-Hungarian bishops were among the last in Europe to accept the new doctrine. In fact, Croatian Bishop Joseph Strossmayer (1815–1905) was the very last bishop in the world to submit formally to the doctrine. After the decision in favor of the doctrine of infallibility had been taken, many Austrian bishops also argued that it should be applied with discretion to avoid public controversy. Voices of ultramontane bishops like Rudigier's, however, were louder in public debates. They raised the issue as often as possible to incite popular religious feeling against liberalism.

In a pamphlet on papal infallibility Rudigier aggressively asserted that any state laws that contradicted God's laws were nonbinding on Austria's Catholics. "Not only are you not guilty if you do not follow these laws," he wrote, "but it would violate the highest law if you did."[34] These words in turn offered liberals ammunition for their assertions about the corrosive effects of this particular brand of "clerical Catholicism" on public life. If Catholics felt free to ignore certain laws, how could they be reliable citizens? Moreover, asked liberals, who were themselves mostly practicing Catholics, what kind of citizens—really what kind of men—would allow their political views to be shaped unquestioningly by the teachings of the foreign pope in Rome? Certainly not men whose independence of mind and rational use of judgment rendered them capable of making decisions for themselves. Clerical Catholicism, as they called it, offered a refuge for weak-willed half-wits and gullible women, not for independent masculine citizens in a modern age. Austria's survival demanded the subjugation of this culture of Catholicism that threatened the very foundations of the state by weakening its citizens' capabilities and making them dependent on Rome.

Despite their flaming rhetoric, the Burgher Ministry's religious policies were hardly in the same league as the punitive culture war *(Kulturkampf)* policies pursued by Bismarck and his liberal allies in Prussia and the newly united Germany. Unlike the German case, where nationalists often defined German identity precisely in terms of an aggressive Protestantism, the cultural identity of the Austrian state was traditionally bound up with Catholic traditions. Moreover, the vast majority of liberal politicians, activists, and voters in the Austrian half of the dual monarchy were also practicing Catholics.[35]

Clerics like Rudigier made it easy for liberal ideologues to blame so-called "ignorant forces" or "forces of darkness" for undermining their enlightened agenda, but in fact a more complex range of factors undermined the success of liberal policies in Austrian society. At the level of local society, organized popular opposition increasingly prevented liberal legislation from taking root successfully. The kind of incident wherein the crowd had prevented the liberal school inspector from doing his job in that mountain village in the Tyrol and had called him a "Lutheran fiend" was not uncommon in the decade after 1867. In December of 1871—during elections to several of the crownland diets—a deranged young man in the Styrian town of Stainz (population of about 1,500) shot the liberal (and Protestant) mayor. Allegedly, when the local priest had said that "an end must be made of liberalism," this particular parishioner had taken him at his word.[36] The *Neue Freie Presse,* mouthpiece of Viennese liberalism, jumped on this incident, arguing in a long editorial that as long as the empire's elite continued to offer financial support and political sympathy to an institution that showed its gratitude by waging war on the government, such horrifying incidents would become normal.

Besides serving as grist for the liberal propaganda mill, these incidents demonstrated the degree to which opponents of the new liberal church and school laws at the ground level understood the laws in specifically cultural terms. To them the laws often represented an attempt by intrusive outsiders to obliterate local customs and traditions, and they framed their local appeals in precisely these terms. Local Catholics continued to use issues like the school laws or the church's proper role in society as a means to galvanize local opposition to liberalism at election time. They may not necessarily have raised voter participation rates much, which in rural districts often remained below 50 percent in the 1870s, but local activists on both sides traded more intense rhetorical barbs in pamphlets published in editions of 5,000 to 10,000.

During the 1860s and 1870s activists founded newspapers and associations. Starting in 1865, for example, Upper Austrians could read the news and follow the activities of their diet in the liberal *Tagespost*. In January 1869, however, Catholic activists in Upper Austria founded their own daily newspaper, the *Linzer Volksblatt*, whose editor was the choirmaster of the local St. Florian Stift. The *Volksblatt* reported local political issues in a Catholic political framework. Where the *Tagespost* described government policy as a welcome means for creating progress and prosperity in Upper Austria, the *Volksblatt* characterized it as alien to "the people" and as an imposition that would be swept away at the next election, along with liberalism in general.[37] As in much of Europe in the first age of mass newspaper readership, the newspaper one read in Upper Austria came to identify the social values to which one subscribed. Catholic activists in Upper Austria also organized a popular political association, the Catholic Patriotic Casino, to compete specifically with the efforts of the Liberal-Political Association in Linz. The casino founded local branches among rural property owners and quickly gained a much larger membership than its liberal counterpart. It soon ended the monopoly on electoral politics in Upper Austria that the liberal elite in Linz had exercised since the rebirth of constitutional life.[38] The two mental universes, liberal and Catholic, constituted "two imagined communities, with increasingly homogenized ideological structures, separate spheres of schooling, associational life and print media—two quasi-'nations,' existing side by side, but apart."[39]

Limits of Liberalism

Yet another emerging culture war during this period placed the new liberal governing elite at odds with emerging working-class organizations. Their conflict reveals the remarkably narrow limits of the liberal worldview in the 1870s, despite liberals' expansive language. How should working-class Austrians contribute to shaping the empire? How might they participate in the construction and elaboration of the new constitutional order? When early working-class political organizations raised these questions, the Burgher Ministry forcefully shelved them, exiling working-class organizations to an uncertain wilderness of illegality for over a decade. There was little agreement among liberals about working-class activism. In the 1860s some influential liberals took a strong interest in nascent working-class movements and fostered self-help and educational organizations. When these movements outgrew the political limits imagined for them by their benefactors, however, their liberal mentors often withdrew their support.

In 1868 mass working-class demonstrations in Vienna called for universal manhood suffrage and the legalization of trade unions. The cabinet intervened against the demonstrations, this time with the full support of the emperor. In general, the police aggressively monitored and frequently shut down meetings of legal working-class associations. The cabinet also adopted harsh emergency measures to deal with what it perceived to be a growing working-class threat to public order, forbidding demonstrations, censoring workers' newspapers, and dissolving several workers' organizations.

Some liberals warned against using state power to disarm workers' organizations. One liberal Viennese newspaper reminded its readers that government persecution of social democracy today might turn "tomorrow against democracy and the next day it will be liberalism's turn."[40] Nevertheless, the liberal government dealt swiftly and ferociously with the workers. None other than Interior Minister Giskra led the charge, perhaps to compensate for the suspicions he knew the emperor continued to harbor about his own political reliability. Addressing a delegation of workers demanding universal manhood suffrage in May 1868, the tanner's son and former 1848 revolutionary warned his working-class brothers: "Do not think that we will introduce mob rule here in Austria. . . . Just because you were born human beings does not mean that you have any right to a vote. You will earn this right [only] when we see that you have a real interest in it, an interest indicated by your payment of income taxes."[41]

This attitude toward workers—that they should earn the right to participate in the state, but that the state would not pursue active policies to promote their social mobility other than financing public education—could be understood partly as a product of liberal fear. Liberals, after all, needed to consolidate the new order against several powerful and hostile reactionary forces ranged against them before they could even consider expanding that order to include the working classes. Many argued, as the *Neue Freie Presse* did after the workers' meeting with Giskra, that universal manhood suffrage would also benefit only reactionary noble-led parties that could too easily trick the uneducated masses into supporting them.[42]

Most liberals took refuge behind the argument that their own primary school legislation offered the workers the surest route to political maturity and the right to participate in public life. "In a country where the working class can barely read, hardly add, and write even less," opined *Der österreichische Ökonomist* (Austrian Economist) in 1869, "the 'worker question' is more dangerous than in those countries that can boast an intelligent fourth estate." Liberal emphasis on the importance of education sought in part to discourage workers from demanding immediate rights of political participation. How could workers be active politically, when they "first and foremost have to learn things just in order to be able to speak in public?" asked *Der österreichische Ökonomist* in 1869?[43] Education in this case, however, turned out not to mean a simple mastery of skills. It also demanded from workers a full acculturation in the dominant values of liberal society, as the following liberal exhortation suggested:

> Where the church catechism, with its commandments to piousness and renunciation, failed to create happiness and welfare for the entire people, the bourgeois catechism with its commandments of work and appropriate remuneration for work, will be able to serve as a basis. In the humanity-freeing, civilizing power of the new discipline, whether one calls it economics or social science, lies its most important meaning.[44]

Workers required education to become economical and thrifty and to value advance planning. The liberal education program would create a *Volk* of sober householders who knew the value of work and the value of money—eventually.

Negative attitudes toward questions of women's enfranchisement among liberal politicians in both Austria and Hungary reinforce this picture of a surprisingly narrow social formation with very little sense of its own political vulnerability. Educated and property-owning women, after all, could arguably have served as effective political allies to their men, and their numbers were increasing rapidly during this period throughout the monarchy. The possible programmatic enfranchisement of educated middle-class women, however, does not seem to have occurred to anyone before the end of the century. It was certainly not a main goal of the regional bourgeois women's movements that developed during the liberal period (1860–1890) in several parts of the monarchy, from Lower Austria and Bohemia to Hungary and Galicia.[45] These, including Vienna's General Austrian Women's Society (Allgemeiner österreichischer Frauenverein) founded in Vienna in 1893 and led by teacher Auguste Fickert, focused their energies on issues of employment, education, professionalization, pension coverage, and reform of marriage law.[46] Not until after 1900 was the issue of women's suffrage more seriously debated as newer mass parties, from the Austrian and Hungarian Social Democrats to the Czech National Socialists and even some activists in the Christian Social movement began to treat women's suffrage as a possible means to expand their voting bases.

During the 1880s some of the liberal-dominated diets even closed existing loopholes that since 1848 had unintentionally allowed some privileged women in their capacities as business- or landowners to vote in communal or diet elections—albeit through male proxies.[47] Arguing in 1889 that respectable women should be protected from election sites where they would "be exposed to the 'influence terrorism' of our increasingly hard fought elections," Lower Austrian deputy Joseph Kopp—one of Austria's most progressive liberals on other issues—labeled the idea of women's suffrage "completely abnormal."[48] The diets in Carniola and Carinthia abolished women's right to vote in 1884; Styria did so in 1904, and Istria in 1908.[49]

In the very same decade when deputies like Kopp intentionally closed off privileged women's remaining opportunities to vote, they were more than happy to encourage their wives and sisters to work for nationalist causes. Since nationalist organizations in Imperial Austria were legally categorized as nonpolitical associations, women were allowed to join their growing networks in the 1880s as active participants and even to found their own branches. The work accomplished by these women was in fact highly political in several ways, as a glance at the texts of the many speeches they gave in these associations amply demonstrates. Moreover, women played hugely influential roles in raising money for nationalist causes by organizing festivals, selling consumer goods whose purchase benefitted nationalist associations, and doing much of the hard work to mobilize their neighbors for various causes. In ideological terms, however, all of these forms of women's mobilization for nationalist causes could be justified as cultural work that befitted their gender.[50]

From Federalism to Culturalism

The controversial Burgher Ministry collapsed in the summer of 1870, brought down by its members' battle fatigue and their complete alienation of their opponents, who eventually boycotted the Parliament. The Burgher Ministry's brief and convulsive rule had left Austria with several critical political-cultural legacies that other political actors would later perfect for their own purposes, especially nationalists and ideologists of empire. The culture wars of the 1870s did not necessarily weaken the fundamental legitimacy of the empire and the Habsburg dynasty. While liberal and Catholic activists in Austria framed political debates in terms of radically incommensurate values—in fact as battles between cultures—they nevertheless competed to place the empire within their own narratives. Catholics activists cited the traditional relationship between dynasty and church to assert a traditionally Catholic vision of empire. Liberals in turn cited the constitution and the successful new parliamentary regime as signs that the empire had become a tool to promote their enlightened and more secular vision.

We now turn to the activists who most effectively built on this example of translating political programs into culture wars: the nationalists. What constituted a nation in the first place, who belonged to it, and who could speak for it were questions without clear answers in the 1860s. For some—especially in the nobility—the nation remained a historic territorial entity within the empire defined by a privileged elite who periodically bargained with the king over the division and exercise of local power. But as we saw in the years surrounding 1848, a nation could also be constituted from a group of people who shared the same cultural traits, the most important of which by far was a common language. Language use was also traditionally a serious concern to the imperial state, which struggled on occasion to mediate between its need to impose a common administrative language for centralizing purposes and its need to be able to communicate with and educate local populations in their vernacular languages. A fundamental law of 1867 had guaranteed:

> All national groups within the state are equal, and each one has the inviolable right to preserve and to cultivate its nationality and language. . . . In those provinces inhabited by several nationalities, public educational institutions should be set up so that without being forced to learn a second language, those nationalities that are in the minority have adequate opportunity for an education in their own language.[51]

These general promises—well in line with traditional Habsburg practice—inadvertently opened up vast new potential spaces for a politics organized around linguistic difference. Linguistic equality was a long way from being realized in practice, and the constitutional laws served as general statements of principle designed to guide subsequent legislation. Much remained unclear. For example, what constituted a legitimate language as opposed to a dialect? How large did a local linguistic minority have to be in order to obtain linguistic rights in a particular crownland? Depending on how one made the argument, "public educational institutions" could mean anything from primary schools to trade schools to secondary schools to universities.

The state's intent to achieve legal equality of *language use* meant that linguistic practice became an increasingly critical factor in public life as political activists sought to identify potential new voting members for their national communities. If nationalists had to convince speakers of a particular language that they belonged to a larger interregional nation, they also had to convince the state that the nation itself constituted a legitimate actor within the empire. The text of the constitution may have referred to national groups ("All national groups within the state are equal, and each one has the inviolable right to preserve and to cultivate its nationality and language"), but it did not define those groups, nor did it make any provision for ascribing a particular nationality to anyone. The law did not allow national communities to serve as actors themselves in the legal system. Complaints about linguistic mistreatment at the hands of the bureaucracy had to be lodged by individuals or by groups of individuals, but could not be brought by nations. This created a significant and ongoing tension centered on the liberal intent of the law to empower individuals who spoke different languages, its interpretation by the courts, and the ways in which nationalist activists sought to transform its meaning by making national communities into legally recognized actors. Over the years, as Gerald Stourzh and those who built on his pioneering work have shown, Austria's courts and bureaucracy supported broader interpretations of the constitutional promises of language equality.[52] It was often imperial institutions that effectively promoted nationalist causes by handing nationalist parties significant victories and eventually by making nations into legitimate legal actors.

To accomplish their aims, nationalists presumed that people's language use meant that they belonged to a national community. This assumption moved institutional and legal practice away from a focus on the rights of individual speakers of languages and toward a definition that attached rights to whole groups (nations). According to this logic, an individual's right to schooling in a particular language, for example, should be understood as a nation's right to schooling in the national language. But national communities and the individuals who allegedly belonged to them did not always share the same understanding of their needs. One reason for the nationalists' focus on the rights of groups was that individuals were unpredictable and changeable in their choices. Nationalists were especially unwilling to trust that individuals who lived in regions where more than one language was in use would make the correct choices about language use and schooling for themselves and their children. Where nationalists wanted children to attend monolingual schools and not, for example, be exposed to a second or third crownland language, parents often desired the opposite for their children—a multilingual education to facilitate social mobility. Nationalists increasingly sought the power of law to force people to make the right choices.[53]

The nationalist compulsion to control people's choices was itself a product of the ways in which political practice evolved after 1867, and the increasing challenges that a developing mass politics posed to politicians. Political conditions in Austria changed radically between the liberal decades of the 1860s and 1870s and the turn of the century. After 1867 Austria experienced four parliamentary electoral reforms (in 1873, 1882, 1888, and 1897).[54] In 1907 Austria adopted universal manhood suffrage and ended the curial system of voting for parliamentary elections altogether. Instead of being about who had the ear of the emperor, as it had traditionally been, Austrian politics became more and more about who could mobilize more voters. This was especially critical since the terms of the 1867 Settlement made it highly unlikely that an older strategy of attaining greater crownland federalism or autonomy had much of a political future, as the following example illustrates.

A short-lived federalist cabinet under Count Karl Hohenwart (1824–1899) replaced the Burgher Ministry in 1871. This cabinet is notable because of an agreement it negotiated with Czech nationalists and their large landowner federalist allies in Bohemia to end their boycott of the diet and Parliament, and to normalize the political situation in Bohemia. Under the terms of this deal, known as the "Fundamental Articles," the Bohemian Diet would recognize both the 1867 Settlement and the fundamental sovereignty of the Austrian Parliament over a limited number of policy areas (defense, commerce, foreign relations). In return the articles would give Bohemia broad autonomy in domestic policy, make the Czech and German languages equal in the administration, and divide Bohemia into Czech- or German-speaking districts for administrative purposes. Once the Bohemian, Moravian, and Silesian diets agreed to the Fundamental Articles, Francis Joseph would be crowned king of Bohemia and the dual monarchy would become a broader federation.

The effort failed. The Moravian Diet agreed only conditionally to the terms of the articles, and the Silesian Diet rejected them completely. More importantly, however, the newly adopted dualist structure of empire made the Fundamental Articles impossible. According to the 1867 Settlement, the Hungarian government had the power to veto any further structural reforms of the empire. Having achieved what they viewed as independence, Hungarian leaders were not about to share their position with other potential states within the Habsburg Empire. There would be no Austria-Bohemia-Galicia-Hungary.

Where Czech nationalists failed in their bid for Bohemian autonomy in 1871, the established Polish conservatives—unencumbered as yet by any effective opposition to their rule in Galicia either from other social classes or from other nationalists—succeeded in negotiating an informal compromise to their advantage. Polish conservatives sought an autonomous status for Galicia—a revival of an independent Poland—similar to that of Hungary after the 1867 Settlement. Here again it is important to point out that the understanding of nation shared by the Polish notables who negotiated with Vienna was not a popular ethnic-based understanding but rather one that maintained the traditional ruling classes in power. Disappointed Polish politicians in the Galician Diet complained in 1867 that the new dualism "did not award our land as much legislative and administrative autonomy as its historical-political past, special nationality, level and dissemination of culture merits."[55]

While a formal constitutional settlement for Galicia remained out of reach, the Vienna government did allow the diet to polonize fully the crownland administration and to return the higher education system to Polish from German.[56] Vienna also created an official cabinet portfolio for a "Galician minister" in all subsequent cabinets. As a result, conservative Polish politicians from the 1870s onward generally supported whatever government held power in Vienna, which in turn rewarded them with a free hand in Galicia. This arrangement came under pressure at the turn of the century when peasant populists and a significant Ukrainian nationalist movement challenged the power of the narrow establishment politicians in Galicia. Making use of imperial structures to gain nationalist advantage, the Ukrainian nationalist movement turned to imperial institutions for help. Ukrainian nationalists demanded that the central state implement precisely those constitutional guarantees of language use in education and administration that nationalist autonomy had allowed Polish nationalists to ignore for three decades.

Liberal and centralist reactions to the short-lived Fundamental Articles for Bohemia illustrate how political conditions produced more ethnic and cultural understandings of nationhood in the 1870s and 1880s. The centralists—generally German-speaking liberals—argued that increased autonomy for any crownland would severely undermine the universal application of Austria's constitutional laws. They also objected to making the Czech and German languages equal in status in the Bohemian administration, asserting that the Czech language was merely a local language whereas German was interregional and international in its status. Implicitly and explicitly the centralist liberals (in 1871 most did not want to call themselves German nationalists because that would have put them on a par with their Czech nationalist opponents) proclaimed their national culture to be of greater intrinsic value than that of the Czech nationalists. But although they were ready to argue for their civilizational superiority, they did not yet argue that Czechs—really Czech-speakers—were incapable of *becoming* Germans nor that Czechs were somehow fundamentally *different* from Germans. In fact, what these centralist liberals found so problematic—indeed galling—was that although the leading Czech nationalists were highly fluent in German, many having experienced a German university education and some having even published important works in German, yet they still chose to equate the cultural value of their Czech language with that of the German language!

During and after the brief fight over the Fundamental Articles a new kind of German nationalism emerged in Bohemia, one that both reacted to and learned from its better-organized and more experienced Czech nationalist counterpart. It involved a self-understanding of being German that as of 1871 could point to the example of a powerful united German Empire just across Austria-Hungary's northern and western borders. The unification of that Germany created mixed reactions among German-speaking circles in Austria-Hungary. Many praised the victory of Prussia and its German allies over the French, seeing in Germany a dynamic example for German-speakers in the Habsburg Monarchy. They did not share a desire to become part of this new German Empire, but they saw it as a natural ally, and its creation helped many to overcome the bitterness they may have still felt about the defeat of 1866.

In the 1860s the German-speaking men and women in Austria who articulated their nationalism in ethnic terms had referred to themselves as liberals or centralists, but not necessarily as German nationalists. Back then, they had asserted that precisely as Germans they could *not* be nationalists in the way that the Czechs, Hungarians, Italians, or Poles were.

Germans, they claimed, stood above the petty pursuit of selfish, sectarian interests in which those other nationalists engaged. Germans were allegedly the best educated of Austria's peoples, paid the most in taxes, and, as we saw above, believed they shared in the most developed high cultural traditions. Their German identity was inseparable from their sense of constituting Austria's privileged *Staatsvolk,* or "state people." The privilege of being the *Staatsvolk* came at a price, however. It allegedly forced them pursue the interests of the whole state against the interests of any particular region or nation within the empire including their own. And as we saw above, many such centralists could not understand why those who used other languages did not want to join the *Staatsvolk* by learning, speaking, and *becoming* German. Speakers of other languages who did learn German would gain—they presumed—a broader perspective on imperial politics that would lead them to abandon their sectarian pursuit of nationalism.

In Bohemia, however, the Czech nationalist politics of language parity mobilized thousands of Bohemians in demonstrations against the government in the 1860s. This Czech nationalist success placed the German-speaking centralist politicians of Bohemia in a difficult position, forcing them to abandon their privileged *Staatsvolk* mentality for an ethnically defined German nationalism. As Bohemian Diet deputy Karl Pickert explained, not without some bitterness toward the state:

> We [Germans] were always the saviors of the state . . . having always represented the Austrian standpoint, while placing our own national interest in the background. We are constantly at a disadvantage against opponents whose nationalism underlies their point of view. . . . We never speak about [our own] national self-interest, but always fight for the interest of the state.[57]

This suggestion of a radically new way of imagining a German nation in Austria was still controversial in the 1870s. Many German-identified liberal activists remained hesitant to exchange their *Staatsvolk* privilege for an openly sectarian politics of nationalism that might put them on a par with their unworthy opponents. In an 1871 letter to his son Ernst, Ignaz von Plener, formerly Finance Minister in the Burgher Ministry (and a deputy from Bohemia), rejected Pickert's nationalist attitude completely.

Arguing that this nationalist turn was entirely unnecessary ("German nationality in Austria . . . is really not in the least threatened despite the Hohenwart Cabinet"), Plener worried that the pursuit of ethnic nationalism "would create enormous ill feeling towards us [at court] and plenty of material for slander of the liberal party [by its enemies in court circles]."[58]

The liberal Plener worried that his party would lose credibility with the emperor if it stooped to the kind of nationalist sectarianism practiced by its more radical opponents. The nationalist Pickert, meanwhile, urged a different understanding of power when he warned the liberals against taking their own voters for granted. For Pickert and his allies, the people—and their numbers—constituted the future key to political power, not the attitude of the emperor toward the party. But who exactly were their own people? And what exactly was their plight? The possible answers to this question were changing swiftly in the 1870s and 1880s.

Ideology, Populism, and Nationhood

Whereas in the 1870s Austrian and Hungarian politicians began to frame ideological struggles as struggles between cultures, by the 1880s many politicians found themselves under extreme pressure to promote their nationalist cultural credentials above their liberal, conservative, democratic, socialist, Catholic or secular, federalist or centralist beliefs. They spoke more often in terms of cultural values and less often in terms of ideological imperatives. In retrospect this transformation seems to have occurred with breathtaking speed.

In overwhelmingly Slovene-speaking Carniola, for example, parliamentary deputy Dragotin Dežman, writer and curator of the Carniolan crownland museum, had a long history of promoting Slovene nationalist and linguistic causes in Carniola. Politically, however, he had aligned himself in the 1860s with the German liberal parties. He strongly believed in liberal cultural values and in what he called a "brotherly unity" between Slovenes and Germans. In 1873, Dežman was hardly alone in this regard. One deputy elected from Ljubljana/Laibach asserted that "in its overwhelming majority, the population of Carniola is *Verfassungstreu*," a contemporary term meaning "loyal to the constitution" and used by the German liberal parties and their media to describe themselves. In the very same year, Richard Forreger, a German liberal deputy representing the Lower Styrian town of Cilli/Celje, began a speech with the statement "I have the honor to have been elected in a land whose population also consists of Slovenes."[59] Twenty years later, however, Forreger had to fight for his political life against populist challengers who questioned his commitment to the German nationalist cause. Similarly in the 1870s when several self-styled "Young Slovene" liberal nationalist deputies gained election to Parliament, their liberal ideological positions had prevented them from joining the conservative Hohenwart Club, traditional home of Catholic conservative Slovene nationalist deputies. In the 1880s, however, as liberals, these Slovene nationalists found themselves isolated in a political wilderness. There was no available political space left for any liberal group to define itself outside of cultural nationalist terms. Nor was there room for political compromise. Politics was becoming so radicalized around nationalism that it was no longer possible for German- or Slovene-identified deputies to admit tolerance for what was now considered to be the enemy nation.

Newcomers to politics in the 1880s offered vigorous challenges to incumbent politicians precisely on the basis of their more radical nationalist credentials. In Bohemia, a more radically nationalist Young Czech party displaced the Old Czechs overnight in the diet and in parliamentary elections of 1891, only to be challenged themselves a decade later by Agrarians and radical National Socialists. In Galicia peasant followers of the charismatic priest and newspaper publisher Stanisław Stojałowski began effectively to challenge the traditional hegemony of the conservative Polish Club in diet and parliamentary elections in the 1890s.[60] In that same decade in Galicia and Bukovina, radical Jewish nationalists and Zionists challenged the local political authority of conservative Jewish political leaders who traditionally backed the powerful Polish Club.[61] Everywhere the addition of new classes of voters to the rolls in parliamentary elections gave populists opportunities to paint traditional incumbents as self-serving, possibly corrupt, and certainly not sufficiently committed to the pursuit of the nation's interests.

Often the success of populist nationalist campaigns derived from their willingness to use openly anti-Semitic accusations against their political opponents. Many of Austria's new voters viewed the emancipation and integration of Jews into society as a social and cultural threat that should be addressed through legislation limiting immigration or participation in the economy. For a few—such as the radical German nationalist Georg von Schönerer and his followers—Jews posed a racial threat to the German nation. For most others, from Lower Austria to Galicia, accusations of Jewish domination of particular trades fueled anti-Semitic populism. For still others, such as the growing Social Catholic movements in the Alpine lands, Jews offered a convenient symbolic for the general dangers of liberal secularism and unrestrained capitalist development that threatened traditional crafts and traditional cultural values.

In Hungary, where liberalism was politically more entrenched than in Austria and where the voting rolls remained far more limited, anti-Semitism served as a language for the unenfranchised to mobilize locally against the power of the established national elite. In 1895, for example, liberal majorities in Hungary's lower and upper houses of Parliament legislated equality among different religions, making Judaism an accepted religion, and introducing obligatory civil marriage.[62] In response, Hungarian Catholics mobilized many unenfranchised Catholics into local organizations dedicated to opposing or overturning liberal legislation. In 1893 in Komárom, a Danube town of 15,000, a local priest, János Molnár, gathered over 1,300 signatures for a petition demanding that Parliament reject civil marriage. Speakers at a Catholic rally in Komárom also attacked Jews as typical avatars of an irreligious modernity in which usury had replaced feudalism.[63]

The liberal media dismissed the signatories with disdain as ignorant commoners, yet the popularity of such petitions demonstrated the degree to which the unenfranchised were becoming politically active. The liberal media also denounced Catholic activists for undermining Hungarian national unity in the face of challenges from ethnic minorities. Liberal politicians argued that religious equality would encourage "new blood" for the Hungarian nation through assimilation. Yet as Robert Nemes points out, if the culture wars of the 1890s removed the last obstacle in the face of a Hungarian-Jewish symbiosis, it also revived anti-Semitism in politics and everyday life.[64]

At the same time, the broad range of social problems that anti-Semitic campaigners attributed to Jews and their recent emancipation also reflected a complete lack of consensus about the precise nature of a Jewish problem that allegedly threatened Austrian or Hungarian society. Moreover, for the anti-Semitic campaigners and voters who shared more traditional economic and religious animosities against Jews, the new racist ideas of a Schönerer made little sense.[65]

Schoolhouse Activists

The larger question remains, however: How did political nationalism become so thoroughly rooted in local societies? How did nationalism come to offer the only route to politicization and political participation for so many people? Through what mechanisms? Nationalist activists in both Austria and Hungary—very different contexts—located schools as the most critical site for their activism. Schools seemed to offer nationalists unlimited opportunities for the indoctrination of new generations into a permanent commitment to a particular national identification. Schools also offered local populations opportunities for community development and individual social mobility. The two impulses did not always go well together.

In terms of the first concern—the opportunity to capture the next generation for the nation—it is noteworthy that when nationalists sought to expand their movements beyond electoral activism, they turned to activism organized specifically around education and schools. In Austria between 1880 and 1890, Czech, German, Italian, and Slovene nationalists founded school associations with thousands of local branches across the monarchy. Their original purpose was to raise money to support the creation and maintenance of private minority language schools in communities where not enough children spoke the second or minority language to warrant a public school in that language.[66] But while working to prevent the so-called loss of children to the nation, these associations also tried to mobilize as many local people as possible into the national community through the school issue. As these groups expanded, they were joined by other nationalist organizations that sought to strengthen the economic base of minority communities in linguistically mixed regions and to provide job training and even welfare benefits where necessary. But the main focus of activism always remained the school.

In Hungary the relationship of nationalists to the school question functioned very differently than it did in Austria, in part because Hungary was a nation-state, and in part because of differences in the structures and goals of the two school systems. The Hungarian School Law of 1868 required six years of daily school attendance from Hungary's school children, as opposed to the original eight-year requirement in Austria.[67] In contrast to Austria, the 1868 law in Hungary did not establish a state school system but instead built it on an existing system of confessional schools and confessional teacher training institutes (although the communes actually paid for the schools). The Hungarian system foresaw the possible creation of state schools only in places where religious schools did not exist. Unlike Austria, where the constitution guaranteed schooling in one's own language and prevented children from being forced to learn the second provincial language, Hungary practiced language policies of Hungarianization, and schools swiftly became the main site for implementation of these policies. They also became the object of nationalist anxiety, among both Hungarian and minority (German, Romanian, Ruthene, Serb, Slovak) political activists. Thus, the cultural politics of the school system—indeed of the very concept of nationhood—developed differently in Hungary than in Austria.

While in Austria nationalists developed cultural definitions of nationhood that emphasized their differences from each other and authenticity within the national community, Hungarian nationalists looked for ways to make assimilation to the Hungarian nation easier and more likely. For the ruling nationalists in Hungary, knowledge of the Hungarian language was a sign of one's commitment to the Hungarian nation—a nation defined in terms of state belonging, but reflected practically in linguistic competence. Hungarian school policy sought to Hungarianize the minorities by teaching them the national language, but not necessarily by changing their cultural background. For this reason, as Joachim von Puttkamer points out, Hungary was also the first European state to introduce a comprehensive civics curriculum, thanks to its distinctive conceptualization of Hungarian nationhood. This occasionally produced confused or unclear understandings of nationhood. A Romanian language version of the Hungarian civics textbook in 1894 explained the civic dimension of Hungarian nationhood in these terms:

"The state in which we live is called Hungary, but the people, of whom we form a part, is called the Romanian people." Only five years later, however, a revised edition of the same textbook dealt with the question substantially differently, avoiding mention of any state/people distinction: "The state in which we live is called Hungary. Hungary is thus our fatherland that we love with our entire hearts."[68]

The policy created some government ambiguity towards educational institutions in other languages. On occasion the government imposed draconian limits on the very existence of such schools. It crippled Slovak language education in 1874, for example, by closing down the Slovak-language secondary schools founded in the 1860s. The following year, for good measure, it also shut down the Matica Slovenská, the Slovak national cultural and scientific center in Turčiansky Svätý Martin, founded in 1863. In 1879 a new law made the teaching of Hungarian a required subject in all primary schools in Hungary. "Pupils will be able to acquire the language in speech and writing by the time they leave school," decreed the minister of education and religion in that same year. Twenty-three years later another minister formulated the government's goals for the law more precisely:

> The sole and supreme goal of Hungarian language teaching in primary schools is that children with non-Hungarian mother tongue can acquire Hungarian speech to a degree to be able to express their thoughts in it clearly, in conformity with their circumstances of living.[69]

The study of Hungarian was to take place during the weekly hours formerly devoted to "Mother tongue" and "writing and reading," leaving almost no time for study of the mother tongue if it was not Hungarian. Counting in mathematics classes should also take place in Hungarian. Geography, history, and citizenship classes in Hungarian soon followed in 1902. Already in 1882 the government had made knowledge of Hungarian a requirement for a teacher's degree; those who had degrees but who did not know the language were given four years to learn it. In 1907, when the more radically nationalist opposition parties came to power, they responded to the demands of their constituents by passing the so-called Lex Apponyi, which required teaching for the first four years of schooling to be carried out solely in Hungarian.[70] This law too had catastrophic effects on what remained of minority language schools in Hungary.

Still, even the Lex Apponyi constituted more of a political concession to the demands of nationalist politicians than an effective intervention in educational policy. As one socialist expert on education noted,

> If the forces active in life come into conflict with the ones active at the school, the impact of the school will be minimal. . . . As long as the family and the social, religious, and communal institutions speak Romanian, the teaching of Hungarian at the primary school will not bring better results than it does today.[71]

Oskár Jászi also considered the law to be utterly ineffective in peasant society, arguing that

> even if in each village . . . the primary school would be a model cultural institution—instead of being a crowded classroom in the hands of one or two underpaid, overworked, and poorly prepared teachers—; still the forcibly applied Hungarian language of instruction would only teach the children a few sentences in Hungarian which life would soon make them forget.[72]

The government simply did not have the money to create effective Hungarianization programs through the schools, and as both radical Hungarian nationalists and left-wing critics pointed out, four years of primary schooling was hardly enough time to teach even pupils from Hungarian-language backgrounds literacy in the language, much less pupils from other language backgrounds.

In the late nineteenth century it was often associations of Hungarian teachers who taught in the multilingual regions of the northeast, east, or south that pressured the government to apply stricter laws to the education system. In 1883 an Upper Hungarian Magyar Education Society was founded to promote Hungarianization of education in Upper Hungary, along with a comparable organization for Transylvania in 1885.[73]

In sum, opposite dynamics steered nationalist activism with regard to schools in Austria and Hungary. In Austria mass mobilization and greater democratization of the political system motivated politicians and organizers to adopt more radical positions in order to outflank opponents within their national communities. The more people gained the vote, the more politicians turned to nationalism to forge unity out of social diversity. Politics in Austria centered on activists' ability to found and maintain minority schools to save children (future voters) who might otherwise be lost to their nation. The government maintained an attitude of neutrality, taking over the funding of minority schools only when those schools achieved the requisite numbers of pupils. In Hungary, however, governments responded to the nationalism of their highly limited voting constituencies by pursuing policies to demonstrate their commitment to achieving greater Hungarianization. In Austria nationalist organizations themselves had to mobilize thousands of people and raise millions of crowns to bear the ambitious costs of their cause: building minority schools. They developed an ever-expanding series of strategies to mobilize new members and raise more funds. They sold consumer goods, they organized informal boycotts, they published guidebooks to funnel tourist business to co-nationals, they published magazines, they commissioned studies, and as we will see below, they used the tools offered them by the decennial census for their endeavors. In Hungary nationalist associations promoted Hungarianization, but they functioned as much to lobby the government as to achieve goals outside of government.

The proliferation of nationalist social and cultural associations in Austria and Hungary also took place in rural and poorer regions such as Galicia and Bukovina in Austria and Transylvania in Hungary. In these regions, however, activists' goals differed somewhat from those promoted by their counterparts farther west. In Galicia and Transylvania nationalist organizations emphasized the necessary educational advancement of the nation—and by extension, social mobility for the individual—rather than basing their policies on fears of losing or gaining members for the nation. Clubs to promote literacy sought to persuade peasants that education could bring them and their children the possibilities of real social mobility and a higher level of prosperity. As early as 1861 in Hungary, for example, a group of Romanian-speaking priests (Greek Catholic and Orthodox), teachers, notaries, and lawyers founded the Transylvanian Association for Romanian Literature and the Culture of the

Romanian People (*Asociațiunea Transilvană pentru Literatura Română și Cultura Poporului Român*, or ASTRA). ASTRA sought primarily to increase literacy among Romanian-speaking peasants by founding small lending libraries, organizing local educational lectures, and supporting Romanian language teachers. Given the narrow social base of educated Romanian-speaking activists, their highly limited financial resources, and especially the constraints placed on their activities by the dominant Hungarian-language press and society, which often saw them as treasonous, ASTRA did not grow appreciably until the 1890s.[74]

In his richly nuanced history of local life on the Hungarian borderlands, Robert Nemes's account of ASTRA activism demonstrates how rarely conditions on the ground fit the nationalist generalities propagated in the metropole. When ASTRA's central committee held its annual convention in Transylvania's Bihor County in 1898, the county's Hungarian press praised the organization's work. Not only did one Hungarian newspaper describe the members as "sober-minded, Romanian-speaking, but Hungarian citizens"; it also went on to explain how ASTRA's activism advanced "the progress of our Hungarian homeland." In Budapest, by contrast, a Hungarian-language newspaper attacked the same meeting as "a Romanian demonstration" that involved people who "regularly trample the Hungarian flag in the mud."[75] There were, in fact, many voices in educated Hungarian society that rejected the kind of knee-jerk reactions of Hungarian nationalists against the cultural activism of minority activists. In 1907, for example, radical poet Endre Ady (1877–1919) used the premier of a Romanian-authored play translated into Hungarian as an opportunity to argue that greater respect be accorded to Romanian cultural aspirations.[76]

In 1880 the Austrian crownland of Galicia counted one school per 2,089 inhabitants, compared to the rest of Austria, which boasted almost twice as many schools per inhabitant. In Bohemia, for example, the number was 1,136. In Tyrol it was 565. Moreover, in Galicia only 49.1 percent of Galician school-aged children actually attended a school, while in the rest of Austria the number stood at 95 percent. These figures were even worse for the eastern districts of Galicia, which were inhabited primarily by Ukrainian-speaking Ruthene peasants of the Greek Catholic religion. The crownland administration in Polish conservative hands had no incentive to promote education among this population, and when it did promote education, it often did so for the purposes of achieving their polonization. Although Ukrainian-speaking parents—like parents elsewhere in Austria and indeed in much of Europe—wanted to use their children's labor at key times of the school year, parents in East Galicia did not necessarily oppose education. After all, the century-long struggle with local lords over the customary use of common lands had taught some peasants the value of an education and the ability to be able to read documents.

Another problem facing Ruthene nationalists was that once peasant children did gain access to education and finished their required six years of schooling, they often forgot what they had learned. The challenge was not simply to create more Ruthene or Ukrainian-language schools, but also to reinforce practices of literacy long after boys and girls had left those schools. In 1867 activists founded a Ruthene nationalist reading society, Prosvita, precisely to encourage pupils to continue literacy practices after the end of their formal schooling. The group's membership grew very slowly in the 1870s, but picked up more rapidly in the 1880s and 1890s. By 1914, there were over 3,000 such clubs.[77]

In Prosvita's publications, rural activists repeatedly narrated their encounters with local skeptics, especially older peasants who rejected their efforts by claiming that "our fathers didn't read and didn't listen to newspapers, and they lived," or "I won't be eating bread from it," or "Am I a lord, that I should read a newspaper?" In response, Prosvita's proponents painted an optimistic picture of steady advance in their publications. In the mid-1880s they claimed that "today more and more people in our land are beginning to read newspapers and books. Before long they'll be laughing at anyone who doesn't read." Many activists also related their work to a new self-consciousness of living in a time of rapid change:

> Shame on you, gentlemen that you are so ignorant! You appeal to the example of your fathers and grandfathers, that somehow they lived, even though they didn't read newspapers. Why, in those days there weren't even any schools, there were no telegraphs and no railways. . . . But today everything has changed, because the world does not stay in one place, but moves forward, and whoever doesn't move forward with it will fall by the wayside.

These activists in Galicia made their knowledge of peasant conditions and peasant activism in other parts of the empire an explicit part of their appeal: "Why are Czech and German peasants so much better off than we are?," they asked. Because "they are all literate and enlightened; each of them, either by himself or together with someone else, receives a newspaper; and it is very rare to find a house without a newspaper or booklets."[78]

Empire, Nation, and the Census

In the 1880s both the Austrian and Hungarian states' different institutional focus on language use gave nationalists new statistical ways of thinking about nationhood.[79] Starting in 1880, both states added critical questions to their decennial census that asked about people's linguistic practices.

In Hungary the census became the primary means with which to measure and evaluate the progress of Hungarianization policies. Given that Hungarian-speakers made up less than 50 percent of Hungary's population (46.6 percent according to the 1880 census), it certainly constituted an ambitious goal to define Hungarian nationhood in terms of language use. In fact the first census the Hungarians took after the 1867 Settlement avoided the question of language use altogether, "out of political prudence."[80] In 1880 the census form asked respondents to list their mother tongue. However, by "mother tongue" they did not necessarily mean the language spoken by the respondent's mother or even, as Ágoston Berecz points out, one's first language. In 1900 and 1910 the Statistical Office qualified the question about mother tongue, describing it as the language that "the respondent considers his own and which he speaks the most fluently and freely." After the 1910 census, policymakers argued that Hungarianization education policies were showing success, since almost 55 percent of Hungarians now claimed Hungarian as their mother tongue. However, it is impossible to know how much of this change to attribute to other issues such as reproductive rates of different populations or rates of migration and emigration. Nevertheless, the degree to which the policymakers and politicians focused on education as the key is reflected in the fact that unlike the Austrian census, the Hungarian census also asked about the respondent's knowledge of other languages. This became another way to document the relative progress of Hungarianization.[81]

In Austria, the allocation of public resources increasingly demanded that the state have accurate knowledge about local language usage. By allowing nationalists to measure and plot geographically both the alleged growth and decline of their imagined national communities, however, the census data itself shaped nationalist ways of conceptualizing nationhood and its territorialization. In Austria the census also provided nationalists with incontrovertible statistical evidence to support their demands for schools in a minority language. This was especially the case after Austria's Supreme Administrative Court ruled in 1884 that communities must provide a school in a particular language if forty or more school-aged children who spoke that language lived within a two-hour walking distance of the local schoolhouse.[82]

For nationalists, however, there was a catch to the Austrian state's intention to measure language use among its peoples. Despite nationalist demands, and despite different practices in Hungary, the state did not ask people to report their "mother tongue" or "nationality" on the census form. Instead the Austrian state invented a special term for the census: "language of daily use." This term downplayed the idea that language use determined identification and instead emphasized language as an instrument of communication. It diminished the claim made by so many nationalists that their nations were the fundamental building blocks of the state. The state also left the determination of what language to report up to the individual—or rather to the male head of a household. Husbands might in fact report different languages for their wives according to this formula—as often happened—and people might change their language of daily use from one census to the next.[83]

Nationalists could not easily discipline people to report what they considered to be the correct answer about language use on the census, often because nationalist presumptions about social life contradicted local experience. For members of some families, identifying oneself in terms of a single language made little practical sense. Some people used diverse languages every day in different situations (family versus commerce); some sought social mobility for their children through bilingualism; some moved from place to place for work, often finding themselves forced to learn a new language in order to survive in their new home. In his well-known memoir, itinerant Austrian factory worker Wenzel Holek, who spoke both Czech and German, observed on his arrival at a glass factory in 1904 that "I got off my bicycle, exhausted [from the trip across the border], listened, and heard Polish, Russian, Czech, and German altogether."[84] This was not an uncommon experience for industrial workers across Europe. Using the term "nationality" to refer to speakers of different languages, Holek nevertheless documented the many ways in which a kind of multilingual normalcy shaped even intimate living arrangements among workers themselves. "The international character of the factory meant that it was not uncommon to find three nationalities together in one apartment," he noted. Holek's sister presided over a household that functioned bilingually in both Czech and German.[85]

Nationalists in Austria, however, did their best to depict the world in terms of mutually exclusive nations whose members' authentic identity and cultural differences from others were reflected in their language use. Activists fought vigorously to make the decennial census into a public display of nationalist loyalty. In towns and villages across the empire, every ten years nationalist agitators resorted to every trick of their trade, scouring every corner of a locality to ferret out those who could possibly report the correct language of daily use. They held public rallies, distributed examples of census questionnaires, and published pamphlets, all designed to obtain maximal support among the local public. Their activism extended to local municipal governments, which increasingly attempted to tilt the census procedure in their own nationalist interest.[86] Once the results were published, nationalist organizations examined them intently: Where had their numbers expanded in the past decade? Where had they declined? Where might they devote their resources most effectively to raise their numbers? The answers to these questions shaped nationalist political strategies, particularly in linguistically mixed frontier regions.[87]

The answers to these questions also produced yet more questions of a sociological nature. How, for example, should expansion or decline of language use in a given region be explained? In cases where labor migration was responsible for expansion or decline, did migrants like Wenzel Holek eventually give up speaking their former language when they moved to a region where it was not spoken? If so, what political or social strategies might prevent this kind of surrender from taking place? Conversely, what about people in mixed-language regions who could communicate to some extent in more one language? Could they be recruited to join one or another nation? What strategies could be used to prevent such people from switching sides—that is, from changing languages or nations?

Nationalists in Austria developed their own answers to these questions, but we must be wary of adopting their understandings of human behavior. In studying nationalism during this period, it helps to avoid seeing people as belonging consistently to one or another defined nation in the way that nationalists did. Instead, we might think more fruitfully in terms of the various situations or events that drove people to identify with one national group or another. Even these identifications did not always last for long. During hard-fought election campaigns, for example, or when the census was taken, people might be galvanized to support a particular nationalist position. But at other times the issue of nationalism may have made little difference in their lives. For the same reasons it also helps to approach questions of identification by thinking more in terms of particular practices that expressed feelings of loyalty or commitment rather than in terms of people's fixed identities.

"Stirring Times in Austria"

One problem for historians is that nationalists' occasional mobilizations of large numbers of people for specific issues made it easy for them to claim that they did indeed speak for existing nations.[88] This in turn makes us more likely to focus on numbers and less likely to see the situational or contextual element influencing nationalist identification. When on 5 April 1897, for example, Prime Minister Count Casimir Badeni (1846–1909) issued language ordinances for Bohemia that mandated equality of the Czech and German languages for the inner civil service, German nationalists throughout the empire argued that the decision affected German speakers' life chances everywhere, not simply in Bohemia. A stunning political crisis ensued as popular demonstrations and riots protested against the law for over a year in several cities, including

Count Casimir Badeni (1846–1909), former governor of Galicia and prime minister of Austria. Badeni's language ordinances unleashed popular protests both within and outside of Parliament. His inability to control the political situation led to his resignation as prime minister in 1897. English engraving after a photograph by J. Henner, 1895. Credit: Private Collection/© Look and Learn/Illustrated Papers Collection/Bridgeman Images.

in Prague, Graz, Salzburg, and Vienna. German-speaking municipal governments in Bohemia, Moravia, Silesia, and the Alpine lands vigorously opposed the ordinances. Egged on by the press, political parties that represented German-speaking regions scrambled to outperform each other in demonstrating an unshakeable nationalist commitment to their voters. Parliament swiftly became unmanageable. Badeni prorogued the Parliament on 2 June, but this did not still opposition.[89]

The media competed to present the stakes of the controversy in as powerful and pathetic a light as possible. One high—or low—point of this campaign came in a report published in the *Deutsche Volkszeitung für den Neutitscheiner Kreis.* On 12 May a headline titled "The Language Ordinances' First Sacrifice" recounted that twenty-three-year-old Karl Buchmann had committed suicide in his parents' apartment, using a hunting rifle. According to the newspaper, the young man, who knew only German and no Czech and who had been seeking a civil service position, feared that under the new laws he could never be employed.[90] Things were just as bad at the level of high politics. When the new parliamentary session opened in September, radical German nationalist Karl Hermann Wolff (1862–1941) insulted Badeni, and the two even fought a duel.[91]

The government was under pressure from the emperor to pass the decennial Settlement agreement with Hungary before the end of the year. Those who opposed Badeni's language ordinances, however, used every tactic they could to obstruct progress on any legislation. Using highly questionable means, the government passed the so-called Lex Falkenhayn to change parliament's order of business. This law allowed it to use force to void the most effective of the interruptive tactics, which it did. The Lex Falkenhayn, however, produced only more violent protest in the streets of Austrian towns and cities. The session of 1897 failed to renew the Settlement with Hungary. Badeni resigned, and his successor, citing paragraph 14 of the constitution, ruled by decree.

The Badeni crisis constituted a critical point in Austrian parliamentary history, but it did not necessarily prove the failure of Austria's institutions. Instead, it demonstrated the degree to which far more people were successfully mobilized into the Austrian political process. The people who protested and rioted did so because they saw contemporary events very much in terms of their own interests. They demonstrated in cities and towns whose institutions would have been untouched by the new language laws. They were not revolutionaries seeking to bring down the regime as in 1848. They were new participants in the parliamentary process who believed that the actions of Badeni—or the reactions of his opponents—threatened to undermine the entire system. Politicians could now call upon their support when necessary. At the same time that demonstrators in Graz or Salzburg protested against a law for Bohemia, it is also true that inside Bohemia the course of events relativized the importance of Vienna for both Czech and German nationalists, thereby making Bohemia a kind of imperial center.[92]

Was the ongoing parliamentary crisis provoked by the language ordinances—the filibustering, the obstruction, the noise-making—a sign of
the fundamental failure of parliamentary government in Austria? Some
historians have pointed out that after a crisis like this, plenty of negotiating proceeded behind the scenes, well out of public view. As Lothar
Höbelt argued, nationalists who could not be seen speaking to each other
in public were nonetheless anxious to maintain a system that gave them
power and influence.[93] The Badeni language ordinances—as necessary as
they might have been to the proper functioning of public life in Bohemia—
could not simply be legislated. They were interpreted as an unfair attack
on the rights of one nation. The same outcome could only be negotiated
among the parties, not legislated over their heads.

This was one recognition that followed the turbulent events of
1897–98. Both the emperor and his high bureaucratic advisors experienced first-hand the extraordinary degree of instability that political
movements—in this case nationalist ones—could produce in public life.
In consequence they sought negotiated solutions to diffuse the mobilizing power of political nationalism. In the next decade they supported
and encouraged attempts by regional political actors to forge structural
compromises that they hoped would remove nationalist issues from the
political arena. In 1905 the first of three such national compromises came
into being in Moravia. The Moravian Compromise divided the Moravian
Diet into Czech, German, and large-landowner voting groups, which
meant that Czech, German, and large landowner voters now voted separately from each other (large landowners seemingly had no nationality).
The school system was divided as well between Czech and German
options, as were several other cultural and economic areas of legislation.[94]
Similar principles underlay the Bukovina Compromise in 1910 and the
Galician Compromise in 1914, although local conditions and concerns
gave each a distinctive shape.[95]

The Badeni crisis also made the emperor far more open to those who
argued that universal manhood suffrage might also diffuse the power of
nationalism by empowering interregional parties like Christian Socials
or even Social Democrats, which focused on broad social and economic
concerns that applied to all of Austria. Finally, to return to the point made
at the outset of this section, the Badeni crisis offers a classic example of

event-driven or situational nationalism. For a few months, the crisis galvanized thousands of people to support a nationalist position actively and to express their position in the streets. Yet this mobilization depended very much on the specifics of the moment. Within a few years interest in nationalist issues—as measured, for example, in membership numbers of nationalist organizations—actually declined. The challenge that nationalist activists could never completely solve was how to keep people in a constant state of excitement about nationhood.

The compromises did offer activists new legal and administrative means to force people to become national, even as it also threatened to remove the burning relevance of nationalism from daily life. In Moravia, for example, citizens had to register as part of the Czech or German group. They did not have the option of identifying themselves as "Austrian" or "Catholic" or "Habsburg loyalist" (some of the options people attempted), nor could they change groups. In Moravia, the compromise divided and duplicated most government functions and services (including voting) between separate Czech and German populations. Nationalists in Moravia also added a law that attempted—not always successfully—to prevent people from sending their children to schools in the language of the "wrong" nation.[96] When people found themselves coerced, they often took their cases to the courts. In the few crownlands that had negotiated national compromises, however, the courts were increasingly bound to support the claims of nationalist groups against the desires of individuals. Here the liberal constitutional guarantee of language rights to the individual gradually became transformed into the right of the national community over its members. This steady legal transformation was the culmination of cultural arguments that had long maintained first, that an individual had a fundamental and authentic national identity, and second, that the cultural gulf between national communities was unbridgeable.[97]

The Empire's Unity in Diversity

Amid growing public discussions of cultural diversity and its nationalist political implications, the dynasty sought renewed legitimation by touting the benefits that imperial unity conferred on its many peoples. Building on strategies we have already encountered in Karl Czörnig's three-volume *Ethnography of the Austrian Monarchy* (1855–1857), the regime celebrated the diversity of its peoples in its own terms, casting this diversity as a strength that benefited all its citizens. In popular geographies and scientific publications, in anthropological exhibitions, in folk art, and in public architecture, the imperial regime articulated a vision of empire meant to reinforce a popular sentiment for unity among its culturally diverse peoples.

When in 1866 Austria lost its traditional political hegemony in Germany, the liberal empire sought a renewed sense of mission in Europe. In the 1870s the exploration of cultural diversity seemed to offer the foundations for a renewed Habsburg civilizing mission directed specifically to eastern and southeastern Europe, including the Balkans. In its earliest incarnation, this new mission for the empire focused its civilizational energies on the existing crownlands of Galicia and Bukovina. Two symbolically important events, the Vienna World's Fair of 1873 and the founding of a university in Czernowitz/Cernăuţi/Cernivci in 1875, offered early elaborations of Austria-Hungary's new civilizational mission to the east and of its ideology of unity in diversity.

On 1 May 1873, Francis Joseph opened the only one of the great nineteenth-century world's fairs to be held in Vienna. The fair was an ambitious undertaking located in Vienna's Prater Park, which had been expanded and rebuilt for the occasion. Covering almost 600 acres, an area five times greater than the Paris Exposition of 1867, the fair's main attractions were housed under a towering steel rotunda some 262 feet high and 354 feet in diameter. The rotunda's size alone made it a miracle of modern technical achievement and an object of speculation among skeptical Viennese who predicted that such a heavy structure would collapse or at least sink into the ground. Inside the rotunda twenty-five countries displayed scientific and cultural wonders, while outside, an additional 194 pavilions, many erected by private companies, housed further exhibits.

In the presence of visiting royalty and local dignitaries, the emperor's brother Archduke Carl Ludwig asserted at the gala opening that the fair would "ensure the recognition of the participation of our fatherland in the promotion of the wellbeing of mankind through work and instruction."[98]

The grand entrance to the Exhibition Palace with rotunda at the Vienna World's Fair, 1873. English engraving for *The Illustrated London News*, 31 May 1873. Credit: Private Collection/© Look and Learn/Illustrated Papers Collection/ Bridgeman Images.

His speech foregrounded particular values of the age—human prosperity achieved through work and education—which liberals believed distinguished their system of values from the values of their aristocratic, religious, or nationalist rivals.

Yet, the world's fair made more claims to Austria's distinctive role than Archduke Carl Ludwig's testimony to cultural and technical accomplishments suggests. The technological marvels that made up the exhibitions were understood specifically as cultural attainments of the individual exhibiting states. By displaying these cultural attainments next to each other, the organizers invited the visitor to compare the achievements of the participating states. How would Austria-Hungary compare to its contemporaries when it came to technological advances? Moreover, the fair's organizers sought actively to cast Austria-Hungary as a cultural bridge between East and West, both through the exhibition's spatial arrangement and in the content of the individual exhibitions. Separate Austrian and Hungarian displays sat at the very center of the fair, directly under the rotunda, along with those from Germany. Russia, the Ottoman Empire, Persia, China, and Japan could be found in the east wing of the building while exhibitions from Britain, France, Italy, the United States, and Brazil made up the west wing. This arrangement appeared to reinforce a growing consensus among journalists and the political classes that Austria-Hungary's new, post-1866 role was to mediate between West and East. Having failed in its efforts to unify Germany under its auspices, the empire turned east for legitimation, reviving Austria's historic role as a bulwark of the Christian West against the Ottoman Empire in order to portray itself as the civilizer of the East. Of course the Chinese, Japanese, and Persian textiles that Westerners viewed at the fair suggested that Eastern civilization had attained a high level, and consumer demand for those textiles and other collectibles tended to confirm that view. Still, contemporaries generally understood differences between points on the compass in terms of different degrees of civilization: the order of the exhibitions suggested that a more civilized west and north could transfer useful knowledge and culture to the less civilized east and south. The press interpreted Western exhibits as more technically advanced and thus deemed them to be culturally more civilized and valuable.[99]

It would have been difficult for Austro-Hungarian visitors to the fair—especially the urban among them—not to transpose this broad civilizational model from the points of the globe to the geography of their own empire. Two decades before, Austrian ethnographers like Czörnig had argued that significant differences in educational or cultural levels within the empire derived largely from differing social conditions and not from innate racial or national differences. In 1873, however, as Matthew Rampley has recently argued, displays of diverse styles of farmhouses from across central and eastern Europe at the fair allowed for other possible impressions about the meanings of cultural differences. On the one hand, the catalog explanations continued Czörnig's tradition, attributing differences in peasant cultures to regional economic conditions and peasant adaptations to them. Yet many observers of the fair offered other possible explanations for differences—particularly as the apparently much more highly civilized western German peasant homes compared to the eastern Moldavian or Galician structures that many

Exhibition of agricultural products from Galicia at the Vienna World's Fair, 1873. Credit: Österreichische Nationalbibliothek.

journalists described as backward, unhygienic, and downright medieval. For their part, some reporters for Galician and Romanian newspapers took offense at the depiction of their peasant cultures, arguing that the displays portrayed Galicia and its people in a poor light, as culturally backward compared to the West.

The complex possibilities inspired by the fair's exhibitions simultaneously undermined and reinforced a range of beliefs about hierarchic differences among societies. If Western states could bring the benefits of civilization to Easterners who wanted to learn, then Easterners (as Czörnig had suggested) were at base fundamentally no different from westerners. Liberal German or Hungarian nationalists who saw themselves as a *Staatsvolk* also argued that anyone could become German and Hungarian—that is civilized—by learning their language and partaking of German or Hungarian high culture. And yet the very discourse of civilizational differences also reinforced the opposite impression at the fair—namely, that the East required civilizing, that its peoples were fundamentally different from those of the West, and that ultimately they could never become like those of the West.

As it turned out the fair was not an international triumph for Austria-Hungary, but more for commercial reasons than because of its presentation of the empire and its peoples. Almost one week to the day after its inauguration, Austria-Hungary—and most of Europe—was plunged into recession by one of the most terrifying stock market crashes of the nineteenth century. Then in July, an outbreak of cholera in the city killed 3,000, keeping more tourists away. By the time it closed, where 20 million had been expected to visit the Fair, only 7 million people had actually shown up.[100] Nevertheless, the Vienna World's Fair had conveyed to those who had come the possibility that the deeper purpose of empire was to bring Western-style civilization to a backwards East, whether at home in Galicia and Bukovina or eventually abroad to the Balkans, specifically to the Ottoman provinces of Bosnia and Herzegovina, which Austria-Hungary occupied only five years later.

Civilization in Halbasien *and the Crisis of Liberalism*

Austrian and Hungarian liberals in the 1870s still believed for the most part in the perfectibility of different peoples through the application of education and cultural and technical advances. Although their laws, institutions, and administrative practices differed from each other— while Austrian policy promoted the equality of languages and peoples, Hungarian policy promoted the long-term assimilation of people to Hungarians—neither Austria nor Hungary inscribed differences among peoples in their legal or administrative codes.

In Austria, a liberal commitment to human perfectibility through education, combined often with an unquestioned—if condescending— belief in the instrumental superiority of German culture, led to the founding in 1875 of the empire's first new university in fifty years. Where did Austria's liberal government choose to locate this new university named for Emperor Francis Joseph? In Czernowitz/Cernăuți/Cernivci, a town of barely 25,000 inhabitants, capital of Bukovina, statistically Austria's most economically impoverished and illiterate crownland, and the farthest east of all the crownland capitals. Never mind that Czech nationalists had agitated for a Czech-language university to be located in Prague or Olmütz/Olomouc and that Italian nationalists demanded an Italian law faculty for Trieste. Never mind that both Czech and Italian nationalists cited the high levels of literacy and civilization their own "peoples" had allegedly attained to justify their demands. Instead, the liberal government and emperor agreed to found a German-language university in Austria's easternmost crownland, one whose largely illiterate and multilingual population spoke combinations of Ruthene, Romanian, Yiddish, German, and Polish.[101]

The new university was largely the product of relentless lobbying by Constantin Tomaszcuk/Tomasciuc, a noble landowner and liberal parliamentary deputy from Bukovina. Tomaszcuk argued that a new university in the east would serve a powerfully integrative function for the empire:

> Austria's unity rests on the common education of all those who through education have managed to raise themselves above the level of the masses. Over time, this common education, this community of ideas has produced an Austrian political nationality.

Tomaszcuk justified the choice of German as the new university's language of instruction, asserting that in the empire, only "German scholarship can claim universality. And only because German scholarship has a universal meaning do the non-German sons of Bukovina strive for a German university." Against those nationalists who might dispute this choice, he added, "Woe to the nation that has to fear the influence of foreign culture. Such a nation will have already consigned itself to a death sentence."[102] The new university did, however, house Austria's first professorships in the Romanian and Ukrainian languages and literatures.

The inauguration of the Francis Joseph University in October 1875 coincided with celebrations of the centenary of Bukovina's annexation to Austria, as well as with the emperor's 1873 silver jubilee. In an essay titled "Ein Culturfest" (A Cultural Festival) liberal journalist and essayist Karl Emil Franzos (1848–1904) glowingly described the inauguration of the new university specifically as a festival of unity. "The struggling elements

Postcard of the main building of the University in Czernowitz/Cernăuți/Cernivci.
Credit: AKON/Österreichische Nationalbibliothek.

of Bukovina could never have found each other peacefully if one particular factor had not been restlessly at work: Germanness." "Germanness,"
he added, did not "oppress the other nationalities, but instead offered
them a reconciling point of unity."[103]

Franzos was just becoming known at the time as the author of a critically acclaimed set of stories and observations about Jewish life in eastern
Europe. Son of a Jewish physician who had studied in Germany, Franzos
grew up in Galicia and Bukovina and graduated in 1867 from the
German-language gymnasium in Czernowitz/Cernăuți/Cernivci.
After studying law in Vienna and Graz, where he joined the German
nationalist fraternity Teutonia, he wrote for the *Neue Freie Presse* and
the *Pester Lloyd*. In 1876 Franzos published his first collection of
short stories set in the eastern part of the empire, with the telling title
Aus Halbasien (From Semi-Asia). Franzos defined his "Semi-Asia" in
cultural terms as a wilderness that stretched "beyond the Silesian border
and beyond the Carpathians," a landscape where "European education
met Asiatic barbarism, European striving toward progress met Asian
indolence, and European humanity met cruel Asiatic conflict among

nationalities and confessions"[104] Franzos's commitment to German culture as a civilizing and unifying agent is best captured in his story "Schiller in Barnow," in which Schiller's poem "Ode to Joy," read in a small Galician town, brings together a Pole, a Ruthene, and a Jew in a friendship that recognizes their common humanity.

In another of Franzos's essays, "From Vienna to Czernowitz," he described his trip to Bukovina for the inauguration of the new university, detailing the exhausting rail journey through the apparently endless bleak and desolate wastelands of Galicia. The mood changed quickly, however, when the train crossed into Bukovina and arrived in Czernowitz/ Cernăuți/Cernivci. Franzos's account of this arrival mixed natural description with moral observation; the influence of civilization is immediately visible to the discerning eye in the landscape:

> The heath is behind us and in front of us the Carpathian foothills rise to meet the train. We cross the foaming Pruth River into the blessed land of Bukovina. Here, the land is better cultivated and the huts are friendlier and cleaner [than in Galicia]. After an hour the train reaches the station in Czernowitz. Splendidly the town is situated on towering heights.

According to Franzos, the arrival in Austria's eastern-most crownland capital is something of a confounding experience. The evidence of the senses appears to contradict the natural geography of the empire: "Whoever arrives [in Czernowitz] is oddly hopeful [again]: he is suddenly back in the West, where education, culture, and white tablecloths may be found." How to explain this conundrum?

> If he wants to know who created this miracle, he should take note of the language spoken by the inhabitants: it is the German language. . . . The German spirit, this best and most powerful magician under the sun, he—and he alone—has set down this blossoming piece of Europe in the middle of this cultural desert of Semi-Asia![105]

That Franzos could make this journey by train was thanks largely to the efforts of the Lemberg-Czernowitz-Iasi railway company. The company had earned a lucrative concession from the liberal government in 1864 specifically to link the Galician and Bukovinan capitals by rail. Once

View of the main railway station concourse in Lemberg/Lwów/Lviv, first opened in 1904. Designed by architect Władysław Sadłowski in the art nouveau style, this larger station replaced the original gothic style structure built in 1861–1862. Credit: Österreichische Nationalbibliothek.

the line was completed in 1866, it was possible to travel by train from Vienna all the way to Czernowitz/Cernăuți/Cernvici.

In 1871, however, just a few years before Franzos's ecstatic description of crossing the Pruth River, the railway bridge there collapsed. An investigation into this incident as well as several other complaints lodged against the Lemberg-Czernowitz-Iasi Company, revealed that the firm had badly cut corners during the construction of the line. The state sequestered the railway while it investigated the alleged wrongdoing of its board chair, Baron Viktor von Ofenheim. In January 1875 the liberal cabinet charged Ofenheim with corruption. The prosecutor alleged that from the moment of the company's founding, Ofenheim had diverted immense sums to himself, while swindling the stockowners. The state also charged Ofenheim with having set up a board made up of strawmen

Railway bridge over the river Pruth near Jaremcze/Yaremche. Drawing by Karl Jeczmieniowski, 1893, as an illustration for the *Kronprinzenwerk* volume on Galicia published in 1898. Credit: Österreichische Nationalbibliothek.

who exercised no oversight and instead had rubber-stamped every one of Ofenheim's decisions. For their services—or their cooperation—each of these directors allegedly received a payment of over 100,000 gulden.

The trial caused a sensational scandal, revealing the degree to which corrupt practices had quickly become the norm among Austria's liberal ruling class in the 1870s. At the high—or low—point of the proceedings the prosecutor called former Minister of the Interior Carl Giskra to the witness stand. Giskra, it turned out, had added his good name to the board, taken a 100,000 gulden payment, and then failed to fulfill his oversight obligations to the company shareholders. The former minister of the interior and hero of 1848 protested his innocence, but under cross examination, Giskra became flustered and eventually blurted out the trial's most memorable line, referring to the 100,000 gulden, that in Austria it was "customary to accept gratuities."[106]

The jury found Ofenheim not guilty of the charges, largely because he managed to frame the trial as a personal vendetta against him by the minister of commerce. Nevertheless, the larger damage had been done to public confidence, especially since the trial followed swiftly on the heels of the stock market crash of 1873. The crash ruined countless small investors who had been persuaded by the immense profits being made in the early 1870s in a largely unregulated stock market to invest their life-savings and pensions in all kinds of inflated ventures, some of which existed only on paper. The liberal cabinet could do little to aid the victims of the crash, many of whom angrily blamed liberalism for their woes. Between the recession ushered in by the crash and the highly public Ofenheim trial a year later, the public reputation of liberals and liberalism lay in tatters.[107]

In a very short period of time, one might argue, the benefits of liberal civilization had been exposed to serious public doubt at the very center of the empire. In symbolic terms, however, the sordid Ofenheim trial also called into question liberalism's achievements precisely in that site—Austria's east—which allegedly stood to benefit most from the spread of liberal culture. Civilization, it seemed, was not the only gift conferred by the West upon the East. The liberals had also made the East a site of corruption, of arrogant chicanery, and worst of all, of downright failure—a fact that Franzos himself and other observers confirmed in their later disappointed critiques of the education available at the university in Czernowitz/Cernăuți/Cernivci. Liberalism had been revealed as simply one more sectarian political party or set of ideologies that benefited only a part of Austro-Hungarian society at the expense of other parts of society. Liberalism itself could no longer muster mass enthusiasm for its cultural claims.

The mantle of civilization in which liberalism had wrapped itself and in which it had hoped to envelope the East did not go unclaimed. If anything, its civilizational mission to the East and South became an even stronger, generalized, and more popular element of an imperial mission that nationalists, religious activists, elite liberals, and the dynasty could all claim as their own.

The Kronprinzenwerk

Between 1885 and 1907 Austro-Hungarian governments subsidized the publication of a twenty-four volume encyclopedia (twenty-one volumes in Hungary) entitled *Die österreichisch-ungarische Monarchie in Wort und Bild* (The Austro-Hungarian Monarchy in Words and Pictures). Known popularly as the *Kronprinzenwerk* (Crown Prince Project), the effort had been inspired by Crown Prince Rudolf in 1883, who also wrote the introduction to the series before his death in 1889. The state contracted 432 experts to produce essays for two different editorial staffs—one for the Austrian version and one for the Hungarian version—on the flora, fauna, geological character, and ethnography of each crownland. The *Kronprinzenwerk* constituted a scientific attempt to document the geographic and cultural diversity of the monarchy's crownlands for a popular subscription audience. Diversity, however, also becomes a strong justification for the civilizational work of the Habsburg Empire, especially in the anthropological and economic sections of the volumes. There the authors continue the implicit and ambivalent work of the displays at the world's fair a decade earlier. Here, the peoples of the empire are unquestionably culturally different from each other, and not merely in terms of their distinctive forms of dress or adornment. The images of peoples drawn by contemporary artists and analyzed by anthropologists often suggest that the differences are racial in character, especially in the case of the Roma, but also with some Balkan or Eastern peoples.[108] The question remains for the reader whether the empire's ability to foster civilization, economic development, or education somehow makes these peoples ultimately equivalent to each other, as with Czörnig's ethnography we encountered earlier, or whether their cultural differences are insuperable and their human capabilities not equivalent to each other.

The *Kronprinzenwerk* also demonstrated the degree to which scientists in several branches of the natural and human sciences in Austria-Hungary sought to demonstrate an underlying logic common to the far-flung and diverse territories ruled by the Habsburgs even as that territorial quality shaped their research. As the brilliantly creative work of historian of science Deborah Coen demonstrates, whole fields of science owed their particular existence to imperial ways of thinking about space, climate, and weather patterns.[109]

"Administration Is Our Only Politics"

In an 1895 interview with a British newspaper, Benjamin von Kállay (1839–1903), Austro-Hungarian minister of finance and administrator of Bosnia-Herzegovina, characterized his imperial mission there in the following words: "to retain the ancient traditions of the land vivified and purified by modern ideas."[110] "Austria," he added, was "a great Occidental Empire, charged with the mission of carrying civilization to Oriental peoples."[111]

At the end of the 1870s, thanks to a rebellion in the neighboring Ottoman Empire, Austria-Hungary became a colonial power by occupying a piece of Ottoman territory. The resulting thirty-year occupation of Bosnia-Herzegovina provided bureaucrats, ideologists, map makers, technicians of all kinds, teachers, and priests (among others) an unparalleled opportunity to realize Austria-Hungary's new civilizing mission in Europe. At the same time, Austria-Hungary's experiences occupying Bosnia-Herzegovina created a consensus around the liberal civilizational concepts of empire long after the liberal movement itself had faded into political obscurity. Many people also saw in Bosnia-Herzegovina an opportunity to fulfill either their own ambitions or, in the cases of Croat, Serb, and south-Slav activists, to fulfill the ambitions of their national movements.

In 1878, when Austro-Hungarian forces marched into the neighboring Ottoman Empire to quell local uprisings in Bosnia and Herzegovina and to forestall Russian interference, they ended up staying there. The subsequent Treaty of Berlin confirmed Austria-Hungary's right to occupy the two Ottoman provinces. For the next thirty years, Austria-Hungary's joint minister of finance had the task of ruling the colonized peoples of Bosnia and Herzegovina. As expressed in the words of its most famous and vigorous governor above, the occupation of Bosnia and Herzegovina epitomized the principles of liberal colonial empire across Europe in the second half of the nineteenth century.

Explaining in a proclamation to the people of Bosnia that "under his mighty scepter many peoples live together, and all freely profess their faith," Emperor King Francis-Joseph announced that "all sons of the land will enjoy equal rights according to the laws."[112] In doing so, he conveyed a similar message to the one Joseph II had hoped to convey to the peoples of Galicia and Bukovina over a century before. Like those earlier attempts, this colonial project sought both to stabilize and to transform Bosnian society by bringing it the benefits of modern innovations while simultaneously strengthening traditional Bosnian society enough to keep it stable and quiescent. From the start, the colonial project in Bosnia-Herzegovina was supported equally by liberals, Catholic activists, and Slavic nationalist politicians, all of whom saw the occupation as beneficial to both Bosnia and the empire but for very different reasons. The invasion, according to one Catholic politician, had "promoted the cause of humanity and civilization" by creating a "productive peace." Another Catholic activist published a work entitled "How Can European Culture Be Implanted in Bosnia?" One Slavic nationalist deputy from Dalmatia asserted that only the idea of a civilizing mission could justify the occupation.[113]

All the benefits of civilization, from legal equality to education to technical modernity, would be bestowed on these wards of empire—of course, at a sensible rate and not too high a cost. At the same time, Austria's proven ability to treat all linguistic and religious groups even-handedly would demonstrate the superiority of the liberal Habsburg multinational ideal over ethnic nationalism as the best vehicle for progress.[114] The effective transmission of a civilizing mission to Europe's East, understood in economic, social, legal, and cultural terms, represented the culmination of a transformed Austrian imperial idea whose role now officially included the export of its work beyond its own borders. The Habsburg idea had traditionally been universal in its pretentions, although aimed at central Europe. In the 1870s, as we have seen, it became an argument for spreading European values to the East. Bosnia-Herzegovina may actually have been located to the south of Austria-Hungary, but in terms of mental maps it lay well to the East.

An army of administrators preaching a liberal colonial message of social modernization and cultural equality to their new subjects followed the Austro-Hungarian army units across the Sava River into Ottoman Bosnia. There they immediately set about interpreting Bosnian society's needs through a lens often framed in liberal presumptions and principles. One challenge for Bosnia's new administrators was how to treat the linguistic and religious diversity they encountered there. In religious terms the local population divided into 40 percent Eastern Orthodox, 35 percent Muslim, and 25 percent Roman Catholic. In linguistic terms all of these groups spoke the same language. In social terms the population was largely agrarian, with much of the land in the hands of Muslim landowners. Habsburg administrators sought to create a model colony in Bosnia, one that through infrastructural, educational, and economic advances could showcase the Habsburg civilizing mission successfully in action. At the same time, the colonial regime hoped to avoid the dangers of political nationalism that appeared increasingly to trouble Austro-Hungarian society in the late nineteenth century.

The difficulty lay in the spiraling dynamic of unity and difference that had helped to produce those very problems back home. Empire and nation could not escape each other, especially in this colonial site. Education produced an increased politicization of particular cultural differences even as it also produced a sense of place within the larger imperial order. The purveyors of education brought in to Bosnia-Herzegovina, for example, were usually teachers who could speak the language of the locals, which generally meant that they were often also Croatian and Serb nationalists. Or they were government bureaucrats who sought to create a non-national Bosnian identification for Bosnian Muslims.[115]

*

While nationalist arguments about cultural differences pervaded public institutions and dominated politics by 1900, their influence nevertheless remained limited to these particular situations. Even in their own view, the nationalists' struggle to create nations was at best partially successful. Moreover, in many situations that encouraged nationalist identification, nationalist activity simultaneously buttressed imperial patriotism and loyalties.

By the beginning of the twentieth century ideologies of nationalism and of empire increasingly depended on each other for coherence. Far from constituting opposed or binary concepts and political projects (as they are usually understood to be), "nationhood" and "empire" both depended on each other for their explanatory coherence. The two made use of similar language and similar ideas. Propagandists for empire increasingly deployed national concepts in their publications and exhibitions, and this should also signal to us the extent to which nationalist discourse had already become a capacious if empty or nonspecific vessel capable of accommodating a broad range of ideas, programs, and visions, many of which served imperial projects as well. The imperial administrators who founded museums of culture and folklore encouraged archeological and anthropological projects in ways that strongly resembled the folklorist efforts of earlier nationalist generations. Their purpose, however, was not to encourage nationalist sectarianism, but to tie local nationalism to imperial loyalties.

Consequently, it is difficult to judge whether nationalist political conflict was in fact weakening the fabric of the empire or perhaps strengthening it. It was certainly changing the empire. By 1900 the state often treated nationalism as a potential threat, but this threat was not a threat to the very existence of the state itself, despite the views of many contemporary observers who formulated it in this way. Nationalists forced the state to come to terms with them in terms of imperial political structures and reforms.

CHAPTER SEVEN

Everyday Empire, Our Empire, 1880–1914

... the Monarchy—not so much our Fatherland as our Empire;
something greater, broader, more all embracing than a Fatherland.
— Joseph Roth, The Emperor's Tomb, 1938

From the 1880s until 1914 Austro-Hungarians engaged more intimately and intensely than ever before with empire in their everyday lives. Practices ranging from school attendance to voting in local elections to participation in rituals of military conscription and in annual empire-wide celebrations of the ruler's birthday made Muslim peasants in rural Bosnia, Czech-speaking businessmen in Bohemia, and Hungarian intellectuals in Budapest into increasingly engaged citizens of an empire that more than ever met their needs. No longer merely bystanders and onlookers, Austrians and Hungarians claimed an explicit stake in their empire. If these were the empire's twilight years, or even its last, long Indian Summer, as the years before the First World War have sometimes been characterized, most of its citizens apparently did not know it.

Structurally, the last decade before the First World War saw the empire emerge from political crises caused by nationalist conflicts in the years around 1900—the Badeni crisis in Austria, and the governmental stalemate in Hungary a few years later. These crises produced a willingness among some elites to develop more flexible models of power-sharing within the empire. Much of the willingness for such compromise took place behind closed doors, however, away from public view.

A New Kind of State for a New Kind of Society

Around 1880 the world changed. Across Europe communications and transport infrastructures expanded at quickening rates, more goods came to more people than ever before, and people now traveled far beyond their accustomed horizons, both physically and mentally. Growing numbers of people left farms or workshops in one corner of the empire for destinations in towns and cities in other parts of the empire, or indeed in other parts of the world.[1] As a result, in a mere twenty years between 1890 and 1910, the populations of Vienna, Budapest, Prague, Lemberg/Lwów/Lviv, Czernowitz/Cernăuţi/Cernivci, Zagreb, Innsbruck, Fiume/Rijeka, Kolozsvár/Klausenburg/Cluj, and Pola/Pula increased over 60 percent. Trieste/Trst, Debreczen, Temesvar/Timosoara, and the industrial regions of northern Moravia and Silesia followed close behind with 50 percent growth, as migrants from both the local countryside and other parts of the empire swelled these centers of manufacture, trade, and government.[2] By 1900 close to 40 percent of all Austro-Hungarians had left their original place of *Heimat* and migrated to their current homes from another part of the monarchy.[3]

Thanks to revolutions in transport and pricing, rail travel within the empire became a commonplace experience for millions. In Hungary, nationalization of the rail system significantly lowered passenger prices in 1889 and raised the annual number of rail travelers from next to nothing to an astonishing seven million in just a few years' time.[4] Well before the turn of the century Galicians could regularly board a train in their capital city of Lemberg/Lwów/Lviv and arrive in Vienna only fourteen hours later—a 500-mile trip that today takes many more hours. Many also traveled beyond the empire's borders to Hamburg in Germany, where they could board a ship to North or South America. In fact, during the period 1876–1910, almost four million men and women migrated overseas, most to Canada, the United States, and Latin America. Hundreds of thousands of those emigrants also returned to Austria-Hungary within a few years, sometimes with new capital or new skills, and always bringing experiences of a wider world.[5]

The revolutions in transport and communication that made such moves possible also transformed the lives of those who stayed behind. By

1900 the inhabitants of most smaller towns and remote villages had access to local and regional newspapers and sometimes to telephone service. By 1910 there were 22,386 primary schools in the Austrian half of the dual monarchy and 16,455 in Hungary. Increasing numbers of people—especially rural youth—actively sought and gained a degree of social mobility through the pursuit of education beyond primary school.[6] This did not necessarily mean education in high schools or technical colleges or universities; instead, they often enrolled in short preparatory courses that offered training in basic secretarial skills, such as typing, filing, and stenography, which enabled candidates to access a range of new low-level white-collar jobs.

After 1900, stubbornly low literacy rates in the most rural regions of the monarchy (especially Galicia, Bukovina, Dalmatia, Croatia, Transylvania, and Bosnia-Herzegovina) began visibly to catch up with higher rates in the more urbanized Bohemian, Austrian, or metropolitan Hungarian lands.[7] In 1910 the average literacy rate in the entire Austrian half of the empire for those over the age of eleven was 83.5 percent, a figure comparable to that of France (85 percent). In Galicia and Bukovina the average stood at 58 percent, in Dalmatia and Istria at 67 percent, while in the rest of Austria it reached 90 percent. In Hungary for the same period the statistical averages for literacy applied to those over the age of six, which also puts them somewhat lower than those for Austria. In terms of language groups in Hungary, German and Hungarian speakers reported the highest literacy rates (at about 70 percent) while for Romanian or Ruthene (increasingly known as Ukrainian by 1900) speakers the averages stood closer to 30 percent.

Thanks both to literacy and also to near universal military conscription, many people also learned about the wider worlds of science, politics, economics, and current events from consuming a rapidly expanding print media. More people than ever also came to see their own futures—or those of their hometowns—in terms of broader interregional interests. For the first time people in rural Dalmatia, Vorarlberg, or the Banat paid attention to political decisions taken in far-away Budapest, Vienna, Prague, or Zagreb. Many sought actively to influence the policies that shaped the futures of their own hometowns.

As the needs and desires of citizens changed, so did the functions and meanings of the state. From schooling to military service to welfare benefits to postal services, the responsibilities of the state increased, and some of these responsibilities became understood as entitlements by their clients. In a period of twenty years, for example, the Austrian and Hungarian governments had created mandatory—although very different—primary education systems; Austria also created obligatory accident insurance (1887) and health insurance (1889) systems for workers and company officials in commerce, industry, and trade. When we add to this the massive state-funded expansion of the railway, telegraph, and postal systems (in 1848 there had been ten telegraph stations in Austria, by 1913 there were 7,282), we can see how the state became a more immediate and present actor in people's lives.[8]

Expanding infrastructures and new public entitlements compelled the governments of Austria and Hungary to add layers of bureaucrats to fulfill new functions, and then more layers to monitor the effectiveness of the first layers. Competence in producing desired outcomes became critical to maintaining political legitimacy, in local town halls and in imperial ministries alike. Parliaments, crownland diets, and town halls now engaged in archival record-keeping on a scale as yet unknown, while enforcing a maze of legal standards for everything from workplace safety to public health to transportation to conditions of emigration.[9] Bureaucracy begat more bureaucracy as popular expectations fueled the state's expansion into the everyday lives of its citizens.

Unlike previous periods of major state growth, such as the 1780s under Joseph II or the neo-absolutist regime of the 1850s, initiatives from the margins of empire drove much of this late nineteenth-century expansion. Developed by locally elected officials and the administrative experts they increasingly consulted, such initiatives—from public hygiene programs and the establishment of hospitals to the creation of parks and public swimming pools—fueled an expansion of bureaucratic functions in villages, towns, and the crownland governments, along with increases in personnel. Both the state-appointed and the local "autonomous" bureaucracies in the communes stretched to fill mounting responsibilities to a growing clientele.[10] They employed more men—and by the late nineteenth century, women as well—from increasingly varied social backgrounds in a range of new positions, from telegraph operators to food inspectors to postal workers to schoolteachers to railway ticket sellers.

The development of local postal savings banks in Austria and Hungary, for example, offered banking services to rural and small-town customers of modest means, who would otherwise not have access to them. Postal workers and elementary school teachers came to symbolize the empire for the general public, since they represented it in the most common daily life interactions, even in the most out of the way rural settings. As one historian wrote of the Hungarian postal system, it "was the state institution that doubtless created the greatest familiarity among ordinary people."[11]

These recognizable professional sectors—postal and telegraph workers along with teachers—were also noteworthy as sites of expanded employment for single women in the late nineteenth century. Hungary first employed women in these areas in 1870.[12] By 1911, the Austrian state employed over fifteen thousand women, most of them in the postal, telegraph, and telephone services, while in 1913 close to 19,000 Austrian women held certificates qualifying them to teach in primary schools.[13]

State growth came at a high cost. By 1900 local infrastructural expansion had created a serious fiscal crisis in the Austrian half of the empire.[14] Who would pay for the new services and local employees? Community and crownland politicians had to face stark constitutional limitations on their ability to raise taxes independently of the imperial state. With several crownland governments and municipalities falling into serious debt, government commissions began to study the problem while economists and administrative experts devised a range of creative reform ideas to find long-term solutions. Experts, philanthropists, and many politicians warned that Austria faced a serious crisis. The government set up commissions to study the problem and to recommend programs that might restructure imperial institutions more effectively.

The expansion of governmental functions also spurred citizens to identify and organize politically around particular occupational interests and seek effective representation in public institutions such as town councils, school boards, or chambers of commerce. This in turn produced all kinds of specialized interest groups—from sugar-beet farmers to telegraph operators to rural insurance salesmen to state bureaucrats themselves—all of whom lobbied local and state governments for particular concessions. Industrial workers, unable to vote in most elections, still flocked to the

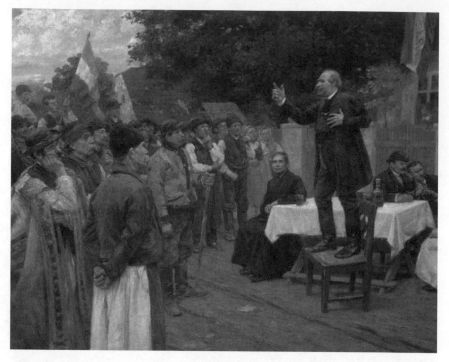

Depiction of an election campaign speech in nineteenth-century Hungary. Painting by Sandor Bihari. Credit: De Agostini Picture Library/A. Dagli Orti/ Bridgeman Images.

Social Democratic Party (founded in 1889) and presented local, regional, and imperial governments with formidable and insistent challenges. Their expanding networks of associations, which covered everything from sports activities to education and social activities like singing, their widely read party-owned newspapers, and their highly disciplined public demonstrations made them effective political actors and helped working-class men gain the vote for parliamentary elections in Austria in 1907.

Governments and parties became far more attentive both to creating and to manipulating popular opinion to mobilize greater levels of public support for their own programs. Consequently politics—at least in its public performative sites—became less about personal negotiations, expert management, or elite relations and more about rituals of mass mobilization. Like the nationalists discussed in Chapter 6, politicians after 1880 increasingly exploited mass media outlets to articulate individual interests in terms of group interests, whether on the basis of class, religion, region, profession, or nation. To borrow a characterization applied to Germans during the same period by historian Margaret Anderson, Austrians and Hungarians learned to "practice democracy," even if their political institutions were not fully democratic in character.[15]

The same forces that galvanized the expansion of the state—rising literacy, freer print media, and movement of people and goods—increased popular pressures for a greater democratization of imperial society. Politicians brought up on the more elite political traditions of previous decades found the democratizing changes of the 1880s perplexing and distasteful. Some could not adapt to a style of mass politics that they found crass and opportunistic. Other men forged innovative populist political practices, what Carl Schorske famously dubbed a "politics in a new key."[16] Like Karl Lueger (1844–1910), the enormously popular Christian Social mayor of Vienna from 1897 until his death, these men had often begun their public careers as liberals. Unwilling to remain passive backbenchers in the liberal system, they mobilized formerly unenfranchised groups (artisans, small business owners, peasants) against incumbent liberal oligarchs in populist mass-based politics. Many turned to anti-Semitism and radical nationalism (or both) as ideological glue to hold together otherwise disparate social and economic interest groups such as artisans in traditional crafts and lower-level white-collar workers employed by expanding new industries.[17]

These politicians successfully reframed popular understandings of liberalism. Painting it as the ideology of a powerful economic, political, and cultural elite, they undermined liberalism's traditional claims to be a force for reform or progress. Part of this strategy meant depicting the empire's Jews as the grateful clients of the dominant liberals, who, after all, were responsible for Jewish emancipation. At the same time, however, the exponents of this new populism carefully combined their critique of the liberal establishment with a powerful insistence on maintaining a system of small property ownership against the growing threat of social democracy in both Austria and Hungary. In most cases the new politicians split the nationalist political movements between traditional liberals and new populists, as with the so-called Young Czech movement that overwhelmed its erstwhile "Old Czech" partners in the parliamentary elections of 1891 in Bohemia. A few years later the populist Catholic Slovene People's Party defeated the more elite urban Slovene liberals in Carniola and South Styria by engaging peasant voters. By 1900, however, those same Young Czechs now found themselves outflanked ideologically and organizationally by the more radical populist appeals of the Czech National Socialists, Agrarians, and Social Democrats.[18] In Galicia, in turn, an establishment conservative elite—which frowned on anything popular, including more ethnically based forms of nationalism—found itself increasingly challenged by the peasant-oriented movement of the priest Stanisław Stojałowski (1845–1911) in the 1890s.

These transformations did not center only on the world of politics, although their effects were plainly felt there. From tiny rural villages to new neighborhoods in sprawling urban metropolises, the rhythms and certainties of daily life changed rapidly.[19] In a 1908 newsletter the prefect of Rann/Brežice, a rural district at the southeastern corner of Styria, addressed topics of public concern that would have been unheard of only a decade earlier. One article promoted the schools as an effective site for addressing children's poor levels of nutrition, warning that children who traveled far from home to attend school needed a good lunch to ensure their physical and psychic development. Another article suggested that the schools also serve as sites to improve children's dental hygiene. A third article advised people (both children and adults) against the misguided practice of throwing stones at that new phenomenon on country lanes, the automobile. Drivers might lose control and hit bystanders! Yet another article warned locals about scams touting emigration to Canada, Argentina, Chile, and the United States. Finally, the prefect distributed instructions about how schools should celebrate the upcoming sixtieth jubilee of Emperor Francis Joseph's reign.[20]

Initiatives for managing or promoting change originated far more often with local activists than with district administrations. In Galicia and Transylvania the 1880s and 1890s witnessed the slow rise of popular, often religiously based peasant self-help organizations to promote reading, agrarian improvement, and economic independence. In Galicia this often meant founding local cooperative stores to compete specifically with

Jewish-run shops and peddlers.[21] Self-help was meant not simply to produce social mobility and increased prosperity but to facilitate effective engagement with the institutions of empire.

Amid stunning social and technical transformations, faith in the virtues of a common empire crucially stabilized and coordinated heterogeneous desires, needs, and practices of millions of Austro-Hungarians. Even at the local level, empire remained the institution on which many activists projected their different visions of the future, especially those who sought to diffuse nationalist political conflicts by imagining new ways to organize the empire. As ideas, both empire and dynasty came to symbolize a reassuring constancy in times of bewildering change; Emperor-King Francis Joseph enjoyed unprecedented popularity. Forgotten were Francis Joseph's brutal crushing of the revolutions of 1848, the decade of absolutism, the postponement of Jewish emancipation, the lost wars, the equivocating over reform. Now a benign grandfatherly Francis Joseph watched over the progressive transformations of society, moderating social radicalism of the politicians when necessary. He appeared increasingly as a martyr to the many personal tragedies that had marred his long reign.[22] The traditional reciprocal dynamic of dynastic obligation and popular loyalty that underlay the very idea of empire also shaped popular attitudes toward the very new kinds of functions created or assumed by the state. The symbolic language of monarchy often cloaked new forms of governance and government obligation in reassuringly familiar terms.

Municipal Autonomy

This revolutionary expansion of the state often originated in the village or municipality, not in the dual capitals of Vienna and Budapest. In 1875 a survey of villages and towns in Galicia demonstrated that in a few short years the empire's liberal communal autonomy laws had already produced something of a social revolution in local political relations. Now, almost every mayor (99.2 percent) and village councilor (99.65 percent) in rural Galicia was a peasant. But in 1875, close to 80 percent of those peasant mayors could also neither read nor write.[23] Not surprisingly, Galician village administration in the 1870s witnessed considerable confusion and new forms of corruption as peasants, freed from the immediate control of hated gentry landowners, began to rule themselves. At the same time, however, the autonomous commune offered Galician peasants—and indeed all Austrian citizens from Vorarlberg to Bukovina—a critical schooling in politics. In Galicia it forced peasants to accustom themselves to common administrative procedure, to written law, and to practices of political mobilization. Eventually in the 1880s and 1890s, these experiences aided the Galician peasants in gaining political representation in the crownland diet from which their former lords had successfully excluded them in the 1870s.

The liberal communal legislation of 1862 (confirmed by the constitutional laws of 1867 and subsequently implemented by the individual crownland diets) gave local property owners the right to shape the development of their communities through elected municipal councils. In 1910, almost fifty years after the passage of the commune law, Austrian jurist Josef Redlich rightly asserted that the commune had "developed into the most important organ, without parallel, of free political activity by the population."[24] Loyalty to and exploitation of these monarchy-wide institutions created durable common bonds among peoples across east-central Europe—bonds that outweighed differences of language, religion, and region and that would even live on in many local institutions of the successor states well after the First World War.

The law created two crucial forms of autonomy for communes in the Austrian half of the empire by separating the remaining noble landed estates from nearby villages and giving the latter full responsibility for regulating communal budgets, municipal development, and implementing education policy. In Galicia this was hardly an unmitigated blessing to the newly autonomous peasant villages; it meant that the noble landowners also paid no taxes to the local commune, a fact that subsequently produced serious indebtedness for many autonomous villages.[25] As part of a larger separation of the judiciary from the administration, the liberal regime also established district courts throughout the Austrian half of the empire where feudal lords had previously provided the only form of justice. Citizens could bring local complaints against each other and against the state to these courts. The law also separated these new communal governments that were responsible to local voters from the top-down state administration that was responsible to the Vienna governments and that had previously controlled municipal development. Under this dual track administrative system, the imperial governments appointed a district prefect to oversee (at a distance) the work of the elected communal governments. The district prefects could also assign government functions such as responsibility for taking the decennial census to the autonomous commune. The autonomous communes, meanwhile, hired their own second track of local civil servants to carry out their expanding responsibilities. The law did not make clear a precise division of function between the state and autonomous tracks, and this occasionally produced an uneasy local cohabitation between state-appointed and autonomous system bureaucrats. Nevertheless, the communes and their bureaucracies largely administered their localities themselves and decided on their own futures.

The local voters who elected Austria's municipal councils consisted of male taxpayers divided into two or three curias, or groups of voters, depending on the amount of taxes they paid. Each curia usually elected the same number of councilors, so that the curia of men who paid the most taxes elected the same number of deputies as did the larger curia of men who paid fewer taxes. The minimum tax payment or level of property ownership for exercising the franchise in a given town or village depended on the overall tax contributions of a community. This produced a much higher threshold for the right to vote in cities like Vienna and the other crownland capitals, and a far lower ones for poorer villages in Galicia or Istria. Taken as a whole, this system not only privileged the wealthier members of a community, but also strongly restricted the right to vote in local elections. In Austria these laws enfranchised somewhere between 10–20 percent of the local population in the 1860s and 1870s. By 1914, seven years after Austrian men over the age of twenty-three had received the vote for Parliament, only 10–25 percent of the population could vote in communal elections, and even fewer for the crownland diets.[26] Thus as in Germany, but not in Britain, far more men could vote in parliamentary elections than in their local municipal elections.

If in Austria a centralized system was devolving increasing power to the communes and crownland governments, in Hungary the opposite took place. Here, local administrative power had traditionally rested with the county *(Comitate)* governments, which were dominated by the local noble gentry. From the eighteenth century on, it was they who had fed opposition to the demands of the Habsburgs, especially during the long periods when the diet was not in session. By empowering a national government in Budapest, however, the 1867 Settlement changed the stakes in this conflict decisively and for the first time also created national support for—or at least acceptance of—imperial structures. A decentralized county administration now made little sense to the men who ran the new national government.

Increasingly after 1867 the Hungarian state in Budapest sought to exercise greater control over county and local government. Many Budapest politicians—representing the national elite who had backed the 1867 Settlement—worried that left to their own devices, county governments could become dangerous centers of opposition, either dominated by radical Hungarian nationalists who rejected the settlement or by ethnic minorities (Slovaks, Romanians, Serbs, Germans) who demanded greater representation in Parliament and more government support for their cultural programs. In legislation in 1870 and 1886 the Hungarian government diminished the power of the county governments while still continuing to rely on them to carry out administrative functions. After 1870 Budapest appointed the highest local administrators—the lieutenants *(Föispán)* to the counties and to the limited number of towns that enjoyed rights of self-government.[27] The *Föispán* chaired the town council together with a vice lieutenant or mayor *(Alispán)*, who was elected by the local council. The town's field of responsibilities, covering infrastructure development, tax collection, and public health and welfare, resembled that of Austrian autonomous communes, but with structural checks placed on their abilities to take autonomous initiatives.[28]

In the 1860s and 1870s local elites elected by the first and second curias dominated politics in Austria, especially in the larger cities. Their interests monopolized policymaking as well as political procedure in the town councils. Only occasionally in these decades did the combination of a freer press, the legalization of political associations, and the grandstanding efforts of parliamentary politicians successfully rally mass opinion behind particular causes.[29] In one outstanding example Czech nationalists mobilized up to 40,000 Bohemians in open-air protest meetings called *tabors* to demand autonomy for their crownland and equality for their language in the years leading up to the failed Fundamental Laws of 1871. Still, such mass demonstrations of popular activism remained exceptional for most of the monarchy in the 1860s and 1870s.[30]

The tendency for a limited number of men to determine town policy was even more exaggerated in Hungary, where the suffrage provisions were considerably more restrictive than in communal franchises in Austria. The Hungarian municipal statutes of 1870 limited the electorate in other ways as well. Those eligible to vote elected only half of the town council in the first place. The voters included men with advanced educational degrees whose tax payments were actually counted double for the purpose of determining voting eligibility. The other half of the council was made up of so-called *Virilisten*, the town's wealthiest taxpayers who automatically held seats and who tended to support the governing parties in Budapest. In the northeastern town of Kassa/Kaschau/Košice over the period 1867–1914, for example, an electorate limited to 1,200 to 1,800 at most determined policy for a town that grew from 22,000 people in 1870 to 45,000 in 1910.[31] Few would confuse this with mass democracy.

Even given suffrage restrictions, the communal autonomy laws brought massive changes to local landscapes across both Austria and Hungary. Communes big and small initiated projects to rehabilitate their infrastructures, to attract or promote more business, to increase trade, and to implement the new school laws. Many municipal councils used the autonomy laws to pursue programs of radical renewal, following the example of Vienna's sparkling new Ringstrasse.

They zealously tore down medieval walls that cramped town growth, filled in disease-prone moats, and transformed reclaimed spaces into public parks with flower beds, tree-lined promenades, and, in some larger towns, broad boulevards. The communes dug up-to-date sewer systems, secured local supplies of drinking water, and paved roads. They built grand public buildings in historicist architectural styles designed to project their municipality's greatness and their town's distinctive achievements. Somewhat ironically, these buildings also accomplished the opposite of their intended effect, contributing to a powerful visual sense of imperial commonality and even uniformity throughout Austria-Hungary, which remains striking even today. From Graz to Prague to

The Vienna Ringstrasse nears completion around 1890. View from the Museum of Natural History toward Parliament on the left, City Hall in the center, with the University of Vienna to the right and the Burgtheater at the far right. Credit: Österreichische Nationalbibliothek.

Zagreb to Budapest to Kolozsvár/Cluj/Klausenburg to Czernowitz/Cernăuți/Cernivci, municipalities generally adopted a neo-Baroque style for public buildings—often also painted an imperial yellow. This was especially the case for the new theaters and opera houses, to which, as Phillip Ther tells us, "local elites in any town of over 50,000 would aspire." The architectural firm of Fellner and Helmer famously built close to fifty theaters and concert halls—but also palaces, hotels, and apartment buildings—across the empire in a common style whose character and function would be immediately and reassuringly recognizable to any visiting observer.[32]

The stylistic similarity of urban architecture in the empire is the subject of a considerable literary nostalgia for empire as well, a literature that dwells on the many lost ways that a particular imperial look and way of life pervaded every region of the monarchy. If every large town showed off a grand theater—of whatever size—or a magnificent new town hall,

Brünn, Stadttheater

1128 Reich's Postkartenverlag, Brünn

14./11 1905

Postcard from ca. 1905 of the city theater in Brünn/Brno designed by the firm of Ferdinand Fellner and Hermann Helmer. The theater first opened in 1882 with an electric lighting system designed by Thomas Edison. Credit: AKON/Österreichische Nationalbibliothek.

even small villages sported at least a coffee house, a tobacconist shop with "the doors . . . painted a bright yellow and black stripes," and possibly a railway station painted yellow and adorned with the Habsburg Double Eagle.[33] "Only much later then was I to realize," wrote Joseph Roth in 1938, memorializing the visual power of empire, "that even landscapes, fields, nations, races, huts and coffee houses of the most widely differing sorts are bound to submit to the perfectly natural dominion of a powerful force with the ability to bring near what is remote, to domesticate what is strange and to unite what seems to be flying apart. I speak of the misunderstood power of the old monarchy which worked in such a way that I was just as much at home in Zlotograd as I was in Sipolje or Vienna."[34]

The grand new boulevards with their magnificent public buildings that added to the luster of historic city centers presented a powerful contrast to the overcrowded and unsanitary housing—also often financed by the rising bourgeoisie—to be found in the expanding working-class suburbs of many cities. In Vienna, Prague, Graz, and Brno/Brünn,

Postcard of the Croatian National Theater in Zagreb designed by the firm of Ferdinand Fellner and Hermann Helmer. The theater was inaugurated in 1895 during a visit of Emperor King Francis Joseph. Credit: AKON/Österreichische Nationalbibliothek.

Postcard of the theater in Graz designed by the firm of Ferdinand Fellner and Hermann Helmer, opened in 1899. Credit: AKON/Österreichische Nationalbibliothek.

new industrial suburbs grew up around the wealthier inner city districts, also in common recognizable styles across the empire. From 1859 to 1917, for example, the Viennese built 460,000 new apartments—a number that hardly kept pace with the size of the population, which doubled between 1870 and 1900, reaching two million in 1910. In Prague between 1890 and 1910 the suburbs grew by over 200,000 people. The ring model served common symbolic social, political, and cultural functions, besides simply producing a similar look. As Wolfgang Maderthaner and Lutz Musner have argued, the Ringstrasse and the Gurtel that circled Vienna's inner suburbs were not simply stage sets for the display of bourgeois values and accomplishments. They also constituted real physical and social barriers that marked social hierarchies "between the luxury housing of the city center and the potentially dangerous working-class districts."[35] The new utilitarian grid layout of the streets and the neo-Baroque tenement blocks that sprang up around the factories in working-class suburbs served critical policing functions as well. As in Baron Haussmann's Paris—a very different kind of project where the grand new boulevards actually traversed the city center—workers in the new suburbs beyond the ring roads could not throw up barricades that had been so easily erected in the narrow irregular streets of historic town centers in 1848.

The expansion of communal infrastructure and services took place in two very different phases. In the first phase, stretching from 1862 until around 1880, the elite businessmen who dominated most town councils sought to develop their communes without incurring what they considered to be unnecessary debt. A typical representative of this attitude was Mayor Anton Strohschneider of the industrial city of Aussig/Ústí in northern Bohemia (population 36,364 in 1880), who asserted, "As long as I am mayor, there will be no public debt!" Strohschneider, like many a town mayor of the 1870s, adamantly refused to consider funding any but the public investments that he and his allies considered to be the most necessary for the town. These involved paving streets in the historic center of town, where its wealthiest inhabitants usually did business or lived, building a government-mandated schoolhouse, or fixing the most egregious sanitation problems.[36] In the industrial town of Beraun/Beroun (population circa 6,000 in 1880), located some twenty miles southwest of Prague, the town council articulated its goals as the "maintenance, stabilization, and conservation of the town's financial assets."[37] Other than repairing some roads and lighting certain streets in the 1870s, the council declined to take on major projects for urban renewal. In Ungarisch Hradisch/ Uherské Hradiště, a southern Moravian town of 3,600 in 1880, the council focused its efforts on administering a brewery, renting out communally owned agricultural land and forests, and leasing town buildings to the government, all for a profit. Except for building primary and secondary schools in the 1870s, the council undertook few infrastructural changes.[38]

When local bourgeois elites in both Austria and Hungary did undertake to expand town infrastructure in the 1860s and 1870s, they shared the expense with philanthropists and charitable associations, seeing these alliances as the most appropriate way to improve the municipality. After an 1831–1832 cholera epidemic in the northwestern Moravian industrial town of Märisch-Schönberg/Šumperk (1880 population of 8,500), and following a recommendation by the town's physician, a local businessman paid to have the old town moat filled in and to build the town's first covered sewer line. Twenty years later the mayor, another businessman, bought the rest of the moat to create a promenade. In 1857 yet another local businessman endowed the town's first hospital. In 1871 the town benefited enormously from a link to the railway network that was funded by a joint-stock company created by eighty of the region's wealthiest industrialists, merchants, and landowners. Meanwhile, a voluntary town beautification association *(Verschönerungsverein)* founded by members of the city council raised money to create a park, a cemetery, a public swimming pool, and a monument to Schiller.[39] Liberal elites, whose own laws had gained for them control over their communes, remade them according to their private understandings of their public responsibility and the common good. This phase of communal development ended abruptly in the late 1870s as far more people mobilized to demand a voice in local government.

Changing the Guard

The political hold on power of liberal visions, ideas, and practices that had dominated policy in the mid-nineteenth century gradually fell apart in the 1880s, not least because of the rise of an increasingly mass-oriented society. Mass patterns of urbanization, consumption, communication, and social organization challenged liberalism's highly limited, individualistic, and hands-off approach to social problems and the exercise of political power. Suffrage reforms for elections to the Imperial Parliament in the 1880s and 1890s drew more people into direct participation in the public life of the empire. Elections now functioned as major social and cultural events that involved all members of communities—even the unenfranchised—in common public rituals, from rallies to riots.

The rise of mass society also created a variety of social problems that Habsburg liberalism appeared completely unprepared to tackle. Men and women from lower-middle and working-class backgrounds, who were educated by the liberal school system, had learned their lessons only too well. They wanted to become active citizens and contributors to empire. Was not the communal government theirs as well? Should it not respond to their economic, social, and cultural needs? Did they not deserve a voice in determining the direction taken by the empire? We see signs of this earthquake already in 1873 when the economic crash unleashed a long-term recession, whose social fallout (unemployment, bankruptcy) liberalism appeared incapable of addressing. The recession undermined the fictional unity of bourgeois politics with which liberal elites had justified their tight control over many town councils in Austria. The liberals characterized local politics as a struggle that pitted a unified class of producers—the local *Bürgertum*—against the intrusion of outsiders like state bureaucrats, the crownland government, or socialist workers who had recently immigrated to the town. This fiction of unity was unable to paper over growing differences within the local middle classes about the nature of desirable economic development and the scope of town services for the less fortunate.[40] Those in charge threw oil on the fires at election time by openly using local contracts or leases on communally held land as forms of political patronage.

As lower-middle-class artisans, small retailers, and white-collar industrial workers challenged the power of bankers, industrialists, and big businessmen, the fiction of bourgeois unity collapsed. After 1873, the smaller producers began to organize their own associations designed to articulate their political interests against the rule of the local business, commercial, and manufacturing elites.[41] In the northern Bohemian industrial city of Aussig/Ústí, for example, the town's artisans organized their own economic association and at election time challenged the dominant liberals in the town hall, holding public meetings (something the liberals shied away from) and mobilizing the local press to articulate their complaints.

The activist challengers framed these elections in terms of fairness and local authenticity. Who, after all, should benefit from the town's development? Who truly represented the real townspeople? They skillfully engaged cultural wedge issues like anti-Semitism, religious difference, or national identification to dislodge their entrenched opponents by accusing them of doing the bidding of shadowy outside forces. In response, the local elite deployed every possible trick of urban patronage to reinforce its political hegemony. Local mayors in Austria and Hungary built political machines based largely on personal relations and patronage to help reelect themselves or their allies. At election time in Beraun/Beroun, the incumbent city councilors suddenly leased town lands to potential supporters, added sidewalks in neighborhoods where they sought electoral goodwill, assigned to potential supporters the local concessions for selling community wood, all of which earned them accusations of bribery from their opponents. In 1887 the incumbents even announced two different dates for the elections, a trick that drew the scrutiny of the crownland government and that eventually annulled the elections.[42]

As citizens of lesser means succeeded in electing majorities for their candidates in the third curia and sometimes even in the second curia, local power began to change hands. In Beraun/Beroun, an opposition party composed largely of artisans accused the elite of too little engagement with the economic interests of the voters. The artisans complained that the council repeatedly awarded building contracts for competing firms in neighboring towns rather than to local ones. As early as 1878 their campaigns began to pay off with electoral victories. Their success derived largely from their mobilization of popular voluntary associations during campaigns, from the local gymnastics association (Sokol) to the singing association (Slavos) to a local veterans' association. Another important factor was the founding and spread of local newspapers that supported the challengers.[43] In all of these cases of apparent conflict, the expansion of civil society actually deepened local attachment to empire by mobilizing new politically active classes to engage in the political process and link their local desires to imperial structures.

Responding to changed electorates, the municipalities expanded their purviews considerably. They organized small lending banks to make credit available to peasants and local small business owners, and they built more schools, courthouses, hospitals, asylums, slaughterhouses, brick factories, and military barracks. They lit their streets—first with gas and later with electricity—while many larger cities and towns built tramway systems to connect working-class suburbs to town centers.[44] As even this partial list implies, the function of communes changed enormously over a short period of time, from the limited administration of community property in the 1860s to the provision of a large array of services to their client electors by the 1880s.

Mobilizing new people into everyday engagement with empire was an unpredictable process that often generated physical violence, as newer stakeholders literally fought traditional elites for the right to shape local policies. Elections produced volatile behavior precisely because everyone understood that they were about choosing what directions the empire should take. Electoral engagement with empire created new forms of resistance—often violent—to the local power of entrenched elites, just as it had in the eighteenth century when peasants sought state help against the crushing power of the local nobility. Now, however, those elites were often the liberals who had created the new system in the first place. On 13 March 1897, a crowd in the majority Polish-speaking and Roman Catholic village of Dawidów in Galicia (population 1,300) attacked an election official, Stanislav Popel, alleging massive electoral fraud. Popel in turn shot one of his peasant attackers, and this provoked the crowd to beat him to death.[45] The two village gendarmes were powerless to control the crowd. The peasants suspected that local officials had created phony lists of eligible electors to nullify the people's voice and hand a fraudulent election victory to the local large landowners. The rules according to which the imperial system functioned produced an expectation of fairness, and in the eyes of local peasants, the large landowners had unfairly violated the rules.

The stunning incident during the election campaign of 1911 in the Galician oil town of Drohobycz described in the introduction pitted the town's Jewish vice mayor, Jacob Feuerstein, a supporter of the powerful Polish conservatives, against Jewish nationalists who had joined forces with local Ruthene nationalists to elect a Zionist-Jewish nationalist candidate. With the support of the Galician government, Feuerstein deployed military units from the nearby fortress at Przemyśl to prevent the Jewish and Ruthene nationalist opponents of his favored candidate from voting. When a crowd of Jews and Ruthene-speakers demanded their right to vote at the district's single polling station, Feuerstein allegedly ordered the troops to fire on the crowd. Twenty-six people died, and dozens more were wounded. A correspondent for the Viennese *Neue Freie Presse* confirmed this account, and also noted that in the hours leading up to the shooting, the troops had behaved in a highly restrained manner in the face of provocations from the crowd.[46] That twenty-six people had been killed demonstrates how high the political stakes could be both for the incumbent groups and the challengers.

The end of a hard-fought election campaign rarely brought an end to bitter animosities in the town councils themselves. Historians of Austria-Hungary have often attributed the high level of conflict—sometimes physical—in local elected bodies to the corrosive power of nationalism. Yet the kinds of conflict most commonly associated with nationalist efforts to cripple the Austrian Parliament after 1897—through obstruction, insult, hurling of objects—in fact characterized the behavior of many village or town councilors in places where nationalism was not at issue. In Ungarisch Brod/Uherský Brod, a town whose municipal government had already been Czechified in the mid-1880s, losing political parties consistently protested municipal election outcomes (in 1900, 1906, and 1911) to the Moravian government, which finally responded in 1913 by actually annulling the 1911 results in both the first and third curias. Sessions of the town council could be stormy, and several councilors routinely brought legal charges of slander—usually unsuccessfully—against their opponents.[47] In mostly Czech-speaking Beraun/Beroun, where the Bohemian government had already nullified election results in 1888 (when the town government had published two different dates for the election), political life remained turbulent. One local historian characterized council sessions in the 1890s as beset by "an atmosphere of intolerance, complete disrespect for opposing opinions, and violations of the most basic forms of etiquette including physical attacks."[48]

Examples drawn from councils like that of Ungarisch Brod/Uherský Brod demonstrate the inherent strength of empire as it was comprehended and experienced at the most local level of Austro-Hungarian society. Political violence was not simply a characteristic of nationalist conflict but reflected the stakes that many people held in the functioning of a political system that they believed gave them the opportunity to shape their town's future in the context of a larger imperial system. During a jarring period of transition in which political reform in Austria enfranchised thousands more people, friction was produced at precisely those sites and in precisely those moments where peoples' stake in their empire mattered most: elections.

Being Modern, Being European (and Paying for It)

Everyone in these fractious municipal governments did increasingly appear to agree that their town should be what they called "modern." It should share in what contemporaries perceived to be general European technological improvements and cultural advances. A town's government had to be constantly prepared to implement reforms and generally to think ambitiously about potential development. To take advantage of the rapid technological and economic transformations underway in the last third of the nineteenth century, towns had to act or risk losing markets and the quotidian benefits of modernity to regional rivals. The placement of a railway link or a military garrison could make or break a town's economic future.

Modernity meant more than a promising economic future. It also meant incorporating the representative elements of a common European modernity in the town's landscape or its appearance. Negotiating with the city government of Cracow on his suburb's possible incorporation into the neighboring metropolis, one suburban mayor insisted: "Of course we would expect lights, paved roads, water lines, police, and all the other things one should expect from a big city." Another local mayor who was engaged in similar negotiations demanded gas lighting, paved roads, the building of a school, and better transportation facilities for his suburb as the price of absorption. Nathan Wood recounts in his study of

Cracow around 1900 how local men of influence there—usually using local newspapers as vehicles—self-consciously crafted a rhetoric of urban modernity, which situated their newly enlarged city squarely in "Europe," thanks to their claims for its "cosmopolitan" and "modern" character, while also requiring perpetual activity to maintain this cherished status.[49] This included constant efforts to gain positive publicity for the city in international media outlets as well as the creation of tourism bureaus, often in conjunction with private initiatives.

Most experienced modernity as imperial in nature. In 1891 several town councilors of Mährisch-Schönberg/Šumperk, who also happened to belong to the cultural association "Kosmos," heard a lecture in their club about the benefits of a recent invention: the telephone. Immediately they began to lobby the Ministry of Commerce for the right to link their town to the early telephone network. At the end of 1892, with the ministry's assent, the council had built a telephone exchange.[50] Not far behind was Ungarisch Brod/Uherský Brod. By 1905 that town boasted thirty-one telephone numbers, all linked to a larger interregional telephone network.[51] In this case both towns linked themselves actively to the imperial center, seeing their interests in the context of their place in this new kind of empire-wide network.

Infrastructure development also meant taking risks such as building barracks, for example, to attract a profitable military garrison. When Mährisch-Schönberg/Šumperk's council did so, it nevertheless failed to attract the desired garrison to the town. Such efforts in the empire's largest cities of Budapest, Prague, Vienna, or Trieste are well known. What is more important to understand, however, is the dizzying array of imperial projects undertaken by small and medium-sized towns in the two decades from 1895 to 1914—projects ranging from new school buildings and hospitals to libraries and theaters, from electric lights to public swimming pools, from new railway stations to tramway systems.

To keep up with their growing responsibilities and functions, communal administrations expanded and diversified, hiring increasing numbers of educated staff. In 1896 the town of Aussig/Ústí already employed a hundred people. As became typical, by 1900 the town had found it necessary to hire a director to supervise the growing personnel, and in 1911 the town inaugurated a new town office building because the old town hall had no space for increased office demand.

The problem in Austria at least was how to pay for all of these modern necessities. Another was how to pay for the expansion of every aspect of town and crownland government. In Austria the central state maintained control over tax policy, but in a fiscally clever concession to federalist demands back in the 1860s, it had also assigned responsibility for maintaining social welfare, cultural institutions, agricultural development, education, transport infrastructure, public buildings, and all their attendant costs to the crownlands and municipalities.[52] The crownlands did have endowed funds dedicated to some of these areas, and they were allowed to add a surcharge to imperial taxes, but by the late 1890s these were woefully insufficient. The municipalities' freedom to develop in the way their citizens' wished became a double-edged sword, as town councilors found themselves desperate to increase reliable funds to pay for development.

What options did cities and towns have to pay for placing themselves at the forefront of imperial development by making themselves modern? They could increase fees or use town monopolies to raise money. Villages, however, did not have those options. Moreover, by 1900 the crownlands themselves were deeply in debt, as they reached the legal limits of surcharges they could add to imperial direct and indirect taxes. In 1905 the average surcharge that the crownlands added to imperial taxes came to 55 percent of Austria's direct taxes.[53] A large portion of crownland debt could also be traced to the increasing obligation in multilingual crownlands to provide educational and cultural institutions in more than one language. For financial expert Ernst Mischler, one culprit was the crippling cost of duplicated linguistic services in Moravia and Bukovina, where national compromises organized voters, school systems, and cultural policy according to language group:

> Each party seeks in the period of its national hegemony to satisfy its national needs as much as possible and it is not seldom (e.g., in several districts in Moravia) that these "needs" are nationally parallel or doubly satisfied, which very often leads to exorbitant expenditure.[54]

As everywhere else in Europe, the central state also expanded the numbers of its competencies and the size of its personnel drastically. The expansion of parliamentary suffrage in Austria between 1867 and 1907 also increased the influence of mass-based political parties. They legislated a wide array of new services for their constituents, and they also sought to influence appointments to the bureaucracy. Local prefectures too needed to hire more technically trained officials in fields as diverse as agricultural inspection, engineering, and health care. It was not simply party activism and patronage requirements that produced this expansion. After the divisive legislative obstruction that had brought down the Badeni government, Prime Minister Ernest von Koerber (1850–1919) tried to shift the focus of politics away from the national to the local.[55] Koerber hoped to bring the state closer to the people by radically increasing the number of prefectures and their expert employees. He was never able to realize his most ambitious reform plans before his fall from power in 1904. Nevertheless, with a government seeking to expand its presence in the countryside and political parties demanding new constituent services, between 1890 and 1911 the annual cost of the Austrian administration rose from 4 million to 18 million crowns.[56]

The Commission for the Promotion of Administrative Reform (*Kommission zur Förderung der Verwaltungsreform*) (1911–1914), which published this statistic, was founded to restructure Austria's administration and to give it more stable financing. The commission held public hearings, solicited suggestions, and issued reports on every aspect of Austria's bureaucracies and their staffs.[57] It considered several proposals to streamline the expanding civil service, including ideas about hiring fewer university-trained officials and more high-school educated clerks.[58] The point was not to cut down the size of Austria's bureaucracy. Rather, the reformers wanted to make it work more efficiently for its expanding clientele and to stabilize its budgets. Yet thanks to the very ways that the current system empowered local interests, it would be very difficult indeed to obtain the support of so many varied groups for any major overhaul of the system.[59]

In Hungary, nationalist activists in the governing parties put an especially high premium on independent Hungary's abilities to make use of the latest technologies and inventions to demonstrate its membership in a European club of so-called modern nations. The government invested enormous sums in the development of rail infrastructure, swiftly creating a highly centralized national system in which all lines ran to or through Budapest. Locally, too, the Budapest city government sought to attract visitors by presenting itself as an eastern "Paris on the Danube." In 1902 the city government created a Tourism and Travel Company that, supported by the Hungarian Ministry of Commerce, swiftly developed a marketing plan to place Budapest firmly within existing European and global travel networks. As Alexander Vari points out, the demands of marketing a relatively new city like Budapest created dilemmas for the city fathers. Lacking the kinds of historic monuments and museums that brought visitors to Vienna, Paris, or London, Budapest had to market its very modernity by simultaneously developing up-to-date forms of spectacle: "Where one cannot find pyramids, sphinxes, a Vatican, artistic masterpieces and beautiful natural landscapes, there the foreigner's stay should be turned into an interesting one through artificial means" wrote one local activist. With projects ranging from a so-called Ice Palace (*Jégpalota*) opened in 1903, where one could enjoy both a hothouse with palm trees and an ice-skating rink, to Danube Festivals (electric city illuminations and evening fireworks), car pageants, bicycle rallies, and even a bullfight, Budapest's town fathers sought to make their city itself into the object of tourist curiosity.[60]

If the decades after 1880 saw considerable Hungarian government investment in constructing urban and national infrastructure, this flurry of building was more a product of nationalist prestige worries than a response to increased participation in public life. In contrast to Austria, both local and parliamentary electorates in Hungary actually contracted during the period 1867–1913, maintaining municipal political power even more firmly than ever in the hands of a very small gentry, upper bourgeois, and noble elite.[61] Hungarian town councils tended to be far less prone to the same political pressures to expand infrastructure and city services to benefit more inhabitants than many of their Austrian counterparts were in the 1880s and 1890s. Those projects that the Hungarians did undertake tended to serve more elite bourgeois neighborhoods, usually in the traditional center of the town, while satisfying aspirations to national glory using both monumental architecture and technological innovation. Manifestations of mass politics—when they happened in Hungary—occurred more often in the streets and in local associational

EZREDÉVES KIÁLLITÁS BUDAPEST 1896.

Opening festivities of the millennium celebrations in Budapest, 1896, organized to celebrate the 1,000-year anniversary of Hungarian settlement in the Carpathian basin. Credit: Alinari/Art Resource, NY.

life than they did in specifically political settings like the municipal and county councils or in the Hungarian Parliament. This also meant that Hungarian political society was not spared the experience of the kind of ideological radicalization that overtook Austrian political life in the 1890s and 1900s.

In the decades around 1900 the attractions of modernity and the goal of demonstrating "progress" on a European scale also found expression in initiatives that went well beyond creating new infrastructures. Demands by workers' organizations, by feminist groups of varied political persuasions, and by educational and life-style reformers all sought to transform crucial elements of society to bring it into line with what they claimed was European progress. From animal protection to medical therapies to eugenics, to vegetarianism (Bohemia and Moravia together boasted twelve vegetarian restaurants in 1913, Vienna had six, and Budapest one), social activists developed radical new perspectives on modern life.[62] For the diverse range of women's organizations that sought to expand women's opportunities in specific forms of employment, for example, women's changing roles in society became a general measure for society's openness to progress.[63]

In Austria, women's sections were also highly visible—indeed proudly featured—in almost all nationalist organizations. Women activists by the thousands repeatedly proved themselves highly effective at organizing events, raising money, and developing new ways to mobilize local support for nationalist causes.[64] At the same time, women's organizations in the white-collar professions agitated for specific improvements, from pensions to work conditions. In the decades around 1900, for example, women civil servants in Austria, who by this point numbered close to 9,000, fought to eliminate severe pay discrimination and to obtain adequate retirement pensions.[65]

In Hungary a school play called *A nők Hódolata* (The Women's Tribute), written for the millennium celebrations of 1896 and to be performed in girls' schools across Hungary, hailed Hungary's modernity in terms of the opportunities it afforded to women. In the play a character named Slander attempts to turn three female characters representing Romanian, German, and Slavic women against "Hungaria." Hungaria, however, wins the day by enumerating the many opportunities that Hungarian society has made available to women of every nation. As teachers, postal workers, and telegraph workers, modern women of the present all take part in the development of the Hungarian nation.[66]

A few major political parties after 1900 supported women's suffrage, most notably the Austrian and Hungarian Social Democrats and the Czech National Socialists. The latter, in alliance with the Czech Progressives and the Young Czech Party successfully ran the nationalist writer Božena Vitková-Kunětická (1862–1934) as a protest candidate in a Prague district for the Bohemian Diet in 1912. Her victory there constituted an important symbolic one, although she was not allowed to take office.[67]

If the rise of new urban ways of life—so-called modernity—in Austria-Hungary's towns and cities brought women new forms of employment and opportunities for nationalist public activism or for petitioning legislative bodies, it also produced new cultural interest in gendered phenomena like prostitution and sexual deviance. As elsewhere in Europe, the rapid growth of an inexpensive illustrated boulevard press in the 1890s encouraged competition among newspapers, which tried to raise their sales by bringing shocking elements of a new, specifically urban world to the attention of the public. Especially in places that sought to attract tourists or that housed military installations, the boulevard press reported enthusiastically about the more shadowy elements of this so-called modernity, including widespread prostitution, increasingly visible homosexual circles, and a breathtaking range of sexually violent crime.[68] As Scott Spector's revealing analysis of one Viennese press scandal in 1907 shows, newspapers sought to expand their readership precisely by detailing highly lurid dangers about which, so the papers claimed, a respectable reading public hardly knew anything.[69] Offering "sensational content" about the scourges of the modern city, a newspaper like the *Illustrierte Österreichische Kriminal-Zeitung* (Illustrated Austrian Criminal Newspaper) in Vienna proclaimed it a duty to inform a swiftly growing readership about the "uncontrolled trollops," "their procurers," and the "ever more self-confident pederasts" in their midst.[70] In Hungary one year later, a contemporary police publication analyzed by Anita Kurimay went farther, actually comparing for its readers the putative motivations of female and male prostitutes:

> There are quite a few among both registered and clandestine [female] prostitutes whose unstoppable licentious blood and exotic desire for men place them among the condemned. This would be almost impossible among male prostitutes. They are all businessmen, who destroy the last drop of human decency by throwing themselves even to perverted bestialities, for money. It is understandable therefore that their moral insanity soon arrives at criminality.[71]

Not surprisingly, Hungarian writers often linked the blossoming of sexual perversion in Budapest precisely to urban growth and the rapid transformation of this city into a "Paris of the East":

> That is why our nice Budapest is a large city. A myriad of nightclubs and cafes further develop and shape the already awakened desires. In turn, all desires of humankind are experienced in the city, including the *wild offshoots of nature*. These wild offshoots are well-known and cunning perversities, which proliferate at the places of love, just like they do within so many families.[72]

In Cracow, according to Nathan Wood, the same newspapers that repeatedly sought to align their town with the "modern" cities of Europe
often related detailed accounts of shocking forms of immorality that
came with being modern. Unspeakable crimes of violence and depraved
sexual desires, not to mention robbery, infanticide, or juvenile delin-
quency, it seems, invariably constituted the price paid by a city for becoming the Paris or London of the East. "Cracow is not really London or
Paris," explained one newspaper, "but terrible poverty here in this little
Cracow gives rise, as in great centers of population, to holes and dens."
By 1910 Cracow had its own illustrated boulevard newspaper, the *Ilus-
trowany Kuryer Codzienny* (Illustrated Daily Courier). In an exposé on
child prostitution in the city, the paper warned smugly that

> considering our complete love for our hometown, considering the
> complete piety reserved for its valuable historical monuments, . . .
> we cannot forget that Cracow . . . is becoming as the years go by a
> truly great city, and it follows that great-city corruption—perhaps in
> a tempo faster than it should—strides alongside its actual growth.[73]

If Austria-Hungary's cities and towns were self-conscious avatars of
modernity, many worried that modernity came at a very high price. But
then, when skillfully magnified by the media, their worries became themselves a recognizable aspect of modernity.

From Service to Patriotism

A very different major reform of the liberal era, the conscription law of
1868, also shaped popular engagement with the empire, creating a significant common experience for millions of male citizens, which did not
necessarily end when their service period ended. As in other contemporary European societies, the new law mobilized young men from all
classes and regions of the monarchy to experience a common military
training and service, usually for a period of three years. In the context of
state-building, historians have treated nineteenth-century conscription
laws as powerful tools for creating a unified sense of a national community by encouraging young men to see the links between their own home
regions and the larger state.[74] Historians have only recently begun to ask

similar questions about the state-building and citizenship-forming roles of common military service for the case of Austria-Hungary.[75] To what extent did the experience of conscription give young men from diverse regions and social backgrounds a common sense of identification with the state they served?

In the first half of the nineteenth century the character, scope, and length of service in the Austrian military varied by region and had been subject to constant changes. Prior to the 1840s, for example, military service in Hungary had sometimes lasted for life, while service in most of the rest of the empire had been limited to fourteen years. Young men had traditionally been recruited by local lottery. However, given formal and informal practices for avoiding service, including exceptions for specific professions, levels of education, social statuses, and the possibility of buying one's way out of service, it was mostly poorer men from rural backgrounds who traditionally made up the rank and file. In 1840, with an eye toward standardizing service throughout the empire, the government reduced the length of service for Hungarians to ten years and in 1845 introduced eight-year service for the entire monarchy.[76]

The law of December 1868 replaced the Habsburg Monarchy's traditional policy of selective conscription with a system that both shortened the length of military service decisively and applied it to the entire male populations of both Austria and Hungary.[77] The law made all men in the empire equally liable for a lottery, although not all numbers were called up in any given year. In fact Austria-Hungary called up a lower percentage of eligible men to service annually than did the other great powers in Europe. Those not called up had to join the reserves, or the separate territorial militias, the Austrian *Landwehr* and the Hungarian *Honvéd*.[78] Educated middle-class recruits who qualified for university admission might volunteer for a single year of active training as reserve officers.[79] This guaranteed the state a high number of reserve officers and gave the Austro-Hungarian reserves a far greater social and religious diversity (and a much higher percentage of Jewish officers) than in neighboring Germany or Russia, where the officer corps remained bastions of aristocratic social exclusivity.

The reform created a military whose universal character made service into a common rite of manhood for eighteen-year-olds across the monarchy. A popular Slovene folk song of the 1870s explained the egalitarian nature of imperial service: "Whether a noble's son or a peasant's son, everyone must be called up."[80] Along with the new system of universal primary schooling, military service constituted the most influential point of contact between the Habsburg state and its male citizens of all classes. This contact may not always have been positive in nature; nevertheless, military service played a major role in inculcating male citizens from every region with a defined set of common practices and imperial ideologies.

Military service had traditionally been treated as a burden to be avoided wherever possible. Service in the modern military, however, offered attractive benefits to the potential peasant or working-class recruit, including three years of regular pay, medical care, food and accommodation, some technical training that could prove useful for a later civilian career, exposure to other languages of the monarchy, and often the experience of serving in several regions of the monarchy.[81]

For the liberal reformers of 1868 military service would not simply become universal in character; it would also become more humane and rational. Several drastic and cruel punishments that had regularly been meted out to recruits without reason were banned, and legal limits were placed on the forms that physical punishment could take. In part, this reform stemmed from a liberal belief—not necessarily shared by military commanders—that the status of citizen-soldier in the empire deserved a new degree of dignity and respect. Nevertheless, as Christa Hämmerle has shown, many older practices continued to characterize barracks life well into the twentieth century, and memoirs and letters from common soldiers often complained of excessive physical punishments applied irrationally to them for no apparent reason.[82]

As in the case of the local, crownland, and imperial bureaucracies, the military also had to develop policies for language use after 1867, especially given Austrian and Hungarian constitutional promises and requirements. For the common Austro-Hungarian military the language of command (Kommandosprache) remained the German language, largely for the sake of military efficiency and imperial unity. The Honvéd, by contrast, used Hungarian as the language of command (as did the Hrvatsko domobranstvo, the Croatian territorial militia), whereas for the Austrian

Landwehr the language was German.[83] Every recruit to the common military had to learn eighty or so German-language commands as part of his common training. In addition, the military used German as the service language *(Dienstsprache)* to communicate between its various institutions.

In 1868, however, conscripts gained the right to be trained in their own languages and to use their own languages within their regiment with each other and with officers up to the rank of captain. This right stemmed from the language-use guarantees in the Austrian constitution, but it applied to the entire Austro-Hungarian military, not simply to its Austria recruits. If a minimum of 20 percent of a regiment's recruits spoke one of the official languages of the empire, that language became one of the regiment's official languages. Recruits also sang songs in their regimental languages when on parade. Officers in each regiment were encouraged to learn the languages spoken by the recruits they commanded. Since the military frequently posted officers to new locations and generally prevented them from serving—at least for a significant amount of time—in their home regions, this language requirement often became a hardship. Officer training rarely included the option of language classes.[84] By 1900 the intersection of these laws and traditions had produced a situation of functional institutional multilingualism, unique among Europe's militaries. Regimental linguistic practice, like other imperial experiences such as primary schooling, nationalized soldiers while simultaneously unifying the military through the common use of the German language, wearing common uniforms, and participating in common traditions.

The system of regimental languages and of the German command language did, however, repeatedly ignite heated debates in both the Austrian and Hungarian parliaments, as well as in the crownland diets. Nationalist politicians often cited specific incidents in which officers had proved incapable of speaking a regimental language with sufficient skill in order to brand the army as too slow to implement fair language practices or to accuse the officers of Germanizing or Hungarianizing recruits. Hungarian politicians regularly demanded equal status for the Hungarian language in the military and an end to German as the sole language of command and service. During the 1880s and 1890s, radical Hungarian nationalists used the language-of-command issue to mobilize political opposition against the liberal nationalists who dominated the Hungarian Parliament, whom they accused of being slaves of a nationally humiliating status quo. Their efforts orchestrated a major constitutional crisis in the years 1903–1906, when the nationalist opposition unseated the governing party in the Hungarian Parliament, but was incapable of forming a government acceptable to Francis Joseph.

Francis Joseph was determined to maintain a single language of command in the military. He threatened to introduce universal manhood suffrage in Hungary as a way to force the new government to compromise in its demands to introduce Hungarian as the language of command. As much as Hungarian nationalists sought to increase their country's independence from Austria in every way, their deep fears of universal manhood suffrage—which would enfranchise high numbers of other linguistic groups as well as hostile social classes—forced them eventually to compromise on this issue.

It wasn't simply the privileged position of German as command and service language that raised the ire of Hungarian politicians. They also argued that regimental language practices based on provisions in the Austrian constitution legitimated the public use of Slovak, Romanian, or Serb. This directly undermined Hungary's policies of linguistic assimilation. For this reason they also sought—unsuccessfully—to strengthen the position of Hungarian as a regimental language for units stationed within Hungary and to prevent other languages from being used in those units.

Local conditions in which soldiers and officers found themselves, garrisoned as they were throughout the empire, undoubtedly also reinforced regimental practices of multilingualism. We have already seen how towns and cities competed for the economic benefits that a military presence might bring them. This practice coexisted with and on occasion could outweigh local politicians' commitment to nationalist activism. In Ljubljana/Laibach when Slovene nationalists replaced German nationalist liberals on the city council in 1882, they moved swiftly to replace German signs and the administrative use of the German language with the Slovene language. The same nationalist city politicians, however, continued to correspond with the officials of the local garrison in German, and they approved bilingual signage in German and Slovene for the barracks. Their pragmatism resulted from an appreciation of how their city was situated within a broader imperial context and of the economic benefits that imperial institutions could bring their city, a fact acknowledged by many other town councils across the monarchy.[85] Yet their positive attitude toward the military presence (despite that military's use of German) also resulted from a strong and popular local patriotism. For many people in Carniola, Slovene nationalism and Austrian patriotism gained coherence from each other even as late as the period of the Balkan Wars (1912–1913), when some Slovene nationalists also supported Serbia's war efforts.[86] Slovene nationalists regularly portrayed themselves as the emperor's most loyal subjects, while Slovene-speaking military veterans demonstrated pride in the particular loyalty of their nation.

The military also played several roles in town social life across the monarchy. Officers from a local barracks often participated in local associations' festival culture in the towns where they were posted, attending balls or fund-raising events. Military bands gave regular public concerts and participated in local religious feast days and dynastic holiday celebrations. Moreover, members of the military could adapt themselves to the cultural demands of local conditions.[87] In Ljubljana/Laibach, in order to appear nationally impartial, for example, officers apparently made an attempt to attend Slovene nationalist festivals and some occasionally spoke publicly in Slovene, while military bands often played Slovene marches.[88]

The diverse effects on the larger population of multilingual practice in the military combined with other common aspects of military service are difficult to assess. Historians who characterized imperial institutions in largely binary terms—they either weakened the monarchy (through popular nationalism) or strengthened it (through popular patriotism)—traditionally viewed the military as a crucial pillar of empire. But the use of regimental languages and increasing nationalist self-consciousness within regiments does not easily fit the traditional trope of the military as a simple centripetal force for empire either. Tamara Scheer is undoubtedly correct to argue that institutional multilingualism had the effect of strengthening both nationalist and imperial patriotic tendencies at the same time.[89] This becomes particularly apparent in the activities and attitudes of veterans in the growing number of their associations around 1900.

When veterans of military service began to memorialize their experiences by creating patriotic veterans' societies in the 1880s and 1890s, both the ways in which and the degree to which conscripts' experiences made them identify with empire become evident. Veterans' societies engaged in social activism and charitable work related to patriotic causes in their local hometowns throughout the empire. Their engagement does not appear to have reflected a specifically militarized attitude so much as it demonstrated veterans' desire to maintain their patriotic activism through community service and a ritualized festive culture.[90] The development of veterans' organizations from below did not go unremarked in government circles, where they quickly became a subject of keen interest. Many in the imperial and royal governments seeking new ways to reinforce loyalty to empire targeted the veterans' associations as a cause that deserved material and moral support.[91]

Laurence Cole's study of veterans' associations points to their proliferation in the final decades of the nineteenth century (in 1890 there were 1,700 in Cisleithania, in 1913 there were 2,750) as a way to understand the personal significance men retrospectively attributed to their military service.[92] The example of veterans can, in turn, help us to understand further the complex role that patriotism played in everyday life in the empire in its last decades, as well as the intricate and often intertwined relationship between patriotism and local forms of nationalist pride. Specific factors of place and situation determined the character, membership, and local function of a veterans' association. Unlike many other kinds of associations—including nationalist ones—veterans' associations usually mobilized a more socially diverse membership into their ranks. A lower-middle-class and sometimes peasant or working-class profile meant that in some regions membership offered veterans a sociable alternative to associations dominated by local liberal notables. Cole demonstrates that in parts of the Austrian littoral and the Tyrol, for example, veterans' organizations often allied with populist Social Catholic parties to undermine the traditional domination of public space by liberal nationalists (in this case Italian). This social dimension to the issue meant, as Cole points out, that in these regions veterans' patriotic culture also "left significant sections of modern society—the liberal bourgeoisie in Trentino and the Littoral, most of the organized working class in Trieste—unmoved."[93]

Politicians and bureaucrats increasingly took note of this growing mass phenomenon, understanding that in an age of mass politics—and nationalist agitation—former soldiers provided a reservoir of active patriotism in Austro-Hungarian public life.[94] Under the Koerber administration (1900–1904), which, as we have seen, sought to reestablish the political viability of the Austrian party system after the chaos and conflict that met the Badeni language decrees, the cabinet even debated creating a veterans' organization for the entire Austrian half of the dual monarchy as a way to strengthen the imperial state idea. At the same time, the Ministry of Defense suggested placing such an organization under state control in order to mobilize its members to undertake policing tasks for the government in case of war. The project of creating a unified, empire-wide veterans' organization ultimately failed, thanks to the veterans' own determination to guard their local autonomy. Regional pride and ethnic identification were critical components of veterans' self-identification, not to mention of their imperial patriotism. Many local and some provincial organizations did not want to see their distinctiveness erased in a larger umbrella organization.[95]

Mass Society and Political Cultures

On 5 November 1905, thousands of Austrians in cities and towns across the empire demonstrated peacefully for universal manhood suffrage. From Innsbruck, Trieste/Trst, and Linz in the west to Cracow and Lemberg/Lwów/Lviv in the east, crownland capitals witnessed unprecedented crowds made up mostly of industrial workers demanding the right to participate in the empire's legislative process. The same happened in smaller provincial towns, especially in Bohemia, Moravia, Upper Austria, and Styria. In Vienna, where only days before another demonstration had produced bloodshed, police allowed marchers to enter the Ringstrasse near the Hofburg Palace and proceed to the Parliament building where, again as police looked on, workers raised red flags on the black-gold flagpoles in front of Austria's Parliament.[96] Only in Prague did the demonstrations turn violent. There protestors built barricades and fought police for almost two days. The governor of Bohemia, Count Charles Coudenhove (1855–1913), begged Vienna for military reinforcements and the power to declare martial law. While the minister of the interior granted the latter request, he also counseled restraint, warning the governor against the possibility of provoking civil war. Later that day Prime Minister Paul Gautsch (1851–1918) sent a message to be published in Prague's newspapers officially sanctioning all peaceful demonstrations and warning that any more violence would incur a suspension of civil rights.[97]

These incidents demonstrate the state's growing willingness to tolerate and even respond to political expression from below, while at the same time seeking to avoid violence. The liberals of 1869 treated workers' demands for suffrage with condescension. Now, however, after thirty years of sectarian nationalist political conflict, some statesmen saw in working-class voters a possible way to channel parliamentary politics into social and economic issues of concern to the entire empire. At the very same time, international events made it harder for the government to ignore workers' demands any longer.

The November demonstrations—along with the occasional violence—took place in the shadow of the 1905 revolution in Russia. In October, after months of social unrest, the Tsar had been forced to concede to a constitution with a legislative parliament. But Austrian workers were not simply reacting to dramatic developments in Russia. Working-class socialists in Austria had been publicly demonstrating for universal manhood suffrage since 1869; at that time, they had been met with the icy disdain of the former 1848 revolutionary, Interior Minister Carl Giskra. In the 1870s and 1880s working-class political organizations had largely been driven underground by draconian legislation drafted in response to fears of anarchist violence. When that legislation ran out, activists founded an Austrian Social Democratic Party on 1 January 1889 at a conference in Hainfeld, under Marxist principles formulated largely by Dr. Viktor Adler (1852–1918). In July of 1889 the new party participated in founding the Second International of Socialist parties in Paris.

Like the empire itself, the Socialist Party that developed in the 1890s was driven by both centralizing *and* federalizing impulses. Laws governing political associations generally hampered the creation of a centralized organization consisting of many regional and local branches. This gave the more independent regional and local party branches considerable influence, to the chagrin of many party leaders. Much of the Socialists' most successful organization thus came in the form of cultural and social organizations—reading clubs, sports clubs, singing clubs, and lecture series. Unlike formally political organizations (and like nationalist associations), such groups could more easily—and legally—organize umbrella organizations. Social Democratic mass rituals, especially the carefully choreographed annual Mayday celebrations, became a critical focus of party attention. Such festivals were the only times when a broad range of people could enact their participation as a popular collective. Austrian leaders like Adler also treated the annual Mayday celebrations as an opportunity to emphasize worker maturity, respectability and dignity in public spaces like Vienna's Ringstrasse, sites not normally occupied by workers.[98]

Unionization in the Austrian half of the dual monarchy grew rapidly in the 1890s, and this also drove a growing Social Democratic belief in the inevitability of a Socialist victory in Austria. A contemporary account gives the following numbers for union membership in Austria: 46,606 in 1892, 135,178 in 1902, and 448,270 in 1906, the year when mass demonstrations for suffrage reform were occurring. Such numbers are closer to French unionization rates than to British or German ones, which were well in the millions during the same period. In Hungary, however, there were 71,173 unionized workers in 1905, mostly in Budapest.[99] Membership in the Austrian Social Democratic Party as in the unions was strongest in industrial regions of Bohemia, Moravia, Silesia, Styria, Lower and Upper Austria, and Trieste. In 1897 the party adopted a federalized structure along linguistic/ethnic lines, in order to deploy its resources more effectively, especially at election time. After this reorganization national groups held their own congresses separately and every other year joined together in a congress of the entire party. This remained the case until 1911, when, under pressure from rival populist parties, the Austrian party officially split into national parties.[100]

The Austrian Social Democratic Party's multinational identity along with its commitment to suffrage reform made it in practical terms a mass party in support of a democratic version of empire. This quality was reinforced at the party's conference in Brünn/Brno in 1899 when for the first time it adopted a program advocating a federal transformation of Austria into a nationally egalitarian and politically democratic state. The Socialists devised this program in part as a way to respond to bourgeois nationalist accusations that their cosmopolitanism made Socialists unsympathetic to nationalist interests.[101] As Jakub Benes argues, Czech-, German-, Italian- and Polish-speaking activists within the movement responded to such accusations by asserting that their democratic approach to politics would serve their national communities far more effectively than would a bourgeois approach.[102]

It is important to see that as they constructed their own approach to nationalist politics, Austrian workers were not victims, much less passive objects of a rampant bourgeois nationalism that dominated debate in the last decades before World War I. Rather, they asserted their own, far more democratically inflected and highly oppositional concepts of nationhood. It is also worth pointing out that by giving Austrian Socialists a programmatic statement about the coexistence of cultural groups in the empire for the first time, the Brünn/Brno program also clearly committed the party to the preservation of the empire, albeit in a more democratized version.

The question of nationhood and socialism was not merely a matter of tactics. In the writings of Austro-Marxists like Otto Bauer and Karl Renner it also became an issue of theoretical importance to the possibility of establishing a truly just society. Just as nationalist ideas about cultural difference had developed in response to specific Austrian and Hungarian laws and constitutional promises, so too was Austro-Marxism shaped by its critical encounters with empire. The Austro-Marxists opposed the idea that nationalist identifications were merely superstructural. By 1900 they believed those differences to be highly ingrained in the material realities of daily life in Austria-Hungary. At the same time, however, they rejected the nationalists' view of political relations among nations within the empire as a zero-sum game. Believing in a voluntary and so-called "personality principle" of nationhood, rather than in a territorial, historic, or ascribed one, Austro-Marxists proposed cultural autonomy and equality for all nations. At the same time they sought to implement economic and social justice for the working class. They rejected nondemocratic solutions like the Moravian Compromise, wherein Czech and German nationalists had agreed to limit suffrage to tax payers and to maintain privileged curial voting within each nation. Instead the Austro-Marxists sought to federalize cultural affairs, while centralizing economic and political policy at the level of a supranational state. Austro-Marxists also argued for a fair division of cultural institutions—and the resources to fund them—among Austria-Hungary's nations. Not all Social Democrats agreed, especially Czech-speakers from Bohemia.[103]

In 1897 an electoral reform added a new voting group, or curia, to the existing four (large landowners, chambers of commerce, urban, rural) that elected Parliament. This one enfranchised men regardless of their income, who were at least twenty-four years of age who could claim at least six month's residency in their district. The new curia elected seventy-two deputies to the Parliament out of a total of 425.[104] Thanks to this reform, the Social Democrats gained an opportunity to compete in elections, and in March of that year the party elected fourteen deputies to the Parliament. Socialist representation in the crownland diets and town councils generally remained much smaller on account of narrower suffrage restrictions, curial voting, and practices of gerrymandering. For this reason suffrage became a potent symbol for the possibility of achieving socialist future, and at the party's 1896 congress Adler proclaimed it to be "the party of suffrage." Under these conditions and in making these claims, the party mobilized massive support across the empire for its suffrage demonstrations in November of 1905.

The demonstrations peaked on 28 November, the day when legislation on universal manhood suffrage would be introduced to Parliament. The Social Democrats planned a general strike for that day (having obtained the agreement of several employers and the government in advance), so that hundreds of thousands of men and women could march in disciplined silence past Parliament and stage comparable demonstrations in cities and towns throughout the empire. Local bourgeois progressives who also supported suffrage reform joined the Socialist demonstrations and helped to create an impression among the workers that their path led inexorably to success and a socialist future for the empire.

The achievement of universal manhood suffrage and the end of the curial system of voting embodied in the reform—and signed by the emperor into law on 26 January 1907—gave Socialists in Austria an enormous sense of accomplishment and bolstered their optimism about the future. This was their reform, not that of the nationalists, and not that of the bourgeoisie. The Social Democrats had singlehandedly destroyed the feudal privileges of the nobility embodied in curial voting and smashed the barriers that had kept them from power. On 14 and 23 May 1907, in the first parliamentary elections conducted after the suffrage reform, the high rates of voter participation—over 80 percent—helped produce an outcome in which overnight the Socialists became the largest single party in Parliament. The Social Democrats had won 23 percent of the popular vote—over a million votes—and had elected eighty-seven deputies, out of 516. The elections in Austria were held in single constituencies rather than under a system of proportional representation, which helps to explain why the Social Democrats had not elected even more deputies. Nevertheless, the massive electoral victory appeared to confirm the most optimistic rhetorical flourishes of the Social Democratic leadership regarding their party's soaring influence. The results also showed socialists that the empire was indeed theirs. This triumph generated a narrative of state ownership unique among comparable labor movements in Germany, France, Italy, and Great Britain.[105]

The elections also confirmed the hopes of the government and even of the emperor that the reform might empower transregional parties intent on strengthening the empire against the regional forces of nationalism. This had been a common argument among Socialist theorists in the years around 1900. Karl Renner repeatedly argued, for example, that universal manhood suffrage would direct voters' attention away from sectarian nationalist issues to economic issues that demanded a statewide perspective.[106]

Suffrage reform did reconfigure Austrian politics significantly on several levels and in ways that tended to make empire as a whole more consequential to voters and their parties. The other main beneficiaries of the

1907 reform, for example, were the regional social Catholic parties, which joined together in Parliament to create an alliance of ninety-six deputies. As John Boyer has cogently argued, Habsburg politics after 1907 developed new norms and expectations that legitimized mass organizations while hastening the disappearance of regionally influential aristocrats whose power had rested on privilege built into the old curial system.[107] Those aristocrats still exercised considerable influence in the crownland diets and municipalities, but their influence was rapidly waning.

That these mass parties appealed to potential constituents primarily as workers or as Catholics, rather than as members of nations, is worth noting because it made them more imperial or empire-wide in their character and attraction. Their political appeals and ideologies sought officially to transcend one national community or another by making the empire and its many peoples the objects of their political agitation. Socialist organizations in particular succeeded to an even greater extent than did most nationalist movements in building sustained popular mass support for their work through networks of social, economic, cultural, and educational organizations. And although the Social Democrats were often far more critical of the institutional sites of authoritarianism that remained to be rooted out of the monarchy than were the social Catholics, both challenged existing power relations in society, and both envisioned the future in terms of a reformed empire.

An Empire with a Future?

Habsburg bureaucrats and party politicians had long demonstrated a flexible creativity in negotiating structural modifications intended to make the empire function more effectively and to give it greater long-term political stability. In the Austrian half of the monarchy the architects of the Moravian (1905), Bukovinan (1910), Galician (1914), and Budweis/Budějovice (1914) Compromises, as well as the authors of the 1907 suffrage reform and the initiators of bureaucratic reform, all developed bold political solutions to diffuse conflicts related to political nationalism. Their work was political, based on situational concerns, and clearly not perfect. Solutions were largely idiosyncratic, and their specifics were shaped by local conditions. One model could not easily be applied to another crownland. In Moravia, for example, the curia of large landowners was even exempt from having to choose a nationality. In Bukovina the compromise informally allowed for a Jewish national voting group, or curia, even though technically Jews could not be considered a nation.[108]

Once placed in action, these compromises frequently produced unanticipated consequences. In the case of the Moravian Compromise, for example, contemporaries and later analysts noted that it unintentionally strengthened nationalist identifications by forcing people previously indifferent to national identification to choose a nation.[109] Moreover, once the compromises were in place, Austria's high courts had to take their new premises and assumptions about nationhood into account in determining legal accountability. In Moravia this meant that individuals gradually lost the right to determine their nationality and that of their children. Once national categorization determined how individuals exercised rights from voting in elections to determining their children's schooling, nationalists demanded that the state enforce objective standards of national belonging to prevent people from switching nations.

In Austria in the decade before 1914 we can see a willingness to negotiate highly distinctive solutions to structural conflicts at the level of the regional crownlands and even—as with the case of the Budweis/Budějovice Compromise—at the level of an individual town. Although no such development approached the scale of the 1867 Settlement with Hungary, nevertheless the Austrian state became in some ways far more decentralized or federalized by region in its last decades—this despite (or in addition to) the exponential growth of the imperial civil service or the ways in which the highest courts insisted on maintaining common legal and administrative standards for all Austria.

Even in Bohemia, the crownland where the nationalist conflict appeared to be the most intransigent, informal negotiations to reach a federalist compromise remained ongoing, if often secretive. Nationalist politicians found it impossible to engage in compromise negotiations with the national enemy without appearing vulnerable to political challenge from even more obstinate fellow nationalists. In July 1913, to much public criticism, Prime Minister Count Karl Stürgkh (1859–1916) had the emperor dissolve the hopelessly deadlocked Bohemian Diet and its executive committee, placing Bohemian affairs in the hands of an administrative committee. For months Bohemia had teetered on the brink of financial crisis, and obstruction from nationalist parties had prevented the diet from solving the budget crisis. Many critics referred to Stürgkh's act as a breach in the constitution—which technically it was—and Czech nationalist deputies responded by blocking the legislative process in the Parliament, thereby compelling its suspension. As historian Lothar Höbelt points out, however, while Czech and German nationalist politicians may have loudly condemned Stürgkh in public, in private they were greatly relieved that he had resolved Bohemia's fiscal quandary for them. By placing the administrative committee in charge of Bohemian affairs, he had ensured there would be no break in public services. In turn, that special administrative committee hired many staff members of the now dissolved provincial executive committee to continue their work.[110] Stürgkh had tacitly relieved Czech and German nationalists from taking responsibility for the crisis. Would this kind of action pave the way for yet another federalist agreement, or would it lead to a revived centralist Austrian state?

Another very different example of imperial state-building also pointed in several possible directions. On 17 February 1910, sixteen months after Francis Joseph publicly announced his decision to annex it to Austria-Hungary, Bosnia-Herzegovina received a constitution and its own elected diet. The process of integrating Bosnia and Herzegovina into the empire, however, involved several complex constitutional maneuvers that required the creation of some legal fictions and the outright disregarding of other constitutional realities. Until its annexation Austria-Hungary's common Ministry of Finance had administered the empire's lone colony—or protectorate. According to Austria-Hungary's foreign minister, Count Alois Lexa von Aehrenthal (1854–1912), annexation had been necessary in 1908 in order to douse Serb nationalist hopes for territorial aggrandizement in Bosnia-Herzegovina, as well as Ottoman hopes for its return to a reformed Ottoman Empire. But internally, how exactly could the territory be integrated?

No constitutional place for Bosnia-Herzegovina existed within the empire, unless Austria or Hungary annexed it directly to its state territory, something to which neither state would agree. One more or less utopian possibility would have been to treat Bosnia-Herzegovina as the territorial basis for a new South Slav Habsburg state that would join the existing two, perhaps with the addition of some territory from both Austria (Carniola, Istria, Dalmatia) and Hungary (Croatia). The heir to the throne, Archduke Francis Ferdinand, might well have favored this kind of solution in light of his sympathies for the ambitions of Habsburg South Slavs and his general opposition to the power of the Hungarians. Hungarian leaders, however, rejected any territorial concessions, not to mention any diminution of their influence that would have resulted from a move from dualism to "trialism." They also opposed the addition to more Slav peoples to Hungary, an inevitable consequence of annexing Bosnia-Herzegovina to Hungary.

The 1910 constitution or provincial statute *(Landesstatut)* for Bosnia-Herzegovina did include a bill of rights, citizenship laws, the creation of a mostly elected parliament or diet, a judicial system, and a civil service, in a way that both bypassed and took account of the rest of the empire's structures. Francis Joseph governed the new territories in his capacity as the ruler of Austria and Hungary. His power in Sarajevo derived not from a separate family claim to Bosnia and Herzegovina, or from Bosnia-Herzegovina's agreement to the Pragmatic Sanction, but rather from his position as emperor-king of Austria-Hungary. Yet under the new constitutional situation Bosnia-Herzegovina existed in a kind of unacknowledged legal limbo, technically part of neither Austria nor Hungary. Although Bosnians elected a diet and town councils that determined their domestic affairs, structurally they had no voice in debates over the common issues that affected the entire monarchy (military, foreign affairs, common finances).[111]

The Bosnian Diet that met in Sarajevo consisted of several voting curias, similar to the crownland diets of the Austrian Empire. However, where linguistic differences now stood at the basis of many elected Austrian institutions, in the Bosnian constitution differences were understood and inscribed primarily in religious terms. The Moravian Compromise of 1905 had created separate Czech and German sections for voting in the urban and rural curias. The Bosnian constitution in turn created separate Eastern Orthodox, Muslim, and Catholic sections of the three main curias (large landowners/highest taxed, urban, rural).[112] Voters in the second two curias had to be male citizens of

Bosnia-Herzegovina who had reached the age of twenty-four and had lived in the country for at least a full year. Unlike the situation in Austria, however, voting was not limited to citizens of the territory. Austrian and Hungarian men over the age of twenty-four who were part of the civil administration or were railway employees or teachers in Bosnia also had the right to vote there.

The framers of the Bosnian constitution adopted almost word for word the language of the Austrian Constitutional Laws of 1867 in enumerating the civil rights of the citizen, but with some exceptions that applied to specific circumstances in the new territories. The law created a Bosnian-Herzegovinan affiliation or citizenship, since no imperial citizenship existed that applied to both Austria and Hungary. The statutes guaranteed equality before the law, as well as freedom of person, of property, and of movement. They also assured the public practice of all recognized religions in the territory. Here the specificity of religious conditions was critical, since the statutes recognized the application of Sharia law for determining civil cases for Muslims. The document also assured the safeguarding of the rights of the different nationalities to use their languages and to protect their national character, but it did not take over the specific language of paragraph 19, with its strong guarantee of the individual's right to use his or her language in schools and public life.[113]

In a detailed analysis of the statute and the circumstances surrounding its drafting, Karl Lamp (1866–1962), law professor at the University of Czernowitz/Cernăuți/Cernivci, warned that this document might well produce unanticipated consequences for Austria-Hungary's future. He thought that the Bosnian Provincial Statutes did little to clarify Bosnia-Herzegovina's constitutional status, especially since neither Austria nor Hungary had modified its constitution—or even its laws—to take account of the 1908 annexation. What exactly was Bosnia-Herzegovina's status, asked Lamp?[114] How would its status influence future constitutional developments in the rest of Austria-Hungary?

We might see the Bosnian constitution aligning with so many other decentralizing and federalist developments. But Lamp believed that the Bosnian statute was a starting point for the monarchy's "cultural work in the new lands [Neuland]" and not an end point, and he argued that "it would be a mistake to locate the effect of the Bosnian Constitution in the direction of further decentralization." Instead, he believed that in the long run, Austria-Hungary's foray into colonial politics would have to produce a greater—if utterly unintended—centralization of the empire as a whole, and a weakening of Austria's and Hungary's independent existences.[115] The pursuit of colonial politics had created new common interests that would have to tie the two states more closely together in the future, especially given the strengthening of the competence of the common ministries that the Bosnian constitution foresaw.[116]

Lamp's analysis did not focus on questions of ethnic groups and their potentially problematic mutual relations. That did not strike him as a critical issue. Rather, he argued that Austria and Hungary would eventually have to forge a closer constitutional union based on issues of constitutional rights and authority raised by the annexation and left unresolved by the 1910 statute. Lamp's analysis also treated Austria-Hungary neither as particularly exceptional by European standards nor certainly as some kind of anachronistic state structure. Instead Lamp analyzed the empire in the context of constitutional anomalies like Alsace-Lorraine in Germany or the long-term challenges faced by European states with overseas colonial holdings

The analysis of legal commentators and scholars like Lamp demonstrates the degree to which countless Austrians and Hungarians in the period after 1900 debated the future directions the empire should take, as well as possible reforms to its structures.[117] In part these discussions resulted from contemporaries' belief that this flourishing society required new rules, structures, and institutions to improve its functioning. Admittedly any comprehensive reform of the empire was impossible, given the constitutional ability of each state to block reform in the other, the disagreements between Hungarian and Austrian politicians over the future of empire, and the proliferation of interest groups who guarded their privileges.

Nevertheless, the excitement and creativity around reform projects demonstrates that Austria-Hungary cannot be written off simply as a doomed anachronism in Europe. The existence of nationalist movements and nationalist conflicts in Austro-Hungarian politics did not weaken the state fatally, and they certainly did not cause its downfall in 1918. Within Austria-Hungary nationalist movements shaped their demands around the institutions and expectations created by empire. As we have seen, from schools to military barracks to interregional commerce to scientific scholarship, it was institutions of empire that constituted the focus of political activity and emotional loyalties. If anything, the tensions created by nationalist and imperial impulses engendered even greater creativity in imagining political. This is especially clear in the extensive political and administrative resources that both the Austrian and Hungarian states expended—often in diametrically opposed ways—to manage, domesticate, and even normalize nationalist politics.

At the same time, we should also note another type of state attempt to manage nationalist politics, one that was a notable failure in every way. Recent work by Mark Cornwall on major treason trials—especially those in the decades before the First World War—illuminates badly mismanaged and misguided attempts by other elements in the state to manage those same tensions around imperial and nationalist politics.[118] If regional compromises that promised greater federalism constituted one response to structural problems, the occasional trumped up treason trial that both violated the strictures of the *Rechtsstaat*, and generally failed to deliver the state's hoped-for verdict, constituted another kind of response. Nevertheless, even these poor imitations of the best known treason trial in Europe, France's Dreyfus Affair, cannot be said to have demonstrated the bankruptcy of the imperial state. Rather, they suggest that within the higher bureaucracy a struggle over democratization was taking place. It was not that large elements of the bureaucracy favored direct rule by the people. Rather, after 1900 as we have seen, the bureaucrats could no longer easily be separated from the elected institutions and the political parties that increasingly appointed them.

*

Historians did not simply invent the idea of an anachronistic empire doomed to die well before the war, thanks supposedly to the weakness of its internal institutions or their inability to face the challenges of modernity. In the decades before 1914 an influential group of participant observers in the empire's military, bureaucratic, and aristocratic elites also spread dire predictions about the inability of the empire to survive. Their memoirs and correspondence about the period before the war betray darkly pessimistic assessments of the empire's immediate future. In particular, the suffrage reforms that culminated in 1907 and empowered mass movements at the expense of the landed aristocracy fueled fears about the potential abilities of Marxist socialism or sectarian nationalism to overwhelm imperial patriotism. In 1898 Prince Karl Schwarzenberg opined that "the so-called individual freedoms must be curtailed. People who think that the wheel cannot be turned back would scarcely be suitable [to carry out this intervention]. In my opinion, Austria can no longer be held together in any other way than by a modernized absolutism." Five years later he complained that "wherever you turn there is decay, and nowhere can be seen that firm will and that firm hand that are so urgently needed." Count Oswald Thun-Salm was more blunt: "In our country an optimist must commit suicide."[119]

In 1902 Count Francis Thun-Hohenstein, one-time governor of Bohemia and prime minister of Austria, complained to Foreign Minister Alois Lexa von Aehrenthal that radicals on both sides—meaning Czech and German nationalists—were so publicly influential that there appeared to be no room in politics for "rational persons" to maneuver. Such statements of fundamental pessimism regarding the viability of the monarchy in the twentieth century abound, particularly among those traditionally charged with running the empire—that is, the aristocrats who still dominated the uppermost ranks of the civil service and the military. Thun was certainly correct that by 1900 many people appeared to profit politically from articulating radically nationalist or social democratic political positions.

But did this in itself spell doom for the empire? There were in fact several different empires at stake by 1900. The one most congenial to men like Aehrenthal, Schwarzenberg, or Thun-Hohenstein and Thun-Salm had already died, thanks to the liberal reforms of the mid-nineteenth century that produced the mass-based reforms of the twentieth. These elites understood very well that the transformations of Austro-Hungarian society in the last decades of the nineteenth century—from the growth of popular politics to the politicization of the bureaucracy—had seriously reduced their power and influence. Many feared too that these transformations also diminished Austria-Hungary's great power status.

This elite mood of existential pessimism in 1914 was one factor that encouraged some members of the General Staff and Diplomatic Corps to risk taking Austria-Hungary to war. Believing that a cataclysm like a war offered them their last opportunity to silence political conflict at home and forestall further damage to the empire's great power status abroad, they embraced it. As the single individual most responsible for war, Chief of the General Staff Conrad von Hötzendorf (1852–1925) himself wrote to Joseph Redlich of his caste's fears, "It is very difficult to improve the internal situation of the monarchy peacefully."[120]

We historians can examine the state of the empire critically without endorsing the rump perspective of an increasingly anachronistic elite as the most apt or even the only way to understand this period.

CHAPTER EIGHT

War and Radical State-Building, 1914–1925

The path of history is in fact not that of a billiard ball, which, once struck, follows a predictable course, but resembles rather the path of a cloud, which also follows the laws of physics but is equally influenced by something that can only be called a coinciding of facts.

— Robert Musil, "The German as Symptom," 1923

In the summer of 1914 Austria-Hungary's citizens—along with most Europeans—suddenly found themselves at war. They were no strangers to war scares, like the one following the annexation of Bosnia-Herzegovina in 1908, but while their Balkan neighbors had been at war on and off since 1912, this new war surprised most Austro-Hungarians. Nonetheless, many groups in society quickly recognized that war offered them opportunities to reshape empire according to their particular visions.

For almost six years, key military leaders such as Chief of the General Staff Conrad von Hötzendorf imagined a Balkan war as an opportunity— perhaps the final opportunity—to turn back the clock on the political democratization of recent years. They would remake the empire along the lines of an apolitical, unified, hierarchic, and disciplined past. This was a past, of course, of their own imagining. Once war became probable in the summer of 1914, political leaders across the spectrum also embraced it. For socialists the war offered the chance to achieve social and political reform in return for the cooperation of the industrial working classes. Nationalist activists also saw in war unique opportunities to attain regional autonomy, increased linguistic rights, or even the reorganization of the empire in return for their national community's patriotic sacrifice. War promised politicians an unparalleled prospect to break the ongoing stalemates in Austria's Parliament and the Bohemian Diet. Moreover, politicians of all stripes were mindful that popular opinion in working-class, peasant, and middle-class communities appeared to accept the necessity of war.[1] Finally and most unexpectedly, wartime conditions created an array of new avenues for local people, from women workers in the cities to peasants in small villages, to assert their own desires for radical social and political change.

In statistical terms the empire mobilized close to 8 million men for military service between August of 1914 and November of 1918. Nearly 1,500,000 were killed either in combat or died in captivity; 3,620,000 were wounded; and over 2 million were captured by enemy forces. The war left few families and communities unaffected. Add to this widespread suffering on the home front caused by malnutrition, exhaustion, disease, and outright starvation, the war's demographic effects were universal.[2] The war impacted Austro-Hungarian society in countless other ways as well.[3] The warfare state's voracious need for labor at a time when most men were conscripted into the military drove increasing numbers of women into industrial workplaces. There, the state frequently subjected them to a harsh military discipline, while making no provision for their family responsibilities. By the last years of the war, women were even brought in to replace men in clerical positions in that most unyieldingly conservative of institutions, the military.[4] While teachers were sent to the front, schools closed their doors, mothers worked long hours in factories, and children scavenged for their survival on the streets or held their absent mothers' place for hours—often overnight—in endless market lines.

The state that demanded enormous sacrifice from men and women on both the military and home fronts also had to assume greater responsibility for their immediate physical needs. People depended on direct state intervention for their daily survival, and many of them adopted the state's own language of patriotic sacrifice to demand provision for themselves. The lack of food and fuel resources meant that in the eyes of its peoples the state constantly failed to fulfill its obligation to provide adequate nutrition, heating fuel, or benefits to the families of fallen soldiers. The failure of the empire's military and bureaucratic rulers to respond to material expectations they themselves raised among the populace produced severe crises of legitimacy. The state answered these crises with new promises to take more effective action, promises it simply could not keep.[5]

Finally, in October 1918, only months after an exhausted Habsburg Empire and its German ally eked out victories over Russia, Italy, and Romania, the empire imploded, and new regional governments in Prague, Zagreb, Lemberg/Lwów/Lviv, Vienna, and Budapest took over what was left of the imperial administration.

The war was not the proverbial final straw that broke a failing empire's back. It did not accelerate an inevitable collapse. It did, however, create heretofore unimaginable new conditions in Austria-Hungary that in just a few years' time made collapse not only possible but also likely. The horrific conditions of war galvanized revolutionary forces everywhere in Europe. A state that could not ameliorate its peoples' intense and dramatic suffering imperiled its popular legitimacy. In Imperial Austria another reason why suffering from shortages led to a breakdown of imperial patriotism was the harsh, extra-legal military dictatorship imposed on the citizens in the first two years of war. Both contemporaries and later historians agreed that this regime was qualitatively more dictatorial than comparable regimes in other belligerent societies. Whether any government could have solved the food supply crisis satisfactorily is doubtful, but in its blatant disregard for normal legal practices Austria-Hungary's governments did much to undermine people's confidence in their regime.[6]

In its radical transformation of the very conditions that create society, the war produced several new rounds of institution-building, both formally from above (food rationing, surveillance, new welfare benefits) and informally from below (popular attempts to organize food distribution and police behaviors). Moreover, contrary to the perceptions of contemporary protagonists and later historians, November 1918 did not mark a radical break with the past. The stakes in our understanding of the periodization surrounding the war are substantial. The world of 1919 was indeed very different from the world of 1914, but the particular political outcome was not ordained at any point during the war until the very end. The new states that replaced the empire struggled to demonstrate their profound difference with empire. The breakup of the empire in October 1918, however, did not create a radical break with imperial institutions, practices, or legal systems. Nor did Austria-Hungary's disappearance change most people's lives. Ongoing crises of food provision,

Austria-Hungary in 1914

housing, and disease haunted Central Europeans for several years following the official end of the war. In several formerly Habsburg-controlled regions new wars broke out and raged among paramilitary and regular military units for years. We can gain greater insight into the character of the 1920s in Central Europe by looking beyond the surface claims made by the successor states to take broad institutional continuities into account. Several states discretely retained imperial laws, imperial structures of rule, imperial judicial systems, and even the same personnel in positions of authority. The differences in kind between empire and nation state, between new regime and old, that seemed so stark to contemporaries who were eager to point them out may not be all that useful to the historian. Despite a rhetoric that insisted on their nation-based character, I argue that many of the states that replaced Austria-Hungary could more usefully be considered little empires, given the ways they administered their populations, legitimated themselves, and conceptualized cultural difference.

July Crises

The assassination of the Habsburg heir to the throne and his wife while on an inspection tour of the Bosnian capital of Sarajevo on 28 June 1914 produced a general European war crisis a month later. Still, it was other crises that apparently occupied the minds of many of Austria's highest officials that month. In July 1914, the Ministry of the Interior asked the crownland governors to report on their projected needs for the 1915–1916 budget. Most of the governors argued that Austria was sliding into a crisis, one that had nothing to do with the Balkans or with the possibility of war. Faced with mounting caseloads brought on by expansion of infrastructure, the increased provision of state services in several languages, and growing public welfare obligations, the governors wanted more personnel with technical training who could fully understand the administrative intricacies of everything from insurance practices to medical technologies. From Trieste the governor's office reported that it had processed 85,913 case files in 1913 as compared to 38,044 in 1900. From Troppau/Opava the governor of Silesia demanded eleven new paid positions, warning ominously that "the non-consideration of my repeated requests" had "damaged state services."[7]

Habsburg bureaucrats could see only one crisis on the horizon, and it had nothing to do with a possible war. The governors who hoped to get what they could from the central state did their best to paint the staffing situation—and the question of sustainable funding that lurked behind it—as an urgent crisis. This crisis had nothing to do with a long-term decline of empire, nor was it fueled by a sense of imminent imperial collapse, nor did the governors paint the state as somehow old-fashioned or anachronistic in character. The governors did not even mention the possibility of war in their calculations of their staff needs for the coming year.

As John Deak argues for the years leading up to 1914, "a series of actions by a vigorous and expanding state apparatus" sought "to push the envelope of state-sponsored modernization further."[8] Precisely these policies went a long way toward legitimating the imperial state in the eyes of its peoples. To continue them in a sustainable way, however, there would need to be major reform. Nationalist politicians also recognized the importance of this legitimating dynamic of the imperial bureaucracy, since they worked hard to influence administrative appointments at every level in the governors' or local prefects' offices. Their own associations' often mimicked the government's practices, making welfare benefits available to the targeted populations they hoped to win for their national communities in mixed-language regions.[9] At the same time, this dynamic pointed to the increasing federalization of Austria. Nationalism may not have been destroying the state, but as we have already seen, after 1900 its influence clearly shaped reform efforts and visions for the future by devolving more powers to the level of the crownlands.

At the very same time, yet another July crisis was brewing at another high level of government, a crisis that by the end of the month had embroiled some of the very same governors who sought more resources to fund staff increases. This second July crisis also had nothing to do with the potential collapse of empire, but it gained strength from the looming possibility of war. It involved military initiatives to take the empire in a very different direction from those advocated by politicians and the bureaucracies.

Since the recent Balkan Wars (1912–1913), and the international crisis created by Austria-Hungary's annexation of Bosnia-Herzegovina in 1908, elements in the military leadership had warned darkly of potentially treasonous behavior among Austria-Hungary's Slavic populations. Their hostility toward Slavic nationalists was not simply a manifestation of an anti-Slav prejudice, although there was plenty of that among the military elite. Rather, this hostility stemmed from the military's conscious separation from—indeed rejection of—civil society and popular politics altogether. That separation in turn was a product of the structural position of the military under the emperor-king's command, and outside of the authority of the civil governments of Austria and Hungary. Those governments had the right to negotiate budgets for the military but they exerted no control over its conduct. The fact that the military had to depend on contentious negotiations between the Austrian and Hungarian delegations for its budgets, and the fact that the Hungarian government often used those negotiations to press for nationalist changes in military policy, only increased military enmity to the entire political system. In its thinking the military elite had become the last significant bastion of a kind of political absolutism that completely rejected a participatory role for society in the running of the state. Political participation in military eyes would always weaken the monarchy by giving voice to unnecessary divisions. The military elite increasingly viewed the bureaucracy as complicit in this negative development, in part because the bureaucracy had become—at least in military eyes—too dependent on the influence and patronage of the political parties.[10]

Military hostility to the bureaucracy had structural origins, since both competed for scarce state resources.[11] In July 1914, as Austria-Hungary went to war, twin crises pitted the governors and the military against each other as each sought to increase their own access to resources from a cash-strapped state. When war came, it altered the power dynamics between the military and the bureaucracy, but it did not diminish the fundamental conflicts between them.

Waging War on Society

When war with Serbia and possibly with Russia became a possibility, the Military High Command (*Armeeoberkommando,* or AOK) swiftly arrogated to itself several critical powers, in order both to reshape domestic institutions during wartime and to impose an apolitical order after the war. Consonant with the military's contempt for civil society, the military did not desire to fight what historians refer to as a total war. It did not seek to remove formal boundaries between civil society and the military, between public obligation and private sacrifice, and it certainly did not seek to mobilize society actively for the war effort. Rather the military sought to prosecute the war in such a way that would make it possible to resurrect the tattered boundaries it believed ought to separate the state from society. According to Jonathan Gumz, the war offered the military an unparalleled opportunity to impose a rigidly militarized and depoliticized regime based on a system of strict hierarchies and discipline, one that several military leaders hoped would remove political conflict—indeed all politics—from governance of the empire forever.[12]

In Austria at least, the civilian government allowed the military to carry out its aims largely by placing itself—and its bureaucracy—under military command. Using paragraph 14 of the Austrian constitution, which empowered the emperor and his ministers to impose legislation when the Austrian Parliament was not in session, the Austrian government quickly curtailed civil rights and imposed new obligations on its citizens, creating what legal historian and politician Josef Redlich originally termed a "military dictatorship."[13] Just days before Austria-Hungary's declaration of war, the Austrian cabinet under Minister President Count Karl Stürgkh put the state on a wartime footing by suspending indefinitely both Parliament and the crownland diets. An order from the dual Austro-Hungarian cabinet also put several constitutional rights such as freedom of speech and free association "temporarily on hold" *(zeitweilig ausser Kraft)*. The Austrian cabinet introduced war censorship and suspended the right to trial by jury, placing civilians suspected of war-related crimes (everything from espionage or hoarding to disturbing public order), under a strict military law (*Standrecht,* or summary justice).[14] In addition, the military now operationalized its secret plans for organizing the domestic front, created in 1906 and modified in 1909 and 1912.

Altogether these measures gave the military control over the Austrian and Austro-Hungarian administration and the power to dismiss and replace civilian bureaucrats in key posts with its own appointments and to replace civilian courts with military courts (and civilian justice with courts martial). Through the related War Production Act (*Kriegsleistungsgesetz*) the AOK was able to militarize several industries and their workers. These measures also enabled the War Ministry to create—almost overnight—a vast new bureaucracy, the War Surveillance Office (*Kriegsüberwachungsamt,* or KÜA), which was designed to spy on Austrians, resident foreigners, displaced people, and POWs held in foreign camps.[15]

The military did not, however, obtain everything it wanted. For one, the Hungarian government guarded its national prerogatives jealously. Under its strongman prime minister, István Tisza, the Hungarian government kept both its parliament and the Croatian *Sabor* open throughout the war.[16] Moreover, since Budapest viewed with suspicion any effort by the military—even the dualist War Ministry—to impose its conditions on Hungarian territory, this led to a frequent duplication of institutions. In Hungary, where special wartime institutions remained nominally under the control of the civilian government, Hungary's

Ministry of Defense created its own War Surveillance Commission (*Hadifelügyleti Bizottság*, or HB).[17] Tisza also insisted on a precise elaboration of what the Austrian KÜA could not do in Hungarian territory, and he complained frequently when the military overstepped its boundaries in the so-called military zones located in Hungary.[18] Hungary's insistence on civilian rule, however, did not protect its citizens from the kind of dictatorial legal provisions that covered Austria. In 1912, for example, the Hungarian government adopted a secret codicil for the wartime deployment of the gendarmerie, one of which ordered that "persons under acute suspicion of espionage should be detained on the day of mobilization."[19] Starting in late July, this provision could be applied wantonly to almost any person in a warzone who belonged to a suspected language group, especially Serb-speakers and Ruthene-speakers. One place where civilian control did make a difference was in wartime press censorship. Budapest controlled all political press matters in Hungary, and the Hungarian press often reported far more freely on the war than Austrian newspapers could.[20]

The military's assumption of vast dictatorial powers constituted a fundamental break in Austro-Hungarian history for several reasons. Despite the fig leaf offered by emergency paragraph 14, or the Hungarian prime minister's obligation to report on the specific uses of emergency measures to the Hungarian Parliament, these changes heralded a radical departure from the normal functioning of the *Rechtsstaat,* or "state of law."[21] They interrupted a system that since the 1860s had tied together popular expectations and administrative responses. The closing of Parliament and the crownland diets in Austria also meant that Austria lost several key legitimizing institutions in the eyes of the public at the moment when it most needed them. The bureaucracy—now subordinated to the military—had to take full responsibility for unpopular wartime measures with little legitimating support from popularly elected officials. On the other hand, this formal distinction does not seem to have been immediately critical in the popular mind, since those hard hit by wartime shortages and militarized discipline nevertheless continued to turn to local mayors, former parliamentary and diet deputies, and party leaders, to make their complaints.

Denunciation and Food Riots as State Building from Below

"This deed has brought shame to all South Slavs. . . . Every good Slovene must reject this assassination on moral and practical grounds." These words written in his diary by a Slovene-speaking student at the gymnasium in Cilli/Celje in the summer of 1914 echo not only the shock experienced by many at the news of the assassination of the heir to the throne and his wife, but also the ways in which imperial loyalties and national identifications actively reinforced each other at the outbreak of the war.[22] Here a young Slovene nationalist articulated his patriotic feelings to the dynasty and empire.

There is no reason to believe that Austro-Hungarians responded much differently to the challenge of war than did their counterparts in Britain, France, Germany, or Russia. As in the other European belligerent countries, the outbreak of war produced visible and spontaneous demonstrations of patriotism in Austria-Hungary if also serious reflection about the possible suffering war might bring. Loyalty and patriotism were amply documented among all of the so-called national communities of the empire, and despite the anti-Slav fears of the AOK, its own reports admitted that there was no resistance to mobilization in Slavic regions of the monarchy.[23] Among young men throughout the empire an excitement for war often prevailed in August 1914, thanks partly to the values they had learned in the mass organizations—religious, nationalist (such as the *Sokol* gymnastics' federations), or Social Democratic—that flourished immediately before the war. There, in the context of peacetime, many of them had developed an enthusiasm for the values of community and sacrifice as a means to overcome the allegedly corrupting and self-serving values often attached to modern urban society.[24]

Yet by ignoring these feelings of patriotism and subjecting some of the empire's Slav populations to unreasonable suspicion, Austria's military rulers blundered badly. They failed utterly to comprehend the key ways in which nationalist pride formed a critical part of imperial patriotism for so many Austrians. "It was more the ruling elite that lost faith in its peoples," Laurence Cole shows, "rather than the other way around."[25] Its fears of disunity—a complete misreading of popular politics—led the

AOK to take preemptive punitive measures against the potential treachery of imagined Slavic fifth columnists, either among Ruthenes in Galicia who allegedly favored Russia or among so-called Serbophiles in western Austria and southern Hungary.[26]

The military's dictatorial state-building efforts from above, however, produced unexpected responses from the population. Most recent histories of the wartime home front stress the ways in which people officially subjected to harsh militarized conditions responded to the new conditions by taking their own initiatives, from personal denunciations to organized food riots. Coercion creates not simply compliance but also confusion. Confusion can lead to new forms of agency, and to new local codes of behavior to ensure survival. Almost from the start the wartime state-building processes involved changes that came from several directions at once in society, and not merely from above. As Maureen Healy argues, when faced with an economy of rationed information, ordinary people in wartime Vienna reacted to government censorship and propaganda by spreading rumors and denouncing their neighbors in an effort to effect their own system of legality and fairness.[27] Thus the efficacy of the military's measures was shaped in no small measure by initiatives taken by ordinary and resourceful Austro-Hungarians.

The first areas in which military and civilian administrators lost control over the application of the new wartime measures was in the local treatment of suspected traitors. On 22 July the Austrian interior ministry issued a decree warning local officials to act forcefully against any people who might respond to a war declaration with Serbophile or anti-military declarations. This was meant to enable local authorities to combat local agents in the pay of Russia or Serbia, as well as possible Socialist opposition to war. While fears about anti-military declarations were soon forgotten, a developing paranoia about Serbophilia, fed largely by popular denunciations, snowballed in multilingual regions like southern Styria or Carinthia, which included both Slovene- and German-speaking populations.[28] German nationalist newspapers in these regions eagerly took advantage of military paranoia to accuse their Slovene nationalist rivals, including several priests, of Serbophile sympathies and to urge gendarmes to investigate them—this despite the obvious fact that, as the high-school diarist from Cilli/Celje quoted above also wrote in his diary, most Slovene nationalists believed—quite accurately—that the heir to the throne had been highly sympathetic to South Slav interests.[29]

"Every loyal Carinthian or Styrian of both [Slovene and German] nationalities should make it his duty to bring everything that appears to him to be even partially Serb-friendly or treacherous to the notice of the gendarmes."[30] Thanks to this directive, the discipline the military confidently believed that it was imposing on local society swiftly escalated into an uncontrollable orgy of denunciation. Neighbors suddenly reported shadowy goings on about each other. Local authorities and gendarmes encouraged growing social chaos by treating every whispered rumor, every innuendo as a serious threat. They more than fulfilled their mandates from above to guard against potential subversives with no regard for the law, thanks in part to the paranoia created by the sudden state of war. Rumors circulated that someone in the village had once said something positive about Serbia during the recent Balkan Wars or had collected money to donate to the Serbian Red Cross. Someone else reported that a local priest had not shown sufficient contrition about the archduke's assassination because he had not immediately hung a black flag from the church. More far-fetched reports of Italian or Serb spies buying up local property or rumors about French cars driving to Russia laden with gold led to the creation of spontaneous citizens' patrols that fired their guns and made citizens' arrests.[31]

In southern Styria gendarmes overreacted to the military's directives to the point that anyone who even questioned their authority could be arrested for Serbophile treachery. On 5 August, for example, acting on their own initiative, gendarmes from Pragerhof interrogated and charged Anton Ravšl, a Slovene-speaking priest from Zirkovetz/Cirkovce (Pettau/ Ptui district), with using his pulpit to glorify the Serbs. It later turned out that it was in fact Ravšl's stubborn denial of the charges that had provoked his arrest: "since you are arguing with me," the gendarme reportedly said, "I'm going to arrest you." Brutalized in prison and labeled a "*Windisch* traitor who should be hanged," the priest was eventually freed on 15 September for lack of evidence.[32] From 27 July until 1 December similar rumors and anonymous tips about a neighbor's questionable convictions or sympathies led to the persecution of over 900 men and women in Styria alone, although as Martin Moll points out, these numbers represent only a fraction of the actual number of those arrested. Of the recorded cases, two thirds originated specifically in linguistically mixed regions where nationalist organizations were strongest, suggesting that local German nationalist activists took this opportunity to finger their local opponents as subversives.[33]

By September the authorities—including Minister President Stürgkh and Governor Clary of Styria—worried that the situation was completely out of hand. What had begun as a military measure to control local society had in fact produced chaos. The high civilian authorities now tried—at first to little avail—to discourage the gendarmes from acting on denunciations without clear evidence. Nevertheless, as later parliamentary investigations would make clear, this wave of denunciations damaged the reputation of the state among the otherwise patriotic citizens who had been targeted. It also saddled the victims with serious long-term consequences, since many who were later declared innocent had lost their local employment thanks to the original accusations. While provincial and local civilian administrators learned some sobering lessons from this experience, they were unable to prevent the military from carrying out even more severe policies against Italian-speakers in Trieste, Trentino, and the littoral in the spring of 1915, when Italy declared war on Austria-Hungary. This time, however, when the Interior Ministry instructed civilian administrators to proceed harshly against the irredentist movement, it also warned its officials that "loyal supporters of the [Austro-Hungarian] state of Italian nationality should be protected from unjustified attacks, and denunciation." Officials should do nothing to "agitate the population," and they should "not vex loyal elements."[34]

The civilian control maintained by Hungary's government over wartime emergency measures failed to prevent similar popular waves of persecution. In fact, early on, it too appears to have encouraged them. Often fed by denunciation, attacks were directed primarily against the Serb-speaking population in Croatian southern Hungary, but also against Ruthene-speakers in northeastern Hungary. On 15 July the dual minster of defense, Alexander Krobatin (1849–1933), warned Hungarian Prime Minister Tisza that in his opinion the local Serb *Sokol*, or gymnastics associations, in Croatia Slavonia were agitators for what he called a "greater Serbian revolutionary movement." A few weeks later Tisza alerted the county lieutenants: "I call your attention with particular emphasis to the attitude to be taken towards the non-Hungarian population. . . . We must show them our strength."[35] When war broke out, gendarmes immediately and haphazardly arrested local *Sokol* leaders and members across southern Hungary, as well as prominent Croatian Serb members of the *Sabor*, despite the latter's alleged parliamentary immunity.[36]

As in Austria, so in Hungary, mob violence and denunciation intensified gendarme policy, lending a mass dimension to the radical policies pursued by both the military and the gendarmes. In Croatia, the opposition Frankist Party had little trouble provoking anti-Serb riots.[37] In Zombor/Sombor, a town of some 30,000 people in the West Vojvodina Bačka region, of whom 12,000 were Serb-speakers, popular demonstrations in early September demanded the removal of all shop signs in the Cyrillic alphabet. When an angry mob chased one Serb-speaking shopkeeper to his home for refusing to remove his Cyrillic sign, he responded by shooting at the demonstrators. The military commander of Zombor/Sombor demanded the shopkeeper's immediate extradition from the mayor and prosecutor, court martialed him, and executed him on the spot. The court martial also designated twelve more affluent hostages from among the Serb-speaking population who would "be arrested and immediately executed by the military authorities" in the case of any obstruction or opposition shown by the local population to the military authorities.[38]

Prime Minister Tisza protested repeatedly against this and other similar episodes of military activism. Writing to Foreign Minister Count Burián (1851–1922) in August 1914, he lamented that "excesses committed by military commanders disregarding government and authorities are increasing. Please do everything possible by all means to stop this madness. I shall be obliged to see his majesty and make this a matter of principle." However the issue was as much popular anti-Serb demonstrations as it was military overzealousness, and the Hungarian government sent vacillating signals to the population, one day arguing for moderation and the next demanding relentless severity.

Soon popular practices of denunciation in both Austria and Hungary created other uncontrollable social dynamics. In many cases, denunciation to the local authorities became an important strategy for citizens who wanted to ensure that they enforced particular wartime rules about everything from food provision to appropriate forms of patriotic behavior. Given the serious manpower shortages that plagued authorities of all kinds—from police to teachers—denunciation became a way for citizens to insist that the short-handed authorities nevertheless enforce the rules the citizens cared about most. Denunciation became a new instrument for upholding general principles of legality and fairness, principles whose implementation was allegedly threatened by a few corrosive individuals in society—food hoarders, black marketers, unscrupulous landlords, delinquent youth—who sought to take advantage of their neighbors' suffering. Particularly in a situation where access to food for daily survival was increasingly limited in urban settings, denunciation reminded the authorities of their responsibilities to the citizens.

Food provision to all Austro-Hungarian cities declined drastically during the war as production plummeted and imports evaporated in the face of a foreign blockade.[39] The increasing shortages were not alleviated by eventual victories over Romania and Russia in 1917 or by military occupations of Serbia and Russian Poland (where the military requisitioned local supplies for its own needs).[40] The immediate loss to the Russians in the fall of 1914 of agricultural Galicia, with its one-third of all Austrian farmland, constituted a terrible blow to Austria's ability to feed its people. So too did a general loss of manpower and draft animals to the military. Even when Austro-Hungarian and German forces reconquered Galicia the following year, its farmlands were devastated and depopulated by the fighting.

Overall, Austrian harvests of wheat and rye in 1915 fell to less than half of the already poor harvest results of 1914. In 1916 and 1917 they fell to 44 percent and 40 percent of 1914 levels. Other food products could not make up for the missing grains, so in many cases producers simply mixed available grains with fillers—anything from potatoes to chestnuts to nettles to sawdust—in order to extend supplies. This in turn diminished the caloric and nutritional value of what little flour or bread was available and caused angry consumers to protest.[41] In February 1918 one letter writer in Prague echoed a general complaint that citizens were treated little better than animals, saying that "we have for supply completely black flour that is not even [fit] for cattle."[42]

Food production remained much higher in agrarian Hungary where in 1916 Hungarian farmers produced an average of 203 kilos of grain per head, compared to 72 kilos in Austria. Before the war Hungary had exported 2.1 million tons of grain and flour annually to Austria. In 1916, however, the Hungarians could barely spare 100,000 tons total for their Austrian partners. In 1915 the Hungarian government also regulated supplies of basic foodstuffs.[43] In response to repeated Austrian complaints, the Hungarian government invariably replied that it could not alleviate food supply problems in Austria since Hungary was also responsible for providing the military—now over three million enlisted men, officers, and animals—with the lion's share of its food and fodder needs.[44]

In February 1915 the Austrian government created a War Grain Control Agency (Kriegsgetreide Verkerhrsanstalt) to oversee wartime distribution of flour and bread products throughout the empire. Socialists Karl Renner and Vinzenz Muchitsch were appointed to the advisory board, and they immediately agitated for a state monopolization of the grain trade. Local Austrian governments also contracted with private firms to create local cartels (Zentralen/ustředny) that rationed supplies of foods, fuels, and other materials such as leather or cotton. Not until November 1916 did the Austrian government create an actual Food Office (Amt für Volksernährung) for all of Austria with socialist representation (Karl Renner) on its board of directors.[45] Starting in April 1915 local governments in Vienna and Prague introduced systems of ration cards that entitled individuals to purchase a specified daily amount of a given product in local markets. In both Vienna and Prague the first items to be rationed in 1915 were flour and bread, followed by sugar, milk, coffee, and lard in the following year.[46] Those Austrian regions that were perceived to have more prosperous agriculture, such as rural Bohemia, were ultimately no better off, since their imagined advantages made them liable to greater provisioning demands from the military.[47]

The worsening crisis in the cities was reflected in the deep decline in amounts of daily-allotted foodstuffs to Vienna, for example, between April 1915 (flour: 100 grams) and November 1918 (35.7 grams). In 1916 all Viennese were technically allowed a ration of one-eighth of a liter of milk. By 1918 there was not enough milk to ration.[48] In Prague the city had to implement a half-ration of bread in April 1918, and by June even this much was not being delivered. Rations for fats in Prague fell to 50 grams for the entire month in April 1918. In general the wartime provisioning of Austrian cities compared extremely poorly to that of Paris, for example, where only sugar was rationed in 1917 and bread only in 1918, or to London, where rationing was not even introduced until early 1918.[49] Austrian officials also complained that even German cities that suffered to a comparable degree nevertheless received greater benefits from the 1918 peace treaties with Russia and Romania.

The situation in Budapest was not much better. Prewar emergency legislation in case of war passed in 1912 and supplemented in 1914 had given the Hungarian government the power to regulate many aspects of the economy including the power to fix maximum prices for basic consumer goods and to order the delivery of all surplus reserves of those goods. Thanks to supply problems already experienced in 1914 by towns in the northeast and southwest (near the fronts) the government introduced food coupons—the first step toward rationing—in March 1915. Bread rationing followed soon thereafter in December 1915.[50]

The real challenge to people, of course, was to obtain the rationed product in the first place. Maureen Healy's insightful analysis of the many ways this system functioned—or failed to function—in Vienna demonstrates the considerable gaps between official allotments and what people could actually procure in cities and towns throughout the empire. In 1917, for example, the governor of Trieste complained to the Ministry of the Interior that deliveries of rationed products like grain, potatoes (which by this time had replaced bread in that city), beans, and fats regularly failed to meet promised amounts. Instead of 2,400 wagons of potatoes, for example, the city had received only 1,680. Thanks to the resulting malnutrition, tuberculosis rates were rising in the city. "The mood of the population," he warned, "which so far has born the manifold hardships of war in an exemplary fashion, cannot be subjected to further burdens."[51] The governor, like others in positions of authority, worried that further burdens could deal a death blow to the popular legitimacy of the state.

The challenging business of procuring food came to take up more and more of people's time, as working women—many subjected to militarized factory discipline—and their children eventually lined up at night in city market squares for a chance to buy at stores that opened the next morning.[52]

In her illuminating study, Claire Morelon quotes an oral testimony of one Praguer who recalled at the age of seven or eight "sitting or lying on the pavement in front of the bakery" with other children his age all night, "so as not to miss their turn in the morning."[53] Healy quotes Social Democrat politician and journalist Max Winter who investigated this phenomenon in Vienna and learned that if one arrived after 3:00 a.m., it meant missing out on food the next day.[54] In an outraged plea to Prime Minister Stürgkh, Winter directly linked the suffering of the soldiers at the front to the state's obligations to their families at home:

> As first officer of the Empire you surely consider yourself to be a pa-
> triot . . . [but] it's a poor patriot who abandons the children whose
> fathers are fighting and dying on the battlefield, endangering their
> health and their lives.[55]

Winter's outrage demonstrates the degree to which questions about the failure of wartime provisioning could swiftly turn into dangerously corrosive challenges to the very justification of empire. Protesting citizens repeatedly demanded guarantees from a range of local and provincial officials to implement the empire's promises to its peoples, even as the authorities increasingly failed to carry out their appointed tasks. Police reports in Prague noted the increased dangers of violent incidents thanks to the practice of all night queuing. "These crowds of people stand in the most lively streets of the city and are so embittered that they could, with the smallest provocation, get violently agitated."[56] Crowds of women angry at the unavailability of certain essential items, for example, might gather spontaneously in groups to march on the local town hall and de-mand what the government owed them. Rumors of food availability in other neighborhoods produced more group marches. The officials they confronted may have sympathized with the women, but they could do little to aid them, and often such groups left dissatisfied to seek out yet another official. Frustration also led very quickly to violence and in the last two years of the war to political protest as well.[57] When desperate city folk began leaving the cities to scavenge nearby rural regions for food, the authorities responded by searching baskets and knapsacks at train sta-tions and confiscating food items they found.[58]

Their foraging trips to the countryside did little to endear city folk to their agrarian neighbors, particularly since socialist newspapers often claimed that the peasantry profited from starvation in the cities. In Bohemia, the Czech nationalist Agrarian Party sought to combat urban resentments against the peasantry that appeared in both the German-language and Czech-language socialist press. To restore a sense of Czech nationalist solidarity between the city and the countryside, the party's charity, *České Srdce* (Czech Heart), developed a program that linked city families to agrarian families and eventually sent urban children on repeated stays in the countryside, a practice Emperor Charles also later promoted as a way to buttress imperial unity. Most importantly, the Agrarian Party press offered a compelling alternate nationalist narrative to explain the situation: Bohemian food supplies were being exported to Germany. Both the military and civilian authorities repeatedly denounced this claim, and the Prague branch of the War Grain Agency even offered a prize to anyone who could provide proof of such shipments to Germany. All of this was of little use, and complaints about food shipments to Germany appeared regularly, even after the end of the war.[59]

Citizens increasingly treated food provisions as a fundamental right. One Viennese letter writer complained angrily that working people "must sacrifice their lives and for that we are left hungry. . . . Every person, whether rich or poor has a right to life."[60] Indeed, letter writers, denouncers, and political activists, increasingly spoke of their work on the home front as a form of sacrifice comparable to that being made by the troops at the military fronts. Public agitation demanding greater fairness and effectiveness in the provision of food and fuel became a critical area of wartime state-building from below that politicians, bureaucrats, even military administrators could not ignore. Politicians like Vienna's Christian Social mayor, Richard Weiskirchner (1861–1926), for example, increasingly positioned themselves on the side of the people against—in this case—the arrogant Hungarians who refused to share their bounty.[61]

The sympathetic agreement of mayors and their deputies also ratcheted up the political stakes by confirming the legitimacy of peoples' claims for food and creating new rights attached to citizenship. As Weiskirchner remarked at one meeting of party leaders from the Vienna

War loan propaganda poster advertising the fifth bond issue (November 1916) through the Živnotenská Bank in Prague. Austria-Hungary helped finance its enormously expensive war effort through a series of eight war bonds issued every six months starting in November 1914. Altogether the loans raised 35.1 billion crowns in Austria and 18.6 billion in Hungary. Credit: Library of Congress, Prints and Photographs Division, WWI Posters.

City Council, back in peacetime "nobody demanded from me that I should get him potatoes. It didn't occur to anyone that I should provide flour or meat; it was never the legal duty of the municipality to do so." The mayor might complain that "it is neither in a statute nor found in law that it is the city's duty to take care of food," but he and the others were responsible for creating the very expectations that had produced their unaccustomed obligations.[62]

The new social contract demanded by citizens in return for their sacrifice required the state at every level to provide them with adequate food. While the state—either the municipal, crownland, or imperial/royal government—may not have been able to satisfy these demands, it nevertheless passed new laws and redoubled its efforts to root out black marketers, those who violated price laws, and those who falsified or watered down food products to show that it took these issues seriously. By responding energetically to the complaints of its citizens, however, the state legitimated their demands, not by providing food but with a flurry of legal discourse and largely ineffective activity. This behavior by the authorities in turn confirmed for many citizens that the problem of food supply must really be a product of clandestine operations by particular groups of suspicious fellow citizens or aliens (usually refugees or Jews). In so doing, they may have deflected the problem momentarily away from the failure of the state, but they nevertheless damaged the unity of imperial society.[63]

Of course denunciation of this kind also offered citizens the opportunity to settle personal scores, but officials quickly became attuned to this kind of complaint. Denunciation also became a strategy to forestall any possible suspicions from falling on the denouncer. Denunciation asserted and demonstrated one's own patriotism against the clearly lacking patriotism of one's neighbors. To whom did it matter in Prague, after all, that the patriotic Czech Women's Aid Committee sported the flags of Bohemia and Prague outside its headquarters but not the black and yellow flag of the empire? In this case both the denouncer and the accused clearly demonstrated their patriotism, but over time, in increasingly antithetical ways.[64]

Another and related product of denunciation practices had an even greater effect on society. It was not simply the outbreak of war that had produced manic suspicions about the possible presence of traitors in Austro-Hungarian society. In military terms the first year of the war went very badly for Austria-Hungary. Almost immediately the Russians successfully occupied most of Galicia and Bukovina, while at the same time Serbia managed to repulse Habsburg invasion attempts. Adding to these woes, Italy and Romania demanded territorial compensation from the empire for maintaining their neutrality, and given the adverse military situation, Germany pressured Austria-Hungary to consider concessions. In the spring of 1915 Italy abandoned its formal stance of neutrality and opened a new front against Austria-Hungary in the southwest, thanks to a treaty with Britain and France that secretly promised Italy large territorial gains on the eastern Adriatic. At this point the situation appeared to be dire, and many believed that the Habsburg Monarchy would soon suffer an ignominious defeat. The military often explained its failures in the first two years of war—massive territorial and POW losses in Galicia in 1914–15, failure to conquer Serbia—by blaming civilian and Slavic nationalist subversion. Certain national groups, the military argued, clearly strove for Austria-Hungary's defeat.

Many German nationalists in Bohemia and Hungarian nationalists in the south adopted this line enthusiastically, warning darkly of Czech or Serb nationalist betrayals, of Czech soldiers shooting in the air instead of at the enemy, and of Czech or Serb desertion altogether.[65] For most of the war Czech nationalists answered such accusations by treating them as fantasies propagated by hostile German nationalists. Citing countless examples of Czech sacrifices that it predicted would earn the Czech nation a better position within the empire after the war, *Národní politika*, the organ of the Czech National Socialist Party, proclaimed in January 1917: "This inner loyalty of ours, the realization that we have capably performed our duties to the empire and the dynasty, must strengthen our firm, unshakeable faith in future justice, even if it is inconvenient to a few German nationalists."[66] In a May 1917 address to parliament, Czech National Socialist deputy Jiří Stříbrný complained of the Prague police chief's anti-Czech bias, speculating that the recent appearance of Russophile leaflets in Prague might actually have been a German nationalist plot abetted by the police to discredit Czech nationalists.[67]

Only a few months later the international situation changed dramatically. Having lost Russia to peace-demanding bolshevism, and increasingly pessimistic about the possibility of negotiating a separate peace with Austria-Hungary, the western allies now began to consider the possibility of a future breakup of the Habsburg Empire. Exiled nationalist politicians from Austria-Hungary, like Thomas Masaryk who had been unsuccessfully trying to make a case for such a breakup for three years, suddenly gained more willing ears for their arguments.[68] In consequence, some Czech nationalists in Bohemia now began to adopt the very same unsubstantiated German nationalist accusations for their own purposes, arguing to the outside world that the Czech nation had in fact opposed the war from the start, that it had always sought independence from Austria, and that Czech nationalists had indeed attempted to subvert the war effort. After the war, Czech nationalist politicians, journalists, and activists praised the wartime Czech desertions and subversion invented by German nationalists, using them to justify the creation of the new state of Czechoslovakia.

Research into these questions has repeatedly established that stories about mass Czech desertions or refusals to fight were in fact myths—often propagated by German nationalists or military leaders—to help the military to deflect attention from its utter incompetence especially in the first years of the war. Historian Richard Lein has demonstrated that a famous defection to the Russians of part of Infantry Regiment Twenty-Eight (from the Prague region) in April 1915 never happened. Eager to hide its own culpability behind spurious accusations of treachery, the Austro-Hungarian military dissolved the regiment based on false accusations of mass Czech desertion.[69] Later Czech nationalist and German nationalist politicians had so much at stake in maintaining these myths that they effectively colluded to prolong their existence well after the war had ended. Many German nationalists blamed Czechs both for Austria-Hungary's military defeat and for the break-up of the empire. At the same time, Czech nationalists after the war played up the myths of their desertions and betrayals because such claims made it appear that they had worked to achieve an independent nation-state since the beginning of the war. Thus, Czech treason became a critical mythological component of the founding of their nation-state.

New Neighbors

Another unplanned for catastrophe tore at the fabric of social relations in the very first weeks of war as thousands of displaced Austrians fled the Russian invasion of Galicia and Bukovina. This massive movement of refugees was both the product and cause of severe chaos and confusion.

The state was completely unprepared for this contingency, partly because of the swiftness of events, partly because it had not expected a successful invasion, and partly because invasion ripped apart local government institutions so thoroughly. Civil servants from Galicia and Bukovina found themselves trying to reconstitute local records on the run and pleading with the state for a resumption of their salaries while destitute and terrified constituents overwhelmed them with their own entreaties.[70] Eventually Galician refugees ended up scattered in Lower Austria (Vienna), Bohemia (Prague), Moravia, northern Hungary, and the Alpine provinces.[71]

Some provincial governments swiftly built temporary camps to hold and feed numbers of people while decisions about their future could be taken. In Bárta/Bardejov/Bartfeld, a town of 6,000 located in northern Hungary on the other side of the Carpathian Mountains from Galicia, over 10,000 Jewish refugees arrived from Galicia in just three days' time in mid-November 1914. These civilians had been struggling on foot, dragging carts since mid-September, when Russian troops had invaded their towns. They were starving, and many suffered from contagious diseases. The town's military commander ordered the arrivals to be transported to the interior of the monarchy. Those with some financial means *(bemittelt)* and those whom the commander described as "intelligent" would be sent to Kassa/Kaschau/Košice, Budapest, Vienna, and Graz. Those without means *(unbemittelt)* would be transported to recently constructed barracks in the Moravian town of Ungarisch Hradisch/Uherský Hradiště. From there they would later be transported to networks of smaller camps still to be built in Bohemia and Moravia. The latter group soon departed for Moravia, but largely on foot, since the train system was overwhelmed with military transport demands.[72]

As this example shows, Austrian and Hungarian refugee policy—as it developed—divided migrants both according to their citizenship status

Evacuated population, Galicia, 1914. Credit: Österreichische Nationalbibliothek.

and according to their financial means. Austrian citizens were the responsibility of the Austrian government and entitled to aid and a daily allowance of 70 Heller from their state (raised to 90 Heller in 1915), to be paid only on Austrian territory. As Austrians, the Galician Jews who made it to Bárta/Bardejov/Bartfeld, for example, were not entitled to aid from Hungary. The second critical division separated refugees who could provide for themselves *(bemittelt)* from those who could not *(unbemittelt)*. Those in the first category had more rights to travel on their own within Austria or Hungary to destinations other than the receiving camps. Those who could not provide for themselves, however, had to be transported to camps in Austria and in the meanwhile hope for help from the international aid organizations such as the American Jewish Joint Distribution Committee, which swiftly set up centers in areas where refugees collected.

Very quickly it became apparent that the distinction between *bemittelt* and *unbemittelt* resulted not only from state fears of contagion and criminality, but also from attempts to maintain morale and then later, from attempts to shape refugee behavior. The government justified the creation of barrack camps by arguing that "in big cities or rural areas . . . every type of control [of these people], especially those of a sanitary nature, would become impossible." Moreover the state hoped to house "people of the same nationality wherever possible in the same area in order to maintain their feeling of *Heimat*."[73] The state used barrack-camps to control morale and hygiene, while instilling normative behaviors for work, leisure, and morality. Refugee experts also worried about the potentially ill effects of barracks life on the morale of the more affluent among the refugees. They often provided them with separate private housing, thus exacerbating class tensions among populations that the state was supposed to treat equally and fairly.[74]

In the summer of 1915 Austria-Hungary reconquered most of Galicia and Bukovina, but in May found itself under attack from Italy. Most Galician refugees were moved from Styria and Lower Austria to camps in Bohemia, and many were sent back to Galicia later that year. In turn, thousands of Italian-speaking refugees from Trentino replaced the Galicians in the Wagna barracks camp (near Leibniz Styria). Thousands more Italian-speakers ended up in camps at Braunnau in Upper Austria or Mitterndorf and Pottendorf in Lower Austria. At the same time some 80,000 Slovene-speakers who fled the western border areas around Görz / Gorica/Goriza and the Isonzo region in the face of Italian invaders also ended up in the camps.[75]

As camps became more permanent fixtures on the Austrian landscape, they offered catchall solutions to a broad range of population control issues—some even unconnected to the war—that went well beyond simply aiding and accommodating refugees. There were camps for interned enemy aliens trapped in Austria-Hungary at the outset of the war, camps for those preemptively evacuated from theaters of war, camps for uncooperative refugees, a special camp for Roma populations, and camps for those removed from border regions under suspicion of political unreliability.[76] In this last category the judgment of a person's unreliability often rested on little more than his or her having belonged to a prewar Italian nationalist association, having been involved in electoral agitation for Italian nationalism, or having attempted to escape military conscription.[77]

The situation was little better for Italian-speaking Austrian refugees who found themselves under Italian occupation or in Italy. Local populations also suffered from food shortages and treated unwanted refugees with great suspicion. In general, and especially after the spectacular Austro-German victory at Caporetto/Kobarid in the fall of 1917, the Italian military treated Italian-speaking Austrians with enormous distrust as *austriacanti,* or Austrophiles. When his forces occupied a border town early in the war, one Italian general already warned Italian-speaking Austrian locals, "My soldiers are convinced that they are conducting a war of liberation, not occupation and woe betide you, if they learn that you are not content to be liberated from Austria."[78]

All these camps rapidly became new locations of wartime human misery. They were poorly planned, hastily constructed, and almost immediately overcrowded with unexpectedly large numbers of refugees, evacuees, and politically suspect people. Their inmates suffered from poor nutrition, disease, exhaustion, mental depression, and dislocation. The Moravian collection camp in Ungarisch Hradisch/Uherský Hradiště, for example, held over 90,000 people at the end of 1916. The Wagna camp, with barracks whose construction had begun in October 1914, held 21,300 people in May of 1915. By the end of 1915, however, the camps in Austria technically had spaces for up to 130,000 people.[79]

Inside the early camps refugees felt more like prisoners than unfortunate loyal citizens deserving aid from their empire. This was partly because some camps were also used to house interned resident enemy aliens, but mostly because of government fears about contagion—especially typhus—and a lack of local officials who could speak Polish, Ruthene, Yiddish, or later Italian or Slovene. Hygiene in the first camps was indeed disastrous. At the Thalerhof camp in Styria alone some 2,000 people died of various illnesses during the war. Medical care was scarce because at least a third of the physicians working for the crownland government had been conscripted by October of 1914.[80] Moreover, administrators faced outbreaks of diseases that had not been seen locally for decades. The almost prison-like conditions in the camps also did little to endear their occupants to the empire. How many things the stay in Mitterndorf has taught us," one refugee from the region around Trento confided bitterly to her diary in 1917; "how much ideas have changed with regard to patriotism."[81] In the face of its own internal humanitarian disaster, which was exacerbated by differences of language among its refugee citizens, the empire lost one of the most crucial battles of the war. It failed to hold the minds and hearts of thousands of displaced ordinary women and men.

Despite strict censorship, news of the desperate conditions in the early camps soon leaked to the press. The Cracow newspaper *Nowa Reforma* published a scathing report by Galician crownland officials. Their visit to Wagna and Thalerhof early in 1915 prompted their demand that the Galician governor's office, reeling from its own recent evacuation to the border town of Biala, intervene with the Ministry of the Interior. While the Interior Ministry denied accusations of maladministration in Wagna, the Styrian government did install a large delousing and bathing unit.[82] Nevertheless, as late as the spring of 1916, parliamentary deputies of the Italian People's Party from Friuli could still demand from the Interior Ministry that refugees from their region be housed in only nearby Carniola and Styria, that barracks be arranged according to people's village of origin, that food should be prepared by people familiar with the local cuisine, that there should be no restrictions on refugees' freedom to come and go from the barracks, and that they should be run more like town welfare institutions than prisons. Above all, the deputies demanded that the barracks should lose "the character of penal colonies that they have assumed in the psychology of the refugees."[83]

Increasingly sensitive to accusations about poor conditions in the refugee and internment camps, the government tried to paint a better picture of conditions there and to dispel recurring rumors that camp inmates, for example, were subjected to involuntary labor or that they were work shy and refused paid labor on nearby farms. When, for example, the neutral American government conveyed complaints to the Austro-Hungarian Ministry of Foreign Affairs about conditions for interned Italian citizens in the Croatian Koprivnica camp in 1916, the ministry assured the Americans that internees often ate more regularly than did local civilians. Camp inmates allegedly received a daily portion of 400 grams of bread, and when meat prices allowed, goulash on Sundays, Mondays, and Thursdays.[84] But even if conditions inside the camps were occasionally better than they were on the outside, imperial officials still found themselves in an impossible situation since such favorable comparisons did little to win them any gratitude.

The government also worried about the psychological health of the inmates. Long-term stays in the barracks might reduce inmates' "normal love of homeland" and eventually create moral havoc in the camps. Given the refugees' often violent separation from their homes and loved ones, and their current lives in unaccustomed surroundings far from home, the government sought ways to rebuild their mental, moral, and cultural state by creating a sense of normalcy for them. One Austrian Ministry of the Interior report concluded in 1915 that it was crucial that refugee mental depression not threaten the mood of the population in the hinterland. "Comfort, distraction, and useful occupation should be offered them, without competing with the local labor market, [along with] instruction for refugee youth." As camps became more permanent in nature, some also built special barracks for food stores, butchers, bakers, public kitchens, hospitals, schools, and even churches to create a greater sense of normal life.[85] But then normal life during the war was a relative concept, rarely possible outside the camps, much less inside.

In the interests of promoting greater wartime solidarity the Wagna administration even published a daily camp newspaper that refugees could purchase for a price of four Heller. The first issue in October 1915 welcomed 4,040 Friulians and 13,460 Istrians in a bilingual (German-Italian) edition, explaining to them that the former Galician inhabitants of the camp had returned to their "native soil." "You are welcome as guests in Green Styria," the newspaper told them, "and German hospitality should alleviate your suffering, which is also our suffering." The newspaper offered (different) serialized novels in both German and Italian, hopeful news from the various fronts, relevant government decrees, humorous war stories, and in the second edition, an invitation to all girls and women over the age of fourteen to register for the Wagna camp needlework school.[86]

In March 1917 we even catch overt glimmers of a kind of imperial patriotic opportunism in the government's report to crownland officials

Women's sewing class in the barracks of the refugee camp at Wagna, 1915. From a propaganda album entitled *Flüchtlingsfürsorge* (Care for the Refugees) published by the Austrian Ministry of the Interior. Credit: Österreichische Nationalbibliothek.

that many refugees who spoke Ruthenian (now referred to more frequently as Ukrainian), Italian, Romanian, Slovene, or Croatian had asked camp administrations to organize German-language school classes for their children, "in order to assure their economic futures." Urging provincial administrators to respond favorably to such requests, Vienna officials argued optimistically that these efforts would "encourage the development of more lively economic and social relations between the borderlands and the hinterlands of the monarchy, and directly deepen people's unified feelings of belonging together."[87] Some officials dared hope that human catastrophe might yet strengthen the post-war empire.

Those refugees whose family or work connections or resources in the west allowed them to settle independently (legally or often illegally) in cities like Budapest, Prague, or Vienna also experienced dislocation and deprivation, as well as extremely hostile attitudes from their new neighbors. Often stores refused to serve them, and municipal governments concerned about infection frequently subjected them to involuntary physical examination. Much of the anti-refugee hostility in the cities was directed at Galician Jews, although there are plenty of documented examples of local contempt directed at Polish-speaking or Ukrainian-speaking refugees as well. In 1917, for example, the Prague city council—citing fears of contagion—even attempted to ban Jewish refugees altogether from using the public tram service, although the measure had to be quickly reversed.[88]

The state met the unprecedented challenges of wartime migration in ways that demonstrated some creativity and care. Nevertheless, given the extraordinary demands of waging total war, it lacked sufficient resources to create even the bare minimum conditions of life for its displaced citizens. The more the state labored to accommodate refugees needs, the less gratitude it earned, either from the displaced themselves, or from their unwilling hosts in the general population. Imperial officials failed to influence the attitudes of locals—themselves already victims of shortages. Why should they welcome refugees whom they viewed as foreigners, sources of contagion, and social disruption and decidedly not as fellow imperial citizens in need?

Propaganda for Empire

In the early years of the war, the state did little to augment its harsh censorship regime (especially in Austria) with positive forms of war propaganda. Later, however, the AOK cultivated the talents of several Austrian journalists, artists, photographers, and film production companies in order to depict the war graphically—and favorably—to the public. In December of 1915 the Austrian KÜA and Hungarian HB also began to hold weekly press conferences in Vienna and Budapest for groups of invited journalists, in the belief that providing some news was more effective in controlling information reaching the home front than providing none at all.[89] Through its War Press Agency (*Kriegspressequartier*, or KPQ) the AOK eventually set up a large propaganda machine in the last two years of the war.

The practices of the KPQ mirrored the corrosive prejudices of the AOK about the peoples of the empire. The KPQ divided reporters into Austrian and Hungarian sections, whose official languages were German and Hungarian, and effectively cut Slavic journalists out of the information loop altogether. Only rarely were journalists actually provided the opportunity to visit the front, and when such visits took place, they were carefully monitored. In the summer of 1915, when Austria-Hungary retook the fortress at Przemyśl in Galicia or conquered Serbia, KPQ-accredited journalists were finally allowed to visit a front. Most field commanders, however, shared Conrad von Hötzendorf's animosity to the press, and only a few saw the cultivation of relations with reporters as a way to burnish their reputations with the public.

Wartime propaganda in the first years of war was a byproduct of private campaigns undertaken by wartime charitable causes or of public efforts to sell war bonds. Most of these campaigns focused on the needs of local men at the front rather than on imperial patriotism. A key challenge was to develop a coordinated set of specific but empire-wide messages for the troops at the front and for the population at home. Eventually the War Archive (*Kriegsarchiv*), which oversaw much propaganda creation, became active in creating propaganda specifically designed to raise domestic morale. In 1916, for example, it produced something like a basic war almanac with photographs of the imperial family and patriotic essays by well-known German-language writers like Arthur Schnitzler or Stefan Zweig. Soon, similar German-language anthologies containing accounts of experiences at specific fronts or battles followed.[90] Some of these publications also appeared in Croatian, Czech, Hungarian, and Polish translation, but for the most part they were directed at a German-speaking public. In the later years of the war, the archive also organized exhibitions of paintings and photographs by artists on war themes in cities across Austria-Hungary including Budapest, Vienna, Graz, Zagreb, Prague, Salzburg, and Innsbruck.

In May 1916 the most ambitious of the war Exhibitions, and by far the largest, opened in Vienna's Prater. In over forty exhibition halls visitors could experience every aspect of the war, from the home front (exhibitions about ersatz foods), to a replica of a front line trench, to artificial limbs devised for wounded veterans.[91] Maureen Healy's brilliant analysis of this exhibition, which ran for over a year, suggests, however, that since the depiction of certain elements of wartime life in the exhibition directly contradicted people's personal experience, the entertainment value of the exhibition far outweighed its potential propaganda value.[92] The same could probably be said for the many wartime propaganda films made at the behest of the regime. In 1915, for example, Vienna and Budapest each sported about 150 cinemas. Smaller cities like Zagreb, Kolozsvár/Cluj/Klausenburg, and Pozsony/Pressburg had far fewer cinemas. By the end of the war Prague had thirty-five. During the war far more impromptu cinemas came into being. Film studios multiplied during the war. They also worked to consolidate Austrian and Hungarian film companies for the purpose of coordinating feature films about the war as well as newsreel footage and propaganda films. It was all entertainment, so people went. It had little effect on peoples' attitude toward the war, in part because, as with the war-exhibitions, the experiences of the audiences starkly contradicted the depictions and claims made about wartime conditions in such propaganda.

Reviving Legitimacy

> It was nine o'clock in a cold November evening. . . . On most evenings the people of Budapest, sick of the monotonous sadness of war news, would hurry past the depressing news stands—but tonight they stopped to look and read. . . . Today for a while they put aside their daily anxiety for those on the front line, their fears and worry for husbands, sons and brothers who were prisoners of war, their anguish for the dead. Today all were overcome by the sense of a great national disaster, by the fear of what was to come and the terror of an unknown future. What was drawing everyone to those brightly lit newsstands was the announcement of the death of Franz Joseph.[93]

On 21 November 1916 the man who had embodied both dynasty and empire for almost seventy years died. Francis Joseph had not always been the beloved grandfather of his people but he had long ago become a crucial symbol of continuity and was venerated as a protector by people of all social, linguistic, religious, and political groups in the empire. Few people in 1916 could have remembered the time before Francis Joseph was the ruler. His death brought anxiety and uncertainty as Austria-Hungary's peoples faced the third and worst winter of the war.

The new emperor-king was Francis Joseph's great nephew, Charles (1887–1922), a young man of twenty-nine years. In 1911 Charles had married Princess Zita of Bourbon Parma, and at the time of Francis Joseph's death the couple had four young children with more on the way. Charles was untested, inexperienced in state affairs, and far less known to his subjects than his uncle, the former heir Francis Ferdinand, had been. He assumed the throne during a war that demanded unprecedented sacrifice from those subjects. It was therefore all the more important for the legitimacy of the dynasty and the continuity of the state that he successfully inhabit the role of imperial father figure by immediately establishing a recognizable, comforting, and popular profile.[94] Like his ancestors Joseph II and Francis II/I, Francis Joseph had filled the unglamorous role of first servant of the state, legendarily rising every day before dawn, and retiring only when there was no unfinished business remaining on his desk. What could Charles's role look like?

Charles and the men around him sought to create a visible public persona for his peoples, although they do not always seem to have been clear about the particular content of those images. The depictions of Charles certainly conveyed his personal piety, his dutiful devotion to his young family, and his willingness to traverse the empire to meet with frontline troops and population. As part of the young emperor-king's efforts to promote a greater connection between the dynasty and the people, he and Zita made highly public—and often filmed—visits to several sites of the fighting from Bukovina to South Tyrol. Zita, too, assumed an active role in several Austrian and Hungarian war charities, and in 1917 Charles was even the subject of a propaganda film entitled *Our Emperor*. Charles was not necessarily comfortable with the idea of using his person to market the empire to his subjects, but he was far more willing than Francis Joseph had been to use new technologies of communication for this purpose during the war.

In fact one of his first filmed actions as king was his coronation. Hungary's leaders insisted that the ceremony in Budapest take place as soon as possible following Francis Joseph's funeral, and after several last-minute changes, it was scheduled for 30 December 1916. To Hungarian leaders it was crucial that the new king undergo the coronation ritual both to bolster his legitimacy in Hungary and to rally the Hungarian populace for the war effort. A coronation also created a highly visible opportunity to reintroduce Charles and his family to his people. One reason for doing so was that from the start of his reign Charles sought to take the empire in some new directions, many of which worried Hungary's political leaders. They feared that Charles was close to many of his Uncle Francis Ferdinand's advisers, whose reputations were decidedly anti-Hungarian, a suspicion confirmed early on when Charles nominated Count Ottokar Czernin (1872–1932), another man associated with Archduke Francis Ferdinand, to be Austria-Hungary's new foreign minister. The swift coronation was meant to diffuse these concerns, while also enabling Hungary's leaders to make their wishes known to the sovereign.

Count Miklós Bánffy (1873–1950), director of the Hungarian State Theaters (1913–1918) and later novelist, was entrusted with the critical design of this first coronation since 1867. Not surprisingly, Bánffy reported difficulties in obtaining craftsmen to create the ambitious decorations for the coronation church. Another problem was that the cameras and lighting required considerable electricity, so difficult to procure in wartime. The coronation ceremonies ultimately came off smoothly, and the new king managed successfully to mount his horse for the cameras and then gallop up the artificial hill that had been prepared outside of the coronation church.

From there he waved a sword in the four directions of the compass. Bánffy also noted that the royal couple, highly conscious of the impression they sought to make on the public, displayed their four-year-old son and heir, Otto, prominently during the ceremony. Only after the coronation church had emptied out, Bánffy recalled, did something happen that might have produced gossip about dire omens for the future, had people known about it. A protective sheet of heavy plate glass that Bánffy had hoisted above the altar to protect the space under the arc lights "split in the heat and crashed like a giant guillotine to the altar . . . below."[95]

Charles hoped to change Austria-Hungary's dangerous wartime political situation by creating new domestic and foreign policy options. He shook up the military command, replacing Archduke Friedrich with himself as commander in chief, and removing Conrad from the general

Newly crowned King Charles IV of Hungary taking an oath outside the Mathias Church in Budapest, 30 December 1916. Credit: Österreichische Nationalbibliothek.

staff. He repeatedly sought both publicly and secretly to sound out the allied powers about the possibility of leaving the war and even of concluding a separate peace. He reestablished constitutional rule in Austria, ending the military dictatorship that had governed Austria since the summer of 1914. He sought significant political allies in Hungary to support an extension of the suffrage and a more tolerant policy toward Hungary's national minorities. In March 1917 he sanctioned the creation of a complaint commission with worker representation for those industrial workers subject to military discipline.[96] In May 1917 Charles reopened the Austrian Parliament, implicitly encouraging politicians to make known their demands for reform of the monarchy. That summer he issued a general amnesty that freed countless prisoners condemned by military tribunals for a range of political offenses, including Friedrich Adler, the Socialist who had assassinated Austrian Prime Minister Stürgkh at his lunch in 1916. The amnesty also freed several leading Czech nationalist parliamentary deputies including Karel Kramář (1860–1937) and Alois

Rašín (1867–1923), who were awaiting trial on trumped-up charges of treason.

By October, the wartime censorship imposed by the AOK was also ended in Austria, replaced by prewar standards of censorship.

Given the inescapable structural reality of the German alliance however, none of these measures, from ending the military dictatorship and liberalizing public life to signaling support for suffrage reform in Hungary, succeeded in creating significant space for maneuver. Liberalization did not unify Austria's politicians behind a new course. Instead, it set them at odds with each other and demonstrated how radicalized their prewar political conflicts had become. There was even less space in foreign affairs, thanks to the German alliance. Despite the promising negotiations he undertook with the allied powers both publicly and secretly, Charles could not extricate himself from the embrace of the German alliance. He could not realistically take Austria-Hungary out of the war. As both he and Czernin learned, the degree to which Austria-Hungary had become both militarily and economically dependent on its German ally in the past two years made the pursuit of an independent foreign policy ultimately impossible.[97]

At his very first Common Cabinet meeting held 12 January 1917, Charles was ready to hear arguments about how to reconstruct the empire in a way that would conciliate the nationalists. Could Austria-Hungary trade Eastern Galicia to Russia in return for Russian Poland, thus allowing the creation of a Ukrainian state in Russia and a Habsburg-dominated Poland? Could the monarchy create a new South Slav entity in Austria that would serve as the basis for transforming dualism (Austria-Hungary) into trialism (Austria-Hungary-Yugoslavia)? Although Tisza strongly opposed any hint of trialism, Charles hoped at least to gain the support of nationalist and Social Democrat politicians for a federal transformation of empire, which would better ensure its long-term survival.[98]

The reestablishment of a more normal political life in Austria constituted a sincere attempt to rebuild political support for the empire among alienated nationalist political parties and groups that had suffered particularly at the hands of the military dictatorship. Not surprisingly, though, the effects of the reopening of Parliament were not what Charles had expected. The freeing up of civic life in Austria produced immediate and massive public complaints about living and working conditions. Opening previously closed channels for political complaints and political opposition resulted in harsh and openly articulated criticism against the regime. More and more, public debate demonstrated that the parties had ratcheted up their demands during the two years of dictatorship and were in no mood to compromise. Parliamentary commissions, for example, immediately initiated investigations into the unfair imprisonment of people during the hysteria surrounding the outbreak of the war. Nationalist parties rushed to publicize their formal reform demands for restructuring the empire. On 30 May Anton Korošec (1872–1940), deputy for the Slovene People's Party and member of the newly constituted Yugoslav Club, read out the so-called May Declaration that called for the unification of South Slavs within a single administrative unit comparable to Austria and Hungary within the monarchy. The Czech Union (of Czech nationalist parties plus most of the Social Democrats) submitted its own program that same day calling for an autonomous Czech and Slovak state within a restructured federation.[99]

If the government had unwittingly encouraged these demands, it did little to respond to them creatively. Charles and the bureaucrat-politicians on whom he largely relied to govern Austria were used to thinking of empire in terms of the priority of the whole. In consequence, they tended not to understand the privileged position of the German language in the civil administration, for example, as a problem. They did not entertain seriously the major demands for autonomy of the nationalist politicians, many of whom contradicted each other by demanding overlapping territories for their particular future federal units. Charles's advisors also did not want to threaten the political relationship with Hungary, whose leaders looked askance at any federalization effort. When the government failed to respond adequately to the May Declaration, the deputies who supported it turned to the people to apply pressure on the government. In Slovene-speaking regions of Carniola, South Styria, Istria, and Trieste/ Trst, for example, a Yugoslav petition movement developed in the fall of 1917 demanding the enforcement of the May Declaration. Typically these petitions opened with phrases like "Long live the Habsburgs and a happy Yugoslavia under their scepter!" and typically members of the local Catholic clergy, which traditionally supported the Habsburgs as well, also lent the petitions their support. From September 1917 to March 1918 in South Styria alone the petitioners collected over 72,000 signatures.[100]

In the north, meanwhile, the government along with its German ally was also willing to concede the creation of a new Polish kingdom—hopefully under the rule of a Habsburg archduke—but it also sought to balance Ukrainian nationalist demands. When in February 1918, for example, Austria-Hungary signed a peace treaty with the new Ukrainian Republic (formerly part of Russia) and offered it an eastern part of occupied (Russian) Poland, Polish nationalists protested vigorously and withdrew their support from the cabinet. In each case nationalist activists maneuvered to advance their own state-building efforts—still inside the nominal framework of a Habsburg Empire—even as their contradicting positions made that framework increasingly tenuous.[101]

As Charles groped his way toward some kind of federalist solution to the nationalist demands of the parties in Austria, Hungary's political rulers showed no interest in any reform that would structurally undermine the authority of their own political nation by empowering the parties of the so-called national minorities. At most, Tisza was willing to make minor concessions to Romanian nationalists. He and his allies would not even consider a suffrage reform to enfranchise war veterans (the so-called heroes' right to vote), as some parties like the Catholic Socials suggested. Even at this late stage in the war Tisza adamantly argued, "This would involve carelessly granting political rights to strata and factors which are not ripe for them."[102] Some members of the establishment opposition shot back that extension of the suffrage might be the only means of saving the regime from revolution:

> It is better if we overcome them when they have the right to vote, than if we exclude them from that right, abandon them to extreme despair and thus undermine the very basis of the state. . . . If the government and the leading circles think that they need not conduct an entirely new social policy for which the first step must be taken now, then there really will be a revolution.[103]

Thanks in large measure to intolerable conditions of hunger and deprivation, the last two years of the war saw rapidly increasing numbers of industrial strikes, political demonstrations, violent incidents, and even mutinies. Up until the end of 1916 industrial strikes had largely been localized, partly because of harsh military discipline in the factories and the knowledge among male skilled workers that they could be sent to the front for any infraction of work discipline. The introduction of the new complaint commissions with worker representation, which could also decide wage rates for militarized industries, soon led workers in other industries to strike for the same rights.[104] Just as with political liberalization, creative solutions like the complaint commissions to wartime problems created only new problems. In 1917 far more strikes involving far more workers than in previous years took place, all with similar demands for better wages, shorter hours, bread, and peace. Socialist leaders who gained significant power through the complaint commissions now found it increasingly difficult to keep their members in line, a fact commented on by local civil administrators in Styria, who noted that "if today the Social Democratic Party, which to a certain extent sides with the government, loses its power over the dissatisfied masses, then it will be even harder to maintain quiet."[105]

In 1918 three massive waves of industrial strikes in January, March, and June paralyzed Austrian and Hungarian industrial output. When it looked as if the peace negotiations with Russia might collapse, a strike broke out in Wiener Neustadt on January 12 and soon spread to other industrial centers in Austria. On 16 January the Social Democratic leadership retroactively sanctioned the work stoppages. On 17 January 20,000 Styrian metal workers went on strike. By 22 January, over 40,000 workers in industrial Styria were on strike, and a demonstration of 15,000 in Graz brought the workers' demands—including a call for immediate peace—to the provincial governor.[106] Although the Socialists just barely retained control over demonstrations in Styria, they failed to do so elsewhere in the empire. Strike actions also spread to industrial workers in Hungary. In Budapest renegade workers called a general strike, and on 19 January industrial workers in Szeged mimicked the Russian revolution by setting up municipal workers' councils.[107]

Fears that peace would fail and food shortages would not be alleviated sparked worker actions. According to an Interior Ministry memorandum to the emperor in February 1918, the strikes "began with complaints about insufficient food supplies, but spread just as quickly into the political realm and evolved finally into a peace demonstration in which 550,000 workers [from around Austria] took part. Strikers included women."[108] The government did its best to stabilize the situation since it did not have the manpower to put down the strikes with force, as all available men were at the front. However, in 1918 there was no solution in sight to the food problem. Even in Hungary food production reached terrifying lows—the yield on potatoes, for example, had fallen from 211 million quintals in 1914 to 90 million in 1918. There were general strikes in Budapest on Mayday and again in June 1918.[109]

Meanwhile the military fared little better. As in other belligerent countries, the Austro-Hungarian military faced increasing desertions, and in 1918, open mutinies. On 30 January in Pola/Pula, Austria-Hungary's main naval facility, dockworkers and some military special forces struck on 22 January. A deputation demanded higher wages, the provision of shoes and clothing, and the return of their families who had been transported to camps in the interior when war with Italy had broken out. After negotiations, the crowd remained dissatisfied and refused to return to work, accusing the deputation of having been bought off.[110] Then in February, sailors of several language groups serving in the Adriatic fleet both in Pola/Pula and further south in Cattaro mutinied outright in sympathy with dock strikes in Pola/Pula and Trieste/Trst. This was merely the best known mutiny. Several took place in larger and smaller garrisons in both Austria and Hungary.[111]

Thousands of returning POWs from Russia also posed a potential security problem, according to the AOK and KÜA. In May 1918 the gendarmerie department in Żółkiew/Zhovka, a town just north of Lemberg/Lwów/Lviv reported to the Austrian Ministries of the Interior and of Defense that "a majority of the returning POW's from Russia had experienced the revolution and was permeated with revolutionary tendencies."[112] This report—like many others—confirmed the earlier suspicions of General Max Ronge, head of the AOK's intelligence bureau, who warned that POWs had been infected in Russia by the "Bolshevik bacillus." In consequence, "what awaits returning POW's is not a jubilant welcome but a thorough examination of heart and conscience." Before receiving their leave, these former POWs were held in so-called returnee camps *(Heimkehrlager)* for medical examinations and ten days of "disciplinary reeducation."[113] The gendarmes from Żółkiew/Zhovka wrote their report primarily to complain that the former POWs in the returnee camps in fact enjoyed far too much freedom to roam the area and openly express their regret in nearby villages for having returned to Austria-Hungary. Of the 120,272 returning POWs screened by May 1918, only 517 were suspected of disloyal activity (that could not be proved) and only 603 deserted (for any number of possible reasons) before their investigation had been finalized.[114]

Strikes, mutinies, and even desertions to the enemy worried the government, but the biggest challenge to the legitimacy of the empire remained its inability to feed its population. As long as the war dragged on, the basic calculus that determined food provision would not change. In fact it could only get worse. Treaties with newly independent Ukraine and with defeated Romania and Russia in 1918 raised sporadic hopes for increased food supplies to reach the cities. The Treaty of Brest-Litovsk with Russia, signed in March 1918, was even known by many as the "bread peace" although little came of it.[115] At the beginning of October, when Styria, for one, could no longer guarantee the provisioning of the crownland for more than a week, the Vienna government gave up its authority and passed the buck to the crownlands, authorizing them to distribute the remaining food reserves.[116]

If nothing could be done to improve the food supply, Charles nevertheless kept trying to relieve public misery in other ways that might rebuild public trust. In August 1917 the government created a new cabinet Ministry for Social Welfare. This new ministry would organize all welfare for the Austrian Empire—especially institutions for children and orphans—under the auspices of the central state, doling out the considerable funds allotted to the orphans and widows fund.[117] From the start the state foresaw using the scientific expertise and popularity developed by existing and private welfare organizations. These, in turn, were largely in the hands of nationalist organizations. Private and parallel Czech and German nationalist Provincial Commissions for Child and Youth Welfare (the *Česká zemská komise pro ochranu dětí a péči o mládež* and the *Deutsche Landesstelle für Kinderschutz und Jugendfürsorge*) had already developed intricate networks of local welfare organizations in Bohemia,

Austria-Hungary with wartime Polish and Balkan Zones of Occupation

particularly institutions that aimed both to protect and to nationalize children.[118]

The new minister for social welfare, economist Viktor Mataja (1857–1934), recognized from the start that his new ministry could be effective only if it mobilized the expertise of these private organizations. In a speech to Parliament he assured deputies, "The new Ministry for Social Welfare ... will in particular strive to attract the enthusiastic cooperation of private associations and autonomous organizations." When the new ministry organized a council charged with developing empire-wide policies on youth welfare, its board consisted mainly of representatives

appointed from Czech, German, Italian, Croat, Polish, and Jewish nationalist organizations.[119] Justifying their bid for influence, one Czech
nationalist on the Youth Welfare Board wrote, "Our deep understanding
of practical life has convinced the [Czech Provincial Commission]
that . . . we can only hope for success with a law written in a national
spirit, which can count on the deepest sympathy and eager cooperation
of the widest masses."[120] In other words, only an institution that gave
power to local nationalists could gain the confidence of the people.

Nationalist activists from private organizations staffed the new Welfare Ministry at all levels, and in Bohemia, the millions of crowns allo-
cated to the ministry were essentially distributed to Czech and German
nationalist welfare associations. But if the state hoped to harness the
nationally segregated private child welfare system to achieve its own
goals, it was mistaken. Clients of the welfare system increasingly identified nationalist organizations rather than the imperial state as the source
of the aid they received.[121] One German nationalist newspaper justified
the close nationalist involvement with the state arguing that the latter
functioned thanks only to the expertise and assistance given it by the
former. In this sense the nationalist associations had become the state:

> One often encounters the claim that the care of war widows and or-
> phans is not the responsibility of private charity, but is solely the task
> of the state. . . . Only who is the state in the final analysis? In fact it is
> only us, in that directly or indirectly, we must provide the state with
> the means that will enable it to fulfill its duties.[122]

The new welfare initiatives tried to help the growing number of vulnerable Austrians where it could, and in doing so, it reinforced the influence
and popularity of regional nationalist forces by allowing them to regulate the distribution of aid and claim credit for it. This would matter a
great deal when, less than a year later, those same regional nationalist
forces proclaimed themselves to be the new state.

Two Last-Minute Journeys

Under these fateful conditions for the empire, two independent observers
undertook informational trips in the late summer of 1918. One of them,

Vienna Socialist and education reformer Robert Scheu traveled privately to Bohemia from July to September to obtain a clearer picture for himself of Czech-German national relations. The other, Count István Tisza, former prime minister of Hungary, traveled to Croatia, Dalmatia, and Bosnia Herzegovina in September to survey the food supply situation. Tisza's journey came at the request of the sovereign, who apparently still hoped that the experience would somehow change Tisza's adamant opposition to the idea of creating a unified South-Slav third administrative unit within the monarchy. Tisza well understood the implicit purpose of his trip, writing, "My actual task is to become informed of the political situation (South-Slav agitation, etc.) and report on it."[123]

To the north in Bohemia Scheu interviewed local businessmen, civil servants, priests, teachers, and local and provincial nationalist politicians like Karel Kramař, as well as ordinary peasants. While the politicians gave Scheu a picture of imminent radical political transformation, the impressions he gathered from the others about the near future were not so clear. Scheu later recounted that he heard remarkably little animosity from Czech peasants toward local Germans, but a lot of complaints about arrogant German-speaking civil servants and German-speaking military officials. One relatively prosperous farmer from the region around Budweis/Budjěovice asserted to Scheu that the Kingdom of Bohemia would now become autonomous, much like the Kingdom of Hungary, and that this step would make Czechs free. This view suggests the degree to which many people imagined a reformed future very much in the framework of the recent past. The end of the war would bring an independent Czech nation-state into being but somehow it would be defined in relation to an ongoing Habsburg imperial whole. In this sense Scheu's report documents the great distance in imagination that existed between the views of politicians who foresaw the end of empire, and the views of the people when it came to imagining the future.

The highpoint of Tisza's trip, meanwhile, came with his arrival in Sarajevo after tours of Croatia, Dalmatia, and Herzegovina. In the Bosnian capital he met with deputies from the Bosnian Diet. They submitted a declaration to him that protested the merciless wartime treatment of the local population, and petitioned the former prime minister for a general amnesty, compensation for war losses, and the restoration of local autonomy. Tisza, however, addressed the parliamentary delegation allegedly in the arrogant tones with which "a feudal lord receives his serfs." In turn, as Bosnia's governor, Stjepan Sarkotić (1858–1939), recounted, "The delegation turned their backs on Count Tisza and left," adding in his own report to Vienna that what Tisza told the Bosnian leaders "was so brusque that I will refrain from transmitting it on the Hughes-Machine." In his own account of the day, Tisza reiterated that the dualist structure of the monarchy and the federalist relationship between Croatia and Hungary were "immovable barriers between which all the plans and endeavors of Bosnia and Herzegovina must move." There could be no South-Slav unit and no trialist solution (Austria-Hungary-Yugoslavia) because this would constitute an abrogation of the 1867 Settlement. Sarkotić described Tisza in this moment as a man "who suddenly notices an abyss at his feet, is caught by vertigo, but cannot make a step either forward or backward." In the face of the abyss, Tisza remained bound by narrow and conventional options for the future, thanks to his all-too-limited understanding of the recent past.[124]

"As If There Had Been No Revolution at All"

With its resources strained to the extreme after four long years, the empire's capacity to inspire hope for a different future—let alone guarantee physical survival in the present—finally collapsed.[125] Just as the military fronts buckled (Bulgaria withdrew from the war in late September, while the Italians broke through in late October, exactly one year after their humiliation at Caporetto/Kobarid), the powerful sense of reciprocal relations that had linked the state to its citizens disintegrated. The empire's inability to feed and care for its citizens and its often harsh wartime treatment of them had exposed its abject failure to fulfill its side of the equation of sacrifice and reward. This failure in turn produced a general indifference to the fate of empire, which allowed regional nationalist authorities to take power from the imperial authorities at the end of October (in Cracow, Lemberg/Lwów/Lviv, Prague, Zagreb, Vienna) and in some cases produced social revolution (Budapest).

No doubt this regional breakup was reinforced by the fact in the summer of 1918 the British, French, and Americans finally, if reluctantly, agreed to the dissolution of the empire and the creation of the new states of Czechoslovakia, Poland, and Yugoslavia. The particular borders of those states were still to be decided. Now in October, however, came the moment for action, as nationalists groped—and often bumbled—their way toward establishing new states.[126]

On 2 October, sensing what was coming, Charles's new prime minister openly promised the Austrian Parliament a federal reorganization of the empire. Few paid attention, however, as the leaders of the Czech, Polish, and Slovene nationalist political parties denied Vienna's right to determine their futures. As early as 5 October a National Council of Slovenes, Croats, and Serbs had constituted itself in Zagreb and declared itself the institutional representative of the South Slav peoples. Two weeks later members of this council refused to attend the Hungarian Parliament and instead formed an executive committee that would act as a government, at least in Croatia. On 11 October the Polish national parliamentary deputies created a national council in Cracow as a first step toward joining Galicia to a new Polish Republic with its capital in Warsaw. On 17 October Romanian nationalist deputies from Bukovina formed a Romanian National Council in Vienna.[127]

National committees were not the only ones scrambling to secure a better future for their regions. In Styria, representatives of business and labor began to negotiate secretly with the object of taking over the crownland administration from the government. They planned to guarantee the food supply by directly bartering Styrian industrial products—from iron, coal, and magnesium to wire and paper—for grains, fats, and meats from neighboring crownlands. The negotiators elected a Committee of Public Welfare co-chaired by a Socialist and a German nationalist (later joined by a Christian Socialist). When committee members made their proposals public on 20 October, they gained considerable public support, the *Grazer Tagblatt* noting for its middle-class readers that "as there is no central office forming in Vienna, we here in the country cannot wait any longer. We must give up on powers that cannot protect us from starvation."[128] Within a week both the central and crownland governments agreed to give Eisler and Kranz full authority as "Commissioners of the Economy." Clearly a federalist devolution of imperial powers was not simply a nationalist phenomenon. Nationalists were often—but not always—simply the political actors best situated to make the argument for independence most persuasively. As things fell apart, however, individual districts even tried to close themselves off from neighboring districts in a kind of "every man for himself" effort to hold onto what resources they had.[129]

In Vienna, Charles tried in vain to slow the growing dissolution of his state by announcing a federalization of the Austrian half of the empire on 16 October:

> Following the desires of its peoples, Austria shall become a federal state in which each national component [Volksstamm] will form its own state organization in its area of settlement. . . . This reorganization, which in no way touches the integrity of the lands of Hungary's holy crown, guarantees every national [single] state its independence. But it will also protect common interests effectively everywhere where the commonality is necessary for the [survival of the] individual [unit]. In particular the union will be given all necessary power so that it may fairly and lawfully to solve the great challenges that result from the repercussions of the war.[130]

It is worth noting the degree to which his manifesto tried to persuade nationalists, who were all moving in different directions, that there was indeed something to be gained from sticking together. Revising an argument in favor of Austria that had famously and persuasively been made by Czech nationalist František Palacký in 1848, Charles emphasized that a common organization was critical to the survival of the individual nations. He also reiterated another argument that supporters of empire had made for the past century and a half, that only empire—one might say as umpire—could guarantee legality, fairness, and impartiality in the coming struggles. This last argument must have seemed ludicrous to those who had survived over four years of a militarized regime that had frequently trampled on the Rechtsstaat. During his brief reign Charles had done much to restore that Rechtsstaat, but he had not been able to do enough.

In immediate practical terms, the manifesto foresaw—and in some cases retroactively validated—the creation of various national councils made up of parliamentary deputies. These in turn were supposed to organize federal state units, determining their relations to each other as well as their affiliation to a central government. Ultimately this is exactly what happened, only without the oversight of a central government and without the precious unity of its peoples cited by Charles in the closing of his hopeful charge.

On 28 October the Czech National Council took control of the Office for Grain in the center of Prague. According to Richard Lein and Claire Morelon, it remains unclear whether this single act constituted a revolutionary assertion of regime change by the National Council or whether it had in fact already been agreed to by Governor Coudenhove, who was out of town that day. Nor is it clear whether the employees of the Grain Office even understood that they were no longer acting for the central government.[131] Crowds gathered that day on Wenceslas Square, where the Grain Office happened to be located, not so much because of this revolutionary takeover, but because many people had seen a poster that mistakenly announced an armistice. This misleading news—in fact Austria-Hungary had merely asked for an armistice—produced popular enthusiasm, which then took on a more specifically nationalist character when it was announced that Austria-Hungary had accepted Woodrow Wilson's conditions regarding the self-determination of the Slav nations.

Only now, according to newspapers and memoirs, did red and white flags, the colors of Bohemia, begin to appear all over the city. Czech nationalist songs were heard in the street, and parliamentary deputies made speeches. The Czech National Committee assumed the responsibilities of a government. The cooperation of local civil servants and the relatively passive behavior of imperial administrators were in part responses to the confusion about authority that the emperor's federalization manifesto of 16 October had already created. Had not Vienna deputized the National Councils to reorganize the empire? Since Bohemian Governor Coudenhove was in Vienna on 28 October, it was his deputy who handed over power to the National Committee, and it is not clear what he thought he was doing. Additionally, according to Lein, the imperial military command was too surprised by events to act.

The first general law issued by the Czech National Committee stated emphatically that "all previous provincial and imperial laws and regulations remain for the time being in effect." As one of the committee's most prominent members, Alois Rašín, later recalled about this moment, "The basic purpose of this law was to prevent any anarchic situation from developing so that our whole state administration would remain and continue on October 29 as if there had been no revolution at all."[132] Analyses of his statement have typically focused on Rašín's expressed commitment to maintaining the social order in this first law ("to prevent any anarchic situation from developing"). The founders of this state were certainly no social revolutionaries, and Bohemia was in a politically fragile condition. I prefer, however, to draw the reader's attention to another of Rašín's phrases, in particular to a single word in that phrase, the word "our." Rašín referred to "*our* whole state administration," and as Gary Cohen has insightfully argued, this statement illustrated the extreme degree to which Czech nationalist politicians viewed the Bohemian administration literally as their own creation, rather than as a foreign imposition that had served an alien empire. Their forefathers had helped to establish these institutions, their own parties had staffed them, and it was through these institutions that they had succeeded in creating a Czech nationalist civil service in Austria long before the war.[133] They might refer to Austria in the coming months and years as an alien empire, but they held onto their national creation. Czech nationalists may have built the most effective and far-reaching "empire within an empire," but Polish nationalists in Galicia, Slovene nationalists in Carniola, and Croatian nationalists in Croatia often expressed similar sentiments, and their local administrators often assumed critical roles in the new states.

In the next weeks and months, both the nationalist politicians and the people of Bohemia, Moravia, and northern Hungary (now to be known as "Slovakia") participated in an orgy of renunciation of empire—largely symbolic—as they took over its systems of administration. From 28 October crowds in Prague and other cities and towns removed the hated symbols of empire, such as imperial eagles, now so closely associated with the miseries of the war, from government buildings, schools, hospitals, and even individual uniforms. As early as 13 November the National Council in Prague created a commission charged with renaming streets and squares.[134] The statue of Field Marshal Radetzky in Prague was draped in black and later transported. Other monuments associated with the Habsburgs, such as the statue of Maria Theresa in Pressburg/Pozsony/Prešporok—soon to receive the invented name of Bratislava—

were simply destroyed.[135] In Prague's Old Town Square a crowd pulled down the seventeenth-century column dedicated to the Virgin Mary. For the nationalists who brought it down, that column represented the Habsburg counterreformation's victory over Bohemia outside Prague at the Battle of White Mountain in 1621, the anniversary of which fell on 7 November, right after the National Council's takeover. Many nationalists believed that in bringing down the column they finally avenged the brutal Habsburg victory of 1621. The meanings of symbols and symbolic acts are often ephemeral, however, and the national symbolic revenge taken against the Marian Column by Prague crowds later proved highly controversial. The association of their religion with Habsburg oppression by the state's new secular leaders created considerable resentment and mistrust for the republic among pious Catholic peasants in the new Czechoslovakia, especially, but not only, in the Slovak east.[136]

Yet, as imperial symbols fell, imperial administrators, police officers, and even many military officers often remained in their posts. Studies of the Interior Ministry, of the police force, and the military all demonstrate that a high degree of continuity in personnel characterized those institutions in the transition from empire to republic.[137] Military and government offices in the new Czechoslovakia were even reluctant to enforce a popular 1919 law that gave preferential treatment in hiring to former Czech legionaries who had served in Russia, Italy, or France. Bosses were as fearful as the empire had been of the possible Bolshevik indoctrination of POWs returning from Russia. The Czech nationalists who had just carried out their own revolution did not want to see their new order upset by any further revolutions.[138]

Similarly, many unpopular wartime laws about censorship, food rationing, and freedom of assembly, as well as *lèse majesté* laws (to punish insults to the head of state), all remained in effect. Many refugees also stayed in Prague, both legally and illegally, and the return of so many soldiers only intensified housing and employment crises. Not only that, but war was in fact still being fought, although against different enemies. Just as they had in 1914, recruits in 1919 left the main railway station (renamed for Wilson) to serve in the east, where Czechoslovakia was now fighting against Hungary and Poland to secure its new borders. The state also housed many of the refugees that poured in from Slovakia in a former wartime internment camp. All of this caused many citizens to ask whether there had in fact been a revolution. Or, more ominously, in the words of one legionary witnessing a long line of women waiting to buy milk in 1920, "Is that what we fought for five years for?"[139]

Criticism in Prague of the similarities between the new regime and the old one was not even limited to Czech nationalists. German nationalists too criticized the current state of affairs—especially the ongoing food and housing shortages and general lawlessness—with contempt as being too "Austrian." The popularity of the adjective "Austrian" to characterize behaviors from general authoritarianism to black marketeering, expressed the desire to distance oneself from the old regime while bemoaning its clear persistence in the new order. In fact, long-term continuity of wartime conditions after the declaration of the republic, and not revolutionary ideology, appears to have been at the root of most people's complaints. Well into the 1920s, neither the recent Bolshevik Revolution in Russia nor the disruptive return of POWs from Russia nor even the return of the rowdy Czech legionaries called up the threat of potential revolutionary upheaval. Instead it was the ongoing crisis of survival even after the war had ended that threatened to overturn social stability. From renewed food riots to industrial strikes (of which there were more in 1919 and 1920 than there had been in 1918) to street violence targeting Jews ("Away with the food control agencies, away with the Jews. Give us groceries. We want potatoes."), the situation did not stabilize until the mid-1920s.[140]

"We Are Standing over a Volcano"

In Vienna the German-speaking deputies of the Parliament, like their Polish, Czech, Ukrainian, and South-Slav colleagues, had created a national council of their own on 21 October 1918, a Provisional National Assembly for German Austria (*Provisorische Nationalversammlung für Deutschösterreich*).[141] On 30 October the Provisional Assembly adopted a temporary constitution for German Austria (*Deutschösterreich*). On 3 November Vienna's representative signed the armistice agreement in Italy that went into effect at 3:00 p.m. the next day. A week later the war officially ended.[142] On 11 November, the day the war ended on the western front, Charles issued a proclamation whose careful wording announced his withdrawal from active participation in state affairs. The next day the Provisional Assembly proclaimed the Republic of German Austria with Social Democrat Karl Renner as its first chancellor in a broad-based co-alition government with Christian Socials and German nationalists. What exactly this German Austria was to be territorially and what its future might look like were even less clear than in the cases of the other successor states. The new republic claimed the German-speaking territo-ries in the west including South Tyrol, along with slices of Bohemia, Moravia, and all of Austrian Silesia. It also claimed the right to merge *(Anschluss)* with Germany (Article 2 of the new constitution). The Allies, however, not only forbade the *Anschluss,* but also gave the German-speaking regions of Bohemia, Moravia, and Silesia to Czechoslovakia, as well as acceding to Italy's demand to place the new Tyrolean border at the Brenner Line, rather than drawing that border along linguistic lines far-ther to the south.

In other parts of Central Europe, however, the end of the Habsburg Empire was experienced in more violent and occasionally social revolu-tionary ways. In some regions, military and revolutionary situations on the ground swiftly left behind the moderating efforts of the national councils that had declared the independence of their nations (Zagreb, Bu-dapest) or forced them to take premature military action (Lemberg/Lwów/Lviv). In the early morning hours of 30 October–1 November, for example, former Habsburg troops loyal to the Ukrainian National Council in Lemberg/Lwów/Lviv occupied the public utilities, interned the Habsburg governor of Galicia, and declared the city to be the capital of a new Ukrainian state. On 9 November the council proclaimed that state, the West Ukrainian People's Republic. Almost immediately, war broke out in Galicia between the forces of the newly declared Polish and Ukrainian Republics. Both sides claimed Lemberg/Lwów/Lviv and the territory of East Galicia, and both sides knew that military control on the ground would be decisive in determining the new states' borders.[143] After two weeks of heavy fighting both within and outside of the city, during which time both sides had agreed to allow the creation of a neutral Jewish militia to protect property in Jewish neighborhoods, victorious Polish forces entered the city early on the morning of 22 November. Angry at

In the Jewish quarter of Lemberg/Lwów/Lviv during the pogrom of November 1918. Credit: Adoc-photos/Art Resource, NY.

the city's Jews for their neutrality, and suspecting that they had secretly aided the Ukrainian side, the Polish military disarmed the Jewish militia and unleashed a grueling three-day pogrom that claimed 73 lives and injured another 443 people.[144] The Polish-Ukrainian War ended in July 1919 with Ukrainian defeat, but fighting in the region did not formally end until March 1923.[145]

On 23 October in Budapest, opposition and socialist parties desperate to forestall a violent social revolution also declared a Hungarian National Council, calling themselves the "true representatives of the Hungarian nation," as opposed to what they characterized as "the nobleman's parliament." While the king worked unsuccessfully with that parliament to form an acceptable new cabinet, the National Council proclaimed a twelve-point program to the people of Hungary, promising a democratic franchise, the vote for women, the abolition of the Upper House of Parliament, a renunciation of the German alliance, an immediate end to the war, the complete independence of Hungary, the abolition of censorship, an agrarian reform to give land to the people, and improvement in the lives of working people. With regard to the other nationalities, the council hoped that the implementation of Wilson's principles of self-determination would not "jeopardize the territorial integrity of Hungary but place it on a firmer footing." At the same time, a Soldiers' Council organized by revolutionary officers threatened a more revolutionary end to the war.[146] Massive demonstrations in Budapest on 28 October demanded that power be given to the National Council under opposition leader Count Mihály Károlyi (1875–1955), and on 30–31 October revolutionary crowds supported by striking workers installed the new government. Hoping to maintain Habsburg legitimacy in Hungary, King Charles quickly confirmed Károlyi as prime minister. The new government of Hungary then repudiated the 1867 Settlement with Austria.

Events in Hungary also led to more fighting with no peace in sight. On the basis of a second armistice signed by Hungary (as an independent state) with the French military commander of the Allied Balkan forces, General Louis Franchet-d'Espèrey (1856–1942), in Belgrade, Hungary was obliged to abandon considerable territory to its neighbors Romania, Czechoslovakia, and Yugoslavia. In March of 1919 the Károlyi government in Budapest fell to a Communist-led coup under Béla Kun (1886–1939), which promised more effective military resistance to the territorial demands of Hungary's neighbors. Despite some successes at first, the Communists eventually failed, and when the Romanians broke through the Hungarian lines on 30 July 1919, Kun fled, and the Romanians occupied Budapest. A counterrevolutionary military that had been organized under the auspices of the French in the south—including paramilitary squads—now inflicted a horrifically violent and radically anti-Semitic counterrevolutionary terror on Hungarian society. Eventually in November the nominal commander of these forces, Austro-Hungarian Admiral Miklós Horthy (1868–1957), entered Budapest on a white horse and excoriated a sinful capital for having betrayed the nation to godless bolshevism. In March 1920 a National Assembly reestablished the Kingdom of Hungary, but instead of inviting Charles to resume his position, something the Allies would not have accepted, the assembly appointed Horthy to be regent.[147]

Even in relatively peaceful Bohemia and Moravia, a new Czechoslovak military had to occupy several German-speaking regions that declared their adherence to a rival state called "German Bohemia" with one capital in the northern industrial city of Reichenberg/Liberec and another in the Silesian crownland capital of Troppau/Opava.[148] Although they accomplished this military occupation without much violence, it nevertheless confirmed the point that postwar territorial boundaries depended far more on the question of who controlled them militarily than on expert or political determinations made by the Allies at the Paris Peace Conference in 1919.

In Zagreb, the Yugoslav National Council decided on 24–25 November to invite Serb troops into Croatia and proposed to join with Serbia in a new state. Very quickly, however, peasants expressed opposition to Serb military administrative practices. Peasant Party leader Stjepan Radić (1871–1928) urged peasants passively to resist the Serb military and the new Yugoslav regime, which he labeled militarist and a continuation of the wartime Habsburg state. Historian John Paul Newman argues that peasants transferred their unwillingness to cooperate with the Habsburg authorities toward the end of the war to the new Yugoslav authorities. This attitude contrasted to those in Dalmatia, where Croatian nationalists and peasants alike tended to welcome the advance of the Serb military, given Italian ambitions to control the region. For precisely these reasons the Italians and Hungarians also supported the creation of an anti-Yugoslav Croatian Legion in Hungary in 1919.[149]

In southern Styria a Slovene National Council constituted itself late in September in Marburg/Maribor (there was also one in Laibach/Ljubljana) and in the next weeks started giving orders in the region. On 26 October the prefect (Bezirkshauptmann) in Gonobitz/Konjice wrote to the governor's office in Graz asking whether the Slovene National Council was one of the new organs created by Emperor Charles's manifesto, and whether its orders should be obeyed. The governor never replied.[150] On 1 November southern Styria's future was settled when Major Rudolf Majster, an officer in the Habsburg military, occupied the military installations in Marburg/Maribor. From Vienna, Austria's new chancellor, Renner, directed the Styrian government to protect Marburg/Maribor for Austria militarily, but the Styrians had no forces with which to challenge Majster. Although American experts later advised the Paris Peace Conference to draw Austria's new border below Marburg/Maribor, the Slovene military presence in that town made it unimaginable that Yugoslavia would surrender it.[151]

✻

The lack of a specific date on which the Habsburg Empire came to an end tells us something important about both the circumstances and the meanings of its fall. War destroyed the empire of the Habsburgs over time by eroding any sense of mutual obligation between people and state; popular and dynastic patriotism withered away, calling into question the very raison d'être of empire. As this brief kaleidoscope account should make clear, however, this process took place in fits and starts in different regions. Moreover, the question of what kind of states would replace empire and where their borders would be located remained for the moment completely unclear. The emerging new states depended for their territorial claims largely on the loyalties and locations of Habsburg troops on whose support they could call late in 1918. Many of these troops who demobilized in remarkably orderly fashion out of the Austro-Hungarian military were swiftly re-mobilized into new national armies. Allied support from the Paris Peace Conference in 1919 or the Balkan forces of Franchet-d'Espèrey no doubt made a difference in setting the borders in some cases. Mostly, however, military force and not democracy, national or otherwise, carried the day, and continued to do so in many regions of Central and Eastern Europe until well into the 1920s.

Epilogue: The New Empires

Why . . . are not badges, postage stamps, etc., in three languages as they are in Switzerland? That would offend no one and would help a lot.
— *Emil Ludwig*, Defender of Democracy, 1936

On 3 November 1921, after his second attempt to regain the Hungarian throne had failed, Charles and a pregnant Zita boarded a British ship in the Danube port of Baja which took them to Galați Romania. From there they sailed into exile on the Portuguese island of Madeira, where their seven young children joined them from Switzerland. On the same day that the last crowned king sailed into exile, Prime Minister István Bethlen presented the Hungarian Parliament with legislation to abolish the Pragmatic Sanction. Three days later the Hungarian Parliament annulled the law that had served for two centuries as the legal basis for a unified Habsburg state. Hungary would remain officially a kingdom, but one with a regent instead of a king. Six months later, on 1 April 1922, impoverished and deathly ill, Charles succumbed to pneumonia at the age of thirty-four.

The Habsburgs no longer ruled in Central Europe. Their empire was the first of the great continental empires to vanish from the map of Europe, its territory taken over by three new states (Czechoslovakia, Poland, Yugoslavia) and four existing states (Austria, Hungary, Italy, and Romania), all of which saw themselves as nation-states. Both contemporaries and later historians understood the post-1918 period as, in Eric Hobsbawm's words, the "apogee of nationalism." "If ever there was a moment when the nineteenth-century 'principle of nationality' triumphed," writes Hobsbawm of this phenomenon, "it was at the end of World War I." This was indeed to be the age of nation states.[1] The age was also called an age of democracy, although by the mid-1920s it was already clear that democratic institutions in much of Europe were at best fragile and at worst too weak to survive.[2] It is worth staying with these dual claims for a moment, as we consider the immediate legacies of empire in Central and eastern Europe.

The failure of democratic practice in much of Europe from the start of the post-war period is much clearer to us, of course, than it was to contemporaries. Many basked in the afterglow of the creation of new states or the territorial rewards given to several existing ones. A specifically nationalist way of understanding the meaning of democracy had triumphed within the nationalist political camps of the former Austrian empire. To nationalists the victory of nationhood by definition constituted a victory for democracy, since they believed that democratic rights pertained as much—if not more—to national communities as they did to individuals. According to this way of thinking, the very existence of nation-states was a direct consequence of their people's democratic battles for national emancipation, battles that had allegedly taken place in the half century before 1918.

During World War I nationalist activists around the world helped to promote this presumed link between a concept of national self-determination and its basis in a general acceptance of democratic values. They did so largely by associating empire as a political structure with force, oppression, and the absence of democratic values. In December 1918, for example, Thomas Garrigue Masaryk, president of the newly created Czechoslovakia, chose the following words to proclaim this dual triumph of democracy and nationhood: "On the whole," he said, "great multinational empires are an institution of the past, of a time when material force was held high and the principle of nationality had not yet been recognized, because democracy had not been recognized."[3] This view presumed that great empires could be held together only by oppressive force. The age of such empires was over, according to Masaryk, precisely because the global triumph of democracy had made them impossible. Given the opportunity to choose, the populations of these empires would want to be organized in nation-states. In that particular sense, the existence of nation-states represented a triumph for democracy and a blow against the anti-national authoritarianism of empire—this despite the fact that claims for independence lodged by colonized peoples outside of Europe went largely unheard in 1919.[4]

But if the victories of nation-states constituted triumphs for democracy, at least within Europe, then the Habsburg Empire had to be remembered negatively as a "prison of the peoples." Politicians, journalists, and historians rushed to propagate stories about the prewar and wartime struggles their nations had fought to free themselves from the fetters of an unjust and tyrannical old regime. In fact, their accounts of oppression may have been too effective. When the architects of Versailles invented the mandate system to assert imperial control over former parts of the Ottoman Empire, some thought that it could be applied equally well to the peoples of eastern Europe. Jan Smuts of South Africa, an influential player at Versailles, actually argued that a mandate system could train east Europeans for full sovereignty at a later date. "The peoples left behind by the decomposition of Russia, Austria, and Turkey," he wrote, "are mostly untrained politically; many of them are either incapable or deficient in the power of self-government."[5]

Focusing on the contrast with a dead empire also allowed nation-state ideologists to gloss over the fact that their survival would soon require them severely to limit civil rights among their own populations, especially among those who could not be assimilated to the dominant nation. The question of culturally different populations trapped inside the borders of the new nation-states wracked the brains of the peacemakers. How to create national self-determination for everyone, even those living under a nation that was culturally different from their own?

The Treaty of Versailles' Option Clause technically offered citizens of the former Habsburg Empire the option of acquiring citizenship in another successor state that better accorded to what the treaty referred as their "race" or "nation." Approximately 180,000 German-speaking families (totaling 540,000 people) from former imperial crownlands outside of the new Austria, for example, sought to opt for citizenship in the Austrian Republic. It turned out, however, that not all options were in fact available to all former citizens of empire. In a sign of just how much had changed so quickly, individuals were not allowed to decide for themselves to which race or nation they belonged. This critical difference separated the new states from the old empire. They may have adopted aspects of Habsburg institutions, administrative practices, or legal codes, but in

East Central Europe in 1925

their identification as nation-states and their determination to ascribe nationality objectively, they transformed the way those older institutions, practices, and laws had functioned. Around 75,000 German-speaking Jews from the successor states—mostly Poland—were infamously denied Austrian citizenship because Austria's Supreme Court and Interior Ministry ruled that they could not be considered "racially" German.[6] Pogroms throughout the former Galicia and the Bohemian Lands made the same point as well at the local level. Jews were often physically intimidated and attacked and their homes and businesses destroyed in order to drive home the message that they could not be considered part of the nation, or rather to confirm what local people had long suspected, that the Jews invariably constituted a subversive foreign element no matter what language they spoke.

Groups that became viewed legally as minorities under the Versailles regime were understood to be inimical to the nation's very existence. Given the ways that this attitude was written into both international and domestic law (the successor states were bound by treaty to respect certain minority rights), it is also not surprising that many politicians in the successor states built careers on representing minority populations. They too employed the arguments of nationhood and difference to demand reparations for their clients or a redrawing of state borders. National governments in turn (Germany, Austria, Hungary, even Italy) encouraged minorities of their peoples allegedly trapped in neighboring countries not to emigrate but to remain in so-called hostile territory (Poland, Romania, Italy, Czechoslovakia, Yugoslavia) in order to enable them in the future to lodge persuasive territorial claims against their neighbors.[7] This logic forced people who spoke a given language like German to identify their interests with the German nation-state, even if they had no historical experience of or interest in that state.

The point here is not to evaluate the peace settlement but instead to consider how the structures and practices inherited from empire lived on in Central and eastern Europe, albeit in very different polities and under very different circumstances. Generally both the new states and the older states—including the newly reduced Austria and Hungary—openly rejected legacies of empire, largely claiming to be radically new kinds of states. They described themselves as nation-states, although with the exception of Hungary, each also housed sizable groups of people whom the state officially categorized as somehow culturally different from the ruling nation. Over a third of the people in the new Poland and Romania, for example, did not even speak the national language or practice what became, for all intents and purposes, the national religions of Roman Catholicism in Poland and Orthodoxy in Romania. The same was true for Czechoslovakia, where religion did not factor into the definition of the nation but language was key. In fact, if one counted Czech- and Slovak-speakers separately rather than as belonging to the same nation, something on which many Slovak nationalists increasingly insisted, then no language group made up 50 percent of the population. Italy, too, had gained hundreds of thousands of German-, Slovene-, and Croat-speakers. Yugoslavia called itself a union of the Slovene, Croat, and Serb peoples, but its centralized political structure gave Serb politicians considerable power over the other linguistic and religious groups, including German-speakers, Macedonians, and Albanian-speakers. In almost each of these cases the census became a tool to force the kind of statistical assimilation of which prewar Hungary could only have dreamed. Even in Czechoslovakia, a wrong answer on the census—claiming to be German when objective standards determined that someone was Czech—could end with a fine or a jail sentence.[8]

Czechoslovakia, Romania, and Poland counted millions of people who belonged to other nations in part because each had occupied and claimed territories for strategic or historic reasons as well as for ethnic ones. Some Polish nationalists sought to reestablish the borders of the eighteenth-century Commonwealth, territory that included large numbers of Ukrainian-, Belorussian-, and Lithuanian-speakers.[9] Czechoslovakia even claimed a stretch of formerly northeastern Hungarian territory inhabited mostly by Ukrainian speakers—the sub-Carpathian Ukraine—so that it would have a strategic border with its ally Romania. The Czechoslovak state treated this region, one of the least prosperous of prewar Hungary, as something of a backwards colony to be improved and modernized by a paternalist rational administration. (The Czechoslovak regime spoke of Sub-Carpathian Ukraine in terms often used by the Paris Peace Conference victors to characterize the new mandates or protectorates in the Middle East.)

Closer to home, so to speak, Czechoslovakia encountered significant problems in Slovakia, where locals often resented the arrival of overbearing administrators and experts from Bohemia and Moravia. By the 1930s many Slovak nationalists sought to achieve federal political autonomy of a kind that imperial Austrians would have found familiar. In the west, too, Czechoslovakia incorporated over two million German-speakers who numbered more than the total number of Slovak speakers in the state. Czech nationalists had argued for half a century that their administrative unit should encompass the historic, not ethnic, borders of Bohemia, Moravia, and Austrian Silesia. They now added that the mountainous German-speaking border regions were critical to the military security of the new state. Despite the minority rights that Czechoslovakia offered its millions of non-national citizens—rights that were more extensive than comparable rights offered by the other new states—the fact remained that Czechoslovakia defined itself as a nation-state. Those who were not part of the nation were ultimately disadvantaged both legally and culturally.[10]

Romania, the existing state that in percentage terms gained the most new territory thanks to the Peace Conference, added significant

Hungarian-, German-, Ukrainian-, and Russian-speaking minorities from Transylvania, Bukovina, and Bessarabia, not to mention Jews who constituted the one minority group that could be found in every region of Romania, old and new. And although the peace treaties obliged a very unwilling Romania to concede rights to minorities and to offer the rights of citizenship to Jews for the first time, Jews remained particularly despised in public life, their persecution tolerated and even encouraged by successive Romanian governments. What is telling from the Romanian example for post-war norms is also the highly centralized control Bucharest exerted over its new territories and its unwillingness to employ Romanian-speaking civil servants from former Hungarian territories or even to empower local Romanian nationalists in Transylvania. Romanian nationalists who had fought for decades before 1918 to maintain their Romanian identification in the face of Hungarianization efforts—especially among the Transylvanian intelligentsia—were shut out of a significant voice in governing their home territory. This story repeated itself in the other successor states as well, from Czechoslovakia to Italy to Yugoslavia. Centralization and mistrust of local activists largely prevented the serious consideration of truly federalist or regional solutions to serious political challenges.[11]

"In theory there is an abyss between nationalism and imperialism," wrote Hannah Arendt in *The Origins of Totalitarianism;* "in practice it can and has been bridged."[12] Each of these self-styled nation states in fact acted like a small empire. Each sought to acquire new territories, well knowing that those territories housed significant numbers of people who did not belong to what was now considered to be the ruling nation. Each ended up with populations that would not or could not be integrated into the state on specifically national terms. Each followed a range of creative strategies to overcome the demographic and cultural challenges posed by minority populations, based on the dreams of radical nationalists in pre-1914 Austria and Hungary, from forced education of children to the extremes of forced assimilation to even expulsion.

No state could admit to the possibility of somehow accommodating the cultural differences it faced in its populations. This was not because of the particularly complex demographic or ethnic makeup of the region formerly known as the Habsburg Empire. Rather, it was a product of the zero-sum way that nationalists had come to treat culture and difference within the Habsburg Monarchy in the half century before the war. Differences between members of the new ruling nations and members of minorities were almost always expressed in terms of insuperable cultural barriers rather than in terms of possible commonalities. When differences were expressed in terms of commonalities, as with the Romanian government's imaginative attribution of authentic Romanian origins to Bukovina Ukrainians or Transylvanian Szeklers, they were imposed by the governing power with no attention to the actual desires of those whom they recategorized.[13]

The new rulers developed their policies based on the belief in deep cultural differences that nationalists had cultivated at least since the 1880s (originally as a response to the Austrian state's unwillingness to categorize its citizens in national terms). For this reason, nationalists—and the new governments they founded—were eager to ascribe nationhood on the basis of objective external factors, an exercise in which the Austrian and Hungarian states had for the most part refused to engage. For this reason they were also eager to take over private minority school systems, theaters, libraries, cultural centers, and financial resources that had belonged to enemy nationalist organizations before the war. When they did offer educational rights to speakers of foreign languages, they did their best to reduce the numbers of eligible pupils through processes of involuntary ascription and by gerrymandering school and political districts. Typical of this kind of behavior was the Romanian government's claim in Bukovina, for example, that Ukrainians were really Romanianized Ukrainians, an assertion that absolved the state of having to offer schooling in the Ukrainian language.[14] Another law in Yugoslavia prevented children with Slavic names from attending a minority school.[15] The Habsburg Empire was gone, but the production of politics around cultural difference as the primary way for people to make claims on their state continued with a vengeance.

In a very different way, imperial belonging continued to structure the memory cultures and in particular the private and often semi-public commemorations of wartime service that developed informally in many border regions of the successor states after 1918. No matter what kind of credence one gave to the loud claims made for nationalist foundation myths in the decade after the War, the fact remained that several thousands of citizens in the successor states had in fact fought in the Habsburg military and their families had lost loved ones to the Austro-Hungarian war effort. How might their sacrifice be commemorated in a world in which the very purpose of that sacrifice had vanished? What kind of memory cultures did people develop at the local level to commemorate their wartime service and that of their relatives and neighbors? In particular in regions such as the Trentino (now in Italy), where, as Laurence Cole has recently argued, a kind of hidden defeat lived on in the face of an ostensible victory, war veterans had to suppress their own experiences of having fought on the losing side and families had to find creative ways to commemorate their war dead.[16]

Finally, not only did imperial ways of thinking shape new state policies and popular practices. They also continued to structure local people's understandings of their new relationships to state power. As the Habsburg state collapsed, several attempts at state-building from below attempted to continue imperial relations in the context of a new Europe. When, for example, the leaders of the German-speaking community of Czernowitz/ Cernăuți/Cernivci faced the end of the Habsburg Empire, they telegraphed a statement of loyalty to the new imperial metropole, Bucharest, in terms that replicated its longstanding relationship to Vienna. The community promised its loyalty to the new rulers and in return expected to be able to continue to foster its local world of schools and cultural and financial institutions, from theaters to credit banks to cooperative stores to churches. Whether the imperial language was German or Romanian mattered far less to the German community than did the mutual relations of imperial obligation the community hoped to continue with its new rulers.[17] As if in answer to this declaration, however, Romanian nationalist historian Ion Nistor (1876–1962) reveled in the end of such relations, arguing in 1918 with regard to Bukovina:

> Today when the national principle is celebrating its greatest triumph, when the old states are tumbling down, and in their ruins are arising rejuvenated national states within the ethnic boundaries of each nation, "Bukovinism" has to disappear. . . . Bukovina has reunited with Romania, within whose boundaries there is no room for *homo bucovinensis,* but only for *civis Romaniae.*[18]

Just what this *civis Romaniae* would come to mean in the next years, however, just as what the new Czechoslovak, Pole, Yugoslav, or Italian would come to mean, was someone who spoke the national language—in this case Romanian—and who practiced a particular national religion—in this case Eastern Orthodox Christianity.

We have tended for many years to define and evaluate the continental empires of Central and eastern Europe in terms dictated to us largely by the successor nation-states and their ideologies For example, the empires' multinational character (the claim that the *Vielvölkerstaat* or multinational state is by definition a problematic state), their so-called authoritarian center-periphery structural relations, their alleged failure to develop a popular shared identity, their supposed suppression of nationalist feeling—all of these are *nationalist* definitions of the characteristics of empires. Yet one could easily change the terms of discussion by redefining the self-styled nation-states simply as little empires. Every nation-state after 1918, for example, was a *Vielvölkerstaat* whose survival demanded the integration of multiethnic populations, the successful—if often authoritarian—attachment of peripheries to centers, and the development of a positive sense of shared identification, even among people who claimed to belong to the same nation. Far from marking the end of the imperial *Vielvölkerstaaten,* 1918 could be said to have witnessed their proliferation.

The critical importance of the contradiction between nationhood and statehood that dominated the interwar years in ways that could not be imagined before 1914 also helps to explain the generally horrific treatment of ethnic minorities during the Second World War as well as the postwar expulsions of imagined "undesirable" populations. All the states that were *Vielvölkerstaaten* invested serious rhetoric and considerable resources into denying that reviled status for themselves while at the same time formulating increasingly radical solutions to the challenges posed by minority populations. Brutal nationalist dictatorship in most cases became the only means to square the circle of populist democracy and ethnic nationhood.

If we can prevent nation-state ideologies from influencing the ways we think about empire, then we may be able to locate and analyze the Habsburg Empire's distinctiveness as a state and society on its own terms. That distinctiveness did not lie in an *inability* or *failure* to unify diverse populations, which is as much a critical story in French, British, German, Irish, Italian, Spanish, Romanian, Czechoslovakian, Polish, and Yugoslavian history as it is an aspect of Imperial Habsburg history. Its distinctiveness may lie in the positive ways that empire sought to negotiate the cultural differences that became a key factor in political life and ultimately in the ways it sought to make political and social institutions organized around such differences function effectively. For this reason, too, we can understand the forms of nationalism that emerged from the empire as highly distinctive, forged in the context of Habsburg imperial institutions and in the possibilities those institutions foresaw. Unmoored from the limits of the institutions that gave them life and shaped their development, however, these forms of political nationalism developed into something else during the interwar years, something simultaneously recognizable yet terrifyingly alien to many of those who remembered life in the empire before 1914.

NOTES

ACKNOWLEDGMENTS

INDEX

NOTES

ABBREVIATIONS

Newspapers and Journals

AHY	*Austrian History Yearbook*
CEH	*Central European History*
JMH	*Journal of Modern History*
SR	*Slavic Review*

Archives

AST	Archivio di Stato Trieste
AVA	Allgemeine Verwaltungs Archiv
HHstA	Haus- Hof, und Staatsarchiv

INTRODUCTION

1 The turnout rate was 80.02 percent. Dieter Nolen and Philip Stöver, ed., *Elections in Europe. A Data Handbook* (Baden Baden: Nomos, 2010), 196.

2 See articles in the liberal *Bregenzer Tagblatt*, 11 June, 1911, 2; and the Czech Christian Social *Čech*, 11 June 1911, 1.

3 *Arbeiter-Zeitung*, 12 June 1911, Vienna, 1–2; *Grazer Volksblatt*, 11 June 1911, 1; *Linzer Volksblatt*, 11 June 1911, 1; *Bukowiner Post*, 11 June, 1911, 1–2; *Stajerc*, 11 June 1911, 1.

4 "Ihr werdet entscheiden!" *Arbeiter-Zeitung*, 11 June 1911, Vienna, 1.

5 Both this incident and the local conflicts that provoked it are detailed authoritatively by Joshua Shanes, *Diaspora Nationalism and Jewish Identity in Habsburg Galicia* (New York: Cambridge University Press, 2012), 268–279. According to Shanes, most witnesses testified that by the time of the shooting the threat of crowd violence had already subsided. I thank Shanes especially for sharing with me an unpublished manuscript that analyzes this particular incident and urban politics in Drohobych/Drohobycz in even greater detail. On Drohobych/Drohobycz see Alison Frank, *Oil Empire: Visions of Prosperity in Austrian Galicia* (Cambridge, MA: Harvard University Press, 2005), 76–77; 119–120; 132–134.

6 On Galician elections, see Harald Binder, *Galizien in Wien: Parteien, Wahlen, Fraktionen und Abgeordnete im Übergang zur Massenpolitik* (Vienna: Verlag der Österreichischen Akademie der Wissenschaften, 2005), 295–308.

7 Historian Deborah Coen has repeatedly drawn scholars' attention to the critical work of amateur and professional scientists in shaping contemporary ideas of empire. See Coen, "Climate and Circulation in Imperial Austria," *Journal of Modern History* 82, no. 4 (December 2010): 839–875; Coen, *The Earthquake Observers: Disaster Science from Lisbon to Richter* (Chicago: University of Chicago Press, 2012). See also Peter Stachel, "Ethnischer Pluralismus und wissenschaftliche Theoriebildung im zentraleuropäischen Raum. Fallbeispiele wissenschaftlicher und philosophischer Reflexion der ethnisch-kulturellen Vielheit der Donaumonarchie, " (PhD diss. Karl-Franzens Universität Graz, 1999). For articles that emphasize the concurrent processes of nationalization of science, *The Nationalization of Scientific Knowledge in the Habsburg Empire 1848–1918*, ed. Mitchell Ash and Jan Surman (Basingstoke: Palgrave Macmillan, 2012).

8 There is a growing literature on the twenty-four volumes of *Die österreichisch-ungarische Monarchie in Wort und Bild* published between 1886 and 1902 in German- and Hungarian- language editions and known as the *Kronprinzenwerk* because of the patronage of Crown Prince Rudolf. See Zoltán Szász, "Das 'Kronprinzenwerk' und die hinter ihm stehende Konzeption," in *Nation und Nationalismus in wissenschaftlichen Standartwerken Österreich-Ungarns, ca. 1867–1918*, Endre Kiss, Csaba Kiss, Justin Stagl, ed. (Vienna: Böhlau, 1997), 65–70; Justin Stagl, "Das 'Kronprinzenwerk'—eine Darstellung des Vielvölkerreiches" in *Das entfernte Dorf. Moderner Kunst und ethnischer Artefakt*, ed. Ákos Moravánsky (Vienna: Böhlau, 2002), 169–182; Regina Bendix "Ethnology, Cultural Reification, and the Dynamics of Difference in the Kronprinzenwerk" in *Creating the Other. Ethnic Conflict and Nationalism in Habsburg Central Europe*, ed. Nancy M. Wingfield (New York: Berghahn, 2003), 149–166; Hans Petschar, *Altösterreich. Menschen, Länder und Völker in der Habsburgermonarchie* (Vienna: Brandstätter, 2011).

9 For a provocative theorization of this point, see Tara Zahra, "Imagined Noncommunities: National Indifference as a Category of Analysis," *SR* 69, no. 1 (2010): 93–119. See also, Pieter Judson, *Guardians of the Nation: Activists on the Language Frontiers of Imperial Austria* (Cambridge, MA: Harvard University Press, 2006).

10 On this point, see Wolfgang Goederle, "Administration, Science, and the Nation: The 1869 Population Census in Austria-Hungary," *AHY* 47 (forthcoming).

11 Two important and influential exceptions by American scholar Gary B. Cohen are: "Nationalist Politics and the Dynamics of State and Civil Society in the Habsburg Monarchy, 1867–1914," *CEH* 40, no. 2 (2007): 241–278, and

"Neither Absolutism nor Anarchy: New Narratives on Society and Government in Late Imperial Austria, *AHY* 29 (1998): 37–61. See also, more recently, John Deak, *Forging a Multinational State: State-making in Imperial Austria from the Enlightenment to the First World War* (Stanford, CA: Stanford University Press, 2015).

12 For examples of the economic argument, Daniel Chirot, ed., *The Origins of Backwardness in Eastern Europe* (Berkeley and Los Angeles: University of California Press, 1989). Elsewhere, however, Chirot criticized the arguments about Eastern European difference. "Who is Western, who is not, and who cares?" *East European Politics and Societies* 13/2 (1999): 244–248. I thank Peter Bugge for this point.

13 Tony Judt, *A Grand Illusion? An Essay on Europe* (New York: New York University Press, 2011), 50.

14 For several disturbing examples of this way of thinking in textbook accounts of European history, Peter Bugge, "Eastern Europe: Myths of Uneven Development," unpublished manuscript presented at the American Historical Association annual meeting, January 2008, Washington, DC. See also Bugge, "The Use of the Middle: *Mitteleuropa* vs. Střední Evropa" in *European Review of History—Revue européenne d'histoire* 6/1 (1999): 15–34; "'Shatter Zones': The Creation and Recreation of Europe's East" in *Ideas of Europe Since 1914. The Legacy of the First World War*, ed. Menno Spiering and Michael Wintle (Basingstoke and New York: Palgrave Macmillan, 2002), 47–68.

15 Larry Wolff, *Inventing Eastern Europe: The Map of Civilization on the Mind of the Enlightenment* (Stanford, CA: Stanford University Press, 1994); Maria Todorova, *Imagining the Balkans* (New York: Oxford University Press, 1997); Peter Bugge "Eastern Europe: Myths of Uneven Development," unpublished lecture; Mark Mazower, *The Balkans: A Short History* (New York: Modern Library, 2002).

16 Most of these works either say very little about the Habsburg Monarchy or repeat truisms about its anachronistic, ramshackle, failing character. For an excellent analysis of this genre, see John Deak, "The Great War and the Forgotten Realm: The Habsburg Monarchy and the First World War," in *Journal of Modern History* 86 (June 2014): 336–380. A notable exception is Christopher Clark's *The Sleepwalkers* (New York: HarperCollins, 2012) which takes seriously developments in the Habsburg Monarchy and the Balkans.

17 Most recently, J. Deak, "The Great War and the Forgotten Realm," makes this point powerfully by examining the wartime nationalist propaganda efforts by many of the men who later became the foremost historians of the region.

18 István Deák, "Comments," *AHY* 3, no. 1 (1967): 303.

19 Gary B. Cohen, *The Politics of Ethnic Survival: Germans in Prague, 1861–1914* (Princeton, NJ: Princeton University Press, 1980); John W. Boyer, *Political Radicalism in Late Imperial Vienna: The Origins of the Christian Social Movement* (Chicago: University of Chicago Press, 1980).

20 Gerald Stourzh, *Die Gleichberechtigung der Nationalitäten in der Verfassung und Verwaltung Österreichs, 1848–1918* (Vienna: Verlag der Österreichischen Akademie der Wissenschaften, 1985); Emil Brix, *Die Umgangssprachen in Altöstereich zwischen Agitation und Assimilation: die Sprachenstatistik in den zisleithanischen Volkszählungen, 1880 bis 1910* (Vienna: Verlag der Österreichischen Akademie der Wissenschaften, 1982); Hannelore Burger, *Sprachenrecht und Sprachengerechtigkeit im österreichischen Unterrichtswesen 1867–1918* (Vienna: Verlag der Österreichischen Akademie der Wissenschaften, 1995); Maria Kurz, "Die Volksschulstreit in der Südsteiermark und in Kärnten in der Zeit der Dezemberverfassung" (PhD diss., University of Vienna, 1986).

21 A few examples follow: on economics, David Good, *The Economic Rise of the Habsburg Empire* (Berkeley and Los Angeles: University of California Press, 1984); Richard Rudolph, *Banking and Industrialization in Austria-Hungary: the Role of the Banks in Industrialization in the Czech Crownlands* (New York: Cambridge University Press, 1976); in anthropology, *Katherine Verdery, Transylvanian Villagers. Three Centuries of Political, Economic, and Ethnic Change* (Berkeley and Los Angeles: University of California Press, 1983); on social and cultural history, essays by Péter Hanák, collectively published in English after his death as *The Garden and the Workshop. Essays on the Cultural History of Vienna and Budapest* (Princeton, NJ: Princeton University Press, 1998); István Deák, *Beyond Nationalism. A Social and Political History of the Habsburg Officer Corps 1848–1918* (New York: Oxford University Press, 1990); Waltraud Heindl, *Gehorsame Rebellen. Bürokratie und Beamte in Österreich, 1780–1848* (Vienna: Böhlau, 1991).

22 See, for example, Rogers Brubaker, Margit Feischmidt, Jon Fox, Liana Grancea, *Nationalist Politics and Everyday Ethnicity in a Transylvanian Town* (Princeton, NJ: Princeton University Press, 2006); Brubaker, *Ethnicity Without Groups* (Cambridge, MA: Harvard University Press, 2004); Benno Gammerl, *Untertanen, Staatsbürger und Andere. Der Umgang mit ethnischer Heterogenität im britischen Weltreich und im Habsburgerreich 1867–1918* (Göttingen: Vandenhoeck & Ruprecht, 2010); Jeremy King, *Budweisers into Czechs and Germans: A Local History of Bohemian Politics, 1848–1948* (Princeton, NJ: Princeton University Press, 2002); King, "The Nationalization

of East Central Europe: Ethnicism, Ethnicity, and Beyond" in *The Politics of Commemoration in Habsburg Central Europe, 1848 to the Present*, ed. Nancy Wingfield and Maria Bucur (West Lafayette, IN.: Purdue University Press, 2001), 112–152.

23 On the problem of national master narratives in Central Europe in the twentieth century, Pavel Kolář, "Die nationalgeschichtlichen master narratives in der tschechischen Geschichtsschreibung der zweiten Hälfte des 20. Jahrhunderts: Entstehungskontexte, Kontinuität und Wandel," in *Geschichtsschreibung zu den böhmischen Ländern im 20. Jahrhundert. Wissenschaftstraditionen, Institutionen, Diskurse*, ed. Christiane Brenner and K. Erik Franzen (Munich: R. Oldenbourg Verlag, 2006), 209–241; Pavel Kolář and Michal Kopeček, "A Difficult Quest for New Paradigms: Czech Historiography after 1989," in *Narratives Unbound: Historical Studies in Post-Communist Eastern Europe*, ed. Sorin Antohi, Balázs Trencsényi and Péter Apor (Budapest: Central European University Press, 2007), 173–248; Gernot Heiss, Árpád von Klimó, Pavel Kolař, Dušan Kováč, "Habsburg's Difficult Legacy. Comparing and Relating Austrian, Czech, Magyar, and Slovak National Historical Master Narratives," in *The Contested Nation: Ethnicity, Class, Religion and Gender in National Histories*, ed. Stefan Berger and Chris Lorenz (Basingstoke: Palgrave Macmillan, 2008), 367–403.

1. THE ACCIDENTAL EMPIRE

Epigraph: From Joseph von Sonnenfels, *Über die Liebe des Vaterlands*, translated by Robert Russell, in Balázs Trencsényi and Michal Kopeček, ed., *Discourses of Collective Identity in Central and Southeast Europe (1770–1945). Texts and Commentaries. Volume I, Late Enlightenment—Emergence of the 'National Idea'* (Budapest and New York: Central European University Press, 2006), 130–131.

1 Michael Hochedlinger and Anton Tantner, eds., *". . . der grösste Teil der Untertanen lebt elend und mühselig." Die Berichte des Hofkriegsrates zur sozialen und wirtschaftlichen lage der Habsburgermonarchie 1770–1771*, Mitteilungen des Österreichischen Staatsarchivs, Sonderband 8 (Vienna: Studien Verlag, 2005). The crownlands to which this conscription was applied in 1770 were Silesia, Styria, Carinthia, Carniola, Görz-Gradisca, Bohemia, Moravia, and Upper and Lower Austria. (See map in Hochedlinger and Tantner, lxxvii.) New conscription systems were introduced later in Galicia (1776), the Innviertel (1779), Tirol and Hungary (1784), Vorderösterreich (1786), and Bukovina (1787).

2 Hochedlinger and Tantner, *Berichte des Hofkriegsrates*, xxxi.

3 Hochedlinger and Tantner, *Berichte des Hofkriegsrates*, lxv, lxvi, xlix.

4 Hochedlinger and Tantner, *Berichte des Hofkriegsrates*, 37.

5 Unlike its Prussian counterpart in the eighteenth century, the Habsburg military did not depend on the nobility for its officer corps and the conscription of its infantry.

6 Hochedlinger and Tantner, *Berichte des Hofkriegsrates*, liv–lv.

7 On the problem of languages, including their emergence, categorization, and institutionalization, see Tomasz Kamusella's encyclopedic *The Politics of Language and Nationalism in Modern Central Europe* (New York: Palgrave Macmillan, 2012).

8 Among the several excellent histories of the Habsburg dynasty, see most recently Paula Sutter Fichtner's *The Habsburgs: Dynasty, Culture, and Politics* (London: Reaktion Books, 2014).

9 The Roman appellation made a claim to a link between this empire and the previous Roman Empire. The terms "Roman" and "Holy," however, also referred to a special relationship to the Catholic Church in Rome, although by the fourteenth century the relationship between popes and emperors often involved complex struggles.

10 On the complexities of the Holy Roman Empire and the Habsburgs relationship to the institution, Charles Ingrao, *The Habsburg Monarchy 1618–1815* (Cambridge: Cambridge University Press, 1994), 16–18.

11 A Habsburg from a different family line had ruled briefly as Emperor Albert II from 1438–1439. Fichtner, *The Habsburgs*, 43–44.

12 The settlement had actually been discussed much earlier by Maximilian and Ferdinand of Aragon, although the precise future division of Habsburg territory remained to be determined. After 1525, however, Ferdinand already governed the Austrian hereditary lands. The Bohemian and Hungarian diets had also insisted that he have princely holdings of his own as a prerequisite for his marriage. Paula S. Fichtner, *The Habsburg Monarchy, 1490–1848* (New York: Palgrave, 2003), 11.

13 The last Habsburg king of Spain, the mentally and physically infirm Charles II, had bequeathed the throne to his grandnephew Philip, third in line to the French throne. The ensuing War of the Spanish Succession pitted the Austrian Habsburgs, Great Britain, the Dutch Republic, Portugal, and the House of Savoy against France. At the conclusion of the war in 1714, the new Spanish king, Philip V, was removed from the French line of succession, thus averting the specter of a union of the French and Spanish kingdoms. Ingrao, *Habsburg Monarchy*, 105–119.

14 Fichtner, *Habsburg Monarchy*, 61; Ingrao, *Habsburg Monarchy*, 128–129.

15 Fichtner, *Habsburg Monarchy*, 63; Ingrao, *Habsburg Monarchy*, 150.

16 Quoted in R. J. W. Evans, *Austria, Hungary, and the Habsburgs: Essays on Central Europe c. 1683–1867* (Oxford: Oxford University Press, 2006), 13. On the concept of composite monarchy, J. H. Elliot, "A Europe of Composite Monarchies," *Past and Present* 137 (1992): 48–71. This type of state constituted a union of distinct territories under the rule of one sovereign by which each territory retained its distinctive laws and customs.

17 The Habsburgs administered Bohemia, Moravia, and Silesia through a special Bohemian chancellery in Vienna, comparable to the Austrian chancellery that managed their hereditary lands. Even if the Kingdom of Bohemia remained a critical territory for the Habsburgs and the Holy Roman Empire, its diet did not have the ability to make the kinds of bold claims for full independence made by its Hungarian counterpart.

18 Charles-Albert of Bavaria's claim rested in part on his marriage to the daughter of the Emperor Joseph I, Maria Amalia, Maria Theresa's cousin and the original beneficiary of Leopold I's legislation to enable the female succession. Charles-Albert was himself a descendant of Habsburg Emperor Ferdinand II (ruled 1619–1637).

19 Maria Theresa's title in Hungary was "king" not "queen."

20 In fact Joseph arrived at the Diet over a week later with Maria Theresa's husband Francis Stephen, on the occasion when he swore fealty to the Hungarian Diet. Many accounts merge the two moments into one. Some also assert that she wore mourning. C. A. Macartney, ed., *The Habsburg and Hohenzollern Dynasties in the Seventeenth and Eighteenth Centuries: Selected Documents*, (London: Macmillan, 1970), 132–136; Paul Lendvai, *The Hungarians: A Thousand Years of Victory in Defeat* (Princeton, NJ: Princeton University Press, 2003), 168.

21 Lendvai, *The Hungarians*, 168.

22 C. A. Macartney, *Hungary: A Short History* (Edinburgh: Edinburgh University Press, 1962), 97.

23 Kaunitz was another highly influential Bohemian in Vienna. His family, originally from Bohemia, had settled in Moravia (Austerlitz/Slavkov). He served as ambassador to France before becoming Maria Theresa's chancellor of state and minister for foreign affairs, a post he held from 1753 to 1792. See the excellent study by Franz Szabo, *Kaunitz and Enlightened Absolutism, 1753–1780* (New York: Cambridge University Press, 1994).

24 For a stimulating interpretation of Prussia and the Seven Years War as well as of the diplomacy of this period, Franz Szabo, *The Seven Years War in Europe, 1756–1763* (London and New York: Routledge, 2013).

25 Larry Wolff, *The Idea of Galicia: History and Fantasy in Habsburg Political Culture* (Stanford, CA: Stanford University Press, 2010), 15. Since Poland

had not acquired the region until the fourteenth century, Wolff points out that Maria Theresa could assuage her conscience somewhat since as King of Hungary she could at least argue that she had a prior claim to the region.

26 Evans, *Austria, Hungary, and the Habsburgs*, 95.

27 Frank Henschel, "'Das Fluidum der Stadt . . .' Lebenswelten in Kassa/Kaschau/Košice zwischen urbaner Vielfalt und Nationalismus 1867–1918" (PhD diss., University of Leipzig, 2013), 139.

28 On early scientific, patriotic, and cultural societies that involved both aristocratic and middle-class members, see Rita Krueger, *Czech, German, and Noble: Status and National Identity in Habsburg Bohemia* (New York: Oxford University Press, 2009).

29 Evans, *Austria, Hungary, and the Habsburgs*, 61.

30 Ibid., 69. "Whereas English nobles, it is alleged, removed their swords on entering a lodge, Austrian bourgeois were lent one to strap on."

31 Krueger, *Czech, German, and Noble*, 94.

32 "Wherever we look in the Austrian government of this period (1740–1790) we find Bohemians" (Evans, *Austria, Hungary, and the Habsburgs*, 95; see also generally, 75–98).

33 Ernst Bruckmüller, *Sozialgeschichte Österreichs* (Vienna: Böhlau, 2001), 253; Evans, *Austria, Hungary, and the Habsburgs*, 68.

34 Lois Dubin, *The Port Jews of Habsburg Trieste: Absolutist Politics and Enlightenment Culture* (Stanford, CA: Stanford University Press, 1999), 15. From a small town of some three to five thousand people in 1700 Trieste doubled its population by mid-century, and by 1775 it sported an economically thriving population of over fifteen thousand people (including suburbs).

35 See the excellent analysis of these discussions in Börries Kuzmany, *Brody. Eine galizische Grenzstadt im langen 19. Jahrhundert* (Vienna: Böhlau, 2011), 49–55, especially 52.

36 Hochedlinger and Tantner, *Berichte des Hofkriegsrates*, 29.

37 Quoted in Derek Beales, *Joseph II*, vol. 2, *Against the World* (Cambridge: Cambridge University Press, 2009), 247.

38 Thanks largely to the delaying tactics of the crownland elites, the new code, actually begun under Maria Theresa, was not completed until 1786 during the reign of Joseph II.

39 See Hannelore Burger, "Passwesen und Staatsbürgerschaft," in *Grenze und Staat. Passwesen, Staatsbürgerschaft, Heimatrecht und Fremdengesetzgebung in der österreichischen Monarchie, 1780–1867*, eds. Waltraud Heindl and Edith Saurer with the assistance of Hannelore Burger und Harald Wendelin (Vienna: Böhlau, 2000), 3–172, here 97.

40 Hochedlinger and Tantner, *Berichte des Hofkriegsrates*, lxvii.

41 Ibid., 29–30.

42 Ibid., 37.

43 Ibid., 61.

44 Ibid., 31–32, 48.

45 Michael O'Sullivan, "A Hungarian Josephenist, Orientalist, and Bibliophile: Count Karl Revicky, 1737–1793," *AHY* 45 (2014): 68. On the academy, its curricula and students, see Paula S. Fichtner, *Terror and Toleration: The Habsburg Empire Confronts Islam, 1526–1850* (London: Reaktion Books, 2009), 117–163.

46 Evans, *Austria, Hungary, and the Habsburgs*, 51.

47 Dubin, *Port Jews*, 13–15.

48 Ibid., 14, 43. Trieste was one of the few locations in the Austrian hereditary lands were Jews were permitted to settle. In 1771 (at a very high financial cost to them) Maria Theresa granted a special diploma to the Jews of Trieste.

49 As one sign of the tenuousness of their power, the Habsburgs moved the Hungarian capital west from Buda to Pressburg/Pozsony in 1536. Not until the late eighteenth century did the dynasty return governing functions back to Buda. Habsburg-occupied Hungary is generally referred to as "Royal" or "Western Hungary." During this same period the Ottoman Empire often supported alternative "prince" rulers for Transylvania.

50 The creation of so-called "military frontiers" in the regions stretching from Croatia in the west to Transylvania in the east helps explain the presence of a considerable population of Orthodox Catholics in otherwise Catholic Croatia. In the western military borders, for example, inhabitants often belonged to village communities that fled en masse, seeking asylum in the Habsburg territories to avoid Ottoman rule.

51 On the county governments in the seventeenth and eighteenth centuries, George Barany, "Ungarns Verwaltung: 1848–1918" in *Die Habsburger Monarchie 1848–1918*, volume II, *Verwaltung und Rechtswesen*, ed. Adam Wandruschka and Peter Urbanitsch (Vienna: Verlag der Österreichischen Akademie der Wissenschaften, 1975), 306–468, especially 314–322.

52 Montesquieu had traveled to Hungary and visited the diet in 1728. He later referred to its politics as being at a stage France had experienced in the early Middle Ages. Gabor Vermes, *Hungarian Culture and Politics in the Habsburg Monarchy 1711–1848* (Budapest and New York: CEU Press, 2014), 89–90. For a brilliant analysis of Hungarian constitutional developments, László Peter, "Die Verfassungsentwicklung in Ungarn," in *Die Habsburgermonarchie 1848–1918*, vol. VII, *Verfassung und Parlamentarismus*

(Vienna: Verlag der Österreichischen Akademie der Wissenschaften, 2000), 239–540; on Montesquieu, 255.

53 Quoted in Evans, *Austria, Hungary, and the Habsburgs*, 21.
54 Evans, *Austria, Hungary, and the Habsburgs*, 174.
55 Ibid., 30.
56 George Barany, "Ungarns Verwaltung," 316–317.
57 Evans, *Austria, Hungary, and the Habsburgs*, 61.
58 Ibid.
59 Beales, *Joseph II*, vol. 2, 66.
60 Ibid., 63.

2. SERVANTS AND CITIZENS, EMPIRE AND FATHERLAND

Epigraph: "Den vollen Genuss der bürgerlichen Rechte erwirbt man durch die Staatsbürgerschaft," *Allgemeine Bürgerliches Gesetzbuch*, 1811, section 5, paragraph 28.

1 Quoted in Derek Beales, *Joseph II*, vol. 2, *Against the World, 1780–1790* (New York: Cambridge University Press, 2009), 486.
2 Quoted in ibid., 204.
3 Quoted in ibid., 486.
4 In his *Pastoral Letter* of 1784 Joseph wrote, for example, that "The Monarch himself [is] accountable to each subject for his management of public money." Quoted in Beales, *Joseph II*, vol. 2, 347, and in William Godsey, "Habsburg Government and Intermediary Authority under Joseph II (1780–1790): The Estates of Lower Austria in Comparative Perspective" in *CEH* 46 (2014): 728.
5 On Joseph II, language, enlightenment, and the rise of a more official use of vernacular languages from Czech or Croatian to Romanian, R. J. W. Evans, "Joseph II and Nationality in the Habsburg Lands" in Evans, *Austria, Hungary, and the Habsburgs: Essays on Central Europe c. 1683–1867* (Oxford: Oxford University Press, 2006), 134–146.
6 On the development of depictions of Maria Theresa both during and after her life, see Werner Telesko, *Maria Theresia: Ein europäischer Mythos* (Vienna: Böhlau, 2012).
7 T. C. W. Blanning, *Joseph II* (New York: Routledge, 1994), 126; Laurence Cole, *Military Culture and Popular Patriotism in Late Imperial Austria* (Oxford: Oxford University Press, 2014), 32–33, 62.
8 Joseph II had a daughter by his first marriage who died at the age of seven.
9 Beales, *Joseph II*, vol. 2, 56, quoted in Godsey, "Habsburg Government and Intermediary Authority," 700.

10 Joseph also decreed that civil servants with university law degrees would dispense justice in towns and villages and even on noble estates throughout the monarchy. The universities (Vienna, Prague, Louvain, Freiburg in Breisgau, Lemberg/Lwów/Lviv, Pest, later Cracow and Padua) had the right to award doctorate degrees. The lyceums (Graz, Innsbruck, Brünn/Brno) had previously had the title of university, but could no longer award doctorates. Heindl, *Gehorsame Rebellen. Bürokratie unf Beamte in Österreich 1780 bis 1848* (Vienna: Böhlau 1990), 69, 97.

11 In 1787 Johann Pezzl estimated the annual cost for a single man with a modest life style in Vienna at 467 florins. Many students financed their studies by serving as tutors to the children of the nobility. Heindl, *Gehorsame Rebellen*, 180.

12 Ibid., 23–24.

13 In the years covered by this chapter (1780–1815), for example, the number of princes and archdukes in this sample ranged between .5 percent and 1 percent of the total. The number of counts ranged from 8.5 percent to 7.6 percent, as did that of barons and freiherr. Those from ennobled civil servant or military backgrounds fell slightly from 45 percent to 41 percent while those from commoner backgrounds rose from 37 percent to 41 percent. The absolute number of positions in this survey rose from 495 in 1781 to 618 in 1811. Heindl, *Gehorsame Rebellen*, 147.

14 See ibid., 226, on separation of workplace and home.

15 Pezzl, quoted in ibid., 227

16 Ibid., 185, and later, especially on *Vormärz* period.

17 Ibid., 22.

18 Beales, *Joseph II*, vol. 2, 46–47; Heindl, *Gehorsame Rebellen*, 26–28.

19 From a decree of March 1786, quoted in Heindl, *Gehorsame Rebellen*, 30.

20 Reproduced in the excellent series of volumes edited by Balázs Trencsényi and Michal Kopeček, *Discourses of Collective Identity in Central and Southeast Europe (1770–1945). Texts and Commentaries. Volume I, Late Enlightenment—Emergence of the 'National Idea'* (Budapest & New York: Central European University Press, 2006), 131.

21 Quoted in Miroslav Hroch, *Na prahu národní existence* (Prague: Naučná literatura - Politologie 1999), 49.

22 Van Swieten was also known as a minor composer and patron of Haydn, Mozart, and Beethoven. His father, Maria Theresa's physician Gerard van Swieten, had been sent by the Empress in 1755 to investigate reports of vampires in Moravia. See his *Abhandlung des Daseyns der Gespenster nebst einem Anhange von Vampyrismus* (Augsburg: Andreas Mayer, 1768). On the history curriculum, see also Heindl, *Gehorsame Rebellen*, 109–111. Heindl

notes, however, that the course was soon ended by Martini, who believed that students acquired enough knowledge of Austrian history in their lower schools. Ibid., 110–111.

23 Quoted in Beales, *Joseph II,* vol. 2, 91.

24 Beales, *Joseph II,* vol. 2, 93–94.

25 Ibid., 95.

26 Ibid., 311. The formula actually required a school to be founded wherever ninety to one hundred school-aged children lived up to a half hour's walk away.

27 According to Beales, Joseph could not help micromanaging. He insisted that students not use the informal second person singular to address each other, that corporal punishment could be used only in limited cases, that teachers were to receive pensions, and that "they were to rank immediately below the magistrates in the hierarchy of the towns." *Joseph II,* vol. 2, 311–312.

28 *Politische Verfassung der deutschen Schulen in den kaiserl. königl. deutschen Erbstaaten* (Vienna: k. und k. Schulbücher Verschleisses bey St. Anna in der Johannes-Gasse, 1812), 150–154.

29 Beales, *Joseph II,* vol. 2, 168.

30 On the British comparison, Beales, *Joseph II,* vol. 2, 170. Laws to anchor these rights firmly in provincial legal codes followed the toleration patents. This meant that tolerance of Protestant, Eastern Orthodox Christian, or Unitarian subjects could not easily be reversed in a later reign.

31 For Jewish population numbers, Beales *Joseph II,* vol. 2, 197–201, taken from Horst Glassl, *Das österreichische Einrichtungswerk in Galizien (1772–1790)* (Wiesbaden: Harrassowitz, 1975), 189–192; P. G. M. Dickson, *Finance and Government under Maria Theresia,* 2 vols. (Oxford: Oxford University Press, 1987), here vol. I, 444; Gabor Vermes cites the number of 75,000 Jews in Hungary and 1,000 in Transylvania for 1772. Gabor Vermes, *Hungarian Culture and Politics in the Habsburg Monarchy 1711–1848* (Budapest and New York: CEU Press, 2014), 25.

32 Bohemia and Silesia, Italian lands 1781; Vienna, Lower Austria, Moravia, 1782; Hungary 1783, Galicia 1785 and 1789. The Galician *Judenpatent* of 1789 was to have applied to the entire monarchy, but Joseph's early death prevented it. Michael Silber, "From Tolerated Aliens to Citizen Soldiers," in Pieter Judson and Marsha Rozenblit, eds., *Constructing Nationalities in East Central Europe* (New York: Berghahn, 2005), 19–36, here 21, 32 (note #8). See also Beales, *Joseph II,* vol. 2, 196–213.

33 Beales, *Joseph II,* vol. 2, 204–205.

34 Neither the Habsburg state nor more Orthodox Jews became involved in the debate or offered opinions on the matter. Silber, "Tolerated Aliens," 21.

35 The sequence of events was that the emperor ordered the conscription and then the Military Council protested. Joseph remained unmoved by these protests and in June 1788 ordered the conscription of Jews from all the Habsburg crownlands. See analysis of the debates in Silber, "Tolerated Aliens," 21–25.

36 Quoted in ibid., 26. Silber notes that the government made some concession to Jewish concerns, such as the provision of separate uniforms free of the mix of fibers prohibited by Jewish law, but that it opposed the creation of separate Jewish units.

37 Ibid., 30. Starting at a much later date during the wars against France, the Prussian military also conscripted Jews.

38 Beales, *Joseph II,* vol. 2, 207–212; see also Michael L. Miller, *Rabbis and Revolution: The Jews of Moravia in the Age of Emancipation* (Stanford, CA: Stanford University Press, 2011), especially 40–52.

39 Paula S. Fichtner, *The Habsburg Monarchy, 1490–1848* (New York: Palgrave, 2003), 82; Beales, *Joseph II,* vol. 2, 316–326.

40 Joseph's law foresaw the possibility of state-sanctioned divorce in certain circumstances and even remarriage within the church. Beales, *Joseph II,* vol. 2, 322–323.

41 The Galician version required the peasants who wanted to move to provide a replacement for their plot. Robin Okey, *The Habsburg Monarchy c. 1765–1918: From Enlightenment to Eclipse* (New York: Palgrave Macmillan, 2002), 42.

42 Beales, *Joseph II,* vol. 2, 252.

43 Quoted in Larry Wolff, The Idea of *Galicia: History and Fantasy in Habsburg Political Culture* (Stanford, CA: Stanford University Press, 2010), 16.

44 Svjatoslav Pacholkiv, "Das Werden einer Grenze: Galizien 1772–1867" in *Grenze und Staat. Passwesen, Staatsbürgerschaft, Heimatrecht und Fremdengesetzgebung in der österreichischen Monarchie, 1780–1867,* Waltraud Heindl and Edith Saurer, ed, unter Mitarbeit von Hannelore Burger und Harald Wendelin (Vienna: Böhlau, 2000), 520–522; Wolff, *The Idea of Galicia,* 22–27.

45 In general on Bukovina in the 1780s and 1790s, Kurt Scharr, "Erfolg oder Misserfolg? Die Durchsetzung des modernen Territorialstaates am beispiel des Ansiedlungswesens in der Bukowina von 1774–1826," in Hans-Christian Maner, ed., *Grenzregionen der Habsburgermonarchie im 18. und 19. Jahrhundert. Ihre Bedeutung und Funktion aus der Perspektive Wiens* (Mainz Contributions to the History of Eastern Europe, Volume I), (Münster: Lit

Verlag, 2005). On the existing social structure and lack of large land-owning nobility, 58.

46 Scharr, "Erfolg oder Misserfolg," 52.

47 Oddly, despite her talents as a jeweler, it seems that she desired to open a milliner's shop. For this story, see Hannelore Burger, "Die Staatsbürgerschaft" in Heindl and Saurer, *Grenze und Staat*, 88–172, here 154–155.

48 To some extent this more consciously open-door immigration policy dated to the 1740s and to Maria Theresa's attempts to replace the valuable lost population of Silesia and its skills.

49 Burger, "Staatsbürgerschaft," 98.

50 That is, cases where claims about marriage or descent were absent from a foreigner's application for citizenship. For a broader critique of the AGBG's gender expectations and the centrality of the concept of family to women's place in law, Gabriella Hauch, *Frau Biedermeier auf den Barrikaden. Frauenleben in der Wiener Revolution 1848* (Vienna: Verlag für Gesellschaftskritik, 1990), 22–24; 60–63.

51 See the assessment by Helmut Rumpler, *Eine Chance für Mitteleuropa. Bürgerliche Emanzipation und Staatsverfall in der Habsburgermonarchie* (Vienna: Überreuter, 2005), 108–111.

52 https://www.ris.bka.gv.at/Dokument.wxe?Abfrage=Bundesnormen &Dokumentnummer=NOR12017706 (accessed 23.10.2015). On the issue of slavery and the Austrian empire, see Alison Frank, "The Children of the Desert and the Laws of the Sea: Austria, Great Britain, the Ottoman Empire, and the Mediterranean Slave Trade in the Nineteenth Century," *American Historical Review* 117, no. 3 (June 2012).

53 Early on, the term was meant to distinguish more between the citizen and the foreigner, and less to emphasize equality among the citizens of the Habsburg realms themselves. On the evolution of the term, Hannelore Burger, "Passwesen und Staatsbürgerschaft," in Heindl and Saurer, *Grenze und Staat*, 95–105.

54 William Godsey argues cogently that while the trend in Joseph II's reign appears to have favored uniformity and a diminishing of the diets' importance, in fact their importance remained substantial especially in particular fiscal matters. "Habsburg Government and Intermediary Authority," 699–740.

55 Harald Wendelin, "Schub und Heimatrecht," in Heindl and Saurer, *Grenze und Staat*, 173–343.

56 See the excellent tables in Wendelin, "Schub und Heimatrecht," 295–323. Women migrants made up only a quarter to a third of those subjected to *Schub* from Vienna, possibly because those who had migrated and then

married assumed the *Heimat* of their husband. Higher percentages of those women subjected to *Schub* on average were expelled to places that were closer to Vienna than were men.

57 Joseph had of course been crowned Holy Roman Emperor in a ceremony in 1765.

58 R. J. W. Evans, *Austria, Hungary, and the Habsburgs: Essays on Central Europe c. 1683–1867* (Oxford: Oxford University Press, 2006), 136–137.

59 The new conscription law was also imposed on Tyrol at this time, where it also drew strong opposition. Okey, *Habsburg Monarchy*, 46. Previous censuses of Hungary had always excluded the nobility from the surveys, something Joseph reversed this time. Beales, *Joseph II*, vol. 2, 478. The results showed the total population of Hungary at over 8 million, whereas it had previously been estimated at 5 million. Similarly the number of nobles came to 200,000 instead of the estimated 30,000. Hungary's population was thus about half that of the monarchy, and the number of nobles was about nine times greater than had been supposed.

60 In technological terms many administrators also doubted that such a survey could even be accomplished. When told, for example, that it would take two hundred trained land surveyors forty years to carry out a land assessment of the entire monarchy, Joseph decided to enlist peasants for the purpose, to whom he distributed instructions and kits. By the end of 1786 these peasant surveyors had already covered 75 percent of the land in Austria (including Bohemia and Galicia). As to the accuracy of the surveys, a Polish assessment made in 1930 actually found that the original one had been largely reliable for Galicia. Beales, *Joseph II*, vol. 2, 492, 566; Okey, *Habsburg Monarchy*, 51.

61 Charles Ingrao, *The Habsburg Monarchy 1618–1815* (Cambridge: Cambridge University Press, 1994), 204–205; Beales, *Joseph II*, vol. 2, 592–597.

62 Okey also estimates that Galician nobles would have lost up to 60 percent of their annual income under this reform. Okey, *Habsburg Monarchy*, 51. Ingrao, *Habsburg Monarchy*, 205, reports that the typical peasant throughout the monarchy devoted 70 percent of his yield to taxes of all kinds.

63 Ingrao estimates rustical peasants constituted 20 percent of peasants in Bohemia. Ingrao, *Habsburg Monarchy*, 205.

64 This is also a place to recall that not all nobles owned estates and that especially in Galicia and Hungary many impoverished nobles were indistinguishable from peasants. Hajo Holborn, *A History of Modern Germany 1648–1840* (New York: Alfred A. Knopf, 1964) 2:289.

65 Still another related problem for the nobility was the fact that despite their smaller incomes under this new system, the state would have expected them

to continue carrying out their duties of record-keeping and administration of justice at the local level.

66 The Habsburg forces won several victories and even captured Belgrade from the Ottomans. This created some popularity for Joseph at home. Beales, *Joseph II*, vol. 2, 580–581.

67 Ingrao, *Habsburg Monarchy*, 207–208.

68 Beales, *Joseph II*, vol. 2, 554.

69 Ibid.

70 Quoted in ibid., 611–612

71 On the particular significance of the crown, and on its return, Vermes, *Hungarian Culture and Politics*, 84, 97.

72 Quoted in Beales, vol. 2, 629.

73 Quoted in ibid., 628.

74 Quoted in Anna M. Drabek, "Patriotismus und nationale Identität in Böhmen und Mähren," in *Patriotismus und Nationsbildung am Ende des Heiligen Römischen Reiches,* ed. Otto Dann, Miroslav Hroch, and Johannes Koll (Köln: SH Verlag, 2003), 156.

75 That crown, like Hungary's crown of St. Stephen, had long been kept in Vienna, and Leopold was about to return it to Prague in a symbolic effort to placate the Bohemian Diet.

76 Drabek, "Patriotismus und nationale Identität," 154.

77 Hugh LeCaine Agnew, "Ambiguities of Ritual: Dynastic Loyalty, Territorial Patriotism and Nationalism in the Last Three Royal Coronations in Bohemia, 1791–1836," *Bohemia* 41 (2000): 1–12.

78 Leopold did establish a chair in the Czech language at the University in Prague.

79 Francis's involvement in more than twenty years of warfare did not reflect any martial aggression on his part. Nor did it betoken any great desire to remake Europe or even to intervene forcefully in France, the way some of his advisors demanded. Unlike his uncle Joseph, Francis was a reluctant warrior, always cautious in nature.

80 Heindl, *Gehorsame Rebellen*, 45–47.

81 Macartney, *The Habsburg Empire, 1790–1918* (London: Weidenfeld and Nicolson, 1969), 152.

82 In 1754 Vienna had counted 175,609 inhabitants. By 1782 the number had grown to 206,120, and in 1807 the city's population was 242,523. Maren Seliger and Karl Ucakar, *Wien Politische Geschichte 1740–1934. Entwicklung und Bestimmungskräfte grossstädtischer Politik,* 2 vols. (Vienna and Munich: Jugend und Volk, 1985), vol. 1, 165.

83 Wolfgang Häusler, "Von der Manufaktur zum Maschinensturm. Industrielle Dynamik und soziale Wandel in Raum von Wien" in *Wien im Vormärz* (Vienna and Munich: Jugend und Volk, 1980), 32–56.

84 Heindl, *Gehorsame Rebellen*, recounts the wartime penury of mid-level civil servants thanks to inflation, 265. See also, however, the account of local economic profit during these years in Troppau/Opava thanks to Napoleon's "Continental System" recounted by Faustin Enns, *Das Oppaland oder der Troppauer Kreis, nach seinen geschichtlichen, naturgeschichtlichen, bürgerlichen und örtlichen Eigenthümlichkeiten*. 4 vols. (Vienna: Carl Gerold, 1835), vol. 1, 152–154.

85 Evans, *Austria, Hungary, and the Habsburgs*, 248 fn. 8.

86 Hugo Schmidt, "The Origin of the Austrian National Anthem and Austria's Literary Effort" in *Austria in the Age of the French Revolution 1789–1815*, ed. Kinley Brauer and William Wright (Minneapolis, MN: Center for Austrian Studies, 1990), 163–183; Laurence Cole, *Military Culture and Popular Patriotism in Late Imperial Austria* (Oxford: Oxford University Press, 2014), 36.

87 Macartney, *Empire*, 182–183. On the patriotic press during this period, Silvester Lechner, *Gelehrte Kritik und Restauration. Metternichs Wissenschaft- und Pressepolitik und die Wiener 'Jahrbücher der Literatur (1818–1849)* (Tübingen: Max Neimeyer Verlag, 1977), 56–60.

88 Macartney, *Empire*, 185.

89 In German, *Der Abschied des Landwehrmannes*. See Werner Telesko, *Kulturraum Österreich. Die Identität der Regionen in der bildenden Kunst des 19. Jahrhunderts* (Vienna: Böhlau 2008), 43.

90 Telesko, *Kulturraum Österreich*, 43–44. The painting became so popular that the emperor commissioned a "Return of the Militiaman" from Krafft in 1817.

91 Brian E. Vick, *The Congress of Vienna: Power and Politics after Napoleon* (Cambridge, MA: Harvard University Press, 2014), chap. 2; Kothgasser, in Walter Spiegl, "Das Glas im Biedermeier," in the excellent exhibition catalog *Bürgersinn und Aufbegehren. Biedermeier und Vormärz in Wien 1815–1848. Katalog der 189. Sonderausstellung des Historischen Museums der Stadt Wien* (Vienna: Museen der Stadt Wien, 1987), 214–217. On literary patriotic texts, see Karen Hagemann, "'Be Proud and Firm, Citizens of Austria!' Patriotism and Masculinity in Texts of the 'Political Romantics' Written during Austria's Anti-Napoleonic Wars," *German Studies Review* 29 (2006): 41–62

92 Macartney, *Empire*, 188.

93 The story is more complicated than the outline given here and also includes elements of betrayal and miscommunication. In 1818 Hofer's family was awarded a patent of nobility by Francis I.

94 Historian Laurence Cole has written several excellent works analyzing the Hofer Myth and its various later uses. See *"Für Gott, Kaiser und Vaterland."* *Nationale Identität der deutschprachigen Bevölkerung Tirols, 1860–1914* (Frankfurt a/M and New York: Campus, 2000), especially 225–322.

95 Krafft, who had painted *The Departure of the Militiaman,* and then *The Return of the Militiaman,* was commissioned by Francis in 1830 to paint this scene of the Emperor's return as part of an historical cycle for the Audience chambers of the Hofburg. Telesko, *Kulturraum Österreich,* 50; also Telesko, "Der Hofburg-Zyklus Johann Peter Kraffts in *Die Wiener Hofburg 1835–1918. Der Ausbau der Residenz vom Vormärz bis zum Ende des "Kaiserforums,"* ed. Werner Telesko (Vienna: Verlag der Österreichische Akademie der Wissenschaften, 2012), 32–36.

96 Brian Vick, "The Vienna Congress as an Event in Austrian History: Civil Society and Politics in the Habsburg Empire at the End of the Wars against Napoleon," *AHY* 46 (2015): 123. Vick offers several examples of popular imperial patriotism from 1815 as well as a complex picture of contemporary (1815) hopes for a future in which the government might again pursue various types of political reform.

97 *Denkbuch für Fürst und Vaterland,* Herausgegeben von Joseph Rossi, 2 vols. (Vienna: J. B. Wallishausser, 1814–1815). I thank Brian Vick for alerting me to the existence of these remarkable volumes.

98 Rossi, *Denkbuch,* I: 82–83.

99 For examples of comparable popular celebrations in urban England in the 1740s, Kathleen Wilson, *The Sense of the People: Politics, Culture, and Imperialism in England 1715–1785* (Cambridge: Cambridge University Press, 1998), especially 140–164.

100 Rossi especially noted the enthusiasm of the people of Trieste, where the festivities also celebrated the return of Austrian rule to the entire Adriatic coastal region (not surprising, given its economic rivalry with Venice). "From the windows one heard nothing but unanimous cries of joy in all the languages used by the inhabitants, 'Long live Kaiser Franz,' 'May Austria rule forever!'" Later he noted that the celebratory parade in Trieste stopped at the governor's palace, where, along with military and civilian leaders, representatives of each of Trieste's many nations had assembled. Rossi, *Denkbuch,* II: 349–350.

3. AN EMPIRE OF CONTRADICTIONS

Epigraph: Moriz von Stubenrauch, *Statistische Darstellung des Vereinswesens im Kaiserthume Österreich* (Vienna, 1857), 2, quoted in Irmgard Helperstorfer, "Die Entwicklung des Vereinswesens im Vormärz," in the Museum catalog of the Historical Museum of Vienna, *Bürgersinn und Aufbgegehren. Biedermeier und Vormärz in Wien 1815–1848* (Vienna: Verlag Jugend und Volk, 1987), 319–325, here 320; and in Brian Vick, "The Vienna Congress as an Event in Austrian History: Civil Society and Politics in the Habsburg Empire at the End of the Wars against Napoleon," *AHY* 46 (2015): 116.

1 The ABGB applied to the Hereditary Lands, although the regime originally planned to apply it to the rest of the empire.

2 Paula Sutter Fichtner, *The Habsburg Monarchy, 1490–1848* (London: Palgrave Macmillan 2003), 114.

3 Several elements of this emerging police state can be traced back to Joseph II, who, as we saw in Chapter 2, had established a court police office under Count Johann Anton Pergen in 1789.

4 David Laven, "Law and Order in Habsburg Venetia, 1814–1835," *Historical Journal* vol. 39, no. 2 (June 1996): 396, 403. "Laws were upheld, and it was an obsession with law which dominated the whole regime; this fact was reflected in the enormous stress placed on its study as the prerequisite for a government career" (ibid., 396).

5 Many observers criticized the fact that the planned independence of the judiciary was never carried out, especially at the local level in regions where patrimonial courts run by local nobles dominated society.

6 Waltraud Heindl, *Gehorsame Rebellen. Bürokratie und Beamte in Österreich 1780 bis 1848* (Vienna: Böhlau, 1991), 51.

7 Ibid., 51. For a detailed analysis of salaries and inflation, see 159–179.

8 Although literacy rates in much of Austria grew substantially during this period, and private technical institutions expanded their numbers and enrollments, state educational policy stagnated. Gary B. Cohen, *Education and Middle-Class Society in Imperial Austria 1848–1918* (West Lafayette, IN: Purdue University Press, 1996), 11–23. On the University environment after the Napoleonic Wars, see Deborah Coen, *Vienna in the Age of Uncertainty: Science, Liberalism, and Private Life* (Chicago: University of Chicago Press, 2007), 35–38.

9 On Austria's 1811 patent system that gave inventors exclusive rights for mechanical inventions for a period of ten years and was revised in 1820 to take account of new technologies in agriculture and chemistry, see David Good, *The Economic Rise of the Habsburg Empire 1750–1918* (Berkeley and Los Angeles: University of California Press, 1984), 64.

10 For Silesian examples of this anti-state use of the term "nation" in the 1830s and 1840s, see Dan Gawrecki, "Regionale und nationale Identitäten in Österreich-Schlesien im langen 19. Jahrhundert," in *Die Grenzen der Nationen. Identitätenwandel in Oberschlesien in der Neuzeit,* ed. Kai Struve and Philipp Ther (Marburg: Verlag Herder Institut, 2002), 111–134.

11 In general on the reform movements and activists on the 1830s, Gabor Vermes, *Hungarian Culture and Politics in the Habsburg Monarchy 1711–1848* (Budapest and New York: CEU Press, 2014), 247–288.

12 István Deák, *The Lawful Revolution. Louis Kossuth and the Hungarians 1848–1849* (New York: Columbia University Press, 1979), 24–26. The translations of the titles and the analysis of the two texts are taken from Deák. On Széchenyi's writings and the reactions they generated, Vermes, *Hungarian Politics and Culture,* 252–260. Vermes argues that although Széchenyi's themes in *Hitel* appear to be economic, in fact the concept of credit produced necessary moral imperatives as well.

13 Deák, *Lawful Revolution,* 26–27, 38–39.

14 For an excellent formulation of this idea of the promise of the strong state and the failures of the weak state, see Konrad Clewing, *Staatlichkeit und nationale Identitätsbildung. Dalmatien in Vormärz und Revolution* (Munich: R. Oldenbourg Verlag, 2001), 69–102.

15 Statistics drawn from Good, *Economic Rise,* 45; Fichtner, *Habsburg Monarchy,* 119; and Don José Marugán y Martín, *Descripcion geográfica, fisica, politica, estadistica, literaria del reino de Portugal y de los Algarbes, comparado con los principales de Europa* (Madrid: en la Imprenta Real 1833), 2:301. According to Marugán, in 1830 Milan counted 150,000 inhabitants, Venice 100,000, Lemberg 50,000, Debreczin 42,000, Triests 40,000, Graz 34,000, Buda 33,000, Brünn/Brno 28,000, Pressburg/Poszonyi 26,000, Koloszvar/Cluj/Klausenburg 25,000, independent Cracow 25,000, Brody 24,000, Zagreb/Agram 17,000, Nagyszeben/Sibiu/Hermannstadt 16,600, Vrsac/Werschetz/Versecz 16,000. Only one European city counted over a million inhabitants (London), while Paris came close. Britain counted eight cities over 100,000, far more than any continental state. Other sources place the population for Trieste well over 40,000 ten years earlier, in 1820.

16 Quoted in Robert Nemes, *The Once and Future Budapest* (Dekalb: Northern Illinois University Press, 2005), 37.

17 For statistics on Trieste, see M. Breschi, A. Kalc, and E. Navarra, "La Nascita di una città. Storia minima della popolazione di Trieste, sec. XVIII–XIX," in R. Finzi and G. Panjek, eds., *Storia economica e sociale di Trieste: Vol. 1: La città dei gruppi 1719–1918,* ed. Finzi and G. Panjek (Trieste: Lint editoriale 2001), 69–237.

18 J. Bromuss [Jan Ohéral], "Bilder aus dem industriellen Leben Brünns (1838)," in *Jung Österreich. Dokumente und Materialien zur liberalen Österreichischen Opposition 1835–1848*, ed. Madeleine Rietra (Amsterdam: Rodopi 1980), 255.

19 For both the eighteenth century and the nineteenth century before the development of the railways, see especially Andreas Helmedach, *Das Verkehrssytem als Modernisierungsfaktor. Strassen, Post, Fuhrwesen und Reisen nach Triest und Fiume vom Beginn des 18. Jahrhunderts bis zum Eisenbahnzeitalter* (Munich: R. Oldenbourg Verlag 2002).

20 Good, *Economic Rise*, 65. Good estimates that in 1847 Austria's primary road system amounted to over 96,000 kilometers (almost 60,000 miles).

21 Nemes, *The Once and Future Budapest*, 116.

22 On the Austrian Lloyd, see Alison Frank, "The Children of the Desert and the Laws of the Sea: Austria, Great Britain, the Ottoman Empire, and the Mediterranean Slave Trade in the Nineteenth Century" in *AHR* 117/2 (2012): 410–444, especially 415. See also Frank, *Invisible Empire: A New Global History of Austria* (Princeton, NJ: Princeton University Press, forthcoming).

23 Clewing, *Staatlichkeit*, 68, 236.

24 Günter Dinhobl, " ' . . . die Cultur wird gehoben und verbreitet.' Eisenbahnbau und Geopolitik in Kakanien," in *Zentren, Peripherien und kollektive Identitäten in Österreich-Ungarn*, ed. Endre Hárs, Wolfgang Müller-Funk, Ursula Reber, Clemens Ruthner (Tübingen and Basel:Francke, 2006), 79–96, here 82.

25 Gerstner was also Professor and first director of the Polytechnic School in Prague. His original plans were approved and then postponed due to the 1809 campaign against Napoleon.

26 This particular project would be financed to the tune of 900,000 gulden by three Viennese bank houses (Sina, Geymüller, Stametz). The final cost was much more.

27 Thanks to a series of technical problems and cost overruns, the line was not completed until 1832, making it by that point the second continental rail project (the first had meanwhile been completed in France [St. Etienne]). In the 1860s this line was converted to a steam engine line.

28 Riepl was professor at the Vienna Technical Hochschul and adviser on the building of Austria's first coke process oven in Witkovice Moravia; later he drafted detailed plans for a railway network for the entire Empire. Burkhard Köster, *Militär und Eisenbahn in der Habsburgermonarchie 1825–1859* (Munich: R. Oldenbourg Verlag, 1999), 54.

29 "Bauperiode und Streckenklassifizierung des Eisenbahnnetzes 1824–1914," in *Die Habsburgermonarchie 1848–1918*, ed. Helmut Rumpler and Martin

Seger, Band IX *Soziale Strukturen*, 2. Teil *Kartenband*, 249. The line to Bochnia was not completed until 1856, but by 1847 it already reached Silesia. For a detailed account of the inauguration of the line from Vienna to Brünn/ Brno, as well as concerns about the early railroads in general, see Chad Bryant, "Into an Uncertain Future: Railroads and Vormärz Liberalism in Brno, Vienna, and Prague," *AHY* 40 (2009): 183–201, especially 186–187.

30 Ibid., 187. By 1845 the Nordbahn was transporting 650,000 people annually, and 109 million kilograms of goods.

31 See the critical discussion of this argument in Good, *Economic Rise*, 65–67. Fichtner offers a more traditional characterization of the relationship: "What was a strategic outpost for the army was not always convenient to centers of trade and manufacture. Such a gross dissonance has persuaded at least some scholars that, in sharp contrast to other European countries, government-built rail links contributed little to the early industrialization of the Habsburg Empire" (*Habsburg Monarchy*, 116). Köster debunks the theory that the construction of the railroads somehow did not follow economic needs. Köster, *Militär und Eisenbahn*, 53–54.

32 Köster, *Militär und Eisenbahn*, 237.

33 Ibid., 77.

34 Dinhobl, *Eisenbahnbau and Geopolitik*, 83; Köster, *Militär und Eisenbahn*, 158.

35 For the example of Ungarisch Hradec/Uherské Hradiště, see Jiri Coupek, "Ungarisch Hradisch—Bürgertum und Stadtpolitik," in *Kleinstadtbürgertum in der Habsburgermonarchie 1862–1914* (Bürgertum in der Habsburgermmonarchie IX), ed. Peter Urbanitsch and Hannes Stekl (Vienna: Böhlau, 2000), 355–381.

36 These challenges included the creation of the alpine Semmering connection, and passage over both the Ljubljana Moor and the dangerous Karst region.

37 For an analysis of the limited forms of self-administration or redress created by the Josephene reforms, see Kai Struve, *Bauern und Nation in Galizien. Über Zugehörigkeit und soziale Emancipation im 19. Jahrhundert* (Göttingen: Vandenhoek & Ruprecht, 2005), 72.

38 Larry Wolff, *The Idea of Galicia: History and Fantasy in Habsburg Political Culture* (Stanford, CA: Stanford University Press, 2010), 33, 36, 134.

39 John-Paul Himka, *Galician Villagers and the Ukrainian National Movement in the Nineteenth Century* (New York: St. Martin's Press, 1988), 15.

40 Struve, *Bauern und Nation*, 75–77. The Stanislau example is taken from the year 1839.

41 Himka, *Galician Villagers*, 21.

42 For these statistics and the following descriptions, Clewing, *Staatlichkeit,* 53–64. Clewing effectively and decisively rejects accusations of a deliberate Austrian policy to isolate Dalmatia from Croatia (ibid., 68).

43 *Memoria statistica sulla Dalmazia. Di Francesco Zavoreo, capitanio ingegnere ex-veneto e direttore provvisorio dei lavori edili e idraulici in pensione* (Venice: Molinari, 1821), quoted in ibid., 122 (emphasis added).

44 Examples cited in ibid., 123 (emphasis added).

45 Hungary and Lombardy were not subject to the school law that regulated education in the rest of the empire. Rumpler, *Mitteleuropa,* 111–113.

46 By 1914, no one could have doubted Austria's accomplishments in this realm as reflected in its impressive literacy statistics compared to other societies in western and central Europe. In 1914, 16.52 percent of the Austrian population was illiterate, compared to 15 percent in France, and 45 percent in Italy. Clewing, *Staatlichkeit,* 114.

47 Ibid., 124, emphasis added.

48 *Visitationsbericht zur Lage der Diözese Zadar,* by Joseph Nowak, archbishop of Zadar, quoted in ibid., 113–114.

49 Ibid., 69–70.

50 Laven, "Venetia," 400.

51 Ibid., 401–402. This sympathetic attitude toward the objects of their attention is reminiscent of reports by local police officials about complaints by local populations during the First World War that we will encounter in Chapter 8.

52 Michal Chvojka, "Buchhändler und Bücherschmuggel ausländische Drückschriften als Politikum im österreichischen Vormärz," *Bohemia* 50 (2010): 351–355. Evans notes that Hungarian society was far freer in terms of censorship than the rest of Austria. Evans, *Austria, Hungary, and the Habsburgs,* 188.

53 Friedrich Engel-Janosi, "Der Wiener juridische-politische Leseverein: seine Geschichte bis zur Märzrevolution," *Mitteilungen des Vereines für Geschichte der Stadt Wien* 4 (1923): 58–66, here 65. Gerhard Pfeisinger notes that discussions in the local coffee houses and theater were more openly political than those in the Johanneum. Pfeisinger, "Der Revolution von 1848 in Graz" (PhD diss., University of Salzburg, 1985), 16, 25–28.

54 Engel-Janosi, "Wiener juridische-politische Leseverein," 58–66.

55 See generally chapter 5, "Was Metternich's Austria a Police State?" in Alan Sked, *Metternich and Austria: An Evaluation* (New York and London: Palgrave Macmillan, 2007), 123–177.

56 Cited in ibid., 126.

57 Faustin Enns, *Das Oppaland oder der Troppauer Kreis, nach seinen geschichtlichen, naturgeschichtlichen, bürgerlichen und örtlichen Eigenthümlichkeiten*, 4 vols. (Vienna: Carl Gerold, 1835).

58 Ibid., II:151–152

59 Ibid., I:vii.

60 "One should not expect a . . . beautiful and inspiring picture of our ancestors here—we don't even know for certain who they were." Ibid, I:vii.

61 Ibid., II:152.

62 Enns, *Das Oppaland*, 2:153–153.

63 Ibid., II:157.

64 Ibid., "Das Troppauer Museum," 2:157–159.

65 See most recently Rita Krueger, *Czech, German, and Noble: Status and National Identity in Habsburg Bohemia* (New York: Oxford University Press, 2009). On the "Ossolineum" in Lemberg/Lwów/Lviv, see Wolff, *The Idea of Galicia*, 81–85; Thomas Weidenholzer, "Bürgerliche Geselligkeit und Formen der Öffentlichkeit in Salzburg 1780–1820," in *Bürger zwischen Tradition und Modernität. Bürgertum in der Habsburgermonarchie VI*, ed. Robert Hoffmann, in cooperation with Gunda Berth-Scalmani and Thomas Hellmuth (Vienna: Böhlau, 1997); Anton Schlossar, *Erzherzog Johann von Oesterreich und sein Einfluss auf das Culturleben der Steiermark. Originalbriefe des Erzherzogs aus den Jahren 1810–1825* (Vienna: Braumüller, 1878), 20; Werner Telesko, *Kulturraum Österreich. Die Identität der Regionen in der bildenden Kunst des 19. Jahrhunderts* (Vienna: Böhlau 2008), 379–381.

66 Zdeněk Hojda, "Patriae et Musis. Počátky Obrazárni Společnosti Vlasteneckých Přátel Umění v Čechách" in *Artis Pictoriae Amatores: Evropa v Zrcadle Pražského Barokního Sběratelství*, ed. Lubomír Slavíček (Prague: Národní galerie v Praze, 1993), 311–316, also cited in Krueger, *Czech, German, and Noble*, 144.

67 Helperstorfer, "Vereinswesen," 320.

68 Otto Hwaletz, "Zur ökonomischen, sozialen und ideologisch-politischen Formierung des industriell-gewerblichen Bürgertums. Das Beispiel der Industrieverein," in *Bürgertum in der Habsburgermonarchie*, vol. I, ed. Bruckmüller et al. (Vienna: Böhlau, 1990), 177–204, here 192–194.

69 Anton von Kraus-Elisago, *Bericht über die dritte allgemeine Gewerbenausstellung* (Vienna, 1846), quoted in Wolfgang Häusler, *Von der Massenarmut zur Arbeiterbewegung; Demokratie und soziale Frage in der Wienerrevolution von 1848* (Vienna and Munich: Jugend und Volk, 1979), 68.

70 Elke Wikidal, "Gewerbe und Industrieausstellungen im österreichischen Vormärz. Ihre Entstehung und Bedeutung im Kontext der industriellen Entwicklung der Zeit," Diplomarbeit, Uni. Wien, 1994.

71 Quoted in Gabriella Hauch, *Frau Biedermeier auf den Barrikaden. Frauen-leben in der Wiener Revolution 1848* (Vienna: Verlag für Gesellschaftskritik, 1990), 45.

72 Krueger, *Czech, German, and Noble*, 100.

73 Laurence Cole, *Military Culture and Popular Patriotism in Late Imperial Austria* (Oxford: Oxford University Press, 2014), 261–262.

74 Clewing, *Staatlichkeit*, 242–244.

75 Franz Petter, *Dalmatien in seinen verschiedenen Beziehungen* (Vienna: Sommer, 1857), 2:13.

76 Frank Henschel, "'Das Fluidum der Stadt . . .' Lebenswelten in Kassa/Kaschau/Košice zwischen urbaner Vielfalt und Nationalismus 1867–1918" (PhD diss., University of Leipzig, 2013), 213, 171. Henschel quotes the author Sándor Márai's enthusiastic account of the discussion culture in Kaschau/Kassa: "Here, newspapers and periodicals were already being printed while in the towns of the Hungarian plains, with few exceptions, people coming together to slaughter pigs constituted the highpoint of the winter season's intellectual life"; Márai also claims that more books were sold here in the early nineteenth century than in Pest (178).

77 Robert Nemes, *Another Hungary: The Nineteenth-Century Provinces in Eight Lives* (Stanford, CA: Stanford University Press, forthcoming), manuscript version, 158.

78 Krueger, *Czech, German, and Noble*, 119.

79 Robert Nemes, *The Once and Future Budapest*, 63.

80 Anna Millo, "Trieste, 1830–1870: From Cosmopolitanism to the Nation," in *Different Paths to the Nation: Regional and National Identities in Central Europe and Italy, 1830–1870*, ed. Laurence Cole (New York: Palgrave Macmillan, 2007), 68.

81 On the industrial associations, Hwaletz, "Industrieverein," 177–204.

82 Some thirteen of these were founded in linguistically non-Hungarian regions of the Kingdom. Friedrich Gottas, "Grundzüge der Geschichte der Parteien und Verbände," in *Geschichte der Habsburgermonarchie 1848–1918*, vol. 8, *Politische Öffentlichkeit und Zivilgesellschaft*, ed. Helmut Rumpler and Peter Urbanitsch (Vienna: Verlag der Österreichischen Akademie der Wissenschaften, 2006), 1133–1168, here 1139.

83 Hauch, *Frau Biedermeier*, 54.

84 See Brian E. Vick, *The Congress of Vienna: Power and Politics after Napoleon* (Cambridge, MA: Harvard University Press, 2014); also Margarete Grandner and Edith Saurer, "Emanzipation und Religion in der jüdischen Frauenbewegung. Die Faszination der Assoziation," in *Geschlecht, Religion und Engagement. Die jüdischen Frauenbewegungen im deutschsprachigen Raum*

19. *und frühes 20. Jahrhundert*, ed. Grandner and Sauer (Vienna: Böhlau, 2005), 8–10, which according to Vick underestimates the number of branches.

85 Nemes, *Another Hungary*, 158.

86 See especially the rich analysis provided by Nemes, *Budapest*, 83–106.

87 For these examples, see Hauch, *Frau Biedermeier*, especially 45–47 and 53–55.

88 Millo, "Trieste," 65–67. Börries Kuzmany, *Brody. Eine galizische Grenzstadt im langen 19. Jahrhundert* (Vienna: Böhlau, 2011), 135–137.

89 On Silesia, see Gawrecki, "Regionale und nationale Identitäten in Österreichisch-Schlesien," 111–134.

90 Krueger, *Czech, German, and Noble*, 96–97, 101.

91 Thirty-three out of a total of 191 appeared in the Hungarian language.

92 Géza Buzinkay, "B. Die ungarische politische Presse" and Lothar Höbelt, "A. Die deutsche Presselandschaft," both in Rumpler and Urbanitsch, *Geschichte der Habsburgermonarchie 1848–1918*, 8:1895–1897 and 8:1880–1883, respectively. See also Gottas "Grundzüge," 8:1137–1138. Nemes notes, however, that during the 1830s and 1840s the readership of Hungarian-language publications grew faster than that of German-language ones in Buda and Pest. By the mid-1830s the circulation of Hungarian-language publications had reached 10,000 as opposed to 5,000 for German-language ones in Buda and Pest. Nemes also points out that many of the same people in Buda and Pest probably read both the Hungarian and German language press. *Once and Future Budapest*, 65.

93 Martin Sekera, "C. Das tschechische Pressewesen," in Rumpler and Urbanitsch, *Geschichte der Habsburgermonarchie 1848–1918*, 8:1977–2036, here 1978–1980.

94 Clewing, *Staatlichkeit*, 57.

95 On the critical role played by famed folklorist Vuk Karadžić in the creation of a South Slav language and the focus on Herzegovina as the locus of its perfect form, see Edin Hajdarpasic, *Whose Bosnia? Nationalism and Political Imagination in the Balkans, 1840–1914* (Ithaca, NY: Cornell University Press, 2015), 20–37.

96 Joachim Hösler, *Von Krain zu Slowenien. Die Anfänge der nationalen Differenzierungs-prozesse in Krain und der Untersteiermark von der Aufklärung bis zur Revolution 1768 bis 1848* (Munich: R. Oldenbourg Verlag, 2006), 246–247.

97 Table reproduced in ibid., 250. See also 1845 statistics, ibid., 249–249.

98 Leopold von Hasner, *Denkwürdigkeiten. Autobiographisches und Aphorismen* (Stuttgart: Cotta, 1892), 17.

99 [Eduard von Bauernfeld], *Pia Desiderata eines österreichischen Schrift-stellers* (Leipzig: Wigand, 1843), 15, 50.

4. WHOSE EMPIRE?

Epigraph: Karl Hickel, "Die Opfer des 13. März 1848 (ein Erinnerungsblatt)" (Prague, 1848), quoted in Jan Randák, "Politische-religiöses Totengedanken zu Beginn der Revolution von 1848/49 in Mitteleuropa," in *Bohemia* 47 no. 2 (2006/07): 317.

1 František Palacký, "Letter to Frankfurt, 11 April 1848," in Balázs Trencsény and Michal Kopeček, eds., *Discourses of Collective Identity in Central and Southeast Europe (1770–1945)* (Budapest and New York: Central European University Press, 2007), 2:327.

2 The uprising in Cracow itself was put down by Austrian troops nine days after its outbreak. In Galicia, some claimed upward of 2,000 casualties. Larry Wolff, *The Idea of Galicia: History and Fantasy in Habsburg Political Culture* (Stanford, CA: Stanford University Press, 2010), 142.

3 Kai Struve, *Bauern und Nation in Galizien. Über Zugehörigkeit und soziale Emancipation im 19. Jahrhundert* (Göttingen: Vandenhoek & Ruprecht, 2005), 81. According to Struve, the leadership of the rebellion had thwarted efforts by the more politically radical Polish nationalist Democrats to engage the peasants in the fall of 1845, fearing that these efforts would alienate the gentry.

4 Ibid., 83. This example comes from a village in East Galicia.

5 Alan Sked, "Austria and the 'Galician Massacres' of 1846: Schwarzenberg and the Propaganda War—An Unknown but Key Episode in the Career of the Austrian Statesman," in *A Living Anachronism? European Diplomacy and the Habsburg Monarchy*, ed. Lothar Höbelt and Thomas G. Otte (Vienna: Böhlau, 2010), 49–118.

6 Struve, *Bauern und Nation,* 80; Wolff, *Galicia,* 183.

7 István Deák, *The Lawful Revolution: Louis Kossuth and the Hungarians, 1848–1849* (New York: Columbia University Press, 1979).

8 Military experts estimated that the use of the railroad had speeded troop transport by eleven to sixteen days, not to mention that the troops arrived rested, not having had to march on foot. Of course conditions on the trains were not exactly comfortable; the men sat crowded together back to back on benches for eight to nine hours, and were barely protected from bad weather. Burkhard Köster, *Militär und Eisenbahn in der Habsburgermonarchie 1825–1859* (Munich: R. Oldenbourg Verlag, 1999), 105.

9 See especially, R. J. W. Evans, "The Habsburgs and the Hungarian Problem, 1790–1848," in Evans, *Austria, Hungary, and the Habsburgs: Essays on*

Central Europe c. 1683–1867 (Oxford: Oxford University Press, 2006), 173–192, especially 182–184.

10 The regime did not hesitate to hold up the example of the bloody Galician events to potentially rebellious noble groups in other crownlands as well. For statements about Lombardy-Venetia, see Alan Sked, *Radetzky. Imperial Victor and Military Genius* (London and New York: I. B. Taurus, 2011), 184–185.

11 In Pest, the fact that some non-noble elements of society were even allowed to vote for the first time also brought a new sense of excitement to the process.

12 In 1847 these three men could all appear to be part of the same broad opposition. In fact their political beliefs soon placed them at odds with each other. Széchenyi was most sympathetic to Vienna, Deák was a moderate, and Kossuth became the symbol of a more radical patriotism.

13 The government outdid the opposition by proposing to lift the hated customs barrier that separated Hungary from the rest of Austria. Many in the opposition saw the customs barrier as an affront to Hungarian national pride, claiming that it kept Hungary in a relationship of "colonial dependence" on the rest of Austria. More sober observers (like Széchenyi) worried that lifting the barrier would hurt nascent Hungarian industries.

14 On the mood in Vienna in the weeks leading up to the revolution, see Wolfgang Häusler, *Von der Massenarmut zur Arbeiterbewegung: Demokratie und soziale Frage in der Wiener Revolution von 1848* (Vienna and Munich: Jugend und Volk, 1979). See also Heinrich Reschauer, *Das Jahr 1848. Geschichte der Revolution,* vol. 1 (Vienna: v. Waldheim, 1872).

15 For the association's program, see Heinrich Reschauer and Moritz Smets, *Das Jahr 1848. Geschichte der Wiener Revolution* (Vienna: v. Waldheim, 1872), 1:126; Ernst K. Sieber, *Ludwig von Löhner: ein Vorkämpfer des Deutschtums in Böhmen, Mähren, und Schlesien im Jahre 1848/1849* (Munich: Lerche 1965), 20–22. Workers in the suburbs had already rioted on 10 and 11 March.

16 "Blue Monday" referred to a day often taken off from work while recovering from the alcohol excesses of the weekend.

17 Häusler, *Massenarmut,* 139–140.

18 Reschauer, *Das Jahr 1848,* 1:175; Gabriella Hauch, *Frau Biedermeier auf den Barrikaden. Frauenleben in der Wienerrevolution 1848* (Vienna: Verlag für Gesellschaftskritik, 1990), 85–86.

19 Evans, *Austria, Hungary, and the Habsburgs,* 252.

20 On Spitzer and the symbolism of what was treated as his martyr's death by many Jews and Christians alike in 1848, see Michael L. Miller's excellent study, *Rabbis and Revolution: The Jews of Moravia in the Age of Emancipation* (Stanford, CA: Stanford University Press, 2011), 219–223; Randák, "Politische-religiöses Totengedanken." See also the discussion below on Jews in 1848.

21 In one case in the confusion of the moment the military actually fired on the small ceremonial civic guard.

22 Häusler, *Massenarmut*, 173–178; R. John Rath, *The Viennese Revolution of 1848* (Austin: University of Texas Press, 1958), 68–73.

23 Archduke Stephen, the "palatine," or royal governor, of Hungary facilitated the process. He had been in Vienna on 13 March, and he was eager to prevent similar social unrest from breaking out in Hungary.

24 For the text, see Trencsényi and Kopeček, *Discourses of Collective Identity*, 2:443–444. See also Deák, *Lawful Revolution*, 71.

25 Deák, *Lawful Revolution*, 70–73.

26 Rudolf Till, "Die Mitgleider der ersten Wiener Gemeinde-Vertretung im Jahre 1848," *Wiener Geschichtsblätter* 4 (1950): 61–72. These conservatives nonetheless demanded the mayor's resignation because of his long-standing association with the Metternich regime.

27 Deák, *Lawful Revolution*, 73–76. The cabinet also included Kossuth as minister of finance, Deák as minister of justice, and Széchenyi as minister of public works and transport.

28 In Lombardy by contrast, the countryside remained peaceful. Sked, *Radetzky*, 134.

29 "Brief aus Linz," *Wiener Zeitschrift für Kunst, Literatur, Theater, und Mode* 59 (1848): 236.

30 For events in revolutionary Graz, see Gerhard Pfeisinger's excellent "Die Revolution von 1848 in Graz" (PhD diss., University of Salzburg, 1985), 55–56.

31 Ibid., 66.

32 Descriptions from the *Cillier Wochenblatt* cited in Joachim Hösler, *Von Krain zu Slowenien. Die Anfänge der nationalen Differenzierungsprozesse in Krain und der Untersteiermark von der Aufklärung bis sur Revolution 1768 bis 1848* (Munich: R. Oldenbourg Verlag, 2006), 271–272.

33 *Klagenfurter Zeitung*, 19 March 1848, 1. On songs and music performed during the March days in Klagenfurt, see Walburga Litschauer, "'Im nächtlichen Dunkel sang der Chor am Platz,' Klagenfurter Musikleben 1848," in the remarkable volume *Musik und Revolution. Die Produktion von*

Identität und Raum durch Musik in Zentraleuropa 1848/49, ed. Barbara Boisits (Vienna: Hollitzer, 2013), 121–133.

34 Hösler, *Von Krain zu Slowenien*, 272.

35 Konrad Clewing, *Staatlichkeit und nationale Identitätsbildung. Dalmatien in Vormärz und Revolution* (Munich: R. Oldenbourg Verlag, 2001), 237.

36 Ibid., 212.

37 See Dominique Kirchner Reill's superb analysis in *Nationalists who Feared the Nation. Adriatic Multi-Nationalism in Habsburg Dalmatia, Trieste, and Venicer* (Stanford, CA: Stanford University Press, 2012).

38 Gualtiero Boaglio, "Das italienische Pressewesen," in *Die Habsburger-monarchie 1848–1918*, ed. Helmut Rumpler and Peter Urbanitsch, vol. 8, *Politische Öffentlichkeit und Zivilgesellschaft* (Vienna: Verlag der Öster-reichischen Akademie der Wissenschaften, 2000), 2279–2340, here 2291.

39 Reill, *Nationalists*, 177, 202–203.

40 Thomas Götz, *Bürgertum und Liberalismus in Tirol 1840–1873. Zwischen Stadt und "Region," Staat und Nation* (Köln: SH Verlag, 2001), 123–125. The Italian-speaking citizens of Trent also petitioned the emperor to remove them from the jurisdiction of the Tyrolean capital of Innsbruck and to at-tach their region to Lombardy.

41 Pieter M. Judson, *Exclusive Revolutionaries: Liberal Politics, Social Expe-rience, and National Identity in the Austrian Empire, 1848–1914* (Ann Arbor: University of Michigan Press, 1996), 26–27; Rita Krueger, *Czech, German, and Noble: Status and National Identity in Habsburg Bohemia* (New York: Oxford University Press, 2009), 204–205.

42 Stanley Z. Pech, *The Czech Revolution of 1848* (Chapel Hill: University of North Carolina Press 1969), 47–62. The one more traditional diet-style de-mand articulated by the petition was for the administrative unification of Bohemia, Moravia, and Silesia under a central administration in Prague.

43 Randák, "Politische-religiöses Totengedanken," 313–314. Randák also de-scribes a Jewish ceremony held on 23 March commemorating the Viennese Martyrs.

44 "Na studentstvo vídenské" quoted in ibid., 316.

45 Struve, *Bauern und Nation*, 86.

46 Ibid, 86–87. Moreover, in contrast to the Polish nationalists' plan, the gov-ernment ordered that for the time being the customary usage of common lands should remain intact.

47 In ibid., 87, Struve points out that one historian estimated that in over six hundred villages the estate owners had already recognized—or had to rec-ognize—the end to feudal obligations.

48 Hösler, *Von Krain zu Slowenien*, 272.

49 Ibid., 324–325.

50 Deák, *Lawful Revolution*, 116–117.

51 "Bürger von Troppau! Unser Kaiser hat gesprochen!" 17 March 1848, Öster-
    reichische Nationalbibliothek, pamphlet collection, http://anno.onb.ac.at
    /cgi-content/anno-plus?aid=flu&datum=0031&page=2&size=45.

52 Oberösterreichisches Landesarchiv, Flugschriftenversammlung B, vol. 10,
    "An die National-Garde Gmundens." See also Bruno König, "Von der Na-
    tionalgarde (1848–1851)," in *Zeitschrift für die Geschichte und Kulturge-
    schichte österreichisch-Schlesiens* (Troppau, 1906), 141–145.

53 "Bürger von Troppau!"

54 Börries Kuzmany, *Brody. Eine galizische Grenzstadt im langen 19. Jahrhun-
    dert* (Vienna: Böhlau, 2011), 139.

55 Miller, *Rabbis and Revolution*, 222.

56 Saul Isaak Kämpf, *Rede gehalten bei der am 23. März 1848 im israelitischen
    Tempel zu Prag stattgefundenen Todtenfeier für die am 13. D. M. in Wien als
    Freiheitsopfer gefallenen Studierenden* (Prague: Buchdruckerei des M. I.
    Landau, 1848), 11.

57 Deák, *Lawful Revolution*, 102; Nemes, *The Once and Future Budapest*
    (DeKalb: Northern Illinois University Press, 2005) 134.

58 Miller, *Rabbis and Revolution*, 254.

59 Ibid., 220.

60 Quoted, along with other examples, in ibid., 255.

61 Hauch, *Frau Biedermeier*, 105.

62 Österreichische Nationalbibliothek: Flugblätter- und Plakate Sammlung,
    1848, "Aufruf eines Mädchens an ihre konstitutionellen Schwestern er köni-
    glichen Stadt Olmütz." Hauch, *Frau Biedermeier*, 102–105; Nemes, *Once
    and Future Budapest*, 141. On Viennese revolutionary songs in general, see
    Erich Wolfgang Partsch, "Revolutionsmusik? Zum Wiener Repertoire im
    Jahre 1848," in Boisits, *Musik und Revolution*, 417–432.

63 Barricade depictions of Vienna in March and October 1848 and of Prague
    in June 1848 clearly show women to be present, although often depicted in
    "helping positions." Pieter M. Judson, *Wien Brennt. Die Revolution 1848
    und ihr liberales Erbe* (Vienna: Böhlau, 1998), 93, 105–106.

64 "Hrdinova milenka. Výjev z boje pro svobodu v Berlíně dne 18 března!" in
    Letáky z roku 1848, ed. Miloslav Novotný (Prague: Národní klenotice, 1948),
    75, quoted in Randák, "Politische-religiöses Totengedanken," 317.

65 Nemes, *Once and Future Budapest*, 138. The government ordered that new
    national flag fly from government buildings, public institutions, and all
    Hungarian ships.

66 Quoted in ibid., 139–141.

67 Reschauer, *Das Jahr 1848*, 1:16, quoted in Hauch, *Frau Biedermeier*, 95. A cockade was a piece of cloth formed like a small rosette and usually worn on the man's hat.

68 Hauch, *Frau Biedermeier*, 98.

69 Ibid.

70 *Schwarz-Roth-Gold*, 11 July 1848.

71 Deák offers several examples in *Lawful Revolution*, including a quotation from Széchenyi that compares activist historian Pál Vasvári to St. Just, 84.

72 Hauch, *Frau Biedermeier*, 145–164; Judson, *Exclusive Revolutionaries*, 39–41. See also the pamphlets in the Österreichische Nationalbibliothek 1848 collection: "Edle deutsche Frauen," "Wai! Gschrirn jetzt fangen die Jüdinen a schon an," "Der Frauenaufruhr im Volksgarten, oder die Waschenanstalt der Wiener Damen"; *Neue politische Strassenzeitung* 2 (31 August 1848). Women's activism was certainly not limited to Pest and Vienna.

73 Struve, *Bauern und Nation*, 88–90. According to Struve, only one of the councils in Galicia was led by a peasant rather than a priest.

74 Judson, *Exclusive Revolutionaries*, 43–44.

75 Quoted in Lothar Höbelt, "Die deutsche Presselandschaft," in Rumpler and Urbanitsch, *Die Habsburgermonarchie 1848–1918*, 8:1821.

76 "Bürger von Troppau!"

77 Martin Sekera, "Das tschechische Pressewesen," in Rumpler and Urbanitsch, *Die Habsburgermonarchie 1848–1918*, 8: 1980, 1992–1993; Höbelt, "Die deutsche Presselandschaft," 1826.

78 Harald Binder, "Das polnische Pressewesen," in Rumpler and Urbanitsch, *Die Habsburgermonarchie 1848–1918*, 8: 2037. See also Binder, "Das ruthenische Pressewesen," in Rumpler and Urbanitsch, *Die Habsburgermonarchie 1848–1918*, 8: 2093.

79 Binder, "Das polnische Pressewesen," 2045–2046.

80 *Constitution*, 20 March 1848.

81 Géza Buzinkay, "Die ungarische politische Presse," in Rumpler and Urbanitsch, *Die Habsburgermonarchie 1848–1918*, 8: 1900–1907.

82 Ibid., 1901–1902.

83 Sekera, "Das tschechische Pressewesen," 1987–1989.

84 Quotation in a heading from a special supplement to the *Laibacher Zeitung*, 20 May 1848, quoted in Hösler, *Von Krain zu Slowenien*, 292.

85 "Oberösterreichisches Landesarchiv, Flugschriftenversammlung B, vol. 5, Die Verhandlungen der am 23. März auf dem Landtage versammeltgewesenen Stände des Erzherzogthums Österreich ob der Enns," sessions of 4 April and 24 July 1848. Among the new deputies from Linz and other

towns were merchants, a lawyer, physicians, an apothecary, a beer brewer, a scythe maker, and a hat maker.

86 "Verhandlungen des provisorischen Landtages des Herzogthumes Steiermark" (Graz 1848), 13 June, 1–3.

87 For a detailed listing of the categories of those who gained the vote, and of the conditions that they had to fulfill, see Deák, *Lawful Revolution*, 97–98.

88 Although Pillersdorf's constitution gave Jews as independent property owners the right to vote in the parliamentary elections, it left the question of their full emancipation—and the necessary legal changes in each crown land, such as the abolition of Moravia's Jew Tax—to a later constitutional committee. See Miller, *Rabbis and Revolution*, 196–206.

89 On the deliberations of the Frankfurt Parliament around the issue of unification that accords more attention than usual to the views of Austria's deputies, see Brian E. Vick, *Defining Germany: The 1848 Frankfurt Parliamentarians and National Identity* (Cambridge, MA: Harvard University Press, 2002).

90 See Karl Oberman, "Die österreichischen Reichstagswahlen 1848. Eine Studie zur Fragen des sozialen Struktur und der Wahlbeteiligung auf der Grundlagen der Wahlakten, " *Mittheilungen des österreichischen Staatsarchiv* 26 (Vienna 1973): 342–374; also the excellent survey by Andreas Gottsmann, "Der Reichstag 1848/49 und der Reichsrat 1861–1865," in Rumpler and Urbanitsch, *Die Habsburgermonarchie, 1848–1918*, 7:569–665, especially 578–582.

91 Gottsmann, "Der Reichstag 1848/49," 584. Oberman and others estimated that most parliamentary deputies in 1848 were elected by about 5 percent of their district's population. In Moravia just over 20 percent of eligible voters participated. In neighboring Silesia the turnout rate was higher at 40 percent, while in Upper Austria it was just under 50 percent. In Trieste turnout reached close to 25 percent. In Lower Austria, with Vienna's above-average number of enfranchised workers, turnout in some districts reached 70 percent, but overall was far lower for the city and its suburbs. Altogether left-wing democrats managed to elect five of Vienna's fifteen deputies, a disappointing number for them, given Vienna's reputation for political radicalism.

92 Pfeisinger, "Graz," 146–147.

93 Galicia as a whole elected three Jewish deputies to the Austrian Parliament, one each from the towns of Brody, Stanislau/Stanislawov/Stanislav, and Tarnopol/Ternopil. One local Yiddish newspaper attacked Brody's choice, asking "How can you elect a man who doesn't know about conditions in our region? We Galicianers need deputies elected from among us, who know

where the show pinches, and where remedies can be sought." Kuzmany, *Brody*, 140.

94 *Der Herold* (Graz), 3 July 1848; Hans Pirchegger, *Geschichte der Steiermark 1740–1919* (Graz and Vienna: Leuschner und Lubensky, 1934), 389.

95 These statistics should be treated with some caution since occupational categories listed are not always clear and many overlap; many deputies also resigned and were replaced in by-elections. Wenzel Dunder, *Denkschrift über die Wiener Oktober-Revolution. Ausführliche Darstellung aller Ereignisse aus ämtlichen Quellen geschöpft, mit zahlreichen Urkunden begleitet* (Vienna: self published, 1849), 37–46; also Gottsmann, "Der Reichstag 1848/49," 587–588, and fn. 57.

96 The high number of noble estate owners elected from Galicia resulted from peasant abstention or noble chicanery. Some peasant delegates abstained from the second round of elections once they realized that noble delegates would be joining with them. Peasants often also asserted that participation with nobles constituted treachery against the emperor. Peasant mistrust also rose when they saw local estate officials administer elections, and when asked to sign the election protocol, many illiterate peasants suspected that they were actually signing a document that local lords would later use against them. See Roman Rosdolsky, *Die Bauern Abgeordneten im konstituierenden österreichischen Reichstag 1848–1849* (Vienna: Europa-Verlag, 1976); Struve, *Bauern und Nation*, 95–98.

97 Struve, *Bauern und Nation*, 98.

98 Eventually the Parliament developed the practice of interrupting its sessions before each vote was to be taken, so that the issues, speeches, and differing positions could be explained to the peasant deputies. Ibid., 99–100.

99 On Kudlich, most recently, Pavel Kladiwa and Andrea Pokludová, *Hans Kudlich (1823–1917). Cesta života a mýtu* (Český Těšín: Finidr, 2012). For the debate around compensation and the participation of the Galician peasant deputies, Struve, *Bauern und Nation*, 101.

100 For the full text of both drafts discussed and quoted below, see http://www.verfassungen.de/at/at-18/kremsier49.htm.

101 Peter Bugge, "Czech Nation Building, National Self Perception, and Politics 1780–1914" (PhD diss., University of Aarhus, 1994), 84.

102 C. A. Macartney, *The Habsburg Empire 1790–1918* (London: Weidenfeld and Nicolson, 1969), 417; Bugge, "Czech Nation Building," 84, on the controversy surrounding this question.

103 The state could confer recognition but only on the basis of individual accomplishment, and no title of recognition could be inherited. Additionally,

in the interest of comparison, we should recall that the empire had already formally abolished "slavery," and that slaves transported on Austrian ships or who reached Austrian soil were considered free, a stipulation articulated most recently in the AGBG of 1811. Alison Frank, "The Children of the Desert and the Laws of the Sea: Austria, Great Britain, the Ottoman Empire, and the Mediterranean Slave Trade in the Nineteenth Century," *American Historical Review* 117, no. 3 (June 2012).

104 The draft made no explicit mention of Jews, but Jewish and non-Jewish activists alike understood paragraph 16's promise of civic rights to all, regardless of confession, as the "Jewish emancipation paragraph." Although parliamentary debates make no mention of it, there was considerable behind-the-scenes lobbying to gain a majority for the paragraph. Palacký, for example, was allegedly unwilling to see the question of Jewish emancipation as comparable to equal rights for Czech speakers, unless it benefitted Czech nationalist interests. For a highly illuminating analysis of the political maneuvering around this paragraph, see Miller, *Rabbis and Revolution*, 214–216.

105 http://www.verfassungen.de/at/at-18/kremsier49.htm, paragraphs 13–15.

106 *Ämtliche Verhandlungs-Protokolle des Gemeindeausschusses der Stadt Wien vom 25. Mai bis 5. Oktober, 1848* (Vienna: no publisher listed, 1848), 43–47; John Boyer, *Political Radicalism in Late Imperial Vienna: Origins of the Christian Social Movement, 1848–1897* (Chicago: University of Chicago Press 1981), 15–16; Judson, *Exclusive Revolutionaries*, 53–55.

107 Oberösterreichisches Landesarchiv, Flugschriftenversammlung B, vol. 5, "Protokoll nr. 1 über die am 24. Juli 1848 von den gesammten Herrn Ständen des Landes ob der Ems mit Zuziehung aller Herren Mitglieder des provisorischen Landes Ausschusses zu Linz gepflogene Verhandlung.

108 Quoted in Götz, *Bürgertum und Liberalismus*, 249.

109 *Verhandlungen des provisorischen Landtages des Herzogthumes Steiermark* (Graz: Leykam, 1848), 17 June, 30.

110 Very few activists in 1848 made the argument with which contemporary Americans are most familiar, that an 'Austrian nation' encompassed the totality of citizens of Austria, regardless of what language they spoke or from what region they came.

111 Quoted in R. J. W. Evans, "Language and State Building: The Case of the Habsburg Monarchy," *AHY* 35 (2004): 13.

112 Anton Orosz, *Worte eines eifrigen und uneigennützigen Staatsdieners, die bei der regulierung der neuen Verhältnisse des Constitutionellen Dalmatien beachtet werden mögen* (Zara: Buchdrücker des Lloyd in Treiste 1848), 55, quoted in Clewing, *Staatlichkeit*, 202–203. Orosz added that of course the

town schools should continue to teach Italian for those who might hope to gain state employment.

113 Hösler, *Von Krain zu Slowenien*, 274.

114 Clewing, *Staatlichkeit*, 249. Dalmatian Slav nationalism also rested on a strongly regional tradition oriented more toward the Adriatic and separated geographically from inland Croatia by mountain ranges. There was considerable disagreement on how to associate Dalmatia with Croatia—some plans maintained Dalmatian autonomy within a new Croatia, even having the diet rotate between meetings in Zagreb and in Dalmatia, for example. Ibid., 219–225.

115 Hösler, *Von Krain zu Slowenien*, 277.

116 Ibid., 278.

117 Tiny Austrian Silesia was often united administratively to Moravia, although treated separately in 1848 by Vienna.

118 Trencsény and Kopeček, *Discourses of Collective Identity*, 2:256–261. The situation was equally complex in Austrian Silesia, which had been technically attached to Moravia. Before 1848, Silesian opponents of the central government referred consistently to a "Silesian nation" without regard to language or ethnicity. During and after the revolution, however, Silesian autonomy came to be understood both in terms of German, Polish, or Czech nationalism, and in terms of proximity to Germany and Russia. See Dan Gawrecki, "Regionale und nationale Identitäten in Österreich-Schlesien im langen 19. Jahrhundert" in *Die Grenzen der Nationen. Identitätenwandel in Oberschlesien in der Neuzeit,* ed. Kai Struve and Philipp Ther (Marburg: Verlag des Herder Instituts, 2002), 111–134, especially 112–119.

119 Hickel, "Die Opfer des 13. März 1848 (ein Erinnerungsblatt) (Prague: 1848)," quoted in Randák, "Politische-religiöses Totengedanken," 317.

120 Many Viennese, for example, experienced the arrival of delegations from all over the monarchy seeking concessions from the emperor in idealistic terms of a fraternity among nations in the spring of 1848. Hauch, *Frau Biedermeier,* 95–97.

121 *Wiener Zeitschrift für Kunst, Literatur, Theater, und Mode* 60–61 (1848): 239.

122 Quoted in Trencsény and Kopeček, *Discourses of Collective Identity,* 2:327. The specific meaning of Palacký's claims are made more complicated for us linguistically by the fact that the word for "Bohemia" (the state) and the word for "Czech" (the language or ethnicity or nation) are essentially the same in Czech.

123 Trencsény and Kopeček, *Discourses of Collective Identity,* 2:326–7.

124 Although Palacký and his allies controlled the agenda of the Slav Congress, it did include some non-Austrian participants for whom a vague pan-Slav agenda (to include Russia) outweighed the Austro-Slav agenda.

125 This was the German nationalist response to a so-called colors incident in Graz, where Slovene nationalists displayed the Slavic red-white-blue colors. Pfeisinger, "1848 in Graz," 103–106. This also explains the enthusiasm in Vienna for Marshal Radetzky—who in fact pursued anti-revolutionary goals—but in northern Italy.

126 Judson, *Exclusive Revolutionaries*, 58–60.

127 Vick, *Defining Germany*, 113. On the particular debates, 110–117 and chapter 4 in general.

128 Abigail Green, *Fatherlands: State-Building and Nationhood in Nineteenth-Century Germany* (Cambridge and New York: Cambridge University Press, 2005), 322.

129 Judson, *Exclusive Revolutionaries*, 62.

130 Upper Austria's Baron Joseph von Lasser asserted that "I see true freedom in the homogeneity of certain basic institutions that guarantee freedom of the individual, freedom of the municipality, and the cohesiveness of the entire empire" (quoted in Judson, *Exclusive Revolutionaries*, 64). Lasser was an important liberal politician in the 1860s and 1870s.

131 In response, centralists proposed a compromise that would divide larger multilingual crownlands like Bohemia into a few sizeable districts drawn on the basis of language use. These districts would then be assigned many of the powers the federalists had conceived of for the crownlands. This suggestion conceded greater autonomy on the basis of language use, but it rejected diet-based crownland federalism.

132 Bugge, "Czech Nation Building," 84–85. Note that in this version a Ruthenian or Ukrainian nation is not mentioned.

133 Hösler, *Von Krain zu Slowenien*, 323.

134 Rogers Brubaker, *Ethnicity without Groups* (Cambridge, MA: Harvard University Press, 2004), 17.

135 Trencsény and Kopeček, *Discourses of Collective Identity*, 2:153.

136 Hösler, *Von Krain zu Slowenien*, 327–329.

137 The victory against Milan was not understood by the Viennese public as a potential threat to the success of the revolution in Austria. Instead, it was perceived patriotically as a victory over rebels and a foreign power that had threatened Austria's integrity.

138 Deák, *Lawful Revolution*, 329.

5. MID-CENTURY MODERN

1 *Allgemeines Reichs-Gesetz-und Regierungsblatt für das Kaiserthum Öster-reich,* II, Stuck, 10, 25, http://alex.onb.ac.at/cgi-content/alex?aid=rgb&datum=1852&page=111&size=45.

2 http://alex.onb.ac.at/cgi-content/alex?aid=rgb&datum=1852&page=111&size=45.

3 Harm Hinrich Brandt, *Der österreichische Neoabsolutismus. Staatsfinanzen und Politik 1848–1860,* 2 vols. (Göttingen: Vandenhoeck & Ruprecht, 1978), 257. "Naked bureaucratic absolutism" is also in Brandt, 256. See also the excellent recent collection Harm Hinrich Brandt, ed., *Der österreichische Neoabsolutismus als Verfassungs- und Verwaltungsproblem: Diskussionen über einen strittigen Epochenbegriff* (Vienna: Böhlau, 2014).

4 In Galicia the issue of the disposal of so-called common lands continued to create conflict between local landowners and peasant communities. See Kai Struve, *Bauern und Nation in Galizien. Über Zugehörigkeit und soziale Emancipation im 19. Jahrhundert* (Göttingen: Vandenhoek & Ruprecht, 2005), 108–112.

5 Solferino was the last European battle at which the sovereigns of each par-ticipating state led their armies: Francis Joseph, Emperor Napoleon II of France, and King Victor Emanuel II of Piedmont/Sardinia.

6 Cited in Robin Okey, *The Habsburg Monarchy c. 1765–1918: From Enlighten-ment to Eclipse* (New York: Palgrave Macmillan, 2002), 189.

7 Friedrich Schütz, *Werden und Wirken des Bürgerministeriums* (Leipzig: Weigand, 1909), 152.

8 Quoted in R. J. W. Evans, *Austria, Hungary, and the Habsburgs. Essays on Central Europe c. 1683–1867* (Oxford: Oxford University Press, 2006), 272.

9 As a member of that committee (whose name suggests a greater degree of social radicalism than its bourgeois members did in fact share), Bach op-posed extending the franchise to workers; he also opposed workers' de-mands for welfare programs. See, for example, Christoph Stölzl, *Die Ära Bach in Böhmen. Sozialgeschichtliche Studien zum Neoabsolutismus 1849–1859* (Munich and Vienna: R. Oldenbourg Verlag, 1971), 250. Friedrich Walter points out the immediacy for Austrian liberals of the Parisian June Days in the summer of 1848. Bach himself barely escaped being lynched in the Vienna uprising of October 1848 (ibid., 250).

10 Under the new system of absolutism, however, cabinet ministers generally did not meet as a collegial group but rather reported individually to a council that advised the emperor directly *(Reichsrat)*.

11 For this entire section, see the insightful analysis of Waltraud Heindl, *Bürokratische Eliten in Österreich 1848–1914* (Vienna: Böhlau, 2013), 42.

12 Evans, *Austria, Hungary, and the Habsburgs*, 281, 282.

13 Bureaucrats dressed in distinctive (and often expensive) uniforms designed in Vienna until 1918. Karl Megner, *Beamte. Wirtschafts- und sozialgeschichtliche Aspekte des k.k. Beamtentums* (Vienna: Verlag der Österreichischen Akademie der Wissenschaften, 1986).

14 Ibid., 335–336.

15 Heindl, *Bürokratische Eliten*, 45.

16 Interestingly, the bureaucrats imposed on recently rebellious Venetia came mostly from other Italian-speaking parts of the monarchy (just not Venice). See Andreas Gottsmann, *Venetien 1859–1866. Österreichische Verwaltung und nationale Opposition* (Vienna, Verlag der Österreichischen Akademie der Wissenschaften, 2005), 31. On accusations that bureaucrats were German, see Markian Prokopovych, *Habsburg Lemberg. Architecture, Public Space, and Politics in the Galician Capital, 1772–1914* (West Lafayette, IN: Purdue University Press, 2009).

17 Heindl, *Bürokratische Eliten*, 38–39.

18 Quoted in ibid., 44–45.

19 Unger, a convert to Christianity from Judaism, later served in the House of Lords, in the liberal Auersperg cabinet of the 1870s, and as president of the Supreme Court *(Reichsgericht)*.

20 See, for example, Waltraud Heindl's account of the uproar in the cabinet produced by an 1852 speech Thun made to the University of Vienna's law faculty in which he openly criticized what he called the "natural law basis" of the 1811 ABGB in Waltraud Heindl, ed., *Die Protokolle des österreichischen Ministerrates 1848–1867 Das Ministerium Buol-Schauenstein*, Vol.1 14. April 1852–13. März 1853 (Vienna: Verlag der Österreichischen Akademie der Wissenschaften, 1975), xix–xxi.

21 C. A. Macartney, *The Habsburg Empire 1790–1918* (London: Weidenfeld and Nicolson, 1969), 441–442. Many policy makers who supported the use of vernacular languages in primary education simply could not imagine the utility of a secondary or university education in a Slavic language.

22 Gary B. Cohen, *Education and Middle-Class Society in Imperial Austria, 1848–1918* (West Lafayette, IN: Purdue University Press, 1996), 25. On Thun's reforms and their relationship to liberalism, see also Deborah Coen, *Vienna in the Age of Uncertainty: Science Liberalism, and Private Life* (Chicago: University of Chicago Press 2007), 66; Heindl, *Bürokratische Eliten*, 59–61.

23 Quoted in Cohen, *Education and Middle-Class Society*, 25.

24 David Good, *The Economic Rise of the Habsburg Empire, 1750–1914* (Berkeley and Los Angeles: University of California Press, 1984), 78–79; Stölzl, *Die Ära*

Bach, 28; Roman Sandgruber, *Ökonomie und Politik. Österreichische Wirtschaftsgeschichte vom Mittelalter bis zur Gegenwart* (Vienna: Ueber-reuter, 2005), 234–235. The bonds could be traded or used to secure loans. Thanks to rising grain prices in the period 1850–1870, many peasants in the west had paid off their share early, by 1860.

25 Struve, *Bauern und Nation,* especially 109–111. Altogether, peasant communities received a total of 1.2 million gulden and ca. 278,000 yoke (almost 400,000 acres) out of a total of 3.6 million yoke (ca. 5.12 million acres) of forest and pasture land that had been common land.

26 Ibid., 110; John-Paul Himka, *Galician Villagers and the Ukrainian National Movement in the Nineteenth Century* (New York: St. Martin's Press, 1988), 40–48.

27 The fact that many peasants borrowed money from their former lords and ended up dependent on them only increased this perception.

28 Stölzl notes the extreme example of the Schwarzenberg family, who went from exercising sovereignty over one and a half million acres with 230,000 subjects in Bohemia, to owning around 440,000 acres. Stölzl, *Die Ära Bach in Böhmen,* 35.

29 Ibid., 36. In social terms nobles also militated against their inclusion in the communes where they had to pay school and communal taxes and where peasants often elected the officials who administered communal taxes. A subsequent law in 1851 permitted noble landowners the choice of withdrawing their property from communes and setting up their own local administration.

30 Bruck believed the tariff system had unintentionally slowed the empire's growth, and he believed (correctly as it turned out) that Austrian manufacturers could compete successfully, especially in Balkan and Ottoman markets.

31 The only non-state-owned line was the Emperor Ferdinand line that connected Vienna to Galicia. Burkhard Köster, *Militär und Eisenbahn in der Habsburgermonarchie 1825–1859* (Munich: R. Oldenbourg Verlag, 1999), 238–240; Good, *Economic Rise,* 81.

32 Good, *Economic Rise,* 81.

33 Good, *Economic Rise,* 83. Good points out that this continental (French) model envisioned an active role for such banks in economic development, a model that differed from the more limited role envisioned for banks by the British. In part, a perception of relative continental backwardness had produced this model.

34 Carl von Czörnig, *Österreichs Neugestaltung 1848–1858* (Stuttgart and Augsburg: Cotta, 1858), 206–208; Macartney, *Empire,* 460.

35 Czörnig, *Österreich*, 208–209. The crownland and regional distribution of chambers of commerce in the 1850s was as follows: one each in the crownlands of Lower and Upper Austria, Salzburg, Carinthia, Carniola, Silesia, Bukovina, and the Voivodina/Banat region. Two each in Styria, Moravia, Dalmatia, and Transylvania. Three each in Galicia, Croatia-Slavonia, and the Littoral (Trieste, Gorizia/Gorica, and Istria). Four in Tyrol. Five each in Bohemia and Hungary. Eight in Venice. Nine in Lombardy. None in the so-called Military Border regions (later Croatia and Hungary).

36 Macartney, *Empire*, 488; see also the important work by Daniel Unowsky, *The Pomp and Politics of Patriotism: Imperial Celebrations in Habsburg Austria, 1848–1916* (West Lafayette, IN: Purdue University Press, 2005), 37.

37 Unowsky, *Pomp and Politics*, 44.

38 Ibid., 41–42. The petition to divide Galicia had over 200,000 signatures and had been circulated by members of the Uniate clergy.

39 Not all Jews, especially Orthodox communities, desired full legal emancipation (although the emperor remained popular with them as well). The Austrian government had emancipated Jews in 1848 (as did the Kremsier constitution) but the Hungarian government had not.

40 On this rumor and generally on the Elisabeth cult in Hungary, see Andras Gerö, *Modern Hungarian Society in the Making: The Unfinished Experience* (Budapest and New York: Central European University Press, 1995), 223–237.

41 Alice Freifeld, "Empress Elisabeth as Hungarian Queen: The Uses of Celebrity Monarchism," in *The Limits of Loyalty: Imperial Symbolism, Popular Allegiance, and State Patriotism in the Late Habsburg Monarchy*, ed. Laurence Cole and Daniel Unowsky (New York: Berghahn, 2007), 143–144.

42 Ibid., 145–146. On Mariazell and the Habsburgs in general, see Alison Frank, "The Pleasant and the Useful: Pilgrimage and Tourism in Habsburg Mariazell," *AHY* 40 (2009): 157–182.

43 On several occasions Elisabeth's image was added to domestic pictures published by newspapers, even though she was increasingly absent from Vienna in the 1870s and 1880s. On this and other aspects of Elisabeth's depiction in the media, see Olivia Gruber Florek, "The Modern Monarch: Empress Elisabeth and the Visual Culture of Femininity, 1850–1900" (PhD diss., Rutgers University, 2012), especially chap. 2.

44 Ernst von Schwarzer, *Geld und Gut in Neuösterreich* (Vienna: Wallihauser, 1857).

45 Ibid., 12.

46 Ibid., 19.

47 Heindl, *Bürokratische Eliten*, 64.

48 Schwarzer, *Geld und Gut,* 8

49 Ibid., 12.

50 See Eugen Weber's classic *Peasants into Frenchmen. The Modernization of Rural France 1870–1914* (Stanford, CA: Stanford University Press, 1976), 67. Also 3–22 and 67–94.

51 Joseph Baron Hammer-Purgstall, "Vortrag über die Vielsprachigkeit" in *Die feierliche Sitzung des kaiserlichen Akademie der Wissenschaften am 29. Mai 1852* (Vienna, 1852), 87–100, here 96.

52 Hammer-Purgstall, Vortrag," 98.

53 Peter Stachel, "Die Harmonisierung national-politischer Gegensätze und de Anfänge der Ethnographie in Österreich," in *Geschichte der österreichischen Humanwissenschaften,* ed. Karl Acham (Vienna: Passagen Verlag, 2002), 323–367. See also Karl Pusman, *Die "Wissenschaften vom Menschen" auf Wiener Boden (1870–1959). Die Anthropologische Gesellschaft in Wien und die anthropologischen Disziplinen im Fokus von Wissenschaftsgeschichte, Wissenschafts- und Verdrängungspolitik* (Vienna and Berlin: Lit Verlag, 2008); Brigitte Fuchs, *"Rasse," "Volk," "Geschlecht." Anthropologische Diskurse in Österreich 1850–1960* (Frankfurt a/M: Campus, 2003).

54 Karl, Freiherr von Czoernig, *Ethnographie der österreichischen Monarchie mit einer ethnographischen Karte in vier Blättern,* 3 vols. (Vienna: Kaiserlich-königlich Hof- und Staatsdrückerei, 1857), 1:v.

55 Quoted in Stölzl, *Die Ära Bach,* 56. Fügner later became a Czech nationalist and was one of the founders of the Czech nationalist gymnastics association, the *Sokol.*

56 Quoted in ibid., 58 fn. 9. On the other hand, Bach evidently believed that the New Year's patent that abrogated the 1849 constitution would incur public demonstrations and violence, something that did not happen.

57 *Augsburger Zeitung,* quoted in ibid., 58–59.

58 Quoted in ibid., 61.

59 Quoted in ibid., 57–58.

60 In Bohemia alone, former liberal deputies Gustav Gross, Eduard Strache, Franz Stradal, and Franz Klier ended up working to build the railways, while others became respected members of Chambers of Commerce. Stölzl, *Die Ära Bach,* 59–61.

61 Leopold von Hasner, *Denkwürdigkeiten. Autobiographisches und Aphorismen* (Stuttgart: Cotta, 1892), 51.

62 Quoted in Thomas Götz, *Bürgertum und Liberalismus in Tirol 1840–1873. Zwischen Stadt und 'Region,' Staat und Nation* (Köln: SH Verlag, 2001), 269. See also Christian Dirninger, "Die Habsburgermonarchie als Beispiel binnenstaatlicher Integration im 19. Jahrhundert," in *Wirtschaftliche*

Integration und Wandel von Raumstrukturen im 19. und 20. Jahrhundert, ed. Josef Wysocki (Berlin: Duncker & Humblot, 1994), 65–100.

63 *Innsbrucker Zeitung* quoted in Götz, *Bürgertum und Liberalismus,* 269.

64 Stölzl, *Die Ära Bach,* 58 fn. 8.

65 Giskra found work as a clerk in the Vienna law offices of liberal Eduard von Mühlfeld. At the end of the 1850s the government allowed Giskra to practice law, but only in Brünn/Brno, not in Vienna. In Moravia Giskra swiftly used his oratorical skills to gain wealthy manufacturers and businessmen as clients, and in 1861 he was elected to the Moravian Diet and from there to the new parliament in Vienna.

66 For this Fischhof quotation: http://www.britannica.com/place/Austria /History#toc33363.

67 Both also gave the commune considerable powers at the expense of the regional diets. See Jiří Klabouch, "Die Lokalverwaltung in Cisleithanien," in *Die Habsburgermonarchi 1848–1918,* vol. 2 *Verwaltung und Rechtswesen,* ed. Adam Wandruszka and Peter Urbanitsch (Vienna: Verlag der Österreichischen Akademie der Wissenschaften, 1975), 270–305. John Deak gives an excellent account in *Forging a Multinational State: State Making in Imperial Austria from the Enlightenment to the First World War* (Stanford, CA: Stanford University Press, 2015), 83–94.

68 Götz, *Bürgertum und Liberalismus,* 253–254.

69 Ibid., 255.

70 Fritz Mauthner, *Prager Jugendjahre: Erinnerungen* (Frankfurt a/M: S. Fischer, 1969), 121; Gerhard Kurz, "Von Schiller zum deutschen Schiller. Die Schillerfeiern in Prag von 1859 und 1905," in *Die Chance der Verständigung. Ansichten und Absätze zu übernationaler Zusammenarbeit in den böhmischen Ländern 1848–1918,* ed. Ferdinand Seibt (Munich: R. Oldenbourg Verlag, 1987), 41; Robert Nemes, *The Once and Future Budapest* (DeKalb: Northern Illinois University Press, 2005), 159.

71 Robert Hoffmann, "Burgerliche Kommunikationsstrategien zu Beginn der liberalen Ära: Das Beispiel Salzburg" in *"Durch Arbeit, Besitz, Wissen und Gerechtigkeit," Bürgertum in der Habsburgermonarchie II,* ed. Hannes Stekl, Peter Urbanitsch, Ernst Bruckmüller, Hans Heiss (Vienna: Böhlau, 1992), 317–336; see also Alfred Hanke, *Die nationale Bewegung in Aussig von 1848– 1914* (Prague: Volk und Reich, 1943), 35–36.

72 Austria's finance ministers sought to reestablish the convertability of the paper gulden into silver by seeking to cut the imperial budget, especially its high military expenditures.

73 F. Schnürer, *Briefe Kaiser Franz Josefs an seine Mutter* (Salzburg: Kösel & Pustet, 1930), 302.

74 The very name of the institution that was to become Austria's parliament, the "Imperial Council" *(Reichsrat),* betrayed the limited capacity the emperor had foreseen for it.

75 This condition was changed in 1872 when voters gained the right to elect parliamentary deputies directly, partly as a way to diminish the ability of recalcitrant federalist diets to boycott the Parliament. Additionally, voters in the rural curia elected deputies in a two-step process reminiscent of 1848.

76 On the electoral system and the division of districts *(Wahlgeometrie),* see Bernd Rottenbacher, *Das Februarpatent in der Praxis. Wahlpolitik, Wahlkämpfe und Wahlentscheidungen in den bömischen Ländern der Habsburgermonarchie 1861–1871* (Frankfurt a/M: Peter Lang, 2001).

77 For how the plan sought to deal with Hungary, see below. This division of the parliament into two also made it possible for the Parliament to meet and legislate for Austria when the Hungarians refused to send representatives to Vienna. The plan originally restored Transylvania to Hungary.

78 See, for example, the excellent analysis by Stefan Malfèr, *Einleitung zu: die Protokolle des österreichischen Ministerrates 1848–1867, V. Abteilung: Die Ministerien Erzherzog Rainer und Mensdorff,* Vol. 2:1 *1. Mai 1861–2. November 1861* bearbeitet von Stefan Malfèr (Vienna: Verlag der Österreichischen Akademie der Wissenschaften, 1981), ix–xxxii.

79 Stenographische Protokolle über die Sitzungen des Hauses der Abgeordneten des österreichischen Reichsrates, (hereafter SPSHA) I, Wahlperiode, I. Session, 2. Session, 2 May 1861, 7.

80 Ibid.

81 On the address debates, see Jonathan Kwan, "'Öffentlichkeit,' Adressdebatten und die Anfänge des Parlamentarismus in der Habsburgermonarchie 1861–1867," in *Hohes Haus! 150 Jahre moderner Parlamentarismus in österreich, Böhmen, der Tschechoslowakei und der Republik Tschechien im mitteleuropäischen Kontext,* ed. Franz Adlgasser, Jana Malínská, Helmut Rumpler, and Luboš Velek (Vienna: Verlag der Österreichischen Akademie der Wissenschaften, 2015), 135–144.

82 Pieter M. Judson, "Forcing Constitutional Change through Parliamentary Practice in 1861," in Adlgasser, *Hohes Haus!,* 119–134.

83 SPSHA, I. Wahlperiode, I. Session, 7. Sitzung am 15. Mai 1861, 116.

84 SPSHA, I. Wahlperiode, I. Session, 13. Sitzung am 11. Juni 1861, 263.

85 Ibid., 267.

86 Heinrich Pollak, *Dreissig Jahre aus dem Leben eines Journalisten,* 3 vols. (Vienna: Alfred Hölder, 1898), 1:68; Franz von Krones, *Moritz von Kaiserfeld. Sein Leben und Wirken* (Leipzig: Duncker & Humblot, 1888), 203ff.; Kurt Wimmer, *Liberalismus in Oberösterreich am Beispiel des liberal-politischen*

Vereins für Oberösterreich in Linz 1869–1909 (Linz: Oberösterreichischer Landesverlag, 1979), 194.

87 Lothar Höbelt, ed., *Der Vater der Verfassung. Aus den Denkwürdigkeiten Anton Ritters von Schmerling* (Vienna: Freiheitliches Bildungswerk, 1993), 157, 52, 136–139; Gottsmann, *Reichstag,* 653ff.

88 For a survey and analysis of the particular issues that divided the Parliament from the cabinet during the period 1861–1865, see Pieter M. Judson, *Exclusive Revolutionaries: Liberal Politics, Social Experience, and National Identity in the Austrian Empire, 1848–1914* (Ann Arbor: University of Michigan Press, 1996), 93–105.

89 He did, however, create a Transylvanian Diet that briefly sent deputies to the Vienna Parliament.

90 Keely Stauter-Halsted, *The Nation in the Village: The Genesis of Peasant National Identity in Austrian Poland, 1848–1914* (Ithaca, NY: Cornell University Press, 2001); Unowsky, *Pomp and Politics,* 46. The 1861 diet was prorogued in 1863 during a Polish nationalist uprising in Russia. Although Polish nationalists in Galicia managed to keep peasants out of the diet in the 1870s, they could not prevent the election of a handful of peasants and thirteen Ruthene nationalists to the Vienna Parliament (who sided generally with centralist German liberals) in the 1870s.

91 On Czech nationalist long-term efforts to change the status quo under Schmerling, Jiří Štaif, "Czech Politics and Schmerling's Electoral Geometry," in Adlgasser, *Hohes Haus!,* 145–156. On emerging divisions within the Czech national party, Bruce Garver, *The Young Czech Party 1874–1901 and the Emergence of a Multi-Party System* (New Haven, CT and London: Yale University Press, 1974), 60–75.

92 Allegedly still maintaining the integrity of the Pragmatic Sanction, Francis Joseph and many former centralists were loathe to use the name "Austria" for the non-Hungarian state or half of the dual monarchy. To them the name "Austria" continued to connote the traditional universal empire, rather than a mere part of it. During the First World War the official name of "Austria" was adopted for this half of the monarchy.

93 There was no Austro-Hungarian constitution, a fact that became structurally problematic only when Austria-Hungary gained a protectorate colony (Bosnia-Herzegovina) that belonged to both. It became structurally even more problematic when Austria-Hungary annexed that protectorate in 1908. For an illuminating discussion, Gerald Stourzh, "Die dualistische Reichsstruktur, Österreichbegriff und Österreichbewusstsein 1867–1918," in *Der Umfang der österreichischen Geschichte. Ausgewählte Studien 1990–2010* (Vienna: Böhlau, 2011), 105–124.

94 Quoted in Andrej Rahten, "Vom Primus zum Volkstribun. Die slowenischen Parlamentarier in den Parlamenten der Habsburgermonarchi," in Adlgasser, *Hohes Haus!*, 192.

95 On the *Nagodba* negotiations, see Macartney, *Habsburg Empire*, 557–558. Francis Joseph agreed that Dalmatia—at the time a part of Austria—could negotiate incorporation into Hungarian Croatia if its diet voted to that effect. The diet, with an Italian nationalist majority, rejected this option, although later with a Croatian nationalist majority, it debated the question. Macartney, *Habsburg Empire*, 645–646.

96 Okey, *Habsburg Monarchy*, 317.

97 Joachim von Puttkamer, *Rumänen und Siebenbürger Sachsen in der Auseinandersetzung mit der ungarischen Staatsidee 1867–1914* (Munich: R. Oldenbourg Verlag, 2003), 36.

98 Ágoston Berecz, *The Politics of Early Language Teaching: Hungarian in the Primary Schools of the Late Dual Monarchy* (Budapest: Central European University Press, 2013), 60.

99 Ibid., 60–61.

100 Percentages cited in Okey, *Habsburg Monarchy*, 315.

101 On the rise of anti-Semitism in local politics in Hungary, see Robert Nemes, "The Uncivil Origins of Civil Marriage: Hungary," in *Culture Wars: Secular Catholic Conflict in Nineteenth-Century Europe*, ed. Christopher Clark and Wolfram Kaiser (Cambridge and New York: Cambridge University Press, 2003), 336–365.

6. CULTURE WARS AND WARS FOR CULTURE

1 The official censuses in both halves of the empire (discussed below in greater detail) defined the following official language categories for the peoples of the monarchy: Czech (referred to after 1880 as Bohemian-Moravian-Slovak), German, Italian (formulated as Italian-Ladino after 1880), Magyar, Polish, Romanian, Ruthene (Ukrainian) Serbo-Croatian (sometimes listed separately), and Slovene. This list hardly exhausts the list of languages used in the empire. Many citizens of the empire spoke what census experts would have called "local languages" or "dialects" such as Ladino in the Tyrol, Yiddish in Galicia and Bukovina, or Moravian dialects in parts of Moravia and Upper Hungary. See *Die Habsburgermonarchie 1848–1918*, vol. 3, *Die Völker des Reiches*, ed. Adam Wandruszka and Peter Urbanitsch (Vienna: Verlag der Österreichischen Akademie der Wissenschaften, 1980), table appearing between pages 38 and 39.

2 Oscar Jászi, *Dissolution of the Habsburg Monarchy* (Chicago: University of Chicago Press, 1929). We encounter this argument—in a somewhat different

form from Jászi's formulation—in the many claims made by the historians, journalists, and politicians who served as ideologists to legitimate the new successor states after 1918 and sought to justify their existence on the basis of the idea that single ethnic nations are the most modern and appropriate basis for political statehood. Given that insistence that ethnic nations should constitute their own states, these writers had a specific interest in linking political weakness to the presence of a multinational population in an empire.

3 Historian Eugen Weber's influential *Peasants into Frenchmen: The Modernization of Rural France 1870–1914* (Stanford, CA: Stanford University Press, 1976) argued famously that only a minority of French citizens during the nineteenth century had been capable of speaking the French language and that a French people had to be created by central state institutions such as schools, military service, and the railroad.

4 One could make a comparable argument for the very different situation that developed in the Ottoman Empire during the same period, where the creation of a concept of Ottoman citizenship and the concurrent breakdown of the *Millet* system that had for centuries managed religious difference and public life often created a strong sense of ethnic and religious conflict in public life. See for example, Michelle U. Campos, *Ottoman Brothers: Muslims, Christians, and Jews in Early Twentieth-Century Palestine* (Stanford, CA: Stanford University Press, 2011), 71–73; 87–92.

5 See the essays by Rogers Brubaker, "Ethnicity without Groups," "Identity" (with Frederick Cooper), "Ethnicity as Cognition," and "Ethnic and Nationalist Violence," in his *Ethnicity without Groups* (Cambridge, MA: Harvard University Press, 2004), 7–115.

6 Here the work of Gerald Stourzh and several of his students on law, legal, and administrative practice especially in the Austrian half of the empire is particularly instructive.

7 *Kikeriki*, 9 January 1868, 1.

8 It is important to distinguish between the kind of acceptable facial hair that included sideburns but a clean-shaven chin—just think of images of Francis Joseph himself—from the unacceptable full beard. For the emperor's and Bach's proscription (and the clean-shaven chin issue), see Ernst Hanisch, "Der Verlust der Bärte. Zur politischen Kultur der Wendehälse," in *"Dürfen's denn das?" Die fortdauernde Frage zum Jahr 1848*, ed. Sigurd Paul Scheichl and Emil Brix (Vienna: Passagen Verlag, 1999), 249–253, especially 250.

9 The six so-called "commoners" were Lower Austrian Johann N. Berger (Minister without Portfolio), Lower Austrian Rudolf Brestel (Finance), Moravian Carl Giskra (Interior), Bohemian Leopold von Hasner (Religion

and Education), Bohemian Eduard Herbst (Justice), and Bohemian Ignaz von Plener (Commerce), although Plener's family had in fact been ennobled thirteen years earlier. The aristocrats in the cabinet were the centralist liberal Prince Karl Auersperg (Prime Minister), Galician conservative Count Alfred Potocki (Agriculture), and Count Eduard Taaffe (Defense and Cabinet Vice Chair, and friend of the emperor).

10 *Konstitutionelle Vorstadt-Zeitung,* 21 December 1867.

11 The quotation is from the program of the Liberal Political Association of Linz. See Kurt Wimmer, *Liberalismus in Oberösterreich am Beispiel des liberal-politischen Vereins für Oberösterreich in Linz 1869–1909* (Linz: Oberösterreichischer Landesverlag, 1979), 172.

12 *St. Pöltener Wochenblatt,* quoted in Erhard Unterberger, "Der Liberalismus in St. Pölten (1870–1918)" (PhD diss., University of Vienna, 1966), 32.

13 Adolf Promber in *Politischer Volkskalender für 1878* (Klagenfurt and Villach, 1877), 1–5.

14 On this *Kulturkampf* especially in Tyrol, see Laurence Cole, "The Counterreformation's Last Stand: Austria," in *Culture Wars: Secular-Catholic Conflict in Nineteenth-Century Europe,* ed. Christopher Clark and Wolfram Kaiser (Cambridge and New York: Cambridge University Press, 2003), 285–312.

15 Carl Schorske, "The Ringstrasse, Its Critics, and the Birth of Urban Modernism," in *Fin-de-Siècle Vienna: Politics and Culture* (New York: Alfred A. Knopf, 1980), 24–115; Nemes, *The Once and Future Budapest* (DeKalb: Northern Illinois University Press, 2005), 107–129; 158–166; Peter Hanak, "Urbanization and Civilization: Vienna and Budapest in the Nineteenth Century," in *The Garden and the Workshop: Essays on the Cultural History of Vienna and Budapest* (Princeton, NJ: Princeton University Press, 1998), 3–43; Markian Prokopovych, *Habsburg Lemberg: Architecture, Public Space, and Politics in the Galician Capital, 1772–1914* (West Lafayette, IN: Purdue University Press, 2009), 83–100; 157–196; Nancy M. Wingfield, *Flag Wars and Stone Saints: How the Bohemian Lands Became Czech* (Cambridge, MA: Harvard University Press, 2007), 17–47; Cathleen Giustino, *Tearing Down Prague's Jewish Town* (Boulder, CO and New York: East European Monographs, 2003). On the liberal cult of Maria Theresa and the erection of monuments to her in Vienna and elsewhere in the empire, Werner Telesko, *Maria Theresa. Ein europäischer Mythos* (Vienna: Böhlau, 2012), 129–176.

16 Werner Telesko, *Kulturraum Österreich. Die Identität der Regionen in der bildenden Kunst des 19. Jahrhunderts* (Vienna: Böhlau, 2008).

17 Cole, "The Counterreformation's Last Stand," 295–296.

18 Ibid., 293–294.

19 From now on the churches controlled only the obligatory religion classes in Austria's elementary schools. Only with great reluctance did the emperor sign this legislation that delivered a blow to the Roman Catholic establishment. In general on the new laws and the reactions they provoked, see Karl Vocelka, *Verfassung oder Concordat? Der publizistische Kampf der österreichischen Liberalen um die Religionsgesetze des Jahres 1868* (Vienna: Verlag der Österreichischen Akademie der Wissenschaften, 1978).

20 Cited in Max Vögler, "Similar Paths, Different 'Nations'? Ultramontanisation and the Old Catholic Movement in Upper Austria, 1870–71," in *Different Paths to the Nation: Regional and National Identities in Central Europe and Italy, 1830–1870,* ed. Laurence Cole (New York: Palgrave Macmillan, 2007), 184.

21 Francis Joseph's confidant in the Bürger Ministry, the aristocratic Count Eduard Taaffe, reported it to him disapprovingly.

22 From an article in the Vienna newspaper *Morgenpost,* 18 October 1867, quoted in Vögler, "Similar Paths, Different 'Nations'?," 184.

23 Kai Struve, *Bauern und Nation in Galizien. Über Zugehörigkeit und soziale Emancipation im 19. Jahrhundert* (Göttingen: Vandenhoek & Ruprecht, 2005), 296.

24 Cole, "The Counterreformation's Last Stand," 294. The new law gave the individual diets leeway in how they implemented the school law, how they determined school funding, and how they created provincial and local school boards. Since the clerical-dominated Provincial School Council refused to provide funds for teachers' salaries until 1910, priests continued to make up the majority of teachers in the Tyrol.

25 On the Sacred Heart cult, Cole, *"Für Gott, Kaiser und Vaterland," Nationale Identität der deutschsprachigen Bevölkerung Tirols, 1860–1914* (Frankfurt a/M: Campus, 2000), 139–224. On pilgrimages in Austria, Alison Frank, "The Pleasant and the Useful: Pilgrimage and Tourism in Habsburg Mariazell," *AHY* 40 (2009): 157–182. For a useful comparison with Catholic popular culture in *Kulturkampf* Germany, David Blackbourn, *Marpingen: Apparitions of the Virgin Mary in Nineteenth-Century Germany* (New York: Alfred A. Knopf, 1994); Jonathan Sperber, *Popular Catholicism in Nineteenth-Century Germany* (Princeton, NJ: Princeton University Press, 1984).

26 Laurence Cole, "Patriotic Celebrations in Late Nineteenth- and Early Twentieth-Century Tyrol," in *Staging the Past: The Politics of Commemoration in Habsburg Central Europe, 1848 to the Present,* ed. Nancy Wingfield and Maria Bucur (West Lafayette, IN: Purdue University Press, 2001), 80.

27 For the text of the *Syllabus,* see http://www.ewtn.com/library/PAPALDOC /P9SYLL.HTM.

28 Cole, "The Counterreformation's Last Stand," 287–289; Nicholas Atkins and Frank Tallett, *Priests, Prelates and People: A History of European Catholicism since 1750* (Oxford: Oxford University Press, 2004), 130. See also Max H. Vögler, "Religion and the Social Question in the Habsburg Hinterland: The Catholic Church in Upper Austria, 1850–1914" (PhD diss., Columbia University, 2006), introduction.

29 Quoted in Wilhelm Wadl, *Liberalismus und soziale Frage in Österreich. Deutschliberale Reaktionen und Einflüsse auf die frühe österreichische Arbeiterbewegung (1867–1879)* (Vienna: Verlag der Österreichischen Akademie der Wissenschaften, 1987), 52.

30 Vögler, "Similar Paths," 184. Pieter M. Judson, *Exclusive Revolutionaries: Liberal Politics, Social Experience, and National Identity in the Austrian Empire, 1848–1914* (Ann Arbor: University of Michigan Press, 1996), 134; Cole, "The Counterreformation's Last Stand," 302.

31 Vögler, "Similar Paths," 185–186.

32 Ibid.

33 Liberal Minister of Education and Religion Karl von Stremayr (1832–1904) explained that the new doctrine had replaced an old, historical, and limited idea of papal authority with one that was "unrestrained and un-restrainable" (*Wiener Zeitung*, 2 August 1870, cited in Vögler, "Similar Paths," 189).

34 Francis Josef Rudigier, *Über die Unfehlbarkeit des Papstes und die Liberalen* (Linz, 1870), quoted in Vögler, "Similar Paths," 191.

35 In parts of Austria the conflict did produce conversions in the hundreds, not to Protestantism but rather to the so-called "Old Catholic" *(Altkatholiken)* movement, a sect that repudiated papal infallibility but otherwise maintained much of traditional Catholic doctrine. Very few Austrians in these years converted to Protestantism, a fact that did not prevent ultramontane radicals like Rudigier from referring contemptuously to the Old Catholics as "New Protestants."

36 *Neue Freie Presse*, 14 December 1871, 1–2. The incident is also mentioned in Walter Rogge, *Österreich seit der Katastrophe Hohenwart-Beust*, 2 vols. (Leipzig & Vienna: Brockhaus, 1879), 1:9.

37 Wimmer, *Liberalismus in Oberösterreich*, 194 n.2; Vögler, "Similar Paths," 184–185.

38 Wimmer, *Liberalismus in Oberösterreich*, 30. Already in the diet elections of 1870 the conservatives shocked the liberals by winning every one of the rural constituencies and even one of the urban ones. For liberal anxieties about the rise of Catholic associations, see the article comparing the growth

of liberal and conservative organizations in *Deutsche Zeitung,* 22 December 1871, *Abendblatt.*

39 Vögler, "Similar Paths," 193.

40 *Neues Wiener Tagblatt,* 15 October 1868.

41 *Für Das Volk,* 20 May and 5 June 1868; [Wilhelm Angerstein], *Österreichs parlamentarische Grössen* (Leipzig: Fr. Luckhardt, 1872), 20; Wadl, *Liberalismus,* 62.

42 *Neue Freie Presse* 13, no. 5 (1868): 1, quoted extensively in Wadl, *Liberalismus und soziale Frage,* 62.

43 Excellent examples from Wadl, *Liberalismus,* 159, 161.

44 From "Die Volkswirtschft und die Volksschule," in *Der österreichische Ökonomist* no. 32, (1869), quoted in ibid., 161.

45 On suffrage, see the works of Birgitta Bader-Zaar, including "Women in Austrian Politics, 1890–1934: Goals and Visions," in *Austrian Women in the Nineteenth and Twentieth Centuries,* ed. David Goode, Margarete Grandner, and Mary-Jo Maynes (New York: Berghahn, 1996), 59–90; "Rethinking Women's Suffrage in the Nineteenth Century: Local Government and the Entanglements of Property and Gender in the Austrian Half of the Habsburg Monarchy, Sweden, and the United Kingdom," in *Constitutionalism, Legitimacy, and Power: Nineteenth-Century Experiences,* ed. Kelly Grotke and Markus Prutsch (Oxford: Oxford University Press, 2014), 107–126; See also these three articles: Renate Flich, "Bildungsbestrebungen und Frauenbewegungen" "'Arbeit, Recht und Sittlichkeit'—Themen der Frauenbewegungen in der Habsburgermonarchie" and Bader-Zaar, "Frauenbewegungen und Frauenwahlrecht," all in *Die Habsburgermonarchie 1848–1918,* vol. 8, *Politische Öffentlichkeit und Zivilgesellschaft,* ed. Helmut Rumpler and Peter Urbanitsch (Vienna: Verlag der Österreichischen Akademie der Wissenschaften, 2006), 941–1028. On specifically Viennese women's movements, Harriet Anderson, *Utopian Feminism: Women's Movements in fin-de-siècle Vienna* (New Haven, CT: Yale University Press, 1992); on bourgeois and working-class women and political movements in Galicia see the highly innovative work by Dietlind Hüchtker, *Geschichte als Performance. Politische Bewegungen in Galizien um 1900* (Frankfurt a/M: Campus, 2014); for a survey of failed women's suffrage efforts in Hungary (after 1900), Judit Acsády, "The Debate on Parliamentary Reforms in Women's Suffrage in Hungary, 1908–1918," in *Suffrage, Gender, and Citizenship: International Perspectives on Parliamentary Reforms,* eds. Irma Sulkunen, Seija-Leena Nevala-Nurmi, Pirjo Markkola (Newcastle: Cambridge Scholars Publishing, 2009), 242–258. On general women's movements in Hungary, Susan

Zimmerman, "Frauenbewegungen und Frauenbestrebungen im König-reich Ungarn," in *Die Habsburgermonarchie, 1848–1918*, vol. 8, *Politische Öffentlichkeit und Zivilgesellschaft*, 1359–1491.

46 On Fickert, see Renate Flich, "Der Fall Auguste Fickert—eine Wiener Lehrerin macht Schlagzeilen," *Wiener Geschichtsblätter* 45, no. 1 (1990): 1–24.

47 For example, Jiří Malíř, "Die Teilnahme von Frauen an den Ergänzung-swahlen in den mährischen Landtag 1865," in *Magister noster. Sborník statí věnovaných in memoriam prof. PhDr. Janu Havránkovi, CSc. (Festschrift in Memoriam Prof. PhD Jan Havránek)*, eds. Michal Svatoš, Luboš Velek, and Alice Velková (Prague: Karolinum, 2005), 419–432.

48 Examples cited in Pieter M. Judson, "The Gendered Politics of German Na-tionalism, 1880–1900," in *Austrian Women*, 1–17, and in Bader-Zaar, "Women in Austrian Politics." Kopp quoted in *Stenographische Protokkole des Landtages für das Erzherzogthum Österreich unter der Enns*, 11 June 1889.

49 Milica Antic Gaber and Irene Selisnik, "Slovene Women's Suffrage Move-ment in a Comparative Perspective," in Sulkunen, Nevala-Nurmi, and Markkola, *Suffrage, Gender, and Citizenship*, 219–242. In Hungary the law of 1886 that restricted the general suffrage further had nevertheless con-firmed the right of women property owners to vote through a male proxy. Acsády, "The Debate on Parliamentary Reforms," 242.

50 Judson, "Gendered Politics"; Heidrun Zettelbauer, *"Die Liebe sei Euer Hel-dentum." Geschlecht und Nation in völkischen Vereinen der Habsburger-monarchie* (Frankfurt a/M: Campus, 2005).

51 Gerald Stourzh, *Die Gleichberechtigung der Nationalitäten in der Verfassung und Verwaltung Österreichs, 1848–1918* (Vienna: Verlag der Österreichischen Akademie der Wissenschaften, 1985), 200–201.

52 See especially Stourzh, *Gleichberechtigung*; also his "Ethnic Attribution in Late Imperial Austria: Good Intentions, Evil Consequences," in *From Vi-enna to Chicago and Back: Essays on Intellectual History and Political Thought in Europe and America* (Chicago: University of Chicago Press, 2007), 157–176; Hannelore Burger, *Sprachenrecht und Sprachengerechtigkeit im österreichischen Unterrichtswesen, 1867–1918* (Vienna: Verlag der Öster-reichischen Akademie der Wissenschaften, 1995); Jeremy King, *Budweisers into Czechs and Germans: A Local History of Bohemian Politics, 1848–1948* (Princeton, NJ: Princeton University Press, 2002).

53 Tara Zahra argues this forcefully in *Kidnapped Soul: National Indifference and the Battle for Children in the Bohemian Lands, 1900–1948* (Ithaca, NY: Cornell University Press, 2008), especially 13–78.

54 The first of these reforms enabled the direct election of parliamentary deputies instead of by the diets. The others expanded the size of the parliamentary suffrage. William Jenks, *The Austrian Electoral Reform of 1907* (New York: Octagon Books, 1974), 15–26.

55 Quoted in Daniel Unowsky, *The Pomp and Politics of Patriotism: Imperial Celebrations in Habsburg Austria, 1848–1916* (West Lafayette, IN: Purdue University Press, 2005), 49–50.

56 Previously German had been imposed as the teaching language in high school and university instruction in Galicia for the past two decades, and much administration of Galicia had also been in German. In general on the autonomy arrangements, see Alison F. Frank, *Oil Empire: Visions of Prosperity in Austrian Galicia* (Cambridge, MA: Harvard University Press, 2005), 35–37; C. A. Macartney, *The Habsburg Empire 1790–1918* (London: Wiedenfeld and Nicolson, 1969), 605–606.

57 Quoted in Gustav Kolmer, *Parlament und Verfassung in Österreich*, 8 vols. (Vienna and Leipzig: Fromme, 1900–1914), 2:122; Judson, *Exclusive Revolutionaries*, 169.

58 Paul Molisch, *Briefe zur deutschen Politik in Österreich von 1848 bis 1918* (Vienna: Braumüller, 1934), 71; Judson, *Exclusive Revolutionaries*, 170.

59 For these and other examples, see Andrej Rahten, "Vom Primus zum Volkstribun. Die slowenischen Parlamentarier in den Parlamenten der Habsburgermonarchi," in *Hohes Haus! 150 Jahre moderner Parlamentarismus in österreich, Böhmen, der Tschechoslowakei und der Republik Tschechien im mitteleuropäischen Kontext*, ed. Franz Adlgasser, Jana Malínská, Helmut Rumpler, and Luboš Velek (Vienna: Verlag der Österreichischen Akademie der Wissenschaften, 2015), 188–190.

60 On Stojatowski and his radicalization, see Struve, *Bauern und Nation*, 192–201. On the general question of peasant challenges to establishment Polish nationalists in Galicia, see also Keely Stauter Halsted, "Rural Myth and Modern Nation: Peasant Commemorations of Polish National Holidays, 1879–1910," in *Staging the Past: The Politics of Commemoration in Habsburg Central Europe, 1848 to the Present*, eds. Nancy M. Wingfield and Maria Bucur (West Lafayette, IN: Purdue University Press, 2001), 153–177.

61 Joshua Shanes, *Diaspora Nationalism and Jewish Identity in Habsburg Galicia* (Cambridge and New York: Cambridge University Press, 2012).

62 Robert Nemes, "The Uncivil Origins of Civil Marriage: Hungary" in *Culture Wars: Secular-Catholic Conflict in Nineteenth-Century Europe*, ed. Christopher Clark and Wolfram Kaiser (Oxford: Oxford University Press, 2003), 313–335.

63 Quoted in ibid., 327.

64 Ibid., 333.

65 On the anti-Semitism of Vienna's and western Austria's Social Catholics, see John Boyer, *Political Radicalism in Late Imperial Vien: Origins of the Christian Social Movement, 1848–1897* (Chicago: University of Chicago Press, 1981) and *Culture and Political Crisis in Vienna: Christian Socialism in Power, 1897–1918* (Chicago: University of Chicago Press, 1995). Boyer sees Karl Lueger's anti-Semitism in instrumental terms, but this does not detract from the often visceral popularity of anti-Semitism for Christian Social constituencies.

66 In 1884 Austria's Supreme Administrative Court established a rule to determine when the state and local community were obliged to support a minority school. The formula was based on the original rule for determining whether a community had to provide a school in the first place. A five-year average of forty school children who lived within a two-hour walking distance of the community was required to warrant public funding of a minority school. Burger, *Sprachenrecht und Sprachgerechtigkeit*, 100–110.

67 After the conclusion of the six years, every Hungarian child was expected to attend three years of "Sunday schooling." Practically speaking, especially in poorer areas of Transylvania, most children who attended school did so for four years. On the Hungarian education system and its practices, the classic is Joachim von Puttkamer, *Schulalltag und nationale Integration in Ungarn. Slowaken, Rumänen und Siebenbürger Sachsen in der Auseinandersetzung mit der ungarischen Staatsidee, 1867–1914* (Munich: R. Oldenbourg Verlag, 2003). Ágoston Berecz, *The Politics of Early Language Teaching: Hungarian in the Primary Schools of the Late Dual Monarchy* (Budapest: CEU Press, 2013) offers an excellent analysis of actual schooling practices and experiences in Transylvania.

68 Quoted in Puttkamer, *Schulalltag*, 302–303.

69 Berecz, *Politics*, 116.

70 Ibid., 116–118.

71 Quoted in ibid., 200–201.

72 Quoted in ibid., 201.

73 On the Hungarian nationalist organizations EMKE in Transylvania and FEMKE in northeastern or Upper Hungary, Joachim von Puttkamer, "Die EMKE in Siebenbürgen und die FEMKE in Oberungarn. Die Tätigkeiten zweier ungarischer Schutzvereine in ihrem nationalen Umfeld," in *Schutzvereine in Ostmitteleuropa. Vereinswesen, Sprachenkonflikte und Dynamiken nationaler Mobilisierung 1860–1939*, ed. Peter Haslinger (Marburg: Verlag Herder Institut, 2009), 158–169.

74 Robert Nemes, *Another Hungary: The Nineteenth-Century Provinces in Eight Lives* (Stanford, CA: Stanford University Press, forthcoming), manuscript version, 219–220.

75 Ibid., 220–221.

76 Ibid., 228.

77 John-Paul Himka, *Galician Villagers and the Ukrainian National Movement in the Nineteenth Century* (New York: St. Martin's Press, 1988), 87.

78 Quotations in this paragraph in ibid., 93–94.

79 On the development and practice of the census in Austria, see Emil Brix, *Die Umgangssprache in Altösterreich zwischen Agitation und Assimilation* (Vienna: Böhlau, 1997); Wolfgang Göderle, "'. . . für Administration und Wissenschaft.' Zensus und Ethnizität: Zur Herstellung von Wissen über soziale Wirklichkeit im Habsburgerreich zwischen 1848 und 1910" (PhD diss., University of Graz, 2014); also Z.A.B. Zeman, "The Four Austrian Censuses and their Political Consequences," in *The Last Years of Austria-Hungary: Essays in Political and Military History, 1908–1918*, ed. Mark Cornwall (Exeter: University of Exeter Press, 1990), 31–39.

80 Berecs, *Politics*, 23. Berecz also provides an excellent analysis of Hungarian census laws and practices, arguing that Magyar officials generally used the census as a gauge, not a tool of assimilation (ibid., 23–30).

81 Of course the statistics did not measure the relative degree of knowledge of another language (ibid., 28–30). For the largely Transylvanian counties he studied, Berecz notes that in 1910 the average rate of knowledge of Hungarian among the Romanian speaking population aged six to twenty-nine ranged between 10 percent and 16 percent (with generally lower numbers when older people are added to the total). Among native German speakers six to twenty-nine years of age in Transylvania, the average rates were considerably higher, between 35 percent and 55 percent (ibid., 234–235).

82 Burger, *Sprachenrecht und Sprachgerechtigkeit*, 100–110.

83 The fact that the state only registered one language of daily use per person was something of a victory for nationalists who sought to downplay the prevalence or significance of multilingualism in Austria.

84 Wenzel Holek, *Vom Handarbeiter zum Jugenderzieher* (Jena: Eugen Dietrichs, 1921), 1, quoted in Caitlin Murdock, *Changing Places: Society, Culture, and Territory in the Saxon-Bohemian Borderlands, 1870–1946* (Ann Arbor: University of Michigan Press, 2010), 47. In this case the factory was located in Dresden.

85 Holek, *Vom Handarbeiter*, 3, 14, cited in ibid., 47.

86 The most egregious (but certainly not exceptional) example of municipal census activism was in the city of Trieste/Trst for the 1910 census. In this

case following a challenge to the results, the government actually decided to re-take the census.

87 See the important study by Peter Haslinger, *Nation und Territorium im tschechischen politischen Diskurs, 1880–1938* (Munich: R. Oldenbourg Verlag, 2010), especially part II, that provides a superb framework to understanding the mechanisms and dynamics of territorialization, including usages of census results. Also Pieter M. Judson, *Guardians of the Nation: Activists on the Language Frontiers of Imperial Austria* (Cambridge, MA: Harvard University Press, 2006), 14–15, 29–33.

88 In 1898 Mark Twain published an account of proceedings in the Austrian Parliament he witnessed during the months of obstruction surrounding the Badeni Language Laws entitled "Stirring Times in Austria, 1898" (*Harper's New Monthly Magazine for March 1898*), 96:530–540.

89 Berthold Sutter, *Die Badenischen Sprachverordnungen von 1897*, 2 vols. (Graz and Köln: Böhlau 1960, 1965).

90 "Das erste Opfer der Sprachenverordnung," in *Deutsche Volkszeitung für den Neutitscheiner Kreis*, 12 May 1897, 6.

91 According to witnesses, Wolff threatened Badeni during the parliamentary session, declaring, "If this is your policy, it is miserable chicanery!" As colleagues tried to hold him back, Wolff continued his insults, referring to "Polish Scoundralism," and some witnesses reported that he called the count a "Polish pig." With the emperor's permission, Badeni sent his seconds to Wolff, and on 25 September Wolff, no stranger to duels—he had fought a Young Czech deputy with swords the previous May—wounded the prime minister in the right arm. "The Badeni Wolff Duel," *New York Times*, 27 September 1897, 5.

92 Markus Krzoska, "Die Peripherie bedrängt das Zentrum. Wien, Prag, und Deutschböhmen in den Badeni-Unruhen 1897," in *Grenzregionen der Habsburgermonarchie im 18. Und 19. Jahrhundert. Ihre Bedeutung und Funktion aus der Perspecktive Wiens*, ed. Hans-Christian Maner (Münster: Lit Verlag, 2005), 145–165.

93 Lothar Höbelt, *Kornblume und Kaiseradler. Die deutschfreiheitliche Parteien Altösterreichs 1882–1918* (Vienna: Verlag für Geschichte und Politik, 1993), especially 180–199. Höbelt provides a masterful and insightful account of behind-the-scenes workings of parliamentary politics in an account that challenges received wisdom about Austrian parliamentarism.

94 On the Moravian Compromise, Horst Glassl, *Nationale Autonomie im Vielvölkerstaat. Der mährische Ausgleich* (Munich: Sudetendeutsche Stiftung, 1977); Zahra, *Kidnapped Souls*, 32–48; Stourzh, *Gleichberechtigung*, 200–228; T. Mills Kelly, "Last Best Chance or Last Gasp? The Compromise

of 1905 and Czech Politics in Moravia," *AHY* 34 (2003): 279–301; *Moravské vyrovnání z roku 1905/Der Mährische Ausgleich von 1905*, eds. Lukás Fasora, J. Hanuš, and Jiří Malíř (Brno: Matice Moravská pro Výzkumné Středisko pro Dějiny Střední Evropy: Prameny, Země, Kultura, 2006), 43–58.

95 On the issue of the compromises taken together (including the Budweis/Budjěovice Compromise), King, *Budweisers*, 138–147. King developed the most sophisticated analysis of the issues relating to national categorization in "Who is who? Separate but Equal in Imperial Austria," unpublished manuscript, (2010). I thank Professor King for sharing his unpublished work with me. On the Bukowina compromise, John Leslie, "Der Ausgleich in der Bukowina von 1910: Zur österreichischen Nationalitätenpolitik vor dem Ersten Weltkrieg," in *Geschichte zwischen Freiheit und Ordnung. Gerald Stourzh zum 60. Geburtstag*, ed. Emil Brix et al. (Graz and Vienna: Verlag Styria, 1991), 113–144; Gerald Stourzh, "The National Compromise in the Bukovina 1909/1910," in *From Vienna to Chicago and Back: Essays on Intellectual History and Political Thought in Europe and America* (Chicago: University of Chicago Press, 2007), 177–189; Börries Kuzmany, "Der Galizische Ausgleich als Beispiel moderner Nationalitätenpolitik?," in *Galizien. Peripherie der Moderne—Moderne der Peripherie*, ed. Elisabeth Haid (Marburg: Verlag Herder-Institut, 2013), 119–137. For a contemporary argument by a noted academic progressive and sociologist of law on the economic necessity of compromise in Bukovina, see Eugen Ehrlich, *Die Aufgaben der Sozialpolitik im österreichischen Osten insbesondere in der Bukowina. Mit besonderer Beleuchtung der Juden und Bauernfrage* (Czernowitz: 1909).

96 This Lex Perek gave nationalists the right to challenge the choices of parents who they believed were sending their children to the wrong school. The law stated that children had to be competent in the language of the school, otherwise they would be "reclaimed" for a school in the other language. The law was written and used by Czech nationalists to prevent parents from obtaining a German language education for their children. It produced an annual "reclamation ritual" in Moravian schools. Zahra, *Kidnapped Souls*, 32–48.

97 Stourzh, "Ethnic Attribution." For two contemporary analyses of this development, Edmund Bernatzik, *Über nationale Matriken* (Vienna: Manz, 1910) and Rudolf von Herrnritt, "Die Ausgestaltung des österreichischen Nationalitätenrechtes durch den Ausgleich in Mähren und der Bukowina," in *Österreichische Zeitschrift für öffentliche Recht*, vol. 1/5–6 (1914): 584–618. I am grateful to Jeremy King for these references.

98 *Vaterland*, 2 May 1873, 1, quoted in Matthew Rampley, "Peasants in Vienna: Ethnographic Display and the 1873 World's Fair," *AHY* 42 (2011): 110.

99 For the structure of the world's fair, see the excellent analysis in Rampley, "Peasants in Vienna."

100 Losses generated by the low attendance were estimated at 20 million gulden.

101 According to the 1880 census (taken only five years after the founding of the university), in Bukovina 14.2 percent of males over the age of six and 8 percent of females could read and write. In Lower Austria by contrast, the numbers were 91 percent and 87 percent, while in Bohemia 89 percent of men and 83 percent of women were literate. Vorarlberg had the highest literacy rates in 1880 with literacy for both men and women at around 95 percent. Other mostly agrarian and poorer regions had lower rates (Istria 28 percent of men and 18 percent of women were literate, while in Galicia 17 percent of men and 10 percent of women were literate). The work of the school system was impressive, however. For Austria as a whole the literacy numbers rose from 1880–1890 from 62 percent for men and 55 percent for women, to 68.5 percent for men and 62.5 percent for women. Friedrich Umlauft, *Die Österreichisch-Ungarische Monarchie. Geographisch-statistisches Handbuch für Leser aller Stände* (Vienna, Pest, Leipzig: A. Hartlebens Verlag, 1897), 780–781. In Hungary—with a different school system—in 1890, by comparison, the literacy rate for the entire population stood at 44 percent with Hungarian (53.6 percent) and German speakers (63 percent) at the high end and Ukrainian (9 percent) and Romanian (14.1 percent) speakers at the lower end. Croatian speakers (42.4 percent) stood near the average with Serb speakers somewhat below (30.9 percent). Puttkamer, *Schulalltag*, 456.

102 Quoted in Kolmer, *Parlament und Verfassung*, vol. 2, 343–345. See also Emanuel Turczynski, "Die Bukovina," in *Deutsche Geschichte im Osten Europeas: Galizien, Bukowina, Moldau*, ed. Isabel Röskau-Rydel (Berlin: Siedler Verlag, 1999), 213–328, here 253.

103 Karl Emil Franzos, "Ein Culturfest," in *Aus Halbasien. Culturbilder aus Galizien, der Bukowina, Südrussland und Rumänien* (Leipzig: Dunder & Humblot, 1876), vol. 1, 324.

104 Franzos, *Aus Halbasien*, 1:iii, 112, 143, quoted in Röskau-Rydel, *Deutsche Geschichte*, 411.

105 Franzos, "Von Wien nach Czernowitz," in *Aus Halbasien*, vol. 1.

106 Heinrich Pollak, *Dreissig Jahre aus dem Leben eines Journalisten*, 3 vols. (Vienna: Alfred Hölder, 1898), 3:78–87.

107 Between 1868 and 1874, 1,005 joint-stock enterprises were founded of which 685 actually existed. All of the Viennese banks founded before 1868 survived the crash while only 8 of the 70 founded in or after that year survived. In the crownlands, 44 of 65 new banks failed. Many parliamentary deputies—and not only liberals—served on one or more of such boards of

directors. Macartney, *Empire*, 608–609. The liberal Auersperg cabinet remained in power for another five years until after the next elections (1879), when the Taaffe cabinet coalition replaced it (1880).

108 On the *Kronprinzenwerk*, Zoltán Szász, "Das 'Kronprinzenwerk' und die hinter ihm stehende Konzeption," in *Nation und Nationalismus in wissenschaftlichen Standartwerken Österreich-Ungarns, 1867–1918*, Justin Stagl, ed. (Vienna: Böhlau, 1997), 65–70; Justin Stagl, "Das 'Kronprinzenwerk'—eine Darstellung des Vielvölkerreiches," in *Das entfernte Dorf. Moderner Kunst und ethnischer Artefakt*, ed. Ákos Moravánsky (Vienna: Böhlau, 2002), 169–182; Regina Bendix, "Ethnology, Cultural Reification, and the Dynamics of Difference in the Kronprinzenwerk," in *Creating the Other: Ethnic Conflict and Nationalism in Habsburg Central Europe*, ed. Nancy M. Wingfield (New York: Berghahn, 2003), 149–166; Hans Petschar, *Altösterreich. Menschen, Länder und Völker in der Habsburgermonarchie* (Vienna: Brandstätter, 2011).

109 Deborah Coen, "Climate and Circulation in Imperial Austria," *Journal of Modern History* 82: 4 (December, 2010): 839–875; *The Earthquake Observers: Disaster Science from Lisbon to Richter* (Chicago: University of Chicago Press, 2012).

110 *Bosnische Post* 48 (17 June 1888): 2.

111 "Round the Near East," Interview with Benjamin von Kállay, *Daily Chronicle* 3 October 1895, quoted in Robert Donia, *Islam Under the Double Eagle* (Boulder, CO and New York: East European Monographs, 1981), 14.

112 Quoted in Robin Okey, *Taming Balkan Nationalism: The Habsburg 'Civilizing Mission' in Bosnia, 1878–1914* (Oxford and New York: Oxford University Press, 2007), 27.

113 Okey, *Taming Balkan Nationalism*, 26.

114 Ibid., 28.

115 On Habsburg efforts to construct a popular Bosnian identification among Muslims, see Edin Hajdarpasic's illuminating *Whose Bosnia? Nationalism and Political Imagination in the Balkans 1840–1914* (Ithaca, NY: Cornell University Press, 2015), especially 161–198.

7. EVERYDAY EMPIRE, OUR EMPIRE

Epigraph: Joseph Roth, *The Emperor's Tomb*, trans. John Hoare (New York: Overlook Press, 2002), 15.

1 For accounts of some of these working-class lives that included both local and global journeys, *Auf der Walz. Erinnerungen böhmischer Handwerkgesellen*, ed. Pavla Vošahlíková (Vienna: Böhlau, 1994).

2 See the excellent work by Andrea Komlosy, *Grenze und ungleiche regionale Entwicklung: Binnenmarkt und Migration in der Habsburgermonarchie*

(Vienna: Promedia, 2003). Komlosy's statistics document those who moved from their legal place of *Heimat*, often a short distance to a nearby parish. See also *Soziale Strukturen. Die Gesellschaft der Habsburgermonarchie im Kartenbild. Verwaltungs-, sozial- und Infrastrukturen. Nach dem Zensus von 1910, Die Habsburgermonarchie 1848–1918*, ed. Helmut Rumpler and Martin Seger (Vienna: Verlag der Österreichischen Akademie der Wissenschaften, 2010), 106–107.

3 Heinz Fassmann, "Die Bevölkerungsentwicklung 1850–1910," in Rumpler and Urbanitsch, *Die Habsburgermonarchie 1848–1918*, vol. 9, *Soziale Strukturen* (Vienna: Verlag der Österreichischen Akademie der Wissenschaften, 2010), 159–184, here 173.

4 Up until 1889, Hungarian rail lines had been used primarily to transport goods. Passenger use had been negligible. János Szulovszky, "Die Dienstleistungsgesellschaft in Ungarn," in ibid., 9:467–491, here 473.

5 For an insightful analysis of emigration and return migration, as well as the complex and often contradictory responses of the Austrian and Hungarian states, see Tara Zahra, *The Great Departure: Emigration from Eastern Europe and the Making of the Free World* (New York: W. W. Norton, 2016), 23–63. When the U.S. immigration bureau began to keep track of return migration in 1908, it estimated that fully 39.5 percent of migrants returned to Austria and 37.9 percent returned to Hungary (in a decade). At least 400,000 emigrants returned to Austria-Hungary from the United States between 1900 and 1910. For statistics, see Senator William P. Dillingham, *Emigration Conditions in Europe: Reports of the Immigration Commission*, 61st Congress (Washington, DC: Government Printing Office, 1911), 351; On emigration from Hungary, see also Julianna Puskás, *Ties that Bind, Ties that Divide* (New York: Holmes and Meier, 2000).

6 In Austria in 1910, 292 classical academic high schools or gymnasia served 95,933 boys, and 24 served 3,254 girls (the largest number in Galicia), and 65 *lycées* serving 10,599 girls. The more mathematically and scientifically oriented 146 *Realschulen* in Austria served 47,562 students. The *Realschulen* tended to offer the second crownland language as a required subject and served as a preparation for careers in commerce and trade. Czech-speakers were proportionally more highly represented in the *Realschulen* than in the gymnasia, where Polish speakers were proportionately more highly represented. See Rumpler and Urbanitsch, *Die Habsburgermonarchie 1848–1918*, 9/2 (*Kartenband*), 220–227. On access to education and social mobility in Austria, see Gary Cohen's insightful study of *Education and Middle-Class Society in Imperial Austria, 1848–1918* (West Lafayette, IL: Purdue University Press, 1996). Cohen demonstrates, for example,

that Austrian secondary schools, technical colleges, and universities enrolled proportions of the population similar to or greater than those in Germany.

7 Margret Friedrich, Brigitte Mazohl, and Astrid von Schlachta, "Die Bildungsrevolution," in Rumpler and Urbanitsch, *Die Habsburgermonarchie 1848–1918*, 9/1:67–107, here 77. See also the charts in ibid., 9/2 (*Kartenband*), 228–229.

8 In its first years, the health insurance provisions covered around 9 percent of the population of Cisleithania. On welfare provision, see Birgit Bolognese-Leuchtenmüller, *Bevölkerungsentwicklung und Berufsstruktur: Gesundheits- und Fürsorgewesen in Österreich, 1750–1918* (Vienna: Verlag für Geschichte und Politik, 1978), 328. Infrastructure spending on railways, telegraph, telephone, and postal services accounted for a third of the Cisleithanian budget by 1910. Josef Wysocki, "Die Österreichische Finanzpolitik," in Rumpler and Urbanitsch, *Die Habsburgermonarchie*, volume 1, *Die Wirtschaftliche Entwicklung* (Vienna: Verlag der Österreichischen Akademie der Wissenschaften,1973), 68–104, here 92.

9 John Deak, *Forging a Multinational State: State-Making in Imperial Austria from the Enlightenment to the First World War* (Stanford, CA: Stanford University Press, 2015), 175–177.

10 The two-track administrative system in Austria and the limited municipal autonomy in Hungary created two kinds of bureaucracies, both of which experienced considerable growth in this period. One type appointed from Budapest, Vienna, or the crownland capitals, and a second type, the "autonomous" bureaucracies, appointed by elected municipal governments in Austria and Hungary. Deak, *Multinational State*, 154–158; Jeremy King, "The Municipal and the National in the Bohemian Lands, 1848–1914," *AHY* 42 (2011): 89–109.

11 Hungary was also one of the earliest states in Europe to introduce mail delivery by truck in 1909. Already since 1896 telegrams had been delivered by bicycle. Szulovszky, "Dienstleistungsgesellschaft," 479.

12 Women civil servants could not be married, and in the early years offices tended to employ the widows or daughters of existing employees. Erna Appelt, "The Gendering of the Service Sector in Late Nineteenth-Century Austria," in *Austrian Women in the Nineteenth and Twentieth Centuries*, ed. David F. Good, Margarete Grandner, and Mary Jo Maynes (New York: Berghahn, 1996), 115–131. On women as telegraph operators, see Sonia Genser, "Von Klingelfeen, Blitzmädels und dem Fräulein vom Amt. Die Geschichte der ersten Frauen im österreichischen Telefon- und telegrafenwesen 1869–1914" (PhD diss., University of Innsbruck, 2003).

13 Friedrich, Mazohl, and von Schlachta, "Die Bildungsrevolution," 74. The Austrian ministries that employed the largest numbers of women were the Ministry of Commerce and the Ministry of the Interior.

14 Although this crisis was debated as one pertaining to local governments, in fact state financing in Austria barely kept pace with spending in the peacetime years before 1914. Wysocki, "Die Österreichische Finanzpolitik," 89–91, 100–101; Deak, *Multinational State*, 226–232.

15 Margaret Lavinia Anderson, *Practicing Democracy: Elections and Culture in Imperial Germany* (Princeton, NJ: Princeton University Press, 2000).

16 Carl E. Schorske, "Politics in a New Key: An Austrian Trio," in *Fin-de-Siècle Vienna: Politics and Culture* (New York: Alfred A. Knopf, 1980), 116–180.

17 There is an enormous and excellent literature on the rise of political, economic, social and cultural forms of anti-Semitism in the various regions of the Habsburg Monarchy around 1900. The classic work on Lueger and the anti-Semitic Social Catholic movement in Vienna and western Austria is John Boyer, *Political Radicalism in Turn of the Century Vienna: Origins of the Christian Social Movement* (Chicago: University of Chicago Press, 1981). An older analysis of the rise of racial anti-Semitism in German nationalist circles is Andrew Whiteside, *The Socialism of Fools: Georg Ritter von Schönerer and Austrian Pan Germanism* (Berkeley and Los Angeles: University of California Press, 1975). On Bohemia and Moravia, see in particular Michal Frankl, *"Emancipace od židů": český antisemitismus na konci 19. Století."* (Prague: Paseka, 2007); Hillel Kieval, *Languages of Community: The Jewish Experience in the Czech Lands* (Berkeley and Los Angeles: University of California Press, 2000), especially "Death and the Nation: Ritual Murder as Political Discourse in the Czech Lands," 181–197; also the recent essays by Daniel Unowsky, Michal Frankl, Marija Vulesica, and Alison Rose in *Sites of European Antisemitism in the Age of Mass Politics, 1880–1918*, ed. Robert Nemes and Daniel Unowsky (Waltham, MA: Brandeis University Press, 2014).

18 On Lueger and his beginnings as a liberal, see ibid. On the Young Czechs and the Czech nationalists political spectrum in general, see Bruce Garver, *The Young Czech Party, 1874–1901, and the Emergence of a Multi-Party System* (New Haven, CT: Yale University Press, 1978). On Slovene nationalist politics, see Peter Štih, Vasko Simoniti, and Peter Vodopivec, *Slowenische Geschichte. Gesellschaft—Politik—Kultur* (Graz: Leykam, 2008), 283–287.

19 For the transformation of urban life in the expanding metropolises, see Wolfgang Maderthaner, "Urbane Lebenswelten. Metropolen und Grosstädte," in Rumpler and Urbanitsch, *Die Habsburgermonarchie 1848–1918*, 9/1:493–538.

20 *Amtsblatt der k.k. Bezirkshauptmannschaft in Rann, Jahrgang 1902–07; 1908–09 Uradni list c.k. okrajnega glavarstva v Brežicah Leto* (Rann/Brezice: 1902–07; 1908–09), 46–47, 72, 73, 79.

21 On these efforts, see Kai Struve, *Bauern und Nation in Galizien. Über Zugehörigkeit und soziale Emanzipation im 19. Jahrhundert* (Göttingen: Vandenhoeck & Ruprecht, 2005), especially148–184; John-Paul Himka, *Galician Villagers and the Ukrainian National Movement in the Nineteenth Century* (New York: St. Martin Press, 1988), especially 86–103.

22 Francis Joseph suffered the death of his two-year-old daughter, Sophie, in 1857, the execution of his brother Max (Emperor Maximilian of Mexico) in 1867, the suicide of his son Rudolf in 1889, the assassination of his wife in 1898, and of course the assassination of his nephew and heir in 1914. On the emperor's popularity later in life, Peter Urbanitsch, "Pluralist Myth and Nationalist Realities: The Dynastic Myth of the Habsburg Monarchy—a Futile Exercise in the Creation of Identity?" *Austrian History Yearbook* 35 (2004): 101–141, here 122–123.

23 Struve, *Bauern und Nation*, 123; Keely Stauter Halsted, *The Nation in the Village: The Genesis of Peasant National Identity in Austrian Poland 1848–1914* (Ithaca, NY: Cornell University Press, 2001). On illiterate mayors, see Chapter 4 of this book.

24 Josef Redlich, *Das Wesen der österreichischen Kommunal-Verfassung* (Leipzig: Duncker & Humblot, 1910), 61–62, quoted in King, "The Municipal and the National," 89.

25 On communal autonomy in Galicia generally and the ways it was shaped by Galician crownland autonomy, see the useful discussion in Alison Frank, *Oil Empire: Visions of Prosperity in Austrian Galicia* (Cambridge, MA: Harvard University Press, 2005), 37–40.

26 In Vienna, the 18.1 percent enfranchised for city elections in 1912 came to 70 percent of the male citizen population over the age of twenty-four. On rates of enfranchisement and participation rates, see Peter Urbanitsch, "Die Gemeindevertretungen in Cisleithanien," in Rumpler and Urbanitsch, *Die Habsburgermonarchie 1848–1918*, vol. 7, *Verfassung und Parlamentarismus*, part 2, *Die regionalen Repräsentativkörperschaften* (Vienna: Verlag der Österreichischen Akademie der Wissenschaften, 2000), 2199–2281, especially 2223–2230.

27 Those towns in Hungary that enjoyed a local autonomy somewhat equivalent to the autonomy enjoyed by all communes in Austria did so by virtue of their traditional status as royally chartered.

28 In general, see Károly Vörös, "Die Munizipalverwaltung in Ungarn im Zeitalter des Dualismus," in Rumpler and Urbanitsch, *Die Habsburgermonarchie*

1848–1918, 7:2345–2382. See also, Barany, "Ungarns Verwaltung," 409–446, and Péter, "Die Verfassungsentwicklung in Ungarn, 476–503, 537–540. For the direct comparison with the Austrian system, see Gary B. Cohen, "Nationalist Politics and the Dynamics of State and Civil Society in the Habsburg Monarchy, 1867–1914," *CEH* 40, no. 2 (2007): 241–278, especially 255–256.

29 On the new associational laws and their effects on Austrian society, Pieter M. Judson, *Exclusive Revolutionaries: Liberal Politics, Social Experience, and National Identity in the Austrian Empire, 1848–1914* (Ann Arbor: University of Michigan Press, 1996), 143–164.

30 Around the same time (1868–1871) Slovene nationalists in Carniola and South Styria mobilized activists at similar open-air *tabor*-like meetings to demand the unification of all Slovene regions into a single crownland. In all, activists held eighteen such *tabors* attended by an average of 5,000–6,000 people each (one near Laibach/Ljubljana attracted close to 30,000 people). Štih, Simoniti, and Vodopivec, *Slowenische Geschichte*, 267.

31 Frank Henschel, "'Das Fluidum der Stadt.' Lebenswelten in Kassa/Kosice/Kaschau zwischen urbaner Vielfalt und Nationalismus, 1867–1918" (PhD diss., University of Leipzig, 2013), 70. Those of the Jewish confession were not eligible to vote in Hungary until 1896, when their religion became officially recognized.

32 Technically, the Ringstrasse construction predated the autonomy laws and given Vienna's unique status, had required the Emperor's assent. On the Ringstrasse and the historicist styles, Schorske, "The Ringstrasse, Its Critics, and the Birth of Urban Modernism" in *Fin-de-Siècle Vienna*, 24–115. On the opera and the firm of Fellner and Helmer (as the leading—but not the only—builders of regional theaters in Central Europe in the late nineteenth century), Philipp Ther, *Center Stage: Operatic Culture and Nation Building in Nineteenth Century Central Europe*, trans. Charlotte Highes-Kreutzmüller (West Lafayette, IN: Purdue University Press, 2014), 196. See also Gerhard Michael Dienes, ed., *Fellner & Helmer. Die Architekten der Illusion. Theaterbau und Bühnenbild in Europa anlässlich des Jubiläums "100 Jahre Grazer Oper"* (Graz: Stadtmuseum, 1999).

33 Joseph Roth, "The Bust of the Emperor," in *Three Novellas*, trans. John Hoare (New York: Overlook Press, 2003), 45. See also Ivo Andric, *The Bridge on the Drina* (London: George Allen & Unwin, 1959), especially the final chapters on the recognizable signs of Habsburg culture that pervade Bosnia after 1878. For a somewhat different set of cultural commonalities in Hungary, see Miklós Bánffy, *The Writing on the Wall: The Transylvanian Trilogy,*

3 vols., trans. Patrick Thursfield and Katalin Bánffy-Jelen (London: Arcadia Books, 2001).

34 Roth, *The Emperor's Tomb*, 38–39.

35 Wolfgang Maderthaner and Lutz Musner, *Unruly Masses: The Other Side of Fin-de-siècle Vienna*, trans. David Fernbach and Michael Huffmnaster (New York: Berghahn, 2008), 34, 42, 52–56. Of Austria-Hungary's largest cities, only Trieste and the Pest half of Budapest, both of which had been built much later than the others, had more modern layouts that did not distinguish in this way between an ancient core and modern suburbs. Galician industry was not centered in Galicia's two cities with populations over 100,000 in 1910, Cracow and Lemberg/Lwów/Lviv. For a comparative view, see Wolfgang Maderthaner, "Urbane Lebenswelten: Metropolen und Grossstädte," in Rumpler and Urbanitsch, *Die Habsburgermonarchie 1848–1918*, 9:499–505.

36 Hans Peter Hye, "Aussig—eine Industriestadt am Rande des Reiches," in *Kleinstadtbürgertum ind der Habsburgermonarchie, 1862–1914*, ed. Peter Urbanitsch and Hannes Stekl (Vienna: Böhlau, 2000), 43.

37 Marie Tosnerova, "Beraun—Im sog fortschreitender Modernisierung," in ibid., 158–159.

38 Jiři Coupek, "Ungarisch Hradisch—Bürgertum und Stadtpolitik," in ibid., 357.

39 František Spurny, "Mährisch Schönberg—Eine Domäne der deutschen Industrie," in ibid., 310–311.

40 John Boyer analyzed this dynamic of a fiction of bourgeois unity superbly in the Viennese context in *Political Radicalism in Turn-of-the-Century Vienna* (Chicago: University of Chicago Press, 1980).

41 See for example, Hye, "Aussig," 42.

42 Tosnerova, "Beraun."

43 Ibid.

44 For several examples, see the essays in Urbanitsch and Stekl, *Kleinstadtbürgertum in der Habsburgermonarchie 1862–1914*.

45 I am grateful to Zoriana Melnyk for bringing this case to my attention in her dissertation research. As Melnyk argues, the Dawidów incident is also noteworthy as the only example in Galicia of election violence that actually involved the death of an official.

46 Joshua Shanes, *Diaspora Nationalism and Jewish Identity in Habsburg Galicia* (Cambridge: Cambridge University Press, 2012), 279.

47 Coupek, "Ungarisch-Hradec," 374–375.

48 Tosnerova, "Beraun," 149–152; 161–162.

49 Of course one local mayor also insisted that Cracow's "modern" building codes should not have to apply to his suburb. Nathan Wood, *Becoming Metropolitan: Urban Selfhood and the Making of Modern Cracow* (Dekalb: Northern Illinois University Press, 2010), 92–93.

50 Spurny, "Mährisch Schönberg," 311. Telephone service came to Austria-Hungary in 1881, and in 1895 the state took over all aspects of service. On the telephone in Austria-Hungary, see Hans Peter Hye, "Technologie und sozialer Wandel," in Rumpler and Urbanitsch, *Die Habsburgermonarchie 1848–1918*, 9:29–30.

51 Coupek, "Ungarisch Hradisch," 370.

52 An insightful analysis of the crownland budgets, their financing, and the ensuing crisis is Hans Peter Hye, "Strukturen und Probleme der Landeshaushalt," in Rumpler and Urbanitsch, *Die Habsburgermonarchie 1848–1918*, 7:1545–1592. Another excellent analysis of this crisis and its origins is Deak, *Forging a Multinational State*, 226–232; 249–258.

53 Deak cites statistics showing that the surcharge equaled 95 percent in Bukovina and 81.5 percent in Galicia. Ernst Mischler, "Der Haushalt der österreichischen Landschaften," *Jahrbuch des öffentlichen Rechts der Gegenwart* 3 (1909): 589; Mischler, "Selbstverwaltung, finanzrechtlich," 236–237, cited in Deak, *Forging a Multinational State*, 230–231.

54 Mischler, "Der Haushalt," 586, cited in Deak, *Forging a Multinational State*, 231.

55 John Deak, "The Great War and the Forgotten Realm: The Habsburg Monarchy and the First World War, *JMH* 86 (June 2014): 368. On Koerber's specific plans for administrative expansion and economic reform, see Fredrik Lindström, "Ernest von Koerber and the Austrian State Idea: A Reinterpretation of the Koerber Plan (1900–1904)," *AHY* 35 (2004): 143–184.

56 During that same period, forty-six new prefectures were created. Statistics from the Commission for Promotion of Administrative Reform cited by Deak in "The Great War," 368.

57 Deak, *Forging a Multinational State*, 249. This commission was only one of several that worked during the last decades before the First World War.

58 Deak, "The Great War," 372.

59 Deak, *Forging a Multinational State*, 242, 250–258.

60 Alexander Vari, "Bullfights in Budapest: City Marketing, Moral Panics, and Nationalism in Turn-of-the-Century Hungary," *AHY* 41 (2010): 149–151; Miklós Hadas, "Modernity and Masculinity: Cycling in Hungary at the End of the Nineteenth Century," in *Gender and Modernity in Central Europe: The Austro-Hungarian Monarchy and its Legacy*, ed. Agatha Schwarz (Ottawa: University of Ottowa Press, 2010), 47–64.

61 Henschel, "'Das Fluidum der Stadt,'" 74; Vörös, "Die Munizipialverwaltung in Ungarn," 2366–2368.

62 Reinhard Farkas, "'Lebensreform' als Antwort auf den sozialen Wandel," in Rumpler and Urbanitsch, *Die Habsburgermonarchie 1848–1918*, 9:1361.

63 Dietlind Hüchtker, *Geschichte als Performance. Politische Bewegungen in Galizien um 1900* (Frankfurt a/M: Campus, 2014), 14–15.

64 On women's labor in nationalist associations, Pieter M. Judson, "The Gendered Politics of German Nationalism in Austria," in *Austrian Women in the Nineteenth and Twentieth Centuries*, ed. David F. Good, Margarete Grandner, and Mary Jo Maynes (New York: Berghahn, 1996), 1–18; Heidrun Zettelbauer, *"Die Liebe sei Euer Heldentum." Geschlecht und Nation in völkischen Vereinen der Habsburgermonarchie* (Frankfurt a/M: Campus, 2005); Hüchtker, *Geschichte als Performance*; Jitka Malečkova, "Nationalizing Women and Engendering the Nation: The Czech National Movement," in Ida Blom, Karen Hagemann, and Catherine Hall, eds., *Gendered Nations: Nationalisms and Gender Order in the Long Nineteenth Century* (Oxford and New York: Berg, 2000), 293–310.

65 Appelt, "The Gendering of the Service Sector," 121 and 126–127.

66 Joachim von Puttkamer, *Rumänen und Siebenbürger Sachsen in der Auseinandersetzung mit der ungarischen Staatsidee 1867–1914* (Munich: R. Oldenbourg Verlag, 2003), 403.

67 Katherine David, "Czech Feminists and Nationalism in the Late Habsburg Monarchy: 'The First in Austria,'" *Journal of Women's History* 3, no. 2 (1991): 26–45.

68 On sensationalist criminal reporting in the Austrian media, see for example Scott Spector, "Where Personal Fate Turns to Public Affair: Homosexual Scandal and Social Order in Vienna, 1900–1910," *AHY* 38 (2007): 15–24; Nancy M. Wingfield, "Echoes of the Riehl Trial in Fin-de-Siècle Cisleithania," *AHY* 38 (2007): 37–47; Daniel Vyleta, *Crime, Jews, and News: Vienna 1895–1914* (New York: Berghahn, 2007).

69 See Scott Spector's brilliant and suggestive article, "The Wrath of the 'Countess Merviola': Tabloid Exposé and the Emergence of Homosexual Subjects in Vienna in 1907," *Contemporary Austrian Studies* 15 (2006): 31–47.

70 Ibid., 36. By the end of its first year in existence, the *Illustrierte Österreichische Kriminal-Zeitung* in Vienna boasted a weekly circulation of 30,000.

71 Cited by Anita Kurimay, "Sex in the 'Pearl of the Danube': The History of Queer Life, Love, and its Regulation in Budapest, 1873–1941" (PhD diss., Rutgers University, 2012), 68. Prostitutes registered with the police were subject to regular medical examination; "clandestine" refers to prostitutes

who avoided police registration. See Nancy M. Wingfield, "The Enemy Within: Regulating Prostitution and Controlling Venereal Disease in Cisleithanian Austria during the Great War," *CEH* 46, no. 3 (2013): 569; Karin J. Jusek, *Auf der Suche nach der Verlorenen. Die Prostitutionsdebatten in Wien der Jahrhundertwende* (Vienna: Löcker, 1994).

72 Cited in Kurimay, "Sex in the 'Pearl of the Danube,'" 16.

73 Cited in Wood, *Becoming Metropolitan*, 178.

74 The argument was made famously by Weber in *Peasants into Frenchmen: The Modernization of Rural France, 1870–1914* (Stanford, CA: Stanford University Press, 1976), 292–303.

75 Christa Hämmerle, "Die k. (u.) k. Armee als 'Schule des Volkes'? Zur Geschichte der allgemeinen Wehrpflicht in der multinationalen Habsburgermonarchie (1866 bis 1914/18)," in *Der Bürger als Soldat. Die Militarisierung europäischer Gesellschaften im langen 19. Jahrhundert. Ein internationaler Vergleich*, Christian Jansen, ed. (Essen: Klartext Verlag, 2004), 175–213.

76 Walter Wagner, "Die k.(u.)k. Armee—Gliederung und Aufgabenstellung 1866–1914," in Adam Wandruszka and Peter Urbanitsch, eds., *Die Habsburgermonarchie 1848–1918*, vol. 5, *Die bewaffnete Macht* (Vienna: Verlag der Österreichischen Akademie der Wissenschaften, 1987), 240–243.

77 On the changing details of military service, length, character, application, and regional diversity, see B. Schmitt, *Armee und Staatliche Integration: Preussen und die Habsburgermonarchie, 1815–1866. Rekrutierungspolitik in den neuen Provinzen: Staatliches Handeln und Bevölkerung* (Paderborn: Ferdinand Schöningh, 2007); Laurence Cole, *Military Culture and Popular Patriotism in Late Imperial Austria* (Oxford: Oxford University Press, 2014); Gunther Rothenberg, *The Army of Francis Joseph* (West Lafayette, IN: Purdue University Press, 1976); István Deák, *Beyond Nationalism: A Social and Political History of the Habsburg Officer Corps* (New York: Oxford University Press, 1990), 56–60; Christa Hämmerle, "Die K&K Armee als Schule des Volks?" Following the reforms, men in Dalmatia became eligible for military service, a fact that produced popular uprisings there.

78 Cole explains that those with the lowest numbers (96,500 men, 50,000 of whom were from Austria) served three years active duty, seven years in the reserves, and two in the *Landwehr* or *Honvéd*. Those with middle-range numbers (20,000) spent two years in either the *Landwehr* or the *Honvéd* followed by ten years in the reserve. Those with the highest numbers received no training but could be called up in times of war for the militias or for the replacement reserves. Cole, *Military Culture*, 114.

79 Ibid., 115. Once they had a year of training, reserve officers took part in annual exercises. Deák, *Beyond Nationalism*, 86–88.

80 From a collection of nineteenth-century Slovene folksongs about military service quoted in Rok Stergar, "Die Bevölkerung der slowenischen Länder und die Allgemeine Wehrpflicht," in *Glanz—Gewalt—Gehorsam. Militär und Gesellschaft in der Habsburgermonarchie (1800 bis 1918)*, ed. Laurence Cole, Christa Hämmerle, and Martin Scheutz (Essen: Klartext, 2011), 135.

81 Ibid., 135; Cole, *Military Culture*, 120.

82 Christa Hämmerle, "'. . . dort wurden wir dressiert und sekiert und geschlagen . . .' Vom Drill, dem Disziplinarstrafrecht und Soldatenmisshandlungen im Heer (1868 bis 1914)," in Cole, Hämmerle, and Scheutz, *Glanz—Gewalt—Gehorsam*, 31–54.

83 Gunther E. Rothenberg, "Toward a National Hungarian Army: The Military Compromise of 1868 and Its Consequences," *Slavic Review* 31 (1972): 805–816; László Péter, "The Army Question In Hungarian Politics 1867–1918," *Central Europe* 4 (November 2006): 88; Catherine Horel, *Soldaten zwischen nationalen Fronten. Die Auflösung der Militärgrenze und die Entwicklung der königlich-ungarischen Landwehr (Honvéd) in Kroatien-Slawonien 1868–1914* (Vienna: Verlag der Österreichischn Akademie der Wissenschaften, 2009).

84 The official languages were Serbo-Croat, Czech-Moravian-Slovak, German, Hungarian, Italian, Polish, Romanian, Ruthene (Ukrainian), and Slovene. Unofficially, Bosnian Serbo-Croatian was treated as a separate language. On regimental languages, see Tamara Scheer, "Die k.u.k. Regimentssprachen: Eine Institutionalisierung der Sprachenvielfalt in der Habsburgermonarchie (1867/8–1914)," in Klaas-Hinrich Ehlers, Martina Niedhammer, Marek Nekula ed., *Sprache, Gesellschaft und Nation in Ostmitteleuropa. Institutionalisierung und Alltagspraxis* (Göttingen: Vandenhoeck & Ruprecht, 2014), 75–92. For individual examples, see Peter Broucek, "Die Mehrsprachigkeit und Sprachenpolitik in den Einheiten der k. und k. Armee in den böhmischen Ländern," in *250 Jahre Fremdsprachenausbildung im österreichischen Militär am Beispiel des Tschechischen*, ed. Josef Ernst (Vienna: Landesverteidigungsakademie, 2003), 16–21; "Rok Stergar, Fragen des Militärwesens in der slowenischen Politik, 1867–1914," *Österreichische Osthefte* 46, no. 3 (2004), 391–422.

85 For other examples, see Nicola Fontana, "Trient als Festungs- und Garnisonsstadt. Militär und Zivilbevölkerung in einer k. u. k. Festungsstadt, 1880–1914," in Cole, Hämmerle, and Scheutz, *Glanz—Gewalt—Gehorsam*, 177–198; Frank Wiggermann, *K.u.K. Kriegsmarine und Politik: Ein Beitrag zur Geschichte der italienischen Nationalbewegung in Istrien* (Vienna: Verlag der Österreichischen Akademie der Wissenschaften, 2004); Wilhelm Steinböck, ed., *Graz als Garnison: Beiträge zur Militärgeschichte der*

steirischen Landeshauptstadt (Graz: Leykam, 1982); Martin Parth, "Die Garnison Graz um 1900," *Historisches Jahrbuch der Stadt Graz* 27, no. 28 (1998): 165–89; Peter Melichar, "Ästhetik und Disziplin: Das Militär in Wiener Neustadt 1740–1914," in *"Die Wienerische Neustadt": Handwerk, Handel und Militär,* ed. Sylvia Hahn and Karl Flanner (Vienna-Köln-Weimar: Böhlau,1994), 283–336. On Galicia, see Piotr Galik, "Miasta Galicyskie jako garnizony armii austro-węgierskiej w prezededniu I wojny światowej," *Acta Uniwersitatis Wratislaviensis* 111 (1993): 113–123.

86 Rok Stergar, "The Evolution of Language Policies and Practices of the Austro-Hungarian Armed Forces in the Era of Ethnic Nationalisms: The Case of Ljubljana-Laibach" (unpublished manuscript, 2015). I am grateful to Professor Stergar for sharing this manuscript with me. See also Stergar, "National Indifference in the Heyday of Nationalist Mobilization? Ljubljana Military Veterans and the Language of Command," *AHY* 43 (2012): 45–58.

87 Fontana, "Trient als Festungs- und Garnisonsstadt," 192–193.

88 Stergar, "Evolution of Language Policies and Practices," 16.

89 Tamara Scheer, "Habsburg Languages at War: 'The Linguistic Confusion at the Tower of Babel Couldn't Have Been Much Worse," in *Languages and the First World War: Communicating in a Transnational War,* ed. Christophe Declercq and Julian Walker (London: Palgrave Macmillan, forthcoming).

90 Hans Haas, "Krieg und Frieden am regionalen Salzburger Beispiel 1914," *Salzburg Archiv* 20 (1995): 303–320; Cole, *Military Culture,* 314.

91 Cole, *Military Culture,* 268–286.

92 For the following discussion, see Cole, *Military Culture,* especially chaps. 3–5. For statistics, 129.

93 Cole, *Military Culture,* 311.

94 As Cole and others have argued, the state's promotion of veterans' associations and their activities did not necessarily constrain, shape, or define the activities in which the veterans engaged, despite the state's efforts.

95 Cole, *Military Culture,* 268–307.

96 Mommsen, *Die Sozialdemokratie und die Nationalitätenfrage im habsburgischen Vielvölkerstaat. Das Ringen um die supranantionale Integration der zisleithanischen Arbeiterbewegung (1867–1907)* (Vienna: Europa-Verlag, 1963), 370.

97 Ibid., 370–371; Karl Ucakar, Demokratie und *Wahlrecht in Österreich: zur Entwicklung von politischer Partizipation und staatlicher Legitimationspolitik* (Vienna: Verlag für Gesellschaftskritik, 1985).

98 On Mayday, see Harald Troch, *Rebellensonntag. Der 1. Mai zwischen Politik, Arbeiterkultur und Volksfest in Österreich (1890–1918)* (Vienna: Europa-Verlag, 1991). The Austrian insistence on celebrating Mayday on

1 May, unlike their German or British comrades who celebrated it on the nearest Sunday, also underlined the willingness of the Social Democratic Party and its members to sacrifice for the demands of their members, especially for the eight-hour day and universal manhood suffrage. For the comparison with Britain and Germany, see Chapter 3.

99 For unionization numbers in Austria, Geoffrey Drage, *Austria-Hungary* (New York: E. P, Dutton, 1909), 112; for Hungary, 851.

100 Wolfgang Maderthaner, "Die Enstehung einer demokratischen Massenpartei: Sozialdemokratische Organisation von 1889 bis 1918," in *Die Organisation der österreichischen Sozialdemokratie, 1889–1995,* ed. Maderthaner and Wolfgang C. Müller (Vienna: Löcker, 1996).

101 During the recent Badeni Crisis (1897–1898), which had spawned demonstrations and violence among Czech and German nationalists, the Socialist parties had refused cooperation with the nationalist bourgeois parties and suffered some loss of support. Thus, the clear articulation of a policy on nationhood and national rights became even more necessary.

102 On nationhood, Jakub Benes offers an innovative analysis in *Workers and Nationalism: Czech and German Social Democracy in Habsburg Austria, 1890–1918* (unpublished book manuscript). I am grateful to Professor Benes for sharing this manuscript with me. See also Karl F. Bahm, "Beyond the Bourgeoisie: Rethinking Nation, Culture, and Modernity in Nineteenth-Century Central Europe," *AHY* 29 Part 1 (1998): 19–36.

103 Otto Bauer, *The Question of Nationalities and Social Democracy,* trans. Joseph O'Donnell (Minneapolis: University of Minnesota Press, 2000); Helmut Konrad, *Nationalismus und Internationalismus. Die österreichische Arbeiterbewegung vor dem ersten Weltkrieg* (Vienna: Europa-Verlag, 1976), 18–40; Konrad, "Arbeiterbewegung und bürgerliche Öffentlichkeit. Kultur und nationale Frage in der Habsburgermonarchie," in *Geschichte und Gesellschaft* 20, no. 4 (1994): 506–518; Hans Mommsen, "Otto Bauer, Karl Renner, und die spozialdemokratische Nationalpolitik in Österreich von 1905 bis 1914," in *Studies in East European Social History,* ed. Keith Hitchens (Leiden: Brill, 1977), vol. 1. It was a Slovene-speaking Social Democratic leader, Etbin Kristan, who first coined the personality principle in 1898.

104 William Jenks, *The Austrian Electoral Reform of 1907* (New York: Octagon Books, 1974), chap. 1; John Boyer, "Power, Partisanship, and the Grid of Democratic Politics: 1907 as the Pivot Point of Modern Austrian History," *AHY* 44 (2013): 148–174; Ernst Bruckmüller and Berthold Sutter, "Der Reichsrat, der Parlament des westlichen Reichshälfte Österreich-Ungarns (1861–1918)," in Bruckmüller, ed. *Parlamentarismus in Österreich* (Vienna: Österreichischer Bundesverlag & Hpt., 2002), 60–109.

105 Geoff Eley, *Forging Democracy: The History of the Left in Europe, 1850–2000* (New York and Oxford: Oxford University Press, 2002), 98.

106 Ucakar, *Demokratie und Wahlrecht*, 290–296.

107 Boyer, "Power, Partisanship, and the Grid of Democratic Politics."

108 Austria's highest Court determined in a case argued before it in 1909 that because language use largely determined nationhood, and the Jews did not use a single language, but rather several languages depending on where they resided, Jews could not be treated as a nation. The negotiators of the Compromise in Bukovina, with a Jewish population of 12 percent, thus had to fashion some form of guaranteed Jewish representation in practice, without creating a formal Jewish voting curia. See Gerald Stourzh's analysis of the Bukovina Compromise and of the court case that determined the Jews could not be treated as a nation, in three important articles: "The National Compromise in the Bukovina 1909/1910," and "Max Diamant and Jewish Diaspora Nationalism in the Bukovina," both in *From Vienna to Chicago and Back* (Chicago: University of Chicago Press, 2007), 177–189 and 190–203. For a contemporary argument by a noted academic progressive and sociologist of law on the economic necessity of compromise in Bukovina, Eugen Ehrlich, *Die Aufgaben der Sozialpolitik im österreichischen Osten insbesondere in der Bukowina. Mit besonderer Beleuchtung der Juden und Bauernfrage* (Czernowitz: 1909).

109 Gerald Stourzh, "Ethnic Attribution in Late Imperial Austria: Good Intentions, Evil Consequences," in Ritchie Robinson and Edward Timms, ed., *The Habsburg Legacy: National Identity in Historical Perspective* (*Austrian Studies* 5) (1994): 67–83. See also the analysis in Jeremy King, *Budweisers into Czechs and Germans: A Local History of Bohemian Politics, 1848–1948* (Princeton, NJ: Princeton University Press, 2002) and Tara Zahra, *National Indifference and the Battle for Children in the Bohemian Lands, 1900–1948* (Ithaca, NY: Cornell University Press, 2008).

110 Stürgkh had also conferred with nationalist party leaders before dissolving the diet. Cohen, "Nationalist Politics," 271; Lothar Höbelt, "Bohemia 1913—a Consensual *Coup d'État?*," *Estates and Representation* 20 (November 2000): 207–214. See also Gerald Stourzh, "Verfassungsbruch im Königreich Böhmen. Ein unbekanntes Kapitel zur Geschichte des richterlichen Prüfungsrechts im alten Österreich," in *Staatsrecht und Staatswissenschaften in Zeiten des Wandels. Festschrift für Ludwig Adamovich*, ed. Ludwig Karl Adamovich and Bernd-Christian Funk (Vienna: Springer, 1992): 675–690.

111 For an illuminating legal analysis of these issues, see Karl Lamp, "Die Verfassung von Bosnien und der Herzegowina vom 17. Februar 1910," in *Jahrbuch des öffentlichen Rechts der Gegenwart*, no. 5 (1911): 137–229.

112 For the specific of who could vote, Lamp, "Die Verfassung," 142–145. Those over the age of thirty who fulfilled the same requirements could also be elected as deputies to the diet, with the exception of civil servants and teachers. In the Muslim section of the large landowners, women had the right to vote by a male proxy. As elsewhere in the monarchy men on active duty in the military, except for military bureaucrats, did not have the right to vote.

113 For an analysis of the new statutes and administrative structures governing Bosnia-Herzegovina, Valerie Heuberger, "Politische Institutionen und Verwaltung in Bosnien und der Hercegovina 1878–1918," in *Die Habsburger-monarchie, 1848–1918*, vol. VII, *Verfassung und Parlamentarismus*, ed. Heinrich Rumpler and Peter Urbanitsch (Vienna: Verlag der Österreichischen Akademie der Wissenschaften, 2000), 2383–2425, especially 2415–2419.

114 Lamp compared Bosnia Herzegovina's status primarily to the *Reichsland* status of Alsace Lorraine in federal Germany as well as to various types of colonies and protectorates. Lamp, "Die Verfassung," 211–215.

115 Ibid., 228–229.

116 In fact Heuberger argues that in 1912 the statutes were reformed in order to devolve some of the central power from the common Austro-Hungarian Finance Ministry to the local government. "Politische Institutionen und Verwaltung," 2420–2423.

117 Robert Kann analyzed and categorized some of the better known and ambitious reform ideas, from those of the Social Democrats to those of Catholic conservatives in *The Multinational Empire: Nationalism and National Reform in the Habsburg Monarchy, 1848–1918* (New York: Columbia University Press, 1950).

118 Cornwall is completing a broad study of treason in the Habsburg Monarchy from 1848 until 1918. See Mark Cornwall, "Loyalty and Treason in Late Habsburg Croatia: A Violent Discourse before the Great War," in *Exploring Loyalty*, ed. Martin Schulze-Wessel and Jana Osterkamp (Göttingen: Vandenhoeck and Ruprecht, forthcoming); "Traitors and the Meanings of Treason in Austria-Hungary's Great War" in *Transactions of the Royal Historical Society* 25 (2015): 113–134.

119 The examples cited here and in the next paragraph quoted by Solomon Wank, "Pessimism in the Austrian Establishment at the Turn of the Century," in *The Mirror of History: Essays in Honor of Fritz Fellner*, ed. Solomon Wank, Heidrun Maschl, Brigitte Mazohl-Wallnig, and Reinhold Wagenleitner (Santa Barbara, CA, and Oxford: ABC-Clio, 1988), 295–314.

120 Quoted in ibid., 306. On Conrad's views in general, see Rothenberg, *The Army of Francis Joseph*, 144–145; Holger Herwig, *The First World War: Germany and Austria-Hungary 1914–1918* (London: Bloomsbury Academic,

1997), 9–11. On the other aristocratic stronghold, the foreign office, William D. Godsey, *Aristocratic Redoubt: The Austro-Hungarian Foreign Office on the Eve of the First World War* (West Lafayette, IN: Purdue University Press, 1999).

8. WAR AND RADICAL STATE-BUILDING

Epigraph: Robert Musil, "The German as Symptom," in *Precision and Soul*, ed. David S. Luft and Burton Pike (Chicago: University of Chicago Press, 1990) 169, quoted in Deborah Coen, "Scaling Down: The 'Austrian' Climate between Empire and Republic," in *Intimate Universality: Local and Global Themes in the History of Weather and Climate*, ed. James Roger Fleming, Vladimir Jankovic, and Deborah Coen (Sagamore Beach, MA: Science History Publications, 2006), 115.

1 Martin Moll, *Die Steiermark im ersten Weltkrieg. Der Kampf des Hinterlandes ums Überleben 1914–1918* (Graz: Styria Premium, 2014), on the Socialist leaders following working-class support for the War, 131.

2 The total estimate for war dead includes approximately 478,000 who died in captivity. John Ellis and Michael Cox, *The World War I Data Book* (London: Aurum Press, 2001), 269. A Carnegie Endowment for International Peace study cited in Leo Grebler, *The Cost of the World War to Germany and Austria-Hungary* (New Haven, CT: Yale University Press, 1940), 147, estimated in addition 467,000 civilian deaths in Austria-Hungary due specifically to the results of the Allied blockade, and not including deaths from the influenza epidemic. Given a total population in 1910 of around 52 million, these statistics point to a 3 percent death rate.

3 An excellent recent analysis of the war economy and the transformations wrought by wartime technological changes is *Wirtschaft, Technik und das Militär. Österreich-Ungarn im Ersten Weltkrieg*, ed. Herbert Matis, Juliane Mikoletzky, and Wolfgang Reiter (Vienna and Berlin: Lit Verlag, 2014).

4 Maureen Healy, "Becoming Austrian: Women, the State, and Citizenship in World War I," *Central European History* 35 (2002): 1–35.

5 See Maureen Healy, *Vienna and the Fall of the Habsburg Empire: Total War and Everyday Life in World War I* (Cambridge: Cambridge University Press, 2004); Cole, *Military Culture and Popular Patriotism in Late Imperial Austria* (Oxford: Oxford University Press, 2013), 318.

6 That Austria's military dictatorship was exceptionally rigid by European standards was Josef Redlich's argument in *Österreichs Regierung und Verwaltung im Weltkrieg* (Vienna: Hölder-Pichler-Tempsky, 1925), 123. Redlich characterized secret meetings between the War Ministry, the Joint Minis-

terial Council, and members of the general staff in 1912 as illegal. At those meetings plans for a Wartime Surveillance Office (later the *Kriegsüberwachungsamt*, or KÜA) had been drawn up. See also Iris [Alon] Rachamimov, "Arbiters of Allegiance: Austro-Hungarian Censors During World War I," in *Constructing Nationalities*, ed. Pieter M. Judson and Marsha Rozenblit (New York: Berghahn, 2005), 157–177, here 162.

7 John Deak, "The Great War and the Forgotten Realm: The Habsburg Monarchy and the First World War," *Journal of Modern History* 86 (June 2014): 369–370.

8 Ibid., 370.

9 Tara Zahra, *Kidnapped Souls: National Indifference and the Battle for Children in the Bohemian Lands, 1900–1948* (Ithaca, NY: Cornell University Press, 2008), 27–29; Pieter M. Judson, *Guardians of the Nation: Activists on the Language Frontiers of Imperial Austria* (Cambridge, MA: Harvard University Press, 2006), 40–41; 44–46.

10 Jonathan Gumz, *The Resurrection and Collapse of Empire in Habsburg Serbia, 1914–1918* (New York: Cambridge University Press, 2009), 10–16; Christoph Führ, *Das k.u.k. Oberarmeekommando und die Innenpolitik in Österreich, 1914–1917* (Studien zur Geschichte der Habsburgermonarchie 7) (Graz, Vienna, Cologne: Böhlau, 1968). For attitudes in the army elite, see also István Deák, *Beyond Nationalism: A Social and Political History of the Habsburg Officer Corps, 1848–1918* (New York: Oxford University Press, 1990); Günther Kronenbitter, *"Krieg im Frieden": Die Führung der k. u. k, Armee und die Grossmachtpolitik Österreich-Ungarns 1906–1914* (Munich: R. Oldenbourg Verlag, 2003).

11 Waltraud Heindl, "Bureaucracy, Officials, and the State in the Austrian Monarchy: Stages of Change since the Eighteenth Century," *AHY* 37 (2006): 35–57.

12 Gumz, *Resurrection and Collapse*, 14. Gumz views the occupation regimes of Austria-Hungary—especially in Serbia—as an opportunity to build utopian societies organized along military lines in which political conflict would be completely absent.

13 Redlich, *Österreichs Regierung*, 123. The government and military also imposed control and reorganization on several key parts of the economy, but this control was less extreme by European standards.

14 Christoph Führ, *Das k.u.k. Oberarmeekommando und die Innenpolitik in Österreich, 1914–1917* (Vienna: Böhlau, 1968), 27; Martin Moll, *Kein Burgfrieden. Der deutsch-slowenische Nationalitätenkonflikt in der Steiermark 1900–1918* (Innsbruck: Studien Verlag, 2007), 184; John Deak, *Forging a Multinational State: State Making in Imperial Austria from the Enlightenment*

to the First World War (Stanford, CA: Stanford University Press, 2015), especially 264–269. The Austrian Parliament had already been closed by Stürgkh in March 1914.

15 Rachamimov, "Arbiters of Allegiance"; Tamara Scheer, *Die Ringstrassenfront. Österreich-Ungarn, das Kriegsüberwachungsamt und der Ausnahmezustand während des ersten Weltkrieges* (Vienna: Republik Österreich, Bundesminister für Landesverteidigung und Sport, 2010). According to Rachamimov, the mail-censorship arm of the KÜA was the envy of Europe.

16 On Tisza, see Gabor Vermes, *István Tisza: The Liberal Vision and Conservative Statecraft of a Magyar Nationalist* (New York: Columbia University Press, 1985).

17 It is worth repeating that while Austria's KÜA answered only to the Dual War Ministry, Hungary's HB answered only to the Hungarian cabinet and parliament.

18 József Galántai, *Hungary in the First World War*, trans. Éva Grusz and Judit Pokoly, rev. Mark Goodman (Budapest: Akadémiai Kiadó, 1989), 72–79.

19 Quoted in ibid., 95.

20 Mark Cornwall, "Das Ringen um die Moral des Hinterlandes." Unpublished manuscript for *Die Geschichte der Habsburgermonarchie*, vol. 11/1, *Die Habsburgermonarchie und der Erste Weltkrieg*, ed. Helmut Rumpler and Anatol Schmidt-Kowarzik (Vienna: Verlag der Österreichischen Akademie der Wissenschaften, forthcoming). I am grateful to Professor Cornwall for sharing this manuscript with me.

21 During the war the prime minister reported on the use of emergency measures to the Parliament eight times. Galántai, *Hungary in the First World War*, 79.

22 Quoted in Arnold Suppan, "Die Untersteiermark, Krain und das Küstenland zwischen Maria Theresia und Franz Josef (1740–1918)," in *Deutsche Geschichte im Osten Europas. Zwischen Adria und Karawanken*, ed. Arnold Suppan (Berlin: Siedler Verlag, 1998), 342.

23 Z. A. B. Zeman, *The Breakup of the Habsburg Empire 1914–1918: A Study in National and Social Revolution* (London: Oxford University Press, 1961), 42.

24 Mark Cornwall, "Das Ringen um die Moral des Hinterlandes;" Mark Cornwall, *The Devil's Wall: The Nationalist Youth Mission of Heinz Rutha* (Cambridge, MA: Harvard University Press, 2012), especially 35–78.

25 Cole, *Military Culture*, 322.

26 On persecutions in Galicia, see Führ, *Das k.u.k. Oberarmeekommando*, 181. On 17 July, for example, at the insistence of Conrad, who was apparently obsessed with the Sokol Slavic gymnastics associations, the Gemeinsame Minsterrat debated applying an exceptional condition to all lands

with South-Slav populations. Oddly, given these debates, on 26 July Styria permitted a Sokol festival to be held. Moll, *Kein Burgfrieden*, 181.

27 Healy, *Vienna and the Fall of the Habsburg Empire*, 122–159, and especially 159. Healy's work led the way as a new kind of history of the home front. On popular wartime initiatives from below and denunciations, see also Tara Zahra, *Kidnapped Souls*, 82–85.

28 Martin Moll's *Kein Burgfrieden* is a superb analysis of the military arrogation of power, the overreaction of local gendarmes, and the results at the local level in Styria, as well as a careful documentation of many individual cases of people arrested in July and August of 1914 as potential Serbophile traitors.

29 Clearly the hysteria offered many German nationalists in South Styria the opportunity to see the state destroy the infrastructure of their Slovene nationalist rivals. Moll, *Kein Burgfrieden*, 462.

30 Quoted in Suppan, "Die Untersteiermark, Krain und das Küstenland," 345; Moll, *Kein Burgfrieden*, 182.

31 Suppan, ibid., 345; Martin Moll, *Die Steiermark im ersten Weltkrieg*, 45–46; Moll's *Kein Burgfrieden* reproduces detailed accounts of hundreds of individual cases in Styria.

32 "Windisch" is a local term referring to Slovene or Slav. Quoted in Moll, *Kein Burgfrieden*, 367.

33 In Styria at least 637 people were imprisoned, and of these cases the vast majority had originated in August of 1914. For statistics, see Moll, *Kein Burgfrieden*, 424–439. In over 200 documented cases the accused was actually found guilty (although later the sentences were often reversed, and those that were not were covered by Emperor King Charles's general amnesty of 2 July 1917).

34 Ibid., 446. For examples of damaged careers, see 451–458.

35 Galántai, *Hungary in the First World War*, 96.

36 Ibid., 95–98. For a case of overzealous military repression at the highest levels in Hungary, and one where Tisza again found it necessary to intervene, see Irina Marin, "World War One and Internal Repression: The Case of Major General Nikolaus Cena," *AHY* 44 (2013): 195–208.

37 John Paul Newman, "Post-Imperial and Postwar Violence in the South Slav Lands, 1917–1923," *Contemporary European History* 19, no. 3 (2010): 256.

38 On this incident and Tisza's protests quoted below, see Galántai, *Hungary in the First World War*, 97–98. See also Marin, "World War I and Internal Repression," 204–205.

39 For an earlier analysis of the food crisis, see Hans Loewenfeld-Rus, *Die Regelung der Volksernährung im Kriege* (Vienna: Hölder-Pichler-Tempsky,

1926). Other analyses include: Peter Heumos, "'Kartoffeln her oder es gibt eine Revolution': Hungerkrawalle, Streiks und Massenproteste in den böhmischen Ländern, 1914–1918," in *Der erste Weltkrieg und die Beziehungen zwischen Tschechen, Slowaken und Deutschen*, ed. Hans Mommsen, Dušan Kováč, Jiří Malíř, and Michaela Marek (Essen: Klartext, 2001), 255–286; Healy, *Vienna*; Claire Morelon, "Street Fronts: War, State Legitimacy and Urban Space, Prague 1914–1920" (PhD diss., University of Birmingham and École Doctorale des Sciences Po, 2015).

40 See the analysis of occupation food policy in Gumz, *Resurrection and Collapse of Empire*, 142–192.

41 Martin Franc, "Bread from Wood: Natural Food Substitutes in the Czech Lands during the First World War," in *Food and War in Twentieth-Century Europe*, ed. Iva Zweiniger-Bargielowska, Rachel Duffett, and Alain Drouart (Farnham: Ashgate, 2011), 73–83; Roman Sandgruber, *Ökonomie und Politik. Österreichische Wirtschaftsgeschichte vom Mittelalter bis zur Gegenwart* (Vienna: Uebrreuter, 1995, 2005), 325; Moll, *Die Steiermark im Ersten Weltkrieg*, 96.

42 Cited in Morelon, "Street Fronts," 137.

43 Galántai, *Hungary in the First World War*, 80–81.

44 Sandgruber, *Ökonomie und Politik*, 324. For a range of statistics on wartime production, consumption, and movement of products, see *Die Habsburgermonarchie 1848–1918*, 11/2, *Weltkriegsstatistik Österreich-Ungarn 1914–1918. Bevölkerungsbewegung, Kriegstote, Kriegswirtschaft*.

45 On the different municipal efforts, see Redlich, *Österreichs Regierung und Verwaltung im Weltkrieg*; on the *Amt für Volksernährung*, see Ottokar Landwehr von Pargenau, *Hunger. Die Erschöpfungsjahre der Mittelmächte 1917/1918* (Vienna and Zürich: Amalthea-Verlag, 1931), 6.

46 Healy, *Vienna and the Fall of the Habsburg Empire*, 43–44; Morelon, "Street Fronts," 136. For Prague see also Eva Drašarova and Jaroslav Vrbata, ed., *Sborník dokumentů k vnitřnímu vývoji v českých zemích za I. Světové války 1914–1918* (Prague Central State Archive 1993–1995), 2:67.

47 Ivan Šedivý, *Češi, české země a Velká valka 1914–1918* (Prague: Nakladelství Lidové Noviny, 2001), 259; Moll, *Die Steiermark im Ersten Weltkrieg*, 85. As Morelon points out, there exists as yet no study that compares food supplies in the different parts of the monarchy ("Street Fronts," 137).

48 Healy, *Vienna and the Fall of the Habsburg Empire*, 45–47. In Graz available milk before the war was 70,000 liters daily; by 1918 it was 14,000 liters daily. Moll, *Die Steiermark im Ersten Weltkrieg*, 91.

49 Healy, *Vienna and the Fall of the Habsburg Empire*, 43–44; see also Thierry Bonzon and Belinda Davis, "Feeding the Cities," in *Capital Cities at War:*

London, Paris, Berlin 1914–1919, ed. Jay Winter and Jean Louis Robert (Cambridge: Cambridge University Press, New Ed., 1997). On Berlin, see Belinda David, *Home Fires Burning: Food, Politics, and Everyday Life in World War I Berlin* (Chapel Hill: University of North Carolina Press, 2000).

50 Galántai, *Hungary in the First World War*, 80–84.

51 AST, Abschrift Pr. A-107, 11 January 1917, from the Statthalter to Ministry of the Interior, Busta 439, Luogotenenza del Littoral, Atti Presidiali. See also Almerigo Apollonio, *La Belle Epoque e il tramonto dell'Impero Asburgico sulle Rive dell'Adriatico (1902–1918)*, vol. 2, *La Grande Guerra (1914–1918)* (Trieste: Deputazione di Storia Patria per la Venezia Giulia, 2014), charts on food shortages, mortality, and inflation, 959–969.

52 In Hungary, for example, the emergency law made men up to age fifty-five as well as women liable for compulsory war work. Galántai, *Hungary in the First World War*, 80–81.

53 Morelon, "Street Fronts," 139.

54 Healy, *Vienna and the Fall of the Habsburg Empire*, especially 31–86. On lining up, 73–82, here 76.

55 Cited in Healy, *Vienna and the Fall of the Habsburg Empire*, 75.

56 Police report from September 1917 quoted in Morelon, "Street Fronts," 173.

57 For excellent analysis of and examples of this phenomenon in Prague, see Morelon, "Street Fronts," 170–186.

58 On legal sanctions against knapsack commerce, see Moll, *Die Steiermark im Ersten Weltkrieg*, 158; on the search for food in the countryside outside of Prague, see Morelon, "Street Fronts," 146–148. For the region near Vienna, see Healy, *Vienna and the Fall of the Habsburg Empire*, 53–56. Outside Vienna this traffic culminated in the so-called potato war of 1918 when an estimated 30,000 women and children were reported swarming the potato region around Vienna.

59 Morelon, "Street Fronts," 152, 159–160; on the *České Srdce* program, see ibid., 153–155.

60 Quoted in Healy, *Vienna and the Fall of the Habsburg Empire*, 52.

61 Ibid., 51, 57. Healy points out that denouncing Hungary's alleged unwillingness to share its food stores did little to endear politicians to their constituents who often saw the politicians as dupes for the clearly much cleverer Hungarians.

62 Quoted in ibid., 59.

63 Ibid., 65–69. Morelon, "Street Fronts," 124–132.

64 Morelon, "Street Fronts," 61.

65 Galántai cites figures of twenty-one and twenty-nine for the number of Serb-speaking soldiers captured by Serbia who asked to join the Serbian

military and those who fled to Serbia from Hungary to avoid conscription into the Austro-Hungarian military in 1914. Another thirteen soldiers allegedly deserted outright to Serbia. *Hungary in the First World War,* 97.

66 Quoted in Zahra, *Kidnapped Souls,* 85.

67 Morelon, "Street Fronts," 161–162.

68 Masaryk had left Austria-Hungary at the outset of the war.

69 Richard Lein, *Pflichterfüllung oder Hochverrat? Die Tschechischen Soldaten Österreich-Ungarns im ersten Weltkrieg* (Vienna: Lit Verlag, 2011). A small number of Czech troops fought for Russia until 1917, when Russia allowed the recruitment of volunteers from among POWs. The formal establishment of a Czech Legion took place both in Russia and France. By 1918 its strength was about 40,000 troops. The legion fought in the Russian Civil War.

70 Deak, *Forging a Multinational State,* 271.

71 On refugees, see Marsha Rozenblit, *Reconstructing a National Identity: The Jews of Habsburg Austria during World War I* (Oxford: Oxford University Press, 2001); Julie Thorpe, "Displacing Empire: Refugee Welfare, National Activism and State Legitimacy in Austria-Hungary in the First World War," in *Refugees and the End of Empire: Imperial Collapse and Forced Migration in the Twentieth Century,* ed. Panikos Panayi and Pippa Virdee (Basingstoke: Palgrave Macmillan, 2011), 102–126; Beatrix Hoffmann-Holter, *"Abreisendmachung": Jüdische Kriegsflüchtlinge in Wien 1914–1923* (Vienna: Böhlau, 1995); David Rechter, "Galicia in Vienna: Jewish Refugees in the First World War," *AHY* 28 (1997): 113–130; Walter Mentzel, "Weltkriegsflüchtlinge in Cisleithanien, 1914–1918," in *Asylland wider Willen. Flüchtlinge in Österreich im europäischen Kontext seit 1914,* ed. Gernot Heiss and Oliver Rathkolb (Vienna and Munich: Jugend und Volk, 1995), 17–44. Manfried Rauchensteiner, *Der erste Weltkrieg und das Ende der Habsburgermonarchie* (Vienna: Böhlau, 2013), 835–853. On refugee issues in Prague, see Morelon, "Street Fronts," 120–132.

72 On this incident, and for a useful elaboration of the work of international aid organizations, see Rebekah Klein-Pejšova, "Beyond the 'Infamous Concentration Camps of the Old Monarchy': Jewish Refugee Policy from Wartime Austria-Hungary to Interwar Czechoslovakia," *AHY* 45 (2014): 154–177. On the experience of Jewish refugees in Hungary more generally, Robert Nemes, "Refugees and Antisemitism in Hungary during the First World War," in *Sites of European Antisemitism in the Age of Mass Politics 1880–1918,* Robert Nemes and Daniel Unwosky, ed. (Waltham, MA: Brandeis University Press, 2014), 236–254.

73 HHstA, MdA, AR, Fach 36, Karton 341, "Instruktion betreffend die Beförderung und Unterbringung von Flüchtlinge aus Galizien und der Bukowina, 15 September 1914."

74 K. K. Ministerium des Innern, *Staatliche Flüchtlingsfürsorge im Kriege 1914/15* (Vienna: kk. Hof und Staatsdrückerei, 1915), 10.

75 Peter Štih, Vasko, Simoniti, and Peter Vodopivec, *Slowenische Geschichte. Gesellschaft—Politik—Kultur,* trans. Michael Kulnik (Graz: Leykam, 2008), 306–307.

76 Some local governments often treated wartime dislocation as an opportunity to deal harshly with Roma populations whom they characterized as work-shy, and over whose movements they could exercise very little control. See, for example, the discussions of possible measures in "Zigeunerunwesen, Bekämpfung, 8 July 1918," AVA, MdI, allg 20, Karton 2120 Zigeuner. Rauchensteiner, *Der erste Weltkrieg,* lists the division of the population by language use into specific camps, 845.

77 See, for example, AST, "Verzeichnis über verfügte Internierungen," 24 March 1917, Busta 443, Luogotenenza del Littoral, Atti Presidiali. The document includes a list of 216 internees from Poland. The reasons for their internment ranged from "generally unreliable because of repeated thievery" to "trafficked with Irredentists, hostile to Austria" to "propagandist for Italian liberal ideas, active in elections."

78 Quoted in Cole, *Military Culture,* 320.

79 *Staatliche Flüchtlingsfürsorge im Kriege,* 11.

80 Moll, *Die Steiermark im Ersten Weltkrieg,* 63.

81 Quoted in Cole, *Military Culture,* 320.

82 On Wagna and Thalerhof, see Moll, *Die Steiermark im Ersten Weltkrieg,* 66–76. In fact, the Styrian government also created mobile delousing and bathing units that could travel from camp to camp.

83 "Wünsche und Vorschläge betreffend die staatliche Flüchtlingsfürsorge für Angehörige des Landes Görz-Gradisca 2 March 1916," in OestA, AVA, MdI, 19 allg, Karton 1955.

84 Verpflegung der feindl. Zivilinternierten in der Monarchie, 26 November 1916, HHstA, MdA, AR, Fach 36, Karton 582.

85 *Staatliche Flüchtlingsfürsorge,* 15; Moll, *Die Steiermark im Ersten Weltkrieg,* 72–73.

86 *Lager-Zeitung/ Gazzetta di Campo,* herausgegeben und geleitet von der k.k. Barackenverwaltung in Wagna bei Leibniz, nr. 1, 4 pages, 14 October 1915; nr. 2, 4 pages, 15 October, 1915.

87 "Kulturelle Flüchtlingsfürsorge, deutscher Sprachunterricht," Vienna 14 March 1917, in AVA, AdR, BMsV, Kriegsflüchtlingsfürsorge, Karton 15.

88 Rozenblit, *Reconstructing National Identity,* 79; Morelon, "Street Fronts," 131.

89 Gustav Spann, "Zensur in Österreich während des 1. Weltkrieges," PhD diss. (Vienna, 1972); Cornwall, "Das Ringen um die Moral."

90 Titles included *Unsere Offiziere* (Our Officers), *Unsere Soldaten*, (Our Soldiers), *Unsere Nordfront* (Our Northern Front), and *Unsere Kämpfe im Süden* (Our Fight in the South). Cornwall, "Das Ringen um die Moral."

91 On ersatz foods in general, see Franz Vojir, "Ersatz Lebensmittel im ersten Weltkrieg in Österreich," in *Wirtschaft, Technik, und das Militär*, 253–284.

92 Maureen Healy, *Vienna and the Fall of the Habsburg Empire*, 87–121.

93 Miklós Bánffy, *The Phoenix Land: The Memoirs of Count Miklós Bánffy*, trans. Patrick Thursfield and Katalin Bánffy-Jelen (London: Arcadia Books, 2003), 3–4.

94 For a superb analysis of the critical theme of the emperor-king as father figure in wartime Viennese popular culture, Healy, *Vienna and the Fall of the Habsburg Empire*, 279–299.

95 Bánffy, *The Phoenix Land*, 32.

96 Moll, *Die Steiermark im Ersten Weltkrieg*, 136.

97 Charles had Czernin seek negotiations with the Allies and with the Americans before they entered the war. At the same time, in a secret letter to be conveyed to the French president in March 1917 by the empress's brother—a letter even Czernin did not know about—Charles declared French claims to Alsace Lorraine to be justified. When Czernin divulged a secret French peace initiative a year later, Clemenceau countered that talks had been originated much earlier by Austria-Hungary, and when Czernin denied it, Clemenceau released the entire text of Charles's letter. While admitting the authenticity of the letter, Czernin claimed the Alsace Lorraine statement had been fabricated. Charles, however, found himself forced to reassure Kaiser Wilhelm II of Germany of his loyalty to his ally, and Czernin had to resign. Robert Kann, *Die Sixtusaffäre und die geheimen Friedensverhandlungen Österreich-Ungarns im Ersten Weltkrieg* (Munich and Vienna: Verlag für Geschichte und Politik, 1966). On Austria-Hungary's changing wartime relationship to the United States, see Nicole Phelps, *US Habsburg Relations from 1815 to the Paris Peace Conference: Sovereignty Transformed* (Cambridge: Cambridge University Press, 2013); Václav Horčička, "The Bilateral Relationship Between Austria-Hungary and the United States from April to December 1917," *AHY* 46 (2015): 261–295.

98 Miklós Komjáthy, ed., *Protokolle des Gemeinsamen Ministerrats des Österreichisch-Ungarischen Monarchie (1914–1918)* (Budapest: Akadémiai Kiadó, 1966), 441–442.

99 On the May Declaration and the declarations of other nationalist groupings in Parliament, Moll, *Die Steiermark im Ersten Weltkrieg*, 147–148; Rauchensteiner, *Der Erste Weltkrieg*, 734–737.

100 Two hundred and fifteen of the 380 municipalities in South Styria supported the petition. Moll, *Die Steiermark im Ersten Weltkrieg,* 147–148; Cornwall, "Das Ringen um die Moral"; Walter Lukan, "Die politische Meinung der slowenischen Bevökerung 1917/1918 im Spiegel der Zensurberichte des Gemeinsamen Zentralnachweisbureaus für Kriegsgefangene in Wien," in *Nacionalismus, společnost a kultura ve střední Evropě 19. a 20. Století,* ed. Jiří Pokorný, Luboš Velek, Alice Velková (Prague: Karolinum, 2007), 246, 259.

101 Rauchensteiner, *Der Erste Weltkrieg,* 912–913; in general see Wolfdieter Bihl, *Österreich-Ungarn und die Friedensschlüsse von Brest-Litovsk* (Vienna: Böhlau, 1970); *Die Besatzung der Ukraine 1918. Historischer Kontext, Forschungsstand, wirtschaftliche und soziale Folgen,* ed. Wolfram Dornik, Stephan Karner (Graz-Vienna-Klagenfurt: Verein zur Forderung der Forschung von Folgen nach Konflikten und Kriegen, 2008).

102 On suffrage struggles in Hungary, see Galántai, *Hungary in the First World War,* 224–226.

103 From a 26 February 1917 speech by Julius Andrássy the Younger (1860–1929) to the Hungarian Parliament, quoted in Galántai, *Hungary in the First World War,* 225.

104 Margarete Grandner, "Die Beschwerdekommissionen für die Rüstungsindustrie Österreichs während des Ersten Weltkrieges. Der Versuch einer 'sozialpartnerschaftlichen' Institution in der Kriegswirkschaft?," in *Historische Wurzeln der Sozialpartnerschaft,* ed. Gerald Stourzh and Margarete Grandner (Vienna: Verlag für Geschichte und Politik, 1986).

105 Quoted in Moll, *Die Steiermark im Ersten Weltkrieg,* 137.

106 Ibid., 141–143.

107 Galántai, *Hungary in the First World War,* 294–295.

108 Quoted in Healy, *Vienna and the Fall of the Habsburg Empire,* 84; Rudolf Neck, ed., *Österreich im Jahre 1918. Berichte und Dokumente* (Munich: R. Oldenbourg Verlag, 1968), 34–35.

109 Galántai, *Hungary in the First World War,* 292–293; 296.

110 AST, "KK Festungskommisär in Pola to Presidium in Trieste," 30 January 1918, Busta 449, Luogotenenza del Littoral, Atti Presidiali.

111 Richard Plaschka, *Matrosen, Offiziere, Rebellen. Krisenkonfrontationen zur See, 1900–1918* (Vienna, Cologne, Graz: Böhlau, 1984); Bruno Frei, *Die Matrosen von Cattaro* (Vienna: Globus Verlag, 1963); Galántai, *Hungary in the First World War,* 299.

112 AST, "Bolschewikische Agitation (Heimkehrer)," MdI, Min für Landesverteidigung, 4 May 1918, Busta 443, Luogotenenza del Littoral, Atti Presidiali.

113 Quoted in Rachamimov, "Arbiters of Allegiance," 171. This article offers an excellent analysis of the state's censorship of POW letters and of the treatment of returning POWs.

114 Ibid., 172.

115 On the "bread peace," Rauchensteiner, *Der Erste Weltkrieg*, 914–920.

116 Moll, *Die Steiermark im Ersten Weltkrieg*, 158.

117 See Tara Zahra's insightful interpretation of the creation and functioning of this new ministry in " 'Each Nation Cares Only For its Own': Empire, Nation, and Child Welfare Activism in the Bohemian Lands, 1900–1918," *American Historical Review* vol. 111, no. 5 (December 2006): 1378–1402, especially 1393. Zahra points out that whereas in Bohemia, Czech and German nationalists often competed for the loyalties of families and children by offering gifts and other incentives, in nation-state Hungary such national competition would have been impossible. There, welfare was organized along liberal nation-state lines to provide only for the neediest cases.

118 On the creation of these networks in Bohemia and Moravia, see Zahra, *Kidnapped Souls*, 95–103.

119 Zahra, "Each Nation," 1381.

120 Ibid., 1394.

121 Ibid., 1379, 1393.

122 *Reichenberger deutsche Volkszeitung*, 16 June 1918, 1–2, cited in ibid., 1400.

123 On Tisza's fact-finding trip, see Galántai, *Hungary in the First World War*, 310–311. On Scheu's trip, Robert Scheu, *Wanderung durch Böhmen am Vorabend der Revolution* (Vienna-Prague-Leipzig: Verlag Ed. Strache, 1919).

124 Quotations in Galántai, *Hungary in the First World War*, 310–311.

125 The quotation is taken from a statement by Czech nationalist leader Alois Rašín in his memoirs quoted in Gary B. Cohen, "Nationalist Politics and the Dynamics of State and Civil Society in the Habsburg Monarchy, 1867–1914," *CEH* 40/2 (2007): 278.

126 On 26 September Thomas Masaryk in Paris proclaimed the Czechoslovak Republic, and on 15 October the French government recognized the new independent state.

127 Irina Livezeanu, *Cultural Politics in Greater Romania: Regionalism, Nation Building and Ethnic Struggle, 1918–1930* (Ithaca, NY: Cornell University Press, 1995), 57. The Romanian National Council had formed in response to Emperor Charles's federalization manifesto issued 16 October and discussed below.

128 Quoted in Moll, *Die Steiermark im Ersten Weltkrieg*, 159.

129 Ibid., 165.

130 The newspapers printed the text of the manifesto two days later. See *Neue Freie Presse*, 18 October 1918, 1.

131 Richard Lein, "Der 'Umsturz' in Prag im Oktober 1918: zwischen Mythen und Fakten," in *Schlaglichter auf die Geschichte der böhmischen Länder vom 16. Bis zum 20. Jahrhundert*, ed. Daivd Schriffl and Niklas Perzi (Vienna: Lit Verlag, 2011), 185–206; Morelon, "Street Fronts," 204–206.

132 Quoted in Gary B. Cohen, "Nationalist Politics and the Dynamics of State and Civil Society in the Habsburg Monarchy, 1867–1914," *CEH* 40, no. 2 (2007): 278.

133 Ibid., 278.

134 Morelon, "Street Fronts," 210.

135 The statue of Maria Theresa by a local artist of some repute was destroyed by Czech Legionnaires in October 1921 over a period of two days while local police looked on. On this incident and on the renaming of the city, see Peter Bugge, "The Naming of a Slovak City: The Czechoslovak Renaming of Pressburg/Pozsony/Prešporok in 1918–1919," *AHY* 35 (2004): 205–227, especially 222.

136 On the Marian Column incident and on Catholic Czech nationalism in the 1920s, see Cynthia Paces' insightful analysis in *Prague Panoramas: National Memory and Sacred Space in the Twentieth Century* (Pittsburgh: University of Pittsburgh Press, 2009), 87–96, 100–114; Cynthia Paces, " 'The Czech Nation Must Be Catholic!' An Alternative Version of Czech Nationalism during the First Republic," *Nationalities Papers* 27, no. 3 (1997): 407–428; Cynthia Paces and Nancy M. Wingfield, "The Sacred and the Profane," in *Constructing Nationalities in East Central Europe*, 107–125; Martin Schulze Wessel, "Tschechische Nation und katholische Konfession vor und nach der Gründung des tschechoslowakischen Nationalstaates," in *Bohemia* 39 (1997): 311–337.

137 Ivan Šedivý, "K otázce kontinuity nositelů státní moci: jmenování vedoucích úředníků v kompetenci ministerstva vnitra v letech 1918–1921," in *Moc, vliv a autorita v procesu vzniku a utváření meziválečné ČSR 1918–1921*, ed. Jan Hájek, Dagmar Hájková, and Luci Merhautová (Prague: Masarykův ústav a Archiv 2008), 184–197; Samuel Ronsin, "Police, Republic, and Nation: The Czechoslovak State Police and the Building of a Multinational Democracy, 1918–1925," in *Policing Interwar Europe: Continuity and Crisis, 1918–1940*, ed. Gerald Blaney (New York: Palgrave Macmillan, 2007), 136–158; Martin Zückert, *Zwischen Nationsidee und staatlicher Realität. Die tschechoslovakische Armee und ihre Nationalitätenpolitik, 1918–1938* (Munich: R. Oldenbourg Verlag, 2006), especially 80–112. In "Street Fronts" Claire Morelon also develops this argument about the continuities in personnel.

138 On questions about Bolshevism and returning POWs throughout Central and eastern Europe, see Hannes Leidinger and Verena Moritz, *Gefangenschaft, Revolution, Heimkehr. Die Bedeutung der Kriegsgefangenproblematik für die Geschichte des Kommunismus in Mittel- und Ostmitteleuropa 1917–1920* (Vienna: Böhlau, 2003). Leidinger and Moritz conclude that individual experience was far more important for radicalization of POWs than was Bolshevik propaganda.

139 Quoted in Morelon, "Street Fronts," 190.

140 In 1918 there were 184 industrial strikes in the Bohemian lands, in 1919 there were 242, and in 1920, 590. After this the number declined. See Heumos, "Kartoffeln her," 271; Morelon, "Street Fronts," 188–190; 223–225.

141 Heading taken from a 22 October speech to the Hungarian Parliament by Károlyi Huszár, quoted in Galántai, *Hungary in the First World War*, 319.

142 Ibid., 325–327.

143 Alison F. Frank, *Oil Empire: Visions of Prosperity in Austrian Galicia* (Cambridge, MA: Harvard University Press, 2005), 205–208. On the war over the Drohobych oil fields, see ibid., 209–228.

144 Carole Fink, *Defending the Rights of Others: The Great Powers, the Jews, and International Minority Protection, 1878–1938* (Cambridge: Cambridge University Press, 2004), 110–112; William Hagen, "The Moral Economy of Popular Violence: The Pogrom in Lwow, 1918" in *Antisemitism and Its Opponents in Modern Poland*, ed. Robert Blobaum (Ithaca, NY: Cornell University Press, 2005), 124–147, especially 127–128, Christoph Mick, "Nationalisierung in einer multiethnischer Stadt. Interethnische Konflikte in Lemberg, 1890–1920," *Archiv für Sozialgeschichte* 40 (2000): 113–146.

145 See the account of the wars in Timothy Snyder, *The Reconstruction of Nations: Poland, Ukraine, Lithuania, Belarus 1569–1999* (New Haven, CT: Yale University Press, 2003), 137–141. Once Poland had defeated the Western Ukrainian Republic, it then faced attack by Soviet Russia.

146 The council proclaimed its program to the Hungarian people on 26 October. Galántai, *Hungary in the First World War*, 321–322.

147 There is a large literature on the white terror in Hungary; see, for example, Bela Bodo, "Militia Violence and State Power in Hungary, 1919–1920," in *Hungarian Studies Review* 33 (2006): 121–167. The degree of Horthy's personal responsibility for the excesses of the White Terror remains in question. On Horthy, see István Deák, "A Hungarian Admiral on Horseback," in Deák, *Essays on Hitler's Europe* (Lincoln and London: University of Nebraska Press, 2001), 148–159; Thomas Sakmyster, *Hungary's Admiral on Horseback: Miklós Horthy, 1918–1944* (New York: Columbia University Press, 1993).

148 Some German nationalists in southern Bohemia also declared their adherence to Upper Austria, and the Linz government sent representatives there to organize an administration of the new territories. On 3 November some German nationalists in southern Moravia declared their adherence to neighboring Lower Austria. On the Czechoslovak occupation of the self-styled "German Bohemia," see AVA, Österreichisches Staatsarchiv, Archiv der Republik, Landesregierung Deutschböhmen 1918–1919, Carton 5, II, IV, VIII, XIV, Karton 6, XIV. See also "Prachatitz (zu Deutschösterreich)," "Winterberg (Tschechoslowaken in der Stadt," and "Bergreichenstein (Besetzung Bergreichenstein durch die Tschechoslowaken)," in *Südbömische Volkszeitung*, 1 December, 1918, 7; "Die Tschechen in Südböhmen," 8 December, 1918, 2; "Tschechische Übergriffe," in *Deutsche Volkszeitung Reichenberg*, 1 December 1918, 4; "Reichenberg von den Tschecho-Slowaken besetzt," 16 December 1918, 1.

149 Newman, "Post-Imperial and Postwar Violence," 258–260.

150 Moll, *Die Steiermark im Ersten Weltkrieg*, 170–171.

151 The American experts determined that ethnic relations were "confused" in this region and that more Slovene speakers preferred to maintain their economic links with Austria to the north. See documents reproduced in Siegfried Beer and Eduard Staudinger, "Grenzziehung per Analogie: Die Miles-Mission in der Steiermark im Jänner 1919: Eine Dokumentation," in *Als Mitteleuropa zerbrach: Zu den Folgen des Umbruchs in Österreich und Jugoslawien nach dem ersten Weltkrieg*, ed. Stefan Karner (Graz: Leykam, 1990).

EPILOGUE

Epigraph: Emil Ludwig, *Defender of Democracy* (New York, 1936; repr. New York: Arno Press and *New York Times*, 1971), 208–209. The quotation refers to the situation in the new Czechoslovak Republic.

1 Eric Hobsbwam, *Nations and Nationalism Since 1780: Programme, Myth Reality* (Cambridge and New York: Cambridge University Press, 1990), 131 and chap. 5.

2 Mark Mazower, *Dark Continent: Europe's Twentieth Century* (New York, Vintage Books, 1998), 3–40.

3 Thomas Garrigue Masaryk, "The Problem of Small Nations and States," in *We Were and We Shall Be: The Czechoslovak Spirit through the Centuries*, eds. Zdenka and Jan Muzner (New York: Frederick Ungar, 1941), 153.

4 Erez Manela, *The Wilsonian Moment: Self-Determination and the International Origins of Anticolonial Nationalism* (New York and Oxford: Oxford

University Press, 2007); Naoko Shimazu, *Japan, Race, and Equality: The Racial Equality Proposal of 1919* (New York and Oxon: Routledge, 1998).

5 Quoted in Margaret Macmillan, *Paris 1919: Six Months That Changed the World* (New York: Random House, 2001), 99. See also Mark Mazower, *No Enchanted Palace: The End of Empire and the Ideological Origins of the United Nations* (Princeton, NJ: Princeton University Press, 2009), 45. Mazower also argues that the ability of the new eastern European states to frame their existence as a necessary and useful strategic buffer against Bolshevism diminished the attractiveness of applying a mandate system to them.

6 On questions of post-war citizenship in German Austria, see the excellent analysis by Ulrike von Hirschhausen, "From imperial inclusion to national exclusion: citizenship in the Habsburg monarchy and in Austria 1867–1923," *European Review of History—Revue européenne d'historire* 16, no. 4 (August 2009): 551–573, especially 559–562. Hirschhausen points out that during the period 1919–1921 different definitions of nationhood could apply in individual cases. When in 1921 Leopold Waber of the German Nationalist Party took over the Ministry of the Interior, however, he applied a clearly racial definition of Germanness to deny naturalization to all Jewish applicants, and the Courts followed his lead. See also Marsha Rozenblit, *Reconstructing a National Identity: The Jews of Habsburg Austria during World War I* (Oxford: Oxford University Press, 2001).

7 See the examples in Annemarie H. Sammartino, *The Impossible Border: Germany and the East, 1914–1922* (Ithaca, NY: Cornell University Press, 2010). On the Minority Rights Treaties and their implementation, see Carole Fink, *Defending the Rights of Others: The Great Powers, the Jews, and International Minority Protection, 1878–1938* (Cambridge and New York: Cambridge University Press, 2004); Tara Zahra, "The Minority Problem and National Classification in the French and Czechoslovak Borderlands," *Contemporary European History* 17, no. 2 (2008): 137–165.

8 See Tara Zahra's analysis of court cases around the Czechoslovak interwar censuses in *Kidnapped Soul: National Indifference and the Battle for Children in the Bohemian Lands, 1900–1948* (Ithaca, NY: Cornell University Press, 2008), 118–141.

9 Timothy Snyder, *The Reconstruction of Nations: Poland, Ukraine, Lithuania, Belarus 1569–1999* (New Haven, CT: Yale University Press, 2003), 52–65.

10 For examples of national ascription and limited rights in interwar Czechoslovakia, see Zahra, *Kidnapped Souls*, chapters four and five. On the character of German nationalism in interwar Czechoslovakia, see also Mark Cornwall, *The Devil's Wall: The Nationalist Youth Mission of Heinz Rutha*

(Cambridge, MA: Harvard University Press, 2012). On Czech imperialism in the Hungarian- and German-speaking borderlands, Daniel Miller, "Colonizing the Hungarian and German Border Areas during the Czechoslovak Land Reform, 1918–1938," *AHY* 34 (2003): 303–318.

11 Irina Livezeanu, *Cultural Politics in Greater Romania: Regionalism, Nation Building and Ethnic Struggle, 1918–1930* (Ithaca, NY: Cornell University Press, 1995), 155–166.

12 Hannah Arendt, *The Origins of Totalitarianism* (New York: Meridian, 1951), 153.

13 Livezeanu, *Cultural Politics,* 63–68, 138–143.

14 Ibid., 49–50; 60–68.

15 Andrej Vovko, "Die Minderheitenschulwesen in Slowenien im Zeitabschnitt des Alten Jugoslawien," in *Geschichte der Deutschen im Bereich des heutigen Slowenien, 1848–1941/ Zgodovina Nemcev na Območju Današnje Slovenije, 1848–1941,* ed. Helmut Rumpler and Arnold Suppan (Vienna: Böhlau, 1988), 255–272. Despite the author's misleading claims about Habsburg "Germanization" in the region, the article offers a useful overview of legal and institutional aspects of Yugoslav education and minority policies.

16 See Laurence Cole, "Divided Land, Diverging Narratives: Memory Cultures of the Great War in the Successor Regions of Tyrol"; Mark Cornwall, "A Conflicted and Divided Habsburg Memory"; and John Paul Newman, "Silent Liquidation? Croatian Veterans and the Margins of War Memory in Interwar Yugoslavia," in *Sacrifice and Rebirth: The Legacy of the Last Habsburg War,* ed. Mark Cornwall and John Paul Newman (New York: Berghahn, 2015), 256–284; 1–12; 197–215.

17 Emanuel Turczynski, "Das Vereinswesen der Deutschen in der Bukowina," in *Buchenland Hundertfünfzig Jahre Deutschtum in der Bukowina,* ed. Franz Lang (Munich: Verlag Südostdeutsches Kulturwerk, 1961), 118–119, reproduces the German Community's memorandum of 17 November 1918.

18 Livezeanu, *Cultural Politics in Greater Romania,* 49.

ACKNOWLEDGMENTS

This book is an argument, a synthesis of ideas that grew directly from encounters with the often provocative, frequently brilliant, regularly quirky, and always inspiring work of other scholars who write the history of central and eastern Europe—many of them dear friends and colleagues. Although based to some extent on my own archival research and previous published work, most of this book builds on the archival work and interpretive virtuosity of others. I could not have undertaken this book without their work, and I thank them for it profusely.

The process of writing this kind of book was completely new to me. It banished me from the archival settings that had given me so much pleasure in the past, but it allowed me to engage more deeply with other people's books. I am grateful to be part of a field that has exploded in the last decades. I had no dearth of books to read for this project during the last eight years—especially brilliant local studies—and there were several I never got to. Still, it remains something of a mystery to me why the field of Habsburg history has produced so few new broad narrative frameworks in which to place usefully all of this diverse new research. This project also forced me repeatedly to confront my own limitations as a historian, most obviously the linguistic ones. Several arguments in this book rest on my readings of historians who write in languages I can read and who have used archival material in Croatian, Hungarian, Polish, Romanian, Serb, Ukrainian, or Yiddish.

When I added writing to my reading, the entire manuscript benefited from repeated critical appraisals by historian friends Belinda Davis and Seth Koven, who have formed with me an ongoing writing group for the last decade. Their unstinting involvement with the construction of every chapter forced me to clarify and improve my arguments, to make them more accessible to non-specialists, and always to find better examples to illustrate my points. Specialist and dear friend Tara Zahra never complained about the many chapters I sent her—usually more than twice—and she never failed to impart insightful criticism and wonderful archival tips. Alison Frank Johnson generously read the entire manuscript and gave me pages and pages of thoughtful notes, saving me from making several crucial errors of fact, interpretation, and style. Historians Maciej Janowski, Adam Kożuchowski, and Endre Sashalmi very liberally advised me in extraordinary detail about how I could improve several chapters, as part of the Warsaw workshop "Recovering Forgotten History: The Image of East-Central Europe in English Language Academic Textbooks."

At a very early phase in the conceptualization of this book Jeremy King kindly shared with me advice and several legal sources I would otherwise never have seen. Scholars Gary Cohen, István Deák, Waltraud Heindl, Marsha Rozenblit, Helmut Walser Smith, Gerald Stourzh, Heidemarie Uhl, and the late Klemens von Klemperer provided personal inspiration, scholarly support, and vigorous debate over the many years it took to write this book. Several other friends, distinguished colleagues, along with former and current students generously shared their unpublished work, gave me tips, or debated particular ideas and interpretations with me over the past decade, including: Mitchell Ash, Brigitta Baader-Zaar, Pamela Ballinger, Ágoston Berecz, Barbara Boisits, William Bowman, Rogers Brubaker, Chad Bryant, Peter Bugge, Matti Bunzl, Jane Burbank, Hannelore Burger, Michelle Campos, Jane Caplan, Holly Case, Sieglinde Clementi, Deborah Coen, Laurence Cole, Fred Cooper, Mark Cornwall, Patrice Dabrowski, John Deak, Dejan Djokic, Astrid Eckert, Paula Sutter Fichtner, Franz Fillafer, Benno Gammerl, William Godsey, Olivia Gruber Florek, Hal Foster, Jon Fox, Robert Gerwarth, Fabio Giomi, Ben Goossen, Andreas Gottsmann, Jonathan Gumz, Edin Haidarpasic, Paul Hanebrink, Peter Haslinger, Gabrielle Hauch, Maureen Healy, Hans Heiss, Tomasz Hen-Konarski, Frank Henschel, Dagmar Herzog, Zdeněk Hojda, Charles Ingrao, Maciej Janowski, Brendan Karch, Markus Krzoska, Börries Kuzmany, Tatjana Lichtenstein, Stefan Malfér, Irina Marin, Zoriana Melnyk, Maria Messner, Caroline Mezger, Erik Middelfort, Martin Moll, Claire Morelon, Dirk Moses, Caitlin Murdock, Norman Naimark, Robert Nemes, Jana Osterkamp, Roberta Pergher, Maya Peterson, Christian Promitzer, Joachim von Puttkamer, Iris Rachamimov, Dominique Reill, Máté Rigó, David Ruderman, Waltraud Schütz, Martin Schulze Wessel, Naoko Shimazu, Alexander Semyonov, Joshua Shanes, Scott Spector, Peter Stachel, Rok Stergar, Lauren Stokes, Ronald Suny, Jan Surman, Werner Telesko, Gregor Thum, Tatjana

Tönsmeyer, Daniel Unowsky, Peter Urbanitsch, Brian Vick, Irina Vushko, Natasha Wheatley, Nancy Wingfield, Marion Wullschleger.

Over the years many others invited me to present the ideas in this book formally in seminars and conferences they organized, enabling me to sharpen certain arguments and helping me to abandon others: David Abraham, Franz Adlgasser, Peter Becker, Harald Binder, James Brophy, Tim Buchen, Moritz Csáky, Sebastian Conrad, R. J. W. Evans, Johannes Feichtinger, Peter Haslinger, Milan Hlavačka, Rudolf Jaworski, Kirsten Jobst, Andrzej Kaminski, Borut Klabjan, Arpad von Klimo, Helmut Konrad, Peter Kracht, Börries Kuzmany, Paul Lerner, Fredrik Lindström, Irina Livezeanu, Oto Luthar, Sue Marchand, Michael L. Miller, Fatima Naquist, Martin Pelc, Markian Prokopovych, Matthew Rampley, Michael Rössner, Malte Rolf, Helmut Rumpler, Annemarie Sammartino, Tamara Scheer, Jeremy Smith, Leonard Smith, Martina Steer, Abigail Swingen, Franz A. J. Szabo, Olaf Terpitz, Philip Ther, Martina Thomsen, Stefan Troebst, Heidemarie Uhl, Luboš Velek, Peter Vodopivec, Thomas Winkelbauer, Larry Wolff, Heidrun Zettelbauer.

Several institutions also supported the writing of this book, including the John Simon Guggenheim Foundation, the National Endowment for the Humanities, and the President and Provost of Swarthmore College. Charles Devlin and I spent five of the most intellectually stimulating, enjoyable, and culinarily remarkable months of our lives at the American Academy in Berlin, where I somehow also found time to draft the first three chapters. Academy librarian Yolande Korb worked miracles on a daily basis, providing me with all of my Austrian research needs in the Prussian north. My good friend Director Peter Haslinger made me a frequent and happy guest at the Herder Institut in Marburg. Martin Pelc introduced me to the charms of Opava and the Silesian University, where I was privileged to serve as European Union guest professor in 2012. My colleagues in the Swarthmore College History Department—especially Farid Azfar, Tim Burke, Bruce Dorsey, Robert S. Duplessis, Lillian Li, Marjorie Murphy, and Robert Weinberg—engaged me in challenging debates about the nature and character of this empire. My new colleagues at the European University Institute, led by Federico Romero, welcomed me into a vigorous and challenging intellectual community. One of the happiest and most unexpected coincidences of joining the EUI faculty is that my dear friend and supportive ally from graduate school Laura Downs is now also my trusted colleague and collaborator. In Florence I also thank my comrade and intellectual partner Lucy Riall for the many new insights I have picked up from co-teaching an annual seminar with her on Empires in Modern Europe. Regina Grafe reminds me daily why modernists like myself need to keep in mind the critical legacies of the early-modern and Spanish Habsburgs. Pavel Kolář stages frequent and stimulating discussions around Habsburg questions in Florence, while brilliantly recreating various regional cuisines of the empire. I also want to thank administrators Theresa Brown and Jen Moore at Swarthmore College, along with Francesca Parenti and Anna Coda at the EUI, for their unfailing and cheerful assistance. Friends Stuart Adair, Leslie Delauter, Nora Johnson, and Diane Shooman kept me going during the inevitable rough patches.

My parents, siblings, and in-laws tactfully stopped asking me long ago about when the book might finally appear. Matt, Dylan, Lucas, Ella, and Callie probably wondered whether their uncle has ever actually finished a project. Kathleen McDermott, my excellent editor at Harvard, helped me through difficult technical challenges—especially those created by the illustrations—while exhibiting more patience over the years than might be thought humanly possible. I thank her especially for having confidently imagined what this book could become, long before I could see it.

Charles Devlin has supported this project with watchful care and energetic enthusiasm for much longer than he ever expected he would have to. The project took him to Berlin for five months in 2011 and then Florence, all the while managing a demanding business in Philadelphia. He learned his Berlin German, and now he's learning Tuscan Italian. I have been fortunate to have his loving companionship on countless research tours of Habsburg sites in several regions of the former empire. I dedicate this book to him with my sincere apologies that after all these years it probably will not become the basis for a major film screenplay.

INDEX

Absolutism in Austria, 29, 46, 109, 219;
  liberal, 6, 220, 248, 251, 256, 266, 277,
  341, 383, 390
Academic Legion (revolutions
  1848/1849), 165, 173, 178–179, 181
Adler, Friedrich, 420
Adler, Viktor, 371–372, 374
Ady, Endre, 307
Aehrenthal, Alois Lexa von, 378, 383
Agram. *See* Zagreb
Agricultural Society, Carniolan, 149
Albanian language, 446
Alexandria, 115
Amsterdam, 11
Anderson, Margaret, 339
Andrássy, Julius, 260–261, 264
Anti Semitism, 67, 268, 300–302, 339, 352,
  405; at the end of the First World War,
  436–439, 445; and revolutions
  (1848/1849), 180
Antwerp, 19
Apony, György, 166
April Laws. *See* Constitution
Architecture: art nouveau, 325; Fellner
  and Helmer (firm), 346, 348; historicist
  (Ringstrasse), 345–346; liberal values
  expressed through, 280–281; monu-
  mental (Hungary), 359; neo-Baroque,
  346, 349; neo-Gothic, 284; visions of
  empire in, 317
Arendt, Hannah, 448
Argentina, 340
Armenian Catholic. *See* Eastern Catholic
Arnstein, banking family, 67, 231
Associations, 30, 41, 101, 104–105, 136,
  139–145, 179, 248–249, 427; agricultural,
  149; auxiliary, 181; beautification
  association (*Verschönerungsverein*),
  350; casinos, 141–143, 288; Catholic,
  283–284, 288; choral, 169; cultural, 356;
  economic, 352; Freemasons, 30–31, 91,
  105, 141; gymnastics (*Sokol*), 352, 394,

397–398, 530–531; industrial, 140–141,
  143, 151, 168; Jacobin societies, 105;
  legislation regarding, 179, 344, 392;
  liberal, 288; local associational context,
  359, 368; nationalist, 291–292, 372, 390,
  410, 426, 428; nationalist school
  associations, 302–308; reading, 133, 143,
  146; and revolutions (1848/1849), 164,
  168–169, 179, 181–184, 195–196, 209–210,
  214; Social Democratic, 338; teachers',
  305; veterans', 352, 369–370; women's,
  143–144, 181–182, 184, 291, 360–361, 405;
  working class, 289
Auersperg, Joseph, 175
Aussig/Ústí, 349, 352, 356
Austria-Hungary 1867 Settlement, 6,
  259–267, 295–296, 314, 344, 377
Austrian Academy of Science, 14, 241
Austrian Civil Law Code (*Allgemeines
  Bürgerliches Gesetzbuch,* ABGB), 36,
  51–52, 76–77, 103, 107, 178, 195
Austrian Lloyd Company, 115
Austrian National Bank, 231
Austrian Netherlands, 23, 53, 79, 83–84;
  on map, 26, 54
Austrian Succession, War of, 26, 28
Austro-Prussian War (1866), 251, 252, 259,
  297, 317
Auxiliary associations, 181

Babenberg family, 21
Bach, Alexander von, 222–224, 234, 275
Badeni, Casimir Felix, 312–313. *See also*
  Badeni Crisis
Badeni Crisis, 312–316, 333, 358, 370
Balkan Wars (1912–1913), 385, 390,
  396
Banat region, 67, 146, 200, 216, 335
Bánffy, Miklós, 419
Bárta/Bardejov/Bartfeld, 408–409
Batschka region, 200
Batthyáni, Lajos, 167